Readings *for* Writers

TWELFTH EDITION

Readings *for* Writers

Jo Ray McCuen-Metherell
Glendale College

Anthony C. Winkler

THOMSON
WADSWORTH

Australia • Brazil • Canada • Mexico • Singapore • Spain
United Kingdom • United States

THOMSON
WADSWORTH

Readings for Writers, **Twelfth Edition**
McCuen-Metherell/Winkler

Publisher: Michael Rosenberg
Senior Acquisitions Editor: Dickson Musslewhite
Development Editor: Laurie Runion
Editorial Assistant: Jonelle Lonergan
Technology Project Manager: Tim Smith
Managing Marketing Manager: Mandee Eckersley
Marketing Assistant: Dawn Giovanniello
Associate MarCom Manager: Patrick Rooney
Senior Project Manager, Editorial Production: Samantha Ross
Print Buyer: Betsy Donaghey
Senior Permissions Editor: Isabel Alves

Production Service: Merrill Peterson, Matrix Productions
Text Designer: Denise Hoffman
Photo Manager: Sheri Blaney
Photo Researcher: Connie Gardner
Cover Designer: Joseph Sherman
Cover Printer: Phoenix Color Corporation
Compositor: International Typesetting and Composition
Printer: RR Donnelly-Crawfordsville
Cover Art: *Brooklyn Bridge Painters* by Eugene de Salignac 1914, Courtesy NYC Municipal Archives

© 2007 Thomson Wadsworth, a part of The Thomson Corporation. Thomson, the Star logo, and Wadsworth are trademarks used herein under license.

ALL RIGHTS RESERVED. No part of this work covered by the copyright hereon may be reproduced or used in any form or by any means—graphic, electronic, or mechanical, including photocopying, recording, taping, web distribution, information storage and retrieval systems, or in any other manner—without the written permission of the publisher.

Printed in the United States of America
1 2 3 4 5 6 7 09 08 07 06

Library of Congress Control Number: 2005931106

ISBN 1-4130-1629-4

Thomson Higher Education
25 Thomson Place
Boston, MA 02210-1202
USA

For more information about our products, contact us at:
Thomson Learning Academic Resource Center
1-800-423-0563

For permission to use material from this text or product, submit a request online at
http://www.thomsonrights.com
Any additional questions about permissions can be submitted by e-mail to
thomsonrights@thomson.com

Credits appear on page 803–808, which constitute a continuation of the copyright page.

*For Allwyn and Cathy—spouses,
silent backers, patient listeners—
with gratitude and love*

Contents

Thematic Table of Contents   xix

Preface   xxiii

PART ONE
Reading and Writing: From Reading to Writing   1

1 Guidelines for Critical Reading   3

KINDS OF READING   3

Andy Rooney   7

- *Education of a Wandering Man* / LOUIS L'AMOUR   10

2 What Is Rhetoric?   17

ROAD MAP TO RHETORIC   17

Grammar and Rhetoric   17
Audience and Purpose   19
The Internal Reader/Editor   19
Levels of English   20
Writing as a Process   23
Writing about Visual Images   24

Exercises   33

ADVICE   37

- *What—and How—to Write When You Have No Time to Write* / DONALD MURRAY   37

EXAMPLES   40

- *I Have a Dream* / MARTIN LUTHER KING, JR.   40
- *Letter to My Husband* / CLEMENTINE CHURCHILL   45
- *Have a Cigar* / JAMES HERRIOT   48

Chapter Writing Assignments   51

vii

viii   Contents

   REAL-LIFE STUDENT WRITING   52
   • *E-Mail from Samoa*   52

3 What Is a Writer's Voice?   55

   ROAD MAP TO WRITER'S VOICE   55
   Voice: Why Did the Chicken Cross the Road?   57
   Vocabulary   57
   Syntax   58
   Attitude   59
   Exercises   60

   ADVICE   61
   • *How to Say Nothing in Five Hundred Words* / PAUL ROBERTS   61

   EXAMPLES   71
   • *Tone: The Writer's Voice in the Reader's Mind* / MORT CASTLE   71
   • *Me* / MARY MacLANE   76
   • *Remarks on the Life of Sacco and on His Own Life and Execution* / BARTOLOMEO VANZETTI   81
   • *Salvation* / LANGSTON HUGHES   83
   • *Killing Ants in the Kitchen at 3 a.m.* / ANTHONY C. WINKLER   86

   Chapter Writing Assignments   88

   REAL-LIFE STUDENT WRITING   89
   • *A Thank-You Note to an Aunt*   89

4 What Is a Thesis?   91

   ROAD MAP TO A THESIS   91
   Finding Your Thesis   91
   Key Words in the Thesis   93
   Characteristics of a Good Thesis   93
   Nine Errors to Avoid in Composing a Thesis   96
   The Explicit versus the Implicit Thesis   99
   Exercises   99

   ADVICE   101
   • *The Thesis* / SHERIDAN BAKER   101

Contents   ix

EXAMPLES   104
- *The Grieving Never Ends* / ROXANNE ROBERTS   104
- *A Good Man Is Hard to Find* / FLANNERY O'CONNOR   111
- *Spring* / EDNA ST. VINCENT MILLAY   123

Chapter Writing Assignments   125

REAL-LIFE STUDENT WRITING   126
- *A Eulogy to a Friend Killed in a Car Wreck*   126

5 How Do I Organize?   129

ROAD MAP TO ORGANIZING   129
   Organizing the Short Essay   129
   Organizing the Long Essay   131
   Planning by Listing Supporting Materials   132
   Organizing with a Formal Outline   133

Exercises   137

ADVICE   139
- *How to Write Clearly* / EDWARD T. THOMPSON   139

EXAMPLES   142
- *My Wood* / E. M. FORSTER   142
- *Rules for Aging* / ROGER ROSENBLATT   146
- *The Catbird Seat* / JAMES THURBER   148
- *That Time of Year (Sonnet 73)* / WILLIAM SHAKESPEARE   156

Chapter Writing Assignments   158

REAL-LIFE STUDENT WRITING   158
- *Note from a Graduate Student to a Department Secretary*   158

6 Developing Paragraphs   161

ROAD MAP TO DEVELOPING PARAGRAPHS   161
   Parts of the Paragraph   162
   Supporting Details   163
   Topic Sentence Developed over More Than One Paragraph   165
   Position of the Topic Sentence   165
   Paragraph Patterns   167

Contents

    Characteristics of a Well-Designed Paragraph   167
    Writing Your Own Paragraphs   170
Exercises   171

ADVICE   **174**
- *Writing Successful Paragraphs* / A. M. TIBBETTS AND CHARLENE TIBBETTS   174

EXAMPLES   **178**
    Paragraphs with the Topic Sentence at the Beginning   178
- *From the Lessons of the Past* / EDITH HAMILTON   178
- *Pain* / WILLIAM SOMERSET MAUGHAM   179
- *I Am Tired of Fighting (Surrender Speech)* / CHIEF JOSEPH OF THE NEZ PERCÉ   180

PARAGRAPHS WITH THE TOPIC SENTENCE AT THE END   **181**
- *Man against Darkness* / W. T. STACE   181
- *What Is a Poet?* / MARK VAN DOREN   182
- *On Disease* / LEWIS THOMAS, M.D.   183
- *The Flood* / ROBERT FROST   184

Chapter Writing Assignments   185

REAL-LIFE STUDENT WRITING   **186**
- *Letter of Application to an Honors Program*   186

PART TWO
Patterns of Development: The Rhetorical Modes   189

7 Narration   195

ROAD MAP TO NARRATION   **195**
    What Narration Does   195
    When to Use Narration   195
    How to Write a Narrative   195
    Warming Up to Write a Narrative   198

EXAMPLES   **199**
- *Shooting an Elephant* / GEORGE ORWELL   199
- *My Name Is Margaret* / MAYA ANGELOU   206

- *Shame* / DICK GREGORY   211
- *James Boswell's Scotland* / TOM HUNTINGTON   215
- *Those Winter Sundays* / ROBERT HAYDEN   228

**ISSUE FOR CRITICAL THINKING AND DEBATE
TERRORISM   229**

- *What Does Islam Say about Terrorism?* / ABDULLAH MOMIN   231
- *"Postscript" to Inside the Kingdom: My Life in Saudi Arabia* / CARMEN BIN LADEN   236

Punctuation Workshop: The Period   244

STUDENT CORNER   245

The Right Moves against Terrorism / SION ARAKELIAN, GLENDALE COMMUNITY COLLEGE   245

How I Write • *How I Wrote This Paper* • *My Writing Tip*   247

Chapter Writing Assignments   248

8 Description   251

ROAD MAP TO DESCRIPTION   251

What Description Does   251
When to Use Description   252
How to Write a Description   252
Warming Up to Write a Description   255

EXAMPLES   256

- *The Libido for the Ugly* / H. L. MENCKEN   256
- *Hell* / JAMES JOYCE   260
- *A Worn Path* / EUDORA WELTY   264
- *Pigeon Woman* / MAY SWENSON   271

**ISSUE FOR CRITICAL THINKING AND DEBATE:
BODY IMAGE   274**

- *Body Image* / CINDY MAYNARD   275
- *Stretch Marks* / ANNA QUINDLEN   282

Punctuation Workshop: The Comma   286

STUDENT CORNER   287

Body Modification—Think about It! / SHELLEY TAYLOR, STATE UNIVERSITY OF NEW YORK, OSWEGO   287

How I Write • *How I Wrote This Essay* • *My Writing Tip*   292

Chapter Writing Assignments   293

9 Process Analysis   295

ROAD MAP TO PROCESS ANALYSIS   295
    What Process Analysis Does   295
    When to Use Process Analysis   296
    How to Write a Process Analysis   296
    Warming Up to Write a Process Analysis   298

EXAMPLES   299
- *This Is a Mortal Wound, Doctor* / THOMAS FLEMING   299
- *Hunting Octopus in the Gilbert Islands* / SIR ARTHUR GRIMBLE   309
- *Hitler's Workday* / WILLIAM SHIRER   313
- *How to Be an Army* / KENNETH PATCHEN   316

ISSUE FOR CRITICAL THINKING AND DEBATE: AGEISM   318
- *Painting: My Parents* / HENRY KOERNER   318
- *The View from Eighty* / MALCOLM COWLEY   319
- *Stay Young* / MARYA MANNES   326

Punctuation Workshop: The Semicolon   330

STUDENT CORNER   331
    Aging / KIMBERLY CAITLIN WHEELER, YALE UNIVERSITY   331
    How I Write • How I Wrote This Essay • My Writing Tip   333
Chapter Writing Assignments   334

10 Illustration/Exemplification   337

ROAD MAP TO ILLUSTRATION/EXEMPLIFICATION   337
    What Illustration/Exemplification Does   337
    When to Use Illustration   338
    How to Use Illustration   339
    Warming Up to Write an Illustration   341

EXAMPLES   342
- *What Is Style?* / F. L. LUCAS   342
- *The Buck Stops Where?* / BARRY PARR   351
- *"Mirror, Mirror, on the Wall..."* / JOHN LEO   356

ISSUE FOR CRITICAL THINKING AND DEBATE: DRUG ABUSE   359
- *Drugs* / GORE VIDAL   361
- *Don't Legalize Drugs* / MORTON KONDRACKE   364

Punctuation Workshop: The Dash   370

Contents   xiii

STUDENT CORNER   371

Drug Use: The Continuing Epidemic / LINDA KUNZE, GLENDALE COMMUNITY COLLEGE   371

How I Write • How I Wrote This Essay • My Writing Tip   373

Chapter Writing Assignments   373

11 Definition   375

ROAD MAP TO DEFINITION   375

What Definition Does   375

When to Use Definition   376

How to Use Definition   376

Warming Up to Write a Definition   379

EXAMPLES   380

- *The Politics of Separation* / WILLIAM A. HENRY III   380
- *The Company Man* / ELLEN GOODMAN   387
- *In Praise of the Humble Comma* / PICO IYER   390
- *Kitsch* / GILBERT HIGHET   394
- *Ars Poetica* / ARCHIBALD MacLEISH   402

ISSUE FOR CRITICAL THINKING AND DEBATE: IMMIGRATION   404

- *Illegal Immigrants Are Bolstering Social Security with Billions* / EDUARDO PORTER   407
- *Wide Open Spaces* / BILL BRYSON   410

Punctuation Workshop: The Apostrophe   415

STUDENT CORNER   416

Immigrants in America / DAVE HERMAN, GEORGIA STATE UNIVERSITY   416

How I Write • How I Wrote This Essay • My Writing Tip   418

Chapter Writing Assignments   419

12 Comparison/Contrast   421

ROAD MAP TO COMPARISON/CONTRAST   421

What Comparison/Contrast Does   421

When to Use Comparison/Contrast   422

How to Use Comparison/Contrast   422

Warming Up to Write a Comparison/Contrast   427

EXAMPLES   428

- *That Lean and Hungry Look* / SUZANNE JORDAN   428
- *Diogenes and Alexander* / GILBERT HIGHET   431
- *Grant and Lee: A Study in Contrasts* / BRUCE CATTON   437
- *Baba and Me* / KHALED HOSSEINI   441

ISSUE FOR CRITICAL THINKING AND DEBATE: THE EXISTENCE OF GOD   449

- *Ten Reasons for Believing in Immortality* / JOHN HAYNES HOLMES   451
- *Breaking the Last Taboo* / JAMES A. HAUGHT   462
- *Children's Letters to God*   471

Punctuation Workshop: The Question Mark   472

STUDENT CORNER   473

The Existence of God / ARA BABAIAN, LOYOLA LAW SCHOOL OF LOS ANGELES   473

How I Write • How I Wrote This Essay • My Writing Tip   474

Chapter Writing Assignments   475

13 Division/Classification   477

ROAD MAP TO DIVISION/CLASSIFICATION   477

What Division/Classification Does   477
When to Use Division/Classification   478
How to Use Division/Classification   478
Warming Up to Write a Division/Classification   480

EXAMPLES   481

- *Move Over, Teams* / PAUL M. MUCHINSKY   481
- *Thinking as a Hobby* / WILLIAM GOLDING   486
- *Kinds of Discipline* / JOHN HOLT   493
- *The Idols* / FRANCIS BACON   496
- *English 101* / BART EDELMAN   499

ISSUE FOR CRITICAL THINKING AND DEBATE: RACISM   501

- *Warriors Don't Cry* / MELBA PATILLO BEALS   503
- *Incidents with White People* / SARAH L. AND A. ELIZABETH DELANY   508

Punctuation Workshop: The Colon   513

STUDENT CORNER   514

Racial Justice: How Far Have We Come? / NANCEY PHILLIPS, CALIFORNIA STATE UNIVERSITY AT LONG BEACH   514

How I Write • How I Wrote This Essay • My Writing Tip   516
Chapter Writing Assignments   518

14 Causal Analysis   519

ROAD MAP TO CAUSAL ANALYSIS   519
What Causal Analysis Does   519
When to Use Causal Analysis   520
How to Use Causal Analysis   520
Warming Up to Write a Causal Analysis   523

EXAMPLES   524
- *A Peaceful Woman Explains Why She Carries a Gun* / LINDA M. HASSELSTROM   524
- *Coming into Language* / JIMMY SANTIAGO BACA   529
- *Why Tigers Become Man-Eaters* / JIM CORBETT   536
- *Why I Went to the Woods* / HENRY DAVID THOREAU   541
- *The Storm* / KATE CHOPIN   548
- *Design* / ROBERT FROST   553

ISSUE FOR CRITICAL THINKING AND DEBATE: THE STATUS OF WOMEN   555
- *The New Feminism* / KATE GUBATA   556
- *The Farce of Feminism* / REBECCA E. RUBINS   560

Punctuation Workshop: The Exclamation Point   563

STUDENT CORNER   564
"Woman" Is a Noun / PAULA REWA, EAST TENNESSEE STATE UNIVERSITY   564
How I Write • How I Wrote This Essay • My Writing Tip   566
Chapter Writing Assignments   567

15 Argumentation and Persuasion   569

ROAD MAP TO ARGUMENTATION AND PERSUASION   569
What Argumentation and Persuasion Do   569
When to Use Argumentation and Persuasion   569
How to Use Argumentation and Persuasion   570
Warming Up to Write an Argument   575

EXAMPLES   576

- *In Defense of Gender* / CYRA McFADDEN   576
- *A Modest Proposal* / JONATHAN SWIFT   580
- *I Want a Wife* / JUDY SYFERS-BRADY   587
- *Sex Predators Can't Be Saved* / ANDREW VACHSS   590
- *Dooley Is a Traitor* / JAMES MICHIE   594

ISSUE FOR CRITICAL THINKING AND DEBATE: HOMELESSNESS   598

- *Painting: Migrant Mother, Nipomo Valley* / *Dorothea Lange*   599
- *Homeless: Expose the Myths* / JOSEPH PERKINS   600
- *The Homeless Lack a Political Voice, But Not American Ideals* / MATT LYNCH   603

Punctuation Workshop: Quotation Marks   606

STUDENT CORNER   607

People Out on a Limb / ANTOINETTE POODT, FURMAN UNIVERSITY   607

How I Write • How I Wrote This Essay • My Writing Tip   609

Chapter Writing Assignments   611

16 Combining the Modes   613

EDITORS' NOTE   613

What Combining the Modes Does   613
When to Combine the Modes   614
How to Use Combined Modes   614

EXAMPLES   616

- *Shrew—The Littlest Mammal* / ALAN DEVOE   616
- *Will Spelling Count?* / JACK CONNOR   620
- *Once More to the Lake* / E. B. WHITE   625

ISSUE FOR CRITICAL THINKING AND DEBATE: SAME-SEX MARRIAGE   631

- *The Case against Homosexual Marriage* / R. ALBERT MOHLER   633
- *Same-Sex Marriage: Just Say No to Prohibition* / SUSAN BLOCK   638

Punctuation Workshop: Using Other Punctuation with Quotation Marks   642

STUDENT CORNER   463

Will Same-Sex Marriages Change the Constitution? / ADAM WINKLER, GEORGIA COLLEGE AND STATE UNIVERSITY   463

How I Write • *How I Wrote This Essay* • *Tips For Writing*   645
Chapter Writing Assignments   646

Image Gallery   647

Terrorism   647
Body Image   650
Ageism   653
Drug Abuse   656
Immigration   659
The Existence of God   662
Racism   665
Status of Women   669
Homelessness   673
Same-Sex Marriage   676

PART THREE
Rewriting Your Writing   679

The Editing Booth   681

REVISING   682

EDITING   685

Rule 1: Make Your Title Descriptive   685
Rule 2: Begin with a Simple Sentence   686
Rule 3: Prune Deadwood   686
Rule 4: Do Not Overexplain   689
Rule 5: Be Specific   690
Rule 6: Avoid Trite Expressions   691
Rule 7: Use the Active Voice   691
Rule 8: Make Your Statements Positive   692
Rule 9: Keep to One Tense   693
Rule 10: Place Key Words at the Beginning or End of a Sentence   693
Rule 11: Prune Multiple *Of*s   693
Rule 12: Break Up Noun Clusters   693
Rule 13: Use Exclamation Points Sparingly   694

Rule 14: Vary Your Sentences   694
Rule 15: Keep Your Point of View Consistent   695
Rule 16: Use Standard Words   695
Rule 17: End with Impact   696

EDITING AN ACTUAL ESSAY   696

PART FOUR
Special Writing Projects   705

ASSIGNMENT 1: THE RESEARCH PAPER   705

Why English Instructors Assign Research Papers   705
How to Choose Your Topic   705
How to Narrow Your Subject   706
The Process of Writing the Paper   707
Preparing "Works Cited" or "References"   712
Writing the Final Copy   712

ANNOTATED STUDENT RESEARCH PAPER:
MODERN LANGUAGE ASSOCIATION (MLA) STYLE   715

Choosing Single Motherhood: A Sign of Modern Times? / STEPHANIE HOLLINGSWORTH   717

ANNOTATED STUDENT RESEARCH PAPER:
AMERICAN PSYCHOLOGICAL ASSOCIATION
(APA) STYLE   745

Development of a Scale to Detect Sexual Harassers: The Potential Harasser Scale (PHS) / LEANNE M. MASDEN AND REBECCA B. WINKLER, DEPAUL UNIVERSITY   747

ASSIGNMENT 2: THE LITERARY PAPER   780

How to Write a Paper about Literature   780
The In-Class Essay on Literature   781

ANNOTATED LITERARY PAPER   783

A Worn but Lightly Traveled Path / DOUGLAS B. INMAN   785

Glossary   795
Credits   803
Index   809

Thematic Table of Contents

- **American Values**
  A Good Man Is Hard to Find, Flannery O'Connor (story)   111
  Aging, Kimberly Caitlin Wheeler (student essay)   331
  Body Image, Cindy Maynard (essay)   275
  Body Modification—Think about It! Shelley Taylor (student essay)   287
  The Buck Stops Where? Barry Parr (essay)   351
  The Case against Homosexual Marriage, R. Albert Mohler (essay)   633
  Choosing Single Motherhood: A Sign of Modern Times? Stephanie Hollingsworth (student research paper)   717
  I Am Tired of Fighting, Chief Joseph of the Nez Percé (speech)   180
  Killing Ants in the Kitchen at 3 a.m., Anthony C. Winkler (poem)   86
  "Mirror, Mirror, on the Wall..." John Leo (essay)   356
  Rules for Aging, Roger Rosenblatt (essay)   146
  Same-Sex Marriage: Just Say No to Prohibition, Susan Block (essay)   638
  Shame, Dick Gregory (essay)   211
  Stretch Marks, Anna Quindlen (essay)   282
  That Lean and Hungry Look, Suzanne Jordan (essay)   428
  The View from Eighty, Malcolm Cowley (essay)   319
  Why I Went to the Woods, Henry David Thoreau (essay)   541

- **Education**
  English 101, Bart Edelman (poem)   499
  Kinds of Discipline, John Holt (essay)   493
  Will Spelling Count? Jack Connor (essay)   620

- **Language**
  Coming into Language, Jimmy Santiago Baca (essay)   529
  Education of a Wandering Man, Louis L'Amour (book excerpt)   10
  How to Say Nothing in Five Hundred Words, Paul Roberts (essay)   61
  How to Write Clearly, Edward T. Thompson (essay)   139
  In Defense of Gender, Cyra McFadden (essay)   576

In Praise of the Humble Comma, Pico Iyer (essay)   390
Move Over, Teams, Paul M. Muchinsky (essay)   481
The Politics of Separation, William A. Henry, III (essay)   380
The Thesis, Sheridan Baker (essay)   101
What Is Style? F. L. Lucas (essay)   342
What—and How—to Write When You Have No Time to Write, Donald Murray (book excerpt)   37
Tone: The Writer's Voice in the Reader's Mind, Mort Castle (essay)   71
Writing Successful Paragraphs, A. M. Tibbetts and Charlene Tibbetts (book excerpt)   174

Literature and the Arts
Ars Poetica, Archibald MacLeish (poem)   402
James Boswell's Scotland, Tom Huntington (essay)   215
Kitsch, Gilbert Highet (essay)   393
What Is a Poet? Mark Van Doren (paragraph)   182
A Worn but Lightly Traveled Path, Douglas B. Inman (student essay)   753

Man and Woman
The Catbird Seat, James Thurber (story)   148
The Farce of Feminism, Rebecca E. Rubins (essay)   560
I Want a Wife, Judy Syfer-Brady (essay)   587
Letter to My Husband, Clementine Churchill (letter)   45
The New Feminism, Kate Gubata (essay)   556
Stay Young, Marya Mannes (essay)   326
The Storm, Kate Chopin (story)   548
That Time of Year (Sonnet 73), William Shakespeare (poem)   156
"Woman" Is a Noun, Paula Rewa (student essay)   564

Philosophy and Religion
Breaking the Last Taboo, James A. Haught (essay)   462
Design, Robert Frost (poem)   553
Dooley Is a Traitor, James Michie (poem)   594
The Existence of God, Ara Babaian (student essay)   473
From the Lessons of the Past, Edith Hamilton (paragraph)   178
Hell, James Joyce (book excerpt)   260
How to Be an Army, Kenneth Patchen (poem)   316

"Postscript" to Inside the Kingdom: My Life in Saudi Arabia, Carmen Bin Laden (book excerpt)   236

Man against Darkness, W. T. Stace (paragraph)   181

My Wood, E. M. Forster (essay)   142

Salvation, Langston Hughes (book excerpt)   83

Spring, Edna St. Vincent Millay (poem)   123

Ten Reasons for Believing in Immortality, John Haynes Holmes (essay)   451

What Does Islam Say about Terrorism? Abdullah Momin (essay)   231

Portrait of the Individual

The Company Man, Ellen Goodman (essay)   387

Diogenes and Alexander, Gilbert Highet (essay)   431

Grant and Lee: A Study in Contrasts, Bruce Catton (essay)   437

Have a Cigar, James Herriot (autobiography)   48

Hitler's Workday, William Shirer (book excerpt)   313

Hunting Octopus in the Gilbert Islands, Sir Arthur Grimble (autobiography)   309

Incidents with White People, Sarah L. and A. Elizabeth Delany (autobiography)   508

Killing Ants in the Kitchen at 3 a.m., Anthony C. Winkler (poem)   86

Me, Mary MacLane (book excerpt)   76

My Name Is Margaret, Maya Angelou (autobiography)   206

Once More to the Lake, E. B. White (essay)   622

A Peaceful Woman Explains Why She Carries a Gun, Linda M. Hasselstrom (essay)   524

Pigeon Woman, May Swenson (poem)   272

Remarks on the Life of Sacco and on His Own Life and Execution, Bartolomeo Vanzetti (notes from a speech)   81

This Is a Mortal Wound, Doctor, Thomas Fleming (book excerpt)   299

Those Winter Sundays, Robert Hayden (poem)   228

A Worn Path, Eudora Welty (story)   265

Science

Development of a Scale to Detect Sexual Harassers: The Potential Harasser Scale (PHS), Leanne M. Masden and Rebecca B. Winkler (APA-style student research paper)   747

Shrew—The Littlest Mammal, Alan DeVoe (essay)   616

On Disease, Lewis Thomas, M.D. (paragraph)   183

Social Problems

Don't Legalize Drugs, Morton M. Kondracke (essay)   364

Drugs, Gore Vidal (essay)   361

Drug Use: The Continuing Epidemic, Linda Kunze (student essay)   371

The Farce of Feminism, Rebecca E. Rubins (essay)   560

The Flood, Robert Frost (poem)   184

The Grieving Never Ends, Roxanne Roberts (essay)   104

Homeless: Expose the Myths, Joseph Perkins (essay)   600

The Homeless Lack a Political Voice, But Not American Ideals, Matt Lynch (essay)   603

I Have a Dream, Martin Luther King, Jr. (speech)   40

Illegal Immigrants Are Bolstering Social Security with Billions, Eduardo Porter (essay)   407

The Libido for the Ugly, H. L. Mencken (essay)   256

A Modest Proposal, Jonathan Swift (essay)   580

Pain, William Somerset Maugham (paragraph)   179

People Out on a Limb, Antoinette Poodt (student essay)   607

Racial Justice: How Far Have We Come? Nanccy Phillips (student essay)   514

The Right Moves against Terrorism, Sion Arakelian (student essay)   245

Sex Predators Can't Be Saved, Andrew Vachss (essay)   590

Shooting an Elephant, George Orwell (essay)   199

Warriors Don't Cry, Melba Pattillo Beals (book excerpt)   503

Why Tigers Become Man-Eaters, Jim Corbett (essay)   536

Wide-Open Spaces, Bill Bryson (book excerpt)   410

Thinking

The Idols, Francis Bacon (essay)   496

Thinking as a Hobby, William Golding (essay)   486

Preface

The lifespan of a textbook is measured in editions and is generally as fleeting as a fruit fly's. Most textbooks do not survive beyond the first edition. When we first developed *Readings for Writers,* we had no inkling that 32 years later it would be entering its twelfth edition. Our basic idea was modest: to produce a rhetorical reader in which every article would be labeled to identify the reason behind its inclusion. Some essays were selected because they gave advice on writing; some because they discussed a particular topic; others because they provided a model of the skill or technique the chapter was intended to teach. Over the years this labeling of readings has been modified but remains the mainspring principle that we have doggedly practiced. Every contribution in the book is intended either to give advice or to serve as an example of a particular rhetorical type or strategy.

The twelfth edition of *Readings for Writers* provides comprehensive coverage of many rhetorical skills and strategies. It contains more than 110 readings, including essays, poems, short stories, excerpts from books, biographies, speeches, paragraphs, and e-mails. Its contributors range from Shakespeare to struggling students to ordinary people with something interesting to say, and its scope of coverage encompasses a breathtaking variety of topics, from how boys in the Gilbert Islands kill octopuses with their teeth to a description of the Auchinleck home of the incomparable biographer James Boswell. It has something for everyone of every taste and every bent.

New to the Twelfth Edition

This twelfth edition is an extension of the first but not its clone. Of all the editions we have produced, this one has the most sweeping changes. Here is what's new for the twelfth edition:

- We have added a four-color Image Gallery to give students a break from text-based writing. The Image Gallery is a collection of images intended to prompt student discussions and assignments. At the end of the modes chapters (7 through 16) we send students to a specific section of the Image Gallery where images related to the theme of the issue for critical thinking and debate can be found. Students are asked either to write about a painting, picture, photograph, or image; to discuss it in a group; or to research a subject suggested by it. The hard fact is that for many of today's students, imagery is the mother's milk of their imagination, as proved by the dismal statistics about how many thousands of hours kids spend in front of the television. If the use of visuals can stimulate students to write better essays, the ends more than justify the means. Including visuals, such as

- paintings and photographs, also gives the instructor a change of pace and some relief from text-centered writing. The assignments triggered by a trip to the Image Gallery result in either an essay, a discussion, or a research project all based on particular images.
- We have changed 17 pieces. Our selections cover the scope of human concerns and range from a description of the fatal duel between Aaron Burr and Alexander Hamilton to the musings of a self-centered teenager whose egotistical writing catapulted her to brief literary fame in 1902. Included among the new pieces are a passionate defense of Islam by a Muslim faithful and a discussion of the sometimes ridiculous extents to which many of us will go to achieve the perfect body image.
- We have changed three of the issues for critical thinking. Out are the issues of *spanking, global warming,* and *separation of church and state*. In are the issues of *body image, immigration,* and *same-sex marriage*. The new pieces chosen are the hot-button issues of today and are discussed by the usual combination of professional and student writers.
- We have added a feature in each of the mode chapters we call the "Punctuation Workshop." Students can drop into any of these workshops to refresh their memories of how to use the most common punctuation marks such as the comma, semicolon, dash, and brackets.

Unchanged in this Edition

Longtime users of *Readings for Writers* might, at this juncture, begin to worry that the changes we have made will require them to retool their syllabi. That, however, is not the case, because the basic structure and intent of the book remain unchanged.

- Unchanged in this twelfth edition is the unique labeling system that identifies the intended function of every anthologized piece as either giving advice about some fundamental principle of writing or as being a model of it.
- Unchanged is the broad sweep of topics, styles, and interests of the included works.
- Unchanged is the popular "Student Corner," which showcases the essays of real students along with their commentary on their own work and their writing tips.
- Each chapter still ends with Chapter Writing Assignments, a Writing Assignment for a Specific Audience, and a Collaborative Writing Project (as well as a new Image Gallery assignment as described earlier).
- Each reading selection is still prefaced by a headnote and followed by questions under the headings of "The Facts," "The Strategies," and "The Issues."

All the changes in this twelfth edition have one aim in common: to make *Readings for Writers* even more practical and easier to use than ever before. Combining the advice of its anthologized experts with the editors' additions, *Readings for Writers* can still be used unaccompanied by any other book.

The Journey Ahead

Learning to write well is comparable to taking a journey. Students travel from topic to topic, picking up tips and techniques as they go, meeting new writers and observing them at work. If there were a metaphorical equivalent for this book, it would be of a trip, perhaps a field trip, where students learn by observing and by practicing what they've learned. Along the way, we send students to an editing workshop and guide their steps with various road signs indicating the direction they should follow. Think of this book, then, not merely as a text with the usual implication of dryness that word suggests, but as a road map that will whisk your students off to far-flung destinations, and then take them back to their own backyard a much better writer than when they began.

Acknowledgments

In this revision, we have been ably guided by the advice of our Development Editor, Laurie Runion; Dickson Musslewhite, Acquisitions Editor; Samantha Ross, Production Project Manager; Sheri Blaney, Photo Manager; and Merrill Peterson, Project Manager. To all of them we offer our heartfelt thanks.

We would also like to gratefully acknowledge the reviewers whose insightful suggestions helped shape this edition:

> Basak Tarkan-Blanco, *Miami Dade College*
> Jeffrey Hotz, *Montgomery College*
> Kathleen Furlong, *Glendale Community College*
> Paul Haeder, *Spokane Falls Community College*
> Melissa McCool, *Mississippi State University*
> Steve Morrison, *South Texas College*
> Ursula Scott, *Daytona Beach Community College*
> LeAnn Smith, *Eastern Illinois University*

Jo Ray McCuen-Metherell
Anthony C. Winkler

PART ONE

Reading and Writing
From Reading to Writing

A veteran English teacher once remarked to us that she had known readers who were not writers, but she had never known writers who were not readers. Neither have we. All writers begin as eager readers and continue to read throughout their lives. Their lifelong pleasure in reading wanes only in the presence of the greater pleasure they take in writing.

You may not be a writer in the sense of making a living from what you write, and you may not even write every day. But like it or not, you read every day, even if it is nothing more than the sign on a passing bus or the words on a billboard. Unless you live in a cave or on a desert island, modern life compels you to read.

All of us begin life as nonreaders. Reading is a skill that begins in childhood and shapes the growth of our intellect in ways that are still not completely understood. And even though we might have learned to read under peculiarly similar or different conditions, we all more or less share a similar reading history.

It began with the delight we felt when we first were taught to read. And once we were able to read on our own, many of us found ourselves swept away into magical worlds. Books took us on exotic journeys to places that existed only on the page and in our heads. We were visited by cats wearing hats, by talking rabbits, and by children who never grow old. We walked down yellow brick roads, sailed a balloon to the moon, and traveled with a crusty pirate in search of buried treasure on a remote island. Reading had planted in our heads a delightful high-definition TV called imagination, and never were colors brighter or images sharper.

But as we grew older a curious thing happened: Reading became associated with schoolwork as we were forced to read textbooks we disliked on subjects we hated. The very act of opening a book became a labor. Soon we were watching television to relax and reading only when we had to because of schoolwork. For many, reading changed from fun to drudgery. A lucky few retained a deep love of reading and will continue throughout their lives to read for fun. Speaking for them, the famous eighteenth-century British historian Edward Gibbon wrote in his *Memoirs*: "My early and invincible love of reading, I would not exchange for the treasures of India."

If you wish to write, you should develop the habit of reading. The skill of writing well is essentially a kind of mimicry, and the more writers we read, the more examples we can choose to imitate. And although reading voraciously is no guarantee that you will write well, your writing is likely to get better if you continue to be an avid reader.

The first part of this book—*Reading and Writing*—covers the preliminary topics of a writing course. Chapter 1 covers critical reading and introduces us to one of America's most prolific writers, himself an avid reader who devoured hundreds of books each year. Chapter 2 examines the role of rhetoric, an ancient discipline that is much misunderstood today. Chapter 3 covers the writer's voice, while Chapters 4, 5, and 6 deal first with the nuts-and-bolts of choosing a thesis topic and organizing a paper, and then with the indispensable craft of paragraph writing.

Among the lessons Part 1 teaches is this: Writing is not an isolated skill that exists apart from the intellect of the individual. It is, instead, ingrained in the whole person. Read widely and your writing is likely to get better as your judgment of good writing matures. You are also likely to rediscover pleasures you once derived from memorable storybooks—pleasures that have no box office charge, no crowds, and require no hardware more elaborate than a library card.

1

Guidelines for Critical Reading

KINDS OF READING

There are at least four different kinds of reading. *Casual reading* is the most common. Everyone does it. The casual reader glances at magazines, newspaper headlines, letters, e-mail messages, and roadside signs. Casual readers read not because they want to, but because they must. Many people, if not most, fall into this category.

Reading for pleasure—whether mystery novels, romances, or tales of adventure—is the second common kind of reading. Reading of this kind is relaxed and uncritical. Many readers do it at bedtime to help them fall asleep. Pleasure readers don't worry about grasping the writer's full meaning as long as they get the gist of it and are transported by the writing to an imaginary world.

Reading for information, the third kind of reading, is practiced by information seekers who use reading as a tool. This type of reading is usually done at work or at school. Doing a job well or completing an assignment on schedule is the primary purpose of reading for information. This type of reading requires attention, understanding, and memorization.

Finally, there is *critical reading*—the kind of reading you must do for your college classes. Critical reading is active reading. You engage in a kind of mental dialogue with the writer. The writer says so-and-so is the case and you reply, "Maybe so, but what about this?" You annotate the margins of the book you're reading with your reactions and comments. You not only try to understand the author's main point, but you also try to deduce any consequences of it. To be a critical reader, you must take the following steps:

1. **Read actively.** Determine the author's main point as well as any secondary effects that stem from it. Ask yourself whether you agree or disagree with the author's opinions. If you disagree, make a note in the margin saying why. If the author makes a mistake of logic or fact, make a note on the page where it occurred.

2. **Demystify the writer.** Many of us have the tendency to regard writers as godlike and to take everything they say as the gospel. But writers are only human and are just as likely to make mistakes as anyone else. Reading

critically begins with kicking the writer off the throne of public esteem and regarding the writer's work as you would any other human production—which is to say, prone to error.

3. **Understand what you read.** Reread difficult passages, looking up in a dictionary all the unfamiliar words. You cannot form an opinion of what you have read unless you understand what the author is saying. Some students find it helpful to summarize aloud any difficult ideas they encounter. Reread any difficult chapter or essay whose meaning you didn't completely comprehend. A difficult-to-understand point usually seems clearer the second time around. For example, Tolstoy's massive novel *War and Peace*, on first reading, seems like a tangled plot cluttered by an overwhelming mass of scenes and characters. On second reading, however, the plot will seem clearer and the scenes and characters more understandable.

4. **Imagine an opposing point of view for all opinions.** If the writer says that the Arab punishment of cutting off the hands of a thief is more humane than the American system of imprisonment, reverse the argument and see what happens. In other words, look for reasons that support the other side. For example, if an essay is passionately against the use of dogs in medical research, try to see the opposing point of view—namely, the benefits of such research to the lives of millions who suffer terrible diseases. A little digging will reveal that insulin, whose introduction has prolonged the lives of millions of diabetics, was discovered through research on dogs. The argument boils down to this question: Does a puppy have the same worth as a human baby?

5. **Look for biases and hidden assumptions.** For example, an atheist arguing for abortion will not attribute a soul to the unborn fetus; a devout Catholic will. To ferret out possible biases and hidden assumptions, check the author's age, sex, education, and ethnic background. These and other personal biographical facts might have influenced the opinions expressed in the work, but you cannot know to what extent unless you know something about the author. (That is the rationale behind the use of biographical headnotes, which accompany the readings in this book.)

6. **Separate emotion from fact.** Talented writers frequently color an issue with emotionally charged language, thus casting their opinions in the best possible light. For example, a condemned murderer may be described in sympathetic language that draws attention away from his or her horrifying crime. Be alert to sloganeering, to bumper sticker philosophizing about complex issues. To the neutral observer, few issues are as simple as black and white. Abortion is a more complex issue than either side presents. Capital punishment is not simply a matter of vengeance versus mercy. The tendency in public debate is to demonize the opposition and reduce issues to emotional slogans. As a critical reader, you must evaluate an argument by applying logic and reason and not be swayed by the emotionality of either side.

7. **If the issue is new to you, look up the facts.** If you are reading about an unfamiliar issue, be willing to fill in the gaps in your knowledge with research. For example, if you are reading an editorial that proposes raising home insurance rates for families taking care of foster children, you will want to know why. Is it because foster children do more property damage than other children? Is it because natural parents are apt to file lawsuits against foster parents? You can find answers to these questions by asking representatives of the affected parties: the State Department of Social Services, typical insurance agencies, foster-parents associations, the county welfare directors association, any children's lobby, and others. To make a critical judgment you must know, and carefully weigh, the facts.

8. **Use insights from one subject to illuminate or correct another.** Be prepared to apply what you already know to whatever you read. History can inform psychology; literature can provide insights into geography. For example, if a writer in psychology argues that most oppressed people develop a defeatist air that gives them a subconscious desire to be subjugated and makes them prey to tyrants, your knowledge of American history should tell you otherwise. As proof that oppressed people often fight oppression unto death, you can point to the Battle of Fallen Timbers in 1794, to the Battle of Tippecanoe in 1811, and to the Black Hawk War of 1832—conflicts in which the Indians fought desperately to retain their territories rather than go meekly to the reservations. In other words, you can use what you have learned from history to refute a falsehood from psychology.

9. **Evaluate the evidence.** Critical readers do not accept evidence at face value. They question its source, its verifiability, its appropriateness. Here are some practical tips for evaluating evidence:

    - **Verify a questionable opinion by cross-checking with other sources.** For example, if a medical writer argues that heavy smoking tends to cause serious bladder diseases in males, check the medical journals for confirmation of this view. Diligent research often turns up a consensus of opinion among the experts in any field.

    - **Check the date of the evidence.** In science especially, evidence varies from year to year. Before 1987, no one really knew exactly how the immune system worked. Then Susumu Tonegawa, a geneticist at the Massachusetts Institute of Technology, discovered how the immune system protects the body from foreign substances by manufacturing antibodies. In 1980, the evidence would say that the working of the immune system was a mystery, but that evidence would be inaccurate in 1987.

    - **Use common sense in evaluating evidence.** For example, if a writer argues that a child's handwriting can accurately predict his or her life as an adult, your own experience with human nature should lead you to reject this conclusion as speculative. No convincing evidence exists to corroborate it.

10. **Ponder the values behind an argument.** In writing the Declaration of Independence, Thomas Jefferson based his arguments on the value that "all men are created equal." On the other hand, Karl Marx based the arguments of his *Communist Manifesto* on the value that the laborer is society's greatest good. Critical reading means thinking about the values implicit in an argument. For instance, to argue that murderers should be hanged in public to satisfy society's need for revenge is to value revenge over human dignity. On the other hand, to argue that democracy can exist only with free speech is to value freedom of speech.

11. **Recognize logical fallacies.** The following logical flaws are among the ones most commonly used in a wide range of arguments: the *ad hominem* attack (attacking the person instead of the point of view or the argument); the *ad populum* appeal (the use of simplistic popular slogans to convince); the *false analogy* (comparing situations that have no bearing on each other); *begging the question* (arguing in circles); *ignoring the question* (focusing on matters that are beside the point); *either/or reasoning* (seeing the problem as all black or all white, with no shades of gray); *hasty generalizaion* (the mistake of inadequate sampling); *non sequitur* (drawing a conclusion that is not connected to the evidence given). For a more detailed discussion of logical fallacies, turn to Chapter 15.

12. **Don't be seduced by bogus claims.** Arguments are often based on unsubstantiated statements. For example, a writer may warn that "recent studies show women becoming increasingly hostile to men." Or, another writer might announce, "Statistics have shown beyond doubt that most well-educated males oppose gun control." You should always remain skeptical of these and similar claims when they are unaccompanied by hard-headed evidence. A proper claim will always be documented with verifiable evidence.

13. **Annotate your reading.** Many of us have the tendency to become lazy readers. We sit back with a book and almost immediately lapse into a daze. One way to avoid being a lazy reader is to annotate your reading—to write notes in the margins as you read. Many students are reluctant to scribble in the margins of a book because they hope to resell it at the end of the term. But this is a penny-wise-and-pound-foolish outlook. Instead of aiming to resell the book, your focus should be on getting the most out of it; annotating is one way to do that. Indeed, to make notes in the margins of books is, in a way, to interact with the reading—almost like chatting with the author. If you can't bring yourself to write directly on the printed page of this book, we suggest you make notes on a separate sheet as you read. Here are some suggestions for annotating your reading:

    - **Write down your immediate impression of the essay.**
        a. Did the subject interest you?
        b. Did the reading leave you inspired, worried, angry, amused, or better informed?
        c. Did the reading remind you of something in your own experience? (Cite the experience.)

d. Did you agree or disagree with the author? (Note specific passages.)
e. Did the reading give you any new ideas?
- **Note the author's style, especially the words or expressions used.**
  a. What specific passages really made you think?
  b. Where did the writer use an especially apt expression or image? What was it? What made it so good?
  c. Where, if any place, did the author write "over your head"?
  d. What kind of audience did the author seem to address? Did it include you or did you feel left out?
- **Make marginal notes that express your response to the author's ideas.**
  a. Supplement the author's idea or example with one of your own.
  b. Underline passages that seem essential to the author's point.
  c. Write any questions you might want to ask the author if he or she were sitting next to you.
  d. Write down any sudden insight you experienced.
  e. Write why you disagree with the author.
  f. Write a marginal explanation of any allusion made by the writer. For example, in the fourth paragraph of this chapter, we wrote, "We were visited by cats wearing hats, by talking rabbits, and by children who never grow old." Did you understand these three allusions? The first is a reference to *The Cat in the Hat* by Dr. Seuss; the second, to *Alice in Wonderland*; the third, to *Peter Pan*.

14. **Finally, be sure you understand the writer's opening context.** The writing may be part of an ongoing debate that began before you arrived and will continue after you've left. Some essays begin by plunging right into an ongoing discussion, taking for granted that the reader is familiar with the opening context. The effect can be mystifying, like hearing an answer but not knowing the question.

Here are the principles of critical reading applied to a brief essay by CBS News commentator Andy Rooney. The annotations in the margins raise questions that we think any reasonable critical reader would ask. At the end of the essay, we provide the answers.

Margin notes:
1. What is the opening context of this article?
2. Who is Fowler?

1   I would choose to have written Fowler's *Modern English Usage*.

2   My book, known far and wide and for all time as Rooney's *Modern English Usage* and comparable in sales to the Bible, would have assured my fame and fortune. Even more than that, if I'd had the kind of command of the language it would take to have written it, I would never again be uncertain about whether to use *further* or *farther*, *hung* or *hanged*, *dived* or *dove*. When I felt lousy and wanted to write

about it, I'd know whether to say I felt *nauseous* or *nauseated*.

> 3. What is his book about?

3   If I was the intellectual guru of grammar, as author of that tome, I would issue updated decrees on usage such as an end to the pretentious subjunctive. Not if I were.

> 4. What do we learn about Fowler's book in this paragraph?

4   I would split infinitives at will when I damn well felt like it, secure in my knowledge that I was setting the standard for when to and when not to. Challenged by some petty grammarian quoting a high school English textbook, I would quote myself and say, as Fowler does, "Those upon whom the fear of infinitive-splitting sits heavy should remember that to give conclusive evidence, by distortions, of misconceiving the nature of the split infinitive is far more damaging to their literary pretensions than an actual lapse could be, for it exhibits them as deaf to the normal rhythm of English sentences."

> 5. What is Rooney doing here?

5   Never again would I suffer indecision over matters like whether it was necessary for me to use an "of" after "a propos." I would not be looking up "arcane" eight or ten times a year. I would not use "like" when I meant "such as."

> 6. What does this quotation tell us about Fowler?

6   The fine difference between sophisticated bits of usage such as syllepsis and zeugma would be clear in my mind. ("She ate an omelet and her heart out" is either syllepsis or zeugma. I am unclear which.)

> 7. What do these terms mean?

7   Having produced the best book on English usage ever written, I would berate the editors of the newly issued *New York Times Manual of Style and Usage* for their insistence that the President of the United States be referred to as merely president except when used as a title immediately preceding his name. In my book he's The President. Corporate chief executives are plain president.

> 8. What is the best book ever written on English usage?

8   I would conduct a nationwide poll to choose a satisfactory gender neutral replacement for both "he" "she," "him" and "her." This would relieve writers of the cumbersome but socially correct necessity of "he or she," "him or her," or the grammatically incorrect "they" or "their" with a singular precedent. ("Someone left their keys.")

> 9. What does this paragraph mean?

9   Eventually, I'd expect Oliver Stone to buy the movie rights to Rooney's *Modern English Usage*. His film would prove it was neither I nor me who murdered the English language.

> 10. What is the significance of either "I nor me"?

Kinds of Reading   9

Answers to Critical Reading Questions on Andy Rooney

1. If you do not know the opening context of this essay, you're likely to miss the writer's intent—although you could probably reconstruct it from his essay. Rooney's essay initially appeared in the 2000 annual awards *Journal of the Screenwriters' Guild* as part of a feature called *A Writer's Fantasy—What I Wish I Had Written*. Various writers, Rooney among them, were asked to select the one work they wish they had written and say why.

2. Henry Watson Fowler (1858–1933) was an English lexicographer and philologist—someone who studies linguistics—who, in collaboration with his younger brother Frank, published in 1906 *The King's English,* a witty book on English usage and misusage. After the death of his brother, Fowler completed the classic Rooney wished he had written, *A Dictionary of Modern English Usage* (1926). Fowler was known for being definitive and blunt in his grammatical and literary opinions.

    He wrote, "Anyone who wishes to become a good writer should endeavor, before he allows himself to be tempted by the more showy qualities, to be direct, simple, brief, vigorous, and lucid"—certainly good advice for anyone who writes.

3. Many people consider *A Dictionary of Modern English Usage* to be the definitive book on English usage and grammar. Grammarians often consult it to settle arguments over the fine points of acceptable usage.

4. We learn in this paragraph that Fowler's book sold as well as the Bible and that its popularity ensured fame and fortune to its writer.

5. He's mocking the rule of the subjunctive, which many people think is an ugly Latin holdover.

6. It gives us a glimpse of the sometimes starchy writing style of Fowler, who is capable of going from clarity and plainness to a scholastic denseness in a single page.

7. These are examples of the kind of arcane topics that Fowler deals with in his book. *Syllepsis* refers to the use of a word in the same grammatical relationship with two other words while disagreeing in case, gender, number, or sense with one of them. An example is "Neither she nor they are coming," where *are* agrees with *they* but not with *she.* Syllepsis is also a figure of speech in which a single word is linked to two others but in different senses, as in this use of *write,* "I write with enthusiasm and a pen." *Zeugma* refers to the linking of one word to two, one of which it does not grammatically fit, as in this use of *were:* "The seeds were devoured but the banana uneaten."

8. Obviously Fowler's, in Rooney's opinion.

9. Rooney is referring here to the quest for a nonsexist, third-person pronoun so that a sentence like "A doctor should take care of his patients" can be written without the sexist bias implicit in the use of "his." In 1858, Charles Crozat Converse, of Erie, Pennsylvania, proposed the use of *thon,* a shortened form of *that one,* as a neutral, third-person pronoun—"A doctor should take care of thon patients"—but the word never caught on.

10. Again, Rooney is spoofing another fusty rule from English grammar—namely, that the verb "to be" takes no object. Rigorous practice of this rule is responsible for the snooty construction one hears over the telephone occasionally: "It is I" or "This is he."

Education of a Wandering Man
Louis L'Amour

Louis L'Amour (1908–1988) was a prolific writer of western stories. Born March 22, 1908, Louis Dearborn LaMoore, in Jamestown, North Dakota, the family's seventh and youngest child, L'Amour dropped out of high school when he was 15 and wandered around the country, earning a living with odd jobs as a lumberjack, elephant handler, and longshoreman. After serving in World War II, L'Amour turned his attention to becoming a writer, publishing pulp short stories in popular magazines. He eventually specialized in western stories, producing more than three books a year until his death in 1988. A voracious reader his entire life, L'Amour kept a running tally of every book he read, recording, for example, the titles of 115 books and plays he read in 1930.

In this chapter from his autobiography, Education of a Wandering Man, *L'Amour shares his thoughts about books, civilizations, writing, and people. The reading is included here to give you an opportunity to exercise your newly learned skill of critical reading. As you read the material, ask yourself what portrait of L'Amour, the man, emerges.*

• • •

1   Only one who has learned much can fully appreciate his ignorance. He knows so well the limits of his knowledge and how much lies waiting to be learned.

2   What had men thought? What had men believed? How did they come by those thoughts and beliefs? How had men learned to govern themselves? Were the processes the same everywhere?

3   Did man build cities because of an inner drive, like that of the beaver to build dams? How much of what we do is free will, and how much programmed in our genes? Why is each people so narrow that it believes that it, and it alone, has all the answers? In religion, is there but one road to salvation? Or are there many, all equally good, all going in the same general direction?

4   I have read my books by many lights, hoarding their beauty, their wit or wisdom against the dark days when I would have no book, nor a place to read.

5   I have known hunger of the belly kind many times over, but I have known a worse hunger: the need to know and to learn.

6   Once, when hitchhiking, I was picked up by a professor from some small college. He noticed I carried a book in my coat pocket, and was curious. It was a Modern Library edition, in the limp bindings they used to have, which sold at the time for 95 cents. This one contained Nietzsche's *Ecce Homo*, and *The Birth of Tragedy*.

7   The professor was a pedantic man of limited imagination and seemed almost offended that I was reading such a book. (I suspected after a few minutes' conversation that he had not read it himself.) He plied me with questions. Obviously I did not fit some category in which he decided I belonged, and when he dropped me off in town, I suspect he was relieved to be rid of me.

8   He kept asking me why I wanted to read such a book. At first, he doubted I was reading it. Where had I heard of Nietzsche?

9   When I told him I thought it was in the preface to a book on Schopenhauer, he was even more disturbed and probably believed I was lying. Fortunately, there seem to be few of his kind, and my subsequent friendships with university professors have proved exciting, stimulating, and fun. Perhaps I was fortunate in that the first group I met was at the University of Oklahoma in the 1930s. At that time I met Kenneth C. Kaufman, Ben Botkin, Walter Stanley Campbell (who also wrote as Stanley Vestal), Carl Coke Rister, Paul Sears, and others. Sears had just written *Deserts on the March,* one of the very first books on ecology, when that word was scarcely known. I believe also that the book was the first best seller to come from a university press. Stuart Chase followed it a bit later with *Rich Land, Poor Land,* also on the subject, in 1936.

10   Having been over a lot of country I had seen what was happening to the land, and was pleased to get a chance to review Sears's book for a farm magazine. Ecology had been getting into some of my stories, principally one titled "Merrano of the Dry Country." It appeared in a pulp magazine and dealt not only with proper usage of the land but with the race question. That story first appeared about forty years ago, or a bit more.

11   The lists of books I read in my earlier years have largely been lost, but my memory for some is clear. It was a knock-about time for me: of going to sea, working in mines, lumber camps, and sawmills, doing whatever was available to make an honest dollar. Many of the activities of young men of the time I missed entirely, or in part. Either I was working, traveling from one place to another, or else I did not have the money to afford it.

12   At the time I thought that I might make a career of fighting. My early training had been good, and in knocking about the country I had picked up a few dollars here and there in small-town boxing rings. For that reason, among others, I never smoked and rarely had a drink. The idea that it might be fun to get drunk never appealed to me, for I had come to believe I could cope with any situation that might arise if I had my wits about me. There was one night in Shanghai when I was in more trouble than one man could handle. Three drunken British sailors pitched in to help, and help they did, but at bitter cost to themselves. Had they been sober, with the right coordination and reflexes, I think they would have made it.

13   Several times while traveling in Asia I hired students to read sight translations of books unavailable, so far as I knew, in English. On occasion this took place on a riverbank. Several times it was in coffee- or teahouses, where we never failed to pick up an interested audience. In one case a rather violent

argument developed between the reader and a listener over a line from an Indian poet, Bhartrihari. I thought the Indus River was about to flow with fresh blood, but after a good deal of shouting and waving of arms and flashing eyes, the listener strode away. When he was well out of hearing, my reader said, "He may be right, at that."

14   (It was Bhartrihari, incidentally, who said of a woman: "She talks to one man, looks at a second, and thinks of a third.")

15   One book always led to another and occasionally my discoveries led to a whole succession of books, but there was no intent in my reading except to learn and to know. Later, when I actually began doing research on various eras of history, from curiosity or because of something I wished to write, all that changed.

16   I read *Crime and Punishment* while in Klamath Falls, Oregon. I had heard much of Dostoevsky but was surprised by this book—surprised and very impressed. Several times I turned back to reread sections of the book. At the time I was working in a sawmill, off-bearing on the green chain. And that, my friends, is purely hard work.

17   When a log is cut into planks, those planks (in this case three inches thick and twelve inches wide) are green, fresh-cut lumber, and heavy. One takes a plank from the chain and puts it aboard a truck standing nearby. Meanwhile, the chain from the saw is bringing more planks, and more and more. If one is strong, reasonably agile, and gets his timing right, he can put in an eight-hour shift without too much trouble, but for hours at a stretch those planks keep coming. That is one description of off-bearing on the green chain.

18   (It has been years since I have been in a sawmill, and it is probably all done by machinery now, as are most of the jobs I used to do. I feel very sorry indeed for any young man without an education in these days, for there is literally nowhere to go.)

19   Also while on that job I read *The Moonstone* by Wilkie Collins, as well as *Plain Tales from the Hills* and *Kim* (for the second time), both by Kipling.

20   We hear a lot of talk these days about violence, but we forget the many generations that have grown up on stories of violence. The bloodiest of all, perhaps, were the so-called fairy tales, but I would have missed none of them and doubt if I did, yet I see little difference between Jack killing a fabled giant and Wyatt Earp shooting it out with an outlaw.

21   It often appears that violence is bad unless it is cloaked with enough tradition. There is much violence in the Bible, and the story could have been told in no other way. Many of Shakespeare's plays end with nearly everybody killed or dead by suicide. If we were to eliminate violence from our reading, we would have to eliminate all history, much of the world's great drama, as well as the daily newspaper.

22   What many people do not understand is that a child in growing up repeats within his early years much of the life history of man upon the earth, and it is necessary that he or she do this to become a human being.

23   At first a baby is simply a small animal that eats and sleeps, but there will come a time when he will want to build a shelter, to find some place he can crawl into, even if it is only a blanket over a chair or a table. Then there will be a time when the child plays capture games, wants a bow and arrow or perhaps a spear or other weapon. By acting out those early years of mankind's history, children put that history behind them. Most violent criminals are cases of arrested development where, for one reason or another, they never grow out of that period.

24   A girl, of course, will play with dolls, playing at being a mother, making a home, and what goes with it. All this is an essential part of growing up, of learning to be a human.

25   Much of this early violence can be sublimated through reading. In my own stories, there is no violence for the sake of violence. I tell it as it happened and, my books are all thoroughly grounded in history. What so many of us who abhor violence often forget is that we have peace and civilized lives because there were men and women who went before us who were willing to fight for our freedom to live in peace.

26   It is always well to remember that many of us sleep safe at night because there are people out there cruising the streets and on call to keep it so. As many have discovered, violence is with us still, and no one is immune to a sudden strike in the night.

27   One of the questions a writer is most often asked is "Where do you get your ideas?" If a person does not have ideas, he had better not even think of becoming a writer. But ideas are everywhere. There are ideas enough in any daily newspaper to keep a man writing for years. Ideas are all about us, in the people we meet, the way we live, the way we travel, and how we think about things. It's important to remember that we are writing about people. Ideas are important only as they affect people. And we are writing about emotion. A few people reason, but all people feel.

28   The raw material is not important. It is what the writer does with the material. One writer will make you laugh, another can make you cry, and a third might write a horror story.

29   At least once a week I get a letter from someone who has material he wants me to shape into a story (wanting, of course, a piece of the action). But a writer builds a readership because those readers like what he does with a story, not because of the material.

30   There are only a certain number of plots, and they are very basic. When Ray Long was editor of *Cosmopolitan* years ago, he gave the same plot to six different writers, and they came up with six vastly different stories.

31   Plots are nothing devious. I have heard some literary or dramatic critics talk of plot in ways that indicated they had no grasp of the idea at all. A plot is nothing but a normal human situation that keeps arising again and again. Shakespeare's work has lived as long as it has because he dealt with normal human emotions—envy, ambition, rivalry, love, hate, greed, and so on. These are basic drives among us humans and are with us forever.

32   Because I have traveled widely it is often suspected I traveled for the purpose of gathering material. That was not the reason. Material is wherever you find it, or can see it. Some of the greatest novels have been written about small areas. Thomas Hardy and William Faulkner, for example, wrote about country districts they knew well. The Brontë sisters (whose name was originally Prunty) wrote about the part of England in which they lived.

33   It is not necessary to travel in order to write good stories; it is only necessary to see, to understand, to reveal.

34   What few realize is that no writer is free to write exactly as he might wish. He is guided, to a great extent, by the tastes of readers and by the choices of editors. Of course, one can write whatever one wishes, but unless it conforms to the tastes of the public at the time, it will stay right on the author's shelf.

35   All manner of weird conjectures have grown up around Edgar Allan Poe, for example, but few have ever understood that he was writing what the public wanted to buy. In the first half of the nineteenth century, over in Europe, Mary Shelley was writing *Frankenstein* and Baudelaire was writing his macabre poetry and prose, while in this country Hawthorne was writing "Rappaccini's Daughter," and Washington Irving was writing *The Legend of Sleepy Hollow*. And this has been true in every age and time.

36   For a while I worked in the big timber but could not bear to see the big ones come down. I topped trees for a time, cleared brush, did whatever was available, but the times were growing worse. When the crash came in '29, we who were on the road hardly noticed the difference.

37   Yet it was a time for decision and I had made mine. If I was ever to get an education beyond my haphazard reading, it must be now.

- Vocabulary

  pedantic (7)   succession (15)   agile (17)
  sublimated (25)   abhor (25)   conjectures (35)
  macabre (35)   haphazard (37)

- Questions for Critical Reading

  1. Paragraphs 2 and 3 consist of a series of questions that L'Amour asked himself. What do these questions tell you about the man?
  2. What lesson is L'Amour teaching in relating the episode with the professor? Why do you think the professor was so surprised? What does his reaction to L'Amour tell you about this unnamed person?
  3. What question would a diligent reader ask about paragraph 13?
  4. What accusation could a modern reader make about L'Amour's attitude toward women?
  5. What theory about criminality does L'Amour espouse in paragraphs 21 through 23?

6. L'Amour claims that there are only so many plots available to a writer and what is important is what the writer does with them. Name two of these basic plots that different writers seem to use over and over again.
7. Read paragraph 32. Based on what you've learned in this chapter, what would a critical reader do after reading this paragraph?
8. How would you characterize the author's attitude toward the land?

For tips on how to revise your work, exit on page 682 to the **Editing Booth!**

2

What Is Rhetoric?

ROAD MAP TO RHETORIC

Rhetoric is the art of putting one's case in the strongest and best possible way. All of the strategies of communicating in speech and writing that we use daily in an attempt to sway each other come under its heading, with practical effects so lasting and widespread that we take them for granted. For instance, when we open a popular cookbook, we expect it to be written clearly, with ordinary words framed into speakable sentences. We do not expect it to be dense and wordy like a piece of legislation. Because of rhetoric, cookbooks are not written like legal contracts; insurance policies do not read like a comic's jokes; and love letters do not sound like State of the Union speeches.

Yet, there is no law requiring that this should be so. It is merely the effect of rhetoric—a combination of audience expectation and writers' desire to please that operates like a force of nature. No doubt there are badly written cookbooks, but few are either published or read; flippant insurance companies go bankrupt; and pompous lovers have trouble finding mates. This desire of writers to please—to communicate with their audiences—is the basic law of rhetoric.

Grammar and Rhetoric

In the minds of some students, grammar and rhetoric are often confused, but they are significantly different. Grammar tells a writer how words should be used and sentences framed. Just as drivers obey the rules of the road, writers follow the rules of grammar. They know that they should not begin a sentence with "one" and then suddenly switch to "you," as in "One must try to do well or you will be embarrassed." That is called a shift in point of view and, like most grammatical lapses, tends to muddy meaning.

While grammar speaks in terms of rules, rhetoric speaks only in terms of effectiveness—and effectiveness is always a relative judgment. If you are writing to a child, for example, you must use simple words and short sentences if you wish to be understood. However, simple words and short sentences may be entirely inappropriate in a paper explaining a complex process to an audience of specialists. When you know the rules of grammar, it is easy to compare two versions of a writing assignment and say if one is more conventionally grammatical than the other. It is far harder to say whether one version is more effectively written than the other.

Judging the effectiveness of a work is, in fact, the chief business of rhetoric. For example, consider this student paragraph:

> During high school, my favorite English course was English literature. Literature was not only interesting, but it was also fun. Learning about writers and poets of the past was enjoyable because of the teachers I had and the activities they scheduled. Teachers made past literature interesting because they could relate the writers back to the time in which they lived. This way I not only learned about English writers but also about English history.

Grammatically, this paragraph is correct; rhetorically, it is empty. It cries out for examples and supporting details. Which writers and poets did the student find so interesting? What activities did the teacher schedule to make them seem so? Without such details, the paragraph is shallow and monotonous.

Here is a paragraph on the same subject, written by a student with a strong sense of rhetoric:

> Picture a shy small-town girl of eighteen, attending college for the first time in a large city. She is terrified of the huge campus with its crowds of bustling students, but she is magnetically drawn to a course entitled "Survey of English Literature," for this awkward girl has always been an avid reader. College for me, this alien creature on campus, was the sudden revelation of a magical new world. I now could read the great English literary masterpieces—Milton's *Paradise Lost,* Shakespeare's *Othello,* Jane Austen's *Pride and Prejudice.* Then I could discuss them in class under the watchful eye of my professor, who encouraged me to dig for ideas and interpret them on my own. As the teacher asked questions, and the students responded to them, I received exciting flashes of insight into the human condition: I understood the loneliness of *Jude the Obscure,* the hardness of life in *Oliver Twist,* and the extravagant beauty of nature as detailed by the Romantic poets. English literature also led me into the mazy paths of history. I learned about the greed for political power as I read about the War of the Roses. I saw how the *Magna Carta,* so reluctantly signed by King John, influenced our present democracy. And Chaucer's tales convinced me that the pageantry of people has not changed much since medieval times. English literature educated me without my being aware of the act of acquiring knowledge. I learned through falling in love with English literature.

The second paragraph is rhetorically more effective than the first because it tells us in richer detail exactly how the author was affected by her English classes.

Audience and Purpose

To write well, you must bear in mind two truths about writing: It has an audience and it is done for a purpose. Many students think that the audience of their writing is a single instructor whose tastes must be satisfied, but this viewpoint is too narrow. The instructor is your audience only in a symbolic sense. The instructor's real job is to be a stand-in for the educated reader. In this capacity, the instructor represents universal standards of today's writing. An English instructor knows writing, good and bad, and can tell you what is good about your work and what is not so good. In this capacity, your instructor can be compared to the working editor of a newspaper, and you, to a reporter.

Purpose, on the other hand, refers to what you hope to accomplish with your writing—the influence you calculate your work will exert on your reader. Contrary to what you might think, earning a grade is not the purpose of an essay. That might be its result, but it cannot be its purpose. A freelance writer who sits down to do an article has expectations of earning money for the effort, but that is not the writer's primary purpose. Instead, purpose refers to the intention—be it grand or simple—the writer had in mind when he or she first put pen to paper. If you are writing an essay about the funniest summer vacation you have ever had, your purpose is to amuse. If you are writing an essay about how amino acids are necessary for life, your purpose is to inform. If you are writing an essay urging mandatory jail terms for sellers of child pornography, your purpose is to persuade.

It follows from this discussion that you must understand the audience and purpose of an assignment if you are to have a context for judging the effectiveness of your words and sentences. Context hints at what might work and what might flop; it warns of perils and points to possible breakthroughs. Anyone knows that a love letter should not be written in the dense sentences of a bank report and that a note of sympathy to a grieving friend should not tell jokes—anyone, that is, who thinks about the audience and the purpose of the written words. As the English writer W. Somerset Maugham put it, "To write good prose is an affair of good manners." Like good manners, good prose is always appropriate. It fits the audience; it suits the purpose. This fitting and suiting of one's writing to audience and purpose are among the chief concerns of rhetoric.

The Internal Reader/Editor

The basic aim of any instruction in rhetoric is to teach you how to distinguish between what is appropriate and inappropriate for different audiences and purposes. You develop a sixth sense of what you should say in an essay for an English instructor, a note addressed to your mother, or an ad seeking a new roommate. We call this sixth sense the *internal reader/editor*. One writer defined it this way: " . . . as it is for any writer, there are two characters in my head: the Writer (me) and a Reader/Editor (also me), who represents anyone who reads what I write. These two talk to each other."

Your internal reader/editor is your sense for judging aptness and effectiveness in writing. This sense improves with practice and exposure to assignments intended for different audiences and purposes. Whether you are penning an essay for a psychology instructor or a letter to a creditor asking for more time to repay a debt, the same internal reader/editor judges the rhetorical and grammatical appropriateness of what you have written.

By the time you are old enough to read this book, your internal reader/editor is already in place and functioning with some sophistication. For example, your reader/editor surely knows that obscenities have no place in an essay, that "ain't" is not appropriate in a formal exam paper, and that a wealth of personal jokes and anecdotes do not belong in an objective paper on science.

Levels of English

Virtually all writing can be subdivided into three levels of English: formal, informal, and technical. Each has its place in the various assignments you will be asked to do. It is your internal reader/editor that must decide on the appropriateness of each for a specific assignment.

Formal English is characterized by full, complex sentences and the use of standard and consistent grammar. It states ideas in an orderly fashion and with an educated vocabulary. It avoids the "I" point of view and does not use contractions such as "can't," "don't," "he'd," or "wouldn't." Here is an example of formal English:

> As the sun rose higher that morning, swarms of canoes, or *canoas* as they were called in the Arawak language, were pushed out to sea through the surf breaking over the glistening white sands of Long Bay. They were all full of excited, painted Indians carrying balls of cotton thread, spears and vividly colored parrots to trade with the vessels lying a short distance off-shore. The Indian craft, probably painted as colorfully as their occupants, must have given the atmosphere of a festive regatta, and trading was brisk and lasted all day until nightfall.
>
> —D. J. R. Walker, *Columbus and the Golden World of the Island Arawaks*

The aim of formal writing is to make a case or present an argument impartially rather than to relate the writer's own views on a subject. The writer takes special care to eliminate the "I" reference and to remain discreetly in the background. Examples are either generalized or in the third person, but never personal. The facts are allowed to speak for themselves; the writer's task is to present them with objectivity.

Formal English is the staple of college writing. You should use it in research papers, scholarly papers, written examinations, and serious letters. Unless instructed to do otherwise, you should also use it in your essays.

Informal English is based on the familiar grammatical patterns and constructions of everyday speech. It uses short sentences, contractions, the "I" point of view, and colloquial expressions. Informal English is commonly found in much journalistic writing and in personal letters, diaries, and light essays. The following student essay is a typical example:

> I drive a truck for a living, and every other week I'm assigned to a senior driver called Harry. Now, Harry is the dirtiest person I've ever met. Let's start with the fact that he never takes a bath or shower. Sitting in the closed cab of a diesel truck on a hot August day with Harry is like being shut up in a rendering plant; in fact, the smell he emanates has, on many occasions, made my eyes water and my stomach turn. I always thought Harry was just dark complexioned until it rained one day and his arms started to streak—I mean this guy is a self-inflicted mud slide. In fact, I could've sworn that once or twice I saw Harry scratch his head and a cloud of dust whirled up above him.

The legitimate topics of informal writing are what the writer thinks or has experienced. It makes free use of the pronoun "I" and draws its material mainly from the writer's personal stock of opinions or memories. Because most of us are thoroughly fascinated with ourselves and have no trouble setting down what we think, informal English is the first kind of writing we are taught. Some assignments, given mainly in English departments, demand its use. For example, you could not write that old standby on your most memorable summer vacation without being subjective, nor should you even try.

Use informal English only in your personal writing and in those special circumstances where you are free to express yourself in your own individualistic style.

Technical English is formal English that uses the vocabulary of a specialized field. It is written most often by engineers, technicians, and scientists. It commonly suffers from wordiness, overuse of abstract nouns, misuse of the passive voice, and improper subordination. Nevertheless, some technical writers are experts at their craft. Here is an example of technical writing:

Installing the ViaVoice Software

1. Insert the ViaVoice CD in your CD-ROM drive to start the installation program. If it does not start automatically, do the following:
   a. Click **Start > Run** from the Windows taskbar.
   b. Type d:setup (where *d* is your CD-ROM drive).
   c. Click OK.
2. Follow the instructions on the screen.

—*IBM ViaVoice for Windows User's Guide*

If you enter a specialized field and have to write about your work, most of your writing will be technical writing.

The level of English you should use in any specific essay will depend on its audience and purpose; that is a judgment your internal reader/editor must make. Let us take an example. Your English teacher asks you to write an essay on the most unforgettable date you've ever had. One student wrote this paragraph:

> My most unforgettable date was with Carolyn, whom I took to a drive-in movie. I chose the drive-in movie as the site of our date because Carolyn was nearly a foot taller than I, and I was embarrassed to be seen out in the open with her. What I did not expect was that my car would break down and I would not only have to get out and try to fix it, but that we would end up walking home side by side like Mutt and Jeff.

The tale that followed was a funny one about the writer's mishaps at the drive-in with Carolyn. He wrote the paragraph and the essay in an informal style because that is exactly what this assignment called for.

If, however, your sociology teacher asks you to write an essay on dating as a courtship ritual in America, you must write a formal essay. Instead of saying what happened to you personally on a date, you must say what is likely to happen on a date. Instead of airing your personal views, you must express the researched ideas and opinions of others. You should not use the pronoun "I" to refer to yourself nor attempt to impose your personality on the material. This does not mean that you should have no opinions of your own—quite the opposite—but you should base your expressed opinions on grounds more substantial than personal experience or unsupported belief. Here is an example of a student paper that follows the rules of objectivity:

> Dating is a universal courtship experience in the life of most American adolescents. The ritual goes back to the earliest chaperoned drawing-room meetings between eligible couples and has evolved to the present-day social outing. But the greatest impact on the ritual, so far as its American practice goes, has been the introduction and popularization of the automobile.

The writer supported her thesis—that the automobile has had a drastic impact on the dating ritual in America—throughout the paper and amply supported it with statistics, facts, and the testimony of experts. Her examples are also generalized rather than personal. Instead of writing that so-and-so happened to me on a date, she wrote that so-and-so is likely to happen to an American couple dating.

All writers will similarly adapt their language to suit the audience and purpose of their writing, using the principles that spring from common sense and the ancient discipline of rhetoric. While much of this adapting may be done unconsciously, it still must be done by all who sincerely wish to communicate with an audience.

Writing as a Process

Learning to write well cannot be mastered by rote the way you might absorb facts about the anatomy of a fish or the chemistry of a nebula. It involves learning a process, and that is always harder to do than memorizing a set of facts. The parts of a bicycle can be memorized from a manual, but no one can learn to ride a bicycle merely by reading a book about it. *Scribendo disces scribere,* says the Latin proverb: "You learn to write by writing." Here, then, are some truths about the writing process uncovered by laboratory research:

- **Composing is a difficult, back-and-forth process.** Many writers compose in a halting, lurching way. A writer will pen a few sentences, pause to go back and revise them, compose several new sentences, and then pause again to reread and further edit before continuing with the paragraph. "In their thinking and writing," says one researcher, "writers 'go back' in order to push thought forward."

    Any professional writer will recognize the truth of this observation, but often it comes as a revelation to students who tend to worry when their own compositions emerge by similar fits and starts. Be assured that this back-and-forth movement is a healthy and normal part of composing. The research even suggests that writers who accept the halting, stumbling nature of composing actually have an easier time with this necessary process of "waiting, looking, and discovering" than those who fight against it.

    Because of this circularity in composing, writing is often described as a *recursive process,* meaning that results are achieved by a roundabout rather than a straight-line path. Often it is necessary to retrace one's trail, to go back to the beginning of a work, to revise earlier sentences and paragraphs before writing new ones. If you find yourself doing something similar in your own writing, be heartened by this truth: That is how the vast majority of writers work. You are merely going through the normal cycle of composing.

- **The topic can make a difference in your writing.** Professional or amateur, few writers are entirely free to choose their own topics. Most are assigned topics by employers, professors, circumstances. Yet, when choice does exist, the lesson from common sense and research is that you should always pick the topic you like best. The fact is that most people write better when they write about a subject that appeals to them.

    It is no mystery why this should be so. We all try harder when we are engaged in a labor of love—whether building our dream house or writing an essay. Unfortunately, in a classroom setting, many students are content to settle for a topic that seems simplest to research or easiest to write about, regardless of whether or not they find it appealing. This is a mistake. When you write for your own enjoyment, you will behave more like an experienced writer than when you force yourself to write about a subject you find boring.

- **Your writing will not automatically improve with each essay.** Writing does not automatically get better with every paper. It is realistic to compare writing to, say, archery. The first arrow might hit the bull's-eye, while the tenth might entirely miss the target. An archer's overall accuracy will gradually improve with practice, but never to the point of absolute certainty for any one arrow. In practical terms, this simply means that you shouldn't brood if you find a later essay turning out worse than an earlier one. Your overall writing skills are bound to improve with experience, even if the improvement isn't reflected in any single essay.

The gist of this chapter may be summed up thus: You can learn to write well, and rhetoric can teach you how. Writing well means doing more than simply scribbling down the first idea that pops into your head. It involves thinking about your audience and purpose and choosing between this level of language and that. It means developing a rhetorical sense about what techniques are likely to work for a particular assignment. All of these skills can be learned from a study of rhetoric.

Writing about Visual Images

Visual images range from works of art found only in museums to photographs published in daily newspapers. They include television images, line drawings, sketches, computer graphics, and a bewitching gallery of exotic scenes and pictures of beautiful people from advertising. So widespread and influential are visual images that many instructors use them as essay topics. This book, for example, contains an image gallery on pages 647–678 whose exhibits you will be asked to interpret or evaluate in the context of the various readings they are meant to illustrate.

If you've never done this kind of writing before, don't worry. Writing about an image is not that different than writing about a pig, a poem, or an adventure. Here are some techniques for writing about artworks, news photographs, cartoons, and advertising images.

Writing about Artworks You do not have to be an art critic to write about a work of art, and you do not have to try to write like one. As in all kinds of writing, it is better for a writer to write from an honest self than to pretend to be someone else. In other words, be yourself always, whether you're writing about a real plum or one in a still-life painting. Here are some steps you can take to write about a work of art:

- **Study the work carefully.** Is it realistic or is it an abstract work with a distorted and imaginary vision? If it is a realistic work—say, a painting of a rural scene—take note of the colors and the way the paint is applied. An artist, by using drab colors and bold strokes of the brush, can suggest a negative feeling about a scene. On the other hand, a scene can be idealized with the use of bright colors and fine brushstrokes. After studying

the work carefully, sum up in a single sentence your overall impression of it. This single sentence will be your thesis.
- **Pay attention to the title of the work.** Many Expressionist painters create images that are purely imaginary and have no equivalent in reality. It often takes a title to help us understand what the images mean. Figure 2.1 is a dramatic example of the importance of title. The painting shows a sinister assembly of men, two of whom have half a skull crammed with what looks like excrement and miscellaneous garbage. In the background are an ugly priest and a Nazi soldier with a bloody sword. It is only after we know the title of the painting, *The Pillars of Society,* that we grasp who these revolting men are meant to be—the emerging Nazi rulers whom the artist was satirizing.

    Another example can be found in Figure 2.2, a lithograph by Kathe Kollwitz of a woman whose hand is raised in a gesture explained by the work's title, *Never Again War.*
- **Use the Internet to research background about the artist and the work.** For example, before writing the paragraph about *Pillars of Society,* we entered the name of the artist George Grosz and the title of his painting in the search engine Google, which gave us the information we needed about the work and its creator. Another example is the lithograph

● **FIGURE 2.1** The Pillars of Society, *1926, by George Grosz*

How admirable are these pillars of society?

FIGURE 2.2
Never Again War!
(Nie Wieder Kreig),
*1924, by Kathe
Kollwitz*

Mothers united against the killing fields of war

of the anti-war woman. Through the Internet we learned that losing a son in World War I and a grandson in World War II made the artist, German Expressionist Kathe Kollwitz (1867–1945), into a committed pacifist and explains much of her work.

- **Check your response to the work of art against the responses of art critics.** We all have a unique eye. If beauty is in the eye of the beholder, so is much of art. Some modernists argue that one reaction to a work of art is as valid as another. Traditionalists take just the opposite point of view, arguing that it is possible for one reaction to be "right" and another "wrong." Most likely the truth lies somewhere in between. It is possible for an interpretation of an artwork to be so far-fetched and unprovable as to come entirely from the viewer's mind rather than from the artwork itself. It is also possible for two contrary interpretations of the same artwork to exist side by side, one no more "right" than the other. In situations like this one, art critics can be helpful. They have the experience and background in evaluating artistic works that enable them to spot what is unique about an artwork and what is imitative.

- **Support your opinions or interpretations of the artwork.** Any opinion you have about an artwork should be supported by details drawn from the work itself. If you say that the portrait of a certain person reflects an air of gloom, you should say why you think that. In support of this opinion, you can point to background colors, a grim facial expression, or perhaps the way the figure slumps.

- **Say how the work made you feel.** An artwork is meant to appeal both to the mind and to the heart. Don't be afraid to express how the work made you feel or to say why you think it affected you as it did. That kind of admission will help a reader better understand your opinions of the work. It is also perfectly allowable to use "I" in an essay interpreting a visual image. As a matter of fact, writing on such a personal topic without the use of "I" would be very difficult to do. You are, after all, expected to say how the work affected *you* and how *you* feel about it. You should not necessarily feel any obligation to like the artwork just because you're writing an essay about it. You may find that you heartily dislike the work. In such a case, what you have to do is to say why. If you did like the work, you should also say why.

In review, here are the steps involved in writing about artworks:

1. State your overall impression of the work in a single sentence.
2. Ground your opinions and impressions of the artwork in details drawn from it.
3. Say how the work affected you.

- Writing Assignment

    Find and make a copy of a work of art that you like. Write three paragraphs about it, interpreting the work of art and saying what about it you especially appreciate. Include a copy of the work of art with your essay.

Writing about News Photographs News photographs, a staple of newspapers and magazines, range from the serene to the horrific. In the hands of a good photographer, the camera can seem to totally capture a subject. That uncanny ability to seemingly X-ray the human soul, coupled with the spontaneity missing in more formal artworks such as paintings, has made photography into a universal language. A photograph of people leaping to their death from a burning skyscraper is globally understandable and universally wrenching, no matter what language we speak. Here are some tips on how to approach writing about a news photo:

- **Begin by researching and describing the context of the photograph.** When was it taken and by whom? Under what circumstances was it shot? Knowing its context puts a photograph in historical perspective and affects your interpretation of it.

FIGURE 2.3 *Third trapped coal miner being rescued.*

A Moment Dramatizing Life

- **Describe the news photograph, clearly stating its details.** Sum up, as well as you can, the facial expressions of people in the shot. The photo in Figure 2.3, for example, taken on July 28, 2002, depicts a jubilant moment in mining history. After being trapped 100 feet beneath the earth in a water-filled cave for more than three days, nine miners were, one by one, lifted to safety. The photo shows the rescue of the third miner. How would you describe the expression on the rescued miner's face?

- **Sum up your interpretation of the meaning of the photograph in one sentence.** This sentence, placed in the opening paragraph, will serve as the thesis of the essay. Many variations are possible, but one summation might be, "The relief of being rescued is visibly etched on the weary face of a miner on July 28, 2002, as he is finally hoisted to the surface after spending more than 78 hours trapped underground in a water-filled cave."

- **Elaborate on the thesis based on evidence from the photo.** You are now ready to write the body of the essay. Focusing on the photograph, you could mention the narrow rescue cage that was rigged to extract the men one at a time from their place of entrapment. You could mention the rescuers' hands reaching protectively for the trapped man and the dark and cramped confines in which the rescue seems to take place. You could describe the weariness reflected in the eyes of the miner who spent the last three days huddled underground without food in a small cave threatened by rising water. All of these details will come from the picture. You can get whatever else you need from studying its context. Again, the Internet is an ideal tool for establishing the context of a photograph.

In review, here are the steps involved in writing about news photos:

1. Establish the context of the photograph, when and where it was taken, and why.
2. Describe the photo in detail.
3. Compose a thesis for the photo.
4. Develop evidence from the photo and its context to support your thesis.

Writing Assignment

Write a couple of paragraphs about a news photograph, explaining its context and giving your interpretation of it. Include a copy of the photo with your written work.

Writing about Cartoons Nothing captures the spirit of an age better than a collection of its best cartoons. They seem to sum up in shorthand the idiosyncrasies of the time. The political cartoon, particularly the caricature—which is a cartoon that exaggerates physical appearance—is actually a good measure of how a particular person is regarded at a particular time. To get an idea of how Teddy Roosevelt was perceived in his day, for example, you need only go to the collection of cartoons that depict him. Here are some tips for writing about cartoons:

- **Make sure you understand the message of the cartoon.** Some cartoons, of course, are merely intended to amuse and have no particular message. Many cartoons mix sugar (humor) with medicine (a message). Look at Figure 2.4 on the next page, for example. Here, a mother vulture is scolding her chick for complaining about being fed regurgitated yak carcass. On one level, this is a funny line from a vulture. But on a deeper level, the cartoon voices a variation on the universal complaint all parents occasionally make—that their kids are ungrateful.

    Another example of this subtlety is in a cartoon that depicts an English teacher standing angrily in front of her class. Behind her on the chalkboard is scrawled, "Homework due today." In front of the teacher stands a young boy who is saying, "I did my homework, but the dog pressed Control-Alt-Delete." What makes this line funny is that it is the computer-age equivalent of "The dog ate my homework."

FIGURE 2.4

The universal childhood hatred of certain foods

"Listen, buster, I didn't sit on your hard little egg in the blazing sun for six weeks just to hear you say, 'Ewww, I don't like regurgitated yak carcass.'"

- **Be aware of the topsy-turvy world of cartoons.** Many cartoons spoof the accepted and habitual views of society, often by turning the world upside down. For example, one cartoon shows the seats of a movie theater filled with an audience of winged bugs waiting for the feature to begin. On the screen is the name of the upcoming movie: "Return of the Killer Windshield." Another—one of our favorites—shows a horrible monster scrambling to get dressed. Looking at his watch worriedly, he is complaining to his wife that he's late and should have already been in a certain boy's closet. The caption of the cartoon? "Monster jobs." The humor of both cartoons comes mainly from the inversion of normalcy, giving us an unusual slant on a familiar situation.

- **State what lesson the cartoon teaches.** Many cartoons teach a lesson. Sometimes the lesson can be obvious, as in the cartoon showing an enormous, savage dog turning to bare its teeth at a tiny cowboy, President Bush, who is tweaking the dog's tail. Painted in a sinister scrawl on the back of the dog is its name: War. The lesson is rather obvious. If you provoke war, it is likely to savagely turn on you. Sometimes the lesson is less obvious. For example, a cartoon featuring two forlorn-looking people standing side by side in the aisle of a library and looking at two different books, one entitled *Self-Improvement,* the other *Self-Involvement,* is teaching a subtle lesson about narcissism. In any case, part of your interpretation of the cartoon is to say what lesson it teaches—if it, indeed, teaches any. Study the cartoon until you get its meaning.

In review, here are the steps involved in writing about cartoons:

1. Make sure you understand the message of the cartoon, if it has one.
2. Be aware of the topsy-turvy world of cartoons.
3. Study the lesson of the cartoon.

- Writing Assignment

   Write a few paragraphs about any cartoon that you particularly like. Be sure to include a copy of the cartoon with your work.

Writing about Advertisements Advertising images, although sometimes bewitching, often have an air of unreality. They glamorize persons, settings, and objects. See Figure 2.5.

Many of the graphic messages in advertisements are either exaggerated or outright lies. We know that it is impossible for anyone to turn a rainy day into a sunny one just by swallowing a pill, that all our worries will not vanish if we take a certain laxative, and that rubbing our faces with a cream will not make wrinkles disappear overnight. Buying a certain mattress will not turn an insomniac into another Rip Van Winkle, nor will driving a new car make you into an overnight sensation with the opposite sex.

- **FIGURE 2.5** *Two white androgynous-looking young men pose on a billboard advertising Gucci designer clothing.*

   The question is, can a piece of clothing change the person inside?

Anyone who writes about advertising images has to exercise both common sense and logic. Common sense will enable you to see through the pitch. Logic will help you to sift through the exaggerated claims made by the hype. Writing about an advertising image requires you to take the following steps:

- **Be sure you know the audience at whom the ad is aimed and the product that is being advertised.** An ad directed at women—for a perfume, for example—often comes with a feminized image. On the other hand, masculine images are typically found in a beer advertisement aimed mainly at men. Strange as it may seem, a few advertisements have been oblique rather than blunt in their hype of a product. Probably the most famous example of this is the advertising campaign for a certain Japanese car. The ads show scenes of pastures and mountain brooks—to the accompaniment of philosophical babble that has little to do with owning a car. Ask yourself what the product is, who uses it, and what it does. Sum up this information in a single sentence and you have your thesis.

- **Pay attention to the language that accompanies the image.** Advertising copy is often written in fragments rather than whole sentences. For example, an ad for a trip to Wales uses the following copy: "Suggested itinerary: London-Nirvana-London. It's a stopover in serenity. A side trip to paradise. Where the wonders of nature and the comforts of home live side by side. Wales. Just two hours from London." One sentence and five fragments make up this copy. Notice any poetic touch used to highlight the image. For example, the most successful advertising slogan of all time consists of two rhyming words: "Think Mink." Advertising copy is also often openly romantic, as in this example: "Somewhere she went from the girl of your dreams to the love of your life. A diamond is forever."

- **Notice any inversion of reality.** Advertisers are notorious for turning reality on its head. If a product is bad for you, the advertising may surround it with an aura of health and well-being. For example, cigarette advertisements used to always show smokers as specimens of perfect, robust health. The typical image associated with Marlboro cigarettes was a rugged cowboy shown on the range herding cattle and occasionally pausing for a "healthful" smoke.

- **Watch out for buzzwords or euphemisms.** A buzzword is a slogan or saying that is associated with the product. The slogan of a certain underarm deodorant was, "Strong enough for a man. But made for a woman." A euphemism is a gentler way of saying something. For example, saying "he passed away" is a euphemism for "he died." Advertisers often combine images with euphemisms as part of their pitch. For example, an advertisement for insurance will talk about sparing your family the heartbreak of final decisions—meaning, finding a place to bury you and a way to pay for it. Personal-hygiene products for women are always euphemistic in their claims. Sometimes, even an image can be euphemistic, as is often the case in some advertisements for laxatives.

- **Use logic to evaluate the extravagant claims of an advertising image.** It is no exaggeration to say that advertisements often tell outright lies. Ad people would probably claim that they do not lie, but merely stress the positives about their product. Yet, anyone with common sense can't help but wonder what to make of a claim like "X toothpaste is used by two out of three dentists." How many dentists were surveyed to come to this conclusion? It might have been three. And what does this claim mean: "Degree antiperspirant deodorant is body-heat activated. Your body heat turns it on." And when an insect repellent advertises that it makes you "invisible to bugs," is that claim meant literally or figuratively?
- **Mention any humor associated with image.** An ad for Toshiba copy machines features a speaking copier: "I print 80 pages per minute and sit near the men's room. She types 80 words per minute and gets the corner office. Is there no balance in the universe?" To discuss this particular image you would have to touch on the humor of the talking copier.

In review, here are the steps involved in writing about advertisements:

1. Be sure you know what's being advertised and to whom.
2. Pay attention to the language that accompanies the image.
3. Notice any inversion of reality.
4. Watch out for buzzwords or euphemisms.
5. Use logic to evaluate the extravagant claims of an advertising image.
6. Mention any humor associated with the image.

Writing Assignment

Write two paragraphs on a magazine or newspaper ad that you particularly dislike. Include a copy of the ad with your work.

Exercises

1. After studying the following passages, suggest the purpose of each and the audience for which it is intended. Give specific examples of language suitable to that audience.

   a. At first our Greg was a model child. Healthy, happy, unfailingly sweet-tempered, he was a total joy as a baby. When he was one year old, he thought that everything mother and father wanted him to do was wonderful. His second birthday passed, and he remained cooperative and adorable. Aha, I thought, the "terrible twos" that everyone complains about must result from inadequate attention and discipline.

   Then Greg turned 2 3/4 years old. Suddenly we had an obnoxious monster in the house. His favorite word was "No!" and he used it constantly. At the simplest request he would stamp his feet and cry. It took a battle to get him to put on clothing he had previously worn happily. Favorite foods were thrown on the floor. It became almost impossible to take him shopping because he would lie down in the store and refuse to move. There was constant tension in the house, and my husband and I became irritable, too. We felt as if we were living on the slopes of a volcano, and we found ourselves giving in to Greg too much in order to avoid the threatened eruptions.

b. Others will debate the controversial issues, national and international, which divide men's minds. But serene, calm, aloof, you stand as the nation's war guardians, as its lifeguards from the raging tides of international conflict, as its gladiators in the arena of battle. For a century-and-a-half you have defended, guarded, and protected its hallowed traditions of liberty and freedom, of right and justice.

Let civilian voices argue the merits or demerits of our processes of government: whether our strength is being sapped by deficit financing indulged in too long; by federal paternalism grown too mighty; by power groups grown too arrogant; by politics grown too corrupt; by crime grown too rampant; by morals grown too low; by taxes grown too high; by extremists grown too violent; whether our personal liberties are as firm and complete as they should be.

These great national problems are not for your professional participation or military solution. Your guidepost stands out like a tenfold beacon in the night: duty, honor, country.

c. To give Eleanor her due, any suspicion as to the slightest inclination on her part toward Mr. Slope was a wrong to her. She had no more idea of marrying Mr. Slope than she had of marrying the bishop, and the idea that Mr. Slope would present himself as a suitor had never occurred to her. Indeed, to give her her due again, she had never thought about suitors since her husband's death. But nevertheless it was true that she had overcome all that repugnance to the man which was so strongly felt for him by the rest of the Grantly faction. She had forgiven him his sermon. She had forgiven him his low church tendencies, his Sabbath schools, and puritanical observances. She had forgiven his pharisaical arrogance, and even his greasy face and oily vulgar manners. Having agreed to overlook such offences as these, why should she not in time be taught to regard Mr. Slope as a suitor?

d. Earthquakes are often accompanied by a roaring noise that comes from the bowels of the earth. This phenomenon was known to early geographers. Pliny wrote that earthquakes are "preceded or accompanied by a terrible sound." Vaults supporting the ground give way and it seems as though the earth heaves deep sighs. The sound was attributed to the gods and called theophany.

The eruptions of volcanoes are also accompanied by loud noises. The sound produced by Krakatoa in the East Indies, during the eruption of 1883, was so loud that it was heard as far as Japan, 3,000 miles away, the farthest distance traveled by sound recorded in modern annals.

e. I beg you to excuse a father who dares to approach you in the interests of his son.

I wish to mention first that my son is 22 years old, has studied for four years at the Zurich Polytechnic and last summer brilliantly passed his diploma examinations in mathematics and physics. Since then he has tried unsuccessfully to find a position as assistant, which would enable him to continue his education in theoretical and experimental physics.

Everybody who is able to judge, praises his talent, and in any case I can assure you that he is exceedingly assiduous and industrious and is attached to his science with a great love.

    f. Letters written by a potential customer asking suppliers for free materials, information, or routine services are among the easiest to write. The customer will usually receive what he or she is asking for since it is to the supplier's advantage to provide it. The potential customer need only be clear and courteous. In writing routine request letters, give all the information the supplier will need in order to be really helpful, keep your request as brief as possible without omitting important details, and express your wishes courteously and tactfully.

2. Write two one-page essays explaining the reasons why you wish to pursue a certain career. Address the first to the personnel manager of an organization that might hire you and the second to your father. Contrast the language and phrasing of each essay and explain the differences between them.

3. Both of the following letters refuse credit to a potential customer. How does the second differ in purpose from the first?

    a. Please accept our regrets that we cannot offer you a 60-day credit for the meeting of your organization here at Pine Lodge in July of 2006. When you held your meeting here last year, we had the embarrassing experience of having to wait six months before you made full payment on your bill. I am sure that you will understand that we cannot take chances on such bad credit risks.

    b. Thank you for choosing Pine Lodge again for your 2006 meeting. We consider it a pleasure to have you, although we must ask you to send us a 25% deposit and to make a full settlement when you check out. This is now our standard arrangement with organizations similar to yours. If these arrangements are satisfactory, we shall do our best to make sure that your group is extended every courtesy and service during its stay.

4. A restaurant owner has sent the following memorandum to the waiters and waitresses working for him. Rewrite the memo to create a more positive tone, without destroying its purpose.

    To: All waiters and waitresses. I've had it with you lazy clowns! This month's profits fell 20% below last year's at this same time. Now, any fool can tell that the problem is your sloppy service to the customers, your excessive breaking of china and glassware, and your horsing around instead of paying attention to such details as keeping the food warm, setting the tables properly, and getting the customer's order straight. So, I'm warning you: either start doing your job right, or you'll find yourselves fired.

5. Assuming an educated audience, label the purpose of each of the following passages: (1) to inspire, (2) to get action, (3) to amuse, or (4) to inform.

    a. Please send us either a check within the next week or an explanation if some problem has arisen. We are eager to cooperate with you.

    b. Conscience is a sacred sanctuary where God alone may enter as judge.

c. In great straits, and when hope is small, the boldest counsels are the safest.
d. Men seldom make passes at girls who wear glasses.
e. The more one comes to know men, the more one admires the dog.
f. "Gavelkind" is the custom of having all of the sons of an estate holder share equally in the estate upon the death of the father. Most of the lands in England were held in gavelkind tenure prior to the Norman Conquest.
g. Seek not the favor of the multitude; it is seldom got by honest and lawful means. But seek the testimony of few; and number not voices, but weigh them.
h. Botticelli isn't a wine, you dunce! Botticelli is a cheese.
i. The Indus River is approximately 1,900 miles long. It rises in the Kailas range of Tibet, flows west across Kashmir, India, and then moves southwest to the Arabian Sea.
j. Flaming manifestoes and prophecies of doom are no longer much help, and a search for scapegoats can only make matters worse. The time for sensations and manifestoes is about over. Now we need rigorous analysis, united effort, and very hard work.

6. Label each of the following passages according to its level of English: formal, informal, or technical. In each case, describe the characteristics that identify the level of writing.

   a. Sometimes I wish I were a mountain stream. If I were a mountain stream, I'd flow down a beautiful green, woodsy, snow-capped mountain. I'd be fed by the cool, melting snow, and I'd shimmer and glisten as the sun warmed my flowing presence. Being a mountain stream, I'd attract only a few select people—those with enough courage and stamina to climb through thickets, across ravines, and up steep paths to my cool, ethereal banks. Those special people could enjoy sitting on my banks to search my clear depths for the solitude, serenity, and peace they're longing to find.

   b. The bony remains of Peking Man all came from a single limestone cave at Chou-k'ou-tien. The bones consist of fifteen crania, six facial bones, twelve mandibles, a miscellaneous collection of postcranial bones, and 147 teeth. Studies of the physical characters of these bones by Davidson Black and Franz Weidenreich disclose that Peking Man was still in an early stage of human development, comparable to the *Homo erectus* of Java.

   The limbs were highly developed and quite modern, indicating that he stood upright and walked on two feet, but the cranium is characterized by low vault, heavy bony features, thick wall, and small cranial capacity (914–1,225 cc., with an average of 1,043 cc., as against Java Man's 860 cc. and modern man's 1,350 cc.). —John T. Meskill

   c. Unlike in nature, where the root feeds the plant, in art, the pinnacle makes possible the base. Drama did not begin with a lot of hacks gradually evolving into Aeschylus and Sophocles; the novel did not start with a slew of James Micheners and Leon Urises building up to Dickens and Joyce. Richardson, Fielding, Sterne, and Smollett started things on a pretty high level; it is they who made the Jacqueline Susanns possible, not the other way around. Public funds for the dissemination of culture are necessary, but unless the most difficult and demanding creations on the individual level are subsidized, no amount of grants to public television to put on The Adams Chronicles will prevent culture and art from withering away or becoming debased, which is the same thing. —John Simon

7. Remember your last significant writing assignment and answer the following questions:
   a. Who was your audience?
   b. What was your purpose?
   c. What level of English did you use?

8. Assuming that choice of topic affects the quality of your writing, choose the topic that most interests you from the following list. In two or three sentences, state why the topic appeals to you. Describe the audience for whom you would like to write about your chosen topic.
   a. The future of working women
   b. Care for the elderly
   c. The cost of owning a house
   d. The pleasures associated with a particular hobby
   e. Preserving our environment
   f. Some aspect of working with computers
   g. Handicapped children
   h. Some aspect of primitive civilization
   i. A favorite painter, sculptor, dancer, or musician
   j. Business ethics
   k. Political reform

Stumped by wordiness? Exit on page 686, at the **Editing Booth!**

ADVICE

What—and How—to Write When You Have No Time to Write

DONALD MURRAY

Donald Murray (b. 1924) is a Pulitzer Prize–winning journalist who has made it part of his life's work to teach others how to write. He writes a much-read weekly column for *The Boston Globe* as well as feature articles for a variety of magazines. Many teachers of composition rely on Murray's books for teaching strategies. Among his most influential books are *Shoptalk: Learning to Write with Writers* (1990); *Expecting the Unexpected: Teaching Myself and Others to Read and Write* (1989); *The Craft of Revision* (2007); and *Crafting a Life in Essay, Story, Poem* (1996). Murray is Professor Emeritus of English at the University of New Hampshire.

Murray, who is known for his practical approach to writing, dispenses some sensible advice, which he summarizes into "ten little habits of mind and craft." While his ideas apply particularly to the full-time writer, they are also practical enough to help the student.

• • •

1   The less time I have for writing, the more important it is that I write. Writing gives me a necessary calm, what Robert Frost called "a momentary stay against confusion." Writing slows down the rush of life, forcing awareness and reflection. As writing increases my awareness, language clarifies that vision. What is vague and general becomes concrete and specific as I find the words. These words connect with other words in phrase and sentence, placing the immediate experience in the context of my life. I read the story of my life by writing it. I also receive the gift of concentration and escape the swirling problems of my life as I follow paragraph and page toward meaning.

2   I write fragments in slivers of time, always with interruptions, and yet, when I look back, I am surprised that the writing caught on the fly has produced a lifetime of productivity. I have come to realize that very little published writing is produced during sustained periods of composition without interruption. You have to arrange a life in which part of your mind is writing all the time; that's when the seeds of writing are sown and then cultivated. The writing is harvested in short periods of time between the busy chores that crowd the day.

3   Graham Greene said, "If one wants to write, one simply has to organize one's life in a mass of little habits." Here are ten little habits of mind and craft that I realize, looking back, made me a productive writer—without long writing days free of interruption.

4   **1. Don't wait for an idea.**

5   If you know what you want to say, you've probably said it before, or it's not worth saying. Writing is thinking, and thought begins not with a conclusion but with an itch, a hint, a clue, a question, a doubt, a wonder, a problem, an answer without a question, an image that refuses to be forgotten. Such fragments are caught on the wing, when I think my mind is somewhere else.

6   My four-year-old grandson told his mother, "I know Grandpa is a writer because he's always writing in his wallet." It is not a wallet, but a container for the 3 X 5 cards that are always in my shirt pocket with three pens. In a shoulder case that is not far from me night and day is the spiral daybook in which I talk to myself, capturing and playing with fragments of language that may become a draft.

2. Listen to your own difference.

People who want to write look at what is being published, but the writers who are published have looked within themselves, found their own vision of the world, heard their own voices. Sandra Cisneros said, "Write about what makes you different."

As I look back, I realize that what made me strange to my family, classmates and teachers, friends and neighbors, colleagues and editors, is what has produced the writing that has been read. In the wonderful way of art, what is most personal, eccentric, individual, becomes most universal. When I have tried to become someone else I have failed; when I have been myself I have succeeded.

3. Avoid long writing sessions.

Most people believe, as I once did, that it is necessary to have long, uninterrupted days in which to write. But there are no such days. Life intrudes. I try to follow the counsel of Horace, Pliny, and so many others through the centuries: nulla dies sine linea—never a day without a line.

How long does it take me to write? My weekly columns take 71 years of living and about forty-five minutes of writing. I write in bursts of twenty minutes, five, fifteen, thirty, sixty; ninety minutes is the maximum amount of writing time that is effective for me.

And how much writing do I produce? I've finished a book averaging 300 words a day. These days I try to average 500 words a day. The important thing is not the time or the words, but the habit, that dailiness of the writing.

4. Break long writing projects into brief daily tasks.

Books are written a page at a time, and I find it helpful—essential—to break a book into units that can be finished in a short morning's writing: lead for Ch. 3, scene in court, description of experiment, interview with source, column on writing time.

5. Write in the morning.

Most writers write in the early morning before the world intrudes. They harvest the product of their subconscious. Each hour of the day becomes less efficient as the writer is not only interrupted, but increasingly aware of all the professional and family concerns that crowd the mind. An 800-word column I can write in 45 minutes in the morning takes me three hours in the afternoon.

6. Know tomorrow's task today.

I set myself a single writing task and know what it is the night before. I don't know what I am going to write, but I assign the writing problem to my subconscious at the end of the morning writing session or before I go to bed, and part of my mind works on it as I go about my living.

7. Seek instructive failure.

Effective writing is the product of instructive failure. You try to say what you cannot yet say, but in the attempt you discover—draft by draft— what you have to say and how you can say it. Failure is essential. Failure occurs when the words race ahead of thought, producing insights that may be developed through revision. The writer should seek to fail, not to say what has been said before, but what has not yet been said and is worth saying.

8. Focus on what works.

Once failure has revealed what you want to say, you should develop the topic by concentrating on what works, rather than focusing on correcting errors. Most errors will not occur if you develop what works and, at the end of the drafting process, you can solve any problems that remain. I revise mostly by layering, writing over—and over—what has been written.

9. Keep score.

As you write, it is important to suspend critical judgment until after a draft is finished. It's helpful to count words—or pages or hours—so that you can tell yourself that you have written without assessing how well you have written until the piece is finished.

10. Let it go.

Hardest of all is to let it go. The draft never equals the dream. The draft will expose your private thoughts and feelings to the world, but when you are published, what you most feared would appear foolish, your readers often find most profound. You have given words to their private thoughts and feelings.

Writing produces writing. When writing you are more aware of the world and your own reaction to it. As a writer, you relive your life hundreds of times, and when you are in your seventies, as I am, you'll come to your writing desk and discover you have even more to say than you imagined when you were 7 years old and dreaming of a writing life.

- Vocabulary

  sustained (2)   daybook (6)   eccentric (9)
  suspend (25)   assessing (25)

EXAMPLES

I Have a Dream

Martin Luther King, Jr.

Martin Luther King, Jr. (1929–1968), American clergyman and black civil rights leader, was born in Atlanta and educated at Morehouse College, Crozer Theological Seminary, and Boston University (Ph.D., 1955). Dr. King, a lifelong advocate of nonviolent resistance to segregation, led a boycott of blacks in Montgomery, Alabama (1955–1956) against the city's segregated bus system and organized a massive march on Washington,

D.C. in 1963, during which he delivered his famous "I Have a Dream" speech. In 1964, he was awarded the Nobel Peace Prize. Dr. King was assassinated on April 4, 1968, on a motel balcony in Memphis, Tennessee, where he had journeyed in support of the city's striking sanitation workers.

In August 1963, more than 200,000 blacks and whites gathered peacefully in Washington, D.C., to focus attention on black demands for civil rights. The marchers gathered at the Lincoln Memorial, where Dr. King delivered this impassioned speech.

• • •

1 Five score years ago, a great American, in whose symbolic shadow we stand today, signed the Emancipation Proclamation. This momentous decree came as a great beacon light of hope to millions of Negro slaves who had been seared in the flames of withering injustice. It came as a joyous daybreak to end the long night of their captivity.

2 But one hundred years later, the Negro still is not free. One hundred years later, the life of the Negro is still sadly crippled by the manacles of segregation and the chains of discrimination.

3 One hundred years later, the Negro lives on a lonely island of poverty in the midst of a vast ocean of material prosperity. One hundred years later, the Negro is still languished in the corners of American society and finds himself an exile in his own land. So we have come here today to dramatize a shameful condition.

4 In a sense we have come to our nation's capital to cash a check. When the architects of our republic wrote the magnificent words of the Constitution and the Declaration of Independence, they were signing a promissory note to which every American was to fall heir. This note was a promise that all men, yes, black men as well as white men, would be granted the unalienable rights of life, liberty, and the pursuit of happiness.

5 It is obvious today that America has defaulted on this promissory note insofar as her citizens of color are concerned. Instead of honoring this sacred obligation, America has given the Negro people a bad check, which has come back marked "insufficient funds."

6 But we refuse to believe that the bank of justice is bankrupt. We refuse to believe that there are insufficient funds in the great vaults of opportunity of this nation. So we have come to cash this check—a check that will give us upon demand the riches of freedom and the security of justice.

7 We have also come to this hallowed spot to remind America of the fierce urgency of now. This is no time to engage in the luxury of cooling off or to take the tranquilizing drug of gradualism. Now is the time to make real the promises of democracy. Now is the time to rise from the dark and desolate valley of segregation to the sunlit path of racial justice. Now is the time to lift our nation from the quicksands of racial injustice to the solid rock of brotherhood. Now is the time to make justice a reality for all of God's children.

8 It would be fatal for the nation to overlook the urgency of the movement and to underestimate the determination of the Negro. This sweltering summer of the Negro's legitimate discontent will not pass until there is an

invigorating autumn of freedom and equality. 1963 is not an end but a beginning. Those who hope that the Negro needed to blow off steam and will now be content will have a rude awakening if the nation returns to business as usual.

9   There will be neither rest nor tranquility in America until the Negro is granted his citizenship rights. The whirlwinds of revolt will continue to shake the foundations of our nation until the bright day of justice emerges.

10   But there is something that I must say to my people who stand on the warm threshold which leads into the palace of justice. In the process of gaining our rightful place we must not be guilty of wrongful deeds.

11   Let us not seek to satisfy our thirst for freedom by drinking from the cup of bitterness and hatred. We must forever conduct our struggle on the high plane of dignity and discipline. We must not allow our creative protest to degenerate into physical violence. Again and again we must rise to the majestic heights of meeting physical force with soul force.

12   The marvelous new militancy which has engulfed the Negro community must not lead us to a distrust of all white people, for many of our white brothers, as evidenced by their presence here today, have come to realize that their destiny is tied up with our destiny and they have come to realize that their freedom is inextricably bound to our freedom. This offense we share mounted to storm the battlements of injustice must be carried forth by a biracial army. We cannot walk alone.

13   And as we walk, we must make the pledge that we shall always march ahead. We cannot turn back. There are those who are asking the devotees of civil rights, "When will you be satisfied?" We can never be satisfied as long as the Negro is the victim of the unspeakable horrors of police brutality.

14   We can never be satisfied as long as our bodies, heavy with the fatigue of travel, cannot gain lodging in the motels of the highways and the hotels of the cities. We cannot be satisfied as long as the Negro's basic mobility is from a smaller ghetto to a larger one.

15   We can never be satisfied as long as our children are stripped of their selfhood and robbed of their dignity by signs stating "for whites only." We cannot be satisfied as long as a Negro in Mississippi cannot vote and a Negro in New York believes he has nothing for which to vote. No, we are not satisfied, and we will not be satisfied until justice rolls down like waters and righteousness like a mighty stream.

16   I am not unmindful that some of you have come here out of excessive trials and tribulation. Some of you have come fresh from narrow jail cells. Some of you have come from areas where your quest for freedom left you battered by the storms of persecution and staggered by the winds of police brutality. You have been the veterans of creative suffering. Continue to work with the faith that unearned suffering is redemptive.

17   Go back to Mississippi; go back to Alabama; go back to South Carolina; go back to Georgia; go back to Louisiana; go back to the slums and ghettos of the Northern cities, knowing that somehow this situation can, and will be changed. Let us not wallow in the valley of despair.

18   So I say to you, my friends, that even though we must face the difficulties of today and tomorrow, I still have a dream. It is a dream deeply rooted in the American dream that one day this nation will rise up and live out the true meaning of its creed—we hold these truths to be self evident, that all men are created equal.

19   I have a dream that one day on the red hills of Georgia, sons of former slaves and sons of former slave-owners will be able to sit down together at the table of brotherhood.

20   I have a dream that one day, even the state of Mississippi, a state sweltering with the heat of injustice, sweltering with the heat of oppression, will be transformed into an oasis of freedom and justice.

21   I have a dream my four little children will one day live in a nation where they will not be judged by the color of their skin but by the content of their character. I have a dream today!

22   I have a dream that one day, down in Alabama, with its vicious racists, with its governor having his lips dripping with the words of interposition and nullification, that one day, right there in Alabama, little black boys and black girls will be able to join hands with little white boys and white girls as sisters and brothers. I have a dream today!

23   I have a dream that one day every valley shall be exalted, every hill and mountain shall be made low, the rough places shall be made plain, and the crooked places shall be made straight and the glory of the Lord will be revealed and all flesh shall see it together.

24   This is our hope. This is the faith that I go back to the South with.

25   With this faith we will be able to hew out of the mountain of despair a stone of hope. With this faith we will be able to transform the jangling discords of our nation into a beautiful symphony of brotherhood.

26   With this faith we will be able to work together, to pray together, to struggle together, to go to jail together, to stand up for freedom together, knowing that we will be free one day. This will be the day when all of God's children will be able to sing with new meaning—"my country 'tis of thee; sweet land of liberty; of thee I sing; land where my fathers died, land of the pilgrim's pride; from every mountain side, let freedom ring"—and if America is to be a great nation, this must become true.

27   So let freedom ring from the prodigious hilltops of New Hampshire.
28   Let freedom ring from the mighty mountains of New York.
29   Let freedom ring from the heightening Alleghenies of Pennsylvania.
30   Let freedom ring from the snow-capped Rockies of Colorado.
31   Let freedom ring from the curvaceous slopes of California.
32   But not only that.
33   Let freedom ring from Stone Mountain of Georgia.
34   Let freedom ring from Lookout Mountain of Tennessee.
35   Let freedom ring from every hill and molehill of Mississippi, from every mountainside, let freedom ring.
36   And when we allow freedom to ring, when we let it ring from every village and hamlet, from every state and city, we will be able to speed up that day

when all of God's children—black men and white men, Jews and Gentiles, Catholics and Protestants—will be able to join hands and to sing in the words of the old Negro spiritual, "Free at last, free at last; thank God Almighty, we are free at last."

● Vocabulary

momentous (1)	manacles (2)	languished (3)
unalienable (4)	hallowed (7)	gradualism (7)
invigorating (8)	degenerate (11)	militancy (12)
inextricably (12)	tribulation (16)	redemptive (16)
sweltering (20)	interposition (22)	nullification (22)
exalted (23)	prodigious (27)	curvaceous (31)

● The Facts

1. The speech begins "Five score years ago. . . ." Why was this beginning especially appropriate?
2. What grievances of black Americans does Dr. King summarize in paragraphs 2 and 3 of this speech?
3. What does Dr. King caution his listeners against in paragraph 11?
4. What attitude toward white people does the speaker urge upon his audience?
5. Although Dr. King speaks out mainly against injustices committed against blacks in the South, he is also critical of the North. What can be inferred from this speech about the living conditions of blacks in the North during the early 1960s?

● The Strategies

1. One critic of this speech has written that its purpose was to intensify the values of the black movement. What characteristic of its style can you point to that might be said to have served this purpose?
2. Paragraphs 4 through 6 of the speech are linked through the use of an extended analogy. What is this analogy?
3. What common rhetorical device does the speech frequently use to emphasize its points?
4. It is often said that speakers and writers use paragraphs differently. How are the paragraphs of this speech especially adapted for oral delivery? What is the most obvious difference between these paragraphs and those a writer might use?
5. What is the function of the brief paragraph 32?

● The Issues

1. "Black" is a term widely used in the United States to designate people whose skin color may range from dark brown to sepia; however, what definition of blackness does our society seem implicitly to use?

2. In your opinion, what is the basis of racial prejudice?
3. Will the United States ever have a black president? Defend your answer.
4. Does prejudice in the United States against black men exceed or equal the prejudice against black women? Explain the difference, if there is one, and justify your answer.
5. What stereotypes do you hold about people of other races? Write them down along with an explanation of how you arrived at them. Share them with your classmates.

Suggestions for Writing

1. Write an essay analyzing the extensive use of metaphors in this speech. Comment on their effectiveness, bearing in mind the audience for whom the speech was intended.
2. Write an essay analyzing the oral style of this speech. Point out specific techniques of phrasing, sentence construction, paragraphing, and so on, that identify this composition as a speech. Suggest how a writer might have phrased some passages if this work had been written to be read rather than heard.

Letter to My Husband
Clementine Churchill

Clementine Churchill (1885–1977) and Winston Churchill, famous prime minister of England during World War II, were married in 1908 and remained mutually devoted until Winston's death in 1965. Their correspondence spanned fifty years during which they endured long and painful absences caused by Winston's roller-coaster political career. Through it all Clementine remained his faithful wife and ardent supporter who often whispered sage advice to her sometimes grouchy husband.

Following the surrender of France to the forces of Hitler on June 22, 1940, England and her new Prime Minister Winston Churchill stood alone against the German military juggernaut. In the weeks of crisis that followed, Churchill drove himself and his colleagues mercilessly, drawing this gentle warning from his "devoted and watchful Clemmie."

• • •

From CSC   10 Downing Street
27 June 1940[1]

1 My Darling,
I hope you will forgive me if I tell you something that I feel you ought to know.
2   One of the men in your entourage (a devoted friend) has been to me & told me that there is a danger of your being generally disliked by your colleagues &

---
[1]This is the only letter extant between WSC and CSC during 1940.

subordinates because of your rough sarcastic & overbearing manner—It seems your Private Secretaries have agreed to behave like schoolboys & "take what's coming to them" & then escape out of your presence shrugging their shoulders—Higher up, if an idea is suggested (say at a conference) you are supposed to be so contemptuous that presently no ideas, good or bad, will be forthcoming. I was astonished & upset because in all these years I have been accustomed to all those who have worked with & under you, loving you—I said this & I was told, "No doubt it's the strain"—

3   My Darling Winston—I must confess that I have noticed a deterioration in your manner; & you are not so kind as you used to be.

4   It is for you to give the Orders & if they are bungled—except for the King the Archbishop of Canterbury & the Speaker you can sack anyone & everyone—Therefore with this terrific power you must combine urbanity, kindness and if possible Olympic calm. You used to quote: —"On ne régne sur les âmes que par le calme"[2]—I cannot bear that those who serve the Country & yourself should not love you as well as admire and respect you—

5   Besides you won't get the best results by irascibility & rudeness. They will breed either dislike or a slave mentality—(Rebellion in War time being out of the question!)

6   Please forgive your loving devoted & watchful
    Clemmie

7   I wrote this at Chequers[3] last Sunday, tore it up, but here it is now.

● Vocabulary

entourage (2)	contemptuous (2)	deterioration (3)
bungled (4)	sack (4)	urbanity (4)
Olympic (4	irascibility (5)	

● The Facts

1. What importance is attached to the return address of this letter—10 Downing Street? Where was the letter written?
2. Why does the letter end with the words, "Please forgive your loving devoted & watchful Clemmie"? What needed to be forgiven?
3. How did Clementine find out that her husband was being overbearing? Is the source to be trusted?
4. What change has Clementine noticed of late in Churchill's behavior? Would a "good wife" notice such a change, or would she be too busy tending to her own problems?
5. What is the nickname used by Mrs. Churchill? Who probably gave her that nickname? What, if anything, does the nickname imply?

---

[2]Translation: Human souls will be reigned only by calm.
[3]Official country residence of British Prime Ministers.

The Strategies

1. How would you characterize the tone of the opening paragraph in this letter? How appropriate is the opening for the content of the letter? What does the opening tell us about the correspondent?
2. What specific accusations from colleagues does Clementine relate to her husband? Does she sugarcoat the issue or does she confront it directly?
3. What words precede the admittance that Clementine, too, had noticed a change in Winston's manner—a growing lack of kindness? What is the purpose of those words?
4. Why does Clementine use a French quotation to support her point? What does the use of this quotation tell us about the writer?
5. What is the implication of the parenthetical statement at the end of paragraph 5? Does it give support to her notion of extracting the best results from one's staff?

The Issues

1. On what did some of Churchill's staff blame his cantankerous attitude? Do you consider this blame realistic or are there more pressing reasons for his personality change? Explain your answer.
2. According to Clementine, what will happen to the minds of persons with grave responsibilities when Churchill is so contemptuous of their ideas? Do you agree with the writer? Why or why not?
3. According to Clementine, what responsibility comes with power? If a leader does not take on this responsibility, what could be the results? What example from history or your personal life proves this point?
4. Do you agree with Clementine that her husband needed to know the rumors circulating about him? Or would she have been a better wife if she had kept quiet? Give reasons for your answer.
5. What general impression do you have of Clementine Churchill? Describe the kind of person she was as reflected in this letter to her husband, the prime minister.

Suggestions for Writing

1. Look up the word "tyrant" in an encyclopedia and write a brief essay on how the word has changed meaning since its Roman inception. Be sure to give appropriate examples of this evolution in language.
2. On the Internet or at the library, find some biographical material on Clementine Ogilvy Churchill. Then write a physical description and a personality sketch of this remarkable woman. You might consider some of the major events that influenced her life, such as the death of her beloved sister Kitty and the influence of her mother, Lady Blanche Ogilvy. If possible, attach a photo of Clementine.

Have a Cigar

James Herriot

James Herriot, pseudonym of James Alfred Wight (1916–1995), was a Scottish-born veterinary surgeon and writer. His books about his veterinary practice in the Dales of England were enormously popular and led to feature films and a television series. His many books include *All Creatures Great and Small* (1972), *All Things Bright and Beautiful* (1974), and *All Things Wise and Wonderful* (1977).

This poignant story, "Have a Cigar," is typical of Herriot's writing in its sharp observations and simple but evocative prose. Herriot is a master at pacing a story and at drawing a powerful and appealing scene with a minimum of words.

• • •

1   I looked again at the slip of paper where I had written my visits. "Dean, 3 Thompson's Yard. Old dog ill." There were a lot of these "yards" in Darrowby. They were, in fact, tiny streets, like pictures from a Dickens novel. Some of them opened off the marketplace and many more were scattered behind the main thoroughfares in the old part of the town. From the outside you could see only an archway, and it was always a surprise to me to go down a narrow passage and come suddenly upon the uneven rows of little houses with no two alike, looking into each other's windows across eight feet of cobbles.

2   In front of some of the houses a strip of garden had been dug out and marigolds and nasturtium straggled over the rough stones; but at the far end the houses were in a tumbledown condition and some were abandoned with their windows boarded up.

3   Number three was down at this end and looked as though it wouldn't be able to hold out much longer.

4   The flakes of paint quivered on the rotten wood of the door as I knocked; above, the outer wall bulged dangerously on either side of a long crack in the masonry.

5   A small, white-haired man answered. His face, pinched and lined, was enlivened by a pair of cheerful eyes; he wore a much-darned woollen cardigan, patched trousers and slippers.

6   "I've come to see your dog," I said, and the old man smiled.

7   "Oh, I'm so glad you've come, sir," he said. "I'm getting a bit worried about the old chap. Come inside, please."

8   He led me into the tiny living-room. "I'm alone now, sir. Lost my missus over a year ago. She used to think the world of the old dog."

9   The grim evidence of poverty was everywhere. In the worn-out lino, the fireless hearth, the dank, musty smell of the place. The wallpaper hung away from the damp patches and on the table the old man's solitary dinner was laid:

a fragment of bacon, a few fried potatoes and a cup of tea. This was life on the old age pension.

10   In the corner, on a blanket, lay my patient, a cross-bred Labrador. He must have been a big, powerful dog in his time, but the signs of age showed in the white hairs round his muzzle and the pale opacity in the depth of his eyes. He lay quietly and looked at me without hostility.

11   "Getting on a bit, isn't he, Mr. Dean?"

12   "Aye, he is that. Nearly fourteen, but he's been like a pup galloping about until these last few weeks. Wonderful dog for his age is old Bob, and he's never offered to bite anybody in his life. Children can do anything with him. He's my only friend now—I hope you'll soon be able to put him right."

13   "Is he off his food, Mr. Dean?"

14   "Yes, clean off, and that's a strange thing because by gum, he could eat. He always sat by me and put his head on my knee at meal times, but he hasn't been doing it lately."

15   When his master spoke, the tail thumped twice on the blankets and a momentary interest showed in the white old eyes; but it quickly disappeared and the blank, inward look returned.

16   I passed my hand carefully over the dog's abdomen. Ascites was pronounced and the dropsical fluid had gathered till the pressure was intense. "Come on, old chap," I said, "let's see if we can roll you over." The dog made no resistance as I eased him slowly on to his other side, but, just as the movement was completed, he whimpered and looked round. The cause of the trouble was now only too easy to find.

17   I palpated gently. Through the thin muscle of the flank I could feel a hard, corrugated mass; certainly a splenic or hepatic carcinoma, enormous and completely inoperable. I stroked the old dog's head as I tried to collect my thoughts. This wasn't going to be easy.

18   "Is he going to be ill for long?" the old man asked, and came the thump, thump of the tail at the sound of the loved voice. "It's miserable when Bob isn't following me round the house when I'm doing my little jobs."

19   "I'm sorry, Mr. Dean, but I'm afraid this is something very serious. You see this large swelling. It is caused by an internal growth."

20   "You mean . . . cancer?" the little man said faintly.

21   "I'm afraid so, and it has progressed too far for anything to be done. I wish there was something I could do to help him, but there isn't."

22   The old man looked bewildered and his lips trembled. "Then he's going to die?"

23   I swallowed hard. "We really can't just leave him to die, can we? He's in some distress now, but it will soon be an awful lot worse. Don't you think it would be kindest to put him to sleep? After all he's had a good, long inning." I always aimed at a brisk, matter-of-fact approach, but the old clichés had an empty ring.

24   The old man was silent, then he said, "Just a minute," and slowly and painfully knelt down by the side of the dog. He did not speak, but ran his hand

again and again over the grey muzzle and the ears, while the tail thump, thump, thumped on the floor.

25 He knelt there a long time while I stood in the cheerless room, my eyes taking in the faded pictures on the walls, the frayed, grimy curtains, the broken-springed armchair.

26 I filled the syringe and said the things I always said. "You needn't worry, this is absolutely painless. Just an overdose of an anaesthetic. It is really an easy way out for the old fellow."

27 The dog did not move as the needle was inserted, and, as the barbiturate began to flow into the vein, the anxious expression left his face and the muscles began to relax. By the time the injection was finished, the breathing had stopped.

28 "Is that it?" the old man whispered.

29 "Yes, that's it," I said. "He is out of his pain now."

30 The old man stood motionless except for the clasping and unclasping of his hands. When he turned to face me his eyes were bright. "That's right, we couldn't let him suffer, and I'm grateful for what you've done. And now, what do I owe you for your services, sir?"

31 "Oh that's all right, Mr. Dean," I said quickly. "It's nothing—nothing at all. I was passing right by here—it was no trouble."

32 The old man was astonished. "But you can't do that for nothing."

33 "Now please say no more about it, Mr. Dean. As I told you, I was passing right by your door." I said goodbye and went out of the house, through the passage and into the street. In the bustle of people and the bright sunshine, I could still see only the stark, little room, the old man and his dead dog.

34 As I walked towards my car, I heard a shout behind me. The old man was shuffling excitedly towards me in his slippers. His cheeks were streaked and wet, but he was smiling. In his hand he held a small, brown object.

35 "You've been very kind, sir. I've got something for you." He held out the object and I looked at it. It was tattered but just recognisable as a precious relic of a bygone celebration.

36 "Go on, it's for you," said the old man. "Have a cigar."

• Vocabulary

dank (9)
dropsical (16)
hepatic (17)
stark (33)
opacity (10)
palpated (17)
carcinoma (17)
ascites (16)
corrugated (17)
clichés (23)

• The Facts

1. What was the name of the old man's dog?
2. Where was the old man's wife?
3. What was wrong with the dog?

4. What kind of dog did the old man own?
5. How much did the veterinarian charge the old man for the visit?

● The Strategies

1. In paragraph 3, the author writes about the old man's house that it looked "as though it wouldn't be able to hold out much longer." Aside from its descriptive effect, what does this observation add to the story?
2. Examine paragraph 9. How does the author drive home to us the stark reality of the old man's poverty?
3. In paragraphs 16 and 17, Herriot uses terms such as "ascites" and "splenic or hepatic carcinoma," which ordinary readers are unlikely to understand. What does he accomplish by using this specialized vocabulary?
4. What is Herriot's attitude toward the old man? How can you tell how Herriot really feels?
5. What is ironic about the old man's offering the veterinarian a cigar?

● The Issues

1. Some critics have accused Herriot of being "a Disney veterinarian." What is your opinion of this accusation? What justification do you think critics have for making it?
2. What is your opinion of the euthanasia of terminally ill animals? Why should not a similar mercy be applied to humans in the same situation?
3. How should dead animals be disposed of? What is your opinion of pet cemeteries that offer formal burial sites with headstones for dead pets?
4. Why do you think Herriot has been such a popular writer? What explanation for his popularity can you infer from this story?
5. This particular story is about the relationship between an old man and his dog. Why do you think the dog has become such a popular pet worldwide?

● Suggestions for Writing

1. Write about any incident that occurred between you and an animal.
2. Write about your favorite pet.

● CHAPTER WRITING ASSIGNMENTS

1. Select any two paragraphs, one from an article in *Reader's Digest* and another from an article in *The New Yorker*. Analyze the differences in the language (diction, phrasing, sentence style, and paragraph length) and speculate on the intended audience of each magazine.
2. Write an essay on the meaning and practice of rhetoric as exemplified in this chapter.

WRITING ASSIGNMENTS FOR A SPECIFIC AUDIENCE

1. To an audience of African American readers, write an essay arguing for or against the idea that race relations in America have gotten better since Dr. King delivered his "I Have a Dream" speech.
2. Write an essay aimed at an audience of eighth graders explaining to them what they can expect to encounter later in high school and college writing courses.

COLLABORATIVE WRITING PROJECT

Dividing a group of students into two teams, have each team poll its members for the writing techniques, tips, and practices they have successfully used over the years to write their essays. Make a list of these after appropriate discussion and explanation. Get together as two groups to compare and discuss the findings. Finally, have each group team write an essay that summarizes what the team has found about the writing process and the way it has been practiced by its members.

REAL-LIFE STUDENT WRITING

E-Mail From Samoa

The following excerpt is from an actual e-mail written by one student to another. The sender, Mark, is writing from the South Pacific island of Samoa, where he had arrived two months before as a Peace Corps volunteer. He was on the island only a month when he and another volunteer fell afoul of local authorities and were expelled from the Peace Corps—in their opinion, unfairly. To appeal their expulsion would have required a trip to Washington, DC, which neither could afford. Instead of returning home as his friend did, Mark decided to stay on the island for as long as he could. He took a job teaching English at a local school while he applied for his visa, which would allow him to remain in Samoa for at least another year. Mark sent this e-mail to his friend, Adam. The two had been classmates in a cross-cultural program in British and American studies.

• • •

```
Mark
From:     Mark Smith
Sent:     Wednesday, January 15, 2004  4:14PM
To:       Adam Johnson
Subject:  Hey What's Up
```

1

3

What Is a Writer's Voice?

ROAD MAP TO WRITER'S VOICE

Most writers do not sit down to write consciously in a certain style. They do, however, try to project a certain voice onto the page. Sometimes the writer assumes this voice deliberately, but often it is chosen for the writer by the psychology of audience and material—by the need and occasion that make the writing necessary.

Here is an example. You are the boss. You sit down to write a memo to your employees, but being the boss goes to your head, and you write:

> Illumination of the overhead fixtures must be extinguished by the final person exiting the premises.

This notice tells the reader two things: First, it tells the reader to turn off the lights before leaving the room; second, it tells the reader that you are the boss and you say so. That is not the only kind of notice you could have written. You might, for example, have written this equivalent:

> The last person to leave this room must turn out the overhead lights.

This makes the point, but you think it also makes you sound awfully humble.

The difference between these two is not one of content, but of tone or style. It is tone of voice when you are composing the memo, for what you tried to do was not write in a certain style but to sound like the boss; to the reader, however, it is your style.

Many writing teachers, with some justification, approach voice and style as if they were always related to the writer's psychology. If you had confidence in your authority as the boss, if you really felt comfortable with your power, you wouldn't think it necessary to sound like God in your every memo. So if you must sound like the Almighty in your memos, perhaps it is because you really don't feel at ease with the idea of being the boss. Many similar mishaps of voice or style in student papers can be traced to a psychological uncertainty about the material, to an unconfident attitude, or even to the writer's feelings about the assignment.

The relationship between feelings and tone is slippery but makes sense. It is only natural that our feelings about a subject or person should spill out onto the page and affect our tone. Here is an example:

> Dear Monty,
>
> I'm really sick and tired of your mess. It's embarrassing to walk into our room with a visitor and see your bed unmade, your clothes scattered all over the floor, and your beer cans making sticky rings on the table. I've told you before about this, but now I want you to know that if you don't shape up, I'm moving out.
>
> Bob

Do you hear the angry tone in that note? On the other hand, listen to the difference in the tone of this e-mail:

> Hi, Everyone,
>
> I have just returned from my backpacking trip through Europe. You won't believe the wonderful experiences I had. At one point I even lost my passport, but the American consulate was very helpful in getting me a temporary one. I met some exciting new friends, who, like me, were camping out or riding the second class compartments of the trains. The world is really a great place. Anyway, I'll wait until I see you to fill in the details. I sure missed you. A bunch.
>
> Irene

The practical effect of tone on our writing is sometimes plainly evident and sometimes not. We would expect, for example, that if we write a letter to a roommate we're mad at, our tone will reflect that anger. Less evident is the effect a feeling of boredom about an assignment might have on our tone. It is only logical to assume that if we're bored with the topic and think it a waste of our time, our tone will be affected for the worse. That is why instructors always urge students to write about topics they like.

Another piece of traditional advice related to tone is the ancient warning instructors often give to student writers to be themselves—and it is genuinely good advice. Don't try to write in a voice that is not truly your own; don't try to put on airs in your writing. If you do, your tone is bound to be affected by the pretense. You will discover, if you have not already, that you do your best writing when you simply sound like your true self.

These psychological considerations aside, we do know—on a more practical level—that voice in writing is influenced by three factors under the writer's control: (1) vocabulary, (2) syntax, and (3) attitude.

Voice: Why Did the Chicken Cross the Road?

Conservative politician (self-righteous)
My fellow conservatives, the chicken crossed to steal a job from a decent, hardworking American. That is what these reckless left-wing chickens do.

Children's book writer (nonsensical)
Did the chicken cross the road? Did he cross it with a toad? Yes, the chicken crossed the road, but why he crossed, I've not been told!

Ernest Hemingway (straightforward)
To die. In the rain. Alone. From an *idée fixe*.

Grandpa (self-important)
In my day, we didn't ask why the chicken crossed the road. Someone told us that the chicken crossed the road, and that was good enough for us.

Karl Marx (philosophical)
It was a historical inevitability.

Sigmund Freud (psychological)
All chickens cross the road for the same reason: sex.

Albert Einstein (ambiguous)
Did the chicken really cross the road or did the road cross under the chicken?

Colonel Sanders (miffed)
Darn! I missed one!

Vocabulary

The English language is a treasure trove of words. It is bursting with synonyms—words that have the same meaning. As you write, you can express the same idea any number of different ways. Often, the choice seems to boil down to expressing yourself either simply or complexly. You can give the facts without frills while remaining quietly in the background or you can mount the pulpit, take on the grandeur of a bishop, and posture.

The second choice is one that we do not recommend. You will do your reader a kindness if you write without putting on airs or pretending to be a know-it-all. Choose your words to inform, not to impress. Faced with a choice between a big, little-known word and a smaller, better-known equivalent, choose the smaller one because more people will understand it. Your overriding aim is to tell your reader what you know about the subject, not to impress. (Yet, oddly enough, sophisticated readers are generally impressed by writing that is plain and to the point.)

Here's an example of a style of writing that even for its day was pompous:

> It is the fate of those who toil at the lower employments of life, to be rather driven by the fear of evil, than attracted by the prospect of good; to be exposed to censure, without hope of praise; to be disgraced by miscarriage, or punished for neglect, where success would have been without applause, and diligence without reward. —Samuel Johnson, *Preface to the Dictionary of the English Language* (1755)

Johnson was a noted scholar and conversationalist who had a definite flair for spoken and written pompousness. If we replace some of the words with their more common equivalents, the passage takes on a different tone:

> It is the lot of those who work at the lower jobs of life, to be rather driven by the fear of evil, than drawn by the likelihood of good; to be open to criticism, without hope of praise; to be shamed by mistakes, or punished for neglect, where success would have been without recognition, and hard work without reward.

Even with the changes in vocabulary, this passage is still hard to follow because it suffers from a second problem—knotty syntax.

Syntax

The arrangement of words in a sentence is known as *syntax*. Because English is so flexible, the same idea can be said in many different ways and in many different kinds of sentences. The considerate writer uses only as many sentences as are needed to get the job done. Most of these sentences will be simple subject-verb-object combinations. For the sake of variety, a few will have a different construction, but mainly, the sentences will be short and easy to read and understand.

In constructing a sentence, your aim should be to express your ideas clearly. It should not be to show off your learning or scholarship. The Johnson passage quoted earlier consists of a single sentence punctuated by commas and semicolons. A little alteration in the syntax—mainly in the use of simpler sentences—makes the ideas in the quotation much easier to understand:

> Those who work at the lower jobs of life are driven by the fear of doing wrong, rather than drawn by the likelihood of doing good. They are open to criticism yet have no hope of praise. They are both shamed by their mistakes and punished for their neglect; yet their success wins no recognition, and their hard work no reward.

Now we have a better idea of what Johnson is trying to say. We may agree or disagree with it, but at least we share a common understanding.

Why, then, did Johnson express himself the way he did if he could have written the same idea more clearly? The answer is because of his *attitude*—the third factor affecting a writer's voice.

Attitude

Your attitude toward yourself and your work is bound to affect your voice. If you regard writing as a means of communication, you will work hard to make your meaning clear. If you regard writing as a reflection of your inner self, you might behave as some people do when they stand in front of a mirror: preen and strut.

The problem with the Johnson passage is that he does not believe what he says, because he knows it is not true. He is, in fact, pretending to feel a humility and modesty he does not have. It is his attitude toward the work that makes his style so self-inflated and pompous. Here are the next two paragraphs from the preface:

> Among these unhappy mortals is the writer of dictionaries; whom mankind have considered, not as the pupil, but the slave of science, the pioneer of literature, doomed only to remove rubbish and clear obstructions from the paths of Learning and Genius, who press forward to conquest and glory, without bestowing a smile on the humble drudge that facilitates their progress. Every other author may aspire to praise; the lexicographer can only hope to escape reproach, and even this negative recompense has been yet granted to very few.
>
> I have, notwithstanding this discouragement, attempted a dictionary of the English language, which, while it was employed in the cultivation of every species of literature, has itself been hitherto neglected, suffered to spread, under the direction of chance, into wild exuberance, resigned to the tyranny of time and fashion, and exposed to the corruptions of ignorance, and caprices of innovation.

Does Johnson really believe that he is a "drudge," a "slave of science," a garbage man "doomed only to remove rubbish and clear obstructions from the paths of Learning and Genius"? Nothing about the man or his life tells us that he saw himself in such lowly terms. He had just completed, after a massive labor of nine years, a dictionary that defined 43,000 words supported by 114,000 quotations from literature. His was not the first dictionary of the English language, but even today it is ranked as the most important. Part of the problem with his preface is that he uses it to show off his learning and scholarship rather than to communicate facts about his dictionary. His attitude affects his voice.

Vocabulary, syntax, and attitude—these are all factors the writer can control. They are important in developing the voice you can use in factual writing. Naturally, they're less important in some other kinds of writing—poetry and fiction, for example—that aim to do more than merely communicate an idea. The lessons we are teaching are meant only for factual writing, which is to prose what the camel is to the desert. For that kind of writing, you must strive for clarity and readability if you wish to please your reader.

CHAPTER 3 • What Is a Writer's Voice?

Exercises

1. How would you characterize the tone of the following paragraph that came from a letter a tenant sent to a landlord?

   If you want your rent this month, you'd better do something about the leaky kitchen faucet. I've told you about this at least five times and still you have done nothing. The dripping at night is driving me mad. I don't know what ever possessed me to rent such a pigsty. But if you don't do something about it, I'm going to go to the city and complain and tell them what a roach-infested dump you're renting to innocent people.

2. Change the voice of the preceding paragraph by rewriting it to reflect a softer tone.

3. How would you characterize the voice in the following excerpts? Describe the vocabulary, syntax, and attitude evident in each passage:
   a. I am 20 years of age today. The past year has been an eventful one to me, and I thank God for all His mercies to me. I trust my life in the future may be spent in His service.
   b. The Internet is a treasure chest of data, facts, statistics, opinions, speculations, and viewpoints—all that comes under the general heading of information.
   c. In clinical psychiatry and psychoanalytical work there are few such heroes, men and women whose intelligence, compassion, and above all, candor, illuminate their deeds, their words, and the failures they inevitably suffer.

4. Write two brief letters on any event that occurred in your school and in which you took part: one to a parent or an authority figure and the other to your best friend.

5. Write a paragraph or two analyzing the differences in the voices you used in the letters you just wrote.

6. What attitude toward medical doctors does the following paragraph reveal? What kind of person might write such a paragraph?

   If I had cancer, I would not submit to chemotherapy. I watched my mom have chemotherapy, and it made her so nauseated and so weak that she often said, "I can't take this anymore." I can't see why it would be beneficial to put what is obviously a strong poison into any human body. Surely, nature has better ways of curing cancer than chemotherapy. Doctors are just too tunnel-visioned to use natural herbs to help cure cancer. They think that only prescriptions you get through pharmaceutical companies can possibly be effective; yet, I know someone who was cured of breast cancer by drinking a quart of carrot juice every day.

7. Which of the two statements that follow reflects the more rational and objective tone toward a photographic exhibit? Identify the vocabulary that makes the difference.
   a. This photographic exhibit is a wonderful gallery of varied portraits—politician, seamstress, drifter, ballet dancer, mother, and much more. Each

portrait has been shot against a starkly white background, which seems to allow no place for the subject to hide and therefore suggests a confrontational intimacy between the photographer and the subject. Because of the backlighting involved, each head appears to sprout a halo that contrasts paradoxically with the shadows on the face, lending a beguiling mystery to the facial features in each frame.

b. After staring at this portrait gallery for almost an hour, I decided that it was all meaningless trash. Who wants to waste time looking at this sort of nightmare? This is not art; it is the revelation of a sick mind. All I could see were men and women photographed against a white wall. Some kind of weird circle of light surrounded their heads, but their faces were dark and wrinkled. The ugliness of these faces really bugged me. I felt depressed to think that this Halloween-type exhibit was considered great modern art and was shown at the local museum.

ADVICE

How to Say Nothing in Five Hundred Words
PAUL ROBERTS

Paul McHenry Roberts (1917–1967) taught college English for over twenty years, first at San Jose State College and later at Cornell University. He wrote several books on linguistics, including *Understanding Grammar* (1954), *Patterns of English* (1956), and *Understanding English* (1958).

Freshman composition, like everything else, has its share of fashions. In the 1950s, when this article was written, the most popular argument raging among student essayists was the proposed abolition of college football. With the greater social consciousness of the early 1960s, the topic of the day became the morality of capital punishment. Topics may change, but the core principles of good writing remain constant, and this essay has become something of a minor classic in explaining them. Be concrete, says Roberts; get to the point; express your opinions colorfully. Refreshingly, he even practices what he preaches. His essay is humorous, direct, and almost salty in summarizing the working habits that all good prose writers must cultivate.

● ● ●

1   It's Friday afternoon, and you have almost survived another week of classes. You are just looking forward dreamily to the weekend when the English instructor says: "For Monday you will turn in a five-hundred-word composition on college football."

2   Well, that puts a good hole in the weekend. You don't have any strong views on college football one way or the other. You get rather excited during the season and go to all the home games and find it rather more fun than not. On the other hand, the class has been reading Robert Hutchins in the anthology and perhaps Shaw's "Eighty-Yard Run," and from the class discussion you

have got the idea that the instructor thinks college football is for the birds. You are no fool. You can figure out what side to take.

After dinner you get out the portable typewriter that you got for high school graduation. You might as well get it over with and enjoy Saturday and Sunday. Five hundred words is about two double-spaced pages with normal margins. You put in a sheet of paper, think up a title, and you're off:

Why College Football Should Be Abolished

College football should be abolished because it's bad for the school and also for the players. The players are so busy practicing that they don't have any time for their studies.

This, you feel, is a mighty good start. The only trouble is that it's only thirty-two words. You still have four hundred and sixty-eight to go, and you've pretty well exhausted the subject. It comes to you that you do your best thinking in the morning, so you put away the typewriter and go to the movies. But the next morning you have to do your washing and some math problems, and in the afternoon you go to the game. The English instructor turns up too, and you wonder if you've taken the right side after all. Saturday night you have a date, and Sunday morning you have to go to church. (You can't let English assignments interfere with your religion.) What with one thing and another, it's ten o'clock Sunday night before you get out the typewriter again. You make a pot of coffee and start to fill out your views on college football. Put a little meat on the bones.

Why College Football Should Be Abolished

In my opinion, it seems to me that college football should be abolished. The reason why I think this to be true is because I feel that football is bad for the colleges in nearly every respect. As Robert Hutchins says in his article in our anthology in which he discusses college football, it would be better if the colleges had race horses and had races with one another, because then the horses would not have to attend classes. I firmly agree with Mr. Hutchins on this point, and I am sure that many other students would agree too.

One reason why it seems to me that college football is bad is that it has become too commercial. In the olden times when people played football just for the fun of it, maybe college football was all right, but they do not play college football just for the fun of it now as they used to in the old days. Nowadays college football is what you might call a big business. Maybe this is not true at all schools, and I don't think it is especially true here at State, but certainly this is the case at most colleges and universities in America nowadays, as Mr. Hutchins points out in his very interesting article. Actually the coaches and alumni go around to the high schools and offer the high school stars large salaries to come to their colleges and play football for them. There was one case where a high school star was offered a convertible if he would play football for a certain college.

Another reason for abolishing college football is that it is bad for the players. They do not have time to get a college education, because they are so busy playing football. A football player has to practice every afternoon from three to six and then he is so tired that he can't concentrate on his studies. He just feels like dropping off to sleep after dinner, and then the next day he goes to his classes without having studied and maybe he fails the test.

(Good ripe stuff so far, but you're still a hundred and fifty-one words from home. One more push.)

Also I think college football is bad for the colleges and the universities because not very many students get to participate in it. Out of a college of ten thousand students only seventy-five or a hundred play football, if that many. Football is what you might call a spectator sport. That means that most people go to watch it but do not play it themselves.

(Four hundred and fifteen. Well, you still have the conclusion, and when you retype it, you can make the margins a little wider.)

These are the reasons why I agree with Mr. Hutchins that college football should be abolished in American colleges and universities.

4   On Monday you turn it in, moderately hopeful, and on Friday it comes back marked "weak in content" and sporting a big "D."

5   This essay is exaggerated a little, not much. The English instructor will recognize it as reasonably typical of what an assignment on college football will bring in. He knows that nearly half of the class will contrive in five hundred words to say that college football is too commercial and bad for the players. Most of the other half will inform him that college football builds character and prepares one for life and brings prestige to the school. As he reads paper after paper all saying the same thing in almost the same words, all bloodless, five hundred words dripping out of nothing, he wonders how he allowed himself to get trapped into teaching English when he might have had a happy and interesting life as an electrician or a confidence man.

6   Well, you may ask, what can you do about it? The subject is one on which you have few convictions and little information. Can you be expected to make a dull subject interesting? As a matter of fact, this is precisely what you are expected to do. This is the writer's essential task. All subjects, except sex, are dull until somebody makes them interesting. The writer's job is to find the argument, the approach, the angle, the wording that will take the reader with him. This is seldom easy, and it is particularly hard in subjects that have been much discussed: College Football, Fraternities, Popular Music, Is Chivalry Dead?, and the like. You will feel that there is nothing you can do with such subjects except repeat the old bromides. But there are some things you can do which will make your papers, if not throbbingly alive, at least less insufferably tedious than they might otherwise be.

Avoid the Obvious Content

7   Say the assignment is college football. Say that you've decided to be against it. Begin by putting down the arguments that come to your mind: it is too commercial, it takes the students' minds off their studies, it is hard on the players, it makes the university a kind of circus instead of an intellectual center, for most schools it is financially ruinous. Can you think of any more arguments, just offhand? All right. Now when you write your paper, make sure that you don't use any of the material on this list. If these are the points that leap to your mind, they will leap to everyone else's too, and whether you get a "C" or a "D" may depend on whether the instructor reads your paper early when he is fresh and tolerant or late, when the sentence "In my opinion, college football has become too commercial," inexorably repeated, has brought him to the brink of lunacy.

8   Be against college football for some reason or reasons of your own. If they are keen and perceptive ones, that's splendid. But even if they are trivial or foolish or indefensible, you are still ahead so long as they are not everybody else's reasons too. Be against it because the colleges don't spend enough money on it to make it worthwhile, because it is bad for the characters of the spectators, because the players are forced to attend classes, because the football stars hog all the beautiful women, because it competes with baseball and is therefore un-American and possibly Communist-inspired. There are lots of more or less unused reasons for being against college football.

9   Sometimes it is a good idea to sum up and dispose of the trite and conventional points before going on to your own. This has the advantage of indicating to the reader that you are going to be neither trite nor conventional. Something like this:

> We are often told that college football should be abolished because it has become too commercial or because it is bad for the players. These arguments are no doubt very cogent, but they don't really go to the heart of the matter.

Then you go to the heart of the matter.

Take the Less Usual Side

10   One rather simple way of getting into your paper is to take the side of the argument that most of the citizens will want to avoid. If the assignment is an essay on dogs, you can, if you choose, explain that dogs are faithful and lovable companions, intelligent, useful as guardians of the house and protectors of children, indispensable in police work—in short, when all is said and done, man's best friends. Or you can suggest that those big brown eyes conceal, more often than not, a vacuity of mind and an inconstancy of purpose; that the dogs you have known most intimately have been mangy, ill-tempered brutes, incapable of instruction; and that only your nobility of mind and fear of arrest prevent you from kicking the flea-ridden animals when you pass them on the street.

11   Naturally personal convictions will sometimes dictate your approach. If the assigned subject is "Is Methodism Rewarding to the Individual?" and you are a pious Methodist, you have really no choice. But few assigned subjects, if any, will fall in this category. Most of them will lie in broad areas of discussion with much to be said on both sides. They are intellectual exercises, and it is legitimate to argue now one way and now another, as debaters do in similar circumstances. Always take the side that looks to you hardest, least defensible. It will almost always turn out to be easier to write interestingly on that side.

12   This general advice applies where you have a choice of subjects. If you are to choose among "The Value of Fraternities" and "My Favorite High School Teacher" and "What I Think About Beetles," by all means plump for the beetles. By the time the instructor gets to your paper, he will be up to his ears in tedious tales about a French teacher at Bloombury High and assertions about how fraternities build character and prepare one for life. Your views on beetles, whatever they are, are bound to be a refreshing change.

13   Don't worry too much about figuring out what the instructor thinks about the subject so that you can cuddle up with him. Chances are his views are no stronger than yours. If he does have convictions and you oppose him, his problem is to keep from grading you higher than you deserve in order to show he is not biased. This doesn't mean that you should always cantankerously dissent from what the instructor says; that gets tiresome too. And if the subject assigned is "My Pet Peeve," do not begin, "My pet peeve is the English instructor who assigns papers on 'my pet peeve.'" This was still funny during the War of 1812, but it has sort of lost its edge since then. It is in general good manners to avoid personalities.

Slip Out of Abstraction

14 If you will study the essay on college football [near the beginning of this essay], you will perceive that one reason for its appalling dullness is that it never gets down to particulars. It is just a series of not very glittering generalities: "football is bad for the colleges," "it has become too commercial," "football is big business," "it is bad for the players," and so on. Such round phrases thudding against the reader's brain are unlikely to convince him, though they may well render him unconscious.

15   If you want the reader to believe that college football is bad for the players, you have to do more than say so. You have to display the evil. Take your roommate, Alfred Simkins, the second-string center. Picture poor old Alfy coming home from football practice every evening, bruised and aching, agonizingly tired, scarcely able to shovel the mashed potatoes into his mouth. Let us see him staggering up to the room, getting out his econ textbook, peering desperately at it with his good eye, falling asleep and failing the test in the morning. Let us share his unbearable tension as Saturday draws near. Will he fail, be demoted, lose his monthly allowance, be forced to return to the coal mines? And if he succeeds, what will be his reward? Perhaps a slight ripple of applause when the third-string center replaces him, a moment of elation in the locker room if the

team wins, of despair if it loses. What will he look back on when he graduates from college? Toil and torn ligaments. And what will be his future? He is not good enough for pro football, and he is too obscure and weak in econ to succeed in stocks and bonds. College football is tearing the heart from Alfy Simkins and, when it finishes with him, will callously toss aside the shattered hulk.

16   This is no doubt a weak enough argument for the abolition of college football, but it is a sight better than saying, in three or four variations, that college football (in your opinion) is bad for the players.

17   Look at the work of any professional writer and notice how constantly he is moving from the generality, the abstract statement, to the concrete example, the facts and figures, the illustrations. If he is writing on juvenile delinquency, he does not just tell you that juveniles are (it seems to him) delinquent and that (in his opinion) something should be done about it. He shows you juveniles being delinquent, tearing up movie theatres in Buffalo, stabbing high school principals in Dallas, smoking marijuana in Palo Alto. And more than likely he is moving toward some specific remedy, not just a general wringing of the hands.

18   It is no doubt possible to be too concrete, too illustrative or anecdotal, but few inexperienced writers err this way. For most the soundest advice is to be seeking always for the picture, to be always turning general remarks into seeable examples. Don't say, "Sororities teach girls the social graces." Say, "Sorority life teaches a girl how to carry on a conversation while pouring tea, without sloshing the tea into the saucer." Don't say, "I like certain kinds of popular music very much." Say, "Whenever I hear Gerber Sprinklittle play 'Mississippi Man' on the trombone, my socks creep up my ankles."

Get Rid of Obvious Padding

19   The student toiling away at his weekly English theme is too often tormented by a figure: five hundred words. How, he asks himself, is he to achieve this staggering total? Obviously by never using one word when he can somehow work in ten.

20   He is therefore seldom content with a plain statement like "Fast driving is dangerous." This has only four words in it. He takes thought, and the sentence becomes:

> In my opinion, fast driving is dangerous.

Better, but he can do better still:

> In my opinion, fast driving would seem to be rather dangerous.

If he is really adept, it may come out:

> In my humble opinion, though I do not claim to be an expert on this complicated subject, fast driving, in most circumstances, would seem to be rather dangerous in many respects, or at least so it would seem to me.

Thus four words have been turned into forty, and not an iota of content has been added.

21   Now this is a way to go about reaching five hundred words, and if you are content with a "D" grade, it is as good a way as any. But if you aim higher, you must work differently. Instead of stuffing your sentences with straw, you must try steadily to get rid of the padding, to make your sentences lean and tough. If you are really working at it, your first draft will greatly exceed the required total, and then you will work it down, thus:

> It is thought in some quarters that fraternities do not contribute as much as might be expected to campus life.
>
> Some people think that fraternities contribute little to campus life.
>
> The average doctor who practices in small towns or in the country must toil night and day to heal the sick.
>
> Most country doctors work long hours.
>
> When I was a little girl, I suffered from shyness and embarrassment in the presence of others.
>
> I was a shy little girl.
>
> It is absolutely necessary for the person employed as a marine fireman to give the matter of steam pressure his undivided attention at all times.
>
> The fireman has to keep his eye on the steam gauge.

22   You may ask how you can arrive at five hundred words at this rate. Simple. You dig up more real content. Instead of taking a couple of obvious points off the surface of the topic and then circling warily around them for six paragraphs, you work in and explore, figure out the details. You illustrate. You say that fast driving is dangerous, and then you prove it. How long does it take to stop a car at forty and at eighty? How far can you see at night? What happens when a tire blows? What happens in a head-on collision at fifty miles an hour? Pretty soon your paper will be full of broken glass and blood and headless torsos, and reaching five hundred words will not really be a problem.

Call a Fool a Fool

23   Some of the padding in freshman themes is to be blamed not on anxiety about the word minimum but on excessive timidity. The student writes, "In my opinion, the principal of my high school acted in ways that I believe every unbiased person would have to call foolish." This isn't exactly what he means. What he means is, "My high school principal was a fool." If he was a fool, call him a fool. Hedging the thing about with "in-my-opinion's" and "it-seems-to-me's" and "as-I-see-it's" and "at-least-from-my-point-of-view's" gains you nothing. Delete these phrases whenever they creep into your paper.

24   The student's tendency to hedge stems from a modesty that in other circumstances would be commendable. He is, he realizes, young and inexperienced,

and he half suspects that he is dopey and fuzzy-minded beyond the average. Probably only too true. But it doesn't help to announce your incompetence six times in every paragraph. Decide what you want to say and say it as vigorously as possible, without apology and in plain words.

25 Linguistic diffidence can take various forms. One is what we call euphemism. This is the tendency to call a spade "a certain garden implement" or women's underwear "unmentionables." It is stronger in some eras than others and in some people than others but it always operates more or less in subjects that are touchy or taboo: death, sex, madness, and so on. Thus we shrink from saying "He died last night" but say instead "passed away," "left us," "joined his Maker," "went to his reward." Or we try to take off the tension with a lighter cliché: "kicked the bucket," "cashed in his chips," "handed in his dinner pail." We have found all sorts of ways to avoid saying "mad": "mentally ill," "touched," "not quite right upstairs," "feebleminded," "innocent," "simple," "off his trolley," "not in his right mind." Even such a now plain word as "insane" began as a euphemism with the meaning "not healthy."

26 Modern science, particularly psychology, contributes many polysyllables in which we can wrap our thoughts and blunt their force. To many writers there is no such thing as a bad schoolboy. Schoolboys are maladjusted or unoriented or misunderstood or in the need of guidance or lacking in continued success toward satisfactory integration of the personality as a social unit, but they are never bad. Psychology no doubt makes us better men and women, more sympathetic and tolerant, but it doesn't make writing any easier. Had Shakespeare been confronted with psychology, "To be or not to be" might have come out, "To continue as a social unit or not to do so. That is the personality problem. Whether 'tis a better sign of integration at the conscious level to display a psychic tolerance toward the maladjustments and repressions induced by one's lack of orientation in one's environment or—" But Hamlet would never have finished the soliloquy.

27 Writing in the modern world, you cannot altogether avoid modern jargon. Nor, in an effort to get away from euphemism, should you salt your paper with four-letter words. But you can do much if you will mount guard against those roundabout phrases, those echoing polysyllables that tend to slip into your writing to rob it of its crispness and force.

Beware of Pat Expressions

28 Other things being equal, avoid phrases like "other things being equal." Those sentences that come to you whole, or in two or three doughy lumps, are sure to be bad sentences. They are no creation of yours but pieces of common thought floating in the community soup.

29 Pat expressions are hard, often impossible, to avoid, because they come too easily to be noticed and seem too necessary to be dispensed with. No writer avoids them altogether, but good writers avoid them more often than poor writers.

30 By "pat expressions" we mean such tags as "to all practical intents and purposes," "the pure and simple truth," "from where I sit," "the time of his life," "to the ends of the earth," "in the twinkling of an eye," "as sure as you're born," "over my dead body," "under cover of darkness," "took the easy way out," "when all is said and done," "told him time and time again," "parted the best of friends," "stand up and be counted," "gave him the best years of her life," "worked her fingers to the bone." Like other clichés, these expressions were once forceful. Now we should use them only when we can't possibly think of anything else.

31 Some pat expressions stand like a wall between the writer and thought. Such a one is "the American way of life." Many student writers feel that when they have said that something accords with the American way of life or does not they have exhausted the subject. Actually, they have stopped at the highest level of abstraction. The American way of life is the complicated set of bonds between a hundred and eighty million ways. All of us know this when we think about it, but the tag phrase too often keeps us from thinking about it.

32 So with many another phrase dear to the politician: "this great land of ours," "the man in the street," "our national heritage." These may prove our patriotism or give a clue to our political beliefs, but otherwise they add nothing to the paper except words.

Colorful Words

33 The writer builds with words, and no builder uses a raw material more slippery and elusive and treacherous. A writer's work is a constant struggle to get the right word in the right place, to find that particular word that will convey his meaning exactly, that will persuade the reader or soothe him or startle or amuse him. He never succeeds altogether—sometimes he feels that he scarcely succeeds at all—but such successes as he has are what make the thing worth doing.

34 There is no book of rules for this game. One progresses through everlasting experiment on the basis of ever-widening experience. There are few useful generalizations that one can make about words as words, but there are perhaps a few.

35 Some words are what we call "colorful." By this we mean that they are calculated to produce a picture or induce an emotion. They are dressy instead of plain, specific instead of general, loud instead of soft. Thus, in place of "Her heart beat," we may write, "her heart pounded, throbbed, fluttered, danced." Instead of "He sat in his chair," we may say, "he lounged, sprawled, coiled." Instead of "It was hot," we may say, "It was blistering, sultry, muggy, suffocating, steamy, wilting."

36 However, it should not be supposed that the fancy word is always better. Often it is as well to write "Her heart beat" or "It was hot" if that is all it did or all it was. Ages differ in how they like their prose. The nineteenth century liked it rich and smoky. The twentieth has usually preferred it lean and cool. The

twentieth century writer, like all writers, is forever seeking the exact word, but he is wary of sounding feverish. He tends to pitch it low, to understate it, to throw it away. He knows that if he gets too colorful, the audience is likely to giggle.

37   See how this strikes you: "As the rich, golden glow of the sunset died away along the eternal western hills, Angela's limpid blue eyes looked softly and trustingly into Montague's flashing brown ones, and her heart pounded like a drum in time with the joyous song surging in her soul." Some people like that sort of thing, but most modern readers would say, "Good grief," and turn on the television.

Colored Words

38 Some words we would call not so much colorful as colored—that is, loaded with associations, good or bad. All words—except perhaps structure words—have associations of some sort. We have said that the meaning of a word is the sum of the contexts in which it occurs. When we hear a word, we hear with it an echo of all the situations in which we have heard it before.

39   In some words, these echoes are obvious and discussible. The word *mother*, for example, has, for most people, agreeable associations. When you hear *mother* you probably think of home, safety, love, food, and various other pleasant things. If one writes, "She was like a mother to me," he gets an effect which he would not get in "She was like an aunt to me." The advertiser makes use of the associations of *mother* by working it in when he talks about his product. The politician works it in when he talks about himself.

40   So also with such words as *home, liberty, fireside, contentment, patriot, tenderness, sacrifice, childlike, manly, bluff, limpid*. All of these words are loaded with associations that would be rather hard to indicate in a straightforward definition. There is more than a literal difference between "They sat around the fireside" and "They sat around the stove." They might have been equally warm and happy around the stove, but *fireside* suggests leisure, grace, quiet tradition, congenial company, and *stove* does not.

41   Conversely, some words have bad associations. *Mother* suggests pleasant things, but *mother-in-law* does not. Many mothers-in-law are heroically lovable and some mothers drink gin all day and beat their children insensible, but these facts of life are beside the point. The point is that *mother* sounds good and *mother-in-law* does not.

42   Or consider the word *intellectual*. This would seem to be a complimentary term, but in point of fact it is not, for it has picked up associations of impracticality and ineffectuality and general dopiness. So also such words as *liberal, reactionary, Communist, socialist, capitalist, radical, schoolteacher, truck driver, undertaker, operator, salesman, huckster, speculator*. These convey meaning on the literal level, but beyond that—sometimes, in some places—they convey contempt on the part of the speaker.

43   The question of whether to use loaded words or not depends on what is being written. The scientist, the scholar, try to avoid them; for the poet, the advertising writer, the public speaker, they are standard equipment. But every

writer should take care that they do not substitute for thought. If you write, "Anyone who thinks that is nothing but a Socialist (or Communist or capitalist)" you have said nothing except that you don't like people who think that, and such remarks are effective only with the most naive readers. It is always a bad mistake to think your readers more naive than they really are.

Colorless Words

44 But probably most student writers come to grief not with words that are colorful or those that are colored but with those that have no color at all. A pet example is *nice,* a word we would find it hard to dispense with in casual conversation but which is no longer capable of adding much to a description. Colorless words are those of such general meaning that in a particular sentence they mean nothing. Slang adjectives like *cool* ("That's real cool") tend to explode all over the language. They are applied to everything, lose their original force, and quickly die.

45 Beware also of nouns of very general meaning, like *circumstances, cases, instances, aspects, factors, relationships, attitudes, eventualities,* etc. In most circumstances you will find that those cases of writing which contain too many instances of words like these will in this and other aspects have factors leading to unsatisfactory relationships with the reader resulting in unfavorable attitudes on his part and perhaps other eventualities, like a grade of "D." Notice also what *etc.* means. It means "I'd like to make this list longer, but I can't think of any more examples."

- **Vocabulary**

contrive (5)	bromides (6)	inexorably (7)
cogent (9)	vacuity (10)	warily (22)
diffidence (25)	euphemism (25)	jargon (27)
polysyllables (27)	elusive (33)	induce (35)

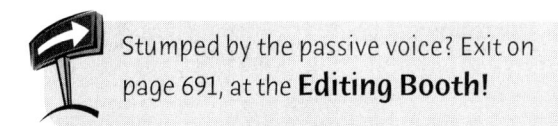

> Stumped by the passive voice? Exit on page 691, at the **Editing Booth!**

EXAMPLES

Tone: The Writer's Voice in the Reader's Mind
MORT CASTLE

Mort Castle (b. 1946) is a dedicated teacher and fiction writer. He has 350 short stories and a dozen books to his credit, including *Cursed Be the Child* (1994), *The Strangers* (1984), and *Moon on the Water* (2000). Castle takes particular pride in the fact that 2,000 of his students, ranging in age from six to ninety-three, have seen their work in print. He is a frequent keynote speaker at writing conferences or workshops. His book, *Writing Horror* (1997), for which he served as editor, has become the "bible" for aspiring horror authors. He is also the executive editor of Thorby Comics, which publishes the popular comic books *Night City, Death Asylum, The Skuler, Blythe: Nightvision,* and *Johnny Cosmic.*

Novice writers often think that tone is used only in speaking, not in writing. By using numerous examples and taking on a humorous tone, Castle convinces us that tone is a key ingredient in the relationship between reader and writer.

• • •

1   Johnny, the new kid, walks into third grade, casually waves to his teacher, Ms. Cruth, and says, "How's it goin', Butthead?"
2   "We do not talk that way in this class, Johnny," says Ms. Cruth. Opting for educational strategy #101: neo-traditional negative reinforcement, but not allowed to hit, she sends Johnny to the corner.
3   The next day, Johnny steps into the classroom, with "Hey, what's up, Ms. Bimbo?"
4   "Corner, Johnny," says Ms. Cruth.
5   The day after, Johnny comes into the classroom. He says, "Good morning, Ms. Cruth."
6   "Go to the corner, Johnny," says Ms. Cruth.
7   "Huh?" Johnny's inquiring mind wants to know, "Why are you sending me to the corner? I did not call you 'Butthead' and I did not call you 'Ms. Bimbo.' and I didn't say one word that might be considered pejorative!"
8   "No," says Ms. Cruth, "but I don't like your tone."
9   When we speak to others, our tone of voice is no less important than our actual words. Call your faithful friend, Fido, into the room, for our experiment in tone. Granted, with the difference in the communicative arts as practiced by human being and canine being, the following analogy is not fully apropos, yet 'twill serve:
10 Talk to your dog. Though your tone is a warm one, you know, "praise the pup, I love my wonderful companionate animal, etc.," don't use real words of praise. Try: "Fido, you double ugly moron, you stinky poo puppy, you drecky wretched doggy dastard!"
11 Fido wags his tail. All is well. I may not get the words, but I know what you mean.
12 In speaking, stressed sounds, vocal cadences, pronunciation, rhythm and pauses, repetition, voice pitch, timbre, and volume, etc. help the listener get the message. The "sincere" tone tells the listener "I'm sorry" truly indicates . . . "I am sorry." Yet, with a sneering, sarcastic tone, those same two words can implicitly say, "I am sorry I did not cause you half the grief, misery, agony, and woe I could have had I only been a trace more imaginative."
13 The "Listen up" tone is for when the mechanic needs to hear that this time, damn it, he'd better find the oil leak.

14   The "cooing selected little nothings" tone can be well suited for the prelude to the proposal moment, whether that be a major commitment proposal or a suggestion of serious messing around.

15   Most kids know the tone that signals, "You'd really better cut it out and this time I mean it!"

16   The conspiratorial tone signals it's "True dirt dishing time."

17   The "ha ha ha ready to happen" tone is for the joke . . .

18   The writer putting words on the page (or computer screen or out there in cyberville) also has a tone of voice. The writer, of course, does not have a speaker's unique tone tools: vocal cords, sinus cavities, lip, tongue, and palette, etc. Nor does the writer have a raised eyebrow to provide a hint, nor a smile, nor a broad hand wave. Instead, tone is achieved by choice and arrangement of our prime building blocks: words.

19   The reader hears—and responds to—that tone of voice as he is reading.

39   That voice, that tone, must be suited to the material so that reader clearly understands what is said, understands on both the literal and the figurative levels.

21   "Let us go then, you and I," T. S. Eliot begins "The Love Song of J. Alfred Prufrock." The tone is somber and formal, made more so, perhaps, by the deliberate grammar fluff of the nominative "I" used instead of the objective "me," an error often made by those hoping to sound "educated": the reader is invited to undertake a desolate and wearying journey. The tone helps to establish the mood of the poem, gives the reader a feeling. But if Eliot had begun (with or without an apology to The Ramones): "Hey ho! Let's go!"

22   Or had he whined in classic Jerry Lewis style, "Look, would you please come on, already? Aw, just come on, okay?"

23   Or in keeping with contemporary "dirty words currently acceptable on Prime Time Network TV": "Let's haul ass!"

24   Well, we would not exactly be anticipating gloom and soul dread as we walk with J. Alfred, would we?

25   Consider the opening of Edgar Allan Poe's familiar "The Tell-Tale Heart":

26   "True!—nervous—very very dreadfully nervous I had been and am, but why will you say that I am mad?"

27   There's an immediate rush of energy with that very first word and exclamation point: A frantic energy. A crazed madman's energy. You hear the protagonist protesting way, way more than a "bit too much" the idea that he is insane. To use today's pseudo-artistic term, the "edgy tone" of the story is established: a barely-in-control-and-soon-to-wig-out tone.

28   The right tone, the proper voice in the reader's mind, lets you say what you want to say the way you want to say it.

29   And the wrong tone . . .

30   In the scene that follows from a deservedly unpublished short story, Mike is visited by his psychopathic brother, Arnold. Mike believes Arnold intends to kill him—and Mike is right.

31   Arnold stepped in. "How are you doing, Mike?" he asked.
32   "I've been doing all right," Mike responded promptly.

33   "That's good," Arnold said.
34   "How about you?" Mike asked.
35   "Well, I guess I have been doing okay," Arnold calmly said.
36   "I'm glad to hear it. It certainly is a snowy day."
37   "I guess everyone talks about the weather but no one does anything about it," Arnold said. "That is my opinion, anyway."
38   "I agree," Mike said.
39   Then Arnold shouted, "It's a perfect day for you to die, you dirty rat!"

40   Except for Arnold's closing outburst, the tone of this passage is mundane, prosaic, no more tense (or interesting) than that of an ordinary, everyday conversation you might overhear in the dentist's waiting room. It is totally unsuited for what is meant to be a moment of high drama.

41   Here's another cutting from a different "wrong tone" story. The protagonist is attempting to get up the nerve to stand before an Alcoholics Anonymous meeting and say for the first time: "My name is Sharon and I am an alcoholic." She sits, biting her nails, and then shakily gets to her feet, . . . flinging her hair back like a galloping filly tossing its mane . . ."

42   Uh-uh. That "mane tossing filly" gives the scene an inappropriate tone. My Girl Friend Flicka. Light-hearted Retro-Range-Romance: Up rides Dale Evans on Buttermilk, meeting her spunky niece from out East, Manda Llewellyn Travis . . . This light hearted tone and the upbeat optimism one feels make for what most critics would judge a wrong tone.

43   That is not to say, of course, that only the "comic tone" can be employed for comic writing, that the "romantic tone" must be used for romance writing, that a horrific tone must be used for horror writing.

44   Let's spend a tone moment with the late Charles Beaumont, one of my all time literary heroes and the writer of many classic short short stories that came to typify what is thought of as "Playboy Magazine horror" in the late 1950s and 1960s.

45   Beaumont's short story is called "Free Dirt":
46   It opens:

> "No fowl had ever looked so posthumous."

47   Seven words—and the tone is established. "Posthumous" gives the sentence an overly formal, almost pompous tone. "Fowl," rather than chicken, is likewise formal. The voice that reads this sentence inside the reader's mind is wryly sardonic, not unlike the voice of the late Alfred Hitchcock. There's humor here, but it's dark humor, the laughter we can hear as we stand by the grave site, and it's perfect for a brief and utterly chilling story, a work of "moral fiction" in the best sense: It teaches in a non-didactic way.

48   The right tone, then, is the one that allows the writer to speak clearly to the reader. The goal, of course, is the essence of the writer-reader relationship: "I get it," the reader implicitly says.

49   You don't want your home builder cracking up with laughter, telling you that you should be swapping one-liners with Leno, when you demand he put

the front door in front, just as the blueprints have it, instead of on the roof—and you don't want your reader snickering, giggling, guffawing, and hoo-ha-ing because your voice in his mind cues him to laugh at your sequel to *A Christmas Carol,* in which Tiny Tim dies of consumption, Bob Cratchit is run over by a hansom cab, and Scrooge gets murdered by Marley's ghost!

Vocabulary

neo-traditional (2)	pejorative (7)	apropos (9)
cadences (12)	pitch (12)	timbre (12)
conspiratorial (16)	figurative (20)	desolate (21)
pseudo-artistic (27)	mundane (40)	prosaic (40)
posthumous (46)	sardonic (47)	non-didactic (47)

The Facts

1. What kind of student is the author portraying through Johnny? How would you react to having such a student in your class?
2. What was wrong with Johnny's third greeting?
3. What analogy does the author use to illustrate the importance of tone over words in speech? What other analogy can you cite?
4. What elements, not used in writing, can a person use to communicate in speech?
5. What is the only arsenal available to writers to establish tone? Does this limited arsenal curtail good writers? Give examples that support your opinion.

The Strategies

1. What rhetorical strategy does the author use to persuade us that his view of tone is correct? Are you convinced? Give reasons for your answer.
2. In what paragraph does the author switch from vocal tone to writing tone? Were you able to follow his shift? If no, why not? If yes, why?
3. Why do you think the author uses the opening line of T. S. Eliot's "J. Alfred Prufrock" as an example of setting a definite tone? Do you think this was a good choice? Why or why not?
4. In paragraph 29, the author does not finish his sentence, but leaves you hanging with ellipsis points. How would you finish this sentence?
5. In what paragraph does the author tell you what the right tone is? What will the reader implicitly say if the author has established the right tone?

The Issues

1. Are there kinds of writing in which no tone is necessary? If you think there are, give examples of this kind of writing.
2. How can mastery of tone help your writing?
3. How can voice and tone be suited to the material on the figurative level? (See paragraph 20.) Explain this idea by using an example.

4. The author assures us that tone does not always need to match the writing genre. For instance, a comic tone might be used for a romance and a romantic tone for a comedy. Cite an example from literature that mixes tone and genre.
5. What tone would most likely suit the following situations?
   a. A mother writes goodbye to her son leaving for war
   b. A college student thanks her sorority sisters for giving her a wild bachelorette party the week before her wedding
   c. A minister encourages his congregation to donate money for some new hymnbooks

Suggestions for Writing

1. Write a letter to one of the following people, using an appropriate tone:
   a. To your boss, announcing that you are quitting the company for a new assignment
   b. To your father, asking for money to pay your car insurance
   c. To your best friend, describing a recent camping trip
   d. To an acquaintance who borrowed money from you and refuses to pay you back
2. Write an essay in which you define tone as you now understand it.

Me

Mary MacLane

Mary MacLane (1881–1929) is an obscure literary figure whose diary, written at the age of 19 and published in 1901, made her an overnight sensation. Fascinated by the eccentric egotism of this young girl, readers alternately labeled her "obscene," "brilliant," or "mad." This frenzy of attention resulted in the diary selling over 80,000 copies in its first month of publication. As a result of this amazing and sudden popularity, MacLane for seven years hobnobbed with Bohemian intellectuals of Chicago, Boston, and New York. Ironically, she never published another significant work after her diary, and she died alone and poor in a Chicago hotel room at the relatively young age of 48—a fate she often dreaded.

The journal entry that follows takes the reader into an unusually intelligent but disturbed mind. What makes the writing so fascinating is that at the turn of the century, girls of Mary's age did not express themselves so freely and with such vehemence. Mary bitterly resented the humdrum life she was forced to lead in Butte, Montana, and she felt completely misplaced in a family of the northwestern plains who simply did not understand her.

• • •

1   I of womankind and of nineteen years, will now begin to set down as full and frank a Portrayal as I am able of myself, Mary MacLane, for whom the world contains not a parallel.

2. I am convinced of this, for I am odd.
3. I am distinctly original innately and in development.
4. I have in me a quite unusual intensity of life.
5. I can feel.
6. I have a marvelous capacity for misery and for happiness.
7. I am broad-minded.
8. I am genius.
9. I am a philosopher of my own good peripatetic school.
10. I care neither for right nor for wrong—my conscience is nil.
11. My brain is a conglomeration of aggressive versatility.
12. I have reached a truly wonderful state of miserable morbid unhappiness.
13. I know myself, oh, very well.
14. I have attained an egotism that is rare indeed.
15. I have gone into the deep shadows.
16. All this constitutes oddity. I find, therefore, that I am quite, quite odd. . . .
17. I was born in 1881 at Winnepeg, in Canada. Whether Winnepeg will yet live to be proud of this fact is a matter for some conjecture and anxiety on my part. When I was four years old I was taken with my family to a little town in western Minnesota, where I lived a more or less vapid and lonely life until I was ten. We came then to Montana.
18. Whereat the aforesaid life was continued.
19. My father died when I was eight.
20. Apart from feeding and clothing me comfortably and sending me to school—which is no more than was due me—and transmitting to me the MacLane blood and character, I can not see that he ever gave me a single thought.
21. Certainly he did not love me, for he was quite incapable of loving any one but himself. And since nothing is of any moment in this world without the love of human beings for each other, it is a matter of supreme indifference to me whether my father, Jim MacLane of selfish memory, lived or died.
22. He is nothing to me.
23. There are with me still a mother, a sister, and two brothers.
24. They also are nothing to me.
25. They do not understand me any more than if I were some strange live curiosity, as which I dare say they regard me.
26. I am peculiarly of the MacLane blood, which is Highland Scotch. My sister and brothers inherit the traits of their mother's family, which is of Scotch Lowland descent. This alone makes no small degree of difference. Apart from this the MacLanes—these particular MacLanes—are just a little bit different from every family in Canada, and from every other that I've known. It contains and has contained fanatics of many minds—religious, social, whatnot, and I am a true MacLane.
27. There is absolutely no sympathy between my immediate family and me. There can never be. My mother, having been with me during the whole of my nineteen years, has an utterly distorted idea of my nature and its desires, if indeed she has any idea of it.

28 When I think of the exquisite love and sympathy which might be between a mother and daughter, I feel myself defrauded of a beautiful thing rightfully mine, in a world where for me such things are pitiably few.

29 It will always be so.

30 My sister and brothers are not interested in me and my analyses and philosophy, and my wants. Their own are strictly practical and material. The love and sympathy between human beings is to them, it seems, a thing only for people in books.

31 In short, they are Lowland Scotch, and I am a MacLane.

32 And so, as I've said, I carried my uninteresting existence into Montana. The existence became less uninteresting, however, as my versatile mind began to develop and grow and know the glittering things that are. But I realized as the years were passing that my own life was at best a vapid, negative thing.

33 A thousand treasures that I wanted were lacking.

34 I graduated from the high school with these things: very good Latin; good French and Greek; indifferent geometry and other mathematics; a broad conception of history and literature; peripatetic philosophy that I acquired without any aid from the high school; genius of a kind, that has always been with me; an empty heart that has taken on a certain wooden quality; an excellent strong young woman's body; a pitiably starved soul.

35 With this equipment I have gone my way through the last two years. But my life, though unsatisfying and warped, is no longer insipid. It is fraught with a poignant misery—the misery of nothingness.

36 I have no particular thing to occupy me. I write every day. Writing is a necessity—like eating. I do a little housework, and on the whole I am rather fond of it—some parts of it. I dislike dusting chairs, but I have no aversion to scrubbing floors. Indeed, I have gained much of my strength and gracefulness of body from scrubbing the kitchen floor—to say nothing of some fine points of philosophy. It brings a certain energy to one's body and to one's brain.

37 But mostly I take walks far away in the open country. Butte and its immediate vicinity present as ugly an outlook as one could wish to see. It is so ugly indeed that it is near the perfection of ugliness. And anything perfect, or nearly so, is not to be despised. I have reached some astonishing subtleties of conception as I have walked for miles over the sand and barrenness among the little hills and gulches. Their utter desolateness is an inspiration to the long, long thoughts and to the nameless wanting. Every day I walk over the sand and barrenness.

38 And so, then, my daily life seems an ordinary life enough, and possibly, to an ordinary person, a comfortable life.

39 That's as may be.

40 To me it is an empty, damned weariness.

41 I rise in the morning; eat three meals; and walk; and work a little, read a little, write; see some uninteresting people; go to bed.

42 Next day, I rise in the morning; eat three meals; and walk; and work a little, read a little, write; see some uninteresting people; go to bed.

43 Again I rise in the morning; eat three meals; and walk; and work a little, read a little, write; see some uninteresting people; go to bed.

what your essay will cover, which is what the thesis should do. Here is an example:

Poor: How life is in a racial ghetto.

Better: Residents of a racial ghetto tend to have a higher death rate, a higher infant mortality rate, and a higher unemployment rate than do residents of the suburbs.

2. **A thesis must not be worded as a question (usually, the answer to the question could be the thesis).** The purpose of the thesis is to spell out the main idea of the essay, which is difficult, if not impossible, to do in a question:

    Poor: Do Americans really need large refrigerators?

    Better: If Americans did their marketing daily, as do most Europeans, they could save energy by using smaller refrigerators.

3. **A thesis should not be too broad.** An overly broad thesis will commit you to write on an idea you may be unable to adequately cover in a short essay. The solution in that case is to rewrite your thesis and begin again, for no matter how hard you work, your essay will otherwise seem labored and abstract:

    Poor: The literature of mythology contains many resurrection stories.

    Better: One of the oldest resurrection myths is the story of the Egyptian god Osiris.

4. **A thesis should not contain unrelated elements.** The expression of a single and unified purpose should be your overriding aim in drafting your thesis. You are trying to prove one point, make one case, dramatize one situation. Veteran writers can, of course, do more than one task in an essay, but this is a skill acquired only with much practice. The beginner is better off framing the thesis to commit the essay to making one point or performing one function. One way to do this is to avoid using a compound sentence as a thesis statement.

    A compound sentence is two independent clauses joined by a conjunction. An independent clause is a grammatical construction that can be punctuated to make sense on its own. Two independent clauses automatically imply two different ideas, which may be hard for the writer to keep separate or treat fairly in a single essay without making a muddle of both. Here is an example:

    Poor: All novelists seek the truth, and some novelists are good psychologists.

    Properly punctuated, each clause expresses a different idea and can stand on its own. "All novelists seek the truth" is one idea. "Some novelists are good psychologists" is the other. Writing an essay on this thesis will require the writer to prove two unrelated points.

    Better: In their attempt to probe human nature, many novelists become excellent psychologists.

5. **A thesis should not contain phrases like "I think" or "in my opinion" because they weaken a writer's argument.** Use the thesis to tell your reader plainly where you stand, what you think, or what you intend to prove in the essay. This is no place to be wishy-washy or uncertain as if you were not quite sure about your opinion or viewpoint. Indeed, if you are not sure about the opinion expressed in your thesis, you should rethink it until you are.

   Poor: In my opinion, smoking should be outlawed because of the adverse health effects of "passive smoking."

   Better: Smoking should be outlawed because of the adverse health effects of "passive smoking."

6. **A thesis should not be expressed in vague language.** With only rare exceptions, it is a general truth that the vague thesis will lead to a vague essay. If the thesis is vaguely worded, it is usually because the writer is uncertain of what to say or has not sufficiently thought through the controlling idea. Should that happen to you, rethink your views on the topic.

   Poor: Religion should not be included in the school curriculum because it can cause trouble.

   Better: Religion should not be included in the school curriculum because it is a highly personal commitment.

7. **A thesis must not be expressed in muddled or incoherent language.** If the thesis is incoherent or muddled, the essay is likely to follow suit. Work on your thesis until it expresses exactly the opinion or viewpoint you intend to cover in the essay.

   Poor: The benefits of clarity and easy communication of a unified language compel a state to adopt codes to the effect that make bilingualism possible but preserving a single official language for transacting business and social intercourse.

   Better: The benefits of clarity and easy communication offered by a single official language in a state are compelling and persuasive.

8. **A thesis should not be expressed in figurative language.** Figurative language has a place in factual writing, but not in a thesis statement. As we have stressed, the thesis is where you plainly state the main point of your essay. Figurative language tends to weaken this healthy plainness and should, therefore, never be used in a thesis.

   Poor: The Amazons of today are trying to purge all the stag words from our language.

   Better: Today's feminists are trying to eliminate the use of sex-biased words from public documents and publications.

9. **A thesis must not be nonsensical.** Above all else, your thesis statement must make sense. You cannot defend the indefensible or argue the unarguable, nor should you waste ink on behalf of a thesis that is absurd. For

example, consider this sentence:

Poor: A good university education is one that is useful, fulfilling, and doesn't require study.

As a thesis, it is virtually useless, even though it does predict, control, and obligate. The problem is that its proposition is plainly nonsense. We cannot conceive of a good university education that doesn't require study. Only a frivolous essay could be written on such a thesis.

Better: A good university education is one that is useful, fulfilling, and challenging.

We are not suggesting that your theses should always advance narrowly orthodox or boringly conventional ideas, but the ideas they contain should be sensible enough to merit discussion by reasonable people.

The Explicit versus the Implicit Thesis

Anyone who has ever listened to a speaker ramble or read a piece of aimless writing can readily appreciate the usefulness of a thesis statement that sets down clearly the writer's main point. However, not all writers find it necessary to be explicit about their main points. Veteran writers know how to make a main point and stick faithfully to it without broadcasting it in a thesis statement. A conspicuous example of this is the essay *Once More to the Lake* reprinted in Chapter 16. In that essay, the writer sticks to the point without ever expressing it in a single thesis sentence.

As a matter of fact, many veteran writers do not need or use a thesis. Yet, they always write with a built-in sense of structure; they do not stray from the point or lose their train of thought. The explicit thesis admittedly has become a requirement of classroom writing, but while it is a useful device for the inexperienced, it can be too simplistic for the professional writer—too much of a formula. Later, as you become a more experienced writer, you too might abandon the use of the explicit thesis. But for now, it is a convention that will help you write better essays.

● Exercises

1. Formulate a thesis for one of the following topics. Use the step-by-step method outlined in the chapter.
    a. Adolescence
    b. Women and the draft
    c. Obligations of parents
    d. The entertainment world
    e. Spectator sports
2. Find a picture that expresses some aspect of today's society, such as violence, youthful idealism, sexual cautiousness, or religious piety; then write a thesis that could serve as an appropriate caption.

3. Underline the key words of the following theses:
   a. Memory entails recall, recognition, and revival.
   b. An argument must present both sides of the question being debated.
   c. The Amish people resist public education because they believe that a simple farm life is best and that formal education will corrupt their young people.
   d. A good farmer cooperates with weather, soil, and seed.
   e. Laura in "Flowering Judas" by Katherine Anne Porter is tortured by doubt, guilt, and disappointment.
   f. The racetracks, the ballparks, the fight rings, and the gridirons draw crowds in increasing numbers.
4. Which of the following theses is the best? Support your choice.
   a. Forest fires are enormously destructive because they ravage the land, create problems for flood control, and destroy useful lumber.
   b. Installment buying is of great benefit to the economy, having in mind the consumer to use a product while paying for it and being like forced savings.
   c. Television is a handicap.
5. The following theses are poorly worded. Analyze their weaknesses in terms of the nine errors discussed earlier, and rewrite each to make it clear and effective.
   a. In my opinion, birth control is the most urgent need in today's world.
   b. Just how far should the law go in its tolerance of pornography?
   c. How Christian missionaries were sent to the Ivory Coast of Africa to introduce Western civilization.
   d. The history of psychology had its inception with Plato and came to full term with Freud.
   e. Strip mining is an environmentally destructive solution to the problem of fuel shortage, and the fuel shortage is caused by our government's foreign policy.
   f. In the United States, the press is the watchdog of society.
   g. Three factors may be singled out as militating against the optimum adjustment that partners in the marriage relationship should experience as money, culture, and education.
   h. Homemaking is the most meaningful work a woman can perform.
   i. The problem with sound pollution is, How much longer can our ears bear the noise?
   j. The noteworthy relaxation of language taboos both in conversation and in print today.
   k. My feeling is that educationalists are just as infatuated with jargon as are sociologists.
   l. Retirement homes need not be depressing places which commercial activities can bring residents together in shared experiences.
   m. The city of New York is in bad shape.
6. From the following pairs of theses, pick out the thesis with the discussible issue. Explain your choice.
   a. (1) The Eiffel Tower is located near the center of Paris.
      (2) Three spectacular crimes have been committed near the Eiffel Tower in Paris.

b. (1) Michelangelo's *David* symbolizes the best qualities of youthful manhood.
   (2) Michelangelo's *David* is carved out of white marble from Carara.
c. (1) The Model-A Ford became popular because it was dependable and uncomplicated.
   (2) Close to a million people still own Model-A Fords today.
d. (1) In Hemingway's *Farewell to Arms,* the knee injury suffered by Frederick Henry symbolizes man's wounded spirit.
   (2) In Hemingway's novel *Farewell to Arms,* Frederick Henry is shot in the knee while driving an ambulance truck.
e. (1) The Greek historian Herodotus claimed that the city of Troy was destroyed in 1250 B.C.
   (2) Troy was an important city because any fortress built on its site could control all shipping traffic through the Dardanelles.
f. (1) Good grammar is the equivalent of good manners.
   (2) According to the rules of grammar, "he don't" is a barbarism.

ADVICE

The Thesis

SHERIDAN BAKER

Sheridan Baker (b. 1918) is Emeritus Professor of English at the University of Michigan and has been a Fulbright lecturer. He has edited several works by the eighteenth-century novelist Henry Fielding, including *Joseph Andrews, Shamela,* and *Tom Jones.* Baker's two rhetorics, *The Practical Stylist* (1962) and *The Complete Stylist* (1976) have been widely used in colleges throughout the United States.

In this excerpt from The Complete Stylist, *Baker advises the student to state clearly, in a sharp-edged thesis, the controlling purpose of the essay.*

• • •

1   You can usually blame a bad essay on a bad beginning. If your essay falls apart, it probably has no primary idea to hold it together. "What's the big idea?" we used to ask. The phrase will serve as a reminder that you must find the "big idea" behind your several smaller thoughts and musings before you start to write. In the beginning was the logos, says the Bible—the idea, the plan, caught in a flash as if in a single word. Find your logos, and you are ready to round out your essay and set it spinning.

2   The big idea behind our ride in the speeding car[1] was that in adolescence, especially, the group can have a very deadly influence on the individual.

---
[1] The example to which the paragraph refers occurred earlier in material that was not printed here.

If you had not focused your big idea in a thesis, you might have begun by picking up thoughts at random, something like this:

> Everyone thinks he is a good driver. There are more accidents caused by young drivers than any other group. Driver education is a good beginning, but further practice is very necessary. People who object to driver education do not realize that modern society, with its suburban pattern of growth, is built around the automobile. The car becomes a way of life and a status symbol. When a teenager goes too fast he is probably only copying his own father.

3   A little reconsideration, aimed at a good thesis-sentence, could turn this into a reasonably good beginning:

> Modern society is built on the automobile. Every child looks forward to the time when he can drive; every teenager, to the day when his father lets him take out the car alone. Soon he is testing his skill at higher and higher speeds, especially with a group of friends along. One final test at extreme speeds usually suffices. The teenager's high-speed ride, if it does not kill him, will probably open his eyes to the deadly dynamics of the group.

4   Thus the central idea, or thesis, is your essay's life and spirit. If your thesis is sufficiently firm and clear, it may tell you immediately how to organize your supporting material and so obviate elaborate planning. If you do not find a thesis, your essay will be a tour through the miscellaneous. An essay replete with scaffolds and catwalks—"We have just seen this; now let us turn to this"—is an essay in which the inherent idea is weak or nonexistent. A purely expository and descriptive essay, one simply about "Cats," for instance, will have to rely on outer scaffolding alone (some orderly progression from Persia to Siam) since it really has no idea at all. It is all subject, all cats, instead of being based on an idea about cats.

The Argumentative Edge

Find Your Thesis

5   The about-ness puts an argumentative edge on the subject. When you have something to say about cats, you have found your underlying idea. You have something to defend, something to fight about: not just "Cats," but "The cat is really man's best friend." Now the hackles on all dog men are rising, and you have an argument on your hands. You have something to prove. You have a thesis.

6   "What's the big idea, Mac?" Let the impudence in that time-honored demand remind you that the best thesis is a kind of affront to somebody. No one will be very much interested in listening to you deplete the thesis "The dog is man's best friend." Everyone knows that already. Even the dog lovers will be uninterested, convinced that they know better than you. But the cat . . .

7   So it is with any unpopular idea. The more unpopular the viewpoint and the stronger the push against convention, the stronger the thesis and the more energetic the essay. Compare the energy in "Democracy is good" with that in "Communism is good," for instance. The first is filled with platitudes, the second with plutonium. By the same token, if you can find the real energy in "Democracy is good," if you can get down through the sand to where the roots and water are, you will have a real essay, because the opposition against which you generate your energy is the heaviest in the world: boredom. Probably the most energetic thesis of all, the greatest inner organizer, is some tired old truth that you cause to jet with new life, making the old ground green again.

8   To find a thesis and put it into one sentence is to narrow and define your subject to a workable size. Under "Cats" you must deal with all felinity from the jungle up, carefully partitioning the eons and areas, the tigers and tabbies, the sizes and shapes. The minute you proclaim the cat the friend of man, you have pared away whole categories and chapters, and need only think up the arguments sufficient to overwhelm the opposition. So, put an argumentative edge on your subject—and you will have found your thesis.

9   Simple exposition, to be sure, has its uses. You may want to tell someone how to build a doghouse, how to can asparagus, how to follow the outlines of relativity, or even how to write an essay. Performing a few exercises in simple exposition will no doubt sharpen your insight into the problems of finding orderly sequences, of considering how best to lead your readers through the hoops, of writing clearly and accurately. It will also illustrate how much finer and surer an argument is.

10   You will see that picking an argument immediately simplifies the problems so troublesome in straight exposition: the defining, the partitioning, the narrowing of the subject. Actually, you can put an argumentative edge on the flattest of expository subjects. "How to build a doghouse" might become "Building a doghouse is a thorough introduction to the building trades, including architecture and mechanical engineering." "Canning asparagus" might become "An asparagus patch is a course in economics." "Relativity" might become "Relativity is not so inscrutable as many suppose." You have simply assumed that you have a loyal opposition consisting of the uninformed, the scornful, or both. You have given your subject its edge; you have limited and organized it at a single stroke. Pick an argument, then, and you will automatically be defining and narrowing your subject, and all the partitions you don't need will fold up. Instead of dealing with things, subjects, and pieces of subjects, you will be dealing with an idea and its consequences.

Sharpen Your Thesis

11   Come out with your subject pointed. Take a stand, make a judgment of value. Be reasonable, but don't be timid. It is helpful to think of your thesis, your main idea, as a debating question—"Resolved: Old age pensions must go"—taking out the "Resolved" when you actually write the subject down. But your resolution will be even stronger, your essay clearer and tighter, if you can sharpen your thesis even further: "Resolved: Old age pensions must go because—."

Fill in that blank and your worries are practically over. The main idea is to put your whole argument into one sentence.

12   Try, for instance: "Old age pensions must go because they are making people irresponsible." I don't know at all if that is true, and neither will you until you write your way into it, considering probabilities and alternatives and objections, and especially the underlying assumptions. In fact, no one, no master sociologist or future historian, can tell absolutely if it is true, so multiplex are the causes in human affairs, so endless and tangled the consequences. The basic assumption—that irresponsibility is growing—may be entirely false. No one, I repeat, can tell absolutely. But by the same token, your guess may be as good as another's. At any rate, you are now ready to write. You have found your logos.

13   Now you can put your well-pointed thesis-sentence on a card on the wall in front of you to keep from drifting off target. But you will now want to dress it for the public, to burnish it, and make it comely. Suppose you try:

> Old age pensions, perhaps more than anything else, are eroding our heritage of personal and familial responsibility.

But is this true? Perhaps you had better try something like:

> Despite their many advantages, old age pensions may actually be eroding our heritage of personal and familial responsibility.

This is really your thesis, and you can write that down on a scrap of paper too.

Vocabulary

obviate (4)   replete (4)   inherent (4)
affront (6)   platitudes (7)   multiplex (12)

EXAMPLES

The Grieving Never Ends

ROXANNE ROBERTS

Roxanne Roberts is an American journalist who occasionally writes for the *Los Angeles Times*.

This essay alerts us to the painful truth about suicide: Often, it can cause lifelong scars that linger to torment those left behind. As the author tells us, twenty years after her father's suicide, she still finds herself cleaning up the emotional debris from that tragic act.

• • •

1. The blood was like Jell-O. That is what blood gets like, after you die, before they tidy up. Somehow, I had expected it would be gone. The police and coroner spent more than an hour behind the closed door; surely it was someone's job to clean it up. But when they left, it still covered the kitchen floor like the glazing on a candy apple.

2. You couldn't mop it. You needed a dustpan and a bucket.

3. I got on my knees, slid the pan against the linoleum and lifted chunks to the bucket. It took hours to clean it all up.

4. It wasn't until I finally stood up that I noticed the pictures from his wallet. The wooden breadboard had been pulled out slightly, and four photographs were spilled across it. "Now what?" I thought with annoyance. "What were the police looking for?"

5. But then it hit me. The police hadn't done it. These snapshots—one of my mother, one of our dog and two of my brother and me—had been carefully set out in a row by my father.

6. It was his penultimate act, just before he knelt on the floor, put the barrel of a .22 rifle in his mouth, and squeezed the trigger.

7. He was 46 years old. I was 21. It has been 20 years since his death and I am still cleaning up.

8. By the time you finish this article, another person in the United States will have killed himself. More than 30,000 people do it every year, one every 15 minutes. My father's was a textbook case: Depressed white male with gun offs himself in May. December may be the loneliest month, April the cruelest, but May is the peak time for suicide. No one knows why, but I can guess: You've made it through another winter, but your world is no warmer.

9. This year, thousands of families will begin the process that ours began that night 20 years ago. Studies show that their grief will be more complicated, more intense and longer lasting than for any other form of death in the family. They will receive less support and more blame from others. Some will never really get over it: Children of suicides become a higher risk for suicide themselves.

10. These are the legacies of suicide: guilt, anger, doubt, blame, fear, rejection, abandonment and profound grieving.

11. Shortly after he died, I remember thinking, "I wonder how I'll feel about this in 20 years?"

12. Twenty years later, my father's suicide is, simply, a part of me. Think of your life as a can of white paint. Each significant experience adds a tiny drop of color: pink for a birthday, yellow for a good report card. Worries are brown; setbacks, gray. Lavender—my favorite color when I was a little girl—is for a pretty new dress. Over time, a color begins to emerge. Your personality.

13. When a suicide happens, someone hurls in a huge glob of red. You can't get it out. You can't start over. The red will always be there, no matter how many drops of yellow you add.

14. The call came about 9 p.m. It was a Friday night in suburban Minneapolis; the restaurant was packed. I was racing from the bar with a tray of drinks for my customers when the manager gestured me to the phone. It's your mother, she said.

15   "Roxanne, he's got a gun. He's in the garage with a gun. You have to come."

16   There had been many, many threats. This was different. There had never been a weapon before.

17   I made many choices that night; some were smart, some stupid, some crazy. I believed my father would indeed kill himself, sooner or later. Looking back, I feel lucky to have survived the night.

18   I drove past the house. He was standing in the shadows of the front yard; I couldn't see if he had the gun. I sped to a phone booth two blocks away and dialed.

19   She answered. "He's in the front yard," I said. "Can you get out?"

20   Five minutes later, she walked up to the car. He was quiet now, she said. She told him she was going to talk to me but would be back. Then she dropped the bombshell: He had held her at gunpoint for two hours before she called me.

21   We attempted rational conversation. We came to what seemed, at the time, a rational decision. We pulled up to the house, and my father came out the front door without the gun. He wanted to talk.

22   Give me the gun, I said. He refused. We can't talk until the gun is gone, we said. He shook his head. Come inside, he asked my mother. She shook her head.

23   He went back in, we drove to a coffee shop nearby. Frantic, we debated what to do next. To this day, I am still astonished that it never occurred to us to get help.

24   It was almost midnight; exhausted, my mother wanted to go home. She would stay the night if he let her take the gun away.

25   The house was silent; the door to the kitchen was shut. Ominous. My mother reached it first. Opened it.

26   "He did it," she whispered and slumped against the wall.

27   There was a time when suicide was considered a noble act of noble men. There was a time when corpses of suicides were dragged through the streets, refused Christian burial, and all the family's worldly goods were seized by the state. There was a time when romantics embraced suicide as a sign of their sensitivity.

28   Now we have long, impassioned debates about "assisted suicide," which pales beside the much larger issue: How do we feel about suicides when there isn't a terminal disease and a supportive family on hand? How do we feel about suicide if a 46-year-old guy just doesn't want to live anymore?

29   How do we feel about someone who's depressed but won't get help? Who blames all his problems on someone else? Who emotionally terrorizes and blackmails the people he loves? Is that OK too?

30   This is what I will tell you: Suicide is the last word in an argument, maybe an argument you never knew you were having. It is meant to be the last scene of the last act of life. Curtain down. End of story.

31   Except it isn't.

32   Tosca jumps off the parapet and I wonder who finds the shattered body. Romeo and Juliet die with a kiss, and I grieve for their parents.

33. The calls began: first to my father's only brother, who lived three blocks away, then to the police. Officers arrived, then detectives and someone from the coroner's office. Someone came into the living room to ask questions. I answered. Yes, he was depressed. Yes, he had threatened suicide. No, there wasn't a note.

34. This was the night of my brother Mike's high school senior prom. The dance was on a boat—we didn't know where—then there was an all-night party and a picnic the next day.

35. The detectives were still in the kitchen when Mike's car turned slowly onto the street and found a sea of police cars, lights flashing.

36. I watched from the front step as my mother ran to him. "Your father shot himself and he's dead," she said, guiding him to the neighbor's house. I watched as the police took the body out, dripping thick drops of blood. I watched my uncle stare blankly when I asked him to help clean up the kitchen.

37. White-lipped, he watched as I scooped up buckets of blood and flushed them down the toilet. I threw him an old sheet and told him to start wiping.

38. Years later, I learned how angry I made him, how he never forgave me for making him do that.

39. I was alone in the kitchen again when I noticed the pictures from my father's wallet. There were two portraits of his children. He loved both pictures. Everybody knew Mike Roberts loved his kids. So why ruin his son's prom night?

40. "You selfish bastard," I thought.

41. "You couldn't have waited one more night?"

42. My mother was never well liked by my father's sisters, and so they concluded that what had happened was my mother's fault. She was having an affair. That's what my father had told them before he died. The fact that she wore an aqua suit to the funeral was proof, wasn't it? (My mother swears there was no affair.)

43. And I? I was on her side. So it was my fault too.

44. After the funeral, we were simply abandoned by my father's family. My mother was still numb, but I was confused and angry. No calls, no help, no kindness. There were no invitations to dinner, not even Thanksgiving or Christmas.

45. Two years later, I found out why: They thought my mother and I killed him.

46. At one of those little get-togethers just after he died, my father's family decided that perhaps my mother and I had cleverly managed to murder my father and make it look like a suicide.

47. A cousin was so skeptical he went to the coroner and asked to see police photos. It was a suicide, the coroner assured him.

48. I vowed never, ever to speak to any of them again. When a distant member of the family—a devoted wife and mother—found her husband dead, sucking the end of an exhaust pipe, I was almost glad.

49. "Good," I thought fiercely. "Now they'll understand that suicide happens in nice families too."

50 Second-guessing is the devil's game, for there are no answers and infinite questions. But it is an inevitable, inescapable refrain, like a bad song you can't get out of your mind. What if, what if, what if. What if we had forced him to get help? Had him committed? What if we had called the police that night? Why didn't we?

51 Part of it was the natural tendency toward privacy. Part of it was arrogance, believing that we knew father best, or at least we could handle whatever he threw at us. I think I knew my father would have charmed the police, sent them away, leaving him furious with me, furious with my mother, dangerous, armed.

52 Maybe that's why. Maybe it was fear. Maybe not. Maybe I wanted him to die.

53 The police were puzzled by a wand of black mascara they found in my father's pocket. Another woman? Proof of an affair? The answer was simple: He used it to touch up the gray on his temples.

54 I don't think he ever really expected to get old. He was the baby, the youngest of five children. He was a very happy child; it was adulthood that he could never quite grasp.

55 He was charming enough to talk his way into job after job. There was the real estate phase, the radio phase, the political hanger-on phase. (In one photo, he is shaking hands with Hubert Humphrey.) No job lasted long; it never occurred to him to do heavy lifting.

56 Things started out well enough: a beautiful teenage bride, two kids and—after his mother died—his childhood home, a little bungalow, to raise his family in.

57 When did things start falling apart? Or were they ever really together?

58 I remember a night when I was 11. One of our cats streaked across the living room. In his mouth was a hamster that had somehow escaped from its cage. We all jumped to the rescue; my father caught the cat at the top of the basement stairs. He was suddenly, unaccountably livid. He shook the cat, and the hamster fell to the floor and scampered free.

59 I will never forget what came next: With all his might, he threw the cat down the stairs.

60 There was a moment of stunned silence, then tears and regret and an emergency trip to the vet. The cat lived. But I think I never fully trusted my father again.

61 The 10 years that followed were filled with sudden rages, explosions. I found out later that he first hit my mother when she was pregnant with me, and continued on and off for two decades.

62 We begged him to get help. We asked his brother and sisters to talk to him. And when, ultimately, I told my mother I thought she needed to leave for her own safety, my father saw that as a betrayal. He didn't speak to me for two months, until the night he died.

63 I lied to the police.

64 I told them there was no suicide note. In fact, there were three. Two were waiting in the living room as we walked into the house.

65 The note to my mother begged for forgiveness but said he simply could not go on the way things were. She has, to this day, no memory of reading it.

66 The note addressed to me opened with a rapprochement. "All is forgiven," read the first line. My eyes filled. No, I said silently, all is not forgiven.

67 The rest of the note instructed me to take care of things.

68 When I went to call the police, I found the third note, addressed to my brother. I cannot recall the specific words, but the short message to an 18-year-old boy was this: Son, you can't trust women.

69 My father had asked me to take care of things. And I was going to take care of things.

70 I stuffed all three notes in my purse and went back out to the living room. A week later, I ripped them to pieces and flushed them down the toilet.

71 When I recently told my brother about this, he was angry and hurt. He asked, quietly, "What made you think you could take something Dad left for me?" Fair question.

72 Here is the answer, Mike. It is simple. I hope you can live with it: I had to. The wishes of the dead do not take precedence over the needs of the living.

73 About a year after my father died, I left Minneapolis. I stumbled through my 20s, met a terrific man and got married, and spent a lot of time thinking about what I wanted to be when I grew up.

74 Nine months after the funeral, my brother moved to California. He was reckless, strong, adrift and almost died three times—once in a motorcycle accident, once in a stabbing and once in a heedless dive into a pool that split open his skull. He returned to Minnesota, subdued and gentle, and went on to a successful computer career. He was, surprisingly, never angry at my father or his family.

75 But he cannot bring himself to marry his girlfriend of 16 years. They live together, in a home they bought together, but he simply does not trust marriage.

76 Two years after the suicide, my mother remarried, changing her friends, her religion, even her first name. She was widowed again—a heart attack—and announced a year later that she was getting married again. Her fiancé was my cousin—her nephew by marriage. He was the son of the aunt who had accused us of murder.

77 "I expect you to be civil to her," my mother told me.

78 We had an ugly fight, and my mother didn't speak to me for months. I went to her wedding but fled to the other side of the room when my aunt approached me.

79 My mother tells me my aunt is very hurt by all this. The cycle continues, in ways I will never fully understand.

80 Four years ago, when my son was a month old, I took him to Minnesota to meet my family.

81 "Take me to Father's grave," I told my brother.

82 It's the first time I'd been there since the funeral. I introduced my beautiful new baby to his grandfather, and my father to his only grandchild.

83 Today, when I stare at the boy who takes my breath away, I think about how much my father missed over the past 20 years, and how much more he will miss. I've more sorrow than anger now.

84 A lot of wonderful things have happened in those years, hundreds of shimmering droplets added to the mix. When I stir the paint now, it is a soft dusky rose. A grownup's color, with a touch of sweetness and a touch of melancholy.

● Vocabulary

| coroner (1) | penultimate (6) | legacies (10) |
| ominous (25) | wand (53) | rapprochement (66) |

● The Facts

1. What did the author discover in her father's wallet?
2. According to the author, how many people commit suicide annually in the United States?
3. When the author drove past the house after her mother called, what did she see?
4. Where was the author's brother, Mike, when the father committed suicide?
5. Whom did the father's relatives blame for the suicide?

● The Strategies

1. What is the thesis of the essay? Write it in one sentence in your own words.
2. Every once in a while the author interrupts the story of the father's suicide with commentary about suicide in general. Why do you think she does this? Does the technique appeal to you? Why or why not?
3. How important is the reference to "assisted suicide" in paragraph 28? What, if anything, does it add to the development of the author's thesis?
4. What figurative language does the author use in her essay? Point out at least one simile and one metaphor. Do you consider these images effective? Give reasons for your answer.
5. How effective is the author's strategy of relating her father's suicide from her own "I" point of view? What does it add to the essay?

● The Issues

1. What is the purpose of this essay on the gloomy subject of suicide? Do you agree or disagree with its purpose?
2. What does the author mean when she says, "He was 46 years old. I was 21. It has been 20 years since his death and I am still cleaning up"?
3. The author refers to the fact that in the past, suicide was considered a noble act, a sinful act, or a romantic act (see paragraph 27). How do you view suicide today? Should everyone embrace your view? Give reasons for your answer.
4. In your opinion, what consequences of the father's suicide seem the worst?
5. What do you think was the basic cause of the father's suicide?

Suggestions for Writing

1. Choose one of the following topics and develop a thesis-oriented essay:
   a. Suicide as an act of desperation
   b. Suicide as an act of selfishness
2. Write an essay about the steps recommended by mental-health professionals to help avert suicide.

A Good Man Is Hard to Find
Flannery O'Connor

Flannery O'Connor (1925–1964) was a Christian humanist writer and a member of the so-called "southern renaissance" in American literature. She was born in Savannah, Georgia, and educated at the Woman's College of Georgia and the State University of Iowa. Her best-known stories, written from an orthodox Catholic perspective, are contained in *A Good Man Is Hard to Find and Other Stories* (1953) and *Everything That Rises Must Converge* (1956).

We do not usually think of a story as having a thesis, but we almost always think of a story as having a point. The point of this story—its thesis—is hinted at in its title, from which it proceeds with grim, irresistible logic. Readers should remember that the racist language used in this selection is partly what labeled O'Connor's stories "Southern Grotesque." Moreover, O'Connor wrote at a time when blacks in the South were often treated in a derogatory manner.

• • •

1   The grandmother didn't want to go to Florida. She wanted to visit some of her connections in east Tennessee and she was seizing at every chance to change Bailey's mind. Bailey was the son she lived with, her only boy. He was sitting on the edge of his chair at the table, bent over the orange sports section of the *Journal*. "Now look here, Bailey," she said, "see here, read this," and she stood with one hand on her thin hip and the other rattling the newspaper at his bald head. "Here this fellow that calls himself The Misfit is loose from the Federal Pen and headed toward Florida and you read here what it says he did to these people. Just you read it. I wouldn't take my children in any direction with a criminal like that aloose in it. I couldn't answer to my conscience if I did."

2   Bailey didn't look up from his reading so she wheeled around then and faced the children's mother, a young woman in slacks, whose face was as broad and innocent as a cabbage and was tied around with a green headkerchief that had two points on the top like a rabbit's ears. She was sitting on the sofa, feeding the baby his apricots out of a jar. "The children have been to Florida before," the old lady said. "You all ought to take them somewhere else for a change so they would see different parts of the world and be broad. They never have been to east Tennessee."

3   The children's mother didn't seem to hear her but the eight-year-old boy, John Wesley, a stocky child with glasses, said, "If you don't want to go to

Florida, why dontcha stay at home?" He and the little girl, June Star, were reading the funny papers on the floor.

4   "She wouldn't stay at home to be queen for a day," June Star said without raising her yellow head.

5   "Yes and what would you do if this fellow, The Misfit, caught you?" the grandmother asked.

6   "I'd smack his face," John Wesley said.

7   "She wouldn't stay at home for a million bucks," June Star said. "Afraid she'd miss something. She has to go everywhere we go."

8   "All right, Miss," the grandmother said. "Just remember that the next time you want me to curl your hair."

9   June Star said her hair was naturally curly.

10   The next morning the grandmother was the first one in the car, ready to go. She had her big black valise that looked like the head of a hippopotamus in one corner, and underneath it she was hiding a basket with Pitty Sing, the cat, in it. She didn't intend for the cat to be left alone in the house for three days because he would miss her too much and she was afraid he might brush against one of the gas burners and accidentally asphyxiate himself. Her son, Bailey, didn't like to arrive at a motel with a cat.

11   She sat in the middle of the back seat with John Wesley and June Star on either side of her. Bailey and the children's mother and the baby sat in front and they left Atlanta at eight forty-five with the mileage on the car at 55890. The grandmother wrote this down because she thought it would be interesting to say how many miles they had been when they got back. It took them twenty minutes to reach the outskirts of the city.

12   The old lady settled herself comfortably, removing her white cotton gloves and putting them up with her purse on the shelf in front of the back window. The children's mother still had on slacks and still had her head tied up in a green kerchief, but the grandmother had on a navy blue straw sailor hat with a bunch of white violets on the brim and a navy blue dress with a small white dot in the print. Her collars and cuffs were white organdy trimmed with lace and at her neckline she had pinned a purple spray of cloth violets containing a sachet. In case of an accident, anyone seeing her dead on the highway would know at once that she was a lady.

13   She said she thought it was going to be a good day for driving, neither too hot nor too cold, and she cautioned Bailey that the speed limit was fifty-five miles an hour and that the patrolmen hid themselves behind billboards and small clumps of trees and sped out after you before you had a chance to slow down. She pointed out interesting details of the scenery: Stone Mountain; the blue granite that in some places came up to both sides of the highway; the brilliant red clay banks slightly streaked with purple; and the various crops that made rows of green lace-work on the ground. The trees were full of silver-white sunlight and the meanest of them sparkled. The children were reading comic magazines and their mother had gone back to sleep.

14   "Let's go through Georgia fast so we won't have to look at it much," John Wesley said.

15   "If I were a little boy," said the grandmother, "I wouldn't talk about my native state that way. Tennessee has the mountains and Georgia has the hills."

16   "Tennessee is just a hillbilly dumping ground," John Wesley said, "and Georgia is a lousy state too."

17   "You said it," June Star said.

18   "In my time," said the grandmother, folding her thin veined fingers, "children were more respectful of their native states and their parents and everything else. People did right then. Oh look at the cute little pickaninny!" she said and pointed to a Negro child standing in the door of a shack. "Wouldn't that make a picture, now?" she asked and they all turned and looked at the little Negro out of the back window. He waved.

19   "He didn't have any britches on," June Star said.

20   "He probably didn't have any," the grandmother explained. "Little niggers in the country don't have things like we do. If I could paint, I'd paint that picture," she said.

21   The children exchanged comic books.

22   The grandmother offered to hold the baby and the children's mother passed him over the front seat to her. She sat him on her knee and bounced him and told him about the things they were passing. She rolled her eyes and screwed up her mouth and stuck her leathery thin face into his smooth bland one. Occasionally he gave her a faraway smile. They passed a large cotton field with five or six graves fenced in the middle of it, like a small island. "Look at the graveyard!" the grandmother said, pointing it out. "That was the old family burying ground. That belonged to the plantation."

23   "Where's the plantation?" John Wesley asked.

24   "Gone With the Wind," said the grandmother. "Ha. Ha."

25   When the children finished all the comic books they had brought, they opened the lunch and ate it. The grandmother ate a peanut butter sandwich and an olive and would not let the children throw the box and the paper napkins out the window. When there was nothing else to do they played a game by choosing a cloud and making the other two guess what shape it suggested. John Wesley took one the shape of a cow and June Star guessed a cow and John Wesley said, no, an automobile, and June Star said he didn't play fair, and they began to slap each other over the grandmother.

26   The grandmother said she would tell them a story if they would keep quiet. When she told a story, she rolled her eyes and waved her head and was very dramatic. She said once when she was a maiden lady she had been courted by a Mr. Edgar Atkins Teagarden from Jasper, Georgia. She said he was a very good-looking man and a gentleman and that he brought her a watermelon every Saturday afternoon with his initials cut in it, E. A. T. Well, one Saturday, she said, Mr. Teagarden brought the watermelon and there was nobody at home and he left it on the front porch and returned in his buggy to Jasper, but she never got the watermelon, she said, because a nigger boy ate it when he saw the initials, E. A. T.! This story tickled John Wesley's funny bone and he giggled and giggled but June Star didn't think it was any good. She said she wouldn't marry a man that just brought her a watermelon on Saturday.

The grandmother said she would have done well to marry Mr. Teagarden because he was a gentleman and had bought Coca-Cola stock when it first came out and that he had died only a few years ago, a very wealthy man.

27   They stopped at The Tower for barbecued sandwiches. The Tower was a part stucco and part wood filling station and dance hall set in a clearing outside of Timothy. A fat man named Red Sammy Butts ran it and there were signs stuck here and there on the building and for miles up and down the highway saying, TRY RED SAMMY'S FAMOUS BARBECUE. NONE LIKE FAMOUS RED SAMMY'S! RED SAM! THE FAT BOY WITH THE HAPPY LAUGH! A VETERAN! RED SAMMY'S YOUR MAN!

28   Red Sammy was lying on the bare ground outside The Tower with his head under a truck while a gray monkey about a foot high, chained to a small chinaberry tree, chattered nearby. The monkey sprang back into the tree and got on the highest limb as soon as he saw the children jump out of the car and run toward him.

29   Inside, The Tower was a long dark room with a counter at one end and tables at the other and dancing space in the middle. They all sat down at a board table next to the nickelodeon and Red Sam's wife, a tall burnt-brown woman with hair and eyes lighter than her skin, came and took their order. The children's mother put a dime in the machine and played "The Tennessee Waltz," and the grandmother said that tune always made her want to dance. She asked Bailey if he would like to dance but he only glared at her. He didn't have a naturally sunny disposition like she did and trips made him nervous. The grandmother's brown eyes were very bright. She swayed her head from side to side and pretended she was dancing in her chair. June Star said play something she could tap to so the children's mother put in another dime and played a fast number and June Star stepped out onto the dance floor and did her tap routine.

30   "Ain't she cute?" Red Sam's wife said, leaning over the counter. "Would you like to come be my little girl?"

31   "No I certainly wouldn't," June Star said. "I wouldn't live in a broken-down place like this for a million bucks!" and she ran back to the table.

32   "Ain't she cute?" the woman repeated, stretching her mouth politely.

33   "Aren't you ashamed?" hissed the grandmother.

34   Red Sam came in and told his wife to quit lounging on the counter and hurry up with these people's order. His khaki trousers reached just to his hip bones and his stomach hung over them like a sack of meal swaying under his shirt. He came over and sat down at a table nearby and let out a combination sigh and yodel. "You can't win," he said. "You can't win," and he wiped his sweating red face off with a gray handkerchief. "These days you don't know who to trust," he said. "Ain't that the truth?"

35   "People are certainly not nice like they used to be," said the grandmother.

36   "Two fellers come in here last week," Red Sammy said, "driving a Chrysler. It was a old beat-up car but it was a good one and these boys looked all right to me. Said they worked at the mill and you know I let them fellers charge the gas they bought? Now why did I do that?"

37   "Because you're a good man!" the grandmother said at once.

38 "Yes'm, I suppose so," Red Sam said as if he were struck with this answer.

39 His wife brought the orders, carrying the five plates all at once without a tray, two in each hand and one balanced on her arm. "It isn't a soul in this green world of God's that you can trust," she said. "And I don't count nobody out of that, not nobody," she repeated, looking at Red Sammy.

40 "Did you read about that criminal, The Misfit, that's escaped?" asked the grandmother.

41 "I wouldn't be a bit surprised if he didn't attact this place right here," said the woman. "If he hears about it being here, I wouldn't be none surprised to see him. If he hears it's two cent in the cash register, I wouldn't be at all surprised if he . . .

42 "That'll do," Red Sam said, "Go bring these people their Co'-Colas," and the woman went off to get the rest of the order.

43 "A good man is hard to find," Red Sammy said. "Everything is getting terrible. I remember the day you could go off and leave your screen door unlatched. Not no more."

44 He and the grandmother discussed better times. The old lady said that in her opinion Europe was entirely to blame for the way things were now. She said the way Europe acted you would think we were made of money and Red Sam said it was no use talking about it, she was exactly right. The children ran outside into the white sunlight and looked at the monkey in the lacy chinaberry tree. He was busy catching fleas on himself and biting each one carefully between his teeth as if it were a delicacy.

45 They drove off again into the hot afternoon. The grandmother took cat naps and woke up every few minutes with her own snoring. Outside of Toombsboro she woke up and recalled an old plantation that she had visited in this neighborhood once when she was a young lady. She said the house had six white columns across the front and that there was an avenue of oaks leading up to it and two little wooden trellis arbors on each side in front where you sat down with your suitor after a stroll in the garden. She recalled exactly which road to turn off to get to it. She knew that Bailey would not be willing to lose any time looking at an old house, but the more she talked about it, the more she wanted to see it once again and find out if the little twin arbors were still standing. "There was a secret panel in this house," she said craftily, not telling the truth but wishing that she were, "and the story went that all the family silver was hidden in it when Sherman came through but it was never found . . ."

46 "Hey!" John Wesley said. "Let's go see it! We'll find it! We'll poke all the woodwork and find it! Who lives there? Where do you turn off at? Hey Pop, can't we turn off there?"

47 "We never have seen a house with a secret panel!" June Star shrieked. "Let's go to the house with the secret panel! Hey Pop, can't we go see the house with the secret panel!"

48 "It's not far from here, I know," the grandmother said. "It wouldn't take over twenty minutes."

49 Bailey was looking straight ahead. His jaw was as rigid as a horseshoe. "No," he said.

50   The children began to yell and scream that they wanted to see the house with the secret panel. John Wesley kicked the back of the front seat and June Star hung over her mother's shoulder and whined desperately into her ear that they never had any fun even on their vacation, that they could never do what THEY wanted to do. The baby began to scream and John Wesley kicked the back of the seat so hard that his father could feel the blows in his kidney.

51   "All right!" he shouted and drew the car to a stop at the side of the road. "Will you all shut up? Will you all just shut up for one second? If you don't shut up, we won't go anywhere."

52   "It would be very educational for them," the grandmother murmured.

53   "All right," Bailey said, "but get this: This is the only time we're going to stop for anything like this. This is the one and only time."

54   "The dirt road that you have to turn down is about a mile back," the grandmother directed. "I marked it when we passed."

55   "A dirt road," Bailey groaned.

56   After they had turned around and were headed toward the dirt road, the grandmother recalled other points about the house, the beautiful glass over the front doorway and the candle-lamp in the hall. John Wesley said that the secret panel was probably in the fireplace.

57   "You can't go inside this house," Bailey said. "You don't know who lives there."

58   "While you all talk to the people in front, I'll run around behind and get in a window," John Wesley suggested.

59   "We'll all stay in the car," his mother said.

60   They turned onto the dirt road and the car raced roughly along in a swirl of pink dust. The grandmother recalled the times when there were no paved roads and thirty miles was a day's journey. The dirt road was hilly and there were sudden washes in it and sharp curves on dangerous embankments. All at once they would be on a hill, looking down over the blue tops of trees for miles around, then the next minute, they would be in a red depression with the dust-coated trees looking down on them.

61   "This place had better turn up in a minute," Bailey said, "or I'm going to turn around."

62   The road looked as if no one had traveled on it in months.

63   "It's not much farther," the grandmother said and just as she said it, a horrible thought came to her. The thought was so embarrassing that she turned red in the face and her eyes dilated and her feet jumped up, upsetting her valise in the corner. The instant the valise moved, the newspaper top she had over the basket under it rose with a snarl and Pitty Sing, the cat, sprang onto Bailey's shoulder.

64   The children were thrown to the floor and their mother, clutching the baby, was thrown out the door onto the ground; the old lady was thrown into the front seat. The car turned over once and landed right-side-up in a gulch off the side of the road. Bailey remained in the driver's seat with the cat—graystriped with a broad white face and an orange nose—clinging to his neck like a caterpillar.

65 As soon as the children saw they could move their arms and legs, they scrambled out of the car, shouting, "We've had an ACCIDENT!" The grandmother was curled up under the dashboard, hoping she was injured so that Bailey's wrath would not come down on her all at once. The horrible thought she had had before the accident was that the house she had remembered so vividly was not in Georgia but in Tennessee.

66 Bailey removed the cat from his neck with both hands and flung it out the window against the side of a pine tree. Then he got out of the car and started looking for the children's mother. She was sitting against the side of the red gutted ditch, holding the screaming baby, but she only had a cut down her face and a broken shoulder. "We've had an ACCIDENT!" the children screamed in a frenzy of delight.

67 "But nobody's killed," June Star said with disappointment as the grandmother limped out of the car, her hat still pinned to her head but the broken front brim standing up at a jaunty angle and the violet spray hanging off the side. They all sat down in the ditch, except the children, to recover from the shock. They were all shaking.

68 "Maybe a car will come along," said the children's mother hoarsely.

69 "I believe I have injured an organ," said the grandmother, pressing her side, but no one answered her. Bailey's teeth were clattering. He had on a yellow sport shirt with bright blue parrots designed in it and his face was as yellow as the shirt. The grandmother decided that she would not mention that the house was in Tennessee.

70 The road was about ten feet above and they could see only the tops of the trees on the other side of it. Behind the ditch they were sitting in there were more woods, tall and dark and deep. In a few minutes they saw a car some distance away on top of a hill, coming slowly as if the occupants were watching them. The grandmother stood up and waved both arms dramatically to attract their attention. The car continued to come on slowly, disappeared around a bend and appeared again, moving even slower, on top of the hill they had gone over. It was a big black battered hearselike automobile. There were three men in it.

71 It came to a stop just over them and for some minutes, the driver looked down with a steady expressionless gaze to where they were sitting, and didn't speak. Then he turned his head and muttered something to the other two and they got out. One was a fat boy in black trousers and a red sweat shirt with a silver stallion embossed on the front of it. He moved around on the right side of them and stood staring, his mouth partly open in a kind of loose grin. The other had on khaki pants and a blue striped coat and a gray hat pulled down very low, hiding most of his face. He came around slowly on the left side. Neither spoke.

72 The driver got out of the car and stood by the side of it, looking down at them. He was an older man than the other two. His hair was just beginning to gray and he wore silver-rimmed spectacles that gave him a scholarly look. He had a long creased face and didn't have on any shirt or undershirt. He had on blue jeans that were too tight for him and was holding a black hat and a gun. The two boys also had guns.

73   "We've had an ACCIDENT!" the children screamed.

74   The grandmother had the peculiar feeling that the bespectacled man was someone she knew. His face was as familiar to her as if she had known him all her life but she could not recall who he was. He moved away from the car and began to come down the embankment, placing his feet carefully so that he wouldn't slip. He had on tan and white shoes and no socks, and his ankles were red and thin. "Good afternoon," he said. "I see you all had you a little spill."

75   "We turned over twice!" said the grandmother.

76   "Oncet," he corrected. "We seen it happen. Try their car and see will it run, Hiram," he said quietly to the boy with the gray hat.

77   "What you got that gun for?" John Wesley asked. "Whatcha gonna do with that gun?"

78   "Lady," the man said to the children's mother, "would you mind calling them children to sit down by you? Children make me nervous. I want all you all to sit down right together there where you're at."

79   "What are you telling us what to do for?" June Star asked.

80   Behind them the line of woods gaped like a dark open mouth. "Come here," said their mother.

81   "Look here now," Bailey began suddenly, "we're in a predicament! We're in. . . ."

82   The grandmother shrieked. She scrambled to her feet and stood staring. "You're The Misfit!" she said, "I recognized you at once!"

83   "Yes'm," the man said, smiling slightly as if he were pleased in spite of himself to be known, "but it would have been better for all of you, lady, if you hadn't of reckernized me."

84   Bailey turned his head sharply and said something to his mother that shocked even the children. The old lady began to cry and The Misfit reddened.

85   "Lady," he said, "don't you get upset. Sometimes a man says things he don't mean. I don't reckon he meant to talk to you thataway."

86   "You wouldn't shoot a lady, would you?" the grandmother said and removed a clean handkerchief from her cuff and began to slap at her eyes with it.

87   The Misfit pointed the toe of his shoe into the ground and made a little hole and then covered it up again. "I would hate to have to," he said.

88   "Listen," the grandmother almost screamed, "I know you're a good man. You don't look a bit like you have common blood. I know you must come from nice people!"

89   "Yes mam," he said, "finest people in the world." When he smiled he showed a row of strong white teeth. "God never made a finer woman than my mother and my daddy's heart was pure gold," he said. The boy with the red sweat shirt had come around behind them and was standing with his gun at his hip. The Misfit squatted down on the ground. "Watch them children, Bobby Lee," he said. "You know they make me nervous." He looked at the six of them huddled together in front of him and he seemed to be embarrassed as if he couldn't think of anything to say. "Ain't a cloud in the sky," he remarked, looking up at it. "Don't see no sun but don't see no cloud neither."

90 "Yes, it's a beautiful day," said the grandmother. "Listen," she said, "you shouldn't call yourself The Misfit because I know you're a good man at heart. I can just look at you and tell."

91 "Hush!" Bailey yelled. "Hush! Everybody shut up and let me handle this!" He was squatting in the position of a runner about to sprint forward but he didn't move.

92 "I pre-chate that, lady," The Misfit said and drew a little circle in the ground with the butt of his gun.

93 "It'll take a half a hour to fix this here car," Hiram called, looking over the raised hood of it.

94 "Well, first you and Bobby Lee get him and that little boy to step over yonder with you," The Misfit said, pointing to Bailey and John Wesley. "The boys want to ast you something," he said to Bailey. "Would you mind stepping back in them woods there with them?"

95 "Listen," Bailey began, "we're in a terrible predicament! Nobody realizes what this is," and his voice cracked. His eyes were as blue and intense as the parrots in his shirt and he remained perfectly still.

96 The grandmother reached up to adjust her hat brim as if she were going to the woods with him but it came off in her hand. She stood staring at it and after a second she let it fall on the ground. Hiram pulled Bailey up by the arm as if he were assisting an old man. John Wesley caught hold of his father's hand and Bobby Lee followed. They went off toward the woods and just as they reached the dark edge, Bailey turned and supporting himself against a gray naked pine trunk, he shouted, "I'll be back in a minute, Mamma, wait on me!"

97 "Come back this instant!" his mother shrilled but they all disappeared into the woods.

98 "Bailey Boy!" the grandmother called in a tragic voice but she found she was looking at The Misfit squatting on the ground in front of her. "I just know you're a good man," she said desperately. "You're not a bit common!"

99 "Nome, I ain't a good man," The Misfit said after a second as if he had considered her statement carefully. "But I ain't the worst in the world neither. My daddy said I was a different breed of dog from my brothers and sisters. 'You know,' Daddy said, 'it's some that can live their whole life out without asking about it and it's others has to know why it is, and this boy is one of the latters. He's going to be into everything!' " He put on his black hat and looked up suddenly and then away deep into the woods as if he were embarrassed again. "I'm sorry I don't have on a shirt before you ladies," he said, hunching his shoulders slightly. "We buried our clothes that we had on when we escaped and we're just making do until we can get better. We borrowed these from some folks we met," he explained.

100 "That's perfectly all right," the grandmother said. "Maybe Bailey has an extra shirt in his suitcase."

101 "I'll look and see terrectly," The Misfit said.

102 "Where are they taking him?" the children's mother screamed.

103 "Daddy was a card himself," The Misfit said. "You couldn't put anything over on him. He never got in trouble with the Authorities though. Just had the knack of handling them."

104   "You could be honest too if you'd only try," said the grandmother. "Think how wonderful it would be to settle down and live a comfortable life and not have to think about somebody chasing you all the time."

105   The Misfit kept scratching in the ground with the butt of his gun as if he were thinking about it. "Yes'm, somebody is always after you," he murmured.

106   The grandmother noticed how thin his shoulder blades were just behind his hat because she was standing up looking down on him. "Do you ever pray?" she asked.

107   He shook his head. All she saw was the black hat wiggle between his shoulder blades. "Nome," he said.

108   There was a pistol shot from the woods, followed closely by another. Then silence. The old lady's head jerked around. She could hear the wind move through the tree tops like a long satisfied insuck of breath. "Bailey Boy!" she called.

109   "I was a gospel singer for a while," The Misfit said. "I been most everything. Been in the arm service, both land and sea, at home and abroad, been twicet married, been an undertaker, been with the railroads, plowed Mother Earth, been in a tornado, seen a man burnt alive oncet," and looked up at the children's mother and the little girl who were sitting close together, their faces white and their eyes glassy; "I even seen a woman flogged," he said.

110   "Pray, pray," the grandmother began, "pray, pray . . ."

111   "I never was a bad boy that I remember of," The Misfit said in an almost dreamy voice, "but somewheres along the line I done something wrong and got sent to the penitentiary. I was buried alive," and he looked up and held her attention to him by a steady stare.

112   "That's when you should have started to pray," she said. "What did you do to get sent to the penitentiary that first time?"

113   "Turn to the right, it was a wall," The Misfit said, looking up again at the cloudless sky. "Turn to the left, it was a wall. Look up it was a ceiling, look down it was a floor. I forget what I done, lady. I set there and set there, trying to remember what it was I done and I ain't recalled it to this day. Oncet in a while, I would think it was coming to me, but it never come."

114   "Maybe they put you in by mistake," the old lady said vaguely.

115   "Nome," he said. "It wasn't no mistake. They had papers on me."

116   "You must have stolen something," she said.

117   The Misfit sneered slightly. "Nobody had nothing I wanted," he said. "It was a head-doctor at the penitentiary said what I had done was kill my daddy but I known that for a lie. My daddy died in nineteen ought nineteen of the epidemic flu and I never had a thing to do with it. He was buried in the Mount Hopewell Baptist churchyard and you can go there and see for yourself."

118   "If you would pray," the old lady said, "Jesus would help you."

119   "That's right," The Misfit said.

120   "Well then, why don't you pray?" she asked trembling with delight suddenly.

121   "I don't want no hep," he said, "I'm doing all right by myself."

122   Bobby Lee and Hiram came ambling back from the woods. Bobby Lee was dragging a yellow shirt with bright blue parrots in it.

123   "Throw me that shirt, Bobby Lee," The Misfit said. The shirt came flying at him and landed on his shoulder and he put it on. The grandmother couldn't name what the shirt reminded her of. "No, lady," The Misfit said while he was buttoning it up, "I found out the crime don't matter. You can do one thing or you can do another, kill a man or take a tire off his car, because sooner or later you're going to forget what it was you done and just be punished for it."

124   The children's mother had begun to make heaving noises as if she couldn't get her breath. "Lady," he asked, "would you and that little girl like to step off yonder with Bobby Lee and Hiram and join your husband?"

125   "Yes, thank you," the mother said faintly. Her left arm dangled helplessly and she was holding the baby, who had gone to sleep, in the other. "Hep that lady up, Hiram," The Misfit said as she struggled to climb out of the ditch, "and Bobby Lee, you hold onto that little girl's hand."

126   "I don't want to hold hands with him," June Star said. "He reminds me of a pig."

127   The fat boy blushed and laughed and caught her by the arm and pulled her off into the woods after Hiram and her mother.

128   Alone with The Misfit, the grandmother found that she had lost her voice. There was not a cloud in the sky nor any sun. There was nothing around her but woods. She wanted to tell him that he must pray. She opened and closed her mouth several times before anything came out. Finally she found herself saying, "Jesus, Jesus," meaning, Jesus will help you, but the way she was saying it, it sounded as if she might be cursing.

129   "Yes'm," The Misfit said as if he agreed, "Jesus thrown everything off balance. It was the same case with Him as with me except He hadn't committed any crime and they could prove I had committed one because they had the papers on me. Of course," he said, "they never shown me my papers. That's why I sign myself now. I said long ago, you get you a signature and sign everything you do and keep a copy of it. Then you'll know what you done and you can hold up the crime to the punishment and see do they match and in the end you'll have something to prove you ain't been treated right. I call myself The Misfit," he said, "because I can't make what all I done wrong fit what all I gone through in punishment."

130   There was a piercing scream from the woods, followed closely by a pistol report. "Does it seem right to you, lady, that one is punished a heap and another ain't punished at all?"

131   "Jesus!" the old lady cried. "You've got good blood! I know you wouldn't shoot a lady! I know you come from nice people! Pray! Jesus, you ought not to shoot a lady, I'll give you all the money I've got!"

132   "Lady," The Misfit said, looking beyond her far into the woods, "there never was a body that give the undertaker a tip."

133   There were two more pistol reports and the grandmother raised her head like a parched old turkey hen crying for water and called, "Bailey Boy, Bailey Boy!" as if her heart would break.

134   "Jesus was the only One that ever raised the dead," The Misfit continued, "and He shouldn't have done it. He thrown everything off balance. If He did

what He said, then it's nothing for you to do but throw away everything and follow Him, and if He didn't, then it's nothing for you to do but enjoy the few minutes you got left the best way you can—by killing somebody or burning down his house or doing some other meanness to him. No pleasure but meanness," he said and his voice had become almost a snarl.

135 "Maybe He didn't raise the dead," the old lady mumbled, not knowing what she was saying and feeling so dizzy that she sank down in the ditch with her legs twisted under her.

136 "I wasn't there so I can't say He didn't," The Misfit said. "I wisht I had of been there," he said, hitting the ground with his fist. "It ain't right I wasn't there because if I had of been there I would of known. Listen lady," he said in a high voice, "if I had of been there I would of known and I wouldn't be like I am now." His voice seemed about to crack and the grandmother's head cleared for an instant. She saw the man's face twisted close to her own as if he were going to cry and she murmured, "Why you're one of my babies. You're one of my own children!" She reached out and touched him on the shoulder. The Misfit sprang back as if a snake had bitten him and shot her three times through the chest. Then he put his gun down on the ground and took off his glasses and began to clean them.

137 Hiram and Bobby Lee returned from the woods and stood over the ditch, looking down at the grandmother who half sat and half lay in a puddle of blood with her legs crossed under her like a child's and her face smiling up at the cloudless sky.

138 Without his glasses, The Misfit's eyes were red-rimmed and pale and defenseless-looking. "Take her off and throw her where you thrown the others," he said, picking up the cat that was rubbing itself against his leg.

139 "She was a talker, wasn't she?" Bobby Lee said, sliding down the ditch with a yodel.

140 "She would of been a good woman," The Misfit said, "if it had been somebody there to shoot her every minute of her life."

141 "Some fun!" Bobby Lee said.

142 "Shut up, Bobby Lee," The Misfit said. "It's no real pleasure in life."

- ## Vocabulary

asphyxiate (10)   sachet (12)   bland (22)
dilated (63)   jaunty (67)   embossed (71)
ambling (122)   parched (133)

- ## The Facts

1. Why didn't the grandmother want to go to Florida? Where did she want to go instead?
2. Why does the family turn off onto the lonely dirt road?
3. What caused the accident?
4. For what crime was The Misfit sent to the penitentiary?
5. Why does he call himself "The Misfit"?

● The Strategies

1. The Misfit is mentioned in the first paragraph. Why does O'Connor introduce him so early?
2. What does the initial dialogue between the grandmother and the children accomplish?
3. In paragraph 70, The Misfit's automobile is described as "a big black battered hearselike automobile." What is O'Connor doing in this description?
4. At a climactic part of the story, the grandmother has a sudden, dramatic recognition of responsibility. When does it occur? Whom does it involve?
5. In paragraph 80, O'Connor writes: "Behind them the line of woods gaped like a dark open mouth." What does this description accomplish? What does it signal to the reader?

● The Issues

1. The Misfit and his cronies commit cold-blooded murder on a family of six. What prerequisite, if any, do you think must exist before a person is capable of murder? If you think there is no prerequisite, do you also think anyone is capable of cold-blooded murder? Justify your answer.
2. What punishment would you regard as just and fitting for The Misfit and his henchmen?
3. Some commentators have said that the children are brats, pure and simple, whereas others have argued that they are rather typical. What is your opinion of the children and their behavior?
4. One interpretation argues that The Misfit is the devil and the grandmother a Christian who confronts him. What is your opinion of this interpretation?
5. What do you think the grandmother meant when she said to The Misfit, "Why you're one of my babies. You're one of my own children!" Why do you think The Misfit killed her when she said that?

● Suggestions for Writing

1. Write an essay analyzing the techniques used by the author to foreshadow the family's fatal encounter with The Misfit. Make specific references to scenes and images and include as many quoted passages as necessary to prove your case.
2. Write an essay interpreting this story. You might begin by asking yourself, "What does the story teach about life?"

Spring

EDNA ST. VINCENT MILLAY

Edna St. Vincent Millay (1892–1950), a graduate of Vassar and one of the most popular poets of her day, lived a Bohemian life during the 1920s in Greenwich Village, New York, writing satirical columns for *Vanity Fair* under a pseudonym. Her first volume of poetry, *Renascence,* was published in 1917 to glowing praise for its vitality. Subsequent volumes include *A Few Figs from Thistle* (1920) and *The Ballad of the Hat Weaver and Other Poems* (1923; Pulitzer Prize). She also wrote verse dramas, many of which were produced by the Provincetown Players. Later volumes of her work include *Fatal Interview* (1931), *Conversation at Midnight* (1937), and *Make Bright the Arrows* (1940). Her former home, "Steepletop" in Austerlitz, New York, which she shared with husband Eugan Jan Boissevain, is a Registered Historic Landmark and the center of the Edna St. Vincent Millay National Society, founded in 1978.

In many poems, the opening sentence presents a theme around which the rest of the poem is organized. In a way, this opening sentence, although strictly speaking not a thesis, fulfills the function of one. This poem is a classic example of what we mean.

• • •

> To what purpose, April, do you return again?
> Beauty is not enough.
> You can no longer quiet me with the redness
> Of little leaves opening stickily.
> 5   I know what I know.
> The sun is hot on my neck as I observe
> The spikes of the crocus.
> The smell of the earth is good.
> It is apparent that there is no death.
> 10 But what does that signify?
> Not only under ground are the brains of men
> Eaten by maggots.
> Life in itself
> Is nothing,
> 15 An empty cup, a flight of uncarpeted stairs,
> It is not enough that yearly, down this hill,
> April
> Comes like an idiot, babbling and strewing flowers.

● Vocabulary

crocus (7)   strewing (18)

● The Facts

1. What quality does April bring with it?
2. In what way do little red leaves open "stickily"?
3. According to the author, what is just as obvious as the fact that at death, the human body is eaten by maggots?
4. What keeps the author dissatisfied with spring?

The Strategies

1. The poem begins with a question. Is the question ever answered? If so, what is the answer?
2. A sharp contrast underlies the poem. What is that contrast?
3. In what way, according to Millay, is the line "brains of men eaten by maggots" symbolic?
4. What metaphors and similes are used in the poem? Explain what they mean.
5. What is the tone of the poem? Is the tone appropriate for the theme?

The Issues

1. What is the theme (thesis) of Millay's poem? State it in one sentence. What do you think has caused the poet to take such a position? Do you agree with it? Why or why not?
2. What is the meaning of the expression "no longer" in line 3?
3. What concrete aspects of spring please the poet? What do these aspects have in common?
4. Why does the author stress the beautiful aspects of spring?
5. Why is it not enough to experience a beautiful spring? What is your personal answer to this poem?

Suggestions for Writing

1. Write an essay on spring and what it means to you.
2. Write an essay refuting Millay's comment that "Life in itself is nothing."

CHAPTER WRITING ASSIGNMENTS

1. Convert one of the following general subjects into a suitable thesis:
    a. college life
    b. parental behavior
    c. unprotected sex
    d. television coverage of crime, war, or natural disasters
    e. meaningful versus meaningless work
    f. youth and age
    g. nostalgia
    h. flag burning
2. Select any issue covered in your local news reports, formulate your position on it in a thesis, and then explain and defend your thesis in an essay.

WRITING ASSIGNMENTS FOR A SPECIFIC AUDIENCE

1. For an audience of third graders, explain in an essay the concept of a thesis and how you make use of it in your own writing.

2. Explain to an audience of business executives how the English education you are presently receiving will make you a better employee.

● COLLABORATIVE WRITING PROJECT

Divide your group into at least three teams, each of which should research the retirement policies of some specific profession or institution of its choice.

Conduct whatever interviews are necessary to learn more about any specific retirement policy. After completing the research, the teams should meet to discuss and debate the fairness of the retirement policies. Finally, each team should write a group essay outlining what it learned about the researched retirement policy as well as its impact on elderly employees.

REAL-LIFE STUDENT WRITING

A Eulogy to a Friend Killed in a Car Wreck

Students sometimes have the unenviable duty of saying a few last words at a funeral or memorial service of friends, relatives, and classmates. Here is a brief eulogy, given by a young man whose best friend was killed in an automobile crash.

• • •

```
He was my best friend. We went to elementary school together,
where we drove our teachers crazy. We grew up in North
Hollywood, both loving the Giants, the 49ers, and the Lakers.
We never missed a Rose Bowl game on TV. We weathered a thunder-
storm in our pup tents in the Sierra Nevadas; we played Blind
Man's Bluff in my parent's swimming pool; we TP'd our girl-
friends' homes; we learned to play the guitar; and we read a
lot of science fiction books together. When I was angry at my
parents, Brett would calm me down. When I felt nervous about
some final exam, Brett encouraged me.

What evil force is this that has taken Brett away without
warning?

                                1
```

Yes, I am angry at the driver who mowed him down; I am angry that God didn't save him. But I am also aware that anger won't bring him back. So, I guess we must all live with the knowledge that Brett was a one-of-a-kind friend—loyal, upbeat, and generous. We'll all remember the good times we had with him. And for those of us who believe in life after death—we look forward to someday meeting him again and hearing him say, "Hey man, how's it goin'?"

2

Stumped by noun clusters? Exit on page 693, at the **Editing Booth!**

5

How Do I Organize?

ROAD MAP TO ORGANIZING

Writers and the way they work fall mainly into two major camps: the organic and the mechanical. The organic writer writes from the subconscious. Such writers often go to sleep thinking about an assignment and wake up the next morning knowing exactly what they intend to write. The mechanical writer, like a carpenter building a house, works from a blueprint or plan. These writers organize their thoughts before writing and plot out their ideas and topics before committing a single word to paper.

We raise this distinction to point out that organizing is not for everyone. It is a technique better suited to the working habits of the mechanical writer. For the organic writer whose subconscious does most of the work, organizing offers little benefit and might even interfere with the process of composing.

Organizing the Short Essay

Short essays (about 300 words long) are usually written in class under the pressure of a time limit. An instructor may assign you to write three paragraphs on some topic you have been studying in class, or you may be asked to write an informal essay on a topic such as why an uninformed person should or should not vote. Obviously, you cannot spend a great deal of time planning what to say in such an essay. Yet, you think some preliminary sketch would be helpful. What can you do?

Make a Jot List A jot list is exactly as it says: a list of those points you mean to cover in the essay. You begin your jot list by scribbling down your main point or thesis. In this case, you think it is better for an ignorant voter to abstain than to cast a vote that amounts to a guess. You express this position in a thesis sentence:

> **Thesis:** To vote for someone whose record you don't know is worse than not voting at all.

Then you add the points you think you ought to cover:

1. If I don't vote, at least the people who know what the candidates stand for will make the decision for me.
2. Uncle John picks candidates by closing his eyes and poking at the ballot with his finger.
3. Voting from ignorance is disrespectful of the democratic process.
4. If I don't know anything about a candidate or an issue, I won't vote. At least that way, I leave the decision up to people who do know.

The jot list has no conventional form. You do not hand it in to your instructor. You can number its entries or arrange them in any other way you please. When you're done writing the essay, you can make a paper plane of the jot list if you like. It is nothing more than a thumbnail sketch of what you want to do.

Sketch Out Your Paragraphs This method of organizing is as simple as a jot list. Sketch out the paragraphs that you intend to write. Most in-class essays require no more than five paragraphs—and usually around three. Here's an example. You have been given the essay topic to write on any aspect of modern popular culture. You choose to write about the movies and why you like them.

Begin by writing down a rough draft of your thesis:

> **Thesis:** The most interesting and entertaining products of modern popular culture are movies.

Next, write down the topics of your beginning paragraphs:

> First paragraph: interesting movies. *Schindler's List, Luther, Alexander.* Why these movies are interesting to me.
> Second paragraph: entertaining movies. *Life Is Beautiful, Chicago, Cheaper By the Dozen.* Why I find these movies entertaining.
> Third paragraph: Our movies are a global influence. They spread our culture and way of life better than literature does.

You don't want to make this list too long because you still have the actual essay to write. But at least you know what topics you have to cover in upcoming paragraphs.

Make a Flowchart This is a more graphic variation of the jot list. Simply make a plan of your entire essay, using specially shaped boxes for supporting ideas and main points. In the example given (Figure 5.1), the triangular shapes indicate supporting details. The rectangular shapes indicate main points, and the diamond shape indicates where transitions need to be inserted.

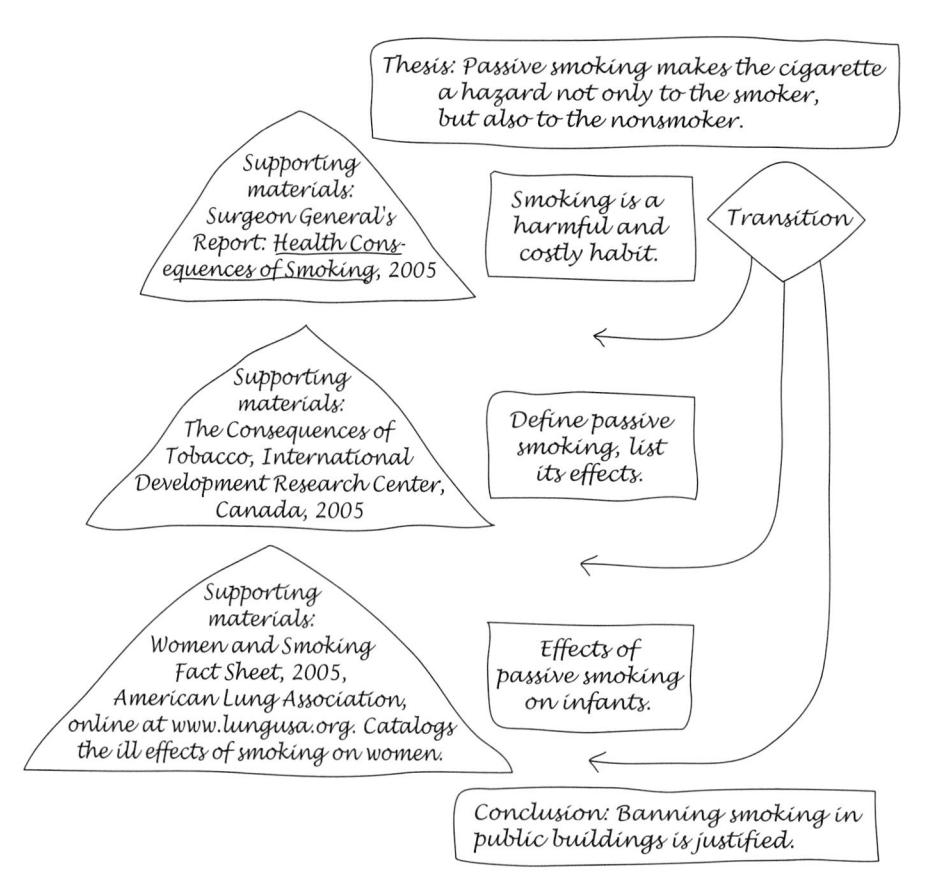

FIGURE 5.1 *Example of Essay Flowchart*

Organizing the Long Essay

The long essay might be a weekend assignment or a research paper completed over the course of several weeks. You might be expected to write an essay five to ten pages long with appropriate and accurate documentation on a topic such as the following: "Why the Shark Is Such a Successful Predator"; "Art Therapy"; or "Initial Critical Reactions to Henry Miller's Novels." Writing about such subjects will require library and Internet research as well as reading periodicals or books found in the libraries of friends and relatives.

The plan of such an essay should function as a guide not only to its writing but also to the research you need to do before you are ready to write. You should consult the plan both as you do the research—modifying it if necessary as you accumulate more supporting materials and possibly change your mind about what you want to say—and as you do the writing. If you find yourself going off in a different direction from the plan during the actual writing, never mind. Follow the lead of inspiration. When you have finished, go back over the rough draft and compare it with your original plan. Be sure that you can justify the switch.

Planning by Listing Supporting Materials

If you have a topic, you can often generate a crude outline of the essay by making a list of the supporting materials you will need for reference. How can you know what supporting materials you need? You find out by asking common-sense questions about the topic. These questions are those that any interested reader would likewise ask.

Here is an example: A student who accompanied her parents on a summer trip to Stonehenge, England, decided to do a paper on the area's mysterious monoliths. Her own tourist pamphlets, bolstered by some preliminary background reading in the college library, led her to this thesis:

> **Thesis:** A visit to Stonehenge, England, taught me that some civilizations of the past have left us some challenging mysteries we can't seem to solve.

These are the questions that naturally occurred to her as she thought about what supporting materials she would need:

- Where is Stonehenge? Give its geographical location.
- What is Stonehenge? Describe the stones so that the reader can visualize their size and arrangement. Try to get across the awesome nature of the stones.
- What was Stonehenge used for? What are the theories of its use?
- Summarize the most popular legends surrounding the history of Stonehenge:
  1. Stonehenge as a sanctuary of the Druids. Look up "Druids" in the encyclopedia. See what role they played in the early history of England (probably Celtic).
  2. The Devil's confrontation with a friar. Find out how this exotic legend got started.
  3. A memorial to the slain knights of King Arthur.
  4. An observatory for tracking the heavens, especially the rising of the moon. This seems to be a realistic explanation. Find out if many sources mention this theory.
- Why is Stonehenge so popular even today? Explain the reasons for its popularity.

These rather straightforward questions gave the writer an idea of the supporting materials she needed to complete the assignment. Asking these questions also resulted in a rough outline of the paper.

Organizing with a Formal Outline

The outline is a summary of what you plan to say in your essay. The outline tells you what you have to do, where you have to go, and when you have gotten there. If you tend to get sidetracked by details or bogged down in vast quantities of information, outlining is a handy way of imposing structure on a long essay.

A convention has evolved for the formal outline, based mainly on the desire to make it readable at a glance. The title of the essay is centered at the top of the page, with the thesis below it. Main ideas are designated by Roman numerals. Sub-ideas branching off the main ideas are indented and designated by capital letters. Examples of these sub-ideas are further indented and designated by Arabic numerals. Indented beneath the examples are supporting details, designated by lowercase letters. In theory, this subdividing could go on forever; in practice, it rarely extends beyond the fourth level. Here is the framework for the formal outline:

Title
   Thesis
      I. Main idea
         A. Sub-idea
            1. Division of sub-idea
               a. Part of division of sub-idea

An outline omits introductory materials, transitions, examples, illustrations, and details; it lists only the major ideas and sub-ideas of the essay. This practice makes sense when you remember that the prime purpose of an outline is to condense the major divisions of a long essay into a form that can be read at a glance. To make the outline as long and complex as the essay itself is self-defeating and pointless labor.

To make an outline, begin with the thesis of your essay and divide it into smaller ideas. It is an axiom of division that nothing can be divided into fewer than two parts. From this, it follows that under every main idea that has been divided, at least two sub-ideas must appear. In other words, for every *I* there must be at least a *II*; for every *A*, at least a *B*. Consider this example:

Temperatures and Mountain Climbers
   Thesis: Extremes in temperatures can have dangerous effects on mountain climbers.
      I. The dangerous effects of excessive heat
         A. Heat exhaustion
         B. Heat stroke
      II. The dangerous effects of excessive cold
         A. Surface frostbite
         B. Bodily numbness

The logic of division will always produce an outline characterized by symmetry. A by-product of this symmetry is evenness in the treatment of all topics. Notice also that each entry is worded in more or less parallel language. This wording underscores the equal importance of the entries and emphasizes the major divisions in the outline.

Creating the Outline Outlining is systematic thinking about your thesis. You examine the essay as a reader might and try to decide what points you need to present, and in what order, to make the topic understandable. For example, let us suppose that you were planning to write an essay on this thesis:

> **Thesis:** Listening is such an important and badly practiced communicative skill that schools should begin offering courses in how to do it better.

The first question a reader is likely to ask is, "Why is listening so important?" The answer should be the development of your first major point.

> I. Listening is an important communicative skill.

What do you mean by "listening is badly practiced"? Common sense suggests that this is the second question likely to occur to an interested reader. The answer could be the development of your second major point.

> II. Listening is a badly practiced communicative skill.

Fill out these two major headings with some secondary points that serve as answers, and you have completed the first part of your outline.

> I. Listening is an important communicative skill.
>   A. We spend most of our communicating time listening.
>   B. We get most of our political information from radio and television.
> II. Listening is a badly practiced communicative skill.
>   A. We typically understand only one-half of what we hear.
>   B. We typically recall only one-quarter of what we hear.

Following this line of thinking, we can deduce some other questions that common sense tells us are likely to occur to a reader: What do you mean by listening? Are all types of listening alike? Answers to these questions can provide us with two more headings:

> III. Listening is an active communicative skill that is divisible into four components.
>   A. Receiving entails decoding the message.
>   B. Attending entails analyzing the message.
>   C. Assigning meaning entails interpreting the message.
>   D. Remembering entails information storage and retrieval.

    IV. Listening is grouped into five major types.
        A. Appreciative listening involves acceptance.
        B. Discriminative listening involves selection.
        C. Comprehensive listening involves generalizing.
        D. Therapeutic listening involves relaxation.
        E. Critical listening involves judgment.

Think about the purpose of the assignment and the questions your thesis is likely to evoke in a reader and you will likewise discover the logical divisions of your essay.

Guidelines for Outlining You should observe the following guidelines in making your outline:

1. **Don't make the outline too long.** One page of an outline is the basis for five pages of developed writing. Your aim is to produce a model of the essay that you can inspect for flaws at a glance.
2. **Don't clutter the sentences of your outline.** Make your entries brief. The idea is to make the outline instantly readable.
3. **Use parallel wording for subordinate entries whenever possible.** Parallel entries are easier to read than nonparallel ones.
4. **Align the entries properly.** Do not allow the second line of an entry to go farther toward the left margin than the line above it.

If you observe these simple guidelines, the outline that results should be easy to read. You should be able to glance at its major entries and immediately spot any flaws in the structure of the essay.

Outlining by Topic/Outlining by Sentence Some outlines are topic outlines in which the entries are not complete sentences, but fragments that sum up the topic. Other outlines are sentence outlines in which the entries are complete sentences. Your decision on whether to use a topic or a sentence outline depends on how complete a breakdown you need. If your subject is simple and all you need are key words to serve as guideposts so that you will not get sidetracked, or if you merely wish to set down some major trends, categories, or stages, then you should use a topic outline. If your subject is a difficult one or in an area that is new to you, you should use a sentence outline. Consider the following topic outline:

The Future of Our Cities

    Thesis: An assessment of the future of our cities reveals two emerging trends.
      I. The megalopolis
          A. Definition
             1. Cluster
             2. System

B. Two major organizational problems
      1. Transcendence
      2. Coordination
II. Shift in decision making
   A. Local decisions
      1. Facts not known
      2. Outside agencies
   B. Federal government
      1. Increase in power
      2. Local restrictions

This topic outline is of no value to a person who is not thoroughly familiar with the problems of city government. A student writing a paper based on such a cryptic outline is bound to have difficulty. Now consider the following sentence outline of the same subject:

The Future of Our Cities

Thesis: An assessment of the future of our cities reveals two emerging trends.

I. The megalopolis is replacing the city.
   A. *Megalopolis* can be defined in two ways.
      1. A megalopolis is a cluster of cities.
      2. A megalopolis is a system of interwoven urban and suburban areas.
   B. Two major organizational problems of the megalopolis will need to be solved.
      1. One problem is how to handle questions that transcend individual metropolitan areas.
      2. Another problem is how to coordinate the numerous activities in the megalopolis.
II. Decision making is shifting from local control to higher echelons of public and private authority.
   A. The growing scale of the urban world often makes local decisions irrelevant.
      1. Local agencies may not know all of the facts.
      2. National policies may supersede local decisions.
   B. The federal government moves into the picture.
      1. The extent of federal involvement increases as the city grows.
         a. Federal long-range improvement plans are used.
         b. Grant-in-aid programs become necessary.
      2. Federal assistance imposes restrictions.
         a. Federal policies make sure that no discrimination takes place in the areas of housing, employment, and education.
         b. Federal representatives check on local installations to make sure that they are up to federal standards.

A good sentence outline supplies all of the basic information you need to write your paper. Without an outline, you run the risk of treating major ideas like details and details like major ideas; furthermore, you may find yourself moving forward, then backtracking, and then moving forward again, resulting in an incoherent paper. Because a careful outline takes into account the relationships among ideas and their degrees of importance, it keeps a novice from producing muddled writing.

We do not wish to mislead you into thinking that every essay you write will be just as easily and neatly outlined as our examples may suggest. In fact, you will most likely find it necessary to revise the outline heavily. You might even end up with three or four scratched-up versions before you are satisfied with the result. As you outline, new ideas will occur to you and clamor to be fitted in somewhere. Old headings will strike you as too obvious to be included. Whether you make a formal outline or simply draw up a sketch of your essay, you are still likely to revise heavily before you are happy with your plan.

● Exercises

1. Write a paragraph outline for one of the following theses:
   a. Inflation has had a deteriorating effect on the purchasing power of the dollar.
   b. The essay exam has several advantages over the objective test.
   c. The first three months of an infant's life are crucial to the development of his or her personality.
2. Create a flowchart for one of the following theses:
   a. Society often uses language to favor one sex over the other.
   b. Economic inflation has political consequences.
   c. Teachers deserve higher salaries.
   d. English should be made the official language of the United States.
3. List the supporting materials you might use for an essay on one of the following topics:
   a. Why people often don't help in a crisis
   b. Multiple-choice versus essay exams as tools of education
   c. Comic strips that have social value
   d. Why modern products are often shoddy
4. Identify the key words in the following theses, specifying two or three subtopics into which they may be divided:
   a. Strong diplomatic ties with China would have several advantages for the United States.
   b. An electrical blackout in any major city of the United States would have disastrous results.
   c. The words *disinterested, inflammable,* and *fortuitous* are often misunderstood.
5. Delete the entry that destroys the logical order in the following outlines:
   a. *Thesis: Because of their cultural traits, the Dobuans are different from other primitive tribes.*
      I. The location and environment of Dobuan Island make it difficult for the Dobuans to find sufficient food.

II. The rituals of marriage set the Dobuans apart from other primitive tribes.

III. The Dobuans' reliance on magic makes them more superstitious than other primitive tribes.

IV. The fact that the Dobuans value treachery and ill will sets them apart from other primitive tribes.

b. *Thesis: The purpose of the California missions was to Christianize the Indians and to strengthen Spain's claim to California.*

I. The mission padres taught the Indians Christian virtues.

II. The padres were concerned with saving the souls of the Indians.

III. The missions were constructed in the form of small cities.

IV. Without its colonists in California, Spain's claim to this territory was weak.

V. Spain was competing with Russia and England for territory in California.

c. *Thesis: American political assassins have acted on nonpolitical impulses.*

I. They are pathetic loners.

II. Their reality is a fantasy world.

III. The victim is usually a surrogate parent image.

IV. The assassin is seeking the same "fame" that the victim has.

V. European assassinations, unlike ours, have been the results of elaborate plots.

6. Scrutinize the following outline for errors of form as well as content. Correct the errors by producing two improved versions—a sentence outline and a topic outline.

a. *Thesis: The adult Moses is one of the most commanding and inspirational figures of the Old Testament.*

I. Moses was a God-intoxicated man.

   A. Moses' faith in God.

   B. He created in the Hebrews a religious faith that was to endure after their life as a nation had died.

      1. The Babylonian and Persian conquests.
      2. The faith endured during the Greek conquest.
      3. The faith endured during the Roman conquest.
      4. Despite their faith, the Hebrews often worshiped foreign gods.
      5. The faith endured during the various diasporas.

II. Moses was a peerless travel guide.

   A. During the long sojourn in the wilderness, Moses showed endless patience.

      1. Enduring constant grumbling on the part of the tribes.
      2. This period of desert wandering symbolizes the age of innocence of any developing nation.
      3. He settled quarrels with great patience.

      B. His earlier flight in order to escape punishment for having killed an Egyptian made him fully acquainted with the Sinai desert.
         1. He knew where to find water.
         2. He knew how to avoid dangerous enemy territory.
         3. He always followed a magical cloud by day and a pillar of fire by night.
  III. Moses was the founder of a complex legal system.
      A. He gave the Hebrews the Torah.
         1. Parts of the Torah dealt with man's relationship to God.
         2. Parts of the Torah dealt with man's relationship to man.
      B. He gave the Hebrews the ordinances.
         1. Some of the ordinances dealt with matters of social justice.
         2. According to one ordinance, a man who knocks out his slave's tooth must let that slave go free.
         3. Others of the ordinances dealt with religious ceremonies.
         4. Some of the ordinances dealt with plans for building a temple.

ADVICE

How to Write Clearly

Edward T. Thompson

Edward Thorwald Thompson (b. 1928) was born in Milwaukee and educated at MIT. Between 1976 and 1984, he was editor-in-chief of *Reader's Digest*. He is currently a consultant to publications.

Whatever you may think of the Reader's Digest—*there are those who love it and those who hate it—you cannot say that its hodgepodge of self-help, optimistic, and heartwarming articles is written in a disorganized way. In fact, the* Digest *is known above all else for its clear (some would say simplistic) style of writing. In the article that follows, a former editor of this venerable, popular publication offers some specific advice on how to organize ideas and express them on paper.*

• • •

1 If you are afraid to write, don't be.

2 If you think you've got to string together big fancy words and high-flying phrases, forget it.

3 To write well, unless you aspire to be a professional poet or novelist, you only need to get your ideas across simply and clearly.

4 It's not easy. But it is easier than you might imagine.

5 There are only three basic requirements:

6 First, you must want to write clearly. And I believe you really do, if you've stayed this far with me.

7   Second, you must be willing to work hard. Thinking means work—and that's what it takes to do anything well.
8   Third, you must know and follow some basic guidelines.
9   If, while you're writing for clarity, some lovely, dramatic or inspired phrases or sentences come to you, fine. Put them in.
10 But then with cold, objective eyes and mind ask yourself "Do they detract from clarity?" If they do, grit your teeth and cut the frills.

Follow Some Basic Guidelines

11 I can't give you a complete list of "do's and don'ts" for every writing problem you'll ever face.
12 But I can give you some fundamental guidelines that cover the most common problems.

1. Outline What You Want to Say

13 I know that sounds grade-schoolish. But you can't write clearly until, before you start, you know where you will stop.
14 Ironically, that's even a problem in writing an outline (i.e., knowing the ending before you begin).
15 So try this method:

- On 3 × 5 cards, write—one point to a card—all the points you need to make.
- Divide the cards into piles—one pile for each group of points closely related to each other. (If you were describing an automobile, you'd put all the points about mileage in one pile, all the points about safety in another, and so on.)
- Arrange your piles of points in a sequence. Which are most important and should be given first or saved for last? Which must you present before others in order to make the others understandable?
- Now, within each pile, do the same thing—arrange the points in logical, understandable order.

16 There you have your outline, needing only an introduction and conclusion.
17 This is a practical way to outline. It's also flexible. You can add, delete or change the location of points easily.

2. Start Where Your Readers Are

18 How much do they know about the subject? Don't write to a level higher than your readers' knowledge of it.
19 CAUTION: Forget that old—and wrong—advice about writing to a 12-year-old mentality. That's insulting. But do remember that your prime purpose is to explain something, not prove that you're smarter than your readers.

3. Avoid Jargon

20 Don't use words, expressions, phrases known only to people with specific knowledge or interests.

21 Example: A scientist, using scientific jargon, wrote, "The biota exhibited a one hundred percent mortality response." He could have written: "All the fish died."

4. Use Familiar Combinations of Words

22 A speech writer for President Franklin D. Roosevelt wrote, "We are endeavoring to construct a more inclusive society." F.D.R. changed it to, "We're going to make a country in which no one is left out."

23 CAUTION: By familiar combinations of words, I do not mean incorrect grammar. That can be unclear. Example: John's father says he can't go out Friday. (Who can't go out? John or his father?)

5. Use "First-Degree" Words

24 These words immediately bring an image to your mind. Other words must be "translated" through the first-degree word before you see the image. Those are second/third-degree words.

First-degree words	*Second/Third-degree words*
face	visage, countenance
stay	abide, remain, reside
book	volume, tome, publication

25 First-degree words are usually the most precise words, too.

6. Stick to the Point

26 Your outline—which was more work in the beginning—now saves you work. Because now you can ask about any sentence you write: "Does it relate to a point in the outline? If it doesn't, should I add it to the outline? If not, I'm getting off the track." Then, full steam ahead—on the main line.

7. Be as Brief as Possible

27 Whatever you write, shortening—condensing—almost always makes it tighter, straighter, easier to read and understand.

28 Condensing, as *Reader's Digest* does it, is in large part artistry. But it involves techniques that anyone can learn and use.

- Present your points in logical ABC order: Here again, your outline should save you work because, if you did it right, your points already stand in logical ABC order—A makes B understandable, B makes C understandable and so on. To write in a straight line is to say something clearly in the fewest possible words.

- Don't waste words telling people what they already know: Notice how we edited this: "Have you ever wondered how banks rate you as a credit risk? ~~You know, of course, that it's some combination of facts about your income, your job, and so on. But actually,~~ many banks have a scoring system...."
- Cut out excess evidence and unnecessary anecdotes: Usually, one fact or example (at most, two) will support a point. More just belabor it.
- And while writing about something may remind you of a good story, ask yourself: "Does it really help to tell the story, or does it slow me down?"

29   (Many people think *Reader's Digest* articles are filled with anecdotes. Actually, we use them sparingly and usually for one of two reasons: either the subject is so dry it needs some "humanity" to give it life; or the subject is so hard to grasp, it needs anecdotes to help readers understand. If the subject is both lively and easy to grasp, we move right along.)

- Look for the most common word wasters: windy phrases.

Windy phrases	*Cut to . . .*
at the present time	now
in the event of	of
in the majority of instances	usually

- Look for passive verbs you can make active: Invariably, this produces a shorter sentence. "The cherry tree was chopped down by George Washington." (Passive verb and nine words.) "George Washington chopped down the cherry tree." (Active verb and seven words.)
- Look for positive/negative sections from which you can cut the negative: See how we did it here: "The answer ~~does not rest with carelessness or incompetence; it~~ lies ~~largely~~ in having enough people to do the job."
- Finally, to write more clearly by saying it in fewer words: when you've finished, stop.

EXAMPLES

My Wood

E. M. FORSTER

E. M. Forster (1879–1969) was a British novelist, essayist, and short-story writer whose work first won wide recognition in 1924 with the publication of his book, *A Passage to India*. In 1946, Forster was made an honorary fellow of King's College, Cambridge, where he lived until his death.

Among his many other works are *Howard's End* (1910) and *Two Cheers for Democracy* (1951), a collection of his essays.

My Wood, a superbly organized short essay, investigates the effect of property ownership on the individual and society.

• • •

1   A few years ago I wrote a book which dealt in part with the difficulties of the English in India. Feeling that they would have had no difficulties in India themselves, the Americans read the book freely. The more they read it the better it made them feel, and a cheque to the author was the result. I bought a wood with the cheque. It is not a large wood—it contains scarcely any trees, and it is intersected, blast it, by a public footpath. Still, it is the first property that I have owned, so it is right that other people should participate in my shame, and should ask themselves, in accents that will vary in horror, this very important question: What is the effect of property upon the character? Don't let's touch economics; the effect of private ownership upon the community as a whole is another question—a more important question, perhaps, but another one. Let's keep to psychology. If you own things, what's their effect on you? What's the effect on me of my wood?

2   In the first place, it makes me feel heavy. Property does have this effect. Property produces men of weight, and it was a man of weight who failed to get into the Kingdom of Heaven. He was not wicked, that unfortunate millionaire in the parable, he was only stout; he stuck out in front, not to mention behind, and as he wedged himself this way and that in the crystalline entrance and bruised his well-fed flanks, he saw beneath him a comparatively slim camel passing through the eye of a needle and being woven into the robe of God. The Gospels all through couple stoutness and slowness. They point out what is perfectly obvious, yet seldom realized: that if you have a lot of things you cannot move about a lot, that furniture requires dusting, dusters require servants, servants require insurance stamps,[1] and the whole tangle of them makes you think twice before you accept an invitation to dinner or go for a bathe in the Jordan. Sometimes the Gospels proceed further and say with Tolstoy that property is sinful; they approach the difficult ground of asceticism here, where I cannot follow them. But as to the immediate effects of property on people, they just show straightforward logic. It produces men of weight. Men of weight cannot, by definition, move like the lightning from the East unto the West, and the ascent of a fourteen-stone bishop into a pulpit is thus the exact antithesis of the coming of the Son of Man. My wood makes me feel heavy.

3   In the second place, it makes me feel it ought to be larger.

4   The other day I heard a twig snap in it. I was annoyed at first, for I thought that someone was blackberrying, and depreciating the value of the undergrowth. On coming nearer, I saw it was not a man who had trodden on the

---

[1]In England.

twig and snapped it, but a bird, and I felt pleased. My bird. The bird was not equally pleased. Ignoring the relation between us, it took fright as soon as it saw the shape of my face, and flew straight over the boundary hedge into a field, the property of Mrs. Henessy, where it sat down with a loud squawk. It had become Mrs. Henessy's bird. Something seemed grossly amiss here, something that would not have occurred had the wood been larger. I could not afford to buy Mrs. Henessy out, I dared not murder her, and limitations of this sort beset me on every side. Ahab did not want that vineyard—he only needed it to round off his property, preparatory to plotting a new curve—and all the land around my wood has become necessary to me in order to round off the wood. A boundary protects. But—poor little thing—the boundary ought in its turn to be protected. Noises on the edge of it. Children throw stones. A little more, and then a little more, until we reach the sea. Happy Canute! Happier Alexander! And after all, why should even the world be the limit of possession? A rocket containing a Union Jack, will, it is hoped, be shortly fired at the moon. Mars. Sirius. Beyond which . . . But these immensities ended by saddening me. I could not suppose that my wood was the destined nucleus of universal dominion—it is so very small and contains no mineral wealth beyond the blackberries. Nor was I comforted when Mrs. Henessy's bird took alarm for the second time and flew clean away from us all, under the belief that it belonged to itself.

5   In the third place, property makes its owner feel that he ought to do something to it. Yet he isn't sure what. A restlessness comes over him, a vague sense that he has a personality to express—the same sense which, without any vagueness, leads the artist to an act of creation. Sometimes I think I will cut down such trees as remain in the wood, at other times I want to fill up the gaps between them with new trees. Both impulses are pretentious and empty. They are not honest movements towards money-making or beauty. They spring from a foolish desire to express myself and from an inability to enjoy what I have got. Creation, property, enjoyment form a sinister trinity in the human mind. Creation and enjoyment are both very good, yet they are often unattainable without a material basis, and at such moments property pushes itself in as a substitute, saying, "Accept me instead—I'm good enough for all three." It is not enough. It is, as Shakespeare said of lust, "The expense of spirit in a waste of shame": it is "Before, a joy proposed; behind, a dream." Yet we don't know how to shun it. It is forced on us by our economic system as the alternative to starvation. It is also forced on us by an internal defect in the soul, by the feeling that in property may lie the germs of self-development and of exquisite or heroic deeds. Our life on earth is, and ought to be, material and carnal. But we have not yet learned to manage our materialism and carnality properly; they are still entangled with the desire for ownership, where (in the words of Dante) "Possession is one with loss."

6   And this brings us to our fourth and final point: the blackberries.

7   Blackberries are not plentiful in this meagre grove, but they are easily seen from the public footpath which traverses it, and all too easily gathered. Foxgloves, too—people will pull up the foxgloves, and ladies of an educational

tendency even grub for toadstools to show them on the Monday in class. Other ladies, less educated, roll down the bracken in the arms of their gentlemen friends. There is a paper, there are tins. Pray, does my wood belong to me or doesn't it? And, if it does, should I not own it best by allowing no one else to walk there? There is a wood near Lyme Regis, also cursed by a public footpath, where the owner has not hesitated on this point. He has built high stone walls on each side of the path, and has spanned it by bridges, so that the public circulate like termites while he gorges on the blackberries unseen. He really does own his wood, this able chap. Dives in Hell did pretty well, but the gulf dividing him from Lazarus could be traversed by vision, and nothing traverses it here. And perhaps I shall come to this in time. I shall wall in and fence out until I really taste the sweets of property. Enormously stout, endlessly avaricious, pseudo-creative, intensely selfish, I shall weave upon my forehead the quadruple crown of possession until those nasty Bolshies come and take it off again and thrust me aside into the outer darkness.

- ### The Facts
1. What intersects Forster's wood and is a source of annoyance to him?
2. What is the first effect Forster's wood had on him?
3. What or whom did Forster discover on his property when he heard a twig snap?
4. According to Forster, what is the effect of property on its owner?
5. What does Forster think he will eventually do with his wood?

- ### The Strategies
1. What are the obvious divisions in the topics and subtopics of this essay? Make an outline showing the thesis, main points, and subtopics of the essay.
2. Read the last sentence of paragraph 2. What is the purpose of this sentence?
3. What is the purpose of paragraph 3?
4. What tone does Forster use throughout this essay? Do you regard his tone as mocking, serious, or ironic? Justify your answer.
5. In paragraph 4, Forster writes: "Happy Canute! Happier Alexander!" What is this figure of speech called? Why is Alexander happier than Canute?

- ### The Issues
1. What point does Forster make obliquely in his discussion about the bird?
2. What effect does ownership have on you? Is Forster exaggerating here, or have you experienced the same effects that he describes?
3. What benefits, if any, do you think society gains from ownership of private property?
4. What do you think Dante meant by "Possession is one with loss"? Interpret this statement.
5. "Our life on earth is, and ought to be, material and carnal." What is your opinion of this statement? How do you think our life on earth ought to be?

Suggestions for Writing

1. Using the Internet as your source, write a paragraph on footpaths in England.
2. In a paragraph or two, comment on the tone of this essay.

Rules for Aging
Roger Rosenblatt

Roger Rosenblatt (b. 1940) is one of *Time*'s most respected editorial writers. His insights into politics and society, as well as his wonderful sense of humor, have delighted his readers for close to two decades. Rosenblatt graduated from Harvard, where he earned a Ph.D. and briefly taught English. He has been featured on television reading his eloquent *Time* essays.

• • •

1   Since older people are as close to perfection as human beings get, I thought it would be generous, from time to time, to use this space to offer guidelines for living to those less old to help them age successfully, or at all. The art of aging requires not doing things more than taking positive action, so this is essentially a list of "nots" and "don'ts."

2   1. *It doesn't matter.* Whatever you think matters, doesn't. This guideline is absolutely reliable and adhering to it will add decades to your life. It does not matter if you are late for anything; if you're having a bad hair day, or a no hair day; if your car won't start; if your boss looks at you cockeyed; if your girlfriend or boyfriend looks at you cockeyed; if you are cockeyed; if you don't get the promotion; if you do; if you have spinach in your teeth or if you lose your teeth in your spinach. It doesn't matter.

3   2. *Nobody is thinking about you.* Yes, I know. You are certain that your friends are becoming your enemies; that your enemies are acquiring nuclear weapons; that your grocer, garbage man, clergyman, sister-in-law, and dog are all of the opinion that you have put on weight; furthermore, that everyone spends two thirds of every day commenting on your disintegration, denigrating your work, plotting your murder. I promise you: Nobody is thinking about you. They are thinking about themselves, just like you.

4   3. *Do not go to your left.* Going to one's left, or working on going to one's left, is a basketball term for strengthening one's weakness. A right-handed player will improve his game considerably if he learns to dribble and shoot with his left hand, and to move to his left on the court. But this is true only for basketball, not for living. In life, if you attempt to strengthen a weakness, you will grow weaker. If, on the other hand (the right), you keep playing to your strength, people will not notice that you have weaknesses.

Of course, you do not believe me. You will go ahead and take singing lessons or write that novel anyway. Trust me.

4. *Give honest, frank, and open criticism to nobody, never.* The following situation will present itself to you over and over: There is a friend, a relative, an employee, an employer, a colleague, whose behavior flaws are so evident to everyone but themselves, you just know that a straightforward, no-punches-pulled conversation with them will show them the error of their ways. They will see the light at once, and forever be grateful that only as good and candid a person as yourself would have sufficient kindness and courage to confront them.

Better still: From the moment you inform them about their bad table manners, their poor choices in clothing, their hygiene, their loudness, their deafness, their paranoia, they will reform on the spot. Their lives will be redeemed, and they will owe their renewed selves and all future happiness to you—honest, frank, and open you.

I implore you: forget about it. When the muse of candor whispers in your ear, swat it, take a long walk, a cold shower, and clear your head. This guideline relates to guideline number two. Nobody is thinking about you, unless you tell them about their faults. Then you can be sure they are thinking of you. They are thinking of killing you.

That's enough wisdom for now. I know younger people will not heed my advice anyway. So the guideline I offer them is: Don't. Go ahead and stay awake worrying what people are thinking about you, work on your weaknesses, and criticize your friends. It doesn't matter.

● Vocabulary

adhering (2)   disintegration (3)   denigrating (3)
paranoia (6)   muse (7)   candor (7)

● The Facts

1. How many rules for aging does Rosenblatt offer? What form do these rules follow?
2. The first rule is pronounced with great authority—"It doesn't matter." What is the author telling us with this rule?
3. In what way is rule #2 related to rule #1?
4. What does the author mean by the image of "going to your left"?
5. What is the implication behind rule #4?

● The Strategies

1. How would you describe the tone of this essay? How does the tone affect the purpose of the essay? Does the essay have a thesis? If so, where is it stated?

2. What is your reaction to the opening sentence of the essay? How did it strike you? Consider such matters as the author's voice, his tone, and his purpose.
3. What is the effect of the "Yes, I know" sentence at the beginning of paragraph 3?
4. Where does the author use parallelism to achieve balance and euphony? Point to specific passages in the essay.
5. Why does the author refer to "the muse of candor" in paragraph 7?

● The Issues

1. What is your personal understanding of the author's statement, "It doesn't matter"? Elaborate on his meaning.
2. Assuming that most human beings are concerned with their own problems more than those of other people, why do they often persist in feeling that their neighbors are plotting against them or making disparaging remarks behind their backs?
3. People say that growing old gracefully is an art. What does that popular saying mean? Do you agree? Give an example of someone you know who has grown old gracefully.
4. Which of Rosenblatt's rules do you think is the most difficult to follow? Why?
5. In giving us rule #3, do you think the author is discouraging forays into new and exciting territories? Might he be keeping older people from trying new hobbies or taking on new responsibilities that might enrich the final years of their lives? Explain your answer.

● Suggestions for Writing

1. Write an essay in which you propose your own rules for aging. You can be humorous like Rosenblatt or dead serious, but use a clear method of organization.
2. Choose one of the following comments and turn it into your thesis for a *brief* essay:
   a. Don't let the opinions of others control your life.
   b. Decide how you will react to unasked-for advice.

   Use a clear pattern of organization for this essay.

The Catbird Seat
JAMES THURBER

James Thurber (1894–1963) was an American humorist, cartoonist, and social commentator. His contributions to *The New Yorker* made him immensely popular. Among his best-known works are *My Life and Hard Times* (1933), *Fables for Our Time* (1940), and *The Thurber Carnival* (1945), from which this selection was taken.

A conventional, well-behaved office clerk suddenly finds his job threatened by an aggressive, loud-mouthed "special adviser to the president." To protect his job, this unobtrusive little man resorts to a most unusual crime.

• • •

1   Mr. Martin bought the pack of Camels on Monday night in the most crowded cigar store on Broadway. It was theatre time and seven or eight men were buying cigarettes. The clerk didn't even glance at Mr. Martin, who put the pack in his overcoat pocket and went out. If any of the staff at F & S had seen him buy the cigarettes, they would have been astonished, for it was generally known that Mr. Martin did not smoke, and never had. No one saw him.

2   It was just a week to the day since Mr. Martin had decided to rub out Mrs. Ulgine Barrows. The term "rub out" pleased him because it suggested nothing more than the correction of an error—in this case an error of Mr. Fitweiler. Mr. Martin had spent each night of the past week working out his plan and examining it. As he walked home now he went over it again. For the hundredth time he resented the element of imprecision, the margin of guesswork that entered into the business. The project as he had worked it out was casual and bold, the risks were considerable. Something might go wrong anywhere along the line. And therein lay the cunning of his scheme. No one would ever see in it the cautious, painstaking hand of Erwin Martin, head of the filing department at F & S, of whom Mr. Fitweiler had once said, "Man is fallible but Martin isn't." No one would see his hand, that is, unless it were caught in the act.

3   Sitting in his apartment, drinking a glass of milk, Mr. Martin reviewed his case against Mrs. Ulgine Barrows, as he had every night for seven nights. He began at the beginning. Her quacking voice and braying laugh had first profaned the halls of F & S on March 7, 1941 (Mr. Martin had a head for dates). Old Roberts, the personnel chief, had introduced her as the newly appointed special adviser to the president of the firm, Mr. Fitweiler. The woman had appalled Mr. Martin instantly, but he hadn't shown it. He had given her his dry hand, a look of studious concentration, and a faint smile. "Well," she had said, looking at the papers on his desk, "are you lifting the oxcart out of the ditch?" As Mr. Martin recalled that moment, over his milk, he squirmed slightly. He must keep his mind on her crimes as a special adviser, not on her peccadilloes as a personality. This he found difficult to do, in spite of entering an objection and sustaining it. The faults of the woman as a woman kept chattering on in his mind like an unruly witness. She had, for almost two years now, baited him. In the halls, in the elevator, even in his own office, into which she romped now and then like a circus horse, she was constantly shouting these silly questions at him. "Are you lifting the oxcart out of the ditch? Are you tearing up the pea patch? Are you hollering down the rain barrel? Are you scraping around the bottom of the pickle barrel? Are you sitting in the catbird seat?"

4   It was Joey Hart, one of Mr. Martin's two assistants, who had explained what the gibberish meant. "She must be a Dodger fan," he had said. "Red Barber announces the Dodger games over the radio and he uses those expressions—picked 'em up down South." Joey had gone on to explain one or two.

"Tearing up the pea patch" meant going on a rampage; "sitting in the catbird seat" meant sitting pretty, like a batter with three balls and no strikes on him. Mr. Martin dismissed all this with an effort. It had been annoying, it had driven him near to distraction, but he was too solid a man to be moved to murder by anything so childish. It was fortunate, he reflected as he passed on to the important charges against Mrs. Barrows, that he had stood up under it so well. He had maintained always an outward appearance of polite tolerance. "Why, I even believe you like the woman," Miss Paird, his other assistant, had once said to him. He had simply smiled.

5   A gavel rapped in Mr. Martin's mind and the case proper was resumed. Mrs. Ulgine Barrows stood charged with willful, blatant, and persistent attempts to destroy the efficiency and system of F & S. It was competent, material, and relevant to review her advent and rise to power. Mr. Martin had got the story from Miss Paird, who seemed always able to find things out. According to her, Mrs. Barrows had met Mr. Fitweiler at a party, where she had rescued him from the embraces of a powerfully built drunken man who had mistaken the president of F & S for a famous retired Middle Western football coach. She had led him to a sofa and somehow worked upon him a monstrous magic. The aging gentleman had jumped to the conclusion there and then that this was a woman of singular attainments, equipped to bring out the best in him and in the firm. A week later he had introduced her into F & S as his special adviser. On that day confusion got its foot in the door. After Miss Tyson, Mr. Brundage, and Mr. Bartlett had been fired and Mr. Munson had taken his hat and stalked out, mailing in his resignation later, old Roberts had been emboldened to speak to Mr. Fitweiler. He mentioned that Mr. Munson's department had been "a little disrupted" and hadn't they perhaps better resume the old system there? Mr. Fitweiler had said certainly not. He had the greatest faith in Mrs. Barrows' ideas. "They require a little seasoning, a little seasoning, is all," he had added. Mr. Roberts had given it up. Mr. Martin reviewed in detail all the changes wrought by Mrs. Barrows. She had begun chipping at the cornices of the firm's edifice and now she was swinging at the foundation stones with a pickaxe.

6   Mr. Martin came now, in his summing up, to the afternoon of Monday, November 2, 1942—just one week ago. On that day, at 3 p.m., Mrs. Barrows had bounced into his office. "Boo!" she had yelled. "Are you scraping around the bottom of the pickle barrel?" Mr. Martin had looked at her from under his green eyeshade, saying nothing. She had begun to wander about the office, taking it in with her great, popping eyes. "Do you really need all these filing cabinets?" she had demanded suddenly. Mr. Martin's heart had jumped. "Each of these files," he had said, keeping his voice even, "plays an indispensable part in the system of F & S." She had brayed at him, "Well, don't tear up the pea patch!" and gone to the door. From there she had bawled, "But you sure have got a lot of fine scrap in here!" Mr. Martin could no longer doubt that the finger was on his beloved department. Her pickaxe was on the upswing, poised for the first blow. It had not come yet; he had received no blue memo from the enchanted Mr. Fitweiler bearing nonsensical instructions

deriving from the obscene woman. But there was no doubt in Mr. Martin's mind that one would be forthcoming. He must act quickly. Already a precious week had gone by. Mr. Martin stood up in his living room, still holding his milk glass. "Gentlemen of the jury" he said to himself, "I demand the death penalty for this horrible person."

7 The next day Mr. Martin followed his routine, as usual. He polished his glasses more often and once sharpened an already sharp pencil, but not even Miss Paird noticed. Only once did he catch sight of his victim; she swept past him in the hall with a patronizing "Hi!" At five-thirty he walked home, as usual, and had a glass of milk, as usual. He had never drunk anything stronger in his life—unless you could count ginger ale. The late Sam Schlosser, the S of F & S, had praised Mr. Martin at a staff meeting several years before for his temperate habits. "Our most efficient worker neither drinks nor smokes," he had said. "The results speak for themselves." Mr. Fitweiler had sat by, nodding approval.

8 Mr. Martin was still thinking about that red-letter day as he walked over to the Schrafft's on Fifth Avenue near Forty-sixth Street. He got there, as he always did, at eight o'clock. He finished his dinner and the financial page of the Sun at a quarter to nine, as he always did. It was his custom after dinner to take a walk. This time he walked down Fifth Avenue at a casual pace. His gloved hands felt moist and warm, his forehead cold. He transferred the Camels from his overcoat to a jacket pocket. He wondered, as he did so, if they did not represent an unnecessary note of strain. Mrs. Barrows smoked only Luckies. It was his idea to puff a few puffs on a Camel (after the rubbing out), stub it out in the ashtray holding her lipstick-stained Luckies, and thus drag a small red herring across the trail. Perhaps it was not a good idea. It would take time. He might even choke, too loudly.

9 Mr. Martin had never seen the house on West Twelfth Street where Mrs. Barrows lived, but he had a clear enough picture of it. Fortunately, she had bragged to everybody about her ducky first-floor apartment in the perfectly darling three-story red-brick. There would be no doorman or other attendants; just the tenants of the second and third floors. As he walked along, Mr. Martin realized that he would get there before nine-thirty. He had considered walking north on Fifth Avenue from Schrafft's to a point from which it would take him until ten o'clock to reach the house. At that hour people were less likely to be coming in or going out. But the procedure would have made an awkward loop in the straight thread of his casualness, and he had abandoned it. It was impossible to figure when people would be entering or leaving the house, anyway. There was a great risk at any hour. If he ran into anybody, he would simply have to place the rubbing-out of Ulgine Barrows in the inactive file forever. The same thing would hold true if there were someone in her apartment. In that case he would just say that he had been passing by, recognized her charming house, and thought to drop in.

10 It was eighteen minutes after nine when Mr. Martin turned into Twelfth Street. A man passed him, and a man and a woman, talking. There was no one within fifty paces when he came to the house, halfway down the block. He was

up the steps and in the small vestibule in no time, pressing the bell under the card that said "Mrs. Ulgine Barrows." When the clicking in the lock started, he jumped forward against the door. He got inside fast, closing the door behind him. A bulb in a lantern hung from the hall ceiling on a chain seemed to give a monstrously bright light. There was nobody on the stair, which went up ahead of him along the left wall. A door opened down the hall in the wall on the right. He went toward it swiftly, on tiptoe.

11 "Well, for God's sake, look who's here!" bawled Mrs. Barrows, and her braying laugh rang out like the report of a shotgun. He rushed past her like a football tackle, bumping her. "Hey, quit shoving!" she said, closing the door behind them. They were in her living room, which seemed to Mr. Martin to be lighted by a hundred lamps. "What's after you?" she said. "You're as jumpy as a goat." He found he was unable to speak. His heart was wheezing in his throat. "I—yes," he finally brought out. She was jabbering and laughing as she started to help him off with his coat. "No, no," he said. "I'll put it here." He took it off and put it on a chair near the door. "Your hat and gloves, too," she said. "You're in a lady's house." He put his hat on top of the coat. Mrs. Barrows seemed larger than he had thought. He kept his gloves on. "I was passing by," he said. "I recognized—is there anyone here?" She laughed louder than ever. "No," she said, "we're all alone. You're as white as a sheet, you funny man. Whatever has come over you? I'll mix you a toddy." She started toward a door across the room. "Scotch-and-soda be all right? But say, you don't drink, do you?" She turned and gave him her amused look. Mr. Martin pulled himself together. "Scotch-and-soda will be all right," he heard himself say. He could hear her laughing in the kitchen.

12 Mr. Martin looked quickly around the living room for the weapon. He had counted on finding one there. There were andirons and a poker and something in a corner that looked like an Indian club. None of them would do. It couldn't be that way. He began to pace around. He came to a desk. On it lay a metal paper knife with an ornate handle. Would it be sharp enough? He reached for it and knocked over a small brass jar. Stamps spilled out of it and it fell to the floor with a clatter. "Hey," Mrs. Barrows yelled from the kitchen, "are you tearing up the pea patch?" Mr. Martin gave a strange laugh. Picking up the knife, he tried its point against his left wrist. It was blunt. It wouldn't do.

13 When Mrs. Barrows reappeared, carrying two highballs, Mr. Martin, standing there with his gloves on, became acutely conscious of the fantasy he had wrought. Cigarettes in his pocket, a drink prepared for him—it was all too grossly improbable. It was more than that; it was impossible. Somewhere in the back of his mind a vague idea stirred, sprouted. "For heaven's sake, take off those gloves," said Mrs. Barrows. "I always wear them in the house," said Mr. Martin. The idea began to bloom, strange and wonderful. She put the glasses on a coffee table in front of a sofa and sat on the sofa. "Come over here, you odd little man," she said. Mr. Martin went over and sat beside her. It was difficult getting a cigarette out of the pack of Camels, but he managed it. She held a match for him, laughing. "Well," she said, handing him a drink, "this is perfectly marvelous. You with a drink and a cigarette."

14   Martin puffed, not too awkwardly, and took a gulp of the highball. "I drink and smoke all the time," he said. He clinked his glass against hers. "Here's nuts to that old windbag, Fitweiler," he said, and gulped again. The stuff tasted awful, but he made no grimace. "Really, Mr. Martin," she said, her voice and posture changing, "you are insulting our employer." Mrs. Barrows was now all special adviser to the president. "I am preparing a bomb," said Mr. Martin, "which will blow the old goat higher than hell." He had only had a little of the drink, which was not strong. It couldn't be that. "Do you take dope or something?" Mrs. Barrows asked coldly. "Heroin," said Mr. Martin. "I'll be coked to the gills when I bump that old buzzard off." "Mr. Martin!" she shouted, getting to her feet. "That will be all of that. You must go at once." Mr. Martin took another swallow of his drink. He tapped his cigarette out in the ashtray and put the pack of Camels on the coffee table. Then he got up. She stood glaring at him. He walked over and put on his hat and coat. "Not a word about this," he said, and laid an index finger against his lips. All Mrs. Barrows could bring out was "Really!" Mr. Martin put his hand on the doorknob. "I'm sitting in the catbird seat," he said. He stuck his tongue out at her and left. Nobody saw him go.

15   Mr. Martin got to his apartment, walking, well before eleven. No one saw him go in. He had two glasses of milk after brushing his teeth, and he felt elated. It wasn't tipsiness, because he hadn't been tipsy. Anyway, the walk had worn off all effects of the whiskey. He got in bed and read a magazine for a while. He was asleep before midnight.

16   Mr. Martin got to the office at eight-thirty the next morning, as usual. At a quarter to nine, Ulgine Barrows, who had never before arrived at work before ten, swept into his office. "I'm reporting to Mr. Fitweiler now!" she shouted. "If he turns you over to the police, it's no more than you deserve!" Mr. Martin gave her a look of shocked surprise. "I beg your pardon?" he said. Mrs. Barrows snorted and bounced out of the room, leaving Miss Paird and Joey Hart staring after her. "What's the matter with that old devil now?" asked Miss Paird. "I have no idea," said Mr. Martin, resuming his work. The other two looked at him and then at each other. Miss Paird got up and went out. She walked slowly past the closed door of Mr. Fitweiler's office. Mrs. Barrows was yelling inside, but she was not braying. Miss Paird could not hear what the woman was saying. She went back to her desk.

17   Forty-five minutes later, Mrs. Barrows left the president's office and went into her own, shutting the door. It wasn't until half an hour later that Mr. Fitweiler sent for Mr. Martin. The head of the filing department, neat, quiet, attentive, stood in front of the old man's desk. Mr. Fitweiler was pale and nervous. He took his glasses off and twiddled them. He made a small, bruffing sound in his throat. "Martin," he said, "you have been with us more than twenty years." "Twenty-two, sir," said Mr. Martin. "In that time," pursued the president, "your work and your—uh—manner have been exemplary." "I trust so, sir," said Mr. Martin. "I have understood, Martin," said Mr. Fitweiler, "that you have never taken a drink or smoked." "That is correct, sir," said Mr. Martin. "Ah, yes." Mr. Fitweiler polished his glasses. "You may describe what you did after leaving the office yesterday, Martin," he said. Mr. Martin allowed less

than a second for his bewildered pause. "Certainly, sir," he said. "I walked home. Then I went to Schrafft's for dinner. Afterward I walked home again. I went to bed early, sir, and read a magazine for a while. I was asleep before eleven." "Ah, yes," said Mr. Fitweiler again. He was silent for a moment, searching for the proper words to say to the head of the filing department. "Mrs. Barrows," he said finally, "Mrs. Barrows has worked hard, Martin, very hard. It grieves me to report that she has suffered a severe breakdown. It has taken the form of a persecution complex accompanied by distressing hallucinations." "I am very sorry, sir," said Mr. Martin. "Mrs. Barrows is under the delusion," continued Mr. Fitweiler, "that you visited her last evening and behaved yourself in an—uh—unseemly manner." He raised his hand to silence Mr. Martin's little pained outcry. "It is the nature of these psychological diseases," Mr. Fitweiler said, "to fix upon the least likely and most innocent party as the—uh—source of persecution. These matters are not for the lay mind to grasp, Martin. I've just had my psychiatrist, Dr. Fitch, on the phone. He would not, of course, commit himself, but he made enough generalizations to substantiate my suspicions. I suggested to Mrs. Barrows, when she had completed her—uh—story to me this morning, that she visit Dr. Fitch, for I suspected a condition at once. She flew, I regret to say, into a rage, and demanded—uh—requested that I call you on the carpet. You may not know, Martin, but Mrs. Barrows had planned a reorganization of your department—subject to my approval, of course, subject to my approval. This brought you, rather than anyone else, to her mind—but again that is a phenomenon for Dr. Fitch and not for us. So, Martin, I am afraid Mrs. Barrows' usefulness here is at an end." "I am dreadfully sorry, sir," said Mr. Martin.

18   It was at this point that the door to the office blew open with the suddenness of a gas-main explosion and Mrs. Barrows catapulted through it. "Is the little rat denying it?" she screamed. "He can't get away with that!" Mr. Martin got up and moved discreetly to a point beside Mr. Fitweiler's chair. "You drank and smoked at my apartment," she bawled at Mr. Martin, "and you know it! You called Mr. Fitweiler an old windbag and said you were going to blow him up when you got coked to the gills on your heroin!" She stopped yelling to catch her breath and a new glint came into her popping eyes. "If you weren't such a drab, ordinary little man," she said, "I'd think you'd planned it all. Sticking your tongue out, saying you were sitting in the catbird seat, because you thought no one would believe me when I told it! My God, it's really too perfect!" She glared at Mr. Fitweiler. "Can't you see how he has tricked us, you old fool? Can't you see his little game?" But Mr. Fitweiler had been surreptitiously pressing all the buttons under the top of his desk and employees of F & S began pouring into the room. "Stockton," said Mr. Fitweiler, "you and Fishbein will take Mrs. Barrows to her home. Mrs. Powell, you will go with them." Stockton, who had played a little football in high school, blocked Mrs. Barrows as she made for Mr. Martin. It took him and Fishbein together to force her out of the door into the hall, crowded with stenographers and office boys. She was still screaming imprecations at Mr. Martin, tangled and contradictory imprecations. The hubbub finally died out down the corridor.

19   "I regret that this has happened," said Mr. Fitweiler. "I shall ask you to dismiss it from your mind, Martin." "Yes, sir," said Mr. Martin, anticipating his chief's "That will be all" by moving to the door. "I will dismiss it." He went out and shut the door, and his step was light and quick in the hall. When he entered his department he had slowed down to his customary gait, and he walked quietly across the room to the W20 file, wearing a look of studious concentration.

● Vocabulary

fallible (2)	appalled (3)	peccadilloes (3)
romped (3)	gibberish (4)	edifice (5)
indispensable (6)	obscene (6)	patronizing (7)
temperate (7)	red herring (8)	ducky (9)
monstrously (10)	wheezing (11)	grossly (13)
bruffing (17)	exemplary (17)	hallucinations (17)
unseemly (17)	catapulted (18)	surreptitiously (18)
imprecations (18)		

● The Facts

1. What is the origin of the colorful expressions that Mrs. Barrows constantly uses?
2. What is Mrs. Barrow's title in the firm of F & S?
3. Why does Mr. Martin finally decide to "rub out" Mrs. Barrows?
4. What shocking disclosures does Mr. Martin reveal to Mrs. Barrows on his surprise visit to her apartment?
5. What is the outcome of Mrs. Barrows's accusations against Mr. Martin?

● The Strategies

1. The organization of the story falls naturally into four divisions: (a) the trial and verdict of Mrs. Barrows, (b) preparation for the crime, (c) change of plan and perpetration of the crime, and (d) result of the crime. Summarize what happens in each of these segments.
2. Early in the story, the author tells us that Mr. Martin plans to kill Mrs. Barrows. Why does this announcement not eliminate suspense from the story?
3. What is the emotional climax of the story?
4. How does Thurber prepare us for Mr. Fitweiler's incredulous reaction to Mrs. Barrows's story about Mr. Martin? Why are we amused but not surprised at Mr. Fitweiler's reaction?

● The Issues

1. What obvious contrasts between Mr. Martin and Mrs. Barrows does Thurber draw?
2. What is your view of the morality of Mr. Martin's actions? Was he justified in his extreme steps or not?

3. How does Mrs. Barrows's character reinforce an ancient sexual stereotype about women? How would you characterize this stereotype?
4. If this story were set in an office today rather than in the 1940s, would it be as believable? Why or why not?
5. Reverse the characters of Mrs. Barrows and Mr. Martin: She is now the fastidious head of the filing department; he the brassy opportunist who has ingratiated himself in the good graces of the boss, Fitweiler. Does the story still work? Why or why not?

- **Suggestions for Writing**

1. Write a short caricature about one of your close friends and exaggerate his or her traits.
2. Write an essay analyzing the humorous devices used by Thurber in the story *The Catbird Seat*. Pay attention to such factors as character, plot reversal, and style.

That Time of Year (Sonnet 73)

WILLIAM SHAKESPEARE

William Shakespeare (1564–1616) is generally acknowledged as the greatest literary genius of the English language. Born in Stratford-upon-Avon, England, he was the son of a prosperous businessman, and probably attended grammar schools in his native town. In 1582, Shakespeare married Anne Hathaway, who was eight years his senior, and who bore him three children. The legacy of his writing includes 36 plays, 154 sonnets, and 5 long poems.

The English or Shakespearean sonnet is composed of three quatrains of four lines each and a concluding couplet of two lines, rhyming abab cdcd efef gg. There is usually a correspondence between the units marked off by the rhymes and the development of the thought. The three quatrains, for instance, may represent three different images or three questions from which a conclusion is drawn in the final couplet. As a result, the sonnet is one of the most tightly organized poetic forms used.

• • •

That time of year thou mayst in me behold
When yellow leaves, or none, or few, do hang
Upon those boughs which shake against the cold,
Bare ruined choirs where late the sweet birds sang.
5   In me thou see'st the twilight of such day
As after sunset fadeth in the west,
Which by and by black night doth take away,
Death's second self, that seals up all in rest.
In me thou see'st the glowing of such fire,

10 That on the ashes of his youth doth lie
    As the deathbed whereon it must expire,
    Consumed with that which it was nourished by.
    This thou perceivest, which makes thy love more strong,
    To love that well which thou must leave ere long.

● The Facts

1. What image does the poet focus on in the first quatrain? What relationship does this image have to the speaker?
2. The speaker shifts to another image in the second quatrain. What is it, and what relationship does it bear to him?
3. Yet another image is introduced in the third quatrain. What is the image, and how does it relate to the speaker? What rather complex philosophical paradox is involved?
4. The final couplet states the poet's thesis (or theme). What is that thesis? State it in your own words.

● The Strategies

1. The entire poem is organized around three analogies. State them in three succinct sentences.
2. The three images in the poem are presented in a particular order. Do you see any reason for this order?
3. In lines 3 and 4, what effect do the words "cold,/Bare ruined choirs" have on the rhythm and meter?
4. In line 2, what would be the result of substituting "hang" for "do hang"?
5. What is the antecedent of "this" in line 13?

● The Issues

1. What can you deduce from this poem about the speaker and his frame of mind?
2. Someone once said, "Youth is wasted on the young." How might that witticism be applied to this poem?
3. Why should a student whose major is, say, business and who has no interest whatsoever in literature be forced to take classes in which poems such as this one are studied?
4. Shakespeare has been called surprisingly modern in his outlook. What about this poem would seem to justify that observation?

● Suggestions for Writing

1. In two or three well-developed paragraphs, give your views on older people.
2. Write an essay about a memorable older person.

● **CHAPTER WRITING ASSIGNMENTS**

1. Write a well-organized essay describing your study habits and methods.
2. Write a well-organized chronological autobiography.
3. Write an essay detailing the steps you follow when you have to complete a writing assignment.
4. Detail in a tightly organized essay any particular procedure or process (e.g., how to tune a car engine) with which you are intimately familiar.

● **WRITING ASSIGNMENTS FOR A SPECIFIC AUDIENCE**

1. Write an essay of appreciation directed at your favorite teacher— from any grade—telling how he or she affected your life.
2. Write an essay, after doing the necessary research, telling an audience of high-school dropouts the opportunities available to them for continuing their education.

● **COLLABORATIVE WRITING PROJECT**

In teams of three, survey the incidence of drug use among a separate and specific segment of your college population. (For example, one team can focus on business majors, another on sociology majors, and so on.) After meeting with the three teams to compare the results, each team should write an essay on its findings.

REAL-LIFE STUDENT WRITING

Note from a Graduate Student to a Department Secretary

The following note was written by a student named Jennifer, who is in the graduate school program of a well-known Catholic university. Katie is the department secretary of the business school. Jennifer is writing to Katie to ask for her help in getting registered in a statistics class. Notice the polite social remarks Jennifer makes before saying what she really wants. Jeff is Katie's new husband. Bailey is Jennifer's boyfriend.

• • •

Hi Katie!

Welcome back from your honeymoon! Hope married life is treating you well. Bailey said he ran into ya'll last night, and Jeff's wig was realistically scary. Wish I could have seen it.

Lucinda sent me to you on an issue I'm having. I keep trying to register for classes in the business school for next quarter, but the system won't let me in! Lucinda said something about how they've changed their criteria. I wonder if I could be using the wrong password. I heard it was due to be changed, but I haven't seen any memo telling us that it had been. Meantime, I need to register for business statistics ASAP! As department secretary, you're my last hope.

Can you help me?

Thanks!

Jennifer

6

Developing Paragraphs

ROAD MAP TO PARAGRAPHS

From ancient times, the primary use of the paragraph has been to signal the introduction of a new idea or the further development of an old one. Here is an example of a paragraph signaling a new idea:

> In the modern formal bullfight or "corrida de toros" there are usually six bulls that are killed by three different men. Each man kills two bulls. The bulls by law are required to be from four to five years old, free from physical defects, and well armed with sharp-pointed horns. They are inspected by a municipal veterinary surgeon before the fight. The veterinary is supposed to reject bulls that are under age, insufficiently armed or with anything wrong with their eyes, their horns or any apparent disease or visible bodily defects such as lameness.
>
> The men who are to kill them are called matadors and which of the six bulls they are to kill is determined by lot. Each matador, or killer, has a caudrilla, or team, of from five to six men who are paid by him and work under his orders. Three of these men, who aid him on foot with capes and at his orders place the banderillas, three-foot wooden sharps with harpoon points, are called peones or banderilleros. The other two, who are mounted on horses when they appear in the ring, are called picadors.
>
> —Ernest Hemingway, *The Bullfight*

The shift in discussion between the first and second paragraph is obvious: Paragraph 1 is about the bulls; paragraph 2 is about the men who will fight and kill them.

A second use of the paragraph is to add significantly to or elaborate on what has been said in a preceding paragraph. Here is an example:

> The oxen in Africa have carried the heavy load of the advance of European civilization. Wherever new land has been broken they have broken it, panting and pulling knee-deep in the soil before the ploughs, the long whips in the air over them. Where a road has been made they

have made it; and they have trudged the iron and tools through the land, to the yelling and shouting of the drivers, by tracks in the dust and the long grass of the plains, before there ever were any roads. They have been inspanned before daybreak, and have sweated up and down the long hills, and across dungas and riverbeds, through the burning hours of the day. The whips have marked their sides, and you will often see oxen that have had an eye, or both of them, taken away by the long cutting whip-lashes. The waggon-oxen of many Indian and white contractors worked every day, all their lives through, and did not know of the Sabbath.

It is a strange thing that we have done to the oxen. The bull is in a constant stage of fury, rolling his eyes, shovelling up the earth, upset by everything that gets within his range of vision—still he has got a life of his own, fire comes from his nostrils, and new life from his loins; his days are filled with his vital cravings and satisfactions. All of that we have taken away from the oxen, and in reward we have claimed their existence for ourselves. The oxen walk along within our own daily life, pulling hard all the time, creatures without a life, things made for our use. They have moist, limpid, violet eyes, soft muzzles, silky ears, they are patient and dull in all their ways; sometimes they look as if they were thinking about things. —Isak Dinesen, *Out of Africa*

In the first paragraph the author points out that oxen have played a key role in civilizing the African continent. In the second paragraph she elaborates on the first by reminding us that the oxen's patient subservience has come at a price.

Parts of the Paragraph

A paragraph generally consists of two main parts: a topic sentence and specific details that support it.

The Topic Sentence This is the sentence that tells us what the writer intends to propose, argue, or demonstrate. In the following paragraph, the topic sentence is underlined.

To all English-speaking peoples the Bible is a national as well as a noble monument, for much of their history is securely rooted and anchored within it. In 17th century England it nurtured the Puritan revolt and paved the way for the Bill of Rights. In 17th and 18th century America it supplied not only the names of our ancestors but the stout precepts by which they lived. They walked by its guidance; their rough places were made plain by their trust in its compassionate promises. It was a lamp to their feet and a light to their path, a pillar of cloud by day and of fire by night. It was the source of the convictions that shaped the building of this country, of the faith that endured the first New England winters and later opened up the Great West. It laid the foundations of our educational system, built our earliest colleges, and dictated the training within our homes. In the words alike of Jefferson and Patrick Henry, John Quincy Adams and Franklin it made better and more useful citizens to their country by reminding a man of his individual responsibility, his own dignity, and his equality with his fellow man. The Bible is, indeed, so imbedded in our American heritage that not to recognize its place there becomes a kind of national apostasy, and not to know and understand it, in these days when we give all for its principles of human worth and human freedom, an act unworthy of us as a people. —Mary Ellen Chase, *The Bible and the Common Reader*

Implied Topic Sentences Some paragraphs have an *implied topic sentence,* also known as a *controlling idea*. Here is an example:

> At graveside, the casket is lowered into the earth. This office, once the prerogative of friends of the deceased, is now performed by a patented mechanical lowering device. A "Lifetime Green" artificial grass mat is at the ready to conceal the sere earth, and overhead, to conceal the sky, is a portable Steril Chapel Tent ("resists the intense heat and humidity of summer and the terrific storms of winter. . . . available in Silver Grey, Rose or Evergreen"). Now is the time for the ritual scattering of earth over the coffin, as the solemn words "earth to earth, ashes to ashes, dust to dust" are pronounced by the officiating cleric. This can be accomplished "with a mere flick of the wrist with the Gordon Leak-proof Earth Dispenser. No grasping of a handful of dirt, no soiled fingers. Simple, dignified, beautiful, reverent! The modern way!" The Gordon Earth Dispenser (at $5) is of nickel-plated brass construction. It is not only "attractive to the eye and long wearing"; it is also "one of the 'tools' for building better public relations" if presented as "an appropriate noncommercial gift" to the clergyman. It is shaped something like a saltshaker. —Jessica Mitford, *The American Way of Death*

The controlling idea of this paragraph is that the funeral industry is guilty of vulgar commercialism. The details amply support that point, and the writer's focus is clear even though she uses no topic sentence. A writer does not have to telegraph a paragraph's meaning in an explicit topic sentence so long as all its details are linked by some organizing theme or focus.

Supporting Details

Good paragraphs are filled with supporting facts, instances, examples, and details. They make a point and then adequately support it. They do not circle the subject, nor do they repeat at the same level of generality what the writer has already said. Here are two examples. In both examples, the topic sentence is underlined. We made up the first example as a dramatic illustration of the repetitive writing often found in bad paragraphs, where the main point is restated over and over at the same level of generality:

> Rotten writing is scarcely a new problem. People have always had bad handwriting. Some old manuscripts are difficult to read because they are so badly written. Old letters are also indecipherable. Some writing from the past looks as if a drunken chicken had walked over it. Strain as much as you might, you just can't tell what the writer meant. Inscriptions of various kinds are just as impossible to read.

Has the point of this paragraph—that "rotten writing is scarcely a new problem"—been proved? It has not. The paragraph simply says that people have always written badly but gives no concrete instances or facts to make this assertion believable.

Here, on the other hand, is a paragraph that begins with the same generalization and then proves it with examples drawn from history:

> Rotten writing is scarcely a new problem. Napoleon's script was so miserable that one of his generals once mistook a letter of his for battle orders. Charles Hamilton, a Manhattan dealer in autographs and manuscripts, contends that Gertrude Stein's oblique prose style may be explained by the fact that compositors often misread her cryptic script. Poet William Butler Yeats often could not read his own work. Horace Greeley, the editor of the old New York *Tribune,* had a notoriously illegible scrawl. He once scribbled a note to a reporter telling him that he was fired for incompetence; so indecipherable was the missive that for years afterwards the man was able to pass it off as a letter of recommendation. —"Nowadays, Writing Is Off the Wall," *Time,* January 1, 1980

Paragraphs with a Final Summing-Up Sentence Some paragraphs begin and end with a generalization. The first generalization is the topic sentence; the second is a summary. Here is an example:

> A language changes because things happen to people. If we could imagine the impossible—a society in which nothing happened—there would be no changes in language. But except possibly in a cemetery, things are constantly happening to people: they eat, drink, sleep, talk, make love, meet strangers, struggle against natural perils, and fight against one another. They slowly adapt their language to meet the changing conditions of their lives. Although the changes made in one generation may be small, those made in a dozen generations may enormously affect the language. The big and little phases of history, fashions, fads, inventions, the influence of a leader, a war or two, an invasion or two, travel to a foreign land, the demands of business intercourse—may alter a language so much that a Rip Van Winkle who slept two or

three hundred years might have trouble making himself understood when he awoke. <u>Even in a relatively quiet society, linguistic change proceeds inexorably.</u> —J. N. Hook and E. G. Mathews, *Modern American Grammar and Usage*

Topic Sentence Developed over More Than One Paragraph

A single topic sentence can also be developed over the course of two or more paragraphs. This development usually occurs when the topic sentence is too broad or complex to be adequately covered in a single paragraph or when the presentation of supporting details in several paragraphs is more emphatic. In the following example, a topic sentence is developed over two paragraphs. The topic sentence is underlined:

> <u>There has always been something so fascinating about the mere fact of fatness that men of all nations and of many degrees of wisdom or lack of it have formulated opinions on its state, its origins, and its correction.</u> Shakespeare's characters are at their most eloquent when the topic is obesity. "Make less thy body and hence more thy grace. Leave gormandizing. Know the grave cloth gape for thee thrice wider than for other men." And, of course, to Julius Caesar, the Bard attributed the notion of the harmlessness of fat companions in warning against "the lean and hungry look" of "yon Cassius."
>
> In *Coming Up for Air,* George Orwell has the narrator, himself a fat man, sum it up: "They all think a fat man isn't quite like other men. He goes through life on a light-comedy plane . . . as low farce." Sometimes the situation is just as sad and much less tolerable. When W. D. Howells was consul at Venice, he was told by a tall, lanky man, "If I were as fat as you, I would hang myself." And Osborn in his otherwise lightly satirical picture-essay, *The Vulgarians,* pontificates, "The fat and the fatuous are interchangeable." —Jean Mayer, *Overweight: Causes, Cost, and Control*

Covering a topic sentence in more than one paragraph allows for a fuller development of the general idea, but it also tempts the writer to stray from the point. Beginning writers will find it safer to use a separate topic sentence for each paragraph.

Position of the Topic Sentence

As the sum of what a paragraph is about, the topic sentence should naturally occupy a prominent position, and in all of our examples so far, the topic sentence has come first. Such a paragraph is said to be organized from the general to the particular: the idea first followed by the particulars. The reverse of this arrangement is the paragraph organized from the particular to the general: The supporting details come first and the topic sentence last. Here is an example:

> The human population already stands at over 4 billion, and at current growth rates that number will double within thirty-eight years. If the growth rate were to continue unchecked, in fact, the global population would reach about 150 billion within two centuries. Yet nearly two-thirds of the existing inhabitants of the earth are undernourished or malnourished, and they are dying of starvation at the rate of more than 10 million every year. <u>There can be little question that unchecked population growth is the most critical social problem in the modern world, with potential consequences in terms of sheer human misery that are almost unimaginable.</u> —Ian Robertson, *Sociology*

This arrangement is an uncommon one and somewhat mannered. Before you can cite details in support of an idea, you must first know the idea. Consequently, it has become traditional for writers to first state the general idea of a paragraph and then cite details in support of it—this pattern conforms to the way people usually think. The paragraph in which the topic sentence appears after the supporting details should be used only as a change of pace, not as a matter of course.

Finally, some paragraphs have topic sentences that come not first or last, but second or third. Paragraphs of this kind are usually found in the middle of an essay. The initial sentences are used to ensure a smooth transition from the preceding paragraph, and then the topic sentence makes its appearance. In the following example, the topic sentence is underlined:

> In our own *way,* we conform as best we can to the rest of nature. <u>The obituary pages tell us of the news that we are dying off, while the birth announcements in finer print, off at the side of the page, inform us of our replacements, but we get no grasp from this of the enormity of scale.</u> There are 3 billion of us on the earth, and all 3 billion must be dead, on schedule, within this lifetime. The vast mortality, involving something over 50 million of us each year, takes place in relative secrecy. We can only really know of the deaths in our households, or among our friends. These, detached in our minds from the rest, we take to be unnatural events, anomalies, outrages. We speak of our own dead in low voices; struck down, we say, as though visible death can only occur for cause, by disease, or violence, avoidably. We send off flowers, grieve, make ceremonies, scatter bones, unaware of the rest of the 3 billion on the same schedule. All that immense mass of flesh and bone and consciousness will disappear by absorption into the earth, without recognition by the transient survivors. —Lewis Thomas, *Death in the Open*

The first sentence is for transition—to connect this paragraph with the one before. The second sentence is the topic sentence. It contains the assertion that the supporting details prove.

Paragraph Patterns

Paragraphs are often written to conform to certain abstract patterns that are partly rhetorical and partly based on some common operations of thinking. You might, for example, write a paragraph drawing a contrast between two animals, two objects, or two people. Or, you might write a paragraph explaining why an incident occurred or predicting what is likely to happen if something is done or left undone. In the first case, you would develop the paragraph by a pattern of comparison and contrast; in the second, by causal analysis.

In Part Two of this book, we will focus extensively on how to write paragraphs by these common patterns. We will explain the paragraph-writing techniques used to compare and contrast, analyze cause, narrate, describe, illustrate, define, classify, and explain process. But for now, we mention these patterns to emphasize this point: No matter what its developmental pattern, any paragraph you write must support its main idea with specific details.

Characteristics of a Well-Designed Paragraph

The characteristics of the well-designed paragraph are *unity, coherence,* and *completeness.*

Unity A paragraph is said to have *unity* when its sentences stick to the topic and do not stray to secondary issues or deal with irrelevancies. Here's an example of a paragraph that lacks unity:

> (1) A fairy tale is a serious story with a human hero and a happy ending. (2) The hero in a fairy tale is different from the hero in a tragedy in that his progression is from bad to good fortune, rather than the reverse. <u>(3) In the Greek tragedy "Oedipus Rex," for example, the hero goes from highest fortune to lowest misery, but in the end he recognizes his error in judgment and maintains a noble posture despite profound suffering. (4) The audience watching him is purged of pity and fear through what Aristotle labeled a "catharsis."</u> (5) The hero in a fairy tale usually has a miserable beginning. (6) He is either socially obscure or despised as being stupid and lacking in heroic virtues. (7) But in the end, he has surprised everyone by demonstrating his courage, consequently winning fame, riches, and love. (8) We clearly see this bad-to-good-fortune progress in stories like "Cinderella," "Sleeping Beauty," and "The Frog Prince."

The topic sentence of the paragraph promises to give a definition of a fairy tale, but part of the paragraph drifts away from the definition. Sentences 3 and 4 (underlined) are entirely beside the point. With the fifth sentence, the writer resumes the announced intent of the paragraph—to define a fairy tale.

The possible causes of this fault are several. Some digressions can be traced to a writer's daydreaming; some to boredom with the topic on hand; some to a desire to impress the reader by introducing an interesting but irrelevant point. The cure is not easy to prescribe. The inexperienced writer needs to remember that the purpose of the paragraph is announced in the topic sentence, and it is this purpose that the other sentences of the paragraph must carry out.

Coherence A paragraph has *coherence* when its sentences are logically connected. However, sentences are not automatically linked simply because they follow one after another on the page. Four devices can be used to ensure paragraph coherence:

1. Transitional words and phrases
2. Pronoun reference
3. Repeated key terms
4. Parallelism

Transitional words and phrases, which point out the direction of the paragraph, are used to link sentences. Here are examples, underlined:

> <u>In addition</u> to the academic traditionalism in schools, there are other problems. First, there is the problem of coordinating education with the realities of the world of work. <u>Second</u>, there is the question of how long the schooling period should be. <u>Despite evidence to the contrary</u>, a case can be made for the notion that we not only overeducate our children, but also take too long to do it.

The underlined words and phrases add coherence to the passage. They join sentences and, consequently, ideas in clear and logical relationships. Without the use of transitional words and phrases, the writing would seem choppy and the relationships between sentences unclear.

Coherence can also be achieved by *pronoun reference.* A noun is used in one sentence or clause and a pronoun that refers to it is used in the next sentence or clause. In the following paragraph the pronouns so used are underlined:

> Twenty years ago women were a majority of the population, but they were treated like a minority group. The prejudice against <u>them</u> was so deep-rooted that, paradoxically, most people pretended that it did not exist. Indeed, most women preferred to ignore the situation rather than to rock the boat. <u>They</u> accepted being paid less for doing the same work as a man. <u>They</u> were as quick as any male to condemn a woman who ventured outside the limits of the roles men had assigned to females: those of toy and drudge.

Key terms may be repeated throughout the paragraph to link sentences. The key terms in the following paragraph are underlined:

> <u>Fantasy</u> is not restricted to one sector of the southern California way of life; it is all-pervasive. Los Angeles restaurants and their parking lots are such million-dollar structures because they are palaces of <u>fantasy</u> in which the upward moving individual comes to act out a self-mythology he or she has learned from a hero of the mass media. Often enough, the establishments of La Cienega Boulevard's Restaurant Row are <u>fantasies</u> of history in their very architecture.

Parallelism is also used to ensure coherence, although not nearly so often as any of the other three devices. The principle behind parallelism is that similar ideas are expressed in structurally similar sentences. Here is a paragraph that uses parallelism to ensure coherence:

> Now, I will not for a moment deny that getting ahead of your neighbor is delightful, but it is not the only delight of which human beings are capable. There are innumerable things which are not competitive. It is possible to enjoy food and drink without having to reflect that you have a better cook and a better wine merchant than your former friends whom you are learning to cold-shoulder. It is possible to be fond of your wife and children without reflecting how much better she dresses than Mrs. So-and-So and how much better they are at athletics than the children of that old stick-in-the-mud Mr. Such-and-Such. There are those who can enjoy music without thinking how cultured the other ladies in their women's club will be thinking them. There are even people who enjoy a fine day in spite of the fact that the sun shines on everybody. All these simple pleasures are destroyed as soon as competitiveness gets the upper hand. —Bertrand Russell, *The Unhappy American Way*

The repetition of "It is possible" and "There are" add bridges that smoothly connect one thought with another.

Completeness A paragraph is complete when it has provided enough details to support its topic sentence. A paragraph is incomplete when the topic sentence is not developed or when it is merely extended through repetition. In either case, the reader is burdened with useless generalizations. The following paragraph is incomplete:

> Withholding tax is a bad way to go about collecting taxes from the people in our country because this system assumes that the American people are incompetent.

This paragraph hints at an argument but then comes to a dead stop. The reader will automatically ask, "In what way or by what means does tax withholding assume that the American people are incompetent?" Without further evidence, the paragraph goes nowhere. Now read the following paragraph:

> Withholding is a bad way to go about collecting tax money, even though the figures may show that it gets results. It is bad because it implies that the individual is incapable of handling his own affairs. The government as much as says, We know that, if left to your own devices, you will fritter away your worldly goods, and tax day will catch you without cash. Or it says, We're not sure you'll come clean in your return, so we will just take the money before it reaches you, and you will be saved the trouble and fuss of being honest. This implication is an unhealthy thing to spread around, being contrary to the old American theory that the individual is a very competent little guy indeed. The whole setup of our democratic government assumes that the citizen is bright, honest, and at least as fundamentally sound as a common stock. If you start treating him as something less than that, you are going to get into deep water. The device of withholding tax money, which is clearly confiscatory, since the individual is not allowed to see, taste, or touch a certain percentage of his wages, tacitly brands him as negligent or unthrifty or immature or incompetent or dishonest, or all of those things at once. There is, furthermore, a bad psychological effect in earning money that you never get your paws on. We believe this effect to be much stronger than the government realizes. At any rate, if the American individual is in truth incapable of paying his tax all by himself, then he should certainly be regarded as incapable of voting all by himself, and the Secretary of the Treasury should accompany him into the booth to show him where to put the X. —E. B. White, *Withholding*

While the reader may not agree with these ideas, the writer has fulfilled his promise to show why he does not like withholding tax. He has provided clear examples and has moved from the general to the specific, keeping in mind the direction of his topic sentence. His paragraph is complete. Make your own paragraphs complete by providing enough detail to support their topic sentences.

It is an essential part of a writer's job to dig up the details necessary to make an essay complete. One source of such details, of course, is the library. Another is the Internet and its various electronic databases.

Writing Your Own Paragraphs

There is no mystery to writing good paragraphs. Begin with a topic sentence that states your opinion or proposes an idea. Back up this sentence with ample supporting details. Stick to the point of the topic sentence. Insert transitions as necessary to keep the text coherent. That, in a nutshell, is all there is to it.

The problems that arise with paragraph writing are usually problems of content rather than of technique. In other words, the writing is affected by the fact that the writer has not done the necessary research and does not understand the topic. Even gifted writers have difficulty writing on topics they know little about. Writing does not begin when you first sit down behind a keyboard. It actually begins when you begin to research your topic. If you are thoroughly grounded in the details of your topic, you'll find that writing paragraphs about it will be surprisingly easy.

Exercises

1. Write a suitable topic sentence for a paragraph that would contain the following supporting details:
   a. (1) Cultivate only the best writers.
      (2) You needn't assume that just because something is in print, it is well written.
      (3) If you fall into the habit of reading hacks or writers that have only a dulled sense for the right word, then you are not helping yourself to become a writer who is fresh and original.
      (4) Read those authors who appear in *The New Yorker,* who get good reviews in magazines like *Time,* and who haven't faded after writing one book or one play.
   b. (1) In primitive tribes this concern was limited to members of the tribe. If a man was not a member, one need not worry about whether one was behaving ethically or unethically toward him.
      (2) But as man started reflecting on his own behavior and how it affected others, he slowly began to realize that his social concerns—his ethics—must include all human beings with whom he came in contact.
      (3) Thus it can be said that a system of ethics evolved in order to ensure that man would be at peace with himself.
   c. (1) Vaccination for German measles has practically eradicated the incidence of birth defects and other complications resulting from that disease.
      (2) Smallpox vaccination has been so effective that the virus lingers only in special labs.
      (3) In the last thirty years, vaccines have all but wiped out polio in our country.
      (4) While a few people fear that some new and terrible disease will crop up for which no vaccine will be powerful enough, we can rejoice in the fact that at least the major child killers of the past have been vanquished.
2. Provide four sentences of supporting details for each of the following topic sentences. (Make sure that the details are on a more specific level than is the topic sentence.)
   a. Many people treat their pets with a lack of respect.
   b. Buying items "on sale" often means buying lower quality.
   c. Advertising in good periodicals is a workable, dignified way to attract a mate. Or advertising for a mate, even in good periodicals, is unsafe and degrading.
   d. A long commute to work can have some advantages.
   e. Today's newspaper cartoons get to the heart of social concerns.

172 CHAPTER 6 • Developing Paragraphs

3. Choose one of the following topics and write a paragraph about it based on a controlling idea rather than on a topic sentence:
    a. Summer camp for disabled children
    b. Typical class reunions
    c. Advantages of coming from a poor family or disadvantages of coming from an affluent family
    d. Stereotyping as revealed in movies
    e. Stopping pollution on an individual level

4. Select one sentence from the following pairs that more clearly consists of supporting details:
    a. (1) Much has been written about the afflictions of growing old.
       (2) The worst aspect of growing old is losing hearing and eyesight.
    b. (1) The average outfit for snow skiing costs $1,000.
       (2) Some popular sports are so expensive that few people can afford to compete in them.
    c. (1) In Little Red Riding Hood the wolf pounces on the innocent little girl, devouring her.
       (2) Children's fairy tales are filled with horrible violence.
    d. (1) Some women feel more comfortable being treated by a female rather than a male gynecologist.
       (2) For many women who are modest to begin with, to be checked for such problems as uterine or breast cancer is less traumatic when the physician is also female.
    e. (1) Too many cooks today have no idea how to prepare homemade corn bread, meat casseroles from scratch, or freshly cooked garden peas.
       (2) The market of "prepared" or "frozen" foods is replacing food that really tastes good with food that is barely appealing to the gourmet's taste buds.

5. In the following paragraphs, draw a line through any sentence that weakens paragraph unity.
    a. I agree with Thomas Jefferson that there is a natural aristocracy among human beings, based on virtue and talent. A natural aristocrat is a person who shows genuine concern for his fellow human beings and has the wisdom as well as ability to help them improve the quality of their lives. He is the kind of person to whom you would entrust your most important concerns because his decisions would be honest rather than self-serving. A natural aristocrat cannot be bought or manipulated. He will not promise what he cannot deliver. But when he makes a promise, he has virtue backed up by talent to fulfill it. Unfortunately, few political leaders today are natural aristocrats, because early in their ambitious careers they get beholden to those powers that helped them up the political ladder.
    b. In medieval society physical strength and animal cunning were the most admired characteristics of human beings, but since the invention of gunpowder, we have come to value other qualities more highly. Now that even a physically weak person can be made strong by carrying a gun, other

ingenuities have become the marks of heroic people. Of course, boxing requires physical strength and animal cunning; yet many people today admire good boxers. The qualities most admired today are intellectual acumen, leadership ability, artistic talent, and social adjustment. I find it distressing that we do not prize goodness as much as we should. After all, Lincoln's outstanding feature was goodness. If a person is not good, he is not admirable. The tournament and personal combat have been replaced by the university, the political arena, the stage, and the personality inventory as testing grounds for heroes.

6. Identify the most obvious means used to establish coherence in the following paragraphs:

   a. In general, relevancy is a facet of training rather than of education. What is taught at law school is the present law of the land, not the Napoleonic Code or even the archaic laws that have been scratched from the statute books. And at medical school, too, it is modern medical practice that is taught, that which is relevant to conditions today. And the plumber and the carpenter and the electrician and the mason learn only what is relevant to the practice of their respective trades in this day with the tools and materials that are presently available and that conform to the building code. —Harry Kemelman, *Common Sense in Education*

   b. The extent of personal privacy varies, but there are four degrees that can be identified. Sometimes the individual wants to be completely out of the sight and hearing of anyone else, in solitude; alone, he is in the most relaxed state of privacy. In a second situation the individual seeks the intimacy of his confidants—his family, friends, or trusted associates with whom he chooses to share his ideas and emotions. But there are still some things that he does not want to disclose, whether he is with intimates or in public. Either by personal explanation or by social convention, the individual may indicate that he does not wish certain aspects of himself discussed or noticed, at least at that particular moment. When his claim is respected by those around him, he achieves a third degree of privacy, the state of reserve. Finally, an individual sometimes goes out in public to seek privacy, for by joining groups of people who do not recognize him, he achieves anonymity, being seen but not known. Such relaxation on the street, in bars or movies or in the park constitutes still another dimension of the individual's quest for privacy. —Alan F. Westin, *Privacy*

   c. The motor car is, more than any other object, the expression of the nation's character and the nation's dream. In the free billowing fender, in the blinding chromium grills, in the fluid control, in the ever widening front seat, we see the flowering of the America that we know. It is of some interest to scholars and historians that the same autumn that saw the abandonment of the window crank and the adoption of the push button (removing the motorist's last necessity for physical exertion) saw also the registration of sixteen million young men of fighting age. It is of deep interest to me that in the same week Japan joined the Axis, De Soto moved its clutch pedal two inches to the left—and that the announcements caused equal flurries among the people. —E. B. White, *The Motor Car*

7. Write a provocative introductory paragraph for an essay on one of the following topics:
   a. Female soldiers fighting in combat
   b. Rationing water or gasoline
   c. Automatic capital punishment for terrorists who take hostages
   d. Purging our language of all words with a sexist bias ("he" as a general pronoun—chairman, congressman, businessman, insurance man)
   e. Job prospects for college seniors
   f. One of today's most serious urban problems

8. Write a brief paragraph that would function as a smooth transition from one to the other of the following pairs of paragraphs:
   a. (1) The first paragraph lists activities of a male executive that are the same as activities for which the homemaker is chided (long phone conversations, coffee klatches with colleagues, unnecessary fancy luncheons).
      (2) The second paragraph indicates the differences between the two sets of activities.
   b. (1) The first paragraph provides statistics to demonstrate that thousands of poor people in America live on pet food.
      (2) The second paragraph argues that we must do something in order to solve the problem of hunger and malnutrition in America.
   c. (1) The first paragraph makes the point that many foreign countries consider Americans wasteful, extravagant, and selfish in their insistence on driving big cars.
      (2) The second paragraph holds the automobile industry responsible for shaping America's taste in cars.

Stumped by trite expressions? Exit on page 691, at the **Editing Booth!**

ADVICE

Writing Successful Paragraphs

A. M. TIBBETTS AND CHARLENE TIBBETTS

Arnold M. Tibbetts (b. 1927) has taught English at the University of Iowa, Western Illinois University, Vanderbilt University, and the University of Illinois, Urbana. His wife, Charlene Tibbetts (b. 1921), has also taught part-time at the University of Illinois, Urbana. The Tibbettses are coauthors of *Strategies of Rhetoric* (1969), from which this excerpt was taken.

The proverbial warning "Don't promise more than you can deliver" applies to writing as well as to everyday life. The basis of a good paragraph, say the authors, is a promise that is made in the topic sentence and then carried out in the specific details. In this excerpt, the authors demonstrate with examples how to make and keep your "paragraph promises."

• • •

1   A paragraph is a collection of sentences that helps you fulfill your thesis (theme promise). Itself a small "theme," a paragraph should be clearly written and specific; and it should not wander or make irrelevant remarks. Each paragraph should be related in some way to the theme promise. Here are suggestions for writing successful paragraphs:

1. Get to the Point of Your Paragraph Quickly and Specifically

2   Don't waste time or words in stating your paragraph promise. Consider this good example of getting to the point—the writer is explaining the ancient Romans' technique for conquering their world:

> The technique of expansion was simple. Divide et impera [divide and conquer]: enter into solemn treaty with a neighbouring country, foment internal disorder, intervene in support of the weaker side on the pretense that Roman honour was involved, replace the legitimate ruler with a puppet, giving him the status of a subject ally; later, goad him into rebellion, seize and sack the country, burn down the temples, and carry off the captive gods to adorn a triumph. Conquered territories were placed under the control of a provincial governor-general, an ex-commander-in-chief who garrisoned it, levied taxes, set up courts of summary justice, and linked the new frontiers with the old by so called Roman roads—usually built by Greek engineers and native forced labour. Established social and religious practices were permitted so long as they did not threaten Roman administration or offend against the broad-minded Roman standards of good taste. The new province presently became a springboard for further aggression. —Robert Graves, *It Was a Stable World*

3   Graves makes his promise in the first nine words, in which he mentions the "simple" technique the Romans had for "dividing" and "conquering" in order to expand their empire. Suppose Graves had started his paragraph with these words:

> The technique of expansion was interesting. It was based upon a theory about human nature that the Romans practically invented. This theory had to do with how people reacted to certain political and military devices which . . .

4   Do you see what is wrong? Since the beginning sentences are so vague, the paragraph never gets going. The writer can't fulfill a promise because he hasn't made one. Another example of a poor paragraph beginning:

> The first step involves part of the golf club head. The club head has removable parts, some of which are metal. You must consider these parts when deciding how to repair the club.

5   Specify the beginning of this paragraph and get to the point quicker:

> Your first step in repairing the club head is to remove the metal plate held on by Phillips screws.

6   This solid, specific paragraph beginning gives your reader a clear promise which you can fulfill easily without wasting words. (Observe, by the way, that specifying a writer's stance—as we did in the last example—can help you write clearer paragraph beginnings.)

2. Fulfill Your Reader's Expectation Established by the Paragraph Promise

7   Do this with specific details and examples—explain as fully as you can. Example:

> The next thing is to devise a form for your essay. This, which ought to be obvious, is not. I learned it for the first time from an experienced newspaperman. When I was at college I earned extra pocket- and book-money by writing several weekly columns for a newspaper. They were usually topical, they were always carefully varied, they tried hard to be witty, and (an essential) they never missed a deadline. But once, when I brought in the product, a copy editor stopped me. He said, "Our readers seem to like your stuff all right; but we think it's a bit amateurish." With due humility I replied, "Well I am an amateur. What should I do with it?" He said, "Your pieces are not coherent; they are only sentences and epigrams strung together; they look like a heap of clothespins in a basket. Every article ought to have a shape. Like this" (and he drew a big letter S on his page) "or this" (he drew a descending line which turned abruptly upward again) "or this" (and he sketched a solid central core with five or six lines pushing outward from it) "or even this" (and he outlined two big arrows coming into collision). I never saw the man again, but I have never ceased to be grateful to him for his wisdom and for his kindness. Every essay must have a shape. You can ask a question in the first paragraph, discussing several different answers to it till you reach one you think is convincing. You can give a curious fact and offer an explanation of it: a man's character (as Hazlitt did with his fives champion), a building, a book, a striking adventure, a peculiar custom. There are many other shapes which essays can take; but the principle laid down by the copy editor was right. Before you start you must have a form in your mind; and it ought to be a form felt in paragraphs or sections, not in

words or sentences—so that, if necessary, you could summarize each paragraph in a single line and put the entire essay on a postcard. —Gilbert Highet, *How to Write an Essay*

8   Highet makes a promise in the first three sentences, and in the remaining sentences he specifically fulfills it.

3. Avoid Fragmentary Paragraphs

9   A fragmentary paragraph does not develop its topic or fulfill its promise. A series of fragmentary paragraphs jumps from idea to idea in a jerky and unconvincing fashion:

> My freshman rhetoric class is similar in some ways to my senior English class in high school, but it is also very different.
>
> In my English class we usually had daily homework assignments that were discussed during the class period. If we were studying grammar, the assignments were to correct grammatical errors in the text. If we were studying literature, we were supposed to read the material and understand its ideas.
>
> In rhetoric class, we do basically the same things, except that in the readings we are assigned, we look much deeper into the purpose of the author.
>
> In my English class . . .

10   Fragmentary paragraphs are often the result of a weak writer's stance.

4. Avoid Irrelevancies in Your Paragraphs

11   The italicized sentence does not fit the development of this paragraph:

> We need a better working atmosphere at Restik Tool Company. The workers must feel that they are a working team instead of just individuals. If the men felt they were part of a team, they would not misuse the special machine tools, which now need to be resharpened twice as often as they used to be. *Management's attitude toward the union could be improved too.* The team effort is also being damaged by introduction of new products before their bugs have been worked out. Just when the men are getting used to one routine, a new one is installed, and their carefully created team effort is seriously damaged.
>
> As with the fragmentary paragraph, the problem of irrelevancies in a paragraph is often the result of a vague writer's stance. The paragraph above does not seem to be written for any particular reader.

● **Vocabulary**

foment (2)   topical (7)

EXAMPLES

Paragraphs with the Topic Sentence at the Beginning

From the Lessons of the Past
EDITH HAMILTON

Edith Hamilton (1867–1963) was an American classicist, educator, and writer. Her writing career began after retirement, and at the age of eighty, she started giving public addresses and lectures. When she was ninety, she was made an honorary citizen of Greece. Among her books are *The Greek Way* (1942), *The Roman Way* (1932), and *Witness to the Truth: Christ and His Interpreters* (1948).

Basic to all the Greek achievement was freedom. The Athenians were the only free people in the world. In the great empires of antiquity—Egypt, Babylon, Assyria, Persia—splendid though they were, with riches beyond reckoning and immense power, freedom was unknown. The idea of it never dawned in any of them. It was born in Greece, a poor little country, but with it able to remain unconquered no matter what manpower and what wealth were arrayed against her. At Marathon and at Salamis overwhelming numbers of Persians had been defeated by small Greek forces. It had been proved that one free man was superior to many submissively obedient subjects of a tyrant. Athens was the leader in that amazing victory, and to the Athenians freedom was their dearest possession. Demosthenes said that they would not think it worth their while to live if they could not do so as free men, and years later a great teacher said, "Athenians, if you deprive them of their liberty, will die."

- **Vocabulary**

reckoning	arrayed	Marathon
Salamis	submissively	tyrant
Demosthenes		

- **The Facts**

  1. Were you convinced of the truth of the topic sentence after reading the paragraph? If so, what convinced you?
  2. In what way are free men superior to those who are submissively obedient to a tyrant?

- **The Strategies**

  1. What is the topic sentence of the paragraph?
  2. Who is the "great teacher" alluded to?

- The Issues
1. Hamilton writes that freedom was basic to the Greek achievement. What does freedom mean to you in a political context?
2. According to Hamilton, it has "been proved that one free man [is] superior to many submissively obedient subjects." Why do you think this is so?

Pain
William Somerset Maugham

English author William Somerset Maugham (1874–1965) wrote short stories, novels, plays, and books of criticism. His most popular plays include *The Circle* (1921), *Our Betters* (1923), and *The Constant Wife* (1927). His best-known novel is his semiautobiographical account of a young physician with a clubfoot, *Of Human Bondage* (1919).

No more stupid apology for pain has ever been devised than that it elevates. It is an explanation due to the necessity of justifying pain from the Christian point of view. Pain is nothing more than the signal given by the nerves that the organism is in circumstances hurtful to it; it would be as reasonable to assert that a danger signal elevates a train. But one would have thought that the ordinary observation of life was enough to show that in the great majority of cases, pain, far from refining, has an effect which is merely brutalising. An example in point is the case of hospital in-patients: physical pain makes them self-absorbed, selfish, querulous, impatient, unjust and greedy; I could name a score of petty vices that it generates, but not one virtue. Poverty also is pain. I have known well men who suffered from that grinding agony of poverty which befalls persons who have to live among those richer than themselves; it makes them grasping and mean, dishonest and untruthful. It teaches them all sorts of detestable tricks. With moderate means they would have been honourable men, but ground down by poverty they have lost all sense of decency.

- Vocabulary

    querulous

- The Facts
1. According to Maugham, why do some people think it necessary to justify pain?
2. What is Maugham's view of pain?
3. Aside from the pain of physical illness, what is another cause of pain?

- The Strategies
1. What analogy does Maugham use in refuting the view that pain elevates?
2. What example does Maugham give to support his view of pain?

3. The paragraph discusses two causes of pain. What transitional word does Maugham use to move the discussion from the one cause to the other?

● **The Issues**

1. Maugham says that he cannot name a single virtue that pain produces. What virtue is pain generally thought to produce?
2. What is the distinction between pain and suffering?
3. Maugham writes that to say pain elevates is as reasonable as asserting that "a danger signal elevates a train." What is fundamentally false about this analogy?

I Am Tired of Fighting (Surrender Speech)
Chief Joseph of the Nez Percé

Chief Joseph (1840?–1904) was the leader of the Nez Percé tribe of the Sahaptin Indians, who lived along the Snake River in Idaho and Oregon. In 1877, under Chief Joseph, the tribe fought the United States government in a desperate attempt to preserve its land. Eventually, the Indians lost their struggle and were forced to retreat to the border of Canada.

I am tired of fighting. Our chiefs are killed. Looking Glass is dead. Toohulsote is dead. The old men are all dead. It is the young men who say no and yes. He who led the young men is dead. It is cold and we have no blankets. The little children are freezing to death. My people, some of them, have run away to the hills and have no blankets, no food. No one knows where they are—perhaps they are freezing to death. I want to have time to look for my children and see how many of them I can find. Maybe I shall find them among the dead. Hear me, my chiefs, I am tired. My heart is sad and sick. From where the sun stands I will fight no more forever.

● **The Facts**

1. According to this speech, what nonmilitary factor contributed most to Chief Joseph's decision to surrender?
2. Who was left among the Nez Percé to say no and yes?

● **The Strategies**

1. On what word do most of the sentences of this paragraph end? What is the effect of this repeated ending?
2. How would you characterize the language used in this speech? Formal? Informal? Colloquial? What effect do you think the speaker achieves in his diction?

3. What are some examples of poetic constructions that add to the stateliness and dignity of this speech? Translate them literally and say what is lost in the translation.

- **The Issues**

1. How are American Indians portrayed in popular literature and films? How has this portrayal affected your impression of them?
2. Historians agree that the Indians got short shrift at the hands of the encroaching white settlers. What responsibility, if any, do the descendants of the victors have to the descendants of the vanquished Indians?

Paragraphs with the Topic Sentence at the End

Man against Darkness
W. T. STACE

Walter Terrence Stace (1886–1967) was an English naturalist and philosopher known for his ability to translate complex theories into terms that appealed to a general reader. An authority on Hegel, Stace was the author of numerous books, among them *A Critical History of Greek Philosophy* (1920) and *The Philosophy of Hegel* (1924).

The picture of a meaningless world, and a meaningless human life, is, I think, the basic theme of much modern art and literature. Certainly it is the basic theme of modern philosophy. According to the most characteristic philosophies of the modern period from Hume in the eighteenth century to the so-called positivists of today, the world is just what it is, and that is the end of all inquiry. There is no reason for its being what it is. Everything might just as well have been quite different, and there would have been no reason for that either. When you have stated what things are, what things the world contains, there is nothing more which could be said, even by an omniscient being. To ask any question about why things are thus, or what purpose their being so serves, is to ask a senseless question, because they serve no purpose at all. For instance, there is for modern philosophy no such thing as the ancient problem of evil. For this once famous question pre-supposes that pain and misery, though they seem so inexplicable and irrational to us, must ultimately subserve some rational purpose, must have their places in the cosmic plan. But this is nonsense. There is no such overruling rationality in the universe. Belief in the ultimate irrationality of everything is the quintessence of what is called the modern mind.

- **Vocabulary**

positivists　　　　　　omniscient　　　　　　subserve
quintessence

182 CHAPTER 6 • Developing Paragraphs

● The Facts

1. What is the basic theme of much modern art and literature?
2. How do the most characteristic philosophies of the modern era view the world?
3. Why is there no such thing in modern philosophy as the ancient problem of evil?

● The Strategies

1. Stace is known for expressing complex ideas with clarity. In this example, how does he make clear the complex views of modern philosophy?
2. From which point of view is this paragraph mainly written? How can you tell?
3. "Begging the question" is the logical name given to an argument that assumes as proven the very thing that is in dispute. Is the attitude of modern philosophy toward evil an example of begging the question? Why or why not?

● The Issues

1. What is your opinion of modern philosophy, as Stace summarizes it, that ascribes everything to irrationality? How does this philosophy square with your own beliefs?
2. What is the ancient problem of evil?
3. What imaginable purpose can evil possibly serve? If evil did not exist, would it have to be invented?

What Is a Poet?

Mark Van Doren

Mark Van Doren (1894–1973), American poet and critic, was born in Illinois and educated at Columbia University, where he later won renown as a dedicated teacher. He was the author of many books, among them *American and British Literature Since 1890* (1939, written with his brother Carl), *Collected Poems, 1922–1938* (1939, Pulitzer Prize), and *The Last Days of Lincoln* (1959).

Here is the figure we have set up. A pale, lost man with long, soft hair. Tapering fingers at the ends of furtively fluttering arms. An air of abstraction in the delicate face, but more often a look of shy pain as some aspect of reality—a real man or woman, a grocer's bill, a train, a load of bricks, a newspaper, a noise from the street—makes itself manifest. He is generally incompetent. He cannot find his way in a city, he forgets where he is going, he has no aptitude for business, he is childishly gullible and so the prey of human sharks, he cares nothing for money, he is probably poor, he will sacrifice his welfare for a whim, he stops to pet homeless cats, he is especially knowing where children are concerned (being a child himself), he sighs, he sleeps, he wakes to sigh again. The one great assumption from which the foregoing portrait is drawn is an assumption which thousands of otherwise intelligent citizens go on. It is the assumption that the poet is more sensitive than any other kind of man, that he feels more than the rest of us and is more definitely the victim of his feeling.

Vocabulary
gullible

The Facts
1. What do we expect a poet to look like?
2. What kind of personality do we expect a poet to have?
3. What one great assumption do we make about poets?

The Strategies
1. What is Van Doren attempting to do in this paragraph? What single word could you use to describe the type of portrait he is sketching?
2. Van Doren writes: "A pale, lost man with long, soft hair. Tapering fingers at the ends of furtively fluttering arms." Grammatically, what do these two assertions have in common? What effect do they contribute to the description?
3. A catalogue is a list of things or attributes. Where in this paragraph does the author obviously use a catalogue?

The Issues
1. Given the characteristics traditionally identified as masculine and feminine, which would you expect a poet to be—more masculine than feminine or vice versa? Why?
2. What, in your mind, is a poet? Does your definition of a poet differ substantially from Van Doren's description? In what way?
3. Of what use is poetry in the modern world?

On Disease
Lewis Thomas, M.D.

Lewis Thomas (b. 1913–1993) was born in New York and educated at Princeton and Harvard. Dr. Thomas was a medical administrator of the Memorial Sloan-Kettering Cancer Center in New York and an essayist who has been praised for his lucid style. His essays have been published in collections such as *The Lives of a Cell* (1974, National Book Award), *The Medusa and the Snail* (1979), *Late Night Thoughts on Listening to Mahler's Ninth Symphony* (1983), and *Etcetera Etcetera* (1990).

We were all reassured, when the first moon landing was ready to be made, that the greatest precautions would be taken to protect the life of the earth, especially human life, against infection by whatever there might be alive on the moon. And, in fact, the elaborate ceremony of lunar asepsis was performed after each of the early landings; the voyagers were masked and kept behind plate glass, quarantined away from contact with the earth until it was a certainty that we wouldn't catch something from them. The idea that germs are all around us, trying to get at us, to devour and destroy us, is so firmly rooted in modern consciousness that it made sense to think that strange germs, from the moon, would be even scarier and harder to handle.

● Vocabulary

asepsis   quarantined

● The Facts

1. What were we all reassured about before the first moon landing was made?
2. What idea about germs is firmly rooted in our consciousness?

● The Strategies

1. What specific detail does the author use to support his assertion that an elaborate ceremony of asepsis was performed after each of the lunar landings?
2. Assuming that the paragraph is representative of the style of the whole essay, for what kind of audience do you think the essay was written?

● The Issues

1. Do you trust medical doctors to the extent that you implicitly follow their advice? Why or why not?
2. Which disease do you fear the most? Why?

The Flood

Robert Frost

Robert Frost (1874–1963) was a lecturer, poet, and teacher. When he was nineteen and working in a mill in Lawrence, Massachusetts, the

Independent accepted and published *My Butterfly, An Elegy*—the poem that began Frost's career as one of America's great poets. Rugged New England farm life was the inspiration for many of his poems.

> Blood has been harder to dam back than water.
> Just when we think we have it impounded safe
> Behind new barrier walls (and let it chafe!),
> 5   It breaks away in some new kind of slaughter.
> We choose to say it is let loose by the devil;
> But power of blood itself releases blood.
> It goes by might of being such a flood
> Held high at so unnatural a level.
> 10 It will have outlet, brave and not so brave.
> Weapons of war and implements of peace
> Are but the points at which it finds release.
> And now it is once more the tidal wave
> That when it has swept by leaves summits stained.
> Oh, blood will out. It cannot be contained.

● Vocabulary

impounded   chafe

● The Facts

1. What interpretation can be given to Frost's mention of a flood of blood?
2. What is meant by the statement "power of blood itself releases blood"?
3. What is the "tidal wave" Frost refers to? Why does it leave summits stained?

● The Strategies

1. In poetry, the stanza serves a purpose similar to that of the paragraph. That being the case, what do you consider the topic sentence of this poem? Is it stated more than once?
2. Both water and blood are mentioned in this poem. Which of these words is used literally and which symbolically?

● The Issues

1. What is the theme of this poem?
2. In writing about blood, Frost says: ". . . Implements of peace/Are but the points at which it finds release." What can this line possibly mean?

CHAPTER WRITING ASSIGNMENTS

1. Select one of the following topics and develop it into a unified, coherent, and complete paragraph:
   a. Carelessness can do more harm than lack of knowledge.
   b. Today the prevailing mood on the campus is one of . . . (fill in the words you think apply).
   c. Many cars are still not designed for safety.
   d. Kissing is an odd, overromanticized act.
   e. A plagiarized paper has several bad effects.
   f. Buying term papers from a commercial source is unethical.

2. List the particular details that you would use to write a convincing paragraph on the following topic sentences:
   a. Sarcastic people are unpleasant to be around.
   b. I like the security of dating the same person (or, I like the freedom of dating different people).
   c. Many rap singers have gotten bad press and a bad name.
   d. Children and fools speak the truth.
   e. Common sense is _____ (define it).

WRITING ASSIGNMENTS FOR A SPECIFIC AUDIENCE

1. Write an essay aimed at an audience of unemployed loggers, arguing the importance of preserving the habitat of the spotted owl even at the cost of logging jobs.

   or

2. Write an essay aimed at an audience of environmentalists, arguing the importance of preserving jobs even at the cost of the spotted owls' habitat.

COLLABORATIVE WRITING PROJECT

Divide your group into four teams. Assign each team to investigate and report on the paragraph-writing techniques practiced by such publications as *Reader's Digest, Atlantic, Consumer Reports,* and the editorial page of your local newspaper. Consider the relationship between the audience of the publication and the kinds of paragraphs it uses. Meet to discuss your findings and then team-write an essay outlining what you have learned.

The Facts

1. Which class of Burmese did Orwell despise most of all?
2. What would likely happen to a white woman who went through the bazaars alone?
3. What is Orwell's opinion of the younger empires that were going to supplant the British Empire?
4. What is invariably the case with stories set in the East?
5. According to Orwell, what is a condition of white rule over the empire?

The Strategies

1. Orwell writes: "They had not shown much interest in the elephant when he was merely ravaging their homes, but it was different now that he was going to be shot." What tone is he using here?
2. Why does Orwell use Latin phrases? What purpose do they have in the story?
3. The story is told in two tenses: the past and the present. What effect does this have on its telling?
4. Orwell encloses some remarks in parentheses in paragraphs 4 and 8. Why are these remarks set off in this way?
5. What analogy does Orwell use in paragraph 10 to describe his feelings about the crowd gathered to see him kill the elephant? Is this an appropriate analogy? Explain.

The Issues

1. What is the value of a role and of role-playing in the relationships of everyday life?
2. What are the obvious disadvantages of role-playing?
3. How would you characterize Orwell's attitude toward the empire he serves?
4. How do you think the author might have behaved, and what do you think he might have done, if other Europeans had been with him when he met the elephant?
5. What circumstances of today's life might similarly make someone, say a student, feel impelled to behave in a way contrary to his or her better judgment?

Suggestions for Writing

1. Analyze and discuss *Shooting an Elephant* as a story about the abstract versus the concrete, the general versus the particular.
2. Write an essay entitled "I Wore a Mask, and My Face Grew to Fit It." Tell how circumstances forced you into playing a part you secretly hated.

My Name Is Margaret

Maya Angelou

Maya Angelou (b. 1928) is novelist, poet, playwright, actress, composer, and singer. Her varied accomplishments have thrown her into the public limelight, where she is greatly admired as a speaker and reader of her own works. She is best known for her single-minded devotion to the cause of tolerance. Many of her novels recount incidents in which her characters must fight ardently to maintain their identity in a world of prejudice. Among her best-known works are *I Know Why the Caged Bird Sings* (1970), from which the selection that follows is taken, *Gather Together in My Name* (1974), *Singin' and Swingin' and Gettin' Merry Like Christmas* (1976), *Heart of a Woman* (1981), and *All God's Children Need Traveling Shoes* (1986). Angelou has also written volumes of poetry, including *Oh Pray My Wings Are Gonna Fit Me Well* (1975) and *I Shall Not Be Moved* (1990). She has become a role model for aspiring female writers of various minority backgrounds.

A black author, admired for her stories dealing with affronts to a black person's pride and sense of dignity, tells of an incident in which a white woman attempts to change the name of the author, who was then working for her.

• • •

1   Recently a white woman from Texas, who would quickly describe herself as a liberal, asked me about my hometown. When I told her that in Stamps my grandmother had owned the only Negro general merchandise store since the turn of the century, she exclaimed, "Why, you were a debutante." Ridiculous and even ludicrous. But Negro girls in small Southern towns, whether poverty-stricken or just munching along on a few of life's necessities, were given as extensive and irrelevant preparations for adulthood as rich white girls shown in magazines. Admittedly the training was not the same. While white girls learned to waltz and sit gracefully with a tea cup balanced on their knees, we were lagging behind, learning the mid-Victorian values with very little money to indulge them. (Come and see Edna Lomax spending the money she made picking cotton on five balls of ecru tatting thread. Her fingers are bound to snag the work and she'll have to repeat the stitches time and time again. But she knows that when she buys the thread.)

2   We were required to embroider and I had trunkfuls of colorful dishtowels, pillowcases, runners and handkerchiefs to my credit. I mastered the art of crocheting and tatting, and there was a lifetime's supply of dainty doilies that would never be used in sacheted dresser drawers. It went without saying that all girls could iron and wash, but the finer touches around the home, like setting a table with real silver, baking roasts and cooking vegetables without meat, had to be learned elsewhere. Usually at the source of those habits. During my tenth year, a white woman's kitchen became my finishing school.

3   Mrs. Viola Cullinan was a plump woman who lived in a three-bedroom house somewhere behind the post office. She was singularly unattractive until

she smiled, and then the lines around her eyes and mouth which made her look perpetually dirty disappeared, and her face looked like the mask of an impish elf. She usually rested her smile until late afternoon when her women friends dropped in and Miss Glory, the cook, served them cold drinks on the closed-in porch.

4   The exactness of her house was inhuman. This glass went here and only here. That cup had its place and it was an act of impudent rebellion to place it anywhere else. At twelve o'clock the table was set. At 12:15 Mrs. Cullinan sat down to dinner (whether her husband had arrived or not). At 12:16 Miss Glory brought out the food.

5   It took me a week to learn the difference between a salad plate, a bread plate and a dessert plate.

6   Mrs. Cullinan kept up the tradition of her wealthy parents. She was from Virginia. Miss Glory, who was a descendant of slaves that had worked for the Cullinans, told me her history. She had married beneath her (according to Miss Glory). Her husband's family hadn't had their money very long and what they had "didn't 'mount to much."

7   As ugly as she was, I thought privately, she was lucky to get a husband above or beneath her station. But Miss Glory wouldn't let me say a thing against her mistress. She was very patient with me, however, over the housework. She explained the dishware, silverware and servants' bells. The large round bowl in which soup was served wasn't a soup bowl, it was a tureen. There were goblets, sherbet glasses, ice-cream glasses, wine glasses, green glass coffee cups with matching saucers, and water glasses. I had a glass to drink from, and it sat with Miss Glory's on a separate shelf from the others. Soup spoons, gravy boat, butter knives, salad forks and carving platter were additions to my vocabulary and in fact almost represented a new language. I was fascinated with the novelty, with the fluttering Mrs. Cullinan and her Alice-in-Wonderland house.

8   Her husband remains, in my memory, undefined. I lumped him with all the other white men that I had ever seen and tried not to see.

9   On our way home one evening, Miss Glory told me that Mrs. Cullinan couldn't have children. She said that she was too delicate-boned. It was hard to imagine bones at all under those layers of fat. Miss Glory went on to say that the doctor had taken out all her lady organs. I reasoned that a pig's organs included the lungs, heart and liver, so if Mrs. Cullinan was walking around without those essentials, it explained why she drank alcohol out of unmarked bottles. She was keeping herself embalmed.

10 When I spoke to Bailey about it, he agreed that I was right, but he also informed me that Mr. Cullinan had two daughters by a colored lady and that I knew them very well. He added that the girls were the spitting image of their father. I was unable to remember what he looked like, although I had just left him a few hours before, but I thought of the Coleman girls. They were very light-skinned and certainly didn't look very much like their mother (no one ever mentioned Mr. Coleman).

11 My pity for Mrs. Cullinan preceded me the next morning like the Cheshire cat's smile. Those girls, who could have been her daughters, were

beautiful. They didn't have to straighten their hair. Even when they were caught in the rain, their braids still hung down straight like tamed snakes. Their mouths were pouty little cupid's bows. Mrs. Cullinan didn't know what she missed. Or maybe she did. Poor Mrs. Cullinan.

12   For weeks after, I arrived early, left late and tried very hard to make up for her barrenness. If she had had her own children, she wouldn't have had to ask me to run a thousand errands from her back door to the back door of her friends. Poor old Mrs. Cullinan.

13   Then one evening Miss Glory told me to serve the ladies on the porch. After I set the tray down and turned toward the kitchen, one of the women asked, "What's your name, girl?" It was the speckled-faced one. Mrs. Cullinan said, "She doesn't talk much. Her name's Margaret."

14   "Is she dumb?"

15   "No. As I understand it, she can talk when she wants to but she's usually quiet as a little mouse. Aren't you, Margaret?"

16   I smiled at her. Poor thing. No organs and couldn't even pronounce my name correctly.

17   "She's a sweet little thing, though."

18   "Well, that may be, but the name's too long. I'd never bother myself. I'd call her Mary if I was you."

19   I fumed into the kitchen. That horrible woman would never have the chance to call me Mary because if I was starving I'd never work for her. I decided I wouldn't pee on her if her heart was on fire. Giggles drifted in off the porch and into Miss Glory's pots. I wondered what they could be laughing about.

20   White folks were so strange. Could they be talking about me? Everybody knew that they stuck together better than the Negroes did. It was possible that Mrs. Cullinan had friends in St. Louis who heard about a girl from Stamps being in court and wrote to tell her. Maybe she knew about Mr. Freeman.

21   My lunch was in my mouth a second time and I went outside and relieved myself on the bed of four-o'clocks. Miss Glory thought I might be coming down with something and told me to go on home, that Momma would give me some herb tea, and she'd explain to her mistress.

22   I realized how foolish I was being before I reached the pond. Of course Mrs. Cullinan didn't know. Otherwise she wouldn't have given me two nice dresses that Momma cut down, and she certainly wouldn't have called me a "sweet little thing." My stomach felt fine, and I didn't mention anything to Momma.

23   That evening I decided to write a poem on being white, fat, old and without children. It was going to be a tragic ballad. I would have to watch her carefully to capture the essence of her loneliness and pain.

24   The very next day, she called me by the wrong name. Miss Glory and I were washing up the lunch dishes when Mrs. Cullinan came to the doorway. "Mary?"

25   Miss Glory asked, "Who?"

26   Mrs. Cullinan, sagging a little, knew and I knew. "I want Mary to go down to Mrs. Randall's and take her some soup. She's not been feeling well for a few days."

27   Miss Glory's face was a wonder to see. "You mean Margaret, ma'am. Her name's Margaret."

28   "That's too long. She's Mary from now on. Heat that soup from last night and put it in the china tureen and, Mary, I want you to carry it carefully."

29   Every person I knew had a hellish horror of being "called out of his name." It was a dangerous practice to call a Negro anything that could be loosely construed as insulting because of the centuries of their having been called niggers, jigs, dinges, blackbirds, crows, boots and spooks.

30   Miss Glory had a fleeting second of feeling sorry for me. Then as she handed me the hot tureen she said, "Don't mind, don't pay that no mind. Sticks and stones may break your bones, but words . . . You know, I been working for her for twenty years."

31   She held the back door open for me. "Twenty years. I wasn't much older than you. My name used to be Hallelujah. That's what Ma named me, but my mistress give me 'Glory,' and it stuck. I likes it better too."

32   I was in the little path that ran behind the houses when Miss Glory shouted, "It's shorter too."

33   For a few seconds it was a tossup over whether I would laugh (imagine being named Hallelujah) or cry (imagine letting some white woman rename you for her convenience). My anger saved me from either outburst. I had to quit the job, but the problem was going to be how to do it. Momma wouldn't allow me to quit for just any reason.

34   "She's a peach. That woman is a real peach." Mrs. Randall's maid was talking as she took the soup from me, and I wondered what her name used to be and what she answered to now.

35   For a week I looked into Mrs. Cullinan's face as she called me Mary. She ignored my coming late and leaving early. Miss Glory was a little annoyed because I had begun to leave egg yolk on the dishes and wasn't putting much heart in polishing the silver. I hoped that she would complain to our boss, but she didn't.

36   Then Bailey solved my dilemma. He had me describe the contents of the cupboard and the particular plates she liked best. Her favorite piece was a casserole shaped like a fish and the green glass coffee cups. I kept his instructions in mind, so on the next day when Miss Glory was hanging out clothes and I had again been told to serve the old biddies on the porch, I dropped the empty serving tray. When I heard Mrs. Cullinan scream, "Mary!" I picked up the casserole and two of the green glass cups in readiness. As she rounded the kitchen door I let them fall on the tiled floor.

37   I could never absolutely describe to Bailey what happened next, because each time I got to the part where she fell on the floor and screwed up her ugly face to cry, we burst out laughing. She actually wobbled around on the floor and picked up shards of the cups and cried, "Oh, Momma. Oh, dear Gawd. It's Momma's china from Virginia. Oh, Momma, I sorry."

38   Miss Glory came running in from the yard and the women from the porch crowded around. Miss Glory was almost as broken up as her mistress. "You mean to say she broke our Virginia dishes? What we gone do?"

39   Miss Cullinan cried louder, "That clumsy nigger. Clumsy little black nigger."

40   Old speckled-face leaned down and asked, "Who did it, Viola? Was it Mary? Who did it?"

41   Everything was happening so fast I can't remember whether her action preceded her words, but I know that Mrs. Cullinan said, "Her name's Margaret, goddamn it, her name's Margaret." And she threw a wedge of the broken plate at me. It could have been the hysteria which put her aim off, but the flying crockery caught Miss Glory right over the ear and she started screaming.

42   I left the front door wide open so all the neighbors could hear.

43   Mrs. Cullinan was right about one thing. My name wasn't Mary.

● Vocabulary

debutante (1)	ludicrous (1)	tatting (2)
sacheted (2)	impudent (4)	barrenness (12)
ballad (23)	shards (37)	crockery (41)

● The Facts

1. In their preparations for adulthood, what did both white girls and black girls have in common?
2. Where did black girls learn to set the table and cook?
3. What kind of housekeeper was Mrs. Viola Cullinan? How does the narrator view her habits?
4. Why does the narrator feel pity for Mrs. Cullinan?
5. Why did the narrator get furious at Mrs. Cullinan? What did the narrator do to vent her anger?

● The Strategies

1. From whose point of view is this story told? How does the point of view affect the narration? How is the narration paced?
2. The narrator calls Mrs. Cullinan's house an "Alice-in-Wonderland house." What kind of image does this label conjure up? Where else in the story does the narrator use an image from Lewis Carroll's *Adventures of Alice in Wonderland*? To what purpose?
3. Although the tale about Margaret's name is essentially a serious matter, there are nevertheless some humorous elements in the narrative. What humorous incidents can you point out? Refer to specific passages.
4. What examples of figurative language does the narrator use in paragraph 11? How effective are they?
5. Why does the narrator never explain who Bailey and Mr. Freeman are? From the context of the story, who do you think they are?

● The Issues

1. The narrator is extremely sensitive about her name. Why is this so? How do you feel about your own name? Does it bother you when someone mispronounces or misspells it?
2. The narrator leaves the ending wide open. What do you think will happen to Margaret following this incident?
3. What does Margaret's decision to write a poem about Mrs. Cullinan indicate?
4. What is the relationship between Miss Glory and Mrs. Cullinan?
5. Describe Miss Glory. Do you think Margaret will ever be like her?
6. What do you think of Miss Glory's attempt to calm down Margaret after Mrs. Cullinan called her "Mary" from the doorway? (See paragraphs 30–32.) How does her reaction differ from Bailey's? Which reaction seems more appropriate to you?

● Suggestions for Writing

1. Narrate an incident in which you reacted to someone who treated you with arrogance or meanness. Make your narrative come to life by using dialogue and vivid details.
2. Narrate an incident from your youth that taught you a lesson in tolerance concerning race, religion, sex, social status, or some other aspect of society. Pace the narration properly and use vivid details.

Shame

DICK GREGORY

Dick Gregory (b. 1932) is a political activist, comedian, and writer. He attended Southern Illinois University, where he was named Outstanding Athlete in 1953. Gregory has been much admired for his interest in social issues such as world famine and for his outstanding ability as a standup comedian. In 1966, he ran for Mayor of Chicago, and in 1968, he was the presidential candidate of the Freedom and Peace Party. Gregory has written several books, including *From the Back of the Bus* (1962), *What's Happening?* (1965), *The Shadow That Scares Me* (1968), *Dick Gregory's Bible Tales* (1974), and his autobiography, *Up from Nigger* (1976). Gregory was one of the first black comedians to break the "color barrier" and perform for white audiences. His popularity is based on his ability to satirize race relations without being derogatory.

Even if you have never felt the poverty described by the narrator in the story that follows, you can probably remember someone from your childhood or adolescence who somehow represented all the romance and beauty you longed for. Ponder the details that make the narrator's experience so heartbreaking.

• • •

1. I never learned hate at home, or shame. I had to go to school for that. I was about seven years old when I got my first big lesson. I was in love with a little girl named Helene Tucker, a light-complected little girl with pigtails and nice manners. She was always clean and she was smart in school. I think I went to school mostly to look at her. I brushed my hair and even got me a little old handkerchief. It was a lady's handkerchief, but I didn't want Helene to see me wipe my nose on my hand. The pipes were frozen again, there was no water in the house, but I washed my socks and shirt every night. I'd get a pot, and go over to Mr. Ben's grocery store, and stick my pot down into his soda machine. Scoop out some chopped ice. By evening the ice melted to water for washing. I got sick a lot that winter because the fire would go out at night before the clothes were dry. In the morning I'd put them on, wet or dry, because they were the only clothes I had.

2. Everybody's got a Helene Tucker, a symbol of everything you want. I loved her for her goodness, her cleanliness, her popularity. She'd walk down my street and my brothers and sisters would yell, "Here comes Helene," and I'd rub my tennis sneakers on the back of my pants and wish my hair wasn't so nappy and the white folks' shirt fit me better. I'd run out on the street. If I knew my place and didn't come too close, she'd wink at me and say hello. That was a good feeling. Sometimes I'd follow her all the way home, and shovel the snow off her walk and try to make friends with her Momma and her aunts. I'd drop money on her stoop late at night on my way back from shining shoes in the taverns. And she had a Daddy, and he had a good job. He was a paper hanger.

3. I guess I would have gotten over Helene by summertime, but something happened in that classroom that made her face hang in front of me for the next twenty-two years. When I played the drums in high school it was for Helene and when I broke track records in college it was for Helene and when I started standing behind microphones and heard applause I wished Helene could hear it, too. It wasn't until I was twenty-nine years old and married and making money that I really got her out of my system. Helene was sitting in that classroom when I learned to be ashamed of myself.

4. It was on a Thursday. I was sitting in the back of the room, in a seat with a chalk circle drawn around it. The idiot's seat, the troublemaker's seat.

5. The teacher thought I was stupid. Couldn't spell, couldn't read, couldn't do arithmetic. Just stupid. Teachers were never interested in finding out that you couldn't concentrate because you were so hungry, because you hadn't had any breakfast. All you could think about was noontime, would it ever come? Maybe you could sneak into the cloakroom and steal a bit of some kid's lunch out of a coat pocket. A bit of something. Paste. You can't really make a meal out of paste, or put it on bread for a sandwich, but sometimes I'd scoop a few spoonfuls out of the paste jar in the back of the room. Pregnant people get strange tastes. I was pregnant with poverty. Pregnant with dirt and pregnant with smells that made people turn away, pregnant with cold and pregnant with shoes that were never bought for me, pregnant with five other people in my bed and no Daddy in the next room, and pregnant with hunger. Paste doesn't taste too bad when you're hungry.

6   The teacher thought I was a troublemaker. All she saw from the front of the room was a little black boy who squirmed in his idiot's seat and made noises and poked the kids around him. I guess she couldn't see a kid who made noises because he wanted someone to know he was there.

7   It was on a Thursday, the day before the Negro payday. The eagle always flew on Friday. The teacher was asking each student how much his father would give to the Community Chest. On Friday night, each kid would get the money from his father, and on Monday he would bring it to the school. I decided I was going to buy me a Daddy right then. I had money in my pocket from shining shoes and selling papers and whatever Helene Tucker pledged for her Daddy I was going to top it. And I'd hand the money right in. I wasn't going to wait until Monday to buy me a Daddy.

8   I was shaking, scared to death. The teacher opened her book and started calling our names alphabetically.

9   "Helene Tucker?"

10 "My Daddy said he'd give two dollars and fifty cents."

11 "That's very nice, Helene. Very, very nice indeed."

12 That made me feel pretty good. It wouldn't take too much to top that. I had almost three dollars in dimes and quarters in my pocket. I stuck my hand in my pocket and held onto the money, waiting for her to call my name. But the teacher closed her book after she called everybody else in the class.

13 I stood up and raised my hand.

14 "What is it now?"

15 "You forgot me."

16 She turned toward the blackboard. "I don't have time to be playing with you, Richard."

17 "My Daddy said he'd . . ."

18 "Sit down, Richard, you're disturbing the class."

19 "My Daddy said he'd give . . . fifteen dollars."

20 She turned around and looked mad. "We are collecting this money for you and your kind, Richard Gregory. If your Daddy can give fifteen dollars you have no business being on relief."

21 "I got it right now, I got it right now, my Daddy gave it to me to turn in today, my Daddy said . . ."

22 "And furthermore," she said, looking right at me, her nostrils getting big and her lips getting thin and her eyes opening wide, "we know you don't have a Daddy."

23 Helene Tucker turned around, her eyes full of tears. She felt sorry for me. Then I couldn't see her too well because I was crying, too.

24 "Sit down, Richard."

25 And I always thought the teacher kind of liked me. She always picked me to wash the blackboard on Friday, after school. That was a big thrill, it made me feel important. If I didn't wash it, come Monday the school might not function right.

26 "Where are you going, Richard?"

27 I walked out of school that day, and for a long time I didn't go back very often. There was shame there.

28   Now there was shame everywhere. It seemed like the whole world had been inside that classroom, everyone had heard what the teacher had said, everyone had turned around and felt sorry for me. There was shame in going to the Worthy Boys Annual Christmas Dinner for you and your kind, because everybody knew what a worthy boy was. Why couldn't they just call it the Boys Annual Dinner, why'd they have to give it a name? There was shame in wearing the brown and orange and white plaid mackinaw the welfare gave to 3,000 boys. Why'd it have to be the same for everybody so when you walked down the street the people could see you were on relief? It was a nice warm mackinaw and it had a hood, and my Momma beat me and called me a little rat when she found out I stuffed it in the bottom of a pail full of garbage way over on Cottage Street. There was shame in running over to Mister Ben's at the end of the day and asking for his rotten peaches, there was shame in asking Mrs. Simmons for a spoonful of sugar, there was shame in running out to meet the relief truck. I hated that truck, full of food for you and your kind. I ran into the house and hid when it came. And then I started to sneak through alleys, to take the long way home so people going into White's Eat Shop wouldn't see me. Yeah, the whole world heard the teacher that day, we all know you don't have a Daddy.

- Vocabulary

    mackinaw (28)

- The Facts

    1. Where did the narrator learn shame?
    2. What did the narrator do for Helene Tucker? How important was she in his life?
    3. According to the narrator, why could he not do well in school? What did the teachers think?
    4. What event at school caused shame to control the narrator's life for a long time? Summarize what happened.
    5. What did the author dislike about the Worthy Boys Annual Christmas Dinner?

- The Strategies

    1. The narration begins in paragraph 3, following two paragraphs of commentary about Helene Tucker, a girl on whom the narrator had a crush. What is the purpose of the preliminary paragraphs?
    2. What dominant impression is always in the background of the narration? Why?
    3. Beginning with paragraph 9, the narrator adds conversation to the narration. What is the effect of this technique?
    4. What is the main theme (lesson about life) revealed in this story? Is it implied or stated?

5. In paragraph 5, what is the purpose of repeating the word "pregnant"? What does the author mean?

- ## The Issues

1. Do you agree with the narrator's comment that "everybody's got a Helene Tucker"? What does Helene Tucker symbolize? Give an example of a Helene Tucker from your own experience.
2. The teacher thought the narrator was a troublemaker. Was he really, or was there another reason for drawing attention to himself?
3. Why did the teacher humiliate the narrator when he announced that his father would donate fifteen dollars? Do you think the teacher should have handled the situation differently? If so, how should she have reacted?
4. The narrator states that he thought the teacher liked him because she always picked him to clean the blackboard on Friday. Why do you think she picked him?
5. Did the narrator do the right thing by not going back to the school often after the shame incident? What kept him away? Do you empathize or do you think the narrator was oversensitive?

- ## Suggestions for Writing

1. Write about an incident in which you or someone you love experienced shame. Use the techniques of pacing, using vivid details, and making a point.
2. Write an essay in which you examine the psychological effects of poverty on children in elementary school.

James Boswell's Scotland
Tom Huntington

Tom Huntington is a journalist and former editor for *American History* and *Historic Traveler* magazines. Huntington first came to prominence with the publication of his article "Finding the London of Sherlock Holmes," as the lead story in the February 1997 issue of *Historic Traveler,* of which he had just become the new editor. Huntington is known for his research about places associated with famous writers. He majored in cinema at the University of Southern California, which probably strengthened his eye for the details of historical settings. Currently he lives in central Pennsylvania.

James Boswell, the author of what many regard as the best biography ever written, Life of Samuel Johnson, *spent much of his life trying to escape Scotland, the country of his birth. Readers who follow Huntington's path to the Auchinleck and Edinburgh of today may wonder why Boswell did not delight in his homeland. The answer is a complex tangle of history and personal circumstance and is partly explained by the smoldering rivalry between Scotland and England. Edinburgh today is quite different and offers many more comforts to the visitor than it did during Boswell's day. As you read, try to imagine what life must have been like in one of the squalid tenement houses of eighteenth-century Edinburgh.*

• • •

1 Late on a sunny afternoon last summer, I visited a deserted churchyard in Auchinleck, a drab little village surrounded by pastureland in Scotland's western district of East Ayrshire. Many of the weathered gravestones were broken or tilted. Two small buildings stood among them: the old parish church and an unpretentious mausoleum, on the side of which I found a coat of arms with the inscription *Vraye Foy*, or True Faith. Otherwise, there was nothing—no statue, no plaque, no marker—to indicate that inside lay the remains of James Boswell, the passionate Scotsman who wrote one of the greatest books of all time, the *Life of Samuel Johnson, LL.D.*

2 Dr. Johnson, as the brilliant 18th-century critic, author and poet was known, produced a huge body of immensely influential literature, including a dictionary that remained the gold standard of English lexicography for the better part of a century. Eccentric and witty, he was the hub of a glittering circle in London that attracted such luminaries as novelist and playwright Oliver Goldsmith, painter Sir Joshua Reynolds, the actor David Garrick and Boswell himself. Johnson was renowned for his barbed aphorisms, many of which—"Patriotism is the last refuge of a scoundrel," "No man but a blockhead ever wrote except for money," "I am willing to love all mankind, except an American"—still circulate.

• *Boswell mausoleum and graveyard*

3   Boswell, a self-described "gentleman of ancient blood," was a lawyer and a writer who knew Johnson well for more than 20 years. He was also kind of genius. His biography of his friend and mentor—published after Johnson's death—created a sensation. Boswell was determined "to tell the whole truth about his subject, to portray his lapses, his blemishes, and his weaknesses as well as his great qualities," says Adam Sisman, winner of the 2001 National Book Critics Circle Award for *Boswell's Presumptuous Task: The Making of the Life of Dr. Johnson*. Nowadays we take such candor for granted, "but in Boswell's time," Sisman adds, it was "a startling innovation."

4   Boswell remains a lively presence on the literary scene. Hardly a week goes by, it seems, without a Boswell sighting somewhere. A *New Yorker* spoof put Boswell to work on the life of Michael Jackson. ("When a boy, he was *already* notably fond of other children, and, as you know, he maintained his fondness for them into middle age.") The *New York Times* has compared journalist Ron Suskind and biographer A. Scott Berg to Boswell and described *Wired* magazine as the "Boswell . . . for the geekerati." The word "Boswell" is even in the dictionary, defined as "one who writes with love and intimate knowledge of any subject." Two Boswell biographies have come out in the past five years, and a host of scholars, critics and other aficionados have taken to calling themselves "Boswellians." One of them, Iain Brown, manuscript curator at the National Library of Scotland, hung a portrait of Boswell in his bathroom at home.

5   My own fascination with Boswell began several years ago, when I bought the *Life* after reading the introduction at a bookstore. Although I've always liked big books, this one was so formidable—1,402 pages—that I decided to try Boswell's much shorter *Journal of a Tour to the Hebrides* first, as a sort of warm-up. By the time I finished that exuberant account of a ten-week holiday Boswell and Johnson spent exploring the islands off Scotland's northwestern coast in 1773, I was hooked. I plunged right into the *Life* and then tackled Boswell's other journals—13 volumes, in all.

6   I was intrigued by Johnson but found Boswell downright enthralling. The astute biographer turned out to be an irresistible character in his own right, a contradictory, needy and sometimes infuriating man who drank too much, talked too much and preserved many of his indiscretions in writing. Among the revelations in his journals: be fathered two illegitimate children before he married, and he remained a compulsive whoremonger throughout his life. He could be a pompous snob or entertain a crowded London theater by imitating a cow. He suffered from debilitating depressions, yet in public was the life of the party. "I admire and like him beyond measure," declared 20-year-old Charlotte Ann Burney, the sister of the famous diarist Fanny Burney. "He . . . puts himself into such ridiculous postures that he is as good as a comedy." The philosopher David Hume described him as "very good-humored, very agreeable, and very mad."

7   One thing he was not agreeable about was Scotland. Boswell's feelings about his homeland were deeply conflicted. He abhorred what he perceived as Scotland's abject provincialism. To rid himself of his Scottish accent, he took diction classes from Thomas Sheridan, father of playwright (*The School for Scandal*) Richard Brinsley Sheridan. Yet Scotland was the place that shaped

him. He spent most of his life there and often boasted "of being descended of ancestors who have had an estate for some hundreds of years."

8   This is why, when I finished Boswell's books, I decided to undertake a sort of literary pilgrimage. I wanted to find what remained of Boswell's Edinburgh, and see Auchinleck, the family estate recently restored from near ruin. I also wanted to visit Boswell's tomb and pay my respects to the great biographer.

9   He was born in Edinburgh in 1740. His father, Alexander, a lawyer and later a judge in Scotland's supreme civil court, was a classical scholar with an unbending sense of propriety that he expected his children to embrace. His mother, Euphemia, was passive and devout, and Boswell was very fond of her. He once recalled that "her notions were pious, visionary and scrupulous. When she was once made to go to the theater, she cried and would never go again."

10   Edinburgh, situated on the shore of the Firth (or bay) of Forth, 400 miles north of London, was Scotland's artistic and social center, and its capital. The nucleus of Boswell's Edinburgh was a stately avenue now known as the Royal Mile. A boulevard lined by tall, straight-faced stone buildings, it descends from Edinburgh Castle on its cliffside perch to the Palace of Holyroodhouse near the base of the weathered peak called Arthur's Seat. The castle was the fortress and palace that has dominated Edinburgh since the 16th century. Holyroodhouse had been the home of Scotland's kings and queens for two centuries until 1707, when the Act of Union made Scotland part of Great Britain.

11   Clustered around the Royal Mile was a tangled maze of alleys and courtyards, where many of Edinburgh's 50,000 inhabitants occupied tall tenements called "lands." The poor lived on the bottom and top floors, the more well-to-do in between. The city, ancient even then (its origins date back to at least the seventh century A.D.), was filthy and smelly. A pall of coal smoke hung over its grimy buildings, and pedestrians had to remain alert for chamber pots being emptied from windows above. The Boswell residence, the fourth floor of a tenement, was just off the Royal Mile near Parliament House, where the Scottish Parliament sat until the Act of Union abolished it.

12   Today Edinburgh is a bustling modern city with a population of 448,000. As my train pulled into Waverley Station, I craned my neck to the castle still perched majestically on its cliffside high above the tracks. From the station a taxi took me up a steep slope to the Royal Mile. Despite the traffic and the tourist shops, the cobblestone street and its stolid, stone-faced buildings retained an unmistakable 18th-century flavor.

13   Boswell's birthplace burned down long ago, but other landmarks remain. I visited Parliament House, opened in 1639 and still the seat for the country's supreme civil court. The exterior was redone in the 1800s, but inside the lofty Parliament Hall, I watched advocates in black gowns and white wigs pace up and down as they talked with clients beneath a magnificent arched-timber ceiling, just as they did in Boswell's day. He often pleaded for his own clients in this hall; on many occasions the presiding judge was his father. Across the square from Parliament House, I admired the High Kirk of St. Giles, a massive, brooding presence capped by buttresses that form a gothic crown. This had

Auchinleck Manor, country home of the Boswells

been Boswell's church, one he connected with his pious mother as well as "the dreary terrors of hell."

14   The Boswells stayed in Edinburgh when the court was in session. In the spring and summer, they lived at their country estate 60 miles away. Auchinleck, a 20,000-acre holdover from feudal times, also provided homes for about 100 tenant farmers. Named after a previous owner, it had been in the Boswell family since 1504. Young James enjoyed riding with his father, planting trees and playing with the gardener's daughter, for whom he developed a mad passion. "Auchinleck is a most sweet, romantic Place," he wrote to a friend. "There is a vast deal of Wood and Water, fine retired shady walks, and every thing that can render the Countrey agreable to contemplative minds."

After Alexander Boswell became a judge at 46, earning the honorary title Lord Auchinleck, he built a fancy new home at his estate. Above the main entrance, he inscribed a quote from Horace: "What you seek is here in this remote place; if you can only keep a balanced disposition"—words he may have meant for his increasingly wayward eldest son.

15   Early on, James had served notice that he was not cut out to follow in his father's strait-laced footsteps. Scots are well known for being torn between dour conformity and impetuous rebelliousness, a contradiction emphatically personified by Boswell father and son. When James was 18, he developed a passion for the theater and fell for an actress a good ten years older. After Lord Auchinleck banished him to the University of Glasgow, Boswell, still under the spell of his Catholic mistress, decided to convert—tantamount to career suicide in Presbyterian Scotland—and ran away to London. There he lost interest in Catholicism, caught a venereal disease and decided he wanted to be a soldier.

16 Lord Auchinleck fetched his son home, and there they made a deal: Boswell could seek a military commission, but first he had to study law. After chafing for two years under his father's oppressive supervision, Boswell returned to London in 1762, intending to fulfill his military dreams. A bookseller there introduced him to Samuel Johnson, then 53 and already a formidable literary figure, who made no secret of his contempt for Scots. "Indeed I come from Scotland but I cannot help it," Boswell stammered. To which Johnson growled: "That, I find, is what a very great many of your countrymen can not help."

17 It was a rocky start to what would eventually become the most famous friendship in English letters. Irma Lustig, who edited two volumes of Boswell's journals for Yale University Press, believes Lord Auchinleck's harshness created in his son "an insatiable need for attention and approval," and in Johnson, almost 32 years his senior, Boswell found an answer to that need. When Boswell "opened his heart," as biographer Frederick Pottle puts it, and told Johnson the story of his life, Johnson was charmed.

18 Lord Auchinleck was anything but charmed. He threatened to sell Auchinleck if James didn't settle down, "from the principle that it is better to snuff a candle out than leave it to stink in a socket." Knuckling under, Boswell went to Holland to continue studying law, then embarked on a postgrad grand tour of the Continent, determined to meet the leading men of his day. Though he failed to obtain an audience with Frederick the Great of Prussia, in Switzerland the brash young Scot wangled an invitation to visit philosopher Jean Jacques Rousseau, and in France he engaged Voltaire in a debate about religion. "For a . . . time there was a fair opposition between Voltaire and Boswell," he noted with satisfaction.

19 While in Rome, Boswell posed for a painting by George Willison, which I found in Edinburgh's National Portrait Gallery. There he was at age 24, round-faced with slight circles under his eyes and the faint suggestion of a smile on his plump lips. He wore a dandyish scarlet-and-yellow-waistcoat beneath a green, fur-trimmed coat; lace peeked out from his cuffs. Above him, an owl perched absurdly on a branch. Somehow the painter captured the mixture of silliness and self-importance that made Boswell so engaging.

20 On the Mediterranean island of Corsica, Boswell got to know Pasquale Paoli, the charismatic patriot leading an insurgency against the Genoese, who then ruled the island. In Paris he learned of his mother's death and departed for Scotland (en route, Boswell noted in his journal, he and Rousseau's mistress had sex 13 times in 11 days). His first important book, *An Account of Corsica* (1768), celebrated Paoli. To Britons of the day, Corsica was an exotic and romantic destination, and Boswell's breezy travelogue made him a minor celebrity known as "Corsica Boswell." Nevertheless, he kept his word to his father and began practicing law. "[He] was a professional writer," notes Irma Lustig, "but he was not, like Johnson, a writer by profession."

21 After entertaining a number of matrimonial schemes involving wealthy women, Boswell again infuriated his father by marrying a poor cousin, Margaret Montgomerie, who was two years older. The couple rented an apartment from

Portrait of James Boswell as a young man

the philosopher David Hume at James's Court, a fashionable Edinburgh address just off the Royal Mile.

22   As it happened, I too stayed in James's Court, at a small hotel. On one of the court's three arched entrances, I saw a plaque green with age noting the connection with Boswell, Johnson and Hume. The building where James and Margaret lived was destroyed by fire in 1857, but others from Boswell's era still stand, tall, gray and unadorned.

23   Johnson stayed with the Boswells after he and James returned from the Hebrides; to Margaret, the ungainly Londoner was the houseguest from hell. "The truth is, that his irregular hours and uncouth habits, such as turning the candles with their heads downwards, when they did not burn bright enough, and letting the wax drop upon the carpet, could not be but disagreeable to a lady," Boswell conceded. She also complained about Johnson's influence over her husband. "I have seen many a bear led by a man," she said in exasperation, "but I never before saw a man led by a bear."

24   During the two decades they would know each other, Boswell and Johnson actually spent little more than a year's time together; their friendship was conducted largely from afar. Even so, the older man became the central figure in

his young admirer's life, a "Guide, Philosopher, and Friend," as Boswell more than once put it. "Be Johnson," he exhorted himself. Though reconciled, for the time being at least, to living in Edinburgh, he tried to visit London for several weeks each spring. "Come to me, my dear Bozzy," Johnson wrote, "and let us be as happy as we can."

25   On Boswell's visits, the two men socialized in taverns, in Johnson's rooms and dining with friends. They discussed topics from literature and politics to religion and gossip, and Boswell took care to preserve the conversations in his journals. One day in 1772 they spoke of marriage, "whether there is any beauty independent of utility," why people swear, "the proper use of riches," public amusements, politics ancient and modern, and various literary topics. Most important perhaps to Boswell was this advice from Johnson: "[N]obody can write the life of a man, but those who have eat and drunk and lived in social intercourse with him."

26   There were occasions for even more talk after Boswell was admitted to the Club, a prestigious group of intellectual heavyweights who met for dinner and gossip every other Friday. Boswell had worried about being blackballed, but Johnson watched out for him. "Sir, they knew that if they refused you, they'd probably never have got in another. I'd have kept them all out," he said. Club meetings meant evenings of scintillating conversation with the cream of Britain's thinkers—historian Edward Gibbon, naturalist Joseph Banks, social philospher Adam Smith and Richard Brinsley Sheridan all eventually became members.

27   The friendship had its rough patches. At times, Boswell felt the lash of Johnson's temper. After one stinging rebuke, Boswell likened himself to "the man who had put his head into the lion's mouth a great many times with perfect safety, but at last had it bit off." Another outburst wounded Boswell so deeply he avoided Johnson for a week. The two men finally reconciled at a dinner. "We were instantly as cordial again as ever," Boswell said.

28   He saved more than a hundred letters from Johnson and quoted them extensively in the *Life*, but their correspondence was erratic. Months might pass in silence, until Boswell roused himself from one of his depressions. Sometimes he requested advice—about his black moods, about his law cases, about his father. Johnson provided thoughtful, penetrating answers, even though the younger man could be every bit as exasperating on paper as he sometimes was in person. On one occasion, Boswell childishly stopped writing just to see how long it would take Johnson to write to him. Other times, he would fret, worried that Johnson was angry. "I consider your friendship as a possession, which I intend to hold till you take it from me, and to lament if ever by my fault I should lose it," Johnson reassured him.

29   There was never any need to doubt Johnson's affection; it was genuine. "Boswell is a man who I believe never left a house without leaving wish for his return," he once said. Among other things, the two were bound by melancholy. Johnson had a morbid fear of madness and he, too, fought depression, while Boswell analyzed his own precarious mental health to the point of obsession. Once, after watching a moth burn in a candle's flame, Johnson said, "That creature was its own tormentor, and I believe its name was Boswell."

- *Boswell's insistence on recording even Johnson's indiscreet comments—"Dr. [Oliver] Goldsmith [left, with Boswell, center, and Johnson] . . . has been loose in his principles, but he is coming right"—both scandalized and delighted his contemporaries.*

30 The Hebrides adventure capped the most settled period of Boswell's life. He was 32 then—reasonably content and cheerful, a busy, respectable advocate making a decent living, with a loving wife and the first of their five children. Eventually, however, he began drinking heavily, losing money at cards, visiting prostitutes. In his profession, he hurled himself into lost causes and earned a reputation for erratic behavior. After his father died in 1782, it was his turn to be the Laird of Auchinleck, a man of distinction. But soon enough the satisfactions of country life began to pall. And then, late in 1784, Samuel Johnson died of congestive heart failure at age 75.

31 The news left Boswell "stunned, and in a kind of amaze." It was well known that he had long intended to write Johnson's biography, and no sooner had the great man breathed his last than a letter reached Edinburgh from a prominent bookseller asking that Boswell do so. But before starting that monumental task, he wrote *The Journal of a Tour to the Hebrides*—perhaps he, too, felt the need of a warm-up—which was published to great acclaim in 1785.

32 Beginning work on the *Life*, Boswell's contempt for Scotland's "coarse vulgarity" and "Presbyterian prejudices" got the better of him. He had long thought about relocating to London for good. Finally, in 1786, he and Margaret

and their children make the move. It was a disaster. Boswell spent much of his time drinking with friends and accomplished only halting progress on the book. Margaret's health deteriorated rapidly. She returned to Auchinleck and soon died there of tuberculosis. Though he had neglected her for years, Boswell was shattered. He wrote in his journal that he longed "to have but one week, one day, in which I might again hear her admirable conversation and assure her of my fervent attachment notwithstanding all my irregularities."

33   Back in London after a dismal interval of mourning at Auchinleck, Boswell resumed work on the *Life*. He wrote by fits and starts, often moving forward only with the gentle prodding of Edmond Malone, a friend and Shakespearean scholar. He did not set out to be innovative, but, says biographer Adam Sisman, he did write consciously for effect. When he was in school in Glasgow, one of his teachers had been Adam Smith, who would later write the landmark economic treatise *Wealth of Nations*. Smith impressed upon Boswell the importance of detail—he said, for example, that he was "glad to know Milton wore latchets in his shoes, instead of buckles." It was a lesson Boswell would never forget. He often said he wanted to write the *Life* like a "Flemish picture," meaning rich in painstaking detail. He was a superb reporter, adept at ferreting tidbits from Johnson's acquaintances, and of course he had shrewdly teased many vivid nuggets out of the man himself, keeping an especially sharp eye for tics and odd behaviors, such as the doctor's shabby personal appearance, his "convulsive starts and odd gesticulations" and his appalling manners at the dinner table. "Let me not be censured for mentioning such minute particulars," he pleaded. "Everything relative to so great a man is worth observing."

34   Boswell also took care to compose his book in what he called "scenes," Sisman points out, skillfully dramatized little playlets piled one atop another. It was a technique all but unprecedented at the time. The result was biography as intimate epic—a stirring narrative with a glamorous supporting cast and the loquacious warts-and-all hero at center stage. Published in 1791, the book was an immediate success. A review in *Gentleman's Magazine* called it "a literary portrait . . . which all who knew the orginal will allow to be THE MAN HIMSELF." The statesman Edmund Burke told King George it was the most entertaining book he had ever read. The massive, two-volume set was expensive—it cost two guineas, four times as much as a typical book—but the first printing of 1,750 copies sold out within months.

35   Boswell enjoyed some brief exaltation, and even took out a boasting ad in London's *Public Advertiser*. "Boswell has so many invitations in consequence of his *Life of Johnson* that he may be *literally* said to *live* upon his deceased friend." But some acquaintances, angered by his "practice of publishing without consent what has been thrown out in the freedom of conversation," avoided his company. Others noticed that once he finished his great work, he lost his bearings. Perhaps the lowest point came when his daughter took him to task for misbehaving with one of her 14-year-old friends. "It seems that after dinner, when I had taken too much wine, I had been too fond," he wrote in his journal, claiming that he had no clear memory of the event.

36   Boswell's final years were grim. He remained in London, carousing and whoring; his health was ruined by repeated venereal infections. Hounded by debts incurred educating his children and buying land in Ayrshire, he complained that he felt "listless and fretful." He died at home from kidney failure and uremia at the age of 54. "I used to grumble sometimes at his turbulence," grieved Malone, "but now miss and regret his noise and his hilarity and his perpetual good humour, which had no bounds."

37   After his death, Boswell's reputation went into a spin. Thanks in no small part to a devastating critique by essayist Thomas Macaulay in 1831, the writer came to be regarded as a toady who had somehow managed to produce a worthy biography that reflected the greatness of its subject, not its author. "Of all the talents which ordinarily raise men to eminence as writers, Boswell had absolutely none," Macaulay wrote. That view began to change only after many of Boswell's papers, including his journals, came to light in the 1920s. They were found in an Irish castle, where they had been taken by a descendant; some had been stuffed into a box used to store croquet equipment. Still more papers turned up later, including the original manuscript of the *Life*. Yale University began publishing the journals in 1950, and the first volume sold almost a million copies. Since then the journals have helped Boswell emerge from Johnson's shadow. "We read him now," says the National Library's Iain Brown, "for the pure pleasure of reading Boswell." What he wrote, and how he wrote, still matter, "Not only did Boswell invent the biography as we know it," notes critic Charles McGrath, "he was also, in effect, the father of feature journalism, and for good and ill he created many of the conventions we still observe. The celebrity profile . . . oral history, documentary reporting . . . the travel yarn, the high-powered-dinner-party piece—the list of forms that he mastered or invented goes on and on."

38   Even as Boswell's reputation was undergoing rehabilitation, Auchinleck was falling into disrepair. By the mid-1960s, when another James Boswell inherited the house, it had so deteriorated that the new owner could not afford to fix it. He sold it, and in 1999 it was given to the Landmark Trust, a charity that rents historic buildings to vacationers. After spending nearly $5 million on renovations, the trust opened Auchinleck to overnight guests two years ago, which is how I was able to stay there last summer.

39   To get to the house, I drove from the village of Anchinleck down a country lane, crossed a small stone bridge and topped a rise. There I found a beautiful mansion standing all by itself in the countryside. Above the entrance, I noticed an elaborately carved pediment "terribly loaded with Ornaments of Trumpets & Maces and the Deuce knows what," as another guest recorded in 1760, and below it Horace's cautionary admonition about keeping a balanced disposition.

40   Exploring outside, at the end of a steep path I stumbled upon a small beach at the edge of the River Lugar, a slow-flowing stream. On the other side, a cliff reared over the black water. It struck me that Boswell had taken Johnson to that very spot, and, so moved by the "romantick scene," had confided to him his family history and gushed about his own distant relationship to King George III.

41   Neil Gow is a local judge and the current chairman of the Auchinleck Boswell Society. On my last day in Scotland, I met him in the churchyard at

- *Boswell became Laird of the Auchinleck estate (the study above, in 2004) upon the death of his father in 1782. Though Boswell installed his wife and children there, he continued to spend most of his time in London: "The country does not at all suit me," he insisted.*

the Boswell mausoleum. A dapper man with a twinkle in his eye, Gow led me inside. Ducking our heads, we descended several stone stairs into a dark, arched space where nine Boswells, including James, his father and Margaret, lay in sepulchers behind unfinished stone. One niche was broken; when Gow beamed his flashlight through the hole, we could see a skull inside. On another sepulcher, I saw the initials J.B. "That's where he is," Gow said. So in the end, I reflected, heritage had won out after all. Here was James Boswell, surrounded by family—including the father he could not please and the wife he so often disappointed. In death, the reluctant Scotsman had done what he could not bring himself to do in life. He had come home for good.

- ## Vocabulary

    unpretentious (1)
    eccentric (2)
    aficionados (4)
    enthralling (6)
    provincialism (7)
    nucleus (10)
    conformity (15)
    erratic (28)

    mausoleum (1)
    luminaries (2)
    curator (4)
    whoremonger (6)
    propriety (9)
    tenements (11)
    impetuous (15)
    loquacious (34)

    lexicography (2)
    aphorisms (2)
    formidable (5)
    abject (7)
    scrupulous (9)
    dour (15)
    matrimonial (21)

● The Facts

1. What experience caused Huntington to become fascinated with Boswell? Which specific event "hooked" him on Boswell and his relationship with Johnson?
2. What was Boswell's attitude about Scotland? Why do you think he felt the way he did about his homeland?
3. How do you feel about someone who hates his homeland?
4. Who were some of the famous people whose acquaintance Boswell sought and made? How was he able to meet these influential people?
5. After many indiscreet love affairs, whom did Boswell finally marry? How did his father react to this marriage? How did the marriage turn out?
6. How would you describe Boswell's final years? Were these the kind of years you would expect to end the life of a writer of his stature? Why or why not?

● The Strategies

1. How does Huntington achieve such an accurate portrayal of Boswell and his surroundings? What techniques serve him best?
2. What was Boswell's strategy in creating the *Life of Johnson*? What were the results of this strategy? How is his work perceived today?
3. Several pictures are attached to this essay. What value, if any, do you find in these pictures?
4. According to Huntington, what has the term "Boswell" come to mean in the literary world today? (See paragraph 4.)
5. What point of view does Huntington use in his essay on Boswell? What advantage does this point of view have for the reader?
6. What rhetorical mode(s) dominate(s) the essay?

● The Issues

1. How would you describe the ups and downs of Boswell's reputation? When was his reputation finally established?
2. What was the relationship between Boswell and his father? How do you think the relationship affected Boswell's character? Be specific in your answer.
3. How would you portray the relationship between Boswell and Johnson? Was it smooth, with Johnson being the wise mentor and Boswell being the student learning at the feet of his great master, or are other sentiments involved? (See paragraph 27.)
4. Which aspects of their two personalities bound Johnson and Boswell together? Suggest the reasons why their friendship bore such tasty literary fruit.
5. How did Boswell's wife feel about Johnson? Do you believe she was justified in her attitude toward this literary genius?
6. What topics of conversation did Johnson and Boswell cover when they were together? Where did most of these conversations take place? Do you

consider the venues suited to fascinating conversations? Give reasons for your answer.
7. What happened to Auchinleck, the manor Boswell inherited from his father? Try to trace its history. What value do you attribute to this property?

Suggestions for Writing

1. Using a library or the Internet as your source, do some research on the life of James Boswell and write a brief essay about his personal indiscretions and how they affected his reputation as a writer.
2. After thinking about the relationship between Boswell and his father, write an essay in which you analyze the relationship between you and your father (if you are a male) or between you and your mother (if you are a female). Focus on matters of control and ambition.

Those Winter Sundays
Robert Hayden

Robert Hayden (1913–1980) was born in Detroit, attended the University of Michigan, and taught at Fisk University. His *Ballad of Remembrance* was awarded a prize at the 1966 World Festival of Negro Arts held in Dakar, Senegal.

The following poem recounts a childhood memory.

• • •

Sundays too my father got up early
and put his clothes on in the blueblack cold,
then with cracked hands that ached
from labor in the weekday weather made
5   banked fires blaze. No one ever thanked him.
I'd wake and hear the cold splintering, breaking.
When the rooms were warm, he'd call,
and slowly I would rise and dress,
fearing the chronic angers of that house,
10 Speaking indifferently to him,
who had driven out the cold
and polished my good shoes as well.
What did I know, what did I know
of love's austere and lonely offices?

Vocabulary

banked (5)   chronic (9)   austere (14)

The Facts

1. What did the narrator's father do on Sundays?
2. How did the narrator react to his father in the morning?
3. How would you characterize the narrator's attitude as he looks back on this time with his father?

The Strategies

1. In what poetic form is this narration framed? (*Hint:* Count the number of lines.)
2. The author writes about his father: "No one ever thanked him." Why do you think he chose to put it this way? Why not simply say "I never thanked him"?
3. The poet writes: "I'd wake and hear the cold splintering, breaking." What kind of figure of speech is this?
4. Examine the sentences in the poem. How many are there? What is the technique of running a sentence across several lines without an endstop or break?

The Issues

1. What kind of work do you suppose the speaker's father did? How can his probable occupation be deduced from the poem?
2. What are "love's austere and lonely offices"? What other examples can you give of them?

Suggestions for Writing

1. Write an analysis of this poem.
2. Narrate an incident from your own childhood that involved your relationship with a parent or other significant adult.

ISSUE FOR CRITICAL THINKING AND DEBATE: TERRORISM

The September 11, 2001, suicide bombing of the World Trade Center in New York and the Pentagon in Washington D.C. was, to most of the horrified Western world, an act of unspeakable wickedness and evil. To some in the Islamic world, it was a deed of heroic martyrdom done in the name of God and one that guaranteed heaven to the self-sacrificing souls responsible for it. After the attack, as the rescuers sifted through the physical rubble, and the talking heads on television combed through the shreds of whys and whats, the irreconcilable divide between the terrorists and us became sharply clear. While we mourned for the victims and prayed for their families, elsewhere in the world some people rejoiced at our sorrow. Even now, when we think about the murderers' cold-bloodedness, their diabolical planning, and their fanatical sacrifice, many of us cannot comprehend the depth of the hate that drove them to invest so much time and energy into slaughtering so many innocents.

Terrorism: A New York City firefighter watches smoke from the remains of the World Trade Center.

Why do they hate us so? We're used to being admired—our material wealth and lifestyle the envy of the world. Our history has repeatedly shown us to be a generous people, donating billions of dollars to help less fortunate nations in the grip of war, famine, pestilence, or economic ruin. When we have won wars, we have always tried to help our former enemies rebuild rather than occupy their territory. Yet, there are millions of people—some Islamic, some not—who hate us with such passion that they are willing, even eager, to sacrifice themselves in murderous and indiscriminate attacks aimed at our destruction. Al-Qaeda, the terrorist organization headed by Osama bin Laden, even now reportedly continues to train assassins and saboteurs, all willing to blow themselves up in an attempt to hurt us. What stuns most Americans is that these people believe that their terroristic attacks are the will of God. Few of us associate God with mass slaughter; even fewer can comprehend the belief that the rewards of paradise will be lavished on such murderers.

The two writers whose opinions are given here represent completely opposite positions on the relationship between terrorism and Islamic beliefs. Neither one expresses doubt about the wickedness of terrorism. But the first writer is a devout Muslim who disavows terrorism while denying that Islam promotes it. The second writer was once married to Osama bin Laden's brother and saw firsthand how women are maltreated in the Islamic world.

Her outlook is a bleak one, for she believes that change of any kind in the attitude of Islamic societies is unlikely.

We're not used to people trying to kill us. To many Americans, that kind of despicable plotting is a fact of life abroad, not life at home. With the horror of 9/11 etched forever in our memories, many of us remain jumpy, for we now know that there are people out there who hate us more than they love life.

What we should do about them is the fundamental question.

What Does Islam Say about Terrorism?
ABDULLAH MOMIN

Abdullah Momin (b. 1971), the pseudonym of Musaddique Thange, was born and raised in India. He holds a graduate degree in Electronics Engineering from the University of Bombay, India, and has been a software professional for the last ten years. He works as a Senior Technical Leader in Roamware India Pvt Ltd. This article was written during his four-year stay in the US (1999 through 2003). He now lives in India with his wife and child.

A careful reading of the essay that follows may surprise you if you have believed blindly that Islam is a cruel, rigid, and oppressive religion. The author has carefully highlighted those verses in the Koran that value human life, that urge protection of the weak and innocent during war, that propose war only to protect those exploited and oppressed by tyrants, that encourage tolerance, and that accept our common origin and the beauty of human diversity. This essay may encourage you to read the entire Koran so that you can evaluate its worth to society.

• • •

1   One of the distinctive characteristics of the times we live in is the overwhelming presence of violence in our societies. Whether it is a bomb going off in a market place, or the hijacking of an aircraft where innocent people are held at ransom to achieve political ends, we live in an age where the manipulation and loss of innocent lives have become commonplace.

2   Such is the all-pervasive nature of indiscriminate violence, that "terrorism" is considered as one of the prime threats to peace and security in our societies.

3   The word "terrorism" came into wide usage only a few decades ago. One of the unfortunate results of this new terminology is that it limits the definition of terrorism to that perpetrated by small groups or individuals. Terrorism, in fact, spans the entire world, and manifests itself in various forms. Its perpetrators do not fit any stereotype. Those who hold human lives cheap, and have the power to expend human lives, appear at different levels in our societies. The frustrated employee who kills his colleagues in cold-blood or the oppressed citizen of an occupied land who vents his anger by blowing up a school bus are terrorists who provoke our anger and revulsion. Ironically, however, the politician who uses age-old ethnic animosities between peoples

to consolidate his position, the head of state who orders "carpet bombing" of entire cities, the exalted councils that choke millions of civilians to death by wielding the insidious weapon of sanctions, are rarely punished for their crimes against humanity.

4   It is this narrow definition of terrorism that implicates only individuals and groups, that has caused Muslims to be associated with acts of destruction and terror, and as a result, to become victims of hate violence and terror themselves. Sometimes the religion of Islam is held responsible for the acts of a handful of Muslims, and often for the acts of non-Muslims!

5   Could it be possible that Islam, whose light ended the Dark Ages in Europe, now propounds the advent of an age of terror? Could a faith that has over 1.2 billion followers the world over, and over 7 million in America, actually advocate the killing and maiming of innocent people? Could Islam, whose name itself stands for "peace" and "submission to God," encourage its adherents to work for death and destruction?

6   For too long have we relied on popular images in the media and in Hollywood films for answers to these pertinent questions. It is now time to look at the sources of Islam and its history to determine whether Islam does indeed advocate violence.

Sanctity of Human Life

7   The Glorious Qur'an says: ". . . take not life, which God hath made sacred, except by way of justice and law: thus doth He command you, that ye may learn wisdom." [Al-Qur'an 6:151]

8   Islam considers all life forms as sacred. However, the sanctity of human life is accorded a special place. The first and the foremost basic right of a human being is the right to live. The Glorious Qur'an says: "...if any one slew a person—unless it be for murder or for spreading mischief in the land—it would be as if he slew the whole people: and if any one saved a life, it would be as if he saved the life of the whole people." [Al-Qur'an 5:32]

9   Such is the value of a single human life, that the Qur'an equates the taking of even one human life unjustly, with killing all of humanity. Thus, the Qur'an prohibits homicide in clear terms. The taking of a criminal's life by the state in order to administer justice is required to uphold the rule of law and the peace and security of the society. Only a proper and competent court can decide whether an individual has forfeited his right to life by disregarding the right to life and peace of other human beings.

Ethics of War

10 Even in a state of war, Islam enjoins that one deals with the enemy nobly on the battlefield. Islam has drawn a clear line of distinction between the combatants and the non-combatants of the enemy country. As far as the non-combatant population is concerned, such as women, children, the old and the infirm, etc., the instructions of the Prophet are as follows: "Do not kill any old person, any

child or any woman"[1]. "Do not kill the monks in monasteries" or "Do not kill the people who are sitting in places of worship."[2] During a war, the Prophet saw the corpse of a woman lying on the ground and observed: "She was not fighting. How then she came to be killed?" Thus non-combatants are guaranteed security of life even if their state is at war with an Islamic state.

Jihad

11   While Islam in general is misunderstood in the western world, perhaps no other Islamic term evokes such strong reactions as the word "jihad." The term "jihad" has been much abused, to conjure up bizarre images of violent Muslims forcing people to submit at the point of the sword. This myth was perpetuated throughout the centuries of mistrust during and after the Crusades. Unfortunately, it survives to this day.

12   The word "jihad" comes from the root word *jahada*, which means to struggle. So jihad is literally an act of struggling. The Prophet Muhammad (peace be upon him) said that the greatest jihad is to struggle with the insidious suggestions of one's own soul. Thus jihad primarily refers to the inner struggle of being a person of virtue and submission to God in all aspects of life.

13   Secondarily, jihad refers to struggle against injustice. Islam, like many other religions, allows for armed self-defense, or retribution against tyranny, exploitation, and oppression. The Glorious Qur'an says: "And why should ye not fight in the cause of God and of those who, being weak, are ill-treated (and oppressed)? Men, women, and children, whose cry is: 'Our Lord! Rescue us from this town, whose people are oppressors; and raise for us from thee one who will protect; and raise for us from thee one who will help!'" [Al-Qur'an 4:75]

14   Thus Islam enjoins upon its believers to strive utmost, in purifying themselves, as well as in establishing peace and justice in the society. Muslims can never be at rest when they see injustice and oppression around them.

15   Martin Luther King, Jr., said: "We will have to repent in this generation not merely for the hateful words and actions of the bad people but for the appalling silence of the good people."

16   Islam enjoins upon all Muslims to work actively to maintain the balance in which God created everything. However, regardless of how legitimate the cause may be, the Glorious Qur'an never condones the killing of innocent people. Terrorizing the civilian population can never be termed as jihad and can never be reconciled with the teachings of Islam.

History of Tolerance

17   Even Western scholars have repudiated the myth of Muslims coercing others to convert. The great historian De Lacy O'Leary wrote: "History makes it clear, however, that the legend of fanatical Muslims, sweeping through the world

---
[1] Narrated in the collection of traditions of Abu Dawud.
[2] Narrated in the Musnad of Imam Ibn Hanbal.

and forcing Islam at the point of sword upon conquered races, is one of the most fantastically absurd myths that historians have ever repeated."[3]

18   Muslims ruled Spain for roughly 800 years. During this time, and up until they were finally forced out, the non-Muslims there were alive and flourishing. Additionally, Christian and Jewish minorities have survived in the Muslim lands of the Middle East for centuries. Countries such as Egypt, Morocco, Palestine, Lebanon, Syria, and Jordan all have significant Christian and/or Jewish populations.

19   This is not surprising to a Muslim, for his faith prohibits him from forcing others to see his point of view. The Glorious Qur'an says: "Let there be no compulsion in religion: Truth stands out clear from Error: whoever rejects evil and believes in God hath grasped the most trustworthy hand-hold, that never breaks. And God heareth and knoweth all things." [Al-Qur'an 2:256]

Islam-The Great Unifier

20   Far from being a militant dogma, Islam is a way of life that transcends race and ethnicity. The Glorious Qur'an repeatedly reminds us of our common origin: "O mankind! We created you from a single pair—male and female—and made you into nations and tribes, that ye may know each other, not that ye may despise each other. Verily, the most honored of you in the sight of God is he who is the most righteous of you. And God has full knowledge and is well acquainted with all things." [Al-Qur'an 49:13]

21   Thus, it is the universality of its teachings that makes Islam the fastest growing religion in the world. In a world full of conflicts and deep schisms between human beings, a world that is threatened with terrorism perpetrated by individuals and states, Islam is a beacon of light that offers hope for the future.

- **Vocabulary**

    distinctive (1)   manipulation (1)   pervasive (2)
    indiscriminate (2)   perpetrated (3)   expend (3)
    revulsion (3)   consolidate (3)   insidious (3)
    sanctions (3)   propounds (5)   enjoins (10)
    verily (20)   universality (21)

- **The Facts**

1. What is the definition of *terrorism* as interpreted by the author? How would you define this term?
2. What does the Koran (Qur'an) declare about killing? What irony does this declaration reveal? Is this irony limited to the Muslim world?

---
[3]*Islam at Crossroads*, London, 1923, page 8.

3. What is the origin of *jihad*? What is its twofold meaning? Why does the author claim that the term has been misunderstood and abused by Westerners?
4. According to the author, what is Islam's view of Muslims forcing their religion on others? Does this view differ from the view of Christianity or other religions?
5. Why, according to this essay, is Islam the fastest-growing religion in the world? What special factors help promote the spread of Islam? Do you consider it a religion worth adopting? Why or why not?

● The Strategies

1. What is the author's thesis, and where is it best stated? Do you think the author has developed his thesis adequately? Support your answer with details from the essay. What major problem, if any, does the essay call out?
2. How does the author attempt to make his essay appealing to readers with a scholarly bent? Does his strategy work? Boost your answer with evidence from the essay.
3. What is the purpose of the questions posed in paragraph 5? How would you answer these questions?
4. What do the subheadings add to the essay? Would the essay be better or worse if they were eliminated?
5. How effective is the parenthetical documentation of the Koran and the parenthetical numbering of footnotes?

● The Issues

1. Has Abdullah Momin's essay in any way changed your mind about terrorism in the world? If yes, state how; if no, state why not.
2. Why does the author consider our view of terrorism too narrow? Do you agree with his assessment? Do you agree that politicians and heads of state can also be terrorists? Give examples to support your point of view.
3. The Koran states that taking human life is justified only when it helps the cause of justice and law. In your view, when is a society justified in taking human life? Give examples when possible.
4. During war, what distinction, if any, do you make between combatants and non-combatants? How should the non-combatants be treated? How should combatants be treated once they have been captured? Why do you think the Koran dictates that neither monks in a monastery nor people praying should be killed in war?
5. Do you see any difference between Muslims and Christians in the matter of forcing their religion on others? Have you had any personal experience with any group—religious or secular—trying to force their way of thinking on you? How do you react to the thought of being forced to champion a certain belief? What, if any, difference do you see between actions that are compulsory and actions that are forced on you?

- **Suggestions for Writing**
  1. Using the Internet and other sources, write an essay on the popular impressions and stereotypes people have of Islam. Suggest how they came by these views.
  2. Write an essay in which you praise those aspects of the Koran that, if followed sincerely, would create a noble, peaceful, caring society.

"Postscript" to Inside the Kingdom: My Life in Saudi Arabia

CARMEN BIN LADEN

Carmen bin Laden (b. 1955) was the sister-in-law of Osama bin Laden, the most wanted terrorist in today's world. Born in Switzerland to a Swiss father and Persian mother, she received international attention when she published her autobiography *Inside the Kingdom,* in which she tells how she fell in love with the rich Yeslam bin Laden, leaving her life in Geneva, Switzerland, to live among the bin Ladens in Jeddah, Saudi Arabia. She traces her growing resentment toward what she considers one of the world's most powerful, secretive, and repressive countries. In order to save her daughters from the fate of other Arabic women, she eventually divorced Yeslam and moved back to Geneva, where she lives with her daughters. Both she and her husband were educated in the United States, a country Carmen loves and admires. The book was originally written for Europeans in French, German, Dutch, Italian, and Spanish.

The essay that follows was written years after Carmen bin Laden experienced her life as a member of the bin Laden family; however, the memories never faded, and she was determined that her own three daughters would live in a free country. For a full account of a wealthy woman's life in a fundamentalist Muslim world, read Carmen bin Laden's shocking autobiography Inside the Kingdom *(2005).*

• • •

1   Three and a half years have gone by since the tragic and dreadful events of September 11, 2001, when so many innocent lives were lost. For the victims' families and loved ones the acute sense of loss and pain continues. My heart goes out to them and I only hope that in some way the passing of time can alleviate their suffering.

2   My daughters live with a daily reminder of that day, for their name has become synonymous with it. Even if one day they marry, their presence will always provoke an echo of hushed whispers and raised eyebrows. If you're born a Bin Ladin, you'll always be a Bin Ladin[*]—I doubt the stigma will ever go away.

---

[*]*Editor's note:* "bin Laden" and "bin Ladin" are both correct spellings of the name.

Many Muslim women are forced to live under suffocating anonynity.

Wafah, Najia, and Noor have been raised with the taste of freedom—with the ability to live, to function, and to make decisions for themselves, believing that their willpower and actions will guide their successes or failures. As free Western women they should be able to be the masters of their own destiny, and yet, after years of struggle to obtain their freedom, my girls are trapped in the prison of their name.

3   In my daily life and my travels with my girls since 9/11, I have witnessed this often. Strolling down Fifth Avenue in Manhattan, Noor, now 17, stopped me, suddenly taken aback. "Mom, what would all these people think of me if they knew my name?" she asked. I realized that she will ask herself that question all her life. The difficulty—the challenge—that my children now face is enormous, making me wonder if they will ever be able to use their intellectual and artistic gifts to pursue their goals and dreams. My wish is that people will understand their burden, and judge them solely on the basis of their talents and abilities.

4   With *Inside the Kingdom*, I had hoped to lighten that burden. I had hoped that by being honest about our story and our struggle to gain freedom I could erase any suspicions about where our loyalties lie. And indeed, as we meet people in America who have read my book, or seen me in interviews, we find ourselves overwhelmed by their warmth and generosity, their genuine understanding and fellowship, and their ability to go beyond the obstacle of our name. Even just blocks away from the awful physical reminder of the attacks on the Manhattan landscape, it seems that the people we meet truly welcome us.

Knowing the greatness of America and the fairness of its people—their willingness to question facts, their ability to perceive and respect individuals, their empathy and warmth—I can say that I am not surprised. I had always known, deep down, that people from the "land of the free" would understand our inextricable dilemma. But I am moved by my daughters' surprise, and I take this opportunity to say that we will always be immensely grateful for this understanding.

5   So many people have come up to me in the street to tell me how brave I have been and how much they admire me. I find myself completely at a loss to respond. I don't see myself as brave. I am a woman who carried out my duty and responsibility as a mother. I defended my children, and I defended our principles, our love of freedom. True courage belongs to women like those who set up clandestine classrooms in Afghanistan so they could teach little girls to read and write in spite of the very real danger that the Taliban authorities would find them and have them whipped and imprisoned, or worse. That is my standard of courage.

6   *Inside the Kingdom* was also my explanation, to my daughters and to the world, of what I perceived in my years of living in Saudi Arabia. I expected questions, even criticisms, about those views. I never imagined that my personal story, and my long struggle to keep my daughters, would give rise to such interest and so many questions. Not a week passes by without my receiving kind letters of sympathy and understanding, all of them moving, and each of them touching my heart. One lady wrote to me, "You made me cry, you made me laugh, and above all, you made me think," I could not have dreamed of a more valuable prize. This flood of warmth has reinforced my respect for the American spirit. I also received letters that echoed my sad experience. I have always been aware of the situation of mothers, less fortunate than I, whose children are trapped in Saudi Arabia, and wondered how I could help. Now I have decided to create an association, to join our forces and to bring their plight to the attention of the general public.

7   After years of living with the constant, chilling fear that I might lose my children, I won the most important personal battle: legal custody. And now I am determined not to be dismissed like a repudiated Saudi wife. The divorce procedure in Geneva courts, which has lasted for more than ten years, has been characterized by misleading statements and outright lies. With the habitual Saudi disdain for judicial systems other than their own, officials of the Bin Laden Organization have refused to appear before the Swiss court. In Yeslam's long effort to hide the vast extent of his wealth, legal requests for evidence from the Saudi Arabian authorities were returned unanswered, or with misleading information. So I found myself obliged to begin a private investigation into the holdings of my husband and the Bin Laden family.

8   The six-year-long investigation that I undertook led me to the discovery of more than a hundred companies many of them offshore. Since 9/11, some of those companies have been closed down. In response to the many unanswered questions and the gravity of the subject matter, I am currently working on a book that will throw unprecedented new light on the secret business of the Bin Laden empire.

9   Generally, as I reflect on my years in Saudi Arabia and my current life in Europe, it seems to me that we are experiencing a clash of cultures between our Western ideals and the values and growing might of Islamic fundamentalism. Fundamentalists have always existed. Thirty years ago, the places they come from started to accumulate the potent wealth of petrodollars. Silently, unnoticed by the West, they began distributing their riches through charities, Koranic schools, mosques, and religious institutions, and their power to influence others began to swell. In 1975 only one country's legal system was based on the Islamic Sharia religious code:** Saudi Arabia. Since then, Iran, Sudan and other countries have adopted Sharia too, and most Muslim countries around the world face insistent demands from powerful—often Saudi-funded—fundamentalist groups, that they, too, establish this harsh, medieval code.

10   The fundamentalists' efforts to impose their values on others are not limited to Muslim countries. I see the signs everywhere. Perhaps because of my background, I am more sensitive to them, or more vigilant. In Canada, I am told, Islamic tribunals in cities such as Toronto seek to regulate divorce, custody, and inheritance issues in the Muslim community—and this is tolerated, under the Arbitration Act of the province of Ontario. This troubles me. In France, some public swimming pools have instituted women-only hours. Throughout Europe, Islamic authorities influence Muslim children to go to school in veils. Girls are deprived of the pleasure of sports, hindered by their veils and cumbersome clothing, and they submit to the strictest form of Islam without speaking out or questioning anything. I find this intolerable. On November 2, 2004, a fanatical fundamentalist assassinated the Dutch filmmaker Theo van Gogh as he strolled through the streets of Amsterdam because he had photographed verses from the Koran printed on women's bodies. I can understand that those images might have shocked some people, but Van Gogh paid with his life for exercising his right to free speech in a democracy. That frightens me.

11   I frequently find myself in situations that illuminate the unbridgeable gulf between our societies. A few months ago, I was a guest speaker at the Oxford Union debating society. After dinner, the cook asked to speak with me. I listened as he told me that I was giving the West a false picture of Islam. He said he had lived in Britain for years, and had become British. He was a practicing Muslim, and he was steeped in both cultures. So I asked him if a practicing Muslim could dissociate the Sharia religious law from his faith in Islam. "Absolutely not," he replied. "Those are the laws of God."

12   So, I asked, "In today's world, we should cut off the hands of thieves?"

13   "That is God's law," he replied, "and it is a deterrent."

14   He had just made my point for me, and I told him so. He had lived for many years in England and he was British, but his archaic, brutal concept of justice and law ran much deeper than that. I knew better than to argue with

---

**Editor's note:* The Sharia is the body of Islamic law that involves strict rules, such as banning alcohol, fasting during Ramadan, praying daily, and minimizing the education of women and their access to the work force.

him; there was no way I could reconcile the complete incompatibility—the clash of thought—that lay between us.

15   This is a small example of a larger issue, and one that is growing in importance. For years, the West didn't see it coming, but now, surely, we must, for it involves our society too. It has become impossible for fundamentalist Muslims to separate the Sharia code from their religious beliefs. For them it simply cannot be done, for the Sharia is an indissociable part of their religion. Any alternative point of view is unacceptable for these zealots, which is why democracy as we know it in the West may not be able to exist in the Muslim world. A fundamentalist cannot allow the ideas that he sees as his religious law to be subjected to scrutiny and debate.

16   In the West, our laws can be reviewed and changed to adapt to our modern world. An unjust and outdated law is questioned. It is noticed, resented, and fought about, sometimes bitterly. Ours is not a perfect society, but it has the strength and flexibility to examine itself and change. We look forward and we seek to improve our laws and our society. To Islamic fundamentalists, Sharia law is immutable. All society must be guided by the way the original community of Muslims in the seventh century lived and thought. Therefore everyone looks backward.

17   What I saw in Saudi Arabia was a culture that refused to evolve. After the tragedy of 9/11, Americans began to ask why they should be so hated. I think the issue goes deeper than Osama Bin Laden's hatred of America. I think he has a larger plan: to propagate what he and many others like him see as the "pure" form of Islam, and to establish it in the Muslim world and beyond, wherever he can.

18   Think of this: There are 1.2 billion Muslims in the world. Not all of them, by any means, are fanatics, and I do not mean to suggest that they are. But even assuming only ten percent of Muslims follow the strongest, most conservative precepts of Islam, that is 120 million people. Of that number, surely no more than ten percent are extremists. But that means 12 million people have been ideologically conditioned to impose their conservative conception of Islam on others. And perhaps ten percent of those extremists are so fanatical that they are prepared to die for their beliefs (because dying for them will earn them eternal paradise). This means that scattered all over the world, a shadow army more than one million people strong is primed to attack Western values and Western culture.

19   The de facto spearhead of this shadow army is my former brother-in-law, Osama Bin Laden. To those who long to obey his every whim, Osama is a hero; to the less zealous, he remains a charismatic figure of a good Muslim.

20   Certain of his popularity among the faithful, Osama Bin Laden had the arrogance to release a video four days before the US presidential election. He confirmed that he had masterminded the 9/11 attacks, and blamed his barbaric action on American policy. He even had the nerve to advise Americans on "the best way to avoid another tragedy." He compared the American government to "a crocodile attacking a helpless child" and threatened to "bleed America." I was outraged. He dared to offend the victims' families by calling the attack that he instigated a "tragedy." But if he considered it tragic, then why did he do it? He admitted that he had ordered the violence, then acted as if it

were someone else's fault—the fault of the victim. He never questioned the rightness of what he did, and showed no remorse for the people he murdered. I could only shake with rage.

21   Osama Bin Laden's attacks are not limited to America. On the morning of March 11, 2004, four bombs exploded on three crowded commuter trains in Spain's capital city of Madrid. At least 173 people were killed, and more than 400 were wounded. This horrible, heartless attack on innocent people heading to work bore the sign of Osama Bin Laden's twisted thinking. Like the others who share his views, he will stop at nothing.

22   Today the fundamentalists are more convinced than ever that they hold the real truth of Islam, and that it is their duty to show their fellow Muslims the true path. I say this with regret: I am convinced that their position won't change any time soon. I have also come to believe that you cannot change a country from the outside. The change must come from within.

23   Will Saudi women, for example, ever *want* the freedoms that Western women fought so hard to get? To overturn the laws in Saudi Arabia that deny women certain basic human rights, the women there would have to *want* freedom. They would have to fight for it. But in my years living among them, I saw no desire in Saudi Arabian women to change their situation.

24   In the twenty-first century, women everywhere should have the freedom to choose how they live their lives. In Saudi Arabia, it seems to me, most women would recoil at the idea of giving their daughters our kind of freedom. They would not want them to learn openness, equality, freedom of thought, or anything that might lead them to question their culture. Most Saudi women don't see the restrictions imposed on them as a repression of their personality. Many of them actually *choose* to remain under the guardianship of men, because they see it as protection. They embrace it, and they perpetuate it. They don't see the bars of the cages they are making for themselves and their children.

25   In Saudi Arabia, the deep-rooted and basic tenets of society are *never* questioned, for anything that is fundamental to Saudi society is based on religion, and religion cannot be doubted. Even the liberal, dissident Saudis—and there are some, both male and female—oppose only details. They demand only practical and convenient changes, such as the right to drive a car. They criticize aspects of the al-Saud regime: that it is corrupt, bloated, parasitical, unworthy in some way. But the real problems in Saudi Arabia go so much deeper. No government arising in that country today would be able to forgo the deep beliefs of Wahabi Islam.

26   We are thus at an impasse: our world, and theirs. They cannot change, and we must not. We should not allow them to use our tolerance to impose their intolerance on us. Today fundamentalists have the power to affect us in places they were previously unable to reach. They can strike us wherever they please. And I fear that this will continue, now and for as long as the powerful families of the oil kingdoms continue to feel it is either their moral duty or it is just politically useful for them to spend hundreds of millions of dollars to spread their beliefs.

27   As a young woman, I was naïvely confident that freedom would come soon to Saudi Arabia. Now I am no longer so sure. Because of my struggle for

my daughters. I have thought so much about life in Saudi Arabia, about what I know of the characteristics of that society. And I ask myself of the hardest question: How can we overcome such a violent clash of cultures?

● Vocabulary

synonymous (2)	provoke (2)	stigma (2)
fellowship (4)	inextricable (4)	dilemma (4)
clandestine (5)	repudiated (7)	disdain (7)
gravity (8)	unprecedented (8)	vigilant (10)
tribunals (10)	illuminate (11)	dissociate (11)
deterrent (13)	archaic (14)	reconcile (14)
indissociable (15)	zealots (15)	scrutiny (15)
immutable (16)	propagate (17)	primed (18)
de facto (19)	spearhead (19)	charismatic (19)
recoil (24)	perpetuate (24)	tenets (25)
parasitical (25)		

● The Facts

1. What fear concerning her daughters' name plagued the writer and drove her to write a book about life in Saudi Arabia? Do you believe the fear is warranted? Give reasons for your answer.
2. What standard of bravery does the author use to label a woman "brave"? Does she consider herself brave when measured by that standard? Why or why not?
3. According to Carmen bin Laden, what is the most important personal battle she won? Why do you think this battle was so important? What similar battles do divorced couples face in the United States? Cite examples of the problems confronted.
4. According to the author, what circumstance supported the Muslim fundamentalists in their urge to spread the conservative Muslim religion to all parts of the world?
5. According to the author, what is Osama bin Laden's ultimate plan? What is your answer to this plan?

● The Strategies

1. What does the title "Postscript" mean with respect to the author's autobiographical work titled *Inside the Kingdom: My Life in Saudi Arabia*? What is the opposite of a "Postscript"?
2. What is the topic sentence of paragraph 10? How does the author support it? What rhetorical mode does she use? How effective is she?
3. What is the purpose of citing the author's experience at the Oxford Union debating society? How does this experience relate to the author's overall thesis?
4. What is the purpose of quoting population statistics in paragraph 18? Do these statistics add useful substance or useless clutter to the essay? Give reasons for your answer.

5. What paradox does the author use in paragraph 20? How effective is it? What does it do to the image of Osama bin Laden? What does being Osama bin Laden's sister-in-law do to the author's argument? Does it help or detract?

The Issues

1. What are the beliefs that aggravate the clash of ideas between Muslim fundamentalism and Western liberalism as described by Carmen bin Laden? What concerns you most about this clash?
2. What is your view of the Muslim punishment code based on "an eye for an eye and a tooth for a tooth"? Do you think it would be effective to cut off the hands of thieves or to kill women caught in adultery? How does the American punishment code differ from that of fundamentalist Islam?
3. What is unhealthy about a country like Saudi Arabia that refuses to evolve? What does the author like about the Western system of laws as opposed to Saudi Arabia's system? Do you agree or disagree with her view? Give reasons for your answer.
4. In paragraph 18, the author indicates that right now a "shadow army" of more than one million people stands ready and eager to attack Western values and culture. Who are the soldiers in this "shadow army"? Do you believe this army exists? If it does, how can we resist it? If it does not, then how should we answer the author's claim?
5. According to the author, what is the only way to change a society that has been led astray in its definition of truth? Do you agree with the author? If so, what test should your fellow students use for finding truth, and how would you go about changing the direction of society? If you do not believe in the author's view of the only way change can occur, then state what stratagem you think might work.

Suggestions for Writing

1. Write a letter to Carmen bin Laden in which you thank her for her candid insights into the world of fundamentalist Islam. Of course, you will not send this letter, but it could stimulate your reflections on inflexible societies and heighten your awareness of how important it is to live in a free society.
2. Write an essay in which you describe certain features of our society that might appall people from more conservative cultures. Consider the violence and sexual explicitness of our films, the total lack of taste in some of the lyrics of our music and its thudding sounds, and the crass materialism we exhibit in the cars we drive and the money we spend on ourselves. You might even compare the veiled look of the Saudi Arabian young women with the clothes that allow Western girls to bare just about every inch of their bodies.

Stumped by deadwood? Exit on page 686, at the **Editing Booth!**

Punctuation Workshop
The Period (.)

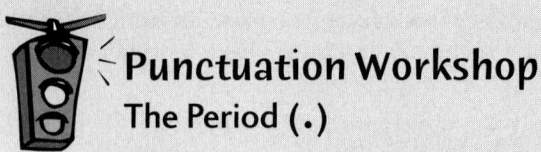

These are the rules for using periods:

1. **Put a period at the end of a sentence:**

    WRONG: We made a dash for the bus we almost missed it. (This is a run-on sentence.)
    RIGHT: We made a dash for the bus. We almost missed it.
    WRONG: I never knew my grandfather, he died when I was three years old. (This is called a comma splice.)
    RIGHT: I never knew my grandfather. He died when I was three years old.

2. **Put a period after most abbreviations:**

Mr.	A.D.	Dr.	Wed.	sq. ft.
Ms.	etc.	Jan.	p.m.	lbs.

    EXCEPTIONS: mph, FM, TV, VCR, NBC, NATO, IRS, DMV

    Dictionaries sometimes give you an option: U.S.A. or USA. When in doubt, consult your dictionary or instructor.

STUDENT CORNER

The Right Moves against Terrorism
Sion Arakelian, Glendale Community College

Terrorism is nothing new to the world. But it is relatively new to us who live in the United States. The 9/11 attack of 2001 is still fresh enough in our memories to draw strong opinions from almost anyone you ask. With the frequent emphasis on security, particularly airport security, we're reminded almost daily that the United States is now in the front lines of the battle against terrorism. Uppermost in everyone's mind is how we're doing and whether what we're doing is right. I believe firmly that the United States must continue its aggressive leadership in the war against terrorism.

As an emigrant from Iran, I know that it is my tendency to hold conservative political views. Many newly arrived immigrants often find themselves siding with the status quo, if only because they also want a piece of the pie. Yet if I look dispassionately on the policies of the government and the steps we're taking to combat terrorism to date, I cannot help but be encouraged and to think that we're on the right road.

The first thing we did right was to proclaim from the beginning that anyone or any country who harbors terrorists we would regard as terrorists themselves. This is an entirely sensible point of view. What our doctrine says is that you do not have to actually throw the bomb yourself to be guilty in a bombing. If you bought the bomb, if you contributed to those who actually acquired the bomb, if you gave comfort and safe haven to the bombers or to those who made the bomb or bought the bomb, you were, in our eyes, equally guilty of an act of terrorism as the bombers themselves. This point of view draws a line in the sand. On one side stand the terrorists and their abettors; on the other side stand the free world and the United Nations. There can be no fudging about which side a country belongs to. You're either for terrorism or against terrorism.

The second thing we did right was taking the war to the enemy, which strangely enough, was of our own creation. As far back as 1978, before the Russians occupied Afghanistan, the United States was secretly sending arms to the rebel forces in Afghanistan known as the mujahedeen. This practice, in turn, created a war that lasted ten years between the Russians and the people of Afghanistan. At the end of this war, the fundamentalists, whom the United States supported, took power and established their own regime. One of their first acts was to establish the rule of the harshest Islamic fundamentalism that removed women from the workplace and wrapped them in the chador. Then they turned against their benefactors—us.

When we went into Afghanistan there was a great outcry about how we were doomed to failure. But that, too, turned out to be the right move. Yes, it is true that Afghanistan has always been a wasteland to invaders. Alexander the Great failed in his invasion of 330 B.C. The Arabs tried in 700 A.D. and failed. The British Empire tried in 1838 and 1878, losing 5,000 men in the first attempt and partly succeeding in the second. Russia sent 115,000 troops in 1979, along with armor and air support. The campaign was going well until we armed the mujahedeen. But in spite of opposition we faced at home and the gloom of the naysayers, we soon had the Taliban, the Al-Qaida and Osama bin Laden on the run. Modern weaponry and air power proved to be more than a match for rugged terrain and inhospitable climate.

Finally, our next right move was involving the world's great peacekeeping organization—the United Nations—from the outset. This alliance made it clear that the United States was not alone in wanting to keep the world a safe, hospitable place. Having the United Nations cooperate with the United States is important in garnering the support of western nations, and it is also an underlying factor in the scheme of safely yet secretly destroying all terrorist forces. These forces are out there, and the United States, as well as the United Nations, knows that. Knowing exactly what to do and how to cut short any harm it may bring to the rest of the world is one of the key problems right now.

Yes, innocent lives may be sacrificed in the battle against terrorism, but were there not thousands who died that tragic day on September 11? People forget that the lives lost were not only American lives but also lives of other nationalities that pledged their allegiance to the United States by way of citizenship. The issue of human rights is at stake here, and if nothing is done by the United States to ensure the safety and security of its citizens, there will be additional harm caused by terrorist forces all over the world. This great country, whose priority is to ensure that its citizens are free to pursue their own individual goals and desires, makes its case known to the rest of the world that world peace will be in grave jeopardy should terrorism continue to rear its ugly head.

How I Write

I tend to wander and wonder before I print out any words on paper. I can do this kind of pre-writing in any environment—in my car, at the breakfast table, or just anywhere I happen to be. Once I start writing at my computer, I need a quiet place without interruptions so that I can concentrate. Since I am from Iran, and English is my second language, I need to concentrate on my writing, and then I also need to spend time revising, editing, and proofreading.

How I Wrote This Paper

I wrote this paper with the intent of getting the message across that this war must take place and also that the United States must prevail in order to uphold world peace and human rights. I wrote this paper after watching several TV programs whose news pundits offered opinions on the war against terrorism. I also consulted several Web sites that had already formed opinions of why the war was taking place and exactly how it would continue to develop. While many of these Web sites led to opinion pieces, some articles to which I referred contained actual facts as to how the United States has dealt with wars in the past. After researching these articles online, I started to form my own opinions about the war and decided to write my paper in favor of the war against terrorism. I created an outline in which I listed my major ideas. Once I thought about these major ideas, the details occurred to me rapidly so that I could develop my essay.

My Writing Tip

If I were to give advice to anyone interested in writing a similar essay, it would be this: Be sure to hold at least a minimal level of interest in the work you are about to write, because success will be difficult to achieve without it. Also, don't leave the paper until you get a measure of pleasure from reading it to yourself. If you don't like it, probably your reader won't like it either.

● CHAPTER WRITING ASSIGNMENTS

1. Write an essay in which you narrate an incident that proves one of the following:
   a. People are often bigoted.
   b. Having good neighbors is important.
   c. Pets are often astoundingly loyal.
   d. Difficulties can be steppingstones to success.

● WRITING ASSIGNMENTS FOR A SPECIFIC AUDIENCE

1. Write a diary entry, listing chronologically the major events of your day. Treat your diary as a confidential, intimate friend to whom you can trust your innermost feelings.
2. Write to your parents, describing to them your college living quarters.

- **COLLABORATIVE WRITING PROJECT**

  Joining three other students in the class, as a group edit a long paper that one of you wrote in a previous semester and for a different class. Each member of the group should have a copy of the paper on which to scribble editing remarks and criticism. Make at least three passes through the manuscript, giving each member of the group an opportunity not only to edit the paper but also to critique it orally. When you're finished, submit the paper to your instructor and request a grade. Was the grade on the edited paper higher than the paper's original grade?

- **IMAGE GALLERY WRITING ASSIGNMENT.**

  Visit pages 647–649 of our image gallery and study all three images dealing with terrorism. Then choose the image that most appeals to you. Answer the questions and do the writing assignment.

8

Description

ROAD MAP TO DESCRIPTION

What Description Does

A description is a word picture. It is the writer's attempt to capture with words the essence and flavor of a scene, person, or thing. No matter what you've heard to the contrary, a sharply drawn description can be every bit as moving as a picture. Focus and concentration contribute more to a vivid description than either the size of the writer's vocabulary or the heedless splattering of adjectives on a page. Here is an example of what we mean. The author, Charles Reade, in this excerpt from *The Cloister and the Hearth,* is describing a medieval inn partly through the eyes, but mainly through the nose, of a weary traveler:

> In one corner was a travelling family, a large one; thence flowed into the common stock the peculiar sickly smell of neglected brats. Garlic filled up the interstices of the air. And all this with closed window, and intense heat of the central furnace, and the breath of at least forty persons.
> They had just supped.
> Now Gerard, like most artists, had sensitive organs, and the potent effluvia struck dismay into him. But the rain lashed him outside, and the light and the fire tempted him in.
> He could not force his way all at once through the palpable perfumes, but he returned to the light again and again like a singed moth. At last he discovered that the various smells did not entirely mix, no fiend being there to stir them around. Odor of family predominated in two corners; stewed rustic reigned supreme in the center; and garlic in the noisy group by the window. He found, too, by hasty analysis, that of these the garlic described the smallest aerial orbit, and the scent of reeking rustic darted farthest—a flavor as if ancient goats, or the fathers of all foxes, had been drawn through a river, and were here dried by Nebuchadnezzar.

The predominant characteristic of this vivid description is its focus. Instead of trying to give us a sweeping view of the dingy inn, the writer zooms in on how bad it smells. The stink of the inn is the dominant impression of this description, and the writer's every word, image, and metaphor aim only to serve up this stench to our nostrils.

When to Use Description

Next to narration, description is probably the most widely used of all the rhetorical modes. In letters, journal entries, reports, and memos we describe places we have visited, people we have met, and adventures that we have had. Over the course of any given week, it is likely that we have painted a word picture, if not in writing, then certainly in speech.

How to Write a Description

There are some well-known techniques of description that all writers use. We recommend that you practice them in your own writing.

Focus on a Dominant Impression Vivid descriptions invariably focus on a single, dominant impression and unremittingly deliver it. Nothing distracts from the dominant impression; every word and image is devoted to rendering it keener and sharper. By *dominant impression,* we mean a feature of the scene that is characteristic of it. Not all scenes have strikingly characteristic features, and writers must often absorb the atmosphere of a place before they can sum it up in a dominant impression. Some scenes, however, will give off a dominant impression that leaps out at you. For example, a freeway at rush hour is anything but a scene of placidity; usually it is a tangled skein of cars jockeying for position or trying to nose from one lane into another. To describe a freeway scene at rush hour, you should word your dominant impression to take in the antics of the drivers, the fumes of the cars, the background grind and roar of traffic. You might write, as your dominant impression, "The San Diego Freeway at rush hour is a bedlam of traffic noise, choking fumes, and aggressive drivers." Then you would support that dominant impression with specific images and details.

Here is a description of the Spanish night that uses this technique:

<u>The Spanish night is so deep and pompous as quite to browbeat the noisier light of day.</u> The buildings, which always look clear-cut and newly built, become, against the dark stress of evening, brilliantly crisp and more brittle than glass. A long line of white buildings will tower up to threaten you with its proud, wave-like bulwarks. At every corner, behind the dark trees that are deep, still areas of water, there will rise up another of those strutting waves out of the depth. In its turn it will draw up, holding itself to full height before it launches a

leonine assault on your puny presence. Then it will hold itself back from you before the superior strength of the next glittering wave that you meet, as you walk through the brittle moonlight. In this way the slowest progress through a town will be running the gauntlet of a whole pack of hungry shadows.

—Sacheverell Sitwell, *Southern Baroque Art*

The paragraph vividly captures the sights and sensations associated with *nightfall* over a Spanish town. At its core is a single, overwhelming impression of night "so deep and pompous as quite to browbeat the noisier light of day." All of the details in the paragraph support this dominant impression.

The dominant impression of your description should be the heart of the person, place, or scene you are attempting to describe. If you are describing an elderly aunt who is dull, use her dullness as your dominant impression. If you are writing a description of a Christmas shopping scene, word your dominant impression to show the frazzled and weary shoppers, the harried salesclerks, the dazzling Christmas lights.

However, you should not account for every speck in the scene you are describing in your dominant impression. For example, among the streaming throngs in the department store at Christmas, there are bound to be a few souls who are calm and composed and seemingly immune to the shopping frenzy. Because these lucky few are not at all representative of the overall scene, you should leave them out lest they water down the description. Similarly, if your sister is mainly a bundle of nerves, that is how you should paint her on the page, even if you have glimpsed her in rare moments of serenity.

Use Images in Your Descriptions Most of us know the basics of imagery, especially the simile and the metaphor. We know that the simile is an image based on an explicit comparison. For example, in *The King of the Birds,* Flannery O'Connor describes the crest of a peabiddy with this simile: "This looks at first like a bug's antennae and later like the head feathers of an Indian." We also know that the metaphor is an image based on an indirect comparison with no obvious linking word such as "as" or "like" used to cement it. For example, in *Once More to the Lake,* E. B. White uses metaphors to describe a thunderstorm: "Then the kettle drum, then the snare, then the bass drum and cymbals, then crackling light against the dark, and the gods grinning and licking their chops in the hills." This is how a thunderstorm seems to the writer—it makes noises like many drums and flashes wicked lights against the hills that look like gods licking their chops. Even though the writer omits the "like" that might have made the comparison explicit, we still get the picture.

In addition to these basic images, which every writer occasionally uses, there are some hard-won lessons about descriptive imagery that can be imparted. The first is this: Vivid images do not miraculously drip off the pen but are usually the result of the writer reworking the material repeatedly. If nothing original or fresh occurs to you after you've sat at your desk for a scant few minutes trying to write a description, all it means is that you did not sit long enough or work hard enough. Reread what you have written. Try to picture in your mind the person, place, or thing you are struggling to describe. Cut a word here; replace another there; persistently scratch away at what you have written and you'll soon be astonished at how much better it gets.

The second lesson about writing vivid images is summed up in the adage "Less is more." Overdoing a descriptive passage is not only possible, it is very likely. If you are unhappy with a description you have written, instead of stuffing it with more adjectives, try taking some out. Here is an example of a bloated and overdone description, from *Delina Delaney* by Amanda McKittrick Ros. The speaker is trying his utmost to describe his feelings as he says goodbye to his sweetheart:

> I am just in time to hear the toll of a parting bell strike its heavy weight of appalling softness against the weakest fibers of a heart of love, arousing and tickling its dormant action, thrusting the dart of evident separation deeper into its tubes of tenderness, and fanning the flame, already unextinguishable, into volumes of blaze.

This is wretched stuff, of course. One can see the writer huffing and puffing at the pen as she tries desperately to infuse her hero's words with passion. She fails awfully from too much effort.

Appeal to All of Your Reader's Senses Most of us are so unabashedly visual that we are tempted to deliver only looks in our descriptions. There is usually much more to a scene than its looks; you could also write about how it sounds, smells, or feels. The best descriptions draw on all kinds of images and appeal to as many senses as are appropriate. Here is an example from Elspeth Huxley's *The Flame Trees of Thika*. The writer is describing a World War I troop train as it leaves an African station at night carrying soldiers to the front:

> The men began to sing the jingle then that was so popular then—"Marching to Tabora"; and the shouts and cheers, the whistles, the hissing and chugging of the engine, filled the station as a kettle fills with steam. Everything seemed to bubble over; men waved from windows; Dick gave a hunting cry; the red hair of Pioneer Mary flared under a lamp; the guard jumped into his moving van; and we watched the rear light of the last coach vanish, and heard the chugging die away. A plume of sparks, a long coil of dancing fireflies, spread across the black ancient shoulder of the crater Menegai; and gradually the vast digesting dark of Africa swallowed up all traces of that audacious grub, the hurrying train.

This description is a mixture of appeals to our senses of sight and hearing. The men sing and cheer, and the engine chugs and hisses. We see Pioneer

Mary's red hair and the sparks from the train's engine. We are regaled with a clever simile, "filled the station as a kettle fills with steam," and treated to a riveting image, "the vast digesting dark of Africa swallowed up all traces of that audacious grub, the hurrying train." Did the author really just sit down and calmly mine this rich descriptive vein without effort? We do not know, but most likely not. If her experience is at all typical, she hit this mother lode of imagery only after persistent and labored digging.

Warming Up to Write a Description

1. Train yourself to be observant. Withdraw to your room or some other familiar place with a note pad and pencil or your laptop and place yourself at an angle where you have a sweeping view. Jot down or type the details of what the place looks like. After you have absorbed the details, formulate a dominant impression of the place and write it down or type it on your laptop. An example might be, "My room always makes me feel cozy because it is filled with mementos from my childhood." Or, "The Hometown Buffet, a restaurant five blocks away from where I live, is a spot where one can breathe in all kinds of smells, hear all kinds of noises, and observe all kinds of people." Next, write only those details that support the dominant impression.

2. Drive through your town or neighborhood, focusing on eyesores that you think the local authorities should correct. Examples might be a huge refuse bin sitting outside a popular coffee house, withered flowers in a planter at the side of a real estate office, or broken-down cars and car parts littering someone's front yard. Take notes that describe the eyesore with sensory details of sight, sound, smell, and touch.

3. Rewrite these undescriptive and dull sentences to make them vivid. Use figurative language whenever possible.
    a. The convalescent hospital smelled unappetizing.
    b. His face bore many wrinkles, indicating his old age.
    c. The protesters were quite loud and active.
    d. The snow falling on the creek is lovely.

    As an added exercise, complete the following sentences to make them vividly descriptive:
    e. The squirrels chased each other up and down the trees as if. . . .
    f. Jasmine's eyes were so deeply green, they looked like. . . .
    g. The suitcase fell off the rack of our car and crashed on the highway, causing. . . .
    h. A cold wind blew from the north, shaking up the trees and bending their trunks back and forth so that from a distance the aspen grove looked like. . . .

EXAMPLES

The Libido for the Ugly

H. L. MENCKEN

Henry Louis Mencken (1880–1956) was an editor, author, and critic. He began his journalism career at the *Baltimore Morning Herald* and later became editor of the *Baltimore Evening Herald*. From 1906 until his death, he was on the staff of the *Baltimore Sun* (or *Evening Sun*). In 1924, with George Jean Nathan, Mencken founded the *American Mercury* and served as its editor from 1925 to 1933. Mencken's writing was chiefly devoted to lambasting the smug, conventional attitudes of the middle class. Among his numerous works is *The American Language*, a monumental study of the American idiom, first published in 1919.

Few writers have such an eye for colorful detail as the incomparable Mencken, at his best when he's railing against physical ugliness or storming against a tradition he dislikes. In the essay that follows, Mencken turns his literary wrath against the ugliness of the industrial heartland of America in the 1920s.

• • •

1 On a Winter day some years ago, coming out of Pittsburgh on one of the expresses of the Pennsylvania Railroad, I rolled eastward for an hour through the coal and steel towns of Westmoreland county. It was familiar ground; boy and man, I had been through it often before. But somehow I had never quite sensed its appalling desolation. Here was the very heart of industrial America, the center of its most lucrative and characteristic activity, the boast and pride of the richest and grandest nation ever seen on earth—and here was a scene so dreadfully hideous, so intolerably bleak and forlorn that it reduced the whole aspiration of man to a macabre and depressing joke. Here was wealth beyond computation, almost beyond imagination—and here were human habitations so abominable that they would have disgraced a race of alley cats.

2 I am not speaking of mere filth. One expects steel towns to be dirty. What I allude to is the unbroken and agonizing ugliness, the sheer revolting monstrousness, of every house in sight. From East Liberty to Greensburg, a distance of twenty-five miles, there was not one in sight from the train that did not insult and lacerate the eye. Some were so bad, and they were among the most pretentious—churches, stores, warehouses, and the like—that they were downright startling; one blinked before them as one blinks before a man with his face shot away. A few linger in memory, horrible even there: a crazy little church just west of Jeannette, set like a dormer-window on the side of a bare, leprous hill; the headquarters of the Veterans of Foreign Wars at another forlorn town; a steel stadium like a huge rat-trap somewhere further down the line. But most of all I recall the general effect—of hideousness without a break. There was not a single decent house within eye-range from the Pittsburgh

suburbs to the Greensburg yards. There was not one that was not misshapen, and there was not one that was not shabby.

3   The country itself is not uncomely, despite the grime of the endless mills. It is, in form, a narrow river valley, with deep gullies running up into the hills. It is thickly settled, but not noticeably overcrowded. There is still plenty of room for building, even in the larger towns, and there are very few solid blocks. Nearly every house, big and little, has space on all four sides. Obviously, if there were architects of any professional sense or dignity in the region, they would have perfected a chalet to hug the hillsides—a chalet with a high-pitched roof, to throw off the heavy Winter snows, but still essentially a low and clinging building, wider than it was tall. But what have they done? They have taken as their model a brick set on end. This they have converted into a thing of dingy clapboards, with a narrow, low-pitched roof. And the whole they have set upon thin, preposterous brick piers. By the hundreds and thousands these abominable houses cover the bare hillsides, like gravestones in some gigantic and decaying cemetery. On their deep sides they are three, four and even five stories high; on their low sides they bury themselves swinishly in the mud. Not a fifth of them are perpendicular. They lean this way and that, hanging on to their bases precariously. And one and all they are streaked in grime, with dead and eczematous patches of paint peeping through the streaks.

4   Now and then there is a house of brick. But what brick! When it is new it is the color of a fried egg. When it has taken on the patina of the mills it is the color of an egg long past all hope or caring. Was it necessary to adopt that shocking color? No more than it was necessary to set all of the houses on end. Red brick, even in a steel town, ages with some dignity. Let it become downright black, and it is still sightly, especially if its trimmings are of white stone, with soot in the depths and the high spots washed by the rain. But in Westmoreland they prefer that uremic yellow, and so they have the most loathsome towns and villages ever seen by mortal eye.

5   I award this championship only after laborious research and incessant prayer. I have seen, I believe, all of the most unlovely towns of the world; they are all to be found in the United States. I have seen the mill towns of decomposing New England and the desert towns of Utah, Arizona and Texas. I am familiar with the back streets of Newark, Brooklyn and Chicago, and have made scientific explorations to Camden, N.J., and Newport News, Va. Safe in a Pullman, I have whirled through the gloomy, God-forsaken villages of Iowa and Kansas, and the malarious tide-water hamlets of Georgia. I have been to Bridgeport, Conn., and to Los Angeles. But nowhere on this earth, at home or abroad, have I seen anything to compare to the villages that huddle along the line of the Pennsylvania from the Pittsburgh yards to Greensburg. They are incomparable in color, and they are incomparable in design. It is as if some titanic and aberrant genius, uncompromisingly inimical to man, had devoted all the ingenuity of Hell to the making of them. They show grotesqueries of ugliness that, in retrospect, become almost diabolical. One cannot imagine mere human beings concocting such dreadful things, and one can scarcely imagine human beings bearing life in them.

6   Are they so frightful because the valley is full of foreigners—dull, insensate brutes, with no love of beauty in them? Then why didn't these foreigners set up similar abominations in the countries that they came from? You will, in fact, find nothing of the sort in Europe—save perhaps in the more putrid parts of England. There is scarcely an ugly village on the whole Continent. The peasants, however poor, somehow manage to make themselves graceful and charming habitations, even in Spain. But in the American village and small town the pull is always toward ugliness, and in that Westmoreland valley it has been yielded to with an eagerness bordering upon passion. It is incredible that mere ignorance should have achieved such masterpieces of horror.

7   On certain levels of the American race, indeed, there seems to be a positive libido for the ugly, as on other and less Christian levels there is a libido for the beautiful. It is impossible to put down the wallpaper that defaces the average American home of the lower middle class to mere inadvertence, or to the obscene humor of the manufacturers. Such ghastly designs, it must be obvious, give a genuine delight to a certain type of mind. They meet, in some unfathomable way, its obscure and unintelligible demands. They caress it as "The Palms" caresses it, or the art of the movie, or jazz. The taste for them is as enigmatical and yet as common as the taste for dogmatic theology and the poetry of Edgar A. Guest.

8   Thus I suspect (though confessedly without knowing) that the vast majority of the honest folk of Westmoreland county, and especially the 100% Americans among them, actually admire the houses they live in, and are proud of them. For the same money they could get vastly better ones, but they prefer what they have got. Certainly there was no pressure upon the Veterans of Foreign Wars to choose the dreadful edifice that bears their banner, for there are plenty of vacant buildings along the track-side, and some of them are appreciably better. They might, indeed, have built a better one of their own. But they chose that clapboarded horror with their eyes open, and having chosen it, they let it mellow into its present shocking depravity. They like it as it is: beside it, the Parthenon would no doubt offend them. In precisely the same way the authors of the rat-trap stadium that I have mentioned made a deliberate choice. After painfully designing and erecting it, they made it perfect in their own sight by putting a completely impossible pent-house, painted a staring yellow, on top of it. The effect is that of a fat woman with a black eye. It is that of a Presbyterian grinning. But they like it.

9   Here is something that the psychologists have so far neglected: the love of ugliness for its own sake, the lust to make the world intolerable. Its habitat is the United States. Out of the melting pot emerges a race which hates beauty as it hates truth. The etiology of this madness deserves a great deal more study than it has got. There must be causes behind it; it arises and flourishes in obedience to biological laws, and not as a mere act of God. What, precisely, are the terms of those laws? And why do they run stronger in America than elsewhere? Let some honest Privat Dozent in pathological sociology apply himself to the problem.

● Vocabulary

lucrative (1)	aspiration (1)	macabre (1)
lacerate (2)	dormer-window (2)	clapboards (3)
eczematous (3)	patina (4)	uremic (4)
malarious (5)	aberrant (5)	inimical (5)
grotesqueries (5)	insensate (6)	libido (7)
inadvertence (7)	enigmatical (7)	dogmatic (7)
Parthenon (8)	etiology (9)	Privat Dozent (9)
pathological (9)		

● The Facts

1. What area of the country does this essay describe?
2. What is the principal occupation of the region?
3. Mencken not only criticizes the architecture of the region, he also suggests an alternative. What sort of architecture does he think is suited to this region?
4. On what does Mencken blame the ugliness he describes?
5. What are Mencken's views of the villages in Europe? In his view, how do they compare with American towns?

● The Strategies

1. A good description focuses on and develops a dominant impression. Examine the second paragraph. What is the dominant impression here?
2. Examine the third paragraph. What dominant impression does Mencken focus on in his description of the buildings?
3. What aspect of the ugliness does paragraph 4 deal with?
4. "I have seen, I believe, all of the most unlovely towns of the world; they are all to be found in the United States." Why does he say unlovely rather than ugly? Which is more effective? Why?
5. "And one and all they are streaked in grime, with dead and eczematous patches of paint peeping through the streaks." What comparison is implied in this metaphor?

● The Issues

1. One of the most vigilant civic groups in the United States today is the environmentalists—men and women determined to preserve historical buildings, wilderness areas, seacoasts, and public parks. What importance do you attribute to the efforts of these people? What do you think would happen if they no longer cared?
2. Mencken seems to feel that although architectural ugliness on any scale is lamentable, it is especially insulting when the edifice is pretentious. Do you agree with Mencken's view? Why or why not?
3. What stretch of highway in the United States is charmingly beautiful and stands in total contrast to Mencken's description of the houses in Westmoreland County? Describe this stretch in detail, focusing on architectural characteristics.

4. Do you agree with Mencken that Americans are psychologically obsessed with ugliness? If you agree, try to find reasons for this obsession. If you disagree, prove that Mencken is wrong by citing instances in which typical Americans have promoted beauty and good taste.

5. If you were to oversee a development of beautiful homes, what aesthetic requirements would you insist on? Describe the development in concrete terms.

Suggestions for Writing

1. Write an essay describing the town or city where you live.
2. Write an analysis of Mencken's diction in this essay, paying particular attention to his use of adjectives.

Hell

James Joyce

James Joyce (1882–1941) is considered by many to be among the most significant novelists of the twentieth century. He was born in Dublin, Ireland, and educated at University College, Dublin. Joyce, a writer who pushed language to its outer limit of comprehensibility, wrote poetry, short stories, and novels. His major novels include *A Portrait of the Artist as a Young Man* (1916), *Ulysses* (written between 1914 and 1921 and published in the United States in 1933), and *Finnegan's Wake* (1939).

Joyce, in this selection from A Portrait of the Artist as a Young Man, *shows us the wreathing fires of hell and persuades us to smell its stench of brimstone and sin. The description that follows is so graphic, so detailed, and so filled with such shuddering imagery, that we almost believe that someone has returned from this dreadful place to tell the tale.*

• • •

1 Hell is a strait and dark and foulsmelling prison, an abode of demons and lost souls, filled with fire and smoke. The straitness of this prisonhouse is expressly designed by God to punish those who refused to be bound by His laws. In earthly prisons the poor captive has at least some liberty of movement, were it only within the four walls of his cell or in the gloomy yard of his prison. Not so in hell. There, by reason of the great number of the damned, the prisoners are heaped together in their awful prison, the walls of which are said to be four thousand miles thick: and the damned are so utterly bound and helpless that, as a blessed saint, saint Anselm, writes in his book on similitudes, they are not even able to remove from the eye a worm that gnaws it.

2 —They lie in exterior darkness. For, remember, the fire of hell gives forth no light. As, at the command of God, the fire of the Babylonian furnace lost its heat but not its light so, at the command of God, the fire of hell,

while retaining the intensity of its heat, burns eternally in darkness. It is a never-ending storm of darkness, dark flames and dark smoke of burning brimstone, amid which the bodies are heaped one upon another without even a glimpse of air. Of all the plagues with which the land of the Pharaohs was smitten one plague alone, that of darkness, was called horrible. What name, then, shall we give to the darkness of hell which is to last not for three days alone but for all eternity?

3 —The horror of this strait and dark prison is increased by its awful stench. All the filth of the world, all the offal and scum of the world, we are told, shall run there as to a vast reeking sewer when the terrible conflagration of the last day has purged the world. The brimstone too which burns there in such prodigious quantity fills all hell with its intolerable stench; and the bodies of the damned themselves exhale such a pestilential odour that as saint Bonaventure says, one of them alone would suffice to infect the whole world. The very air of this world, that pure element, becomes foul and unbreathable when it has been long enclosed. Consider then what must be the foulness of the air of hell. Imagine some foul and putrid corpse that has lain rotting and decomposing in the grave, a jellylike mass of liquid corruption. Imagine such a corpse a prey to flames, devoured by the fire of burning brimstone and giving off dense choking fumes of nauseous loathsome decomposition. And then imagine this sickening stench, multiplied a millionfold and a millionfold again from the millions upon millions of fetid carcasses massed together in the reeking darkness, a huge and rotting human fungus. Imagine all this and you will have some idea of the horror of the stench of hell.

4 —But this stench is not, horrible though it is, the greatest physical torment to which the damned are subjected. The torment of fire is the greatest torment to which the tyrant has ever subjected his fellow creatures. Place your finger for a moment in the flame of a candle and you will feel the pain of fire. But our earthly fire was created by God for the benefit of man, to maintain in him the spark of life and to help him in the useful arts, whereas the fire of hell is of another quality and was created by God to torture and punish the unrepentant sinner. Our earthly fire also consumes more or less rapidly according as the object which it attacks is more or less combustible so that human ingenuity has even succeeded in inventing chemical preparations to check or frustrate its action. But the sulphurous brimstone which burns in hell is a substance which is specially designed to burn forever and for ever with unspeakable fury. Moreover our earthly fire destroys at the same time as it burns so that the more intense it is the shorter is its duration: but the fire of hell has this property that it preserves that which it burns and though it rages with incredible intensity it rages for ever.

5 —Our earthly fire again, no matter how fierce or widespread it may be, is always of a limited extent: but the lake of fire in hell is boundless, shoreless and bottomless. It is on record that the devil himself, when asked the question by a certain soldier, was obliged to confess that if a whole mountain were thrown into the burning ocean of hell it would be burned up in an instant like

a piece of wax. And this terrible fire will not afflict the bodies of the damned only from without but each lost soul will be a hell unto itself, the boundless fire raging in its very vitals. O, how terrible is the lot of those wretched beings! The blood seethes and boils in the veins, the brains are boiling in the skull, the heart in the breast glowing and bursting, the bowels a redhot mass of burning pulp, the tender eyes flaming like molten balls.

6   —And yet what I have said as to the strength and quality and boundlessness of this fire is as nothing when compared to its intensity, an intensity which it has as being the instrument chosen by divine design for the punishment of soul and body alike. It is a fire which proceeds directly from the ire of God, working not of its own activity but as an instrument of divine vengeance. As the waters of baptism cleanse the soul with the body so do the fires of punishment torture the spirit with the flesh. Every sense of the flesh is tortured and every faculty of the soul therewith: the eyes with impenetrable utter darkness, the nose with noisome odours, the ears with yells and howls and execrations, the taste with foul matter, leprous corruption, nameless suffocating filth, the touch with redhot goads and spikes, with cruel tongues of flame. And through the several torments of the senses the immortal soul is tortured eternally in its very essence amid the leagues upon leagues of glowing fires kindled in the abyss by the offended majesty of the Omnipotent God and fanned into everlasting and ever increasing fury by the breath of the anger of the Godhead.

7   Consider finally that the torment of this infernal prison is increased by the company of the damned themselves. Evil company on earth is so noxious that even the plants, as if by instinct, withdraw from the company of whatsoever is deadly or hurtful to them. In hell all laws are overturned: there is no thought of family or country, of ties, of relationships. The damned howl and scream at one another, their torture and rage intensified by the presence of beings tortured and raging like themselves. All sense of humanity is forgotten. The yells of the suffering sinners fill the remotest corners of the vast abyss. The mouths of the damned are full of blasphemies against God and of hatred for their fellow sufferers and of curses against those souls which were their accomplices in sin. In olden times it was the custom to punish the parricide, the man who had raised his murderous hand against his father, by casting him into the depths of the sea in a sack in which were placed a cock, a monkey and a serpent. The intention of those lawgivers who framed such a law, which seems cruel in our times, was to punish the criminal by the company of hateful and hurtful beasts. But what is the fury of those dumb beasts compared with the fury of execration which bursts from the parched lips and aching throats of the damned in hell when they behold in their companions in misery those who aided and abetted them in sin, those whose words sowed the first seeds of evil thinking and evil living in their minds, those whose immodest suggestions led them on to sin, those whose eyes tempted and allured them from the path of virtue. They turn upon those accomplices and upbraid them and curse them. But they are helpless and hopeless: it is too late now for repentance.

Vocabulary

strait (1)	similitudes (1)	offal (3)
conflagration (3)	prodigious (3)	pestilential (3)
fetid (3)	noisome (6)	execrations (6)
parricide (7)	allured (7)	upbraid (7)

The Facts

1. How thick are the walls of hell?
2. What peculiar characteristics does the fire of hell have?
3. What is the greatest physical torment that the damned of hell suffer?
4. What is the source of the fire in hell?
5. How were parricides punished in olden times?

The Strategies

1. Examine carefully this description of hell. What is its overall structure? How are its paragraphs deployed?
2. Examine paragraph 4. How is it developed? What is its purpose?
3. What is the purpose of mentioning the "earthly prisons" in paragraph 1?
4. Examine paragraph 5. How is this paragraph structured? What technique does the writer use to make his description so vivid?
5. In the novel *A Portrait of the Artist as a Young Man,* the preacher delivers this description of hell in a sermon. Identify at least one technique that the preacher uses to involve his listeners in the description.

The Issues

1. For the most part, modern minds have rejected the medieval view of a physical hell, where the damned suffer such tortures as heat, cold, foul smell, laceration, and persecution from demons. What, if anything, has replaced this notion of hell?
2. In your view, why do many people believe in paradise and hell? What disadvantage or advantage does the lack of belief in these places provide?
3. What effect do you think this sermon on hell might have on young boys listening to it? What is your opinion of the technique used?
4. Is torture as a means of punishment ever justified in a civilized society? Why or why not?
5. A portion of Dante's hell was reserved for those who encouraged others to sin. Where in this excerpt does Joyce express a similar idea? Why do both Dante and Joyce call down a harsh judgment on those who aid and abet evil?

Suggestions for Writing

1. Write an essay on hell as it is described here, arguing for or against a belief in its existence.
2. Write a brief description of heaven following the example of this selection.

A Worn Path

EUDORA WELTY

Eudora Welty (1909-2001) is an American novelist and short-story writer whose tales about eccentric but charming characters from small Mississippi towns have won her a large audience. The best known of her stories have been collected in *A Curtain of Green* (1941), *The Wide Net* (1943), and *The Golden Apples* (1949). Among her novels are *Delta Wedding* (1946), *The Ponder Heart* (1954), and *The Optimist's Daughter* (1972). In 1983, she delivered the *William E. Massey Sr. Lectures in American Civilization* at Harvard, which were published as *One Writer's Beginnings* (1984).

In this story, a woman, undaunted by age and hardships, presses on toward her goal—to get the medicine her sick grandchild must have in order to survive.

• • •

1   It was December—a bright frozen day in the early morning. Far out in the country there was an old Negro woman with her head tied in a red rag, coming along a path through the pinewoods. Her name was Phoenix Jackson. She was very old and small and she walked slowly in the dark pine shadows, moving a little from side to side in her steps, with the balanced heaviness and lightness of a pendulum in a grandfather clock. She carried a thin, small cane made from an umbrella, and with this she kept tagging the frozen earth in front of her. This made a grave and persistent noise in the still air, that seemed meditative, like the chirping of a solitary little bird.

2   She wore a dark striped dress reaching down to her shoetops, and an equally long apron of bleached sugar sacks, with a full pocket; all neat and tidy, but every time she took a step she might have fallen over her shoelaces, which dragged from her unlaced shoes. She looked straight ahead. Her eyes were blue with age. Her skin had a pattern all its own of numberless branching wrinkles and as though a whole little tree stood in the middle of her forehead, but a golden color ran underneath, and the two knobs of her cheeks were illuminated by a yellow burning under the dark. Under the red rag her hair came down on her neck in the frailest of ringlets, still black, and with an odor like copper.

3   Now and then there was a quivering in the thicket. Old Phoenix said, "Out of my way, all you foxes, owls, beetles, jack rabbits, coons, and wild animals! . . . Keep out from under these feet, little bobwhites. . . . Keep the big wild hogs out of my path. Don't let none of those come running my direction. I got a long way." Under her small black-freckled hand her cane, limber as a buggy whip, would switch at the brush as if to rouse up any hiding things.

4   On she went. The woods were deep and still. The sun made the pine needles almost too bright to look at, up where the wind rocked. The cones dropped as light as feathers. Down in the hollow was the mourning dove—it was not too late for him.

5   The path ran up a hill. "Seem like there is chains about my feet, time I get this far," she said, in the voice of argument old people keep to use with themselves. "Something always take a hold on this hill—pleads I should stay."

6   After she got to the top she turned and gave a full, severe look behind where she had come. "Up through pines," she said at length. "Now down through oaks."

7   Her eyes opened their widest and she started down gently. But before she got to the bottom of the hill a bush caught her dress.

8   Her fingers were busy and intent, but her skirts were full and long, so that before she could pull them free in one place they were caught in another. It was not possible to allow the dress to tear. "I in the thorny bush," she said. "Thorns, you doing your appointed work. Never want to let folks past—no sir. Old eyes thought you was a pretty little green bush."

9   Finally, trembling all over, she stood free, and after a moment dared to stoop for her cane.

10 "Sun so high!" she cried, leaning back and looking, while the thick tears went over her eyes. "The time getting all gone here."

11 At the foot of this hill was a place where a log was laid across the creek.

12 "Now comes the trial," said Phoenix.

13 Putting her right foot out, she mounted the log and shut her eyes. Lifting her skirt, leveling her cane fiercely before her, like a festival figure in some parade, she began to march across. Then she opened her eyes and she was safe on the other side.

14 "I wasn't as old as I thought," she said.

15 But she sat down to rest. She spread her skirts on the bank around her and folded her hands over her knees. Up above her was a tree in a pearly cloud of mistletoe. She did not dare to close her eyes, and when a little boy brought her a little plate with a slice of marble-cake on it she spoke to him. "That would be acceptable," she said. But when she went to take it there was just her own hand in the air.

16 So she left that tree, and had to go through a barbed-wire fence. There she had to creep and crawl, spreading her knees and stretching her fingers like a baby trying to climb the steps. But she talked loudly to herself: she could not let her dress be torn now, so late in the day, and she could not pay for having her arm or her leg sawed off if she got caught fast where she was.

17 At last she was safe through the fence and risen up out in the clearing. Big dead trees, like black men with one arm, were standing in the purple stalks of the withered cotton field. There sat a buzzard.

18 "Who you watching?"

19 In the furrow she made her way along.

20 "Glad this not the season for bulls," she said, looking sideways, "and the good Lord made his snakes to curl up and sleep in the winter. A pleasure I don't see no two-headed snake coming around that tree, where it come once. It took a while to get by him, back in the summer."

21 She passed through the old cotton and went into a field of dead corn. It whispered and shook, and was taller than her head. "Through the maze now," she said, for there was no path.

22 Then there was something tall, black, and skinny there, moving before her.
23 At first she took it for a man. It could have been a man dancing in the field. But she stood still and listened, and it did not make a sound. It was as silent as a ghost.
24 "Ghost," she said sharply, "who be you the ghost of? For I have heard of nary death close by."
25 But there was no answer, only the ragged dancing in the wind.
26 She shut her eyes, reached out her hand, and touched a sleeve. She found a coat and inside that an emptiness, cold as ice.
27 "You scarecrow," she said. Her face lighted. "I ought to be shut up for good," she said with laughter. "My senses is gone. I too old. I the oldest people I ever know. Dance, old scarecrow," she said, "while I dancing with you."
28 She kicked her foot over the furrow, and with mouth drawn down shook her head once or twice in a little strutting way. Some husks blew down and whirled in streamers about her skirts.
29 Then she went on, parting her way from side to side with the cane, through the whispering field. At last she came to the end, to a wagon track, where the silver grass blew between the red ruts. The quail were walking around like pullets, seeming all dainty and unseen.
30 "Walk pretty," she said. "This is the easy place. This is the easy going."
31 She followed the track, swaying through the quiet bare fields, through the little strings of trees silver in their dead leaves, past cabins silver from weather, with the doors and windows boarded shut, all like old women under a spell sitting there. "I walking in their sleep," she said, nodding her head vigorously.
32 In a ravine she went where a spring was silently flowing through a hollow log. Old Phoenix bent and drank. "Sweetgum makes the water sweet," she said, and drank more. "Nobody know who made this well, for it was here when I was born."
33 The track crossed a swampy part where the moss hung as white as lace from every limb. "Sleep on, alligators, and blow your bubbles." Then the track went into the road.
34 Deep, deep the road went down between the high green-colored banks. Overhead the live-oaks met, and it was as dark as a cave.
35 A black dog with a lolling tongue came up out of the weeds by the ditch. She was meditating, and not ready, and when he came at her she only hit him a little with her cane. Over she went in the ditch, like a little puff of milkweed.
36 Down there, her senses drifted away. A dream visited her, and she reached her hand up, but nothing reached down and gave her a pull. So she lay there and presently went to talking. "Old woman," she said to herself, "that black dog come up out of the weeds to stall you off, and now there he sitting on his fine tail, smiling at you."
37 A white man finally came along and found her—a hunter, a young man, with his dog on a chain.
38 "Well, Granny!" he laughed. "What are you doing there?"
39 "Lying on my back like a June-bug waiting to be turned over, mister," she said, reaching up her hand.

40   He lifted her up, gave her a swing in the air, and set her down, "Anything broken, Granny?"

41   "No sir, them old dead weeds is springy enough," said Phoenix, when she had got her breath. "I thank you for your trouble."

42   "Where do you live, Granny?" he asked, while the two dogs were growling at each other.

43   "Away back yonder, sir, behind the ridge. You can't even see it from here."

44   "On your way home?"

45   "No sir, I going to town."

46   "Why, that's too far! That's as far as I walk when I come out myself, and I get something for my trouble." He patted the stuffed bag he carried, and there hung down a little closed claw. It was one of the bobwhites, with its beak hooked bitterly to show it was dead. "Now you go on home, Granny!"

47   "I bound to go to town, mister," said Phoenix. "The time come around."

48   He gave another laugh, filling the whole landscape. "I know you colored people! Wouldn't miss going to town to see Santa Claus!"

49   But something held Old Phoenix very still. The deep lines in her face went into a fierce and different radiation. Without warning she had seen with her own eyes a flashing nickel fall out of the man's pocket on to the ground.

50   "How old are you, Granny?" he was saying.

51   "There is no telling, mister," she said, "no telling."

52   Then she gave a little cry and clapped her hands, and said, "Git on away from here, dog! Look! Look at that dog!" She laughed as if in admiration. "He ain't scared of nobody. He a big black dog." She whispered, "Sick him!"

53   "Watch me get rid of that cur," said the man. "Sick him, Pete! Sick him!"

54   Phoenix heard the dogs fighting and heard the man running and throwing sticks. She even heard a gunshot. But she was slowly bending forward by that time, further and further forward, the lids stretched down over her eyes, as if she were doing this in her sleep. Her chin was lowered almost to her knees. The yellow palm of her hand came out from the fold of her apron. Her fingers slid down and along the ground under the piece of money with the grace and care they would have in lifting an egg from under a sitting hen. Then she slowly straightened up, she stood erect, and the nickel was in her apron pocket. A bird flew by. Her lips moved. "God watching me the whole time. I come to stealing."

55   The man came back, and his own dog panted about them. "Well, I scared him off that time," he said, and then he laughed and lifted his gun and pointed it at Phoenix.

56   She stood straight and faced him.

57   "Doesn't the gun scare you?" he said, still pointing it.

58   "No sir, I seen plenty go off closer by, in my day, and for less than what I done," she said, holding utterly still.

59   He smiled, and shouldered the gun. "Well, Granny," he said, "you must be a hundred years old, and scared of nothing. I'd give you a dime if I had any money with me. But you take my advice and stay home, and nothing will happen to you."

60   "I bound to go on my way, mister," said Phoenix. She inclined her head in the red rag. Then they went in different directions, but she could hear the gun shooting again and again over the hill.

61   She walked on. The shadows hung from the oak trees to the road like curtains. Then she smelled wood-smoke, and smelled the river, and she saw a steeple and the cabins on their steep steps. Dozens of little black children whirled around her. There ahead was Natchez shining. Bells were ringing. She walked on.

62   In the paved city it was Christmas time. There were red and green electric lights strung and crisscrossed everywhere, and all turned on in the day time. Old Phoenix would have been lost if she had not distrusted her eyesight and depended on her feet to know where to take her.

63   She paused quietly on the sidewalk, where people were passing by. A lady came along in the crowd, carrying an armful of red-, green-, and silver wrapped presents; she gave off perfume like the red roses in hot summer, and Phoenix stopped her.

64   "Please, missy, will you lace up my shoe?" She held up her foot.

65   "What do you want, Grandma?"

66   "See my shoe," said Phoenix. "Do all right for out in the country, but wouldn't look right to go in a big building."

67   "Stand still then, Grandma," said the lady. She put her packages down carefully on the sidewalk beside her and laced and tied both shoes tightly.

68   "Can't lace 'em with a cane," said Phoenix. "Thank you, missy. I doesn't mind asking a nice lady to tie up my shoes when I gets out on the street."

69   Moving slowly and from side to side, she went into the stone building and into a tower of steps, where she walked up and around and around until her feet knew to stop.

70   She entered a door, and there she saw nailed up on the wall the document that had been stamped with the gold seal and framed in the gold frame which matched the dream that was hung up in her head.

71   "Here I be," she said. There was a fixed and ceremonial stiffness over her body.

72   "A charity case, I suppose," said an attendant who sat at the desk before her.

73   But Phoenix only looked above her head. There was sweat on her face; the wrinkles shone like a bright net.

74   "Speak, up, Grandma," the woman said. "What's your name? We must have your history, you know. Have you been here before? What seems to be the trouble with you?"

75   Old Phoenix only gave a twitch to her face as if a fly were bothering her.

76   "Are you deaf?" cried the attendant.

77   But then the nurse came in.

78   "Oh, that's just old Aunt Phoenix," she said. "She doesn't come for herself—she has a little grandson. She makes these trips just as regular as clockwork. She lives away back off the Old Natchez Trace." She bent down. "Well, Aunt Phoenix, why don't you just take a seat? We won't keep you standing after your long trip." She pointed.

79. The old woman sat down, bolt upright in the chair.
80. "Now how is the boy?" asked the nurse.
81. Old Phoenix did not speak.
82. "I said, how is the boy?"
83. But Phoenix only waited and stared straight ahead, her face very solemn and withdrawn into rigidity.
84. "Is his throat any better?" asked the nurse. "Aunt Phoenix, don't you hear me? Is your grandson's throat any better since the last time you came for the medicine?"
85. With her hand on her knees, the old woman waited, silent, erect and motionless, just as if she were in armor.
86. "You mustn't take up our time this way, Aunt Phoenix," the nurse said. "Tell us quickly about your grandson, and get it over. He isn't dead, is he?"
87. At last there came a flicker and then a flame of comprehension across her face, and she spoke.
88. "My grandson. It was my memory had left me. There I sat and forgot why I made my long trip."
89. "Forgot?" The nurse frowned. "After you came so far?"
90. Then Phoenix was like an old woman begging a dignified forgiveness for waking up frightened in the night. "I never did go to school—I was too old at the Surrender," she said in a soft voice. "I'm an old woman without an education. It was my memory fail me. My little grandson, he is just the same, and I forgot it in the coming."
91. "Throat never heals, does it?" said the nurse, speaking in a loud, sure voice to Old Phoenix. By now she had a card with something written on it, a little list. "Yes. Swallowed lye. When was it—January—two—three years ago—"
92. Phoenix spoke unasked now. "No, missy, he not dead, he just the same. Every little while his throat begin to close up again, and he not able to swallow. He not get his breath. He not able to help himself. So the time come around, and I go on another trip for the soothing medicine."
93. "All right. The doctor said as long as you came to get it you could have it," said the nurse. "But it's an obstinate case."
94. "My little grandson, he sit up there in the house all wrapped up, waiting by himself," Phoenix went on. "We is the only two left in the world. He suffer and it don't seem to put him back at all. He got a sweet look. He going to last. He wear a little patch quilt and peep out, holding his mouth open like a little bird. I remembers so plain now. I not going to forget him again, no, the whole enduring time. I could tell him from all the others in creation."
95. "All right." The nurse was trying to hush her now. She brought her a bottle of medicine. "Charity," she said, making a check mark in a book.
96. Old Phoenix held the bottle close to her eyes and then carefully put it into her pocket.
97. "I thank you," she said.
98. "It's Christmas time, Grandma," said the attendant. "Could I give you a few pennies out of my purse?"
99. "Five pennies is a nickel," said Phoenix stiffly.

270   CHAPTER 8 • Description

100   "Here's a nickel," said the attendant.

101   Phoenix rose carefully and held out her hand. She received the nickel and then fished the other nickel out of her pocket and laid it beside the new one. She stared at her palm closely, with her head on one side.

102   Then she gave a tap with her cane on the floor.

103   "This is what come to me to do," she said. "I going to the store and buy my child a little windmill they sells, made out of paper. He going to find it hard to believe there such a thing in the world. I'll march myself back where he waiting, holding it straight up in this hand."

104   She lifted her free hand, gave a little nod, turned round, and walked out of the doctor's office. Then her slow step began on the stairs, going down.

● Vocabulary

meditative (1)	illuminated (2)	bobwhites (3)
limber (3)	appointed (8)	furrow (19)
maze (21)	nary (24)	strutting (28)
husks (28)	pullets (29)	sweetgum (32)
lolling (35)	radiation (49)	ceremonial (71)
lye (91)		

● The Facts

1. In paragraph 1, to what piece of antique furniture is Phoenix Jackson's walk compared? What characteristic is Welty trying to get across? Later on in the narrative, where is the same piece of furniture alluded to again? Why?
2. What is the purpose of the old woman's journey?
3. Essentially this is the story of a courageous woman. What part of the trip is especially difficult for her? How does she manage this obstacle?
4. What details indicate that Phoenix Jackson is slightly senile and therefore not always in touch with reality?
5. What excuse does the old woman offer for not remembering what errand she is on?

● The Strategies

1. What is the plot structure of the story? What is the conflict in the plot? When is the conflict resolved?
2. Analyze Phoenix's language. What is conveyed through her speech?
3. Point out some instances of humor. What kind of humor is used?
4. During what decade would you judge this story to have taken place? What clues to your answer are given in the story?
5. In paragraph 85, we read: "With her hand on her knees, the old woman waited, silent, erect and motionless, just as if she were in armor." What meaning do you attribute to this passage?

The Issues

1. In Egyptian mythology, the phoenix was a bird of great splendor that consumed itself by fire every 500 years and rose renewed from its own ashes. In what way is Phoenix Jackson like this bird?
2. The narrative abounds in descriptive passages. What is the dominant impression in paragraph 2? Are any details included that do not support this impression? What other descriptive passages can you identify?
3. Why does Phoenix keep talking to herself? What do her monologues add to the total portrait of her?
4. What is the meaning of the episode in which Phoenix steals the nickel? Does the act offend our sense of honesty? Explain your answer.
5. What significance can you attribute to the fact that the journey takes place at Christmas time?
6. Phoenix Jackson's journey is in the literary tradition of the mythological quest. What aspects of the story place it in that tradition?

Suggestions for Writing

1. Using your imagination, describe Phoenix's journey home. Make your scenes descriptive by providing details that support a dominant impression.
2. Write an essay in which you describe a loving relationship between a grandparent and a grandchild or between a person and a pet.

Pigeon Woman

May Swenson

May Swenson (1919–1989) poet, playwright, and lecturer, was born in Logan, Utah, and educated at Utah State University. She resided in New York City until her death. She published a number of collections of poetry including her last volume, *New and Selected Things Taking Place* (1978).

The meaning of Pigeon Woman *emerges from the irony contained in a strange old lady's fantasy.*

• • •

      Slate, or dirty-marble-colored,
      or rusty-iron-colored, the pigeons
      on the flagstones in front of the
      Public Library make a sharp lake
5   into which the pigeon woman wades
      at exactly 1:30. She wears a
      plastic pink raincoat with a round
      collar (looking like a little
      girl, so gay) and flat gym shoes,

10 her hair square-cut, orange.
    Wide-apart feet carefully enter
    the spinning, crooning waves
    (as if she'd just learned how
    to walk, each step conscious,
15 an accomplishment); blue knots in the
    calves of her bare legs (uglied marble),
    age in angled cords of jaw
    and neck, her pimento-colored hair,
    hanging in thin tassels, is gray
20 around a balding crown.
    The day-old bread drops down
    from her veined hand dipping out
    of a paper sack. Choppy, shadowy ripples
    the pigeons strike around her legs.
25 Sack empty, she squats and seems to rinse
    her hands in them—the rainy greens and
    oily purples of their necks. Almost
    they let her wet her thirsty fingertips—
    but drain away in an untouchable tide.
30 A make-believe trade
    she has come to, in her lostness
    or illness or age—to treat the motley
    city pigeons at 1:30 every day, in all
    weathers. It is for them she colors
35 her own feathers. Ruddy-footed
    on the lime-stained paving,
    purling to meet her when she comes,
    they are a lake of love. Retreating
    from her hands as soon as empty,
40 they are the flints of love.

Vocabulary

crooning (12)   pimento (18)   motley (32)
purling (37)   flints (40)

The Facts

1. What is the dominant impression conveyed by this "pigeon woman"? In terms of her looks, what role could she play in a fairy tale?
2. As the poem develops, how do our feelings change about the woman?
3. Describe the fantasy that gives purpose to the woman's life.
4. What is the meaning of the final stanza?
5. Is this woman an impossible figment of the poet's imagination or does she represent a kind of reality? Comment.

Issue: Body Image   273

- ## The Strategies

1. How does the level of language used contribute to the description of the woman?
2. How do you explain the image of the pigeons as a lake?
3. What are the "blue knots in the / calves of her bare legs"? Comment on the effectiveness of this image.
4. What is the meaning of the metaphor "her own feathers" in the next-to-last stanza?
5. Interpret the metaphor "the flints of love" in the final line.

> Stumped by ready-made phrases? Exit on page 688, at the **Editing Booth!**

- ## The Issues

1. Various public, as well as private, agencies have been concerned with the plight of the poor, especially women who have been labeled "bag ladies," "crazy drifters," or "old female transients." What suggestions do you have for dealing with this alienated group of our population? Are we doing enough, or should we do more?
2. What is it that keeps this woman from giving up on life? What do you consider the driving force that keeps most people who lead desperate lives from committing suicide?
3. The woman in the poem chooses to feed a flock of pigeons. What other activities could give meaning to such a person's life?
4. How would you describe the male counterpart of the pigeon woman? Include the details of his appearance.
5. What measures do you suggest for reducing the number of street vagrants in our major cities?

- ## Suggestions for Writing

1. Write an essay comparing the pigeon woman with Phoenix Jackson from the previous story.
2. Imagine the loneliness that comes from being old and alone. Describe this loneliness in terms of specific, concrete details.

ISSUE FOR CRITICAL THINKING AND DEBATE: BODY IMAGE

A study conducted by the *Journal of American Medicine* found that 31% of Americans are certifiably obese based on a widely used body mass index. Using the same index, some two thirds of American adults can be classified as overweight.

Nearly 9 million American children between the ages of 6 and 19 weigh more than they should. The extremely obese—people who exceed their expected weight by more than 100 pounds—represent the fastest-growing segment of the overweight population, having quadrupled over the past 20 years until they now account for one in 50 adults or nearly 4 million people.

It is paradoxical that our society, which is so overpopulated with fat people, should also place such a high value on physical appearance. We are obsessed with the way we look. Images abound everywhere in the mass media of svelte and sculptured bodies at work and at play pushing a variety of exercise equipment, miracle diets, and body oils. Dieting is a multibillion-dollar business. In the last decade, huge companies have been built on the new psychology of first impressions that places a higher premium on physical attractiveness than on talent or personality. "Extreme makeover" programs that pool the resources of various plastic surgeons, cosmetic dentists, and personal trainers to transform ugly ducklings into sleek swans proliferate on television. This endless parade of comely flesh would give any alien observer watching from afar the mistaken impression that most Americans are attractive and physically fit instead of chronically overweight chubbies. One study found that many of us tend to grossly underestimate our actual weight and even people who are obese often think themselves trimmer than they really are. All this flesh and self-deception brings a high cost in health problems such as diabetes, heart attack, and stroke.

Because of our obsession with the ideal body, the image merchants market services that did not exist in such profusion fifty years ago. Personal trainers will help you develop a stomach that boasts a six-pack of abs or arms strung with eye-catching biceps and triceps. You can have your tongue, belly button, or even your nipples pierced. You can wallpaper your back with a tattoo that blares your self-confidence to the world, dye your hair a psychedelic color, and dress as outlandishly as you please so long as you stay within the conventions of your particular business (we have, for example, never met a green-haired banker). This kind of body image transformation, the hucksters argue, not only allows you to stand out from the crowd but can also advance your career.

The discussion that follows brings to the table a quasi-scientific as well as a commonsensical approach. First is a survey and an essay by Cindy Maynard, a dietician who teaches young people to accept their bodies and to focus on achieving a healthy lifestyle rather than on attempting to imitate the ideal body images of popular film stars. Second is an article in which Pulitzer Prize–winning journalist Anna Quindlen lays out the very sensible reasons why she joined a gym. Third is a student essay from a psychology major explaining the reasons why young people go for piercings and tattoos. The chapter ends with a writing assignment that requires a trip to the Image Gallery.

Nothing is definitively resolved here, nor would one expect it to be. How we see ourselves is even more complex a phenomenon than how others see us. In the end the only solution may come from that old adage: Be yourself—whether you're fat, thin, in between, or truly an out-and-out hunk or hottie.

• What do you think about body piercing and tattoos? Are these the best ways to acquire a distinctive personality?

Body Image
Cindy Maynard

Cindy Maynard is a health and medical writer and a registered dietitian living in San Diego. She often writes for *Current Health* magazine, a weekly publication. Her advice on body image has helped many young people to escape the trap of seeing themselves as physically unattractive or even repulsive.

According to the author, "body image dissatisfaction is so epidemic in our society that it's almost considered normal." Teenagers, whose self-confidence is already battered by the constant drumbeat of advertisements touting the ideal body, are especially sensitive to the charge of being fat. The essay that follows opens with a questionnaire that tests the reader's body image I.Q. and then offers helpful tips on how to view the body in a healthy way.

• • •

Body Image Questionnaire: How Do You Measure Up?

When you look in the mirror, what do you see? When you walk past a shop window and catch a glimpse of your body, what do you notice first? Are you proud of what you see, or do you think, "I'm too short, I'm too fat, If only I were thinner or more muscular"? Most people answer negatively. Take the following quiz and see how your Body Image I.Q. measures up. Check the most appropriate answer:

1. Have you avoided sports or working out because you didn't want to be seen in gym clothes? Yes_____ No_____
2. Does eating even a small amount of food make you feel fat? Yes_____ No_____
3. Do you worry or obsess about your body not being small, thin or good enough? Yes_____ No_____
4. Are you concerned your body is not muscular or strong enough? Yes_____ No_____
5. Do you avoid wearing certain clothes because they make you feel fat? Yes_____ No_____
6. Do you feel badly about yourself because you don't like your body? Yes_____ No_____
7. Have you ever disliked your body? Yes_____ No_____
8. Do you want to change something about your body? Yes_____ No_____
9. Do you compare yourself to others and "come up short"? Yes_____ No_____

If you answered "Yes" to three or more questions, you may have a negative body image.

Mirror, Mirror

1   Girls are overly concerned about weight and body shape. They strive for the "perfect" body and judge themselves by their looks, appearance, and above all thinness. But boys don't escape either. They are concerned with the size and strength of their body. There has been a shift in the male body image. Boys live in a culture that showcases males as glamorous "macho" figures who have to be "tough," build muscles and sculpt their bodies—if they want to fit in. They think they have to be a "real" man, but many admit being confused as to what that means or what's expected of them. This confusion can make it harder than ever to feel good about themselves.

2   Some sports can contribute to a negative body image. The need to make weight for a sport like wrestling or boxing can cause disordered eating. But other boys say sports make them feel better about themselves. Jon, a 15-year-old, states, "Guys are in competition, especially in the weight room. They say, "I can bench 215 lbs.' and the other guy says, 'Well, I can bench 230 lbs.' If you're stronger, you're better." Daniel, age 16, shares, "Guys are into having the perfect body. But if you feel good about your body, you automatically feel good about yourself."

- Since weight-loss pills and regimens are a multi-million-dollar business, can they be trusted?

3   Most of our cues about what we should look like come from the media, our parents, and our peers. This constant obsession with weight, the size of our bodies, and longing for a different shape or size can be painful.

4   Where do these negative perceptions come from? Here are just a few of the factors contributing to negative perceptions and obsessions about our bodies.

Mission Impossible

5   The media play a big part. Surrounded by thin models and TV stars, teenage girls are taught to achieve an impossible goal. As a result, many teenage girls intensely dislike their bodies and can tell you down to the minutest detail what's wrong with them. Most teens watch an average of 22 hours of TV a week and are deluged with images of fat-free bodies in the pages of health, fashion, and

teen magazines. The "standard" is impossible to achieve. A female should look like, and have the same dimensions as Barbie, and a male should look like Arnold Schwarzenegger. Buff Baywatch lifeguards, the well-toned abs of any cast member of *Melrose Place* or *Friends,* and music-video queens don't help.

6   Take a look at the ten most popular magazines on the newspaper racks. The women and men on the covers represent about .03 percent of the population. The other 99.97% don't have a chance to compete, much less measure up. Don't forget it's a career with these people. They're pros. Many have had major body make-overs and have a full-time personal trainer. Most ads are reproduced, airbrushed, or changed by computer. Body parts can be changed at will.

7   The images of men and women in ads today do not promote self-esteem or positive self image. They're intended to sell products. In the U.S. billions of dollars are spent by consumers who pursue the perfect body. The message "thin is in" is sold thousands of times a day through TV, movies, magazines, billboards, newspapers and songs. Advertising conveys the message "You're not O.K. Here's what you need to do to fix what's wrong." Girls and boys believe it and react to it. In a 1997 Body Image Survey, both girls and boys reported that "very thin or muscular models" made them feel insecure about themselves.

8   Western society places a high value upon appearance. Self-worth is enhanced for those who are judged attractive. Those who are deemed unattractive can feel at a disadvantage. The message from the media, fashion, and our peers can create a longing—a longing to win the approval of our culture and fit in at any cost. And that can be disastrous to our self-esteem.

9   Parents can give mixed messages, too, especially if they're constantly dieting or have body or food issues of their own. How we perceive and internalize these childhood messages about our bodies determines our ability to build self-esteem and confidence in our appearance.

10   The diet/fitness craze is mind-boggling. It's not just dieting, it's diet foods and diet commercials. Everybody's counting fat grams. Listen to the conversation in the lunch room, locker room, or on the bus to school. The talk centers around dieting, fat thighs, or tight "abs" and how many pounds can be lost with the latest diet. This kind of intense focus on food and fat can lead to abnormal eating habits or disordered eating, a precursor to eating disorders, which is taking it to the extreme.

11   Awareness of eating disorders got a big boost in 1995 when Princess Di began talking openly about her struggles with bulimia. Actress Tracy Gold, still struggling with her eating disorder, continues to help others by discussing her eating disorder with the media. Recently many organizations have initiated an effort to expand awareness of eating disorders and promote a positive body image and self-esteem.

Body Image, Body Love

12   Why is a positive body image so important? Psychologists and counselors agree that a negative body image is directly related to self-esteem. The more negative the perception of our bodies, the more negative we feel about ourselves.

13 Being a teenager is a time of major change. Besides the obvious changes in size and shape, teens are faced with how they feel about themselves. Body image and self-esteem are two important ways to help promote a positive image.

14 When most people think about body image they think about aspects of physical appearance, attractiveness, and beauty. But body image is much more. It is the mental picture a person has of his/her body as well as their thoughts, feelings, judgments, sensations, awareness, and behavior. Body image is developed through interactions with people and the social world. It's our mental picture of ourselves; it's what allows us to become ourselves.

15 Body image influences behavior, self-esteem, and our psyche. When we feel bad about our body, our satisfaction and mood plummet. If we are constantly trying to push, reshape, or remake our bodies, our sense of self becomes unhealthy. We lose confidence in our abilities. It's not uncommon for people who think poorly of their bodies to have problems in other areas of their lives, including sexuality, careers, and relationships.

16 A healthy body image occurs when a person's feelings about his/her body are positive, confident and self-caring. This image is necessary to care for the body, find outlets for self-expression, develop confidence in your physical abilities, and feel comfortable with who you are.

17 Self-esteem is a personal evaluation of your worth as a person. It measures how much you respect yourself:

physically (how happy you are with the way you look)
intellectually (how well you feel you can accomplish your goals)
emotionally (how much you feel loved)
morally (how you think of yourself as a person)

18 How you see yourself affects every part of your life. High self-esteem makes for a happier life. It allows you to be your own person and not have others define you.

19 Self-esteem, self-confidence, and self-respect are all related. Self-esteem is also defined as the judgments people make about themselves and is affected by self-confidence and respect. Self-confidence is believing in our ability to take action and meet our goals. Self-respect is the degree to which we believe we deserve to be happy, have rewarding relationships, and stand up for our rights and values. All these factors affect whether or not we will have a healthy body image.

20 To begin to achieve healthy images of ourselves and our bodies is a challenge. Here are some things you can do to start feeling better about your body and yourself.

Making Peace with Your Body and Self

21 When you look in the mirror, make yourself find at least one good point for every demerit you give. Become aware of your positives.

22 Decide which of the cultural pressures—glamour, fitness, thinness, media, peer group—prevent you from feeling good about yourself. How about not buying fashion magazines which promote unrealistic body images?

23   Exercise gets high marks when it comes to breeding positive body feelings. It makes us feel better about our appearance, and improves our health and mood.

24   Emphasize your assets. You have many. Give yourself credit for positive qualities. If there are some things you want to change, remember self-discovery is a lifelong process.

25   Make friends with the person you see in the mirror. Say, "I like what I see. I like me." Do it until you believe it.

26   Question ads. Instead of saying, "What's wrong with me?" say, "What's wrong with this ad?" Write the company. Set your own standards instead of letting the media set them for you.

27   Ditch dieting and bail on the scale. These are two great ways to develop a healthy relationship with your body and weight.

28   Challenge size-bigotry and fight size discrimination whenever you can. Don't speak of yourself or others with phrases like "fat slob," pig out," or "thunder thighs."

29   Be an example to others by taking people seriously for what they say, feel, and do rather than how they look.

30   Accept the fact that your body's changing. In teen years, your body is a work in progress. Don't let every new inch or curve throw you off the deep end.

31   You know you are successful when you look at your image in the mirror and instead of asking, "What's wrong with me?" You can, "There's nothing really wrong with me." And little by little you'll find you can stop disliking your body. When Clister Smith age 15, was asked how we can like our bodies better, he said, "Quit worrying about what others think of you. If you want to change your body, do it for yourself and not for anyone else."

32   This is the starting point. It is from this new way of looking at a problem that we can begin to feel better about ourselves. Make this the time to accept the natural dimensions of your body instead of drastically trying to change them. You can't exchange your body for a new one. So the best thing is to find peace with the one you have. Your body is where you're going to be living the rest of your life. Isn't it about time you made it home?

● Vocabulary

cues (3)
airbrushed (6)
bulimia (11)
dimensions (36)
obsession (3)
internalize (9)
initiated (11)
perceptions (4)
precursor (10)
plummet (15)

● The Facts

1. What is the purpose of the questionnaire preceding the rest of the essay? Do you consider it useful? Give reasons for your answer.
2. How do boys and girls differ in their views of their bodies? What do both views have in common?

3. From what source do most of us receive our cues about the way we should appear to others? In your opinion, are these cues valid or are there other, more important, sources of validation? Explain your answer.

4. Why, according to Maynard, don't the ads in today's magazines promote a good self-image in their readers? Do you agree with Maynard's view? Why or why not?

5. According to Maynard, which of the steps in making peace with your body receives "high marks"? Why is this so?

The Strategies

1. What about the author's writing style strikes you? Is it embroidered and complex or simple and straightforward? Consider the length of paragraphs and the sentence structure.

2. Many of the paragraphs consist of one or two declarative sentences that are not developed the way more sophisticated works develop a topic sentence. What advantage do these staccato statements have? What is your reaction to the style of this essay?

3. Where do you think the author got her idea for the heading "Mirror, Mirror" at the start of the essay? How effective is this heading? What other heading can you suggest?

4. What purpose does the question in paragraph 4 serve? Is the question ever answered in the essay? If so, how? If not, why not?

5. Why does the author keep using the personal pronoun "you" in writing this essay? Would a less personal approach be more effective?

The Issues

1. Do you agree with the author that certain sport requirements can cause boys to suffer from a poor self-image? What is your feeling about today's emphasis on weight lifting, jogging, and training on gym equipment?

2. Why does the author use the title "Mission Impossible" in her second segment? What is the impossible mission to which she refers? Do you agree with her? Give reasons for your answer.

3. How does the author view diets and diet foods? State your own view about how dieting fits into your lifestyle.

4. Who was Princess Di, and how did she help the cause of eating disorders? What was the contribution of Tracy Gold? What do both of these women have in common?

5. Of the many tips offered under the heading "Making Peace with Your Body and Self," which do you consider the most helpful? Do you agree with the author that following all of the tips is only a beginning? Support your answers with reasons.

Suggestions for Writing

1. Looking at yourself in the mirror, find those outer and inner qualities you like best about yourself. Then write an essay titled "The Person I See When I Look

in the Mirror." Do not allow negative thoughts to influence your description. This essay is supposed to present you at your best.

2. Write an essay describing a piece of TV advertising that you do *not* consider a threat to your self-image. Indicate clearly why this ad does not make you feel inferior or abnormal.

Stretch Marks
Anna Quindlen

Anna Quindlen (b. 1953) is a Pulitzer Prize–winning journalist, novelist, and writer of children's books. Her trademark sense of humor has delighted audiences all over the United States. Currently she is writing articles for *Newsweek* magazine. However, she also wrote op-ed columns for *The New York Times* that eventually were reprinted in a book titled *Living Out Loud* (1987), from which the essay below has been excerpted.

Readers who hate exercise but value its benefits in promoting good looks and good health will enjoy the humorous manner in which Quindlen recounts her experiences at the gym. As you read, ask yourself how Quindlen manages to make you laugh at an experience that could be irksome.

• • •

1 For most of my life I have pursued a policy toward my body that could best be characterized as benign neglect. From the time I could remember until the time I was fifteen it looked one way, and from the time I was fifteen until I was thirty it looked another way. Then, in the space of two years, I had two children and more weight changes than Ted Kennedy, and my body headed south without me.

2 This is how I began to work out. I work out for a very simple reason, and it is not because it makes me feel invigorated and refreshed. The people who say that exercise is important because it makes you feel wonderful are the same people who say a mink coat is nice because it keeps you warm. Show me a women who wears a mink coat to keep warm and who exercises because it feels good and I'll show you Jane Fonda. I wear a mink coat because it is a mink coat, and I work out so that my husband will not gasp when he runs into me in the bathroom and take off with an eighteen-year-old who looks as good out of her clothes as in them. It's as simple as that.

3 So I go to this gym three times a week, and here is how it works. First I go into the locker room. On the wall is an extremely large photograph of a person named Terri Jones wearing what I can only assume is meant to be a bathing suit. The caption above her body says Slim Strong and Sexy.

It is accurate. I check to make sure no one else is in the locker room, then I take my clothes off. As soon as I've done this, one of two people will enter the locker room: either an eighteen-year-old who looks as good out of her clothes as in them who spontaneously confides in me that she is having an affair with a young lawyer whose wife has really gone to seed since she had her two kids, or a fifty-year-old woman who has had nine children, weighs 105 and has abdominal muscles you could bounce a quarter off and who says she can't understand why, maybe it's her metabolism, but she can eat anything she wants, including a pint of Frusen Glädjé Swiss chocolate almond candy ice cream, and never gain a pound. So then I go out and exercise.

4   I do Nautilus. It is a series of fierce-looking machines, each designed, according to this book I have, to exercise some district muscle group, which all happen in my case never to have been exercised before. Nautilus was allegedly invented by Arthur Jones, husband of the aforementioned slim strong and sexy Terri, who is his seventeenth wife, or something like that. But I think anyone who comes upon a Nautilus machine suddenly will agree with me that its prototype was clearly invented at some time in history when torture was considered a reasonable alternative to diplomacy. Over each machine is a little drawing of a human body—not mine, of course—with a certain muscle group inked in red. This is so you can recognize immediately the muscle group that is on fire during the time you are using the machine.

5   There is actually supposed to be a good reason to do Nautilus, and it is supposed to be that it results in toning without bulk: that is, you will look like a dancer, not a defensive lineman. That may be compelling for Terri Jones, but I chose it because it takes me only a little more than a half hour—or what I like to think of as the time an average person burning calories at an average rate would need to read *Where the Wild Things Are, Good Night, Moon* and *The Cat in the Hat* twice—to finish all the machines. It is also not social, like aerobics classes, and will not hold you up to widespread ridicule, like running. I feel about exercise the same way that I feel about a few other things: that there is nothing wrong with it if it is done in private by consenting adults.

6   Actually, there are some of the Nautilus machines I even like. Call it old-fashioned machisma, but I get a kick out of building biceps. This is a throwback to all those times when my brothers would flex their arms and a mound of muscle would appear, and I would flex mine and nothing would happen, and they'd laugh and go off somewhere to smoke cigarettes and look at dirty pictures. There's a machine to exercise the inner thigh muscles that bears such a remarkable resemblance to a delivery room apparatus that every time I get into it I think someone is going to yell *push!* and I will have another baby. I feel comfortable with that one. On the other hand, there is another machine on which I am supposed to lift a weight straight up in the air and the most I ever manage is to squinch my face up until I look like an infant with bad gas: My instructor explained to me that this is because women have no upper body strength, which probably explains why I've always found it somewhat difficult to carry a toddler and an infant up four flights of stairs with a diaper bag over one shoulder while holding a Big Wheel.

7   Anyhow, the great thing about working out is that I have met a lot of very nice men. This would be a lot more important if I weren't married and the

mother of two. But of course if I were single and looking to meet someone, I would never meet anyone except married men and psychopaths. (This is Murphy's Other Law named after a Doreen Murphy, who in 1981 had a record eleven bad relationships in one year.) The men I have met seem to really get a kick out of the fact that I work out not unlike the kick that most of us get out of hearing very small children try to say words like hippopotamus or chauvinist. As one of the men at my gym said. Most of the people here are guys or women who are uh well hmm umm.

8   "In good shape," I said.

9   "I wouldn't have put it like that," he answered.

10   Because I go to the gym at the same time on the same days, I actually see the same men over and over again. One or two of them are high school students, which I find truly remarkable. When I was in high school, it was a big deal if a guy had shoulders, never mind muscles. So when I'm finished I go back into the locker room and take a shower. The eighteen-year-old is usually in there, and sometimes she'll say something like, "Oh, that's what stretch, marks look like." Then I put on my clothes and go home by the route that does not pass Dunkin Donuts. The bottom line is that I really hate to exercise, but I have found on balance that this working out is all worth it. One day we were walking down the street and one of the guys from my gym—it was actually one of the high school guys, the one with the great pecs—walked by and said "How ya doing?" My husband said. Who the hell is that guy? And I knew that Nautilus had already made a big difference in my life.

● **Vocabulary**

benign (1) spontaneously (3) abdominal (3)
allegedly (4) prototype (4) toning (5)
bulk (5) machisma (6) squinch (6)
psychopaths (7) chauvinist (7)

● **The Facts**

1. What reason does the author give for working out at the gym? How does her reason differ from reasons given by the experts? What reason would you give for working out?

2. How often does the author go to the gym? Does she spend enough time there to keep herself trim? If you exercise regularly, what is your schedule and how effective is it? Do you recommend it to others? Give reasons for your answer.

3. Who are the two women the author meets in the locker room, and what is the significance of each encounter? Do you empathize with the author's reaction to these women or do you think she is being mean-spirited? Explain your view.

4. What brand of exercise machine does the author use? How does she view this brand? What comparison does she draw? What does she like about it?

a young lawyer whose wife has really gone to seed since she had her two kids, or a fifty-year-old woman who has had nine children, weighs 105 and has abdominal muscles you could bounce a quarter off and who says she can't understand why, maybe it's her metabolism, but she can eat anything she wants, including a pint of Frusen Glädjé Swiss chocolate almond candy ice cream, and never gain a pound. So then I go out and exercise.

4   I do Nautilus. It is a series of fierce-looking machines, each designed, according to this book I have, to exercise some district muscle group, which all happen in my case never to have been exercised before. Nautilus was allegedly invented by Arthur Jones, husband of the aforementioned slim strong and sexy Terri, who is his seventeenth wife, or something like that. But I think anyone who comes upon a Nautilus machine suddenly will agree with me that its prototype was clearly invented at some time in history when torture was considered a reasonable alternative to diplomacy. Over each machine is a little drawing of a human body—not mine, of course—with a certain muscle group inked in red. This is so you can recognize immediately the muscle group that is on fire during the time you are using the machine.

5   There is actually supposed to be a good reason to do Nautilus, and it is supposed to be that it results in toning without bulk: that is, you will look like a dancer, not a defensive lineman. That may be compelling for Terri Jones, but I chose it because it takes me only a little more than a half hour—or what I like to think of as the time an average person burning calories at an average rate would need to read *Where the Wild Things Are, Good Night, Moon* and *The Cat in the Hat* twice—to finish all the machines. It is also not social, like aerobics classes, and will not hold you up to widespread ridicule, like running. I feel about exercise the same way that I feel about a few other things: that there is nothing wrong with it if it is done in private by consenting adults.

6   Actually, there are some of the Nautilus machines I even like. Call it old-fashioned machisma, but I get a kick out of building biceps. This is a throwback to all those times when my brothers would flex their arms and a mound of muscle would appear, and I would flex mine and nothing would happen, and they'd laugh and go off somewhere to smoke cigarettes and look at dirty pictures. There's a machine to exercise the inner thigh muscles that bears such a remarkable resemblance to a delivery room apparatus that every time I get into it I think someone is going to yell *push!* and I will have another baby. I feel comfortable with that one. On the other hand, there is another machine on which I am supposed to lift a weight straight up in the air and the most I ever manage is to squinch my face up until I look like an infant with bad gas: My instructor explained to me that this is because women have no upper body strength, which probably explains why I've always found it somewhat difficult to carry a toddler and an infant up four flights of stairs with a diaper bag over one shoulder while holding a Big Wheel.

7   Anyhow, the great thing about working out is that I have met a lot of very nice men. This would be a lot more important if I weren't married and the

mother of two. But of course if I were single and looking to meet someone, I would never meet anyone except married men and psychopaths. (This is Murphy's Other Law named after a Doreen Murphy, who in 1981 had a record eleven bad relationships in one year.) The men I have met seem to really get a kick out of the fact that I work out not unlike the kick that most of us get out of hearing very small children try to say words like hippopotamus or chauvinist. As one of the men at my gym said. Most of the people here are guys or women who are uh well hmm umm.

8   "In good shape," I said.

9   "I wouldn't have put it like that," he answered.

10   Because I go to the gym at the same time on the same days, I actually see the same men over and over again. One or two of them are high school students, which I find truly remarkable. When I was in high school, it was a big deal if a guy had shoulders, never mind muscles. So when I'm finished I go back into the locker room and take a shower. The eighteen-year-old is usually in there, and sometimes she'll say something like, "Oh, that's what stretch, marks look like." Then I put on my clothes and go home by the route that does not pass Dunkin Donuts. The bottom line is that I really hate to exercise, but I have found on balance that this working out is all worth it. One day we were walking down the street and one of the guys from my gym—it was actually one of the high school guys, the one with the great pecs—walked by and said "How ya doing?" My husband said. Who the hell is that guy? And I knew that Nautilus had already made a big difference in my life.

● **Vocabulary**

benign (1)
allegedly (4)
bulk (5)
psychopaths (7)

spontaneously (3)
prototype (4)
machisma (6)
chauvinist (7)

abdominal (3)
toning (5)
squinch (6)

● **The Facts**

1. What reason does the author give for working out at the gym? How does her reason differ from reasons given by the experts? What reason would you give for working out?

2. How often does the author go to the gym? Does she spend enough time there to keep herself trim? If you exercise regularly, what is your schedule and how effective is it? Do you recommend it to others? Give reasons for your answer.

3. Who are the two women the author meets in the locker room, and what is the significance of each encounter? Do you empathize with the author's reaction to these women or do you think she is being mean-spirited? Explain your view.

4. What brand of exercise machine does the author use? How does she view this brand? What comparison does she draw? What does she like about it?

5. How does the author offer proof that her exercising was worth all the pain and effort involved?

The Strategies

1. How is the title of the essay connected with the rest of the essay? What other title can you suggest?
2. The first two paragraphs offer an argument for going to the gym. What rhetorical mode begins with paragraph 3? What sentence clearly hints at the mode? What other modes are used throughout the essay? Point to specific paragraphs.
3. Quindlen's essay is filled with humor. How does the author achieve humorous passages? Is the humor gentle or barbed? Choose some examples and explain why they make you laugh.
4. Where in the essay does the author use figurative language? What is the effect? Find at least three figures of speech and explain them.
5. How does Quindlen come full circle in writing about why she started to exercise? How does her technique add or detract from the essay?

The Issues

1. What is your opinion of today's exercise craze? Has our country gone too far in creating so many expensive gyms with trainers to facilitate proper body building? Would an hour's walk every day be just as good? Explain how your feel about the importance of exercise in your life.
2. If you are a male, what about a woman attracts you to her in the long run? If you are a female, what about a man attracts you to him in the long run? How important are looks in a lasting relationship? Be honest in your appraisal.
3. What is your opinion about women who build up their biceps, pecs, and obliques, and about men who try to look like those body builders who hang out at beaches?
4. According to the author, one of the benefits of working out is that you meet nice men. What about meeting nice women? Discuss the social possibilities involved in joining some kind of gym or sports club.
5. To what extent is Quindlen's attitude about her body the result of a culture obsessed with youth? What are some real dangers associated with this obsession?

Suggestions for Writing

1. Write an essay in which you explain your attitude about body image and the importance of looking attractive and healthy. Support your essay with specific details.
2. Write an essay in which you make fun of one or more of your insecurities, such as hating to wear a bathing suit, fearing parties where you have to meet strangers, or feeling hesitant about speaking up in class to answer questions or give a report.

Punctuation Workshop
The Comma (,)

1. **Put a comma before *and, but, for, or, nor, yet, so* when they connect two independent clauses:** He played the guitar, and his brother played the saxophone.

2. **Put a comma between more than two items in a series:** Isaac ordered a salami sandwich, a salad, and ice cream.

    Treat an address or date as items in a series: He was born March 5, 1951, in Stoneham, Massachusetts.

    Omit commas if only the month and year are used in a date: The revolution began in May 1980.

3. **Use a comma after an introductory expression or an afterthought:** Well, that certainly was stressful.

4. **Use a comma after a dependent clause that begins a sentence:** Skating across the pond, she fell and broke her ankle.

5. **Put commas around the name of a person spoken to:** Be careful, Professor Gomez, not to slip.

6. **Put a comma around any expression that interrupts the flow of the sentence:** The poor, however, can't live only on food stamps.

7. **Put commas around material that is not essential to meaning:** Joseph Pendecost, who is a tile expert, will lecture on artistic kitchens.

    But if the clause is essential to meaning, no commas are needed: The man who is a tile expert will lecture on artistic kitchens. (No other man will lecture except the tile expert.)

8. **Use commas to separate a speaker from dialogue:** "Forget him," the mother said.

9. **Use commas as necessary to prevent misreading:**

    Woman: without her, man is nothing.
    Woman, without her man, is nothing.

STUDENT CORNER

Body Modification—Think about It!
Shelley Taylor, State University of New York, Oswego

Not long ago I heard a rumor that Barbie, that icon of glamour and favorite doll of girls from several generations, is getting a butterfly tattoo for her 40th birthday—or is it her 45th? Well, no matter, she hasn't aged a day in her life. She has to keep up with the latest fashion statements. After all, her future and reputation are at stake.

Almost everywhere you look these days you can see people with some sort of body alterations. The vast majority of these alterations are body piercings and tattoos. On a walk through a school campus or a shopping mall, for instance, you are bound to see ears adorned by multiple earrings, jeweled drops cascading down eyebrows, and glittering nose studs. There are yin yang symbols etched on ankles, cartoon characters inked on arms, and roses and names of loved ones permanently stamped on wrists (some other pictures aren't quite as "nice.") These are just examples of things you can SEE; many other body parts, including tongues, bellybuttons (well, I guess you CAN see those), and genitals, are routinely pierced, and tattoos can appear practically anywhere.

Actually, throughout history, people from various cultures have decorated their bodies with piercings and tattoos. In 1992, a 4,000-year-old body of a tattooed man was found in an Austrian glacier. From 4000 to 2000 B.C., Egyptians identified tattooing with fertility and nobility. Body piercing has been used as a symbol of royalty and courage, as well as other lauded attributes. In some societies, body piercing and tattoos have long been used in initiation rites and as socialization symbols.

Piercing is performed without anesthesia by either a spring-loaded ear-piercing gun or piercing needles, ranging in diameter from six to eighteen gauge. A tattoo is created by an electric needle, which injects colored pigment into small, deep holes made in the skin. Far too often, however, more crude and less-sanitary methods are used. Even under the best conditions, the process is painful. The discomfort of getting a tattoo has been compared to that of hair removal by electrolysis.

So, why is body alteration so popular? Why do people do this to themselves? The reason most often cited is that individuals feel a need to express themselves in a creative way. They want to tell the world "who they are" (or who they wish they were). The vast majority of body piercings and tattoos are performed on adolescents, many of whom consider what they wear and how they look to be as important as food and water. Modifying their bodies is their way of being non-traditional and "different."

Interestingly enough, however, being different is the last thing they really want to do. If their peers, especially those who comprise the "in-crowd," are doing something, they feel that they need to do it, too. They want to share a *common* identity, to belong to the group, to fit in. The media plays a big role in all of this. Models, sports idols, members of their favorite music groups, all endorsed by magazines, television, and movies, show off their body piercings and tattoos proudly, as the latest and "coolest" thing.

Teens DO strive to be different from their parents and anyone in the older generation. Body alterations are one way for them to say, "I'm growing up and making decisions on my own." This becomes, in a way, a rite of passage, declaring that they are changing and becoming mature. They are seeking their own place in society and a sense of empowerment. They are celebrating their growth toward and into adulthood.

Many would argue that changing their appearance is a relatively harmless way for adolescents to meet the need to search for their identities and to explore less traditional paths. After all, purple hair, hole-filled jeans, and sparkling navel jewels can hardly be compared with drugs and violence. Dress styles come and go, just as they have for centuries, and continue to make the world more interesting and less boring, if nothing else.

The very fact that fads pass so quickly, however, should give one pause when he or she is considering body alterations. While hair color and apparel can be changed easily, a piercing or a tattoo is a physical change that is harder to discard. Body piercing can be relatively temporary in the long run, unless certain types of infection or scarring occur, but its immediate implications can have far-reaching results. A tattoo, however, is permanent. It is not something a person can just take off and throw away when it is no longer in style or desirable. Obviously, this fact points out the utter foolishness of having the name of a boyfriend or girlfriend (or even a spouse) adorning some part of your body forever. What a way to complicate your future!

The question of appearance is an important one. Whether we like it or not, we cannot disregard how we are perceived by others. This factor makes a huge difference in our lives. It takes only ten to fifteen seconds for someone to create a first impression that can affect his or her life for years to come. Nowhere is this truer than in the job market. A prospective employer will take note of your appearance, before giving you a chance to answer a single question or tell about your qualifications. Tattoos and body piercings do not project the type of image that is valued in the conservative business community. Consequently, those who choose to have these body alterations will probably have fewer job opportunities than those who decide not to.

Health is a major issue that must be considered. There are potential health risks involved with the initial process of body piercing and tattooing. Take the tongue, for instance. Tongues swell to twice their normal size when first punctured. This often interferes with eating and effective breathing. Infections, blood clots, drooling, and damaged taste buds and nerves can also develop. Even broken teeth, choking, or impeded speech are possible. Other piercings can cause problems as well. Pierced navels take up to 12 months to heal and are painful, especially when irritated by waistbands. Nipple piercing may cause infection, an allergic reaction to the ring, or scarred milk ducts, which permanently interfere with breast-feeding. The cartilage in the upper ear heals slowly and may become infected. Piercing can cause permanent scarring and keloid formation. An allergic reaction to metal can result in contact dermatitis.

This is just the beginning. Even more serious side-effects can occur. Piercing can be responsible for endocarditis, urethral rupture, and a serious infection of the penis foreskin that can result in disability or death. Piercings and tattoos present the risk of chronic infection, hepatitis B and C, tetanus, and theoretically HIV, especially when proper sterilization and safety procedures are not followed. Black henna tattoos can cause significant rashes and allergies, which can lead to kidney failure and even death. These are especially dangerous to young children.

This brings me to another point. It is illegal for commercial tattoo and body-piercing businesses to administer body modification to a person younger than eighteen years of age unless a parent or guardian signs a consent form. An unfortunate response to this law is the practice of "homemade" tattoos and piercings. Adolescents are getting these body alterations from friends or other amateurs who make their own tools with the use of pens, erasers, and paper clips and perform the procedures under unsanitary conditions. Very young children are being influenced to "be cool" like the older kids they look up to and want to emulate, often with tragic consequences. Not long ago, in an elementary school in Fort Worth, Texas, ten third graders tried to give themselves tattoos using razor blades.

Literally, then, body modification can be a matter of life and death. This is true in another way, which some may not be aware of. As I alluded to before, this practice can represent symbols of group identity. This is often associated with gangs. Members of gangs apply tags or marks to show that they belong to their particular group. Middle-school students (grades five to eight) acquire most of these tags, as a part of gang initiation. Specific color and clothing combinations and tattoos are examples of such tagging. Tattoos are usually applied by fellow gang members.

I worked for a short time in a detention facility for adjudicated youth, ages twelve to eighteen, who had each been convicted of at least one crime. As part of our training, we attended a seminar given by a law officer who had spent years studying gang operations and working with individual gang members. He informed us that graffiti, artwork, specific colors, styles of clothing, music, and dances were all part of the messages that gangs send to their own members and to those who belong to rival gangs.

They establish territory and warn other groups of violent repercussions if this territory is not respected. Even dance moves and hand signals have significant meaning. He told of a rock music performer who was murdered by the "Bloods" because he did the "Crip Walk" (or was it the other way around?) and made "disrespectful" signs with his fingers while on a public stage. Immediately I thought of the thousands of kids who are permanently marked with gang tattoos and the danger that this places them in. It is a known fact that prisoners with these tattoos are in fear for their lives while they are incarcerated with other criminals who have come out of rival gangs.

This fear of gang reprisal, along with the tendency of employers and law officials to associate tattoo markings with crime-related activities, has caused many to try to get their tattoos removed. Often these people are gang members who want out. Yet, of the 10 million Americans who have tattoos, almost half want their tattoos removed—for a variety of reasons. Clinics that offer tattoo removal are springing up everywhere, not only in the U.S., but in other countries as well, especially those in Central and South America. The demand is still more than can be accommodated at this time. Tattoo removal is expensive and is also a very long and painful process. Laser treatments cost thousands of dollars each and have been likened to hot bacon grease streaming down the skin. After multiple sessions, there is still a shadow on the skin while the laser-transmitted pigment enters the lymph system. Other methods of removal involve cutting the skin off with a scalpel or sanding the tattoo off with a wire brush. Many times, total success is not achieved.

So how do you decide what is right for you? Just be sure to consider everything very carefully. As you can see, there is a lot to think about. Take your time. Don't rush out and do something drastic without asking a lot of questions. Are you doing this for yourself or because you want to be like your friends? After all, it is your body. Are the benefits worth all of the risks involved? Are there career plans to consider? How do you think you will want to look in ten years or so? That reminds me—if you decide to go ahead with this, don't gain weight. A cute little frog tattooed onto a size 4 stomach can look pretty scary after it has stretched and grown, twenty, thirty, or more pounds later.

Remember that this decision will most likely affect the rest of your life. That makes it extremely important, wouldn't you say? Whether you are a teenager, a young adult, or a middle-aged person who has always dreamed of doing something fun and outrageous, don't forget to look at all sides of this issue. It will be well worth the trouble. At the risk of being unoriginal, I would like to end with a quotation from one of those very wise anonymous writers for *The College Chalkboard* Web site: "Ponder before you pierce, and think before you ink." I couldn't have said it better myself.

How I Write

Before I actually begin writing, I do a lot of reflective thinking and organizing in my mind. I decide what information I am going to include and try to get a rough idea of the order and format I want to use. I usually sketch out an outline that I can follow. When actually writing the piece, I sit down at the computer and start typing, referring constantly to my outline. I edit and make changes as I go along until I am satisfied with the result. After I have finished, I read through my work several times to do further editing.

How I Wrote This Essay

While working on this piece, I used the Internet to look up a few sites and articles on my subject, to get an idea about current research, others' opinions, etc. I searched my memory for incidents in my own experience and illustrations that were relevant to the issue. Finally, I synthesized and integrated all of this information so as to formulate my own thoughts, feelings, and insights.

My Writing Tips

- Start your writing with something that will capture the attention of your reader—such as an interesting story or illustration, an amazing fact, or a dynamic statement.
- Be imaginative, descriptive, and creative.
- Avoid using redundant words and phrases in your writing.
- Make sure that your grammar and spelling are correct and that your ideas are presented as clearly as possible.
- Be sincere. Always be present in your work. Anyone can write down a bunch of facts, but your own insights and personality can make the words come to life.
- Leave your reader with something to think about. (I personally think the introduction and conclusion are the crucial parts of an essay.)

● CHAPTER WRITING ASSIGNMENTS

1. Write an essay in which you describe one of the following places:
   a. The most peaceful place you know
   b. The most disturbing place you have ever been to
   c. The most boring place you know
2. Write an essay describing a particularly vivid dream. Begin by thinking of and writing down a dominant impression for the scenes you saw in your dream. Using that dominant impression as your thesis, write a description that is supported by specific details.

● WRITING ASSIGNMENTS FOR A SPECIFIC AUDIENCE

1. Write a diary entry, describing the major events of your day. Treat your diary as a confidential, intimate friend to whom you can trust your innermost feelings.
2. Write to your parents, describing to them your college living quarters or a letter to a friend describing your favorite spot on campus.

● COLLABORATIVE WRITING PROJECT

Joining three other students in the class, go—pen and notebook in hand—to a place on campus. Sit and observe your environment for five minutes, trying to absorb details you normally would not notice. Then spend another ten to fifteen minutes writing a list of these details in your notebook. Exchange your list with those of the other students in your group. Because we can assume that four pairs of eyes are better than one, you should now have enough details to develop an essay vividly describing the spot you observed, beginning with a dominant impression and supporting that impression with the details you observed. Once you have completed your essay, compare it with the essays of the other members in your group.

- **IMAGE GALLERY ASSIGNMENT**

Visit pages 650–652 of our image gallery and study all three images dealing with body image. Then choose the image that most appeals to you. Answer the questions and do the writing assignment.

9

Process Analysis

ROAD MAP TO PROCESS ANALYSIS

What Process Analysis Does

An essay that gives instructions on how to do something or describes how something was done is developed by *process analysis*. Many best-sellers have been written in this mode, all bearing such telltale how-to titles as *How to Make a Million in Real Estate* or *How to Learn Spanish the Easy Way*. Historians such as Will Durant use process analysis to tell us how Spartan warriors were trained, how Christianity became the dominant religion of Western civilization, and how the Battle of Normandy was won. Like narration, process analysis presents information in chronological order, commonly in the form of instructions. Here, a student explains the process of cooking vegetables in a microwave oven:

> If you follow these seven easy steps, you will have the pleasure of eating vegetables cooked al dente the way they are done in the finest restaurants where nouvelle cuisine is the rage:
>
> First, choose three vegetables that normally take approximately the same time to cook (for instance, carrots, broccoli, and summer squash). For aesthetic purposes it is a good idea to choose vegetables of different colors.
>
> Second, slice the vegetables into bite-size pieces or slices, depending on which is easier.
>
> Third, arrange the pieces in alternating circles on a ceramic quiche plate.
>
> Fourth, add butter, salt, and pepper to taste.
>
> Fifth, pour one-half cup of water over the vegetables.
>
> Sixth, place a piece of plastic wrap over the plate and seal the sides.
>
> Last, cook the vegetables in the microwave oven for four minutes on "high." The vegetables will be crisply delicious and ready to serve the most discriminating of palates. Best of all, the vitamins will be preserved.

Although process analysis is a simple rhetorical mode and is fairly straightforward to write, it is often done badly and with irksome consequences. Anyone who has ever struggled to understand an inept manual meant to explain some necessary but practical chore can attest to the importance of clear process writing.

When to Use Process Analysis

Although found in all kinds of writing, process explanations are common in science and technology, where they vary from instructions on how to perform a simple test for acidity to how to diagnose a high-risk pregnancy with ultrasound. Many of your classes will require you to write various process explanations: A political-science teacher may ask you to describe how a bill is passed in Congress; a geology teacher, how glaciers are formed; a botany teacher, how flowers are reproduced. Process explanations can range from a historical blow-by-blow account of Custer's Last Stand to an anthropological explanation of how ancient tribes buried their dead.

How to Write a Process Analysis

The first and most important step in writing a process essay is to select an appropriate subject. Decide whether your overall purpose is to give instructions or to inform. If you intend, say, to instruct readers in how to organize a volunteer team to nab graffiti writers or how to study for the SAT, your purpose is to give instructions. On the other hand, if you want to list the circumstances that led to the collapse of the dot com companies in 2001 or the sequence of events that led to the resignation of President Richard Nixon, your purpose is to inform. In writing either kind of essay, you must know and be able to cite appropriate details.

State Your Purpose in a Clear Thesis The second step in writing your process essay is to begin with a thesis that plainly states your overall aim. "It is possible for you to acquire a competitive spirit" is an example of a thesis that leaves your reader in the dark and is singularly unhelpful to you, the writer. On the other hand, the thesis "You can acquire a competitive spirit by practicing five personality traits" establishes an agenda for the writer and tells the reader what to expect—a recital and description of the five traits. Similarly, "I want to inform you how juveniles are imprisoned," tells your reader practically nothing. Contrast it with this more helpful thesis: "Juveniles face four legal steps before they can be imprisoned."

A convenient and simple way to make the steps of your explanation stand out is to number them 1, 2, 3, etc. For example, in an explanation to a nonswimmer of *how* to become drownproof, the logical sequence of steps is as follows:

1. Take a deep breath.
2. Float vertically in the water.

3. Lift the arms to shoulder height and give scissors kicks while flapping the arms down in a winging motion.
4. Raise the head out of the water and exhale.

This sequence of steps is the only one that works, so your explanation must cover it accurately.

Organize the Sequence of Steps Logically Next, you should arrange the steps in the most logical order. Essays that cover simple how-to tasks such as changing a tire or baking a cake are best organized chronologically. On the other hand, essays on broader topics, such as how to build self-esteem in a child, how to make a marriage work, or how Stalin rose to power, are best organized in order of importance.

Regardless of which arrangement you use, you should single out and explain each step clearly. It often helps to sketch out the steps exactly as they will occur in your chosen order. For example, let us say that your parents won a court case against a landlord for discriminating against them because of their ethnic origin. Using your familiarity with their case, combined with further research, you decide to write a paper on how to file an antidiscrimination housing suit. Here are your steps, outlined chronologically:

1. File the complaint with the local Fair Housing Council.
2. Explain your reasons for filing to the investigator who hears your complaint.
3. If the investigation uncovers evidence of discrimination, state or federal authorities will formally accuse the landlord of discrimination. (If your case has no merit, the matter will probably fizzle out here.)
4. Choose between appearing before an administrative hearing officer or hiring an attorney to file a lawsuit in civil court.
5. Either the case will be solved through a settlement or the state will impose a punitive fine to compensate for damages.

Once you have outlined these steps clearly, all you have to do is flesh out the essay with necessary facts and details.

Explain Everything The devil is said to be in the details, and that is clearly the case in process essays. Always assume that your reader is uninformed about your subject. Explain everything. Don't be vague, as maddeningly unhelpful manuals often are. If your essay is giving specific directions about how to do something, simply address the reader directly, as in a command: "Next, [you] fold the paper along the dotted line.... Then, [you] write your personal number in the upper left-hand corner," and so on.

It also helps to carefully signal the succession of described steps with words such as "first," "second," "next," "then," and "finally." Within each step, using words such as "before," "after," and "while" can help the reader keep track of the discussion. It might even be helpful to mention a previous step before going on to the next. For example, in a process essay about how juveniles are imprisoned, the first step might be for the police to bring the youth to a screening office. If so, you might introduce the second step this way, "If after the screening has taken place the case still cannot be informally resolved, the second step is to arrange a date for a court hearing."

As we said, process essays are usually straightforward and relatively simple to write. Most require no poetic or metaphoric language—a manual so written would drive consumers over the brink—and generally demand nothing more of a writer than a sensible grasp of facts and the ability to explain them in understandable sequence.

Warming Up to Write a Process Analysis

1. Choosing one of the following how-to processes, write down in chronological order or in order of importance the steps involved in completing the task. Do not omit a step.
   a. How to trim a Christmas tree
   b. How to intelligently read a newspaper
   c. How to make your college professors like you
   d. How to get ready for a long-distance bicycle race
   e. How to ask for a dinner date, or how to turn down a dinner date
2. Choosing one of the following how-it-happened processes, write down the major steps that led up to it.
   a. How a friend of yours got hooked on an illegal drug such as cocaine or ecstasy
   b. How a serious accident that involved you or a loved one occurred
   c. How Saddam Hussein was finally caught and detained so that he would face a trial.
   d. The stages of AIDS
3. From each group, choose the best topic for a process essay.
   a. 1. How to fly a commercial airplane
      2. How to wash a car
      3. How to write a novel
      4. How to speak Chinese
   b. 1. How the world came into being
      2. How your great-grandfather became a millionaire
      3. The stages of international economic bankruptcy
      4. How the United Nations functions

> Stumped by ending an essay? Exit on page 696, at the **Editing Booth!**

EXAMPLES

This Is a Mortal Wound, Doctor
THOMAS FLEMING

Thomas Fleming (b. 1927) is a distinguished historian and the author of numerous critically acclaimed bestselling novels, such as *The Officers' Wives* (1981), which tells the story of three West Point officers. Fleming is also the author of the CBS miniseries *Liberty! The American Revolution*. In 1994 Fleming was elected a Fellow of the Society of American Historians. He writes frequently for *American Heritage* magazine and is contributing editor of the *Quarterly Journal of Military History*. His nonfiction account of America's most famous political clash—*Duel: Alexander Hamilton, Aaron Burr, and the Future of America* (2000)—finds its place on most library and bookstore shelves. It is the source from which the essay below has been excerpted. His most recent book, *Mysteries of My Father* (2005) is a memoir of Fleming's relationship with his father. Fleming resides in New York City.

That two great statesmen like Alexander Hamilton and Aaron Burr would ever have agreed to fight a duel like ordinary gunslingers in a western movie will seem to many modern readers a little short of preposterous. But in 1804, when this duel was fought, a man's honor was more than his name; it was his passport to society and had to be defended at all costs. As you read, note the careful piling up of events as the author leads us through the process of this fateful duel, with the details of that historic and deadly encounter providing plenty of suspense.

* * *

I

1   That same night, July 10th, in his New York City house, Nathaniel Pendleton* was writing the regulations for tomorrow's duel. He dated the paper July 11th—perhaps a sign of his inner agitation or of the way that date loomed in his mind. The parties were to leave New York for the dueling ground at 5:00 a.m. The distance was to be ten paces—about thirty feet. The pistols were not to exceed eleven inches in the barrel. The choice of positions would be determined by a coin toss.

---

*Nathaniel Pendleton, a friend and legal colleague of Hamilton, who acted as his second, his assistant.

2   The previous day, William P. Van Ness had written his own set of regulations, which agreed with Pendleton's almost verbatim. Oarsmen had been hired by the seconds to row the three miles across the Hudson to Weehawken. For a doctor, both sides had agreed to call on Hamilton's family physician, David Hosack.[1] There was nothing more for anyone to do but try to get some sleep.

3   The night was hot and muggy—typical New York weather for July. How or if Hamilton slept in his Cedar Street house has gone unrecorded. We know Burr threw himself down on a couch in the Richmond Hill library. William P. Van Ness, John Swartout, and Matthew Davis found him there in the predawn darkness, sleeping soundly. He dressed quickly in black pantaloons, half boots, and a coat of dark bombazine. They hurried down to the shore of the Hudson, where a boat was waiting for the colonel and Van Ness. Duelists generally did not breakfast. It was widely believed that food in the stomach would lead to rapid infection if a bullet penetrated that organ.

4   Van Ness and Burr reached the dueling ground first, and began clearing away tree limbs and underbrush. No one had exchanged shots on this grassy ledge below the cliffs known as the Palisades for some time. The outcropping was about six feet wide and eleven yards long. At one corner was a granite boulder. Nearby stood a large cedar tree. The site had become a dueling ground because of its inaccessibility. There was no path leading down the cliff face from the village of Weehawken. Walkers along the Hudson shore could only reach it at low tide. The future town of Hoboken, two and a half miles to the south, was unborn. The isolation was a virtual guarantee against an interruption of the deadly business transacted there.

5   Hamilton set out from another dock in what is now Greenwich Village, not far from the country house of New York merchant William Bayard, a client and friend. The General and Nathaniel Pendleton may have been delayed by the necessity to collect Dr. Hosack. They seem to have arrived on the Weehawken shore considerably after Burr and Van Ness. The physician stayed down on the water's edge with the boatmen while the General and his second clambered up a narrow path to find Burr and Van Ness in their shirt sleeves, clearing away nature's debris. The two parties greeted each other in gentlemanly fashion. The seconds conferred on the regulations and found they were in agreement. They had already decided to use the Church pistols.**

6   Burr put on his coat and waited at a distance. Hamilton stayed at a roughly equal distance on the other side of the seconds while they tossed a coin to see who would have the choice of positions and who would give the order to fire. Pendleton won both tosses. By now it was approaching seven o'clock. The July sun had begun beating down on the river, creating an intense glare. The sun itself was still low enough in the sky to strike the dueling ground at an angle. Pendleton chose to position Hamilton with his back to the cliff, facing the light. Some people have criticized him for this move, but

---

**Pistols belonging to John Barker Church, Hamilton's brother-in-law.

Pendleton probably thought Burr was a better target, outlined against the glistening river. Hamilton had said he was going to throw away his first fire, but he had not decided on his second round, if Burr insisted on one.

II

7 The two seconds now loaded the pistols with powder and a "smooth ball," as the regulations required. The inside of the guns' barrels was also smooth. This made a handgun, with its short barrel, though precision made, even more inaccurate than a musket. Inside and outside the barrel, the spinning bullet was subject to forces over which the gun wielder had no control. A rifled barrel, prohibited by the dueling code, would give a marksman far more accuracy. Beyond thirty yards, a smoothbore pistol was almost a useless weapon, and even at that range it was extremely unpredictable. These ballistics were part of the reason why the duel was not always a fatal encounter.

8 With the pistols loaded, the duelists took their positions, and their seconds walked over to hand each his weapon. As Pendleton gave General Hamilton his gun, he asked: "Do you want the hair spring set?"

9 "Not this time," Hamilton replied.

10 Pendleton stepped back and walked out of the line of fire. He briefly explained the rules they were following. First he would ask them if they were ready. If they answered in the affirmative, he would say "Present!" Thereafter, each could fire whenever he pleased.

11 Both men nodded. At this point, according to Burr and William P. Van Ness, General Hamilton raised his pistol "as if to try the light," and asked them to pardon him. He said the "direction of the light" made it hard for him to adjust his eyes. With his left hand, he drew spectacles from his pocket and put them on.

12 Pendleton asked if they were ready. "Yes," both said.

13 "Present!" Pendleton said.

14 By this time, both men had assumed the duelist's stance, the right foot about twenty-six inches in front of the left foot, the face positioned over the right shoulder, the stomach sucked in, the right thigh and leg covering the left leg. The goal was to present as little body surface as possible. Even the pistol was wielded with protection in mind; it was held somewhat to the left, where it could deflect a bullet.[2]

15 Both men leveled their pistols and the guns boomed within seconds of each other. Van Ness thought Hamilton fired first. He spun his head to see if Burr was hit. At that instant the colonel fired and almost simultaneously his body seemed to jerk as if Hamilton's bullet had struck him. Later, Van Ness would discover Burr had stepped on a stone as he assumed the oblique position and as he fired he must have pressed his foot on it.

16 Pendleton thought Burr fired first. His eyes remained on Hamilton and the Virginian saw his arm jerk upward as he pulled the trigger. To his horror he realized the General was hit. A swirl of gunsmoke enveloped both duelists. For a moment, time, perception, understanding froze. Still clutching his pistol,

Hamilton pitched forward on his face. The oversize lead ball had penetrated his right side a little above the hip, torn through his liver and diaphragm, and lodged in his vertebrae.

17   The vice president uttered a small sound of dismay and started toward him. Pendleton shouted: "Dr. Hosack!" Van Ness rushed forward and led Burr down the path toward the water. One account has him shielding Burr with an umbrella so that the boatmen and Dr. Hosack, who were rushing up the same path, could not testify that they had seen him there. When Burr and Van Ness reached their boat, the vice president hesitated. "I must go and speak to him," he reportedly said. Van Ness persuaded him this was out of the question and the boatmen soon had them out on the river.[3]

18   Dr. Hosack found Hamilton half sitting on the ground in Nathaniel Pendleton's arms. "This is a mortal wound, Doctor," he gasped. A second later he lost consciousness and Hosack thought he was going to die on the spot. The doctor pulled up his bloody shirt and saw at a glance that Hamilton was probably right. Hosack could find no pulse, nor was Hamilton breathing. He put his hand on the General's heart and found no motion there. Hosack thought Hamilton was "irretrievably gone."

19   Against the cliff the air was dense with heat and humidity. Hosack decided the only hope was to get the General on the water as soon as possible. Together he and Pendleton carried him down the path to the point where the land fell steeply to the water's edge. As they labored, an anguished Pendleton told Hosack about Hamilton's refusal to fire at Burr. With the help of the oarsmen they got the wounded man into the boat and pulled off. Hosack began rubbing Hamilton's face with spirits of hartshorne. He applied this invigorating potion to his neck and chest and wrists and palms, and even tried to get some into his mouth.

20   About fifty yards from shore, Hamilton gave a great sigh and began breathing again. The hartshorne, along with the cooler air on the river, had restored him to life. His eyes wandered across the water and around the boat and he muttered: "My vision is indistinct." Gradually, his pulse returned to near normal, his breathing became regular. Hosack tried to examine the wound but even a slight touch caused Hamilton such pain, he "desisted."

III

21   As Hamilton's sight returned, he saw John Barker Church's pistol case open in the bottom of the boat, with the gun he had used lying outside it. "Take care of that pistol," he said. "It is undischarged and still cocked—it may go off and do harm." Attempting to turn his head to Pendleton, who was sitting behind him in the stern, Hamilton added: "Pendleton knows I did not intend to fire at him."

22   "Yes," Pendleton said. "I have already told Dr. Hosack that."

23   Hamilton fell silent. After a few minutes with the only sound the grunts of the sweating oarsmen, Dr. Hosack began asking the wounded man how he felt—nauseous, dizzy? He was trying to get some idea what organs the bullet had struck. Hamilton told him he had lost all feeling in his body from the

waist down. He could not move his legs. Hosack tried to rearrange his legs hoping circulation would be restored, but Hamilton reported no improvement. Once or twice he asked Hosack to take his pulse, which the doctor reported was still fairly normal.

24   As they approached the shore, Hamilton told Pendleton and Hosack to send for his wife. He asked them to break the news to her gradually. "Give her hopes," he said.

25   A moment later they were alongside the dock from which they had set out. Looking up, Hamilton found his friend William Bayard gazing down at him. A servant had seen Hamilton and Pendleton and Hosack setting out in the dawn and told Bayard, who immediately knew where they were going. Bayard already feared the worst. As the boat approached he saw only Hosack and Pendleton sitting up. When the merchant saw Hamilton lying in the bottom of the boat he burst into tears.

26   Hosack told Bayard to prepare a bed for his wounded friend. Bayard was so overwhelmed by grief, he was almost useless. His whole family was soon weeping and wailing. Pendleton and Dr. Hosack almost joined them. In his account of this part of the return from Weehawken, the doctor noted that only Hamilton kept his composure.

IV

27   When they finally got the General to a bed on the second floor of Bayard's lamentation-filled house, Hamilton seemed almost comatose. But Dr. Hosack revived him with some wine and water. With help from others, the doctor undressed him and administered a strong "anodyne"—a painkiller. He rubbed it on the parts of Hamilton's body where he complained of pain, particularly his back. The drug did little to assuage the wounded man's agony.

28   Dr. Hosack sent for Dr. Wright Post, professor of anatomy at Columbia College and one of the New York's leading physicians. Dr. Post soon arrived but he only confirmed Dr. Hosack's opinion that the wound was mortal.

29   Several hours later, the French consul sent surgeons from two men of war in New York harbor in the hope that their experience with gunshot wounds might help. But they too concluded that General Hamilton was a dying man.

30   The General had no doubts about his diagnosis. His thoughts were already focused on the next world. He asked the Bayards to send a servant to Benjamin Moore, Episcopal bishop of New York and president of Columbia College. The bishop came as requested, but was unhappy to learn that Hamilton had been wounded in a duel, an activity Moore considered sinful. Worse, the dying man had never joined the Episcopal church. When Moore learned that Hamilton wanted to receive holy communion, the Bishop demurred. This reception of the body and blood of Jesus, in a consecrated water of bread, was for Christians a central act of faith, and could not be administered casually. The bishop departed, declaring he wanted to give the dying man "time for reflection."

31   Hamilton asked Bayard to summon another clergyman, the Reverend John M. Mason, pastor of the Scotch Presbyterian Church. This was the faith

that had stirred Hamilton in his youth, when a Presbyterian minister had befriended the orphaned boy on St. Croix. Mason hurried to Bayard's house. But the minister sadly informed Hamilton that his church forbade him to give communion privately. It could only be done at the altar, in the course of a Sunday ceremony. He tried to assure Hamilton that communion was only a "pledge" of the forgiveness of sin that Jesus had purchased by his death on the cross. The same forgiveness was available to Hamilton by faith.

32   The dying man did not find this idea satisfactory and pleaded for someone to persuade Bishop Moore to return as soon as possible. Meanwhile, around noon, Elizabeth Hamilton arrived. In obedience to the General's wishes, no one had told her the truth about his condition. She believed Hamilton was suffering from stomach spasms. But a few minutes with her husband must have revealed everything. When Betsy grew frantic and grief, Hamilton reminded her in a strong, firm voice: "Remember, Eliza, you are a Christian."[4]

33   The news that General Hamilton was dying of a mortal wound inflicted by Vice President Burr spread swiftly through New York. Oliver Wolcott, Jr., who was preparing to leave the city to join his wife in Connecticut rushed to Bayard's house but was advised that a visit to the General's bedside was out of the question. Returning home, Wolcott scribbled a distressed letter to his wife, telling her that he would be delayed. One line exposed the central truth of the tragedy. Wolcott wrote that Hamilton had convinced himself that while dueling was criminal, "peculiar reasons . . . rendered it proper for him to expose himself to Col. Burr in particular."[5]

34   About 1:00 p.m. Bishop Moore returned to the Bayard House and spoke with Hamilton. As the bishop recalled it later that day, Hamilton said: "My dear sir, you perceive my unfortunate situation, and no doubt have been made acquainted with the circumstances which led to it. It is my desire to receive the communion at your hands. I hope you will not conceive there is any impropriety in my request." Hamilton added that for some time it had been "the wish of my heart" to join the church. He did not explain why he had never gotten around to it.

35   The Bishop lectured him. Hamilton was putting him in a "delicate" situation. He wanted to relieve "a fellow mortal in distress." But he had to uphold the law of God, which required him to "unequivocally condemn" dueling. Hamilton humbly assured the bishop that he agreed with him and he viewed his trip to Weehawken "with sorrow and contrition." The Bishop sternly asked him, if he regained his health, to promise never to fight another duel. Hamilton said that was his "deliberate intention."

36   Mollified, the bishop asked the General if he repented of his past sins and had a "lively faith" in God's mercy through Jesus Christ. Was he disposed "to live in love and charity with all men"? Hamilton lifted his hands and vowed he could answer yes to all these questions. He said he had "no ill will" toward Colonel Burr. He had met him with a "fixed resolution" not to do him any harm. He forgave him for "all that happened"—the challenge and the duel.

37   The bishop gave Hamilton holy communion. He said the dying man received it" with great devotion" and "his heart afterwards appeared perfectly at rest."[6] Dr. Hosack gave a somewhat amended version of his patient's condition. He said Hamilton, as he writhed in agony, repeatedly muttered: "My beloved

wife and children."[7] The General spent the rest of the day in terrific pain. That night he had what Dr. Hosack called "some imperfect sleep," no doubt helped by the ounce of laudanum that the physician gave him.

V

38 In Richmond Hill, a half mile away from the Bayard house, Vice President Burr was hearing things, perhaps from his servants, perhaps from friends who had contacts with visitors to the Bayards. He scribbled a letter to William Van Ness: "There is in circulation a report which is ascribed to Mr. Pendleton & which he must forthwith contradict." Almost certainly Burr was referring to Hamilton's determination to throw away his first fire. Pendleton had already told this to Dr. Hosack and probably to Bayard and some of the visitors.

39 If Van Ness could not come to Richmond Hill, Burr was ready to visit him in the city, even though the latter "would you know, not be very pleasant."[8] Already the vice president was discovering that the reaction to Hamilton's death was drastically altering his assumption of what he could achieve in the duel.

VI

40 In the morning Hamilton's pain was less but his other symptoms—the inability to move his legs or feel his body from the waist down—were "aggravated." Hosack hesitated to give him a purgative because of the stomach and bowel problems from which Hamilton had been suffering. No doubt the doctor was disinclined to try any of the other so-called heroic methods common in the medicine of his time such as bloodletting and blistering because he knew the case was hopeless.

41 Sometime during the previous day or night, Elizabeth Hamilton had brought the seven Hamilton children down from The Grange. They accompanied her to their father's bedside. Hamilton gazed for a moment at their weeping faces and closed his eyes until they were led from the room. What could he say to them? The distraction on his daughter Angelica's face must have been especially painful. His passion for fame had inflicted a second even more terrible wound on her psyche.[9]

42 Bishop Moore visited Hamilton later in the morning. With a faltering voice, the dying man again expressed his confidence in God's mercy through Jesus. The bishop stayed by the bedside for the next hours, as Hamilton's life signs ebbed. He was joined by a grief-stricken Angelica Schuyler Church. The man she loved more than her husband or any other person on earth did not try to say anything intimate. Her presence was enough, for both of them.

43 From Aaron Burr, in nearby Richmond Hill came a letter to Dr. Hosack.

> Mr. Burr's respectful Compliments. He requests Dr. Hosack to inform him of the present state of Genl. H. and of the hopes which are entertained of his recovery.
>
> Mr. Burr begs to know at what hours of the [day] the Dr. may most probably be found at home, that he may repeat his inquiries. He would

take it very kind if the Dr. would take the trouble of calling on him as he returns from Mr. Bayard's.[10]

44 At round the same time, a grief-stricken Nathaniel Pendleton was writing a letter to Rufus King, who had left New York for Massachusetts a few days before the duel took place. "Before you read this, our dear and excellent friend Hamilton will be no more." Aware that Hamilton had consulted King about the clash, Pendleton omitted most of the details, simply saying: "Burr's first shot was fatal." He described the probable course of the bullet through Hamilton's body and mournfully reported: "I have just left him and the doctors say he cannot outlive the day." Pendleton added that he did not have time to discuss the reflections that were crowding upon his mind "on this . . . public and private calamity." He would only add that the news had already "occasioned a strong public sensation which will be much increased when he is dead."[11]

VII

45 Late on the previous day, a friend had told Governor Morris that Hamilton was dead, killed by Aaron Burr. The statesman rushed from Morrisania to New York on the morning of July 12th, to be told that Hamilton was still alive in Bayard's house. Hurrying there, he found Hamilton "speechless"—comatose and obviously dying. "The scene is too powerful for me," Morris later told his diary. "I am obliged to walk in the garden to take breath."[12]

46 Regaining his self-control, Morris returned to the bedside, where he was joined by several other Hamilton friends. At two o'clock in the afternoon, the General died. Bishop Moore reported that he expired "without a struggle, and almost without a groan." Tears streaming down his face, one friend turned to Morris and said: "If we were truly brave we would not accept a challenge. But we are all cowards."[13] Morris morosely observed that the friend was one of the bravest men alive, but he doubted if he would "so far brave public opinion as to refuse a challenge." Dr. Hosack found words from the Roman poet Horace (mourning the death of another general) swirling through his head.

> Incorrupta fides, nudaque veritas,
> Quando ullum invenient parem?
> Multis ille bonis flebilis occidit.
>
> When will incorruptible Faith and naked Truth
> Find another his equal?
> He has died wept by many.[14]

Works Cited

1. *The Papers of Alexander Hamilton,* NY: Columbia UP, 1961–79. Ed. Goebel Julius Jr. Vol. 26, 60.
2. Steinmetz. *The Romance of Duelling,* 81–84.
3. *PAH,* Vol. 26, 341.
4. *PAH,* Vol. 26, 317; 347.

5. Ibid., 317.
6. Ibid., 315–16.
7. Ibid., 347.
8. Ibid., 341.
9. Ibid., 347.
10. Ibid., 312.
11. *Pendleton Papers*. New York Historical Society. Pendleton to Rufus, 1804.
12. Morris, *Diary and Letters of Gouverneur Morris*, Vol. 2, 455–56.
13. Ibid., 458.
14. *The Papers of Alexander Hamilton,* NY: Columbia UP, 1961–79. Ed. Goebel Julius Jr. Vol. 26, 347.

Vocabulary

loomed (1)　　　　　verbatim (2)　　　　　seconds (2)
pantaloons (3)　　　　bombazine (3)　　　　outcropping (4)
debris (5)　　　　　　smoothbore (7)　　　　ballistics (7)
wielded (14)　　　　　deflect (14)　　　　　oblique (15)
perception (16)　　　　irretrievably (18)　　　desisted (20)
comatose (27)　　　　assuage (27)　　　　　demurred (30)
impropriety (34)　　　unequivocally (35)　　　contrition (35)
mollified (36)　　　　forthwith (38)　　　　purgative (40)
ebbed (42)　　　　　calamity (44)　　　　　morosely (46)
incorruptible (46)

The Facts

1. What were the regulations mentioned in paragraph 1? What role did Nathaniel Pendleton and William Van Ness play in the ensuing drama?
2. Who reached the dueling grounds first and what did they proceed to do? Why was their action necessary? What made this grassy knoll an ideal spot for duels?
3. When Pendleton gave the signal to present, what conflicting stories were given about what happened? How has history resolved this dispute?
4. What were Hamilton's first words as Dr. Hosack hurried to give him medical help? What did these words indicate?
5. What comment did Hamilton make about the pistol lying in its open case at the bottom of the boat? What was the importance of this comment?
6. Once Hamilton was placed in bed at his friend Bayard's home, what did his own physician do in a last-ditch effort to save Hamilton's life? Was he successful?
7. Before dying, what important spiritual request did Hamilton make? Was the request granted? Discuss your reaction to how Hamilton's request was treated.

The Strategies

1. What clues tell the observant reader that this essay is in actuality a chapter from a book? What advantages or disadvantages does excerpting this passage have for the reader?

2. How does the author proceed to give the reader a vivid and accurate picture of the famous historical confrontation between Hamilton and Burr?
3. What does the author accomplish in paragraphs 7 through 15? What was your reaction as you read these paragraphs?
4. How does the author create a temporary sense of relief concerning Hamilton's physical state? Provide an example from the essay.
5. What effect is created by recording Hamilton's dying words?
6. What is the effect of Burr's letter to Dr. Hosack (see paragraph 43)? How did you respond to this letter? Did you find it a message of concern for a colleague or a message of concern for self? Give reasons for your answer.

The Issues

1. Here is a summary of the events (not mentioned in the excerpt) that led to the duel between Alexander Hamilton and Aaron Burr: Burr knew that Hamilton had supported Burr's candidacy for the vice-presidency of the United States only because Burr was connected to Thomas Jefferson as the presidential candidate. When Burr was nominated for governor of New York, Hamilton blocked him from this position. At one point, Burr accused Hamilton of having called him "a dangerous man," and challenged the other man to a duel when Hamilton did not deny the charge. How do you believe this confrontation between politicians would be resolved today? What is your opinion of this duel?
2. What surprising fact about the geography of the duel comes to light in this essay? Where is the place today? What major geographical changes, if any, has your neighborhood experienced over the years?
3. How do you interpret the conversation between Pendleton and Hamilton (see paragraphs 8 and 9). What is the meaning of Hamilton's answer "not this time"?
4. Paragraph 17 hints that Burr was dismayed by seeing Hamilton fall to the ground. In fact, he reportedly told Van Ness, his second, "I must go and speak to him." But Van Ness persuaded Burr that speaking to Hamilton was out of the question. Do you agree with Van Ness, or do you believe that the gentlemanly approach would have been for Burr to speak to Hamilton? If you disagree with Van Ness, what should Burr have said? Why do you think Van Ness dissuaded Burr from speaking to the man he had just shot?
5. What was Hamilton's attitude toward having his wife receive the news of his serious wound? What does his attitude reveal? Did his strategy work? How do you know?
6. How were you affected by the first response of the two clergymen called to give Hamilton holy communion before he died? Did you consider their attitudes understandable or did you see them in another light? Explain your answer.
7. If Hamilton had survived the gunshot, what physical condition would he have probably faced? If you were in this condition, would you have chosen to live or die? Give reasons for your answer.

8. After reading the essay, what opinion do you have of Alexander Hamilton? What opinion do you have of Aaron Burr? What is your opinion of the importance of this event in American history?

● Suggestions for Writing

1. After researching the biographies of Alexander Hamilton and Aaron Burr on the Internet or at the library, write an essay in which you contrast these two famous men. Consider such aspects as their births, their talents, and their personalities.
2. Write an essay in which you trace the historical reasons for accepting duels as a way of resolving disputes. Is the famous biblical narrative of David and Goliath one of the earliest duels?

Hunting Octopus in the Gilbert Islands
Sir Arthur Grimble

Sir Arthur Grimble (1888–1956) was a British colonial government official and writer. After receiving an education from Magdalene College at Cambridge, he joined the colonial service in the Pacific and was posted to the Gilbert and Ellice islands, where he remained in various positions from 1914 until 1933. From 1933 to 1948, he worked as administrator and then governor of the Windward Islands, retiring from the colonial service in 1948. In retirement, Grimble developed a talent for narrating his island experiences on radio for the British Broadcasting Corporation. The result was a series of talks that became so popular that they were published under the title of *A Pattern of Islands* (1952), from which the following excerpt was taken.

Grimble relates an amusing story of watching two young boys hunting just off a reef in the Gilbert Islands. His curiosity about what the boys were doing got him into a predicament from which he could not escape without taking part in their sport. In the course of telling this riveting story, Grimble gives us a process explanation of how the Gilbertese hunt and kill octopus.

● ● ●

1 The Gilbertese happen to value certain parts of the octopus as food, and their method of fighting it is coolly based upon the one fact that its arms never change their grip. They hunt for it in pairs. One man acts as the bait, his partner as the killer. First, they swim eyes-under at low tide just off the reef, and search the crannies of the submarine cliff for sight of any tentacle that may flicker out for a catch. When they have placed their quarry, they land on the reef for the next stage. The human bait starts the real game. He dives and tempts the lurking brute by swimming a few strokes in front of its cranny, at first a little beyond striking range. Then he turns and makes straight for the cranny, to give himself into the embrace of those waiting arms. Sometimes nothing happens. The beast will not always respond to the lure. But usually it strikes.

2   The partner on the reef above stares down through the pellucid water, waiting for his moment. His teeth are his only weapon. His killing efficiency depends on his avoiding every one of those strangling arms. He must wait until his partner's body has been drawn right up to the entrance of the cleft. The monster inside is groping then with its horny mouth against the victim's flesh, and sees nothing beyond it. That point is reached in a matter of no more than thirty seconds after the decoy has plunged. The killer dives, lays hold of his pinioned friend at arms' length, and jerks him away from the cleft; the octopus is torn from the anchorage of its proximal suckers, and clamps itself the more fiercely to its prey. In the same second, the human bait gives a kick which brings him, with quarry annexed, to the surface. He turns on his back, still holding his breath for better buoyancy, and this exposes the body of the beast for the kill. The killer closes in, grasps the evil head from behind, and wrenches it away from its meal. Turning the face up towards himself, he plunges his teeth between the bulging eyes, and bites down and in with all his strength. That is the end of it. It dies on the instant; the suckers release their hold; the arms fall away; the two fishers paddle with whoops of delighted laughter to the reef, where they string the catch to a pole before going to rout out the next one.

3   Any two boys of seventeen, any day of the week, will go out and get you half a dozen octopus like that for the mere fun of it. Here lies the whole point of this story. The hunt is, in the most literal sense, nothing but child's play to the Gilbertese.

4   As I was standing one day at the end of a jetty in Tarawa lagoon, I saw two boys from the near village shouldering a string of octopus slung on a pole between them. I started to wade out in their direction, but before I hailed them they had stopped, planted the carrying-pole upright in a fissure and, leaving it there, swum off the edge for a while with faces submerged evidently searching for something under water. I had been only a few months at Tarawa, and that was my first near view of an octopus-hunt. I watched every stage of it from the dive of the human bait to the landing of the dead catch. When it was over, I went up to them. I could hardly believe that in those few seconds, with no more than a frivolous-looking splash or two on the surface, they could have found, caught and killed the creature they were now stringing up before my eyes. They explained the amusing simplicity of the thing.

5   "There's only one trick the decoy-man must never forget," they said, "and that's not difficult to remember. If he is not wearing the water-spectacles of the Men of Matang,[1] he must cover his eyes with a hand as he comes close to the kika (octopus), or the sucker might blind him." It appeared that the ultimate fate of the eyes was not the thing to worry about; the immediate point was that the sudden pain of a sucker clamping itself to an eyeball might cause the bait to expel his breath and inhale sea-water; that would spoil his buoyancy, and he would fail then to give his friend the best chance of a kill.

---

[1]"Men of Matang" is the Gilbertese phrase for white foreigners.

6   Then they began whispering together. I knew in a curdling flash what they were saying to each other. Before they turned to speak to me again, a horrified conviction was upon me. My damnable curiosity had led me into a trap from which there was no escape. They were going to propose that I should take a turn at being the bait myself, just to see how delightfully easy it was.

7   And that is what they did. It did not even occur to them that I might not leap at the offer. I was already known as a young Man of Matang who liked swimming, and fishing, and laughing with the villagers; I had just shown an interest in this particular form of hunting; naturally, I should enjoy the fun of it as much as they did. Without even waiting for my answer, they gleefully ducked off the edge of the reef to look for another octopus—a fine fat one—mine. Left standing there alone, I had another of those visions . . .

8   It was dusk in the village. The fishers were home, I saw the cooking-fires glowing orange-red between the brown lodges. There was laughter and shouted talk as the women prepared the evening meal. But the laughter was hard with scorn. "What?" they were saying, "Afraid of a kika? The young Man of Matang? Why, even the boys are not afraid of a kika!" A curtain went down and rose again on the Residency; the Old Man was talking: "A leader? You? The man who funked a schoolboy game? We don't leave your sort in charge of Districts." The scene flashed to my uncles: "Returned empty," they said. "We always knew you hadn't got it in you. Returned empty . . ."

9   Of course it was all overdrawn, but one fact was beyond doubt; the Gilbertese reserved all their most ribald humour for physical cowardice. No man gets himself passed for a leader anywhere by becoming the butt of that kind of wit. I decided I would rather face the octopus.

10   I was dressed in khaki slacks, canvas shoes and a short-sleeved singlet. I took off the shoes and made up my mind to shed the singlet if told to do so; but I was wildly determined to stick to my trousers throughout. Dead or alive, said a voice within me, an official minus his pants is a preposterous object, and I felt I could not face that extra horror. However, nobody asked me to remove anything.

11   I hope I did not look as yellow as I felt when I stood to take the plunge; I have never been so sick with funk before or since. "Remember, one hand for your eyes," said someone from a thousand miles off, and I dived.

12   I do not suppose it is really true that the eyes of an octopus shine in the dark; besides, it was clear daylight only six feet down in the limpid water; but I could have sworn the brute's eyes burned at me as I turned in towards his cranny. That dark glow—whatever may have been its origin—was the last thing I saw as I blacked out with my left hand and rose into his clutches. Then, I remember chiefly a dreadful sliminess with a herculean power behind it. Something whipped round my left forearm and the back of my neck, binding the two together. In the same flash, another something slapped itself high on my forehead, and I felt it crawling down inside the back of my singlet. My impulse was to tear at it with my right hand, but I felt the whole of that arm pinioned to my ribs. In most emergencies the mind works with crystal-clear impersonality. This was not even an emergency, for I knew myself perfectly safe.

But my boyhood's nightmare was upon me. When I felt the swift constriction of those disgusting arms jerk my head and shoulders in towards the reef, my mind went blank of every thought save the beastliness of contact with that squat head. A mouth began to nuzzle below my throat, at the junction of the collar-bones. I forgot there was anyone to save me. Yet something still directed me to hold my breath.

13   I was awakened from my cowardly trance by a quick, strong pull on my shoulders, back from the cranny. The cables around me tightened painfully, but I knew I was adrift from the reef. I gave a kick, rose to the surface and turned on my back with the brute sticking out of my chest like a tumour. My mouth was smothered by some flabby moving horror. The suckers felt like hot rings pulling at my skin. It was only two seconds, I suppose, from then to the attack of my deliverer, but it seemed like a century of nausea.

14   My friend came up between me and the reef. He pounced, pulled, bit down, and the thing was over—for everyone but me. At the sudden relaxation of the tentacles, I let out a great breath, sank, and drew in the next under water. It took the united help of both boys to get me, coughing, heaving and pretending to join in their delighted laughter, back to the reef. I had to submit there to a kind of war-dance round me, in which the dead beast was slung whizzing past my head from one to the other. I had a chance to observe then that it was not by any stretch of fancy a giant, but just plain average. That took the bulge out of my budding self-esteem. I left hurriedly for the cover of the jetty, and was sick.

● Vocabulary

quarry (1)   pellucid (2)   pinioned (2)
proximal (2)   annexed (2)   ribald (9)
singlet (10)   funk (11)   limpid (12)
herculean (12)   constriction (12)

● The Facts

1. What two roles in hunting octopus do the hunting partners separately play?
2. What weapon do the Gilbertese use to kill the octopus?
3. What danger does the decoy man face in the octopus hunt?
4. Why did the author consent to take part in the sport of octopus hunting?
5. After the hunt was over, what did the author do?

● The Strategies

1. What do you think is the most prominent feature of the style of this piece?
2. What can you infer about Grimble's attitude toward octopuses from the words he uses to describe them?
3. In describing the reaction (see, particularly, paragraph 8) that might follow his refusal to take part in the octopus hunt, what simple device does Grimble use to make the scene humorous?

4. In paragraph 13, Grimble writes that he was awakened from his "cowardly trance." What is your opinion of this characterization? What effect does it and other self-deprecatory remarks have on the tone of the story?
5. This process explanation of how the Gilbertese hunt octopus consists of two major parts. What are they, and how effective do you find them?

● **The Issues**
1. In spite of the deprecating remarks Grimble makes about his lack of courage, what picture of him emerges from this tale?
2. How does the portrait that Grimble draws of the octopus match your own knowledge of that creature?
3. Had Grimble not been a colonial official assigned to the Gilbert Islands, what do you think his reaction would have been to the invitation from the boys to join the octopus hunt?
4. Based on this story, what can you infer about the Gilbertese and their culture?
5. Imagine yourself in Grimble's place. What would you have done when the Gilbertese boys invited you to take part in the octopus hunt?

● **Suggestions for Writing**
1. Write a process essay depicting the steps involved in any sporting event you've experienced.
2. Write an essay showing how you got entangled in doing something you did not really want to do.

Hitler's Workday
WILLIAM SHIRER

William Shirer (1904–1993) was a journalist and author who covered the Third Reich for CBS radio during the 1930s and 1940s. Between 1942 and 1948, he wrote a syndicated column for the *New York Herald Tribune* and worked for the Mutual Broadcasting System before becoming a full-time writer. His monumental *The Rise and Fall of the Third Reich* (1960) won the National Book Award and became a controversial best-seller, with some critics accusing him of oversensationalizing his subject. Among his many other books are *Berlin Diary: The Journal of a Foreign Correspondent* (1941) and a two-volume memoir, *Twentieth-Century Journey* (1976 and 1984).

Taken from Berlin Diary, *this process excerpt, dated November 5, 1939, gives a step-by-step recounting of a typical workday in the life of Nazi dictator Adolf Hitler. Shirer was then a correspondent for CBS and relied on information provided by unnamed informants.*

● ● ●

Berlin, *November 5*

1   CBS wants me to broadcast a picture of Hitler at work during war-time. I've been inquiring around among my spies. They say: He rises early, eats his first breakfast at seven a.m. This consists usually of either a glass of milk or fruit-juice and two or three rolls, on which he spreads marmalade liberally. Like most Germans, he eats a second breakfast, this one at nine a.m. It's like the first except that he also eats a little fruit. He begins his working day by wading into state papers (a job he detests, since he hates detail work) and discussing the day's program with his adjutants, chiefly S. A. Leader Wilhelm Brückner and especially with his deputy, Rudolf Hess, who was once his private secretary and is one of the few men he trusts with his innermost thoughts. During the forenoon he usually receives the chiefs of the three armed services, listens to their reports and dictates decisions. With Göring he talks about not only air-force matters but general economic problems, or rather results, since he's not interested in details or even theories on this subject.

2   Hitler eats a simple lunch, usually a vegetable stew or a vegetable omelet. He is of course a vegetarian, teetotaler, and non-smoker. He usually invites a small circle to lunch, three or four adjutants, Hess, Dr. Diettrich, his press chief, and sometimes Göring. A one-percent beer, brewed specially for him, is served at this meal, or sometimes a drink made out of kraut called "Herve," flavoured with a little Mosel wine.

3   After lunch he returns to his study and work. More state papers, more conferences, often with his Foreign Minister, occasionally with a returned German ambassador, invariably with some party chieftain such as Dr. Ley or Max Amann, his old top sergeant of the World War and now head of the lucrative Nazi publishing house Eher Verlag, which gets out the Völkische Beobachter and in which Hitler is a stockholder. Late in the afternoon Hitler takes a stroll in the gardens back of the Chancellery, continuing his talk during the walk with whoever had an appointment at the time. Hitler is a fiend for films, and on evenings when no important conferences are on or he is not overrunning a country, he spends a couple of hours seeing the latest movies in his private cinema room at the Chancellery. News-reels are a great favourite with him, and in the last weeks he has seen all those taken in the Polish war, including hundreds of thousands of feet which were filmed for the army archives and will never be seen by the public. He likes American films and many never publicly exhibited in Germany are shown him. A few years ago he insisted on having *It Happened One Night* run several times. Though he is supposed to have a passion for Wagnerian opera, he almost never attends the Opera here in Berlin. He likes the Metropol, which puts on tolerable musical comedies with emphasis on pretty dancing girls. Recently he had one of the girls who struck his fancy to tea. But only to tea. In the evening, too, he likes to have in Dr. Todt, an imaginative engineer who built the great Autobahn network of two-lane motor roads and later the fortifications of the Westwall. Hitler, rushing to compensate what he thinks is an artistic side that was frustrated by non-recognition in his youthful days in Vienna, has a passion for architects' models and will spend hours

fingering them with Dr. Todt. Lately, they say, he has even taken to designing new uniforms. Hitler stays up late, and sleeps badly, which I fear is the world's misfortune.

● Vocabulary
teetotaler (2)   lucrative (3)

● The Facts
1. What time does Hitler eat his breakfast?
2. How many breakfasts does Hitler eat?
3. With whom does Hitler usually eat lunch? What is he likely to have for lunch?
4. What kind of entertainment is Hitler particularly fond of?
5. What particular movie did Hitler run several times a few years ago?

● The Strategies
1. What logical method of organization does Shirer use in recounting Hitler's workday?
2. In writing a process essay, a writer will often use some common words and phrases to indicate steps in the process. What are some of these words and phrases that Shirer uses?
3. Shirer was a lifelong journalist. What characteristic of this piece reveals his journalistic training?
4. In paragraph 3, Shirer writes that when Hitler is "not overrunning a country" he likes to watch movies. How would you characterize the tone of that observation?
5. In paragraph 2, Shirer says of Hitler that he is "of course a vegetarian, a teetotaler, and non-smoker." What do you think Shirer implies by writing "of course"?

● The Issues
1. Shirer says that he has been inquiring among his spies. How would you characterize the kind of information his spies uncovered?
2. Based on this entry, what can you infer about Shirer's personal attitude toward Hitler?
3. What do you think of the ethics of the request made to Shirer—to find out the personal details of a world leader's daily life?
4. Shirer says that "Hitler stays up late, and sleeps badly." Why do you think he fears this as "the world's misfortune"?
5. What picture of Hitler and his work habits emerges from this journal entry?

Suggestions for Writing

1. Write a journal entry that chronicles in step-by-step sequence how you spend a typical day.
2. Write a process essay showing the steps involved in keeping a journal.

How to Be an Army
KENNETH PATCHEN

Kenneth Patchen (1911–1972) was an American poet and graphic artist who became famous in poetry circles for pioneering the technique of reading poetry to the accompaniment of jazz music. During his career as a poet, he received many literary awards, including a Guggenheim fellowship in 1936 and a National Foundation on Arts and Humanities Award in 1967. Collections of his works include *Poems of Humor and Protest* (1960) and *The Collected Poems of Kenneth Patchen* (1969). He also wrote a novel, *Sleepers Awake* (1946). His paintings have been exhibited in various cities and at university galleries.

The unusual amalgamation of figures on page 317 is a concrete poem. Concrete poetry emerged as a form during the 1950s to protest against the aridness of a tradition demanding that poets follow certain stanza, meter, and rhyme forms. Concrete poetry depends on visual effects instead of mere words to deliver its message, suggesting meaning through iconographic pictures and word arrangements.

• • •

The Facts

1. How would you summarize the content of this poem in one sentence?
2. Why does the poet choose shoes as the first element necessary to the process of waging war?
3. What is the meaning of the equation presented?

The Strategies

1. The artwork in the poem resembles the drawings of elementary school children. Why do you suppose the author did not choose more sophisticated drawings?
2. What irony exists between the words "and a faith in the right" and the drawings that follow those words?
3. What technique does the author use to stress certain concepts more than others? How effective is this technique?

HOW TO BE AN ARMY

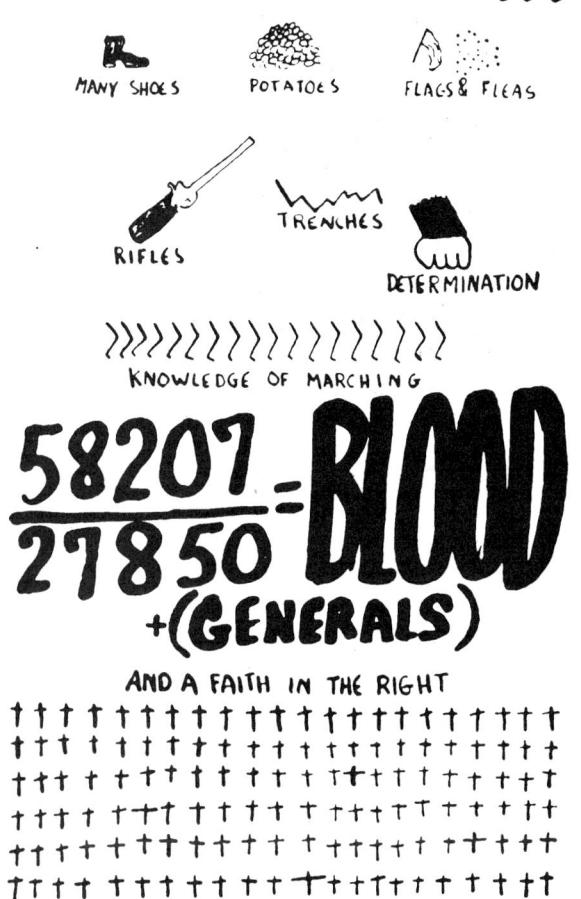

MANY SHOES   POTATOES   FLAGS & FLEAS

RIFLES   TRENCHES   DETERMINATION

KNOWLEDGE OF MARCHING

$$\frac{58207}{27850} = BLOOD + (GENERALS)$$

AND A FAITH IN THE RIGHT

††††††††††††††††††††††
†††††††††††††††††††††††
††††††††††††††††††††††††
†††††††††††††††††††††††
††††††††††††††††††††††††
†††††††††††††††††††††††

- ### The Issues

1. Under what circumstances would you be willing to go to war and possibly lose your life in battle?
2. Of all the ingredients listed in the poem, which one do you consider the most important to waging a successful war?
3. What ingredient for dealing with a third world war seems to be missing from the poem?

- ### Suggestions for Writing

1. Write an essay detailing the steps involved in any kind of military or job training in which you have been involved.
2. Write a process analysis of how an army leader could boost troop morale before heading into combat.

ISSUE FOR CRITICAL THINKING AND DEBATE: AGEISM

The painting *My Parents,* by Henry Koerner, symbolically sums up the issue of ageism in its portrayal of two elderly people deep in a woods. Lost in thought, the man is walking on a separate path away from the woman, who sits near a tree and stares down the narrow trail that unwinds and ominously ends ahead of her. The painting—actually a portrait of Koerner's parents who were exterminated by the Nazis—reminds us that aging also brings infirmity and befuddlement, which intensify the separations that occur naturally at the end of life. Koerner wrote that he spent many days walking with his parents peacefully through the woods of Vienna before World War II and that the painting was meant to commemorate that experience. Yet, in this portrayal, the painting is unrepresentative of growing old today because many of our elderly spend their last days not in an idyllic woodland, but in a grimy apartment or a cheap room. The photograph of British pensioners (senior citizens subsisting on a pension) protesting (see page 320) illustrates this point.

The essayists in this section address ageism from quite different perspectives. As the title of Malcolm Cowley's essay reminds us, he was past eighty when he wrote the book from which this excerpt comes, and he finds philosophical

- My Parents, *Henry Koerner*
  Is old age really a walk in the park?

consolations in growing old. He is not embittered, but a stoical, observant elder. Food tastes wonderful when you are old, he tells us; napping drowsily in the sun is blissful. On the other hand, the view from Marya Mannes is sharp-edged and petulant. When she wrote this essay, she was facing old age, not immersed in it, and from this perspective, she rails against the pressures of growing old and the futility of trying to smother the years under creams and lotions. She is right, too, when she reminds us that a dignified beauty awaits those who gracefully accept the battle scars of aging.

Ageism, unlike other issues, will ultimately and personally affect every reader of this book who achieves life expectancy. It is an issue that is progressively becoming not only more common, but more pressing. Unprecedented numbers of baby boomers are aging, making America inevitably older and grayer. According to the 2000 census, 37.7 million Americans were between the ages of 45 and 54. The median age (the most common age of the population) in 1820 was 16.7 years; by 1980, it had jumped to 30; in the 1990 census, it was 32.9 years. In the 2000 census it was 35.3 years, the highest it has ever been.

If you die young or in your middle years, you will escape the consequences of ageism. Otherwise, ageism will surely and eventually affect your life. Indeed, how you treat the elderly today when you are young might well foreshadow how the young will treat you when you yourself are numbered among the elderly.

The View from Eighty

MALCOLM COWLEY

Malcolm Cowley (1898–1989), American critic and poet, was born in Belsano, Pennsylvania, and educated at Harvard. After World War I, Cowley lived abroad for many years among the so-called "lost generation" of writers, eventually writing about them in *Exile's Return* (1934) and *Second Flowering* (1973). He was the literary editor of *The New Republic* from 1930 to 1940 and numbers among his published works *A Dry Season* (poems, 1942), *Blue Juanita: Collected Poems* (1964), and *The View from Eighty* (1981), from which this excerpt was taken.

The View from Eighty *is a heartening and refreshing reminder that old age does not necessarily entail the loss of literary style, vigor, and wit. Using examples to show how the aged see the world, Cowley writes with the same freshness and liveliness that have characterized all of his works.*

• • •

1   Even before he or she is 80, the aging person may undergo another identity crisis like that of adolescence. Perhaps there had also been a middle-aged crisis, the male or the female menopause, but for the rest of adult life he had taken himself for granted, with his capabilities and failings. Now, when he

British pensioners protesting
Is a government duty bound to care for the elderly?

looks in the mirror, he asks himself, "Is this really me?"—or he avoids the mirror out of distress at what it reveals, those bags and wrinkles. In his new makeup he is called upon to play a new role in a play that must be improvised. André Gide, that long-lived man of letters, wrote in his journal, "My heart has remained so young that I have the continual feeling of playing a part, the part of the 70-year-old that I certainly am; and the infirmities and weaknesses that remind me of my age act like a prompter, reminding me of my lines when I tend to stray. Then, like the good actor I want to be, I go back into my role, and I pride myself on playing it well."

2   In his new role the old person will find that he is tempted by new vices, that he receives new compensations (not so widely known), and that he may possibly achieve new virtues. Chief among these is the heroic or merely obstinate refusal to surrender in the face of time. One admires the ships that go down with all flags flying and the captain on the bridge.

3   Among the vices of age are avarice, untidiness, and vanity, which last takes the form of a craving to be loved or simply admired. Avarice is the worst of those three. Why do so many old persons, men and women alike, insist on hoarding money when they have no prospect of using it and even when they have no heirs? They eat the cheapest food, buy no clothes, and live in a single

room when they could afford better lodging. It may be that they regard money as a form of power; there is a comfort in watching it accumulate while other powers are dwindling away. How often we read of an old person found dead in a hovel, on a mattress partly stuffed with bankbooks and stock certificates! The bankbook syndrome, we call it in our family, which has never succumbed.

4   Untidiness we call the Langley Collyer syndrome. To explain, Langley Collyer was a former concert pianist who lived alone with his 70-year-old brother in a brownstone house on upper Fifth Avenue. The once fashionable neighborhood had become part of Harlem. Homer, the brother, had been an admiralty lawyer, but was now blind and partly paralyzed; Langley played for him and fed him on buns and oranges, which he thought would restore Homer's sight. He never threw away a daily paper because Homer, he said, might want to read them all. He saved other things as well and the house became filled with rubbish from roof to basement. The halls were lined on both sides with bundled newspapers, leaving narrow passageways in which Langley had devised booby traps to catch intruders.

5   On March 21, 1947, some unnamed person telephoned the police to report that there was a dead body in the Collyer house. The police broke down the front door and found the hall impassable, then they hoisted a ladder to a second-story window. Behind it Homer was lying on the floor in a bathrobe; he had starved to death. Langley had disappeared. After some delay, the police broke into the basement, chopped a hole in the roof, and began throwing junk out of the house, top and bottom. It was 18 days before they found Langley's body, gnawed by rats. Caught in one of his own booby traps, he had died in a hallway just outside Homer's door. By that time the police had collected, and the Department of Sanitation had hauled away, 120 tons of rubbish, including besides the newspapers, 14 grand pianos and the parts of a dismantled Model T Ford.

6   Why do so many old people accumulate junk, not on the scale of Langley Collyer, but still in a dismaying fashion? Their tables are piled high with it, their bureau drawers are stuffed with it, their closet rods bend with the weight of clothes not worn for years. I suppose that the piling up is partly from lethargy and partly from the feeling that everything once useful, including their own bodies, should be preserved. Others, though not so many, have such a fear of becoming Langley Collyers that they strive to be painfully neat. Every tool they own is in its place, though it will never be used again; every scrap of paper is filed away in alphabetical order. At last their immoderate neatness becomes another vice of age, if a milder one.

7   The vanity of older people is an easier weakness to explain, and to condone. With less to look forward to, they yearn for recognition of what they have been: the reigning beauty, the athlete, the soldier, the scholar. It is the beauties who have the hardest time. A portrait of themselves at twenty hangs on the wall, and they try to resemble it by making an extravagant use of creams, powders, and dyes. Being young at heart, they think they are merely revealing their essential persons. The athletes find shelves for their silver trophies, which are polished once a year. Perhaps a letter sweater lies wrapped in a

bureau drawer. I remember one evening when a no-longer athlete had guests for dinner and tried to find his sweater. "Oh, that old thing," his wife said. "The moths got into it and I threw it away." The athlete sulked and his guests went home early.

8   Often the yearning to be recognized appears in conversation as an innocent boast. Thus, a distinguished physician, retired at 94, remarks casually that a disease was named after him. A former judge bursts into chuckles as he repeats bright things that he said on the bench. Aging scholars complain in letters (or one of them does), "As I approach 70 I'm becoming avid of honors, and such things—medals, honorary degrees, etc.—are only passed around among academics on a quid pro quo basis (one hood capping another)." Or they say querulously, "Bill Underwood has ten honorary doctorates and I have only three. Why didn't they elect me to. . .?" and they mention the name of some learned society. That search for honors is a harmless passion, though it may lead to jealousies and deformations of character, as with Robert Frost in his later years. Still, honors cost little. Why shouldn't the very old have more than their share of them?

9   To be admired and praised, especially by the young, is an autumnal pleasure enjoyed by the lucky ones (who are not always the most deserving). "What is more charming," Cicero observes in his famous essay *De Senectute*, "than old age surrounded by the enthusiasm of youth! . . . Attentions which seem trivial and conventional are marks of honor—the morning call, being sought after, precedence, having people rise for you, being escorted to and from the forum. . . . What pleasures of the body can be compared to the prerogatives of influence?" But there are also pleasures of the body, or the mind, that are enjoyed by a greater number of older persons.

10   Those pleasures include some that younger people find hard to appreciate. One of them is simply sitting still, like a snake on a sunwarmed stone, with a delicious feeling of indolence that was seldom attained in earlier years. A leaf flutters down; a cloud moves by inches across the horizon. At such moments the older person, completely relaxed, has become a part of nature—and a living part, with blood coursing through his veins. The future does not exist for him. He thinks, if he thinks at all, that life for younger persons is still a battle royal of each against each, but that now he has nothing more to win or lose. He is not so much above as outside the battle, as if he had assumed the uniform of some neutral country, perhaps Liechtenstein or Andorra. From a distance he notes that some of the combatants, men or women, are jostling ahead—but why do they fight so hard when the most they can hope for is a longer obituary? He can watch the scrounging and gouging, he can hear the shouts of exultation, the moans of the gravely wounded, and meanwhile he feels secure; nobody will attack him from ambush.

11   Age has other physical compensations besides the nirvana of dozing in the sun. A few of the simplest needs become a pleasure to satisfy. When an old woman in a nursing home was asked what she really liked to do, she answered in one word: "Eat." She might have been speaking for many of her fellows. Meals in a nursing home, however badly cooked, serve as climactic moments

of the day. The physical essence of the pensioners is being renewed at an appointed hour; now they can go back to meditating or to watching TV while looking forward to the next meal. They can also look forward to sleep, which has become a definite pleasure, not the mere interruption it once had been.

12   Here I am thinking of old persons under nursing care. Others ferociously guard their independence, and some of them suffer less than one might expect from being lonely and impoverished. They can be rejoiced by visits and meetings, but they also have company inside their heads. Some of them are busiest when their hands are still. What passes through the minds of many is a stream of persons, images, phrases, and familiar tunes. For some that stream has continued since childhood, but now it is deeper; it is their present and their past combined. At times they conduct silent dialogues with a vanished friend, and these are less tiring—often more rewarding—than spoken conversations. If inner resources are lacking, old persons living alone may seek comfort and a kind of companionship in the bottle. I should judge from the gossip of various neighborhoods that the outer suburbs from Boston to San Diego are full of secretly alcoholic widows. One of those widows, an old friend, was moved from her apartment into a retirement home. She left behind her a closet in which the floor was covered wall to wall with whiskey bottles. "Oh, those empty bottles!" she explained. "They were left by a former tenant."

13   Not whiskey or cooking sherry but simply giving up is the greatest temptation of age. It is something different from a stoical acceptance of infirmities, which is something to be admired. At 63, when he first recognized that his powers were failing, Emerson wrote one of his best poems, "Terminus":

> It is time to be old,
> To take in sail: The god of bounds,
> Who sets to seas a shore,
> Came to me in his fatal rounds,
> And said: "No more!
> No farther shoot
> Thy broad ambitious branches, and thy root.
> Fancy departs: no more invent;
> Contract thy firmament
> To compass of a tent."

14   Emerson lived in good health to the age of 79. Within his narrowed firmament, he continued working until his memory failed; then he consented to having younger editors and collaborators. The givers-up see no reason for working. Sometimes they lie in bed all day when moving about would still be possible, if difficult. I had a friend, a distinguished poet, who surrendered in that fashion. The doctors tried to stir him to action, but he refused to leave his room. Another friend, once a successful artist, stopped painting when his eyes began to fail. His doctor made the mistake of telling him that he suffered from a fatal disease. He then lost interest in everything except the splendid Rolls-Royce, acquired in his prosperous days, that stood in the garage. Daily he wiped the dust from its hood.

He couldn't drive it on the road any longer, but he used to sit in the driver's seat, start the motor, then back the Rolls out of the garage and drive it in again, back twenty feet and forward twenty feet; that was his only distraction.

15   I haven't the right to blame those who surrender, not being able to put myself inside their minds or bodies. Often they must have compelling reasons, physical or moral. Not only do they suffer from a variety of ailments, but also they are made to feel that they no longer have a function in the community. Their families and neighbors don't ask them for advice, don't really listen when they speak, don't call on them for efforts. One notes that there are not a few recoveries from apparent senility when that situation changes. If it doesn't change, old persons may decide that efforts are useless. I sympathize with their problems, but the men and women I envy are those who accept old age as a series of challenges.

16   For such persons, every new infirmity is an enemy to be outwitted, an obstacle to be overcome by force of will. They enjoy each little victory over themselves, and sometimes they win a major success. Renoir was one of them. He continued painting, and magnificently, for years after he was crippled by arthritis; the brush had to be strapped to his arm. "You don't need your hand to paint," he said. Goya was another of the unvanquished. At 72 he retired as an official painter of the Spanish court and decided to work only for himself. His later years were those of the famous "black paintings" in which he let his imagination run (and also of the lithographs, then a new technique). At 78 he escaped a reign of terror in Spain by fleeing to Bordeaux. He was deaf and his eyes were failing; in order to work he had to wear several pairs of spectacles, one over another, and then use a magnifying glass; but he was producing splendid work in a totally new style. At 80 he drew an ancient man propped on two sticks, with a mass of white hair and beard hiding his face and with the inscription "I am still learning."

17   Giovanni Papini said when he was nearly blind, "I prefer martyrdom to imbecility." After writing sixty books, including his famous *Life of Christ,* he was at work on two huge projects when he was stricken with a form of muscular atrophy. He lost the use of his left leg, then of his fingers, so that he couldn't hold a pen. The two big books, though never to be finished, moved forward slowly by dictation; that in itself was a triumph. Toward the end, when his voice had become incomprehensible, he spelled out a word, tapping on the table to indicate letters of the alphabet. One hopes never to be faced with the need for such heroic measures.

18   "Eighty years old!" the great Catholic poet Paul Claudel wrote in his journal. "No eyes left, no ears, no teeth, no legs, no wind! And when all is said and done, how astonishingly well one does without them!"

• Vocabulary

improvised (1)
succumbed (3)
condone (7)
prerogatives (9)
nirvana (11)

infirmities (1)
lethargy (6)
querulously (8)
indolence (10)
climactic (11)

avarice (3)
immoderate (6)
deformations (8)
exultation (10)

The Facts

1. What kind of crisis does the aging person undergo?
2. What are the virtues of old age? What are its main vices?
3. What is the Langley Collyer syndrome? Why do old people suffer so often from it? What part does society's treatment of the elderly play in this syndrome?
4. Why are some old people so vain?
5. What pleasures do the old revel in?

The Strategies

1. Aside from examples that illustrate what it is like to be old, what kind of supporting detail does Cowley use? What does its use add to the essay?
2. What is the function of the question in paragraph 6?
3. Old people, says Cowley, suffer chronically from avarice, untidiness, and vanity. He gives extended examples of the second and third of these, but not of the first. How does he support his view that the old are often avaricious? What rhetorical logic lies behind this omission of examples?
4. What extended analogy does Cowley use to describe how the young appear to the old? How effective is this analogy?
5. In this excerpt, Cowley gives anecdotes about aging in others, rather than in himself. Do you think this a better tactic than focusing on his own experiences? Why or why not?

The Issues

1. Has Cowley overlooked any vices or virtues associated with old age? Make a written list of the characteristics of old age you wish to avoid and then a second list of characteristics you wish to develop.
2. What is your answer to the question posed in paragraph 3: "Why do so many old persons, men and women alike, insist on hoarding money when they have no prospect of using it and even when they have no heirs?" Do you agree with Cowley's suggestion that perhaps they regard money as a form of power, or are there other reasons for the avarice?
3. What about old age do you fear most? What do you plan to do in order to alleviate your fear?
4. In "Rabbi Ben Ezra," the famous Victorian poet Robert Browning wrote these lines:

> Grow old along with me!
> The best is yet to be,
> The last of life, for which the first was made:
> Our times are in His hand Who saith, "A whole I planned,
> Youth shows but half, trust God: see all, nor be afraid."

What parallels do you see in this excerpt and in Cowley's essay?

5. What kind of person do you imagine yourself to be at age eighty? Describe in detail what kinds of clothes you will wear, how you will spend your time, and what philosophy will guide your existence.

• Suggestions for Writing

1. Some sociologists have suggested that because women generally outlive men, marriage laws should be relaxed to allow the elderly to practice polygyny (wherein a man has more than one wife or mate) as a way of reducing the number of lonely widows. Express your views on this issue in an essay in which you use examples to support your thesis.
2. Write an essay giving examples of the way age has affected an elderly friend or relative.

Stay Young

Marya Mannes

Marya Mannes (1904–1990) was an American novelist, poet, and essayist who worked as a staff writer for *Reporter* magazine. Her books include *The New York I Know* (1961), *But Will It Sell* (1964), *Subverse* (poems, 1964), and *Out of My Time* (1971).

1   Like all people in the middle span, I am aware of death and saddened by its advance forces of disintegration. I do not like the signs in flesh and muscle and bone of slow decline, even if they are yet unaccompanied by pain. To one in love with physical beauty, its inevitable blurring by years is a source of melancholy.

2   Yet I feel sure that while the flesh may retreat before age, the man or woman can advance if he goes towards death rather than away from it, if he understands the excitement implicit in this progression from the part to the whole. For that is, really, what it should be: a steady ascent from personal involvement—the paths and rocks and valleys and rises of the foothills—to the ultimate height where they fuse into one grand and complex pattern, remote and yet rewarding. It is like coming into clearer air. And if that air becomes in course too rare to breathe, the final breath is one of total purity.

3   It is because of these convictions that I protest against the American tyranny of youth. There is beauty and freshness in youth (if there is less and less innocence), but it is an accident of time and therefore ephemeral. There is no "trick" in being young: it happens to you. But the process of maturing is an art to be learned, an effort to be sustained. By the age of fifty you have made yourself what you are, and if it is good, it is better than your youth. If it is bad, it is not because you are older but because you have not grown.

4   Yet all this is obscured, daily, hourly, by the selling barrage of youth: perhaps the greatest campaign for the arrested development of the human being

ever waged anywhere. Look young, be young, stay young, they call from every page and on every air wave. You must be young to be loved. And with this mandate, this threat, this pressure, millions of goods are sold and millions of hours are spent in pursuit of a youth which no longer exists and which cannot be recaptured.

5   The result of this effort is, in women, obscene; in men, pathetic. For the American woman of middle age thinks of youth only in terms of appearance and the American man of middle age thinks of youth only in terms of virility.

6   If obscene seems a strong word to use for old women who try to look young, I will be more explicit. It is quite true and quite proper that better eating habits, better care and less drudgery have made American women look ten years younger than their mothers did at the same age. One of the pleasing phenomena of our life is the naturally young and pretty grandmother, almost as lithe and active as her daughter. But I am talking of the still older woman, past her middle fifties, often alone, often idle, who has the means to spend the greater part of her leisure in beauty salons and shops and weight reducing parlors, resisting age with desperate intensity. They do not know it, but the fact of this resistance nullifies the effects of the effort. The streets of American cities are full of these thin, massaged, made-up, corseted, tinted, over-dressed women with faces that are repellent masks of frustration; hard, empty, avid. Although their ankles are slender and their feet perched on backless high-heeled slippers, they fool no one, and certainly no man. They are old legs and old feet. Although their flesh is clear and fairly firm in the visible areas, it is kneaded flesh, and fools no one. The hips are small indeed, but the girdle only emphasizes their stiff aridity. And the uplift bra, the platinum hair, the tight dress? Whom do they fool? The woman herself, alone. And the obscenity in all this is that she uses the outward techniques of sexual allure to maintain her youth when she is no longer wanted by men. And she does it because she has been told to do it by the advertising media. She has been sold a bill of goods.

7   Let me hastily say at this point that it is the solemn duty of all women to look as well as they can and to maintain through life the grooming that makes them pleasing to others. Towards this end, the advertisers have performed a signal service to Americans. But they have over-reached themselves, and us. Instead of saying "Be Yourself," they say, "Be Young." Instead of saying "Relax," they say "Compete!" In doing this, they deprive the maturing woman of a great joy, an astounding relief: the end, not of sex, heaven knows, but of sexual competition. By the time a woman is fifty she is either wanted as a woman of fifty or not really wanted at all. She does not have to fool her husband or her lover, and she knows that competition with women far younger than she is not only degrading but futile.

8   It is also an axiom that the more time a woman spends on herself, the less she has for others and the less desirable she is to others. If this goes for young women—and I believe it does—it goes doubly for older women, who have—if they knew it—more to give.

9   When I go to Europe and see the old people in villages in France or Italy, for instance, I am struck at once by the age of all women who are no longer young, pitying their premature withering; and at the same time startled by the occasional beauty of their old faces. Lined and grooved and puckered as they may be, their hair grizzled or lank, there is something in their eyes and in their bones that gives age austerity and makes their glossy contemporaries at a bridge table here seem parodies of women. They show that they have lived and they have not yet found the means to hide it.

10   I remember also that as a child and a young girl I never thought of my mother in terms of age. Whatever it was at any time, she looked it; and nobody then told her to lose weight or do something about her hair because she was far too interesting a human being to need such "ameliorations." It would, indeed, have been an impertinence. My mother had no illusions of beauty: she was too concerned with music and her husband and her children to be concerned, in detail, with herself. I don't doubt that, given today's aids, she could have looked younger and smarter than she did. But she would have lost something. The time and effort spent in improving her looks would have been taken from music and from love. With her unruly eyebrows plucked to a thin line, her face made-up, her plump, small body moulded into girdles, an important part of her would have vanished: her identity.

11   It is this that the older women of America are losing. At club gatherings, at hotels, at resorts, they look identical. What lives they have led have been erased from their faces along with the more obvious marks of age. They have smoothed and hardened into a mould. Their lotions have done well.

12   It could be said that if they maintain the illusion of youth to themselves only, no harm is done and some good. But I wonder if all self-deceptions do not harm, and if their price is not loss of self.

13   I wonder too whether one of the reasons for wild, intemperate, destructive youth might not be this same hard finish, this self-absorption, of the women to whom they might otherwise turn. I cannot imagine going for counsel and comfort to a mother or aunt or grandmother tightly buttressed by latex and heavily masked by makeup. Where is the soft wide lap, the old kind hands, the tender face of age?

14   None of us with any pride in person and any sense of aesthetics can allow ourselves to crumble into decay without trying to slow the process or at least veil its inroads. But that is not the major battle. The fight is not for what is gone but for what is coming; and for this the fortification of the spirit is paramount, the preservation of the flesh a trivial second.

15   Let the queen bee keep her royal jelly. Or so I keep telling myself.

Vocabulary

ephemeral (3)
allure (6)
ameliorations (10)
inroads (14)

nullifies (6)
axiom (8)
intemperate (13)
paramount (14)

repellent (6)
austerity (9)
aesthetics (14)

The Facts

1. According to the author, what must a man or woman do to advance with old age?
2. In what terms do American women think of youth? In what contrasting terms do American men think of youth?
3. What does the author think advertisers should be saying to women? Instead, what are they actually saying?
4. In what countries is the author often struck by the natural beauty of older women who do not try to hide their ages?
5. What price do women pay for their attempts at deceiving themselves and the world about how old they are?

The Strategies

1. The author opens her essay with a frank admission about her sadness in the face of aging. What does this admission add to the essay?
2. What evidence does the author offer to support her assertions about the obscene efforts women make to avoid looking their age? How convincing do you find this evidence?
3. Given what the author has written in paragraph 6 about American women who desperately labor to look younger, what rhetorical strategy is implicit in her description of European women in paragraph 9?
4. Why do you think the author included the anecdote about her mother in paragraph 10?
5. What does the final sentence of the essay imply about the author? Why is this an apt implication on which to end this essay?

The Issues

1. What do you think is entailed in the author's advice that a person should go "towards death rather than away from it"?
2. What difference, if any, do you think the feminist movement has made in easing the unrealistic pressures on aging women?
3. From this essay, what can you infer are the causes behind what the author calls "the American tyranny of youth"?
4. What pressures, if any, are exerted upon the young by the culture of youth? Or are the young exempt from such pressures? Explain.
5. Why does it necessarily follow, as the author alleges, that there is scant comfort available from aging aunts, mothers, and grandmothers who try hard to avoid looking their age?

Suggestions for Writing

1. Write an essay discussing how you would like to be treated when you are old.
2. In an essay, explore the potential benefits a successful feminist revolution could have on the present tyranny of youth.

Punctuation Workshop
The Semicolon (;)

1. Put a semicolon between two closely related independent clauses not joined by *and, but, for, or, nor, yet, so:*

    The bakery was closed on Sunday; we settled for crackers.

    Oatmeal contains antioxidants; it is good for the heart.

    The scout lifted his binoculars; a yellow object was floating in the water.

    Some grapes are seedless; others are not.

2. Put a semicolon in front of *however, therefore, nevertheless, then,* and *therefore* when these adverbial conjunctions connect two independent clauses:

    I love e-mail; however, I don't want just anyone to have access to my e-mail address.

    Most people have bad habits they constantly try to break; therefore, psychologists keep getting new patients.

    The gate gave a tired squeak; then, it suddenly flew open.

    Notice that a semicolon precedes the adverbial conjunction, but a comma follows it. Actually, you can write acceptably without ever using semicolons because a period can always be used instead.

3. Use semicolons to separate items in a series already separated by commas:

    Her garden consists of flowers, common and exotic; vegetables, native as well as imported; and species of herbs found nowhere else on the island.

STUDENT CORNER

Final Draft: Aging
Kimberly Caitlin Wheeler, Yale University

There is a general perception in our society that once you reach middle age, you are "Over the hill and going down." As people get older, their value, unlike that of wine, is perceived to decrease. Thus the elderly are "worthless" members of society: They contribute nothing, but take much. This prejudice against the elderly and even the middle aged, ageism, is a big problem in our youth-oriented culture. Ageism does not end with mere perceptions, but also begets action. There are problems with age discrimination both in the entertainment industry and the workplace, but neither problem can be solved without a change in attitude towards the elderly.

Ageism is extremely noticeable within the entertainment industry. Most television programs and movies cater to the younger members of society. The shows portray young characters who are usually facing age-specific problems, such as starting a career or raising a family. Those who have reached retirement and have raised their families are often ignored or are peripheral characters. There are virtually no shows that sympathetically portray the interests of the elderly. One consequence of this is that people begin to perceive the elderly through the eyes of the media—as valueless members of society.

The entertainment industry has some economic justifications in producing only shows geared towards a younger audience. Research has shown that the 18–44 age group has more spending money than members of older age groups. Older age groups are actually wealthier, but they are less likely to spend money frivolously. They are not as receptive to advertisements and product trends. Because members of the 18–44 age group are more likely to spend their money, advertisers who pay for television shows want shows that members of this age group are watching, and support "younger" shows. Likewise, film studios, eager to make box office money, tend to produce shows designed for a more youthful audience.

Age discrimination also appears in the workplace. Employers are often unwilling to hire or keep workers that have reached a certain age. They perceive these workers as incompetent and lacking ambition. For example, the European Union recently implemented a policy of not hiring workers over the age of 35. This policy is unjustified. For most jobs, mature employees bring added skill and experience that can actually improve their performance. The one exception to this rule is in the area of technological advances. In today's workplace, where computers are an essential means of performing tasks, and the Internet forms the hub of office communication, those trained in a less technological age may find themselves at a disadvantage. In a survey done by Great Britain's Motorola Company, 22% of people ages 16–24 had had no Internet training, compared to 78% of people over the age of 65. Those over 65 were also less enthusiastic about technology or comfortable using high-tech equipment or online services. Thus many older workers lack skills that are essential in a high-tech work environment. This often offsets their advantages of experience and dedication.

Solutions to the problems that create age discrimination do exist, but before they can be implemented, it is necessary to overcome the prejudice against older people in this country. The general perception of the elderly as worthless and burdensome members of the society needs to change. Older people should be valued for their knowledge, experience, and successes. Once the attitude has changed, it is possible to effect the solutions for the entertainment industry and the workplace. If older people are perceived as valued customers and quality shows are created for them, they are more likely to watch them and spend their money. Likewise, if mature workers were trained in the use of advanced technology, this skill would add to their other resources of experience and knowledge. Life doesn't have to go downhill at age 40; it should become a time to reap the rewards of previous successes, a time to enjoy maturity.

How I Write

When I first get a topic, I like to take a few days and think about it. I may do some preliminary research, but what I usually do is just think, and jot down any ideas that come to me. This is a technique known to some as "procrastination" but it really is useful. When I have thought for a few days, I do some research, to find facts and figures to support my ideas, or to derive ideas. I usually go to the library for books or periodicals. For a contemporary topic such as this, I like to turn to the Internet. Once I get books, I skim them for discussions of my topic, then take notes at my computer. I print out these notes, then sit down, away from the computer with a pencil, my notes, and a notebook, and plan my paper. My first step is to come up with a rough outline—usually two or three points to talk about. I then read through my material and find information that directly relates to the points that I may use in my paper later. I cut out my notes, divide them into piles that relate to each point, then tape them together in the order I want to use them. Once this is accomplished, I can begin writing the paper.

    I always write the paper from scratch at the computer, because I type faster than I write and it is easier to make changes later. I like to listen to music while I write for several reasons. I usually listen to classical music, which is supposed to boost your IQ and focus. Music also helps when you're writing in a crowded dorm room. With headphones on, it is easier to block out the distracting conversations of my roommates. I also use earplugs sometimes. When I am typing and my fingers or brain cramp up, I take a short break and literally run around the room. Or I get a drink of water or have a short conversation with someone. When I return to writing, my brain is refreshed and ready to go. After I've finished writing, I look at the paper. If it is too short, I look for things I could explain more fully; and if it is too long, I look for things to cut. Then I print the paper out to proofread for obvious errors. At this point, I like to put it down for a while and do something else. Then I can come back to it and see what really needs to be revised and changed. Sometimes it is a few sentences, and sometimes it is the entire focus of the paper. After revising, I spell check and proofread again before printing it out and turning it in. Then I stop thinking about it until I get it back from the professor.

How I Wrote This Essay

For this paper, because I was writing at home, I used a slightly different approach. Because this topic was such a contemporary one, I turned first to the Internet for research. I typed "ageism" into several different search engines, then browsed the pages offered to see what looked interesting or relevant. I printed out the pages that appeared to be most useful, then sat down on the couch with my pencil, my notebook, and my Web pages. I came up with main points, found some statistics to use in my paper, then began writing. I stopped a few times in the middle—for dinner, and to check my e-mail—but I eventually finished it. Then I printed it out to proofread. I marked my revisions, then went back to the computer and changed them.

My Writing Tip

Always write your body paragraphs first. I often don't know exactly what my thesis is until I'm done with the paper, so I always write an introduction and conclusion last. This also makes it easier to begin to write—usually the most difficult thing about writing a paper!

● CHAPTER WRITING ASSIGNMENTS

Write a process analysis about one of the following topics:

1. How to cook your favorite dish
2. How you celebrate a favorite holiday
3. How you reconciled two friends who were not speaking to each other
4. How you study for a big test

● WRITING ASSIGNMENTS FOR A SPECIFIC AUDIENCE

1. Explain to an audience of third graders how to write a process analysis.
2. Explain to an audience of business executives how the English education you are currently receiving will make you a better employee.

● COLLABORATIVE WRITING PROJECT

Divide your group into at least three teams, each of which should research the retirement policies of some specific profession or institution of its choice. Conduct whatever interviews are necessary to learn more about any specific retirement policy. After the research is completed, the teams should meet to discuss and debate the fairness of the retirement policies. Finally, each team should write a group essay outlining what it has learned about the researched retirement policy as well as its impact on elderly employees.

● IMAGE GALLERY ASSIGNMENT

Visit pages 653–655 of our image gallery and study all three images dealing with ageism. Then choose the image that most appeals to you. Answer the questions and do the writing assignment.

10
Illustration/Exemplification

ROAD MAP TO ILLUSTRATION/EXEMPLIFICATION

What Illustration/Exemplification Does

To illustrate means to give examples that clarify what you are trying to say. Short or long, illustrations are especially useful for embodying abstract ideas or sharpening ambiguous generalizations. They might consist of one item or a list of items that exemplify something, as in this paragraph, which illustrates what the author means by the "Discipline of Nature or of Reality":

> A child, in growing up, may meet and learn from three different kinds of discipline. The first and most important is what we might call the Discipline of Nature or of Reality. When he is trying to do something real, if he does the wrong thing or doesn't do the right one, he doesn't get the result he wants. If he doesn't pile one block right on top of another, or tries to build on a slanting surface, his tower falls down. If he hits the wrong key, he hears the wrong note. If he doesn't hit the nail squarely on the head, it bends, and he has to pull it out and start with another. If he doesn't measure properly when he is trying to build, it won't open, close, fit, stand up, fly, float, whistle, or do whatever he wants it to do. If he closes his eyes when he swings, he misses the ball. A child meets this kind of discipline every time he tries to do something, which is why it is so important in school to give children more chances to do things, instead of just reading or listening to someone talk (or pretending to)....
>
> —John Holt, "Kinds of Discipline"

On the other hand, an illustration might consist of one extended example rather than a list. Here is an example:

> Even the shrewdest of men cannot always judge what is useful and what is not. There never was a man so ingeniously practical as Thomas Alva Edison, surely the greatest inventor who ever lived, and we can take him as our example.

In 1896 he patented his first invention. It was a device to record votes mechanically. By using it, congressmen could press a button and all their votes would be instantly recorded and totaled. There was no question but that the invention worked; it remained only to sell it. A congressman whom Edison consulted, however, told him, with mingled amusement and horror, that there wasn't a chance of the invention's being accepted, however unfailingly it might work.

A slow vote, it seemed, was sometimes a political necessity. Some congressmen might have their opinions changed in the course of a slow vote where a quick vote might, in a moment of emotion, commit Congress to something undesirable.

Edison, chagrined, learned his lesson. After that, he decided never to invent anything unless he was sure that it would be needed and wanted and not merely because it worked.

—Isaac Asimov, *Of What Use?*

When to Use Illustration

The illustration is typically used to support an assertion or point. On every page, in almost every paragraph, writers who wish to communicate their meaning must back up their assertions with appropriate examples. It is not enough to generalize that such and such is the case, as you might do in a casual chat. To make your assertions believable, you must back them up with specific instances. Illustration is often practiced in combination with other modes of development, such as definition, description, classification, causal analysis, and so forth. In the following paragraph, for instance, two examples are used to define "romantic recognition":

> Romantic recognition. Two examples will do. When we were flying from Erivan, the capital of Armenia, to Sukhum, on the Black Sea, a Soviet scientist, who spoke English, tapped me on the shoulder and then pointed to a fearsome rock face, an immeasurable slab bound in the iron of eternal winter. "That," he announced, "is where Prometheus was chained." And then all my secret terror—for a journey among the mountains of the Caucasus in a Russian plane is to my unheroic soul an ordeal—gave way for a moment to wonder and delight, as if an illuminated fountain had shot up in the dark. And then, years earlier, in the autumn of 1914, when we were on a route march in Surrey, I happened to be keeping step with the company commander, an intelligent Regular lent to us for a month or two. We were passing a little old woman who was watching us from an open carriage, drawn up near the entrance to a mansion. "Do you know who that is?" the captain asked; and of course I didn't. "It's the Empress Eugenie," he told me; and young and loutish as I was in those days, nevertheless there flared about me then, most delightfully, all the splendor and idiocy of the Second Empire, and I knew that we, every man Jack of us, were in history, and knew it once and for all.
>
> —J. B. Priestly, *Romantic Recognition*

Here, an illustration is used to help describe the humility of John Masefield, the English poet:

> This quality of his can best be illustrated by his behavior that night. When the time came for him to read his poems, he would not stand up in any position of pre-eminence but sheltered himself behind the sofa, in the shade of an old lamp, and from there he delivered passages from "The Everlasting Mercy," "Dauber," "The Tragedy of Nan," and "Pompey the Great." He talked, too, melodiously, and with the ghost of a question mark after each of his sentences as though he were saying, "Is that right? Who am I to lay down the law?" And when it was all over, and we began to discuss what he had said, all talking at the top of our voices, very superficially, no doubt, but certainly with a great deal of enthusiasm, it was with a sudden shock that I realized that Masefield had retired into his shell, and was sitting on the floor, almost in the dark, reading a volume of poems by a young and quite unknown writer.
>
> —Beverley Nichols, *Twenty-Five*

Illustration is especially effective as support for a persuasive argument. For example, the bland assertion that animal experimentation is necessary to the advancement of science will persuade more forcefully when coupled with an example of how an infant's life was saved by a surgical procedure learned in practice on laboratory animals.

An illustration can also be visual: a picture, chart, map, line drawing, graph, or spreadsheet. Such visual illustrations are used widely in scientific and technical writing.

How to Use Illustration

1. **An illustration must be real and specific.** It must not consist simply of a restatement of what you've already said. Here is an example of a paragraph whose "illustration" is merely a rewording of a preceding statement:

   > Before being sold to the American colonies, many slaves had acquired a knowledge of Wolof and Mandingo, the creolized English that had come into use along the Guinea coast as a trade language. For example, many slaves were conversant in both of these languages.

   Although the writer uses "for example," what follows is not an authentic illustration but only further commentary. Here is an improvement:

   > Before being sold to the American colonies, many slaves had acquired a knowledge of Wolof and Mandingo, the creolized English that had come into use along the Guinea coast as a trade language. For example, when a runaway slave who could speak no English was arrested in Pennsylvania in 1731, his white interrogators had no difficulty in finding another Wolof-speaking slave to act as an interpreter.

The illustration now supports the assertion that many slaves came to America already knowing creolized English.

2. **An illustration should be clearly introduced and contextually linked to the point it is intended to support.** If you reread the preceding paragraphs in this section, you will notice that the writers generally use some introductory phrases such as "take him as our example," "two examples will do," or "for example." Such phrases are needed when the context of the paragraph does not alert the reader that an illustration is to follow. On the other hand, if it is clear from the context that an illustration is to follow, no introductory phrase is necessary:

> While viruses and bacteria cause most of the common diseases suffered by people who live in the developed world, protozoa are the major cause of disease in undeveloped tropical zones. Of these diseases, the most widespread are malaria, amoebic dysentery, and African sleeping sickness.

The first sentence makes it plain that malaria, amoebic dysentery, and African sleeping sickness are examples of diseases caused by protozoa in the tropical zones.

Beware, however, of plunging too abruptly into an illustration:

> The idea that art does not exist among the lower animals is a primitive notion. The bower birds of Australia decorate their bowers with shells, colored glass, and shining objects. Some paint their walls with fruit pulp, wet powdered charcoal, or paste of chewed-up grass mixed with saliva. One kind of bower bird even makes a paintbrush from a wad of bark to apply the paint.

Notice how this passage is improved with a transition:

> The idea that art does not exist among the lower animals is a primitive notion. <u>A perfect illustration of art in the animal kingdom is the art of the amazing bower birds of Australia.</u> These birds decorate their bowers with shells, colored glass, and shining objects. Some paint their walls with fruit pulp, wet powdered charcoal, or paste of chewed-up grass mixed with saliva. One kind of bower bird even makes a paintbrush from a wad of bark to apply the paint.

Some illustrations need to be followed by commentary that interprets them for the reader. Here is an example:

> In 1796 Edward Jenner observed that people who came down with cowpox were protected against the far more serious infection of smallpox; therefore, he decided to infect people with cowpox to keep them

from getting smallpox. In 1881 Louis Pasteur accidentally left a culture of chicken cholera out on a shelf. Two weeks later, having returned from a vacation, he injected the culture into some laboratory animals and found to his surprise that the animals, instead of getting cholera, had become immune to the disease. These two experiences illustrate the beginnings of genetic engineering, a science that is now on the verge of splicing out from a virulent microbe the genes that cause disease. Millions of seriously ill people hope to be cured from deadly viruses through the miracles of genetic engineering.

The last two sentences of the paragraph interpret by telling us that the examples cited were illustrations of early genetic engineering. Whether or not you should use an introductory phrase, a concluding phrase, or simply imbed your illustration within the context of the paragraph is mainly a matter of common sense. Use phrases to introduce your illustrations only if they are necessary. In every case, you should ask yourself whether you have made your point clearly enough to be instantly understood. If the answer is no, then you should add whatever sentence or phrase is necessary to complete your illustration.

3. **An illustration should always be relevant to the point you are making.** If it is not, you should leave it out. Again, much of this judgment is a matter of common sense. But sometimes we get paragraphs that read like this:

   My stepfather is a stodgy person. For example, he contributes money every year to the Audubon fund. He serves as an usher in church and is a Scoutmaster for my half brother's troop. He is active in a club that devotes its time to restoring old buildings in our town.

Not being instances of "stodginess," the examples given do not support the writer's assertion. It is better to avoid illustrations entirely than to cite irrelevant ones that do not support your point.

Warming Up to Write an Illustration

1. Following are five different theses that could well be developed through examples. Sketch out three examples for two theses of your choice. Be sure that each example supports the thesis.
   a. If you shop wisely, you can save large amounts of money.
   b. My mom and dad hear and see things differently.
   c. Sometimes imperfections are beautiful.
   d. Not being covered by medical insurance can be disastrous.
   e. My boyfriend (or girlfriend or spouse) always thinks of romantic things to do.

2. Answer the following questions by listing an example that clarifies the answer to the question.
   a. What makes a snowy landscape beautiful?
   b. What are some typical elements of authority against which teenagers rebel?
   c. Why do most people admire firefighters?
   d. What makes our national parks so valuable?
   e. What are the worst aspects of homelessness?
3. Provide an appropriate example to illustrate each of the following facts.
   a. Being a dentist requires ultimate patience.
   b. The President of the United States is not always a role model.
   c. E-mail is one of the great inventions of the last decade.
   d. Modern medicine has created miracle cures.
   e. Saying goodbye can be heart wrenching.

EXAMPLES

What Is Style?

F. L. LUCAS

F. L. Lucas (1894–1967) was, for many years, a distinguished scholar and lecturer at Cambridge. In his teaching, he placed particular emphasis on the classics and on good writing. Lucas tried his hand at virtually every literary form; yet, his best work was in the field of literary criticism, where he was prolific. Among his principal works are *The Decline and Fall of the Romantic Ideal* (1934), *Greek Poetry for Everyman* (1951), *Greek Drama for Everyman* (1954), and *The Art of Living* (1959).

Style belongs to that category of things about which people commonly say: I don't know what it is but I know what I like. We all think that we can recognize and appreciate style when we see it, but few of us would undertake defining it. In this essay, originally published in March 1960, F. L. Lucas tackles the concept of style, drawing many examples from what some famous people have written and said about it. He also suggests that writers who have good style write for their readers with honesty, courtesy, and brevity.

• • •

1 When it was suggested to Walt Whitman that one of his works should be bound in vellum, he was outraged—"Pshaw!" he snorted, "—hangings, curtains, finger bowls, chinaware, Matthew Arnold!" And he might have been equally irritated by talk of style; for he boasted of "my barbaric yawp"—he would not be literary; his readers should touch not a book but a man. Yet

Whitman took the pains to rewrite *Leaves of Grass* four times, and his style is unmistakable. Samuel Butler maintained that writers who bothered about their style became unreadable but he bothered about his own. "Style" has got a bad name by growing associated with precious and superior persons who, like Oscar Wilde, spend a morning putting in a comma, and the afternoon (so he said) taking it out again. But such abuse of "style" is misuse of English. For the word means merely "a way of expressing oneself, in language, manner, or appearance"; or, secondly, "a good way of so expressing oneself"—as when one says, "Her behavior never lacked style."

2   Now there is no crime in expressing oneself (though to try to impress oneself on others easily grows revolting or ridiculous). Indeed one cannot help expressing oneself, unless one passes one's life in a cupboard. Even the most rigid Communist, or Organization-man, is compelled by Nature to have a unique voice, unique fingerprints, unique handwriting. Even the signatures of the letters on your breakfast table may reveal more than their writers guess. There are blustering signatures that swish across the page like cornstalks bowed before a tempest. There are cryptic signatures, like a scrabble of lightning across a cloud, suggesting that behind is a lofty divinity whom all must know, or an aloof divinity whom none is worthy to know (though, as this might be highly inconvenient, a docile typist sometimes interprets the mystery in a bracket underneath). There are impetuous squiggles implying that the author is a sort of strenuous Sputnik streaking around the globe every eighty minutes. There are florid signatures, all curlicues and danglements and flamboyance, like the youthful Disraeli (though these seem rather out of fashion). There are humble, humdrum signatures. And there are also, sometimes, signatures that are courteously clear, yet mindful of a certain simple grace and artistic economy—in short, of style.

3   Since, then, not one of us can put pen to paper, or even open his mouth, without giving something of himself away to shrewd observers, it seems mere common sense to give the matter a little thought. Yet it does not seem very common. Ladies may take infinite pains about having style in their clothes, but many of us remain curiously indifferent about having it in our words. How many women would dream of polishing not only their nails but also their tongues? They may play freely on that perilous little organ, but they cannot often be bothered to tune it. And how many men think of improving their talk as well as their golf handicap?

4   No doubt strong silent men, speaking only in gruff monosyllables, may despise "mere words." No doubt the world does suffer from an endemic plague of verbal dysentery. But that, precisely, is bad style. And consider the amazing power of mere words. Adolf Hitler was a bad artist, bad statesman, bad general, and bad man. But largely because he could tune his rant, with psychological nicety, to the exact wave length of his audiences and make millions quarrelsome-drunk all at the same time by his command of windy nonsense, skilled statesmen, soldiers, scientists were blown away like chaff, and he came near to rule the world. If Sir Winston Churchill had been a mere speechifier, we might well have lost the war; yet his speeches did quite a lot to win it.

5   No man was less of a literary aesthete than Benjamin Franklin; yet this tallow-chandler's son, who changed world history, regarded as "a principal means of my advancement" that pungent style which he acquired partly by working in youth over old Spectators; but mainly by being Benjamin Franklin. The squinting demagogue, John Wilkes, as ugly as his many sins, had yet a tongue so winning that he asked only half an hour's start (to counteract his face) against any rival for a woman's favor. "Vote for you!" growled a surly elector in his constituency. "I'd sooner vote for the devil!" "But in case your friend should not stand. . .?" Cleopatra, the ensnarer of world conquerors, owed less to the shape of her nose than to the charm of her tongue. Shakespeare himself has often poor plots and thin ideas; even his mastery of character has been questioned; what does remain unchallenged is his verbal magic. Men are often taken, like rabbits, by the ears. And though the tongue has no bones, it can sometimes break millions of them.

6   "But," the reader may grumble, "I am neither Hitler, Cleopatra, nor Shakespeare. What is all this to me?" Yet we all talk—often too much; we all have to write letters—often too many. We live not by bread alone but also by words. And not always with remarkable efficiency. Strikes, lawsuits, divorces, all sorts of public nuisance and private misery, often come just from the gaggling incompetence with which we express ourselves. Americans and British get at cross-purposes because they use the same words with different meanings. Men have been hanged on a comma in a statute. And in the valley of Balaclava a mere verbal ambiguity, about which guns were to be captured, sent the whole Light Brigade to futile annihilation.

7   Words can be more powerful, and more treacherous, than we sometimes suspect; communication more difficult than we may think. We are all serving life sentences of solitary confinement within our own bodies; like prisoners, we have, as it were, to tap in awkward code to our fellow men in their neighboring cells. Further, when A and B converse, there take part in their dialogue not two characters, as they suppose, but six. For there is A's real self—call it A1; there is also A's picture of himself—A2; there is also B's picture of A—A3. And there are three corresponding personalities of B. With six characters involved even in a simple tête-à-tête, no wonder we fall into muddles and misunderstandings.

8   Perhaps, then, there are five main reasons for trying to gain some mastery of language:

> We have no other way of understanding, informing, misinforming, or persuading one another.
>
> Even alone, we think mainly in words; if our language is muddy, so will our thinking be.
>
> By our handling of words we are often revealed and judged. "Has he written anything?" said Napoleon of a candidate for an appointment. "Let me see his style."
>
> Without a feeling for language one remains half-blind and deaf to literature.

Our mother tongue is bettered or worsened by the way each generation uses it. Languages evolve like species. They can degenerate; just as oysters and barnacles have lost their heads. Compare ancient Greek with modern. A heavy responsibility, though often forgotten.

9 Why and how did I become interested in style? The main answer, I suppose, is that I was born that way. Then I was, till ten, an only child running loose in a house packed with books, and in a world (thank goodness) still undistracted by radio and television. So at three I groaned to my mother, "Oh, I *wish* I could read," and at four I read. Now travel among books is the best travel of all, and the easiest, and the cheapest. (Not that I belittle ordinary travel—which I regard as one of the three main pleasures in life.) One learns to write by reading good books, as one learns to talk by hearing good talkers. And if I have learned anything in writing, it is largely from writers like Montaigne, Dorothy Osborne, Horace Walpole, Johnson, Goldsmith, Montesquieu, Voltaire, Flaubert and Anatole France. Again, I was reared on Greek and Latin, and one can learn much from translating Homer or the Greek Anthology, Horace or Tacitus, if one is thrilled by the originals and tries, however vainly, to recapture some of that thrill in English.

10 But at Rugby I could not write English essays. I believe it stupid to torment boys to write on topics that they know and care nothing about. I used to rush to the school library and cram the subject, like a python swallowing rabbits; then, still replete as a postprandial python, I would tie myself in clumsy knots to embrace those accursed themes. Bacon was wise in saying that reading makes a full man; talking, a ready one; writing, an exact one. But writing from an empty head is futile anguish.

11 At Cambridge, my head having grown a little fuller, I suddenly found I *could* write—not with enjoyment (it is always tearing oneself in pieces)—but fairly fluently. Then came the War of 1914–18; and though soldiers have other things than pens to handle, they learn painfully to be clear and brief. Then the late Sir Desmond MacCarthy invited me to review for the New Statesman: it was a useful apprenticeship, and he was delightful to work for. But I think it was well after a few years to stop; reviewers remain essential, but there are too many books one cannot praise, and only the pugnacious enjoy amassing enemies. By then I was an ink-addict—not because writing is much pleasure, but because not to write is pain; just as some smokers do not so much enjoy tobacco as suffer without it. The positive happiness of writing comes, I think, from work when done—decently, one hopes, and not without use—and from the letters of readers which help to reassure, or delude, one that so it is.

12 But one of my most vivid lessons came, I think, from service in a war department during the Second World War. Then, if the matter one sent out was too wordy, the communication channels might choke; yet if it was not absolutely clear, the results might be serious. So I emerged, after six years of it, with more passion than ever for clarity and brevity, more loathing than ever for the obscure and the verbose.

13   For forty years at Cambridge I have tried to teach young men to write well, and have come to think it impossible. To write really well is a gift inborn; those who have it teach themselves; one can only try to help and hasten the process. After all, the uneducated sometimes express themselves far better than their "betters." In language, as in life, it is possible to be perfectly correct—and yet perfectly tedious, or odious. The literate last letter of the doomed Vanzetti[1] was more moving than most professional orators; 18th Century ladies, who should have been spanked for their spelling, could yet write far better letters than most professors of English; and the talk of Synge's Irish peasants seems to me vastly more vivid than the latter styles of Henry James. Yet Synge averred that his characters owed far less of their eloquence to what he invented for them than to what he had overheard in the cottages of Wicklow and Kerry.

> CHRISTY: It's little you'll think if my love's a poacher's, or an earl's itself, when you'll feel my two hands stretched around you, and I squeezing kisses on your puckered lips, till I'd feel a kind of pity for the Lord God in all ages sitting lonesome in His golden chair.
> PEGEEN: That'll be right fun, Christy Mahon, and any girl would walk her heart out before she'd meet a young man was your like for eloquence, or talk at all.

14   Well she might! It's not like that they talk in universities—more's the pity.

15   But though one cannot teach people to write well, one can sometimes teach them to write rather better. One can give a certain number of hints, which often seem boringly obvious—only experience shows they are not.

16   One can say: Beware of pronouns—they are devils. Look at even Addison, describing the type of pedant who chatters of style without having any:

> Upon enquiry I found my learned friend had dined that day with Mr. Swan, the famous punster; and desiring him to give me some account of Mr. Swan's conversation, he told me that he generally talked in the Paronomasia, that he sometimes gave it to the Plocé, but that in his humble opinion he shone most in the Antanaclasis.

17   What a sluttish muddle of *he* and *him* and *his!* It all needs rewording. Far better repeat a noun, or a name, than puzzle the reader, even for a moment, with ambiguous pronouns. Thou shalt not puzzle thy reader.

18   Or one can say: Avoid jingles. The B.B.C. news bulletins seem compiled by earless persons, capable of crying around the globe: "The enemy is *reported* to have seized this *important port,* and reinforcements are hurrying up in *support.*" Any fool, once told, can hear such things to be insupportable.

19   Or one can say: Be sparing with relative clauses. Don't string them together like sausages, or jam them inside one another like Chinese boxes or the receptacles of Buddha's tooth. Or one can say: Don't flaunt jargon, like

---

[1] See p. 81—Ed.

Addison's Mr. Swan, or the type of modern critic who gurgles more technical terms in a page than Johnson used in all his *Lives* or Sainte-Beuve in thirty volumes. But dozens of such snippety precepts, though they may sometimes save people from writing badly, will help them little toward writing well. Are there no general rules of a more positive kind, and of more positive use?

20   Perhaps. There *are* certain basic principles which seem to me observed by many authors I admire, which I think have served me and which may serve others. I am not talking of geniuses, who are a law to themselves (and do not always write a very good style, either); nor of poetry, which has different laws from prose; nor of poetic prose, like Sir Thomas Browne's or De Quincey's which is often more akin to poetry; but of the plain prose of ordinary books and documents, letters and talk.

21   The writer should respect truth and himself; therefore honesty. He should respect his readers; therefore courtesy. These are two of the cornerstones of style. Confucius saw it, twenty-five centuries ago: "The Master said, The gentleman is courteous, but not pliable: common men are pliable, but not courteous."

22   First, honesty. In literature, as in life, one of the fundamentals is to find, and be, one's true self. One's true self may indeed be unpleasant (though one can try to better it); but a false self, sooner or later, becomes disgusting—just as a nice plain woman, painted to the eyebrows, can become horrid. In writing, in the long run, pretense does not work. As the police put it, anything you say may be used as evidence against you. If handwriting reveals character, writing reveals it still more. You cannot fool all your judges all the time.

23   Most style is not honest enough. Easy to say, but hard to practice. A writer may take to long words, as young men to beards—to impress. But long words, like beards, are often the badge of charlatans. Or a writer may cultivate the obscure, to seem profound. But even carefully muddied puddles are soon fathomed. Or he may cultivate eccentricity, to seem original. But really original people do not have to think about being original—they can no more help it than they can help breathing. They do not need to dye their hair green. The fame of Meredith, Wilde or Bernard Shaw might now shine brighter, had they struggled less to be brilliant; whereas Johnson remains great, not merely because his gifts were formidable but also because, with all his prejudice and passion, he fought no less passionately to "clear his mind of cant."

24   Secondly, courtesy—respect for the reader. From this follow several other basic principles of style. Clarity is one. For it is boorish to make your reader rack his brains to understand. One should aim at being impossible to misunderstand—though men's capacity for misunderstanding approaches infinity. Hence Molière and Po Chu-i tried their work on their cooks; and Swift his on his men-servants—"which, if they did not comprehend, he would alter and amend, until they understood it perfectly." Our bureaucrats and pundits, unfortunately, are less considerate.

25   Brevity is another basic principle. For it is boorish to waste your reader's time. People who would not dream of stealing a penny of one's money turn not a hair at stealing hours of one's life. But that does not make them less

exasperating. Therefore there is no excuse for the sort of writer who takes as long as a marching army corps to pass a given point. Besides, brevity is often more effective; the half can say more than the whole, and to imply things may strike far deeper than to state them at length. And because one is particularly apt to waste words on preambles before coming to the substance, there was sense in the Scots professor who always asked his pupils—"Did ye remember to tear up that fir-r-st page?"

26 Here are some instances that would only lose by lengthening.

> It is useless to go to bed to save the light, if the result is twins. (Chinese proverb.)
>
> My barn is burnt down—
> Nothing hides the moon. (Complete Japanese poem.)
>
> Je me regrette.[2] (Dying words of the gay Vicomtesse d'Houdetot.)
>
> I have seen their backs before. (Wellington, when French marshals turned their backs on him at a reception.)
>
> Continue until the tanks stop, then get out and walk. (Patton to the Twelfth Corps, halted for fuel supplies at St. Dizier, 8/30/44.)

27 Or there is the most laconic diplomatic note on record: when Philip of Macedon wrote to the Spartans that, if he came within their borders, he would leave not one stone of their city, they wrote back the one word—"If."

28 Clarity comes before even brevity. But it is a fallacy that wordiness is necessarily clearer. Metternich when he thought something he had written was obscure would simply go through it crossing out everything irrelevant. What remained, he found, often became clear. Wellington, asked to recommend three names for the post of Commander-in-Chief, India, took a piece of paper and wrote three times—"Napier." Pages could not have been clearer—or as forcible. On the other hand the lectures, and the sentences, of Coleridge became at times bewildering because his mind was often "wiggle-waggle"; just as he could not even walk straight on a path.

29 But clarity and brevity, though a good beginning, are only a beginning. By themselves, they may remain bare and bleak. When Calvin Coolidge, asked by his wife what the preacher had preached on, replied "Sin," and, asked what the preacher had said, replied, "He was against it," he was brief enough. But one hardly envies Mrs. Coolidge.

30 An attractive style requires, of course, all kinds of further gifts—such as variety, good humor, good sense, vitality, imagination. Variety means avoiding monotony of rhythm, of language, of mood. One needs to vary one's sentence length (this present article has too many short sentences; but so vast a subject grows here as cramped as a djin in a bottle); to amplify one's vocabulary; to diversify one's tone. There are books that petrify one throughout, with the

---

[2] "I shall miss myself."—Ed.

rigidly pompous solemnity of an owl perched on a leafless tree. But ceaseless facetiousness can be as bad; or perpetual irony. Even the smile of Voltaire can seem at times a fixed grin, a disagreeable wrinkle. Constant peevishness is far worse, as often in Swift; even on the stage too much irritable dialogue may irritate an audience, without its knowing why.

31 Still more are vitality, energy, imagination gifts that must be inborn before they can be cultivated. But under the head of imagination two common devices may be mentioned that have been the making of many a style—metaphor and simile. Why such magic power should reside in simply saying, or implying, that A is like B remains a little mysterious. But even our unconscious seems to love symbols; again, language often tends to lose itself in clouds of vaporous abstraction, and simile or metaphor can bring it back to concrete solidity; and, again, such imagery can gild the gray flats of prose with sudden sun-glints of poetry.

32 If a foreigner may for a moment be impertinent, I admire the native gift of Americans for imagery as much as I wince at their fondness for slang. (Slang seems to me a kind of linguistic fungus; as poisonous, and as short-lived, as toadstools.) When Matthew Arnold lectured in the United States, he was likened by one newspaper to "an elderly macaw pecking at a trellis of grapes"; he observed, very justly, "How lively journalistic fancy is among the Americans!" General Grant, again, unable to hear him, remarked: "Well, wife, we've paid to see the British lion, but as we can't hear him roar, we'd better go home." By simile and metaphor, these two quotations bring before us the slightly pompous, fastidious, inaudible Arnold as no direct description could have done.

33 Or consider how language comes alive in the Chinese saying that lending to the feckless is "like pelting a stray dog with dumplings," or in the Arab proverb: "They came to shoe the pasha's horse, and the beetle stretched forth his leg"; in the Greek phrase for a perilous cape—"stepmother of ships"; or the Hebrew adage that "as the climbing up a sandy way is to the feet of the aged, so is a wife full of words to a quiet man"; in Shakespeare's phrase for a little England lost in the world's vastness—"in a great Poole, a Swan's nest"; or Fuller's libel on tall men—"Ofttimes such who are built four stories high are observed to have little in their cockloft"; in Chateaubriand's "I go yawning my life"; or in Jules Renard's portrait of a cat, "well buttoned in her fur." Or, to take a modern instance, there is Churchill on dealing with Russia:

> Trying to maintain good relations with a Communist is like wooing a crocodile. You do not know whether to tickle it under the chin or beat it over the head. When it opens its mouth, you cannot tell whether it is trying to smile or preparing to eat you up.

34 What a miracle human speech can be, and how dull is most that one hears! Would one hold one's hearers, it is far less help, I suspect, to read manuals on style than to cultivate one's own imagination and imagery.

35 I will end with two remarks by two wise old women of the civilized 18th Century.

36   The first is from the blind Mme. du Deffand (the friend of Horace Walpole) to that Mlle. de Lespinasse with whom, alas, she was to quarrel so unwisely: "You must make up your mind, my queen, to live with me in the greatest truth and sincerity. You will be charming so long as you let yourself be natural, and remain without pretension and without artifice." The second is from Mme. de Charrière, the Zélide whom Boswell had once loved at Utrecht in vain, to a Swiss girl friend: "Lucinde, my clever Lucinde, while you wait for the Romeos to arrive, you have nothing better to do than become perfect. Have ideas that are clear, and expressions that are simple." ("Ayez des idées nettes et des expressions simples.") More than half the bad writing in the world, I believe, comes from neglecting those two very simple pieces of advice.

37   In many ways, no doubt, our world grows more and more complex; sputniks cannot be simple; yet how many of our complexities remain futile, how many of our artificialities false. Simplicity too can be subtle—as the straight lines of a Greek temple, like the Parthenon at Athens, are delicately curved, in order to look straighter still.

- ## Vocabulary

  curlicues (2)
  tallow-chandler (5)
  annihilation (6)
  replete (10)
  verbose (12)
  pedant (16)
  endemic (4)
  demagogue (5)
  tête-à-tête (7)
  postprandial (10)
  odious (13)
  aesthete (5)
  gaggling (6)
  degenerate (8)
  pugnacious (11)
  averred (13)

- ## The Facts

  1. According to the author, why did "style" get a bad name?
  2. What are the two basic principles of good writing style? What other principles follow from the second?
  3. What are some other gifts associated with an attractive style, as listed in paragraph 30?
  4. What are two common literary devices that have made many a style? According to paragraph 32, who has a particular gift for these devices?
  5. Lucas ends his essay with some pertinent advice from two women. Who are they, and what is their advice?

- ## The Strategies

  1. What is the difference between "expressing" and "impressing" as discussed in paragraph 2?
  2. In paragraph 4, Lucas states that skilled statesmen, soldiers, and scientists were "blown away like chaff" by Adolf Hitler's "windy nonsense." What would happen to Lucas's style if you substituted "drowned" for "blown away"?

3. Paragraph 5 alludes to Benjamin Franklin, John Wilkes, Cleopatra, and Shakespeare as people who owed their charm or success to their verbal style. Whom else can you add to the list? Give reasons for your choices.
4. In paragraph 9, Lucas suggests that people learn to write by reading good books. What purpose is served by the list of nine authors that follows?
5. What is the rhetorical function of paragraph 34?

● The Issues

1. What is the difference, if any, between "class" and "style" when each word is used to designate an individual's personal conduct and mode of living?
2. The author says that we all express a self no matter how hard we may try to efface it. Does it not follow, then, that we all have "style"? Why or why not?
3. Lucas comes from a highly elitist background in which privilege and status dictated advancement and social preferment. How does his definition of style implicitly reflect this background? Or does it?
4. What is your opinion of the adage "Style is the man"? How does it apply or not apply to Lucas's idea of style?
5. Lucas implies that growing up in a world undistracted by radio and television helped him to develop early as a writer and reader. What effect, if any, have radio and television had on your own development as a reader and writer?

● Suggestions for Writing

1. Lucas's essay was first published as a magazine article in March 1960. Write an essay quoting and evaluating particular passages and opinions to which a modern reader, especially a feminist, might take offense.
2. Write an essay explaining the effect you think the media have had on your own development as a reader and writer. Say how this effect might have been overcome or lessened.

The Buck Stops Where?
BARRY PARR

Barry Parr is a freelance journalist who lives and writes in the San Francisco Bay area.

You will enjoy the humor in Parr's recital of anecdotes involving many of our best-loved presidents. One way to approach this essay is to note what past leaders of our nation got away with compared to the more recent occupants of the White House. Have we become more scrutinizing, or have the media become more invasive? This essay was reprinted from the October 1996 issue of America West.

● ● ●

1   "It's been my experience," observed Honest Abe, "that people who have no vices have very few virtues."

2   Such a wise and tolerant perception would make a fine sound bite in an election year. But rest assured, no one will touch it, for the sad truth is that a little dab of vice makes for a more interesting campaign than a whole vat of virtue. An unflattering image, a well-delivered sound bite, a silly gaffe or a youthful indiscretion raked through the muck all attract far more attention than a lifetime of honest public service.

3   Doubtless, voters in the early days of the republic were no less hungry for all the sottish details—and, indeed, our public leaders were no less inclined to provide them. But for better or worse—probably for better—our forefathers (and foremothers) simply didn't have the technology that we have today for efficiently disseminating a public figure's flaws, shenanigans and peccadilloes to an eager and expectant nation.

4   Could George Washington—who was totally toothless by age 57—have weathered the merciless barrage of jokes on late-night TV? Would daytime television talk-show hosts have ever allowed Lincoln to get beyond his early career as a stripped-down, frontier wrestler?

5   And what would the news media—which have shown more than a passing interest in Bill Clinton's jogging shorts and pale thighs—have made of John Quincy Adams's daily constitutional of skinny-dipping in the Potomac River? When on one occasion a rascal stole his clothes, our sixth president was forced to hail a passing boy, requesting him to ring at the White House to obtain a change of clothes from the first lady.

6   The news media have not played the game on an equal footing with all the presidents. They could tiptoe around the White House with utmost discretion during the sometimes ribald Kennedy tenure, and yet quail with shock when Jimmy Carter fessed up, with boy-like candor, that he had known lust in his heart.

7   Protest trumpeted mightily across the land when Lyndon Johnson lifted his pet beagle by the ears, but the gentlemen of the press were more bemused than outraged when visitors plucked bald spots on Zachary Taylor's old war horse, Whitey, in an effort to collect souvenirs. (Taylor had pastured poor Whitey on the White House lawn.)

8   No one batted an eye while President Grant smoked up the Oval Office with his daily allotment of 20 cigars, and yet, Andrew Jackson's wife, Rachel, was driven to despair (and Old Hickory believed even unto death) by gleefully mean-spirited rumors that she smoked a pipe.

9   We are all too familiar with hullabaloos that arise over completely trivial matters—the hole in presidential candidate Adlai Stevenson's shoe, for instance, or Richard Nixon's 5 o'clock shadow in his famous Kennedy debate (both of which have been blamed for costing their election bids). But the reverse is also true: The most stupendous of presidential stunts has sometimes gone almost totally unnoticed. Somewhat less than obscure is the tale of when Harry S. Truman buzzed the White House. After taking off from Washington, D.C., in May 1946, Truman reportedly bid his pilot to detour through the no-fly

zone that surrounds the presidential mansion. After spotting his family and friends gathered on the roof—where he'd apparently summoned them for a surprise—"Give em Hell" Harry ordered his pilot to dive. As the plane nosed down and accelerated into a steep descent, Truman was delighted to see their excited waves of recognition suddenly dissolve into a wild scramble for cover. Truman apparently enjoyed the prank so much that he ordered a second round, before proceeding onward to Independence, Missouri.

10   Decidedly less spectacular are some of the incidental diversions of Thomas Jefferson, probably our most intellectually accomplished president. A cultured violinist, superb architect and successful lawyer, Jefferson spoke six languages and held his own with the best philosophers of his day, but he still found time for puttering around with other pursuits of a more practical nature. Not only did he invent the chaise lounge, the swivel chair and a successful prototype of an indoor toilet—all considered essential fixtures in the White House to this day—but he also introduced his country to waffles and ice cream, and was reputed to be the first man in America to grow a tomato. (JFK once remarked at one of his famous state dinners—glittering events that garnered cultivated crowds of poets, novelists, musicians, Nobel laureates, Harvard lecturers and heads of states—that the last time so much brilliance had gathered in the White House was when Jefferson ate his supper there, alone.)

11   "Public opinion in this country is everything," Abe Lincoln once noted, indicating that the primal force we now know as "spin" was operating full tilt even in the 19th century. Spin doctors made hay out of Lincoln's humble birth by celebrating him as "The Log Cabin President." Yet, the same "Washington insiders" dealt a dirty hand to his successor, Andrew Johnson, and for much the same humble origins. A tailor and the son of a tailor, Johnson never received a formal education, and first learned to write as a young man, tutored by his patient and sterling wife, Eliza McArdle Johnson. The contempt that fueled his impeachment charges was to no small degree inspired by the vicious snobbery rampant in Washington's higher society. (It bears noting, too, that the egalitarian 1960s never did warm up to Richard Nixon, even after it was revealed that the supreme commander of the United States of America, when a youth, had taken a summer job at the Slippery Gulch Rodeo in Prescott, Arizona, where he worked as a barker for the wheel of chance.)

12   Spin doctors are an ingenious bunch, and even can score points—or deduct them—from something so trivial as a presidential snack. The public was charmed by Gerald Ford's habit of toasting his own muffin for breakfast. We feel somewhat closer to Grover Cleveland to learn that his favorite meal was a plate of corned beef and cabbage. Ronald Reagan's fondness for jelly beans sparked a nationwide run on that commodity. And who can resist smiling with benign indulgence upon learning that U. S. Grant enjoyed nothing better for breakfast than a cucumber in vinegar? On the other hand, Nixon seems to have inspired almost universal condemnation for enjoying a luncheon of cottage cheese with ketchup. Nixon's advisers seem to have been particularly inept at the science of managing spin. The nation expressed almost universal shock and displeasure at the saltiness of his language on the Watergate tapes.

Yet, we are almost universally inclined to view the "oaths" of the Jackson era as, well, something rather quaint. (At Jackson's funeral, his pet parrot had to be removed from the room for peppering the solemnities with a barrage of fine 19th century cusses.) And, of course, "Give'em Hell" Harry Truman is actually venerated for the pungency of his discourse. ("I never did give anybody hell," Truman once snapped. "I just told the truth, and they thought it was hell.")

13   Some presidents have survived public-relations disasters that would ring the death knell with today's voters. Warren Harding routinely parted with pieces of White House china, which he used as chips in friendly poker games. Probably the second most famous act of William Howard Taft—who stood 6 feet 2 inches and weighed up to 350 pounds during his presidential tenure—was becoming stuck in the White House bathtub. (His most famous act? Starting the presidential custom of throwing out the first pitch of the baseball season.) And, of course, we could never stand for a modern president to be as cavalier as Andrew Jackson over matters of security. At his inaugural reception, a rowdy crowd of thousands poured into the White House on open invitation, gobbling and drinking the refreshments in record speed and heatedly demanding more, while Old Hickory himself was forced to escape to a local hotel for the night. On another occasion, the Hero of New Orleans invited the public to enjoy a gigantic cheese, which measured 4 feet in diameter and 2 feet thick, and weighed 1,400 pounds. Milling throngs pressed with knives through the White House entry and ravenously hacked it to pieces, devouring some on the spot and carrying away hunks wrapped in newspapers. The hallowed halls stunk of cheese for weeks thereafter.

14   Despite the all-too-human behavior of many of our leaders, there is indeed something almost shiningly virtuous in any man or woman who has the courage to survive the toss and gore of a presidential campaign amid the fickle court of public opinion. Our next president, whoever that might be, could do worse than take heart from the wry, but wise, observations of Harry Truman, who knew firsthand the glory, and the thankless strain, of life at the top.

15   "A politician," said he, "is a man who understands government, and it takes a politician to run a government. A statesman is a politician who's been dead 10 or 15 years."

16   I believe it also was Truman who noted, "If you want a friend in this life, get a dog."

- **Vocabulary**

    sound bite (2)   dab (2)   vat (2)
    gaffe (2)   sottish (3)   peccadilloes (3)
    pungency (12)

- **The Facts**

    1. Who made the following observation: "It's been my experience that people who have no vices have very few virtues"?

2. What kept our forebears from hearing about the indiscretions of their leaders?
3. Which American president had his clothes stolen while skinny dipping in the Potomac?
4. What prank did President Truman organize while his friends and family gathered on the roof of the White House, where he had summoned them?
5. Which president spoke six languages, played the violin, and was an architect as well as a lawyer?
6. Who said, "A statesman is a politician who's been dead 10 or 15 years"?

The Strategies

1. What pre-writing strategy do you think the author used to develop this essay?
2. In addition to comparing contemporary presidents with those of the past, what rhetorical strategy does the author use? How important is it to his subject?
3. The author seems to poke fun at U.S. presidents. Does his attitude make you respect these presidents less? Why or why not?
4. How does the author portray the presidents he mentions? Are they well-rounded, three-dimensional people? Is the author's description superficial? State how his descriptions relate to the purpose of the essay.
5. What is the meaning of the title? Explain how it fits the essay.

The Issues

1. What kind of president would you prefer—one who is exemplary and virtuous in every respect or one who has a few vices? Describe the morality of your ideal president.
2. Why are people intrigued by the vices of public figures?
3. Are the news media excessive in their quest for scandalous news about public figures? Why should Americans have the right to know all the details of the lives of important people, especially those who lead our country?
4. Do public figures have a duty to curb their tongues and to behave like gentlemen or gentlewomen so long as they hold public office?
5. What does the author mean when he states that "spin doctors are an ingenious bunch, and even can score points—or deduct them—from something so trivial as a presidential snack"? Give an example from recent news in which this kind of spin was created.

Suggestions for Writing

1. Write an essay describing an important trait you admire in your favorite American president. Give examples of the trait you have chosen.
2. Write an essay in which you deplore the way the news media intrude into the private lives of public figures. Give examples of this kind of intrusion.

"Mirror, Mirror, on the Wall..."
JOHN LEO

John Leo (b. 1935), associate editor of *Time,* was born in Hoboken, New Jersey, and educated at the University of Toronto. He has been associated with *Commonweal, The New York Times,* the *Village Voice,* and more recently as editor and columnist for *U.S. News and World Report.*

In the following brief essay from Time, *Leo discusses and gives examples of the relativity of beauty.*

• • •

1   The poet may insist that beauty is in the eye of the beholder; the historian might argue that societies create the image of female perfection that they want. There has always been plenty of evidence to support both views. Martin Luther thought long, beautiful hair was essential. Edmund Burke recommended delicate, fragile women. Goethe insisted on "the proper breadth of the pelvis and the necessary fullness of the breasts." Hottentot men look for sharply projecting buttocks. Rubens favored a full posterior, and Papuans require a big nose. The Mangaians of Polynesia care nothing of fat or thin and never seem to notice face, breasts or buttocks. To the tribesmen, the only standard of sexiness is well-shaped female genitals.

2   An anthropologized world now knows that notions of what is most attractive do vary with each age and culture. One era's flower is another's frump. Primitive man, understandably concerned with fertility, idealized ample women. One of the earliest surviving sculptures, the Stone Age Venus of Willendorf, depicts a squat woman whose vital statistics—in inches—would amount to 96–89–96. This adipose standard stubbornly recurs in later eras. A 14th-century treatise on beauty calls for "narrow shoulders, small breasts, large belly, broad hips, fat thighs, short legs and a small head." Some Oriental cultures today are turned on by what Simone de Beauvoir calls the "unnecessary, gratuitous blooming" of wrap-around fat.

3   The Greeks were so concerned with working out precise proportions for beauty that the sculptor Praxiteles insisted that the female navel be exactly midway between the breasts and genitals. The dark-haired Greeks considered fair-haired women exotic, perhaps the start of the notion that blondes have more fun. They also offered early evidence of the rewards that go to magnificent mammaries. When Phryne, Praxiteles' famous model and mistress, was on trial for treason, the orator defending her pulled aside her veil, baring her legendary breasts. The awed judges acquitted her on the spot.

4   Romans favored more independent, articulate women than the Greeks. Still, there were limits. Juvenal complains of ladies who "discourse on poets and poetry, comparing Vergil with Homer. . . . Wives shouldn't read all the classics—there ought to be some things women don't understand."

5   In ancient Egypt, women spent hours primping: fixing hair, applying lipstick, eye shadow and fingernail polish, grinding away body and genital hair with pumice stones. It worked: Nefertiti could make the cover of *Vogue* any month she wanted. For Cleopatra, the most famous bombshell of the ancient world, eroticism was plain hard work. Not a natural beauty, she labored diligently to learn coquettishness and flattery and reportedly polished her amatory techniques by practicing on slaves.

6   If Cleopatra had to work so hard at being desirable, can the average woman do less? Apparently not. In the long history of images of beauty, one staple is the male tendency to spot new flaws in women, and the female tendency to work and suffer to remedy them. In the Middle Ages, large women rubbed themselves with cow dung dissolved in wine. When whiter skin was demanded, women applied leeches to take the red out. Breasts have been strapped down, cantilevered up, pushed together or apart, oiled and siliconed and, in 16th-century Venice, fitted with wool or hair padding for a sexy "duck breast" look, curving from bodice to groin. In the long run, argues feminist Elizabeth Gould Davis, flat-chested women are evolutionary losers. Says she: "The female of the species owes her modern mammary magnificence to male sexual preference."

7   Still, a well-endowed woman can suddenly find herself out of favor when cultural winds change. The flapper era in America is one example. So is Europe's Romantic Age, which favored the wan, cadaverous look. In the 1820s, women sometimes drank vinegar or stayed up all night to look pale and interesting. Fragility was all. Wrote Keats: "God! she is like a milkwhite lamb that bleats / For man's protection."

8   Victorians took this ideal of the shy, clinging vine, decorously desexed it, and assigned it to the wife. According to one well-known Victorian doctor, it was a "vile aspersion" to suggest that women were capable of sexual impulses. Inevitably that straitlaced era controlled women's shapes by severe compression of the waistline, without accenting breasts or hips.

9   Those womanly curves reasserted themselves at the turn of the century. During the hourglass craze, Lillie Langtry seemed perfection incarnate at 38–18–38. Since then, the ideal woman in Western culture has gradually slimmed down. Psyche, the White Rock girl,[1] was 5 ft. 4 in. tall and weighed in at a hippy 140 lbs. when she first appeared on beverage bottles in 1893. Now, *sans* cellulite, she is 4 in. taller and 22 lbs. lighter.

10   In psychological terms, the current slim-hipped look amounts to a rebellion against male domination: waist-trimming corsets are associated with male control of the female body, and narrow hips with a reluctance to bear children. Says Madge Garland, a former editor of *British Vogue*: "The natural shape of the female body has not been revealed and free as it is today for 1,500 years." W. H. Auden once complained that for most of Western history, the sexy beautiful women have seemed "fictionalized," set apart from real life. In the age of the

---

[1] Psyche has been the emblem of White Rock–brand soft drinks and mixes since the nineteenth century.—Ed.

natural look, a beauty now has to seem as though she just strolled in from the beach at Malibu. Like Cheryl Tiegs.

- **Vocabulary**

  frump (2)
  coquettishness (5)
  decorously (8)
  cellulite (9)

  adipose (2)
  amatory (5)
  aspersion (8)

  gratuitous (2)
  cantilevered (6)
  incarnate (9)

- **The Facts**

  1. What kinds of women did primitive man idealize?
  2. What was the Greeks' standard of beauty?
  3. According to feminist Elizabeth Gould Davis, to what do women owe their "modern mammary magnificence"?
  4. What kind of feminine beauty was favored during Europe's Romantic Age?
  5. What does the modern, slim-hipped look signify in psychological terms?

- **The Strategies**

  1. What notion do most of the examples in this essay support? Where is this notion stated?
  2. Much of the detail about beauty is given not in full-blown examples, but in sketchy references to the opinions of famous people. What are such references called?
  3. In paragraph 3, what does the anecdote about Phryne exemplify?
  4. The author quotes Goethe, Simone de Beauvoir, Juvenal, Elizabeth Gould Davis, John Keats, Madge Garland, and W. H. Auden. What effect does all this opinion sampling have on the tone of the essay?
  5. In paragraph 6, the author writes: "In the long history of images of beauty, one staple is the male tendency to spot new flaws in women, and the female tendency to work and suffer to remedy them." How does the author proceed to support and document this view?

- **The Issues**

  1. Paragraph 2 alludes to an "anthropologized world." How would you define this world? What significance lies in this label?
  2. What, for you, constitutes a beautiful female? A beautiful male? Refer to specific examples from history, from the current scene, or from your personal encounters.
  3. How do you feel about the present emphasis on an athletic female body? Is it justified, or does it diminish some other innately feminine characteristic? Give reasons for your answer.

4. Even if you agree with the poet that beauty is in the eye of the beholder, argue that true beauty must follow certain standards. Suggest what these standards might be when applied to, say, a painting or a sculpture.

5. In paragraph 8, the author describes the typical Victorian wife as a woman who must never be perceived as having sexual impulses. How does the typical Victorian wife compare with the women we observe in the movies or on TV today? Give examples to support your view.

● Suggestions for Writing

1. Write an essay that specifies your idea of human beauty. Give convincing examples to illustrate your point.

2. Write an essay in which you argue that human beauty is in the eye of the beholder.

ISSUE FOR CRITICAL THINKING AND DEBATE: DRUG ABUSE

Ours is a society awash in a transcontinental tidal surge of drugs. We awake to the kick of caffeine, soothe our nerves with tobacco, ease our tension headaches with aspirin, wind down the day with alcohol, and swallow an antihistamine to help us sleep—all perfectly legal, respectable, and even expected.

But there is a dark side to this epidemic of drug use. Over 400 thousand of us perish annually from the effects of tobacco. Some 23 million of us regularly take illegal drugs, ranging from marijuana to cocaine to heroin. A causal relationship exists between drug addiction and criminal wrongdoing, with a significant proportion of those arrested for felonies—in some cities as much as 70%—testing positive for drug use (Skolnick, Jerome H., "Making Sense of the Crime Decline," *Newsday,* 2 Feb. 1997: Electric Library. 27 Nov. 1999. http://www.elibrary.com). The exact incidence of drug usage and addiction among the general population is unknown, although the National Household Survey on Drug Abuse (NHSDA) found that in 2001 an estimated 15.9 million Americans were illicit drugs users (Office of Applied Studies, National Household "Illicit Drug Use." Available online at http://www.samhsa.gov/oas/NHSDA/2k1NHSDA/vol1/Chapter2.htm).

The political response to the spreading tide of illegal drugs has been predictable: Conservatives urge heightened efforts at the interdiction of illegal drugs, mandatory drug testing, stiffer prison terms for pushers, and a crackdown on recreational users. Liberals and libertarians advocate an agenda of education and rehabilitation and, probably the most controversial measure of all, the legalization of drug use. It is this last proposal that has set off the latest and most vehement round of debate.

Making the case for legalization, and doing so in his usual caustic style, is the novelist and writer Gore Vidal. His argument is not new, but it is refreshingly

Can drugs ever be the answer to despair, depression, and boredom?

presented. Prohibition increases the allure of drugs, argues Vidal, and it is only because our society is so devoted to the concepts of sin and punishment that we reject out of hand this simple solution. Equally emphatic in his refutation of the case for legalization is editorial writer Morton Kondracke. He makes his case with an array of statistics from which he infers the direst possible consequences of legalization. The Student Corner essay argues that only early education about the dangers can stem the tide of drug abuse.

England and a few other European countries have experimented with the legalization of drugs, and with some success, but no society as complex and variegated as ours has ever attempted to legalize drugs on such a vast scale as would be involved if the liberals were to win this argument. The consequences of legalization might ultimately be anyone's guess. Given the strong moral strain that permeates American political thinking, however, we think Vidal is right, and that unless drug abuse becomes incalculably worse than it is today, legalization will likely remain a topic for academic debate rather than be adopted as national policy by any present or future administration.

Drugs
Gore Vidal

Gore Vidal (b. 1925), is a writer of novels, plays, short stories, book reviews, and essays. His major novels include *The City and the Pillar* (1948), *Julian* (1964), *Myra Breckenridge* (1968), *1876* (1976), *Burr* (1980), *Creation* (1981), *Lincoln* (1984), and *Eighteen Seventy-Six* (1988).

1. It is possible to stop most drug addiction in the United States within a very short time. Simply make all drugs available and sell them at cost. Label each drug with a precise description of what effect—good and bad—the drug will have on the taker. This will require heroic honesty. Don't say that marijuana is addictive or dangerous when it is neither, as millions of people know—unlike "speed," which kills most unpleasantly, or heroin, which is addictive and difficult to kick.

2. For the record, I have tried—once—almost every drug and liked none, disproving the popular Fu Manchu theory that a single whiff of opium will enslave the mind. Nevertheless many drugs are bad for certain people to take and they should be told why in a sensible way.

3. Along with exhortation and warning, it might be good for our citizens to recall (or learn for the first time) that the United States was the creation of men who believed that each man has the right to do what he wants with his own life as long as he does not interfere with his neighbor's pursuit of happiness (that his neighbor's idea of happiness is persecuting others does confuse matters a bit).

4. This is a startling notion to the current generation of Americans. They reflect a system of public education which has made the Bill of Rights, literally, unacceptable to a majority of high school graduates (see the annual Purdue reports) who now form the "silent majority"—a phrase which that underestimated wit Richard Nixon took from Homer who used it to describe the dead.

5. Now one can hear the warning rumble begin: if everyone is allowed to take drugs everyone will and the GNP will decrease, the Commies will stop us from making everyone free, and we shall end up a race of Zombies, passively murmuring "groovie" to one another. Alarming thought. Yet it seems most unlikely that any reasonably sane person will become a drug addict if he knows in advance what addiction is going to be like.

6. Is everyone reasonably sane? No. Some people will always become drug addicts just as some people will always become alcoholics, and it is just too bad. Every man, however, has the power (and should have the legal right) to kill himself if he chooses. But since most men don't, they won't be mainliners either. Nevertheless, forbidding people things they like or think they might enjoy only makes them want those things all the more. This psychological insight is, for some mysterious reason, perennially denied our governors.

7. It is a lucky thing for the American moralist that our country has always existed in a kind of time-vacuum: we have no public memory of anything that happened before last Tuesday. No one in Washington today recalls what happened during the years alcohol was forbidden to the people by a Congress

that thought it had a divine mission to stamp out Demon Rum—launching, in the process, the greatest crime wave in the country's history, causing thousands of deaths from bad alcohol, and creating a general (and persisting) contempt among the citizenry for the laws of the United States.

8   The same thing is happening today. But the government has learned nothing from past attempts at prohibition, not to mention repression.

9   Last year when the supply of Mexican marijuana was slightly curtailed by the Feds, the pushers got the kids hooked on heroin and deaths increased dramatically, particularly in New York. Whose fault? Evil men like the Mafiosi? Permissive Dr. Spock? Wild-eyed Dr. Leary? No.

10   The Government of the United States was responsible for those deaths. The bureaucratic machine has a vested interest in playing cops and robbers. Both the Bureau of Narcotics and the Mafia want strong laws against the sale and use of drugs because if drugs are sold at cost there would be no money in it for anyone.

11   If there was no money in it for the Mafia, there would be no friendly playground pushers, and addicts would not commit crimes to pay for the next fix. Finally, if there was no money in it, the Bureau of Narcotics would wither away, something they are not about to do without a struggle.

12   Will anything sensible be done? Of course not. The American people are as devoted to the idea of sin and its punishment as they are to making money—and fighting drugs is nearly as big a business as pushing them. Since the combination of sin and money is irresistible (particularly to the professional politician), the situation will only grow worse.

Vocabulary

exhortation (3)   perennially (6)   repression (8)

The Facts

1. What specific proposal does Vidal make for selling drugs?
2. According to Vidal, to whom is the Bill of Rights unacceptable?
3. What lesson about repression does Vidal say the government has largely forgotten?
4. Which two groups, according to Vidal, have a vested interest in prolonging the ban against drugs?
5. What dismal prophecy does Vidal make at the conclusion of his argument? How has his prophecy stood the test of time?

The Strategies

1. Vidal opens his argument with a blunt declaration of his position and without any softening up of the opposition with statistics or background material. What do you think the reaction to this opening would be if this were an essay written by a student? Why?
2. Vidal admits to having used almost every drug and having liked none. How does this frank admission affect his argument?

3. What one word in paragraph 5 dates this essay as from another era?
4. What is the rhetorical purpose of paragraphs 5 and 6?
5. Aside from its blunt tone, what characteristic of this essay would make it unsuitable as a student submission in a writing class?

The Issues

1. What do you think is the likely effect of a governmental attitude that says all drugs are bad for you?
2. What do you think would happen if all drugs were legalized?
3. Vidal says that "forbidding people things they like or think they might enjoy only makes them want those things all the more." Do you think this a truth or a cliché? Why?
4. If the government of the United States sprays marijuana crops with a herbicide that then poisons an unknowing user, who is morally responsible?
5. Do you agree with Vidal that the American people are hooked on the idea of sin and punishment? Why or why not?

Suggestions for Writing

1. Write an essay relating any encounter you have had with, or have heard someone else tell about, drugs.
2. Attack or defend Vidal's opinions in an essay.

- Will one wrong choice easily ruin a life?

Don't Legalize Drugs

MORTON M. KONDRACKE

>Morton Kondracke (b. 1939) is an American journalist who has worked for *Newsweek* and the *New Republic*. Kondracke is a regular commentator on the National Public Radio program "All Things Considered" and writes a monthly column for *The Wall Street Journal*. He is the author of *Gerald R. Ford* (1976), one in a series of short biographies.

1   The next time you hear that a drunk driver has slammed into a school bus full of children or that a stoned railroad engineer has killed 16 people in a train wreck, think about this: if the advocates of legalized drugs have their way, there will be more of this, a lot more. There will also be more unpublicized fatal and maiming crashes, more job accidents, more child neglect, more of almost everything associated with substance abuse: babies born addicted or retarded, teenagers zonked out of their chance for an education, careers destroyed, families wrecked, and people dead of overdoses.

2   The proponents of drug legalization are right to say that some things will get better. Organized crime will be driven out of the drug business, and there will be a sharp drop in the amount of money (currently about $10 billion per year) that society spends to enforce the drug laws. There will be some reduction in the cost in theft and injury (now about $20 billion) by addicts to get the money to buy prohibited drugs. Internationally, Latin American governments presumably will stop being menaced by drug cartels and will peaceably export cocaine as they now do coffee.

3   However, this is virtually the limit of the social benefits to be derived from legalization, and they are far outweighed by the costs, which are always underplayed by legalization advocates such as the Economist, Princeton scholar Ethan A. Nadelmann, economist Milton Friedman and other libertarians, columnists William F. Buckley and Richard Cohen, and Mayors Keith Schmoke of Baltimore and Marion Barry of Washington, D.C. In lives, money, and human woe, the costs are so high, in fact, that society has no alternative but to conduct a real war on the drug trade, although perhaps a smarter one than is currently being waged.

4   Advocates of legalization love to draw parallels between the drug war and Prohibition. Their point, of course, is that this crusade is as doomed to failure as the last one was, and that we ought to surrender now to the inevitable and stop wasting resources. But there are some important differences between drugs and alcohol. Alcohol has been part of Western culture for thousands of years; drugs have been the rage in America only since about 1962. Of the 115 million Americans who consume alcohol, 85 percent rarely become intoxicated; with drugs, intoxication is the whole idea. Alcohol is consistent chemically, even though it's dispensed in different strengths and forms as beer, wine, and "hard" liquor; with drugs there's no limit to the variations. Do we legalize crack along with snortable cocaine, PCP as well as marijuana, and LSD and

"Ecstasy" as well as heroin? If we don't—and almost certainly we won't—we have a black market, and some continued crime.

5   But Prohibition is a useful historical parallel for measuring the costs of legalization. Almost certainly doctors are not going to want to write prescriptions for recreational use of harmful substances, so if drugs even are legalized they will be dispensed as alcohol now is—in government-regulated stores with restrictions on the age of buyers, warnings against abuse (and, probably, with added restrictions on amounts, though this also will create a black market).

6   In the decade before Prohibition went into effect in 1920, alcohol consumption in the United States averaged 2.6 gallons per person per year. It fell to 0.73 gallons during the Prohibition decade, then doubled to 1.5 gallons in the decade after repeal, and is now back to 2.6 gallons. So illegality suppressed usage to a third or a fourth of its former level. At the same time, incidence of cirrhosis of the liver fell by half.

7   So it seems fair to estimate that use of drugs will at least double, and possibly triple, if the price is cut, supplies are readily available, and society's sanction is lifted. It's widely accepted that there are now 16 million regular users of marijuana, six million of cocaine, a half million of heroin, and another half million of other drugs, totaling 23 million. Dr. Robert DuPont, former director of the National Institutes of Drug Abuse and an anti-legalization crusader, says that the instant pleasure afforded by drugs—superior to that available with alcohol—will increase the number of regular users of marijuana and cocaine to about 50 or 60 million and heroin users to ten million.

8   Between ten percent and 15 percent of all drinkers turn into alcoholics (ten million to 17 million), and these drinkers cost the economy an estimated $117 billion in 1983 ($15 billion for treatment, $89 billion in lost productivity, and $13 billion in accident-related costs). About 200,000 people died last year as a result of alcohol abuse, about 25,000 in auto accidents. How many drug users will turn into addicts, and what will this cost? According to President Reagan's drug abuse policy adviser, Dr. David I. McDonald, studies indicate that marijuana is about as habit-forming as alcohol, but for cocaine, 70 percent of users become addicted, as many as with nicotine.

9   So it seems reasonable to conclude that at least four to six million people will become potheads if marijuana is legal, and that coke addicts will number somewhere between 8.5 million (if regular usage doubles and 70 percent become addicted) and 42 million (if DuPont's high estimate of use is correct). An optimist would have to conclude that the number of people abusing legalized drugs will come close to those hooked on alcohol. A pessimist would figure the human damage as much greater.

10   Another way of figuring costs is this: the same study (by the Research Triangle Institute of North Carolina) that put the price of alcoholism at $117 billion in 1983 figured the cost of drug abuse then at $60 billion—$15 billion for law enforcement and crime, and $45 billion in lost productivity, damaged health, and other costs. The updated estimate for 1988 drug abuse is $100 billion. If legalizing drugs would save $30 billion now being spent on law

enforcement and crime, a doubling of use and abuse means that other costs will rise to $140 billion or $210 billion. This is no bargain for society.

11   If 200,000 people die every year from alcohol abuse and 320,000 from tobacco smoking, how many will die from legal drugs? Government estimates are that 4,000 to 5,000 people a year are killed in drug-related auto crashes, but this is surely low because accident victims are not as routinely bloodtested for drugs as for alcohol. Legalization advocates frequently cite figures of 3,600 or 4,100 as the number of drug deaths each year reported by hospitals, but this number too is certainly an understatement, based on reports from only 75 big hospitals in 27 metropolitan areas.

12   If legalization pushed the total number of drug addicts to only half the number of alcoholics, 100,000 people a year would die. That's the figure cited by McDonald. DuPont guesses that, given the potency of drugs, the debilitating effects of cocaine, the carcinogenic effects of marijuana, and the AIDS potential of injecting legalized heroin, the number of deaths actually could go as high as 500,000 a year. That's a wide range, but it's clear that legalization of drugs will not benefit human life.

13   All studies show that those most likely to try drugs, get hooked, and die—as opposed to those who suffer from cirrhosis and lung cancer—are young people, who are susceptible to the lure of quick thrills and are terribly adaptable to messages provided by adult society. Under pressure of the current prohibition, the number of kids who use illegal drugs at least once a month has fallen from 39 percent in the late 1970s to 25 percent in 1987, according to the annual survey of high school seniors conducted by the University of Michigan. The same survey shows that attitudes toward drug use have turned sharply negative. But use of legal drugs is still strong. Thirty-eight percent of high school seniors reported getting drunk within the past two weeks, and 27 percent said they smoke cigarettes every day. Drug prohibition is working with kids; legalization would do them harm.

14   And, even though legalization would lower direct costs for drug law enforcement, it's unlikely that organized crime would disappear. It might well shift to other fields—prostitution, pornography, gambling or burglaries, extortion, and murders-for-hire—much as it did in the period between the end of Prohibition and the beginning of the drug era. As DuPont puts it, "Organized crime is in the business of giving people the things that society decides in its own interest to prohibit. The only way to get rid of organized crime is to make everything legal." Even legalization advocates such as Ethan Nadelmann admit that some street crimes will continue to occur as a result of drug abuse—especially cocaine paranoia, PCP insanity, and the need of unemployable addicts to get money for drugs. Domestic crime, child abuse and neglect surely would increase.

15   Some legalization advocates suggest merely decriminalizing marijuana and retaining sanctions against other drugs. This would certainly be less costly than total legalization, but it would still be no favor to young people, would increase traffic accidents and productivity losses—and would do nothing to curtail the major drug cartels, which make most of their money trafficking in cocaine.

16   Legalizers also argue that the government could tax legal drug sales and use the money to pay for anti-drug education programs and treatment centers. But total taxes collected right now from alcohol sales at the local, state, and federal levels come to only $13.1 billion per year—which is a pittance compared with the damage done to society as a result of alcohol abuse. The same would have to be true for drugs—and any tax that resulted in an official drug price that was higher than the street price would open the way once again for black markets and organized crime.

17   So, in the name of health, economics, and morality, there seems no alternative but to keep drugs illegal and to fight the criminals who traffic in them. Regardless of what legalization advocates say, this is now the overwhelming opinion of the public, the Reagan administration, the prospective candidates for president, and the Congress—not one of whose members has introduced legislation to decriminalize any drug. Congress is on the verge of forcing the administration to raise anti-drug spending next year from $3 billion to $5.5 billion.

18   There is, though, room to debate how best to wage this war. A consensus is developing that it has to be done both on the supply side (at overseas points of origin, through interdiction at U.S. borders and criminal prosecution of traffickers) and on the demand side (by discouraging use of drugs through education and treatment and/or by arrest and urine testing at workplaces). However, there is a disagreement about which side to emphasize and how to spend resources. Members of Congress, especially Democrats, want to blame foreigners and the Reagan administration for the fact that increasing amounts of cocaine, heroin, and marijuana are entering the country. They want to spend more money on foreign aid, use the U.S. military to seal the borders, and fund "nice" treatment and education programs, especially those that give ongoing support to professional social welfare agencies.

19   Conservatives, on the other hand, want to employ the military to help foreign countries stamp out drug laboratories, use widespread drug testing to identify—and, often, punish—drug users, and spend more on police and prisons. As Education Secretary William Bennett puts it, "How can we surrender when we've never actually fought the war?" Bennett wants to fight it across all fronts, and those who have seen drafts of a forthcoming report of the White House Conference for a Drug Free America say this will be the approach recommended by the administration, although with muted emphasis on use of the U.S. military, which is reluctant to get involved in what may be another thankless war.

20   However, DuPont and others, including Jeffrey Eisenach of the Heritage Foundation, make a strong case that primary emphasis ought to be put on the demand side—discouraging use in the United States rather than, almost literally, trying to become the world's policeman. Their argument, bolstered by a study conducted by Peter Reuter of the RAND Corporation, is that major profits in the drug trade are not made abroad (where the price of cocaine triples from farm to airstrip), but within the United States (where the markup from entry point to street corner is 12 times), and

that foreign growing fields and processing laboratories are easily replaceable at low cost.

21   They say that prohibition policy should emphasize routine random urine testing in schools and places of employment, arrests for possession of drugs, and "coercive" treatment programs that compel continued enrollment as a condition of probation and employment. DuPont thinks that corporations have a right to demand that their employees be drug-free because users cause accidents and reduce productivity. He contends that urine testing is no more invasive than the use of metal detectors at airports.

22   "Liberals have a terrible time with this," says DuPont. "They want to solve every problem by giving people things. They want to love people out of their problems, while conservatives want to punish it out of them. What we want to do is take the profits out of drugs by drying up demand. You do that by raising the social cost of using them to the point where people say, 'I don't want to do this.' This isn't conservative. It's a way to save lives."

23   It is, and it's directly parallel to the way society is dealing with drunk driving and cigarette smoking—not merely through advertising campaigns and surgeon general's warnings, but through increased penalties, social strictures—and prohibitions. Random testing for every employee in America may be going too far, but testing those holding sensitive jobs or workers involved in accidents surely isn't, nor is arresting users, lifting driver's licenses, and requiring treatment. These are not nosy, moralistic intrusions on people's individual rights, but attempts by society to protect itself from danger.

24   In the end, they are also humane and moral. There is a chance, with the public and policy-makers aroused to action, that ten years from now drug abuse might be reduced to its pre-1960s levels. Were drugs to be legalized now, we would be establishing a new vice—one that, over time, would end or ruin millions of lives. Worse yet, we would be establishing a pattern of doing the easy thing, surrendering, whenever confronted with a difficult challenge.

● Vocabulary

maiming (1)
extortion (14)
bolstered (20)
strictures (23)
carcinogenic (12)
curtail (15)
coercive (21)
susceptible (13)
interdiction (18)
invasive (21)

● The Facts

1. What parallels do advocates of drug legalization love to draw, according to the author?
2. What important differences between drugs and alcohol does the author cite?
3. According to the author, what is the addictive difference between marijuana and cocaine?
4. Which group of potential users, according to studies cited by the author, is most likely to get hooked on drugs?

5. What alternative proposals do some legalization advocates offer, and how does the author respond to them?

● The Strategies

1. The author begins his argument by conceding that some things will get better if drugs are legalized. Because he is adamantly against the legalization of drugs, what is the benefit of this admission to his argument?
2. The author writes: "Of the 115 million Americans who consume alcohol, 85% rarely become intoxicated; with drugs, intoxication is the whole idea." What logical objection to this statement might an advocate of drug legalization make?
3. What is the thesis of the author's argument, and where is it stated?
4. In paragraphs 6 and 7, the author deduces probable drug addiction and usage from statistics about alcohol consumption before and after Prohibition. What is your opinion of the logic underlying this deduction?
5. In evaluating statistics and studies cited by the author from various agencies and institutes, what kinds of questions should a cautious reader ask before accepting their validity?

● The Issues

1. Which of the author's arguments against the legalization of drugs do you find the most persuasive? Why?
2. The author says that tobacco smoking kills 320,000 people every year. Given this statistic, what is your opinion about the legalization of tobacco?
3. The author quotes an authority who claims that whereas liberals want to love people out of their problems, conservatives want to punish them. Based on your reading of these two articles, what other differences can you discern between the liberal and conservative mindset?
4. What is your opinion about mandatory drug testing in schools and places of employment?
5. Which drugs would you decriminalize, given the power and the opportunity? Why?

● Suggestions for Writing

1. Write an essay arguing for or against the banning of cigarette smoking in public places.
2. Defend or attack the proposal to decriminalize the use of marijuana.

Punctuation Workshop
The Dash (—)

Not to be confused with a hyphen, the dash is a flexible punctuation mark.

1. Use a dash to announce an abrupt break or change in thought:

   All of us need redemption—or is it acceptance?

   Light reveals the world to us—a world often tarnished.

   Let me tell you about kayaking—no, I mean canoeing.

2. Use a dash to set off parenthetical elements you want to emphasize.

   The new pope—with the help of the Vatican—repeatedly emphasizes religious liberty.

   Strong personal feelings—love, admiration, fear—are often easier to admit in a letter rather than face to face.

3. Use a dash to emphasize a list.

   Tortured, undecided, fearful—my father embodied all of these character traits.

Do not overuse dashes as easy substitutes for commas, periods, or other punctuation marks.

STUDENT CORNER

Drug Use: The Continuing Epidemic
Linda Kunze, Glendale Community College

Brakes squeal as the late model Mercury Sable speeds down the street. Onlookers stare in amazement while the driver recklessly maneuvers in and out of traffic. Suddenly, the car jumps the curb and slams head on into a power pole. Moments later, police arrive to find the young female driver dead behind the steering wheel. In her hand she clutches the six-tenths of a gram of rock cocaine she had just purchased.

No, this scenario is not the opening scene from the latest big screen action adventure. Sadly, it is a true story and just another example of the death and destruction caused by the continued popularity and use of illicit drugs. The National Institute of Drug Addiction reports that drug users function at 67% of their capacity and have three times as many accidents as those who do not use drugs. With some 6 million Americans using cocaine and over 20 million regularly using marijuana, the problem is widespread and pervasive.[1]

Drug use is far from new. It has been a major problem in America for decades. According to Linda Villarosa, author of *Body & Soul*, heroin and cocaine (two powerfully addictive drugs) were first introduced to consumers back at the turn of the century as ingredients in many over-the-counter medical remedies and soft drinks. In time, when the addictive properties of these narcotics were discovered, heroin, cocaine, and many other harmful drugs were outlawed, but this action came far too late. The overpowering problem of drug abuse and addiction had already begun to spread across America.

Today, almost every adult American is aware of the dangers involved with the use of illegal substances. However, this knowledge has not stopped the rapid increase of drug abuse in this nation. According to the Substance Abuse and Mental Health Services Administration (SAMHSA),

---

[1] Drugs In the Workplace, August 8, 2003. <http://www.cob.fsu.edu/jmi/articles/drugs.asp> June 21, 2005.

an estimated 90.8 million adults 18 or older have used marijuana at least once in their lifetimes. Some 2.1 million persons age 12 or older have used ecstasy at least one time over the past year. Of this number, some 50.3% also used between two and four other illegal drugs. (Substance Abuse and Mental Health Statistics, SAMHSA, <http://www.drugabusestatistics.samhsa.gov> updated June 16, 2005) Drug dependency and addiction are becoming far too common in this country, and it is so tempting to close our eyes and turn our backs to the drug epidemic and just wish it away.

Unfortunately, denying the problems caused by the ever-growing use and abuse of narcotics will not save anyone from the torments of drug abuse and addiction. Although there are no easy answers to this age-old problem, early education seems to be the only truly effective weapon the nation has against this equal-opportunity destroyer known as drug abuse.

For education to be an effective deterrent to drug abuse, it must begin as early as grade school, because according to Schools Without Drugs, a recent pamphlet published by the United States Department of Education, "One out of every six 13-year-olds has used marijuana (at least once) and fifty-four percent of high school seniors have tried some type of illicit drug by the time they are ready to graduate." Children must be taught the dangers of drug abuse and strategies to avoid the use of these substances, prior to junior and senior high school where availability and peer pressure make drug use all too acceptable and easy to fall for.

The news is not all bad, however. In fact, in 2004 drug use declined significantly among eighth-graders from 9.7% to 8.4%. What makes this statistic heartening is that the decline was across-the-board for all drugs. While abuse will not go away overnight, the numbers show that if we persevere in our attempts at the elimination of illegal drugs, sooner or later we will achieve some positive effects. With this in mind, we must continue to educate everyone, young and old, on the evils of illegal drugs and remain persistent in the fight against their use. We all deserve a drug-free future.

How I Write

I always sit down and brainstorm—usually alone—before I write anything. In other words, I mull over ideas to see how they might work. I have never been gifted in the art of formal outlines, but I do jot down any idea that can be developed successfully. I like to work at home, with country music playing in the background.

How I Wrote This Essay

I located as many sources on drug abuse as time permitted. I then narrowed my sources down to the amount needed. I wrote one draft and put it away for a week. After the week was up, I reread my paper, changing what I didn't like and improving what I did like. The introduction is always the hardest for me to write. Everything else flows from there.

My Writing Tip

Write what you know and develop your own style. Always give yourself enough time to do the assignment well because a shoddy assignment leads only to embarrassment.

● CHAPTER WRITING ASSIGNMENTS

1. Write an essay in which you provide illustrations from history, physics, biology, psychology, or literature to prove one of the following maxims:
   a. "Every man is the architect of his own fortune." (Seneca)
   b. "The injury of prodigality leads to this, that he who will not economize will have to agonize." (Confucius)
   c. "The foundation of every state is the education of its youth." (Diogenes)

    d. "The pull of gravity exerts far more influence than one might think." (Anonymous)
    e. "Satire is the guerrilla weapon of political warfare." (Horace Greeley)
2. Choose one of the following terms and write an essay giving examples of it.
    a. romance
    b. tyranny
    c. education
    d. humility
    e. prejudice
    f. law

WRITING ASSIGNMENTS FOR A SPECIFIC AUDIENCE

1. Addressing yourself to a group of eighth graders, write an essay about racism using examples from your own experience or that of acquaintances and friends.
2. Give examples to back up this statement: It was the best day of my life.

COLLABORATIVE WRITING PROJECT

Form a group with six other students. Brainstorm on the topic of drug use among students. Ask yourself these questions: Which students do I know who are habitual drug users? How do drugs affect their academic performance? How do I feel about drug use on campus? Are all drugs equally bad? Do all drugs necessarily lead to addiction or to the use of more potent and addictive drugs?

    After gathering opinions from other students and making notes, write an essay on one of the following topics, backing up your stand with examples:

1. What differences exist between alcohol and a drug like marijuana?
2. Is it possible for someone to use marijuana recreationally and still function in daily society? Why or why not?
3. What kind of impact has the war against drugs had on society's use of drugs?
4. How do drugs affect you personally?

IMAGE GALLERY WRITING ASSIGNMENT

Visit pages 656–658 of our image gallery and study all three images dealing with drug abuse. Then choose the image that most appeals to you. Answer the questions and do the writing assignment.

11
Definition

ROAD MAP TO DEFINITION

What Definition Does

Definition means spelling out exactly what a word or phrase means. Articles, essays, and entire books have been written for the sole purpose of defining some abstract or disputed word, term, or phrase. Here is an example of a paragraph that defines *plot*.

> Let us define a plot. We have defined a story as a narrative of events arranged in their time-sequence. A plot is also a narrative of events, the emphasis falling on causality. "The king died and then the queen died," is a story. "The king died, and then the queen died of grief," is a plot. The time sequence is preserved, but the sense of causality overshadows it. Or again: "The queen died, no one knew why, until it was discovered that it was through grief at the death of the king." This is a plot with a mystery in it, a form capable of high development. It suspends the time sequence, it moves as far away from the story as its limitations will allow. Consider the death of the queen. If it is a story we say, "and then?" If it is a plot we ask, "why?" That is the fundamental difference between these two aspects of the novel. A plot cannot be told to a gaping audience of cavemen or to a tyrannical sultan or to their modern descendant the movie-public. They can only be kept awake by "and then-and then." They can only supply curiosity. But a plot demands intelligence and memory also.
>
> —E. M. Forster, "Aspects of the Novel"

In the preceding paragraph, the author not only defines *plot,* he distinguishes it from *story.* When he is done, we get a sense not only of what a plot is, but of what it is not.

When to Use Definition

What do words and phrases mean? Especially for abstract words and phrases, the answer is not always simple. It would be easy enough to explain to a Martian what the word *pencil* means because, as a last resort, we can produce one and wave it under the creature's antennas. But how do we explain the meaning of *love* to this alien? Or the meaning of *human rights?* Or even the meaning of *sovereignty?* None of these words overlays an object or thing to which we can point. Each is an idea or concept and, therefore, definable only by experience or words. The problem is that it is difficult, if not impossible, to find two people who have had such an identical experience with *love* or *human rights* or *sovereignty* that they will instantly agree on a common meaning. This is where words rush in to fill the gap.

Definitions are especially useful, then, if your essay hinges on one of these disputed abstractions. If you were writing an essay on *love,* for example, you could not take it for granted that your reader knows what you mean by that word. You would have to define it. You would have to write your definition in such a way as to make it instantly clear to your particular audience.

How to Use Definition

1. **Begin your definition by saying what the term means.** The traditional method is to first place the term in a general class and then show how it differs from others found there. Known as a *lexical definition,* this is the method of defining used by dictionaries. Here is an example:

    A *library* is a repository for artistic and literary materials.

    Repository is identified as the general class to which *library* belongs, but a specialization in artistic and literary materials distinguishes it from other repositories.

    Here are some more examples of lexical definitions:

    A *motor scooter* is a two-wheeled vehicle with small wheels and a low-powered gasoline engine geared to the rear wheel.

    An *oligarchy* is government by the few, especially a small group of people, such as one family.

    Education is the process of systematic instruction in order to impart knowledge or skill.

    Mercy is the kind and compassionate treatment of an offender.

    This is a useful and preliminary way of saying what a term means. First show where the term belongs, then distinguish it from others in that same class. Consciously and unconsciously, we practice this method of defining every day.

2. **Expand your definition, if necessary, with an etymological analysis of the term.** The *etymology* of a word is an explanation of its roots, of what it originally meant, and is often useful in shedding light on how the

current meaning of a word evolved. Here is an example of an etymological analysis that helps us to understand the meaning of the word *bible:*

> In the derivation of our word Bible lies its definition. It comes from the Greek word *biblion,*[1] which in its plural *biblia* signifies "little books." The Bible is actually a collection of little books, of every sort and description, written over a long period of time, the very earliest dating, in part at least, as far back as 1200 B.C. or perhaps even earlier; the latest as late as A.D. 150. In its rich and manifold nature it might be called a *library* of Hebrew literature; in its slow production over a period of many centuries it might be termed a survey of that literature to be understood as we understand a *survey* of English literature, in which we become familiar with types of English prose and poetry from Anglo-Saxon times to our own.
>
> —Mary Ellen Chase, "What Is the Bible?"

3. **Clarify your definition by stating what the word is not or does not mean.** For instance, the meaning of *mythology* can be clarified by the statement that it is not merely "a story filled with lies." Likewise, *liberty* can be clarified by showing that it does not simply mean "doing anything one wants at any time." In the following paragraph, the term *empirical medicine* is partially defined by what it is not:

> By the practice of empirical medicine we mean that conclusions are reached as a result of experience and observation. Diagnoses are made and cures are found as a result of practical experience. Empirical medicine is not the practice of medicine based on scientific theories or knowledge but on what works. Because of its disregard for scientific knowledge, empirical medicine is often considered charlatanry by academicians.

In essays, the overriding aim of a defining paragraph is usually to clarify the meaning of a certain term. Occasionally, however, the technical or dictionary meaning of a word or phrase may not be what the writer is trying to convey. Indeed, some definitions may be philosophical or poetic, as in the following example:

> Home is where you hang your hat. Or home is where you spent your childhood, the good years when waking every morning was an excitement, when the round of the day could always produce something to fill your mind, tear your emotions, excite your wonder or awe or delight. Is home that, or is it the place where the people you love live, or the place where you have buried your dead, or the place where you want to be buried yourself? Or is it the place where you come in your last desperation to shoot

---

[1]*Biblos* was the name given to the inner bark of the papyrus, and the word *biblion* meant a papyrus roll, upon which the Bible was originally copied.

yourself, choosing the garage or the barn or the woodshed in order not to mess up the house, but coming back anyway to the last sanctuary where you can kill yourself in peace?

—Wallace Stegner, The Big Rock Candy Mountain

4. **Expand your definition with examples.** A well-chosen example can add volumes of clarity to your meaning. In the following paragraph, the author tells us what she thinks the word *manhood* means in America:

> America has defined the roles to which each individual should subscribe. It has defined "manhood" in terms of its own interests and "femininity" likewise. An individual who has a good job, makes a lot of money and drives a Cadillac is a real man, and conversely, an individual who is lacking in these "qualities" is less of a man. The advertising media in this country continuously inform the American male of his need for indispensable signs of his virility—the brand of cigarettes that cowboys prefer, the whiskey that has a masculine tang or the label of the jock strap that athletes wear.
>
> —Frances M. Beal, "Double Jeopardy: To Be Black and Female"

Whether or not you agree with this definition, you can at least grasp the author's meaning from her examples.

5. **To define a complex term properly, you may need to practice a combination of techniques: You may have to cite examples, analyze etymology, and/or provide a lexical definition.** Here is a paragraph in which the writer uses all three devices to define *idiopathic diseases:*

examples

etymology

lexical definition

> We have a roster of diseases which medicine calls "idiopathic," meaning that we do not know what causes them. The list is much shorter than it used to be; a century ago, common infections like typhus fever, tuberculosis, and meningitis were classed as idiopathic illnesses. Originally, when it first came into the language of medicine, the term had a different, highly theoretical meaning. It was assumed that most human diseases were intrinsic, due to inbuilt failures of one sort or another, things gone wrong with various internal humors. The word "idiopathic" was intended to mean, literally, a disease having its own origin, a primary disease without any external cause. The list of such disorders has become progressively shorter as medical science has advanced, especially within this century, and the meaning of the term has lost its doctrinal flavor; we use "idiopathic" now to indicate simply that the cause of one particular disease is unknown. Very likely, before we are finished with medical science, and with luck, we will have found that all varieties of disease are the result of one or another sort of meddling, and there will be no more idiopathic illness.
>
> <div style="text-align: right;">—Lewis Thomas, <i>The Medusa and the Snail</i></div>

Remember that your definition is incomplete if it leaves gaps in the meaning of a term or fails to clearly answer the question, "What does this mean?" Keep that question in mind when you write a definition and do your utmost to answer it until your meaning is unmistakably clear to your reader.

As you write your defining essays, beware of the most common student error—the circular definition. To say that "taxation is the act of imposing taxes" is repetitious. Better to say "Taxation is the principle of levying fees to support basic government services." Provide examples and details until you have answered the question "What is it?"

Warming Up to Write a Definition

1. Getting together with three or four of your classmates, sit down and discuss the best definition for each of the following terms. If needed, you may use a dictionary. Once you have agreed on the best definition, write it on a sheet of paper, using only one sentence. Refine the written definition until it could serve as a thesis statement for an essay.
    a. kleptomania
    b. astrology
    c. organ transplant
    d. terrorism
    e. deportation

2. In the following paragraph, the word *renaissance* needs to be defined for readers who are not familiar with it. Define the term by using at least three other words in the passage that explain what the word means. Write down your definition so that it could be used as the thesis of an essay about any community experiencing what Harlem is going through.

> Harlem, a community in northern Manhattan that hit bottom in the 1980s when poverty, neglected housing and drug-related crime took their toll, is enjoying a lively second *renaissance*. Some Harlemites dismiss the resurgence as little more than a real estate boom, because the neighborhood's magnificent 19th-century townhouses are being snapped up at a rapid rate. You'll also hear that the cultural scene doesn't compare with the Harlem's first flowering, in the 1920s, which was animated by extraordinary creativity in politics, the arts and especially the written word. But if it's true there are no stand-ins today for fiery W. E. B. DuBois, gentle Langston Hughes, or patrician Duke Ellington, the second renaissance is still taking shape . . . Highbrow, mainstream, pop, hiphop, avant-garde—Harlem's cultural and artistic revival is evident on nearly every block.
>
> —From Peter Hellman, "Coming Up Harlem," *Smithsonian,* November 2002

3. In the blank provided, check those definitions that are *not* correct; then provide the correct definition.

   a. _____ *Charismatic* means disgusting.
   b. _____ *Desolation* means a feeling of despair.
   c. _____ A *skeptic* is one who is gullible.
   d. _____ *Suburban* means out in the country.
   e. _____ A *turret* is a tower or steeple.
   f. _____ To *pay homage* means to ridicule.
   g. _____ A *residue* is an evil citizen.
   h. _____ *Genetic* means inherited.
   i. _____ To *scrutinize* means to study or pore over.
   j. _____ *Sovereignty* means debauchery.

EXAMPLES

The Politics of Separation
WILLIAM A. HENRY III

William A. Henry III (1950–1994) was a journalist with a reputation for fearlessness in his exposure of cultural missteps. He received a Pulitzer Prize for his 1975 coverage of school desegregation in Boston. In 1990, he won an Emmy Award for the best film documentary for "Bob Fosse: Steam Heat," which PBS broadcast as part of its *Great Performances* series. As an investigative journalist, Henry has chronicled many decades of cultural problems and animosities—from conflicts in the Middle East to the desegregation of public schools. Among Henry's best-known books is *In Defense of Elitism* (1994), where he discusses the importance of our Western European heritage. The essay that follows was written for a special issue of *Time* magazine in the fall of 1993.

Written more than a decade ago, Henry's essay deals with issues that divided our nation when the essay was written and are still dividing us today. To understand the essay fully will require concentration and perhaps more than one reading.

• • •

1   On the eve of the funeral of Chicano hero Cesar Chavez last April, UCLA Chancellor Charles Young announced that the school had decided against creating a separate Chicano studies department. No other ethnic group had its own department, a university task force on the subject noted, and there was not enough academic substance to justify adding that one. Within days, however, 300 students—equivalent to a tenth of the school's Chicanos and about 1% of total

enrollment—staged a protest that escalated into a window-breaking skirmish with police. Next came a hunger strike by five students and one faculty member. In June UCLA backed down, creating the Cesar Chavez Center for Interdisciplinary Instruction in Chicana (in deference to women) and Chicano Studies.

2   Four hundred miles up the coast, at the University of California, Berkeley, "students of color"—notably those of Asian and Hispanic descent—have grown into a majority that demands to see its diversity reflected in textbooks and the faculty. After a debate admittedly more political than scholarly, the school now requires all undergraduates, whatever their ethnicity or major, to study at least three out of five cultural groups: Asians, Latinos, Native Americans, African Americans, and Europeans. The explicit goal: to move away from an "Anglocentric" curriculum toward one that validates other cultures, however slim their connection with America's past, as equally and essentially American.

3   Curriculum changes like these—which really amount to a rethinking of what is required to be an informed citizen—have become commonplace since the twin phenomena of political correctness and prescribed multiculturalism emerged into national consciousness at the end of the '80s. Like much else in American culture, the changes have been most visible first in California, the place where the face of the nation is changing most rapidly. There, Hispanic and Asian presences have both fueled and complicated the p.c. and multicultural debates that initially arose out of polar conflicts between blacks and whites or men and women.

4   With America moving toward an era when there may be no ethnic majority, with whites just another minority, multicultural and p.c. demands are spreading to previously unbesieged institutions. Ethnic studies have been mandated at such heartland schools as the University of Wisconsin and Texas A&M. At Yale, funds unavailable to most extracurricular groups underwrote student performances of Hispanic culture, while nearly half the student body petitioned for more courses on the Asian-American experience.

5   Now the focus of p.c. multiculturalism seems to be shifting from curriculum battles—so many have already been won—to the suppression of "hate speech," which is loosely defined as anything that any recognized minority or victim group chooses to find offensive. A chief tenet of political correctness is that minority groups must support each other, rather like union members refusing to cross a picket line. The very use of the term "of color"—which embraces blacks, historically antagonistic Asian ethnicities, Native Americans and Hispanics, many of whom are ethnically white—implies that these disparate groups are bonded simply by not being of Northern European descent. Often such coalitions add up to a majority, but they cling to rights based on minority status. When white male conservatives feel harassed, multiculturalists retort that they are enabling these fellow students to share in the sense of disenfranchisement, enriching their understanding of the world.

6   One thing is certain: there are a million ways to give p.c. offense. At the University of Nebraska, graduate student Chris Robinson kept a 5 in.-by-7 in. desktop photograph of his wife wearing a bikini—until two female coworkers complained that it constituted sexual harassment and got the department

chairman to order it removed. The Universities of Wisconsin and Minnesota, bowing to pressure from Native Americans and allies, adopted the "nickname rule." This dictum bars sports teams from playing nonleague games with schools using American Indians as symbols.

7   At the University of Pennsylvania, black students who disliked a student's columns challenging affirmative action and the character of Dr. Martin Luther King, Jr., stole 14,000 copies of the *Daily Pennsylvanian* and said they were combating "institutional racism." At Duke University, gays who did not like a student columnist's opinion that theirs was "a dirty, sinful lifestyle that doesn't deserve any special rights" blocked his way to class and shouted epithets. At neither Penn nor Duke were the perpetrators disciplined. During the academic year that ended in June, there were 12 major incidents of U.S. campus papers stolen or destroyed because their contents transgressed political correctness. This form of censorship hits most at "alternative" newspapers—a term that in the '60s and early '70s automatically denoted a leftist competitor to the main campus organ, but that today means one leaning to the right. More than 100 such papers challenge what they see as liberal orthodoxy. The climate of political correctness has diverted the eternal spirit of adolescent rebellion clear across the political spectrum.

8   What does it mean to be p.c.? To qualify, one must be pro-feminist, pro-gay rights, pro-minority studies, mistrustful of tradition, scornful of Dead White European Males, and deeply skeptical toward the very idea of a "masterpiece," because it implies that one idea, culture, or human being can actually be better than another. One must believe in a consumerist approach to education: whatever the student wants is what the curriculum ought to be. Academics must recognize that ignorance of student wishes in favor of one's own scholarly interests is wickedly élitist.

9   At a deeper level, to be p.c. means to debunk the enduring intellectual values of American life. For the generations that fought World War II and the cold war, those values were pluralism, freedom of individual opportunity, integration and free speech. The goal of universities, cultural institutions, and most journals of scholarship and opinion was to open the American experience—ipso facto a virtuous and desirable one—to all comers, regardless of race, creed, color or, later on, gender. American culture was considered so good that no one should be denied a chance at it, and no one should be assumed unable to appreciate or comprehend it.

10 For much of the generation that attends American universities today, almost all those comforting assumptions are either suspect or condemned. In place of integration has come a renewed separatism or tribalism. Women's studies, assorted ethnic studies and, increasingly, gay studies are premised on the idea that people derive their identity less from their individuality than from some group. Strength comes from clustering with the like-minded rather than from grappling with differences. In place of individual opportunity, consequently, p.c. thinking emphasizes the betterment of the group. In place of pluralism and intellectual freedom, it champions the normative rights of the community. In place of freedom of speech has come a demand for freedom from

speech, if that speech is deemed offensive by any victim group. And in place of the assumption that America represents the highest aspirations of mankind is a conviction that the U.S. was, and to a considerable degree still is, an oppressor nation, its history a chronicle of injustice and deceit. Some conservative critics point to p.c. and multicultural rhetoric as proof that the American campus is the last bastion of Marxism. Much p.c. analysis is indeed tinged with scorn for capitalism and its correlative, the proverbial marketplace of ideas. But the movement has more to do with the social contract, with how people interact, than with any economic theory.

11 The pageant of American history has always looked rather different to the descendants of slaves than it does to descendants of slave owners. Not surprisingly, it also appears less than festive to the descendants of conquered natives, exploited migrant workers, or Chinese railroad coolies. To them the vital history lesson is not the myth embodied in the Statue of Liberty but the reality of immigration laws that sharply restricted the chances of Hispanics and Asians. They value less the dazzling engineering feat of the transcontinental railroad than the abuse of laborers. They see the culture that shaped America not as a desirable legacy to be embraced, but as at best an alien heritage and at worst a tainted pattern for élitism. As their numbers grow, they want other Americans to see things the same way.

12 It is this redefinition of the American past that makes p.c. and multiculturalism so distressing to the mainstream. Patriotism and national pride are at stake. In effect, the movements demand that mainstream white Americans aged 35 and over clean out their personal psychic attics of nearly everything they were taught—and still fervently believe—about what made their country great. Like the black and women's movements before them, the new movements rely heavily on the unwelcome rhetoric of guilt.

13 Proponents insist that the new thinking promotes only innocuous inclusion. University of Chicago literature professor Gerald Graff's *Beyond the Culture Wars*, a 1993 American Book Award winner, acknowledges that he favors "feminism, multiculturalism and other new theories and practices that have divided the academy" but insists that this can be a moderate position. Writes Graff: "The curriculum is already a shouting match, and one that will only become more angry and polarized if ways are not found to exploit rather than avoid its philosophical differences. It is important to bring heretofore excluded cultures into the curriculum, but unless they are put in dialogue with traditional courses, students will continue to struggle with a disconnected curriculum, and suspicion and resentment will continue to increase."

14 Persuasive as Graff can be, his book fights a battle that is largely won. Stanford's acrimonious debate on a compulsory course in Western civilization took place five years ago. Most campuses have long since rejected the idea of an immutable "canon" of indispensable Western classics in favor of recognizing the reality that, long before p.c., curriculum has always evolved in response to the changing marketplace of students. A generation or two ago, it demanded validation of America's cultural maturity. Today it demands diversity. The 1991 Heath anthology of American literature, widely used in colleges, begins

with Indian chants and Spanish voyager poems, rather than Pilgrim ruminations. Next year's update adds more "Native American oral narratives." The Heath editors treat literature as of mainly anthropological value. The volume abounds in work by Asians, Hispanics and especially blacks and women—there is more by Charlotte Perkins Gilman than by Hemingway—and conspicuously stints Wasps and Jews.

15   If at times excessive, the p.c. and multicultural movements arose out of real concerns. Says Siby Philips, a senior at the University of Texas: "Multiculturalism came about because a lot of people are ignorant about people of color, gay and lesbian people, or whatever. These groups feel like they are marginalized. It's more than validation for certain groups. It's validation for the whole of society rather than just some part of it." Many distinguished scholars, however, see firsthand evidence that the p.c. and multicultural movements are leading to a more general separatism, a fragmentation of the centrist consensus that built America. To study anyone's culture but one's own—unless one is white, in which case it is necessary to learn about the oppressed others—is to commit an act of identity suicide. Beyond this loss of interest in universal ideas, often expressed as disbelief that anything is actually universal, Duke political scientist James David Barber sees a growing attitude that reason and factuality themselves are European cultural artifacts. Says Barber: "I think a lot of 'impressionism'—a detestation of reason in favor of emotion—is happening now." Scholars who agree with Barber note that p.c. thinkers consider a claim of harassment essentially unchallengeable, regardless of fact, because the only meaningful perception of grievance is that of the alleged victim.

16   The pressures of p.c. and multiculturalism are by no means limited to the campus. They are almost as intense among cultural institutions, charities, and the media, which increasingly earmark jobs for Hispanics, Asians, or other target groups. After the San Diego Opera was cited by a state arts agency for not having enough Hispanic employees, it set aside for only Hispanic candidates its next opening for a publicist. The September convention of the National Gay and Lesbian Journalists Association turned into a recruitment center for major national media seeking to diversify newsrooms. Insiders say the National Book Awards and even the Pulitzer Prizes have at times bowed to political correctness rather than pure merit, seeking to honor blacks, Hispanics, and women.

17   The same principles often lead to strictures on content. When the Guthrie Theater revived *The Front Page*, it debated whether to edit out racist language. Jewish leaders told the Oregon Shakespearean Festival, albeit unsuccessfully, that *The Merchant of Venice* was irredeemably anti-Semitic and should never be produced.

18   The greatest intellectual danger of political correctness is its assumption that there are some ideas too dangerous to be heard, some words too hurtful to be allowed, some opinions no one is ever again permitted to hold. It assumes that all advances in the rights of the downtrodden are final victories, and that questioning those victories is tantamount to colonialism, night riding and the sword.

Henry III / The Politics of Separation

19   Children are taught to fear sticks and stones but chant that names will never hurt them. Names, and the ideas behind them, do hurt people. Political correctness argues that the price of peace in a racially diverse America may be suppressing ideas that cause such pain. Perhaps that could mean a more civilized nation. Up to now, though, America's genius has not been in its civility, but rather in its raucous barroom brawl in search of the truth.

● Vocabulary

escalated (1)	Anglocentric (2)	unbesieged (4)
tenet (5)	disparate (5)	disenfranchisement (5)
dictum (6)	epithets (7)	perpetrators (7)
orthodoxy (7)	élitist (8)	pluralism (9)
ipso facto (9)	normative (10)	oppressor (10)
pageant (11)	tainted (11)	innocuous (13)
polarized (13)	exploit (13)	acrimonious (14)
immutable (14)	canon (14)	indispensable (14)
validation (14)	stints (14)	marginalized (15)
centrist (15)	artifacts (15)	

● The Facts

1. What are the two issues under discussion in the essay? Explain the two issues as you understand them. What are your personal beliefs about these two issues?
2. What did some students "of color" demand at the University of California, Berkeley? What was the outcome of their demand? Why were they able to make such a demand?
3. According to the author, what kind of nation are we becoming in terms of racial balance? What change has occurred?
4. Where is the focus of political correctness now headed? What was the earlier focus?
5. What two examples of politically incorrect behavior are cited in paragraph 6? Were the feelings of being offended warranted? Why or why not?
6. According to the essay, what are the qualifications for being politically correct? What other qualifications can be cited?
7. What did some Jewish leaders attempt to have the Oregon Shakespeare Festival do in order to avoid racist language? They did not succeed in their effort. Why not?

● The Strategies

1. To what kind of audience is the style of this essay best suited? General readers? Sophisticated readers? Who, if anyone, might lose interest in reading this text?
2. Where does the author define the "deeper level" of being p.c.? Explain what he means.

3. What is the purpose of the quotation from Gerald Graff's *Beyond the Culture Wars*? (See paragraph 13.) In what paragraph does Henry expose the danger of accepting Graff's view of p.c.?
4. What connects the title of this essay to the essay's content?
5. How does the author support his statement that "there are a million ways to give p.c. offense"? How effective is this technique?

● The Issues

1. What is the effect of an increase in minorities of all kinds on U.S. campuses? Does it complicate the matter of political correctness? Does it affect the development of curriculum?
2. In 1993, when Henry wrote his essay, the move was away from curriculum battles to political correctness. Is p.c. still emphasized today? Where and to what extent?
3. What worries the author about the direction in which freedom of speech is moving? Do you consider this worry still justified today? Give examples to support your answer.
4. What does the author mean when he states (paragraph 11) that "the pageant of American history has always looked rather different to the descendants of slaves than it does to descendants of slave owners"? What other points of view does he mention? Explain his theory.
5. What, according to the author, is the greatest danger of political correctness? Do you see this danger as a reality, or have we kept p.c. under control? Give examples to support your answer.
6. According to one student, Siby Philips, how did multiculturalism come about? Do you agree with Philips? If not, what do you think gave impetus to the multiculturalism issue?

● Suggestions for Writing

1. Collaborate with a classmate to analyze the Trudeau cartoon at the end of the essay. Then write your own separate interpretations of the cartoon.
2. Write an essay in which you list the major dangers that could emerge from multiculturalism; then point out how to avoid these dangers. Consider the danger of having various cultures band together to the exclusion of others. Consider also the danger of certain cultural groups being regarded as superior to others, leading to the kind of class distinctions that existed in the past.

The Company Man

ELLEN GOODMAN

Ellen Goodman (b. 1941) is a Pulitzer Prize–winning newspaper columnist and editor. Born in Newton, Massachusetts, Goodman is considered part of the "Eastern Establishment," having graduated from Radcliffe and having worked for the *Boston Globe* since 1967. Her column, "At Large," is eagerly read by thousands of fans, who praise her for having intelligence combined with common sense. She has published several volumes of her columns, including *Close to Home* (1975) and *Value Judgments* (1993). She also authored the influential book *Turning Points* (1979), in which she examined the changes in men and women's lives as a result of the feminist movement.

Like many essays that define, this one delivers a definition almost in passing. Goodman tells the sad story of a "company man" who literally worked himself to death, and in the process she ends up defining the term company man. *We have all known company men and women, all of whom share a compulsive devotion to work. Some of us know, if not from experience then from hearsay, company men and women who have neglected family and friends for the job, only to become ill or even to die from work-related stress.*

• • •

1   He worked himself to death, finally and precisely, at 3:00 a.m. Sunday morning. The obituary didn't say that, of course. It said that he died of a coronary thrombosis—I think that was it—but everyone among his friends and acquaintances knew it instantly. He was a perfect Type A, a workaholic, a classic, they said to each other and shook their heads—and thought for five or ten minutes about the way they lived.

2   This man who worked himself to death finally and precisely at 3:00 a.m. Sunday morning—on his day off—was fifty-one years old and a vice-president. He was, however, one of six vice-presidents, and one of three who might conceivably—if the president died or retired soon enough—have moved to the top spot. Phil knew that.

3   He worked six days a week, five of them until eight or nine at night, during a time when his own company had begun the four-day week for everyone but the executives. He worked like the Important People. He had no outside "extracurricular interests," unless, of course, you think about a monthly golf game that way. To Phil, it was work. He always ate egg salad sandwiches at his desk. He was, of course, overweight, by 20 or 25 pounds. He thought it was okay, though, because he didn't smoke.

4   On Saturdays, Phil wore a sports jacket to the office instead of a suit, because it was the weekend.

5   He had a lot of people working for him, maybe sixty, and most of them liked him most of the time. Three of them will be seriously considered for his job. The obituary didn't mention that.

6   But it did list his "survivors" quite accurately. He is survived by his wife, Helen, forty-eight years old, a good woman of no particular marketable skills, who worked in an office before marrying and mothering. She had, according to her daughter, given up trying to compete with his work years ago, when the children were small. A company friend said, "I know how much you will miss him." And she answered, "I already have."

7   "Missing him all these years," she must have given up part of herself which had cared too much for the man. She would be "well taken care of."

8   His "dearly beloved" eldest of the "dearly beloved" children is a hard-working executive in a manufacturing firm down South. In the day and a half before the funeral, he went around the neighborhood researching his father, asking the neighbors what he was like. They were embarrassed.

9   His second child is a girl, who is twenty-four and newly married. She lives near her mother and they are close, but whenever she was alone with her father, in a car driving somewhere, they had nothing to say to each other.

10 The youngest is twenty, a boy, a high-school graduate who has spent the last couple of years, like a lot of his friends, doing enough odd jobs to stay in grass and food. He was the one who tried to grab at his father, and tried to mean enough to him to keep the man at home. He was his father's favorite. Over the last two years, Phil stayed up nights worrying about the boy.

11 The boy once said, "My father and I only board here." At the funeral, the sixty-year-old company president told the forty-eight-year-old widow that the fifty-one-year-old deceased had meant much to the company and would be missed and would be hard to replace. The widow didn't look him in the eye. She was afraid he would read her bitterness and, after all, she would need him to straighten out the finances—the stock options and all that.

12 Phil was overweight and nervous and worked too hard. If he wasn't at the office, he was worried about it. Phil was a Type A, a heart attack natural. You could have picked him out in a minute from a lineup.

13 So when he finally worked himself to death, at precisely 3:00 a.m. Sunday morning, no one was really surprised.

Vocabulary

obituary (1)   conceivably (2)

The Facts

1. What was the exact time of Phil's death? How often is the time stated, and why?
2. The medical cause of Phil's death is given as "coronary thrombosis," but what was the real cause?
3. What is meant by the phrase (paragraph 3) "Important People"? Do you recognize these people in your own sphere?
4. What did the widow mean when she answered "I already have" when a friend said, "I know how much you will miss him"? (See paragraph 6.)
5. In paragraph 7, we are told that the widow would be "well taken care of." What is the meaning of this phrase?

The Strategies

1. What is the relationship of the title to the content of the essay? What synonyms for the title are mentioned in the essay?

2. What kind of evidence does the author use to support her definition? Cite specific examples from the text. After reading the essay, do you feel you know what a "company man" is? Give reasons for your answer.
3. What level of reading difficulty does this essay present? To what kinds of audiences would it appeal?
4. How do the opening and closing of the essay function rhetorically?
5. What is the purpose in quoting Phil's son in paragraph 11?

● **The Issues**

1. What familiar warning to modern America does this essay give? Do you believe that the warning is warranted, or is the author being too alarmist?
2. How do you suggest that an ambitious father reconcile his duties at work with his responsibility to family? Suggest specific steps to follow.
3. What can a family do to prevent the father's becoming too involved in his work?
4. Why is it that the second child, a girl, has nothing to say to her father? Does this situation seem realistic?
5. Why is the story of the youngest child particularly tragic? How could the tragedy have been prevented?

● **Suggestions for Writing**

1. Write an essay about your father or another man you know well. Try to capture the essence of his character and your relationship with him.
2. Following Goodman's style, write an essay titled *The Company Woman*. Use personal experiences or your own imagination to develop the examples.

In Praise of the Humble Comma
PICO IYER

Pico Iyer is a freelance writer and contributing editorial writer for *Time*. He has also written numerous books about exotic places and countries, among them *The Lady and the Monk: Four Seasons in Kyoto* (1992), *Falling off the Map: Some Lonely Places of the World* (1994), *Cuba and the Light* (1996), and *Global Soul: Jet Lag, Shopping Malls, and the Search for Home* (2000).

This essay appeared as the featured essay on the back page of Time *(June 13, 1988). Its purpose is to define punctuation in general and the comma specifically. Iyer suggests that punctuation marks are highly underrated because they give writing elegance as well as clarity, often keeping it from becoming a jumble of words strung across a page.*

● ● ●

1   The gods, they say, give breath, and they take it away. But the same could be said—could it not?—of the humble comma. Add it to the present clause, and, all of a sudden, the mind is, quite literally, given pause to think; take it out if you wish or forget it and the mind is deprived of a resting place. Yet still the comma gets no respect. It seems just a slip of a thing, a pedant's tick, a blip on the edge of our consciousness, a kind of printer's smudge almost. Small, we claim, is beautiful (especially in the age of the microchip). Yet what is so often used, and so rarely recalled, as the comma—unless it be breath itself?

2   Punctuation, one is taught, has a point: to keep up law and order. Punctuation marks are the road signs placed along the highway of our communication—to control speeds, provide directions and prevent head-on collisions. A period has the unblinking finality of a red light; the comma is a flashing yellow light that asks us only to slow down; and the semicolon is a stop sign that tells us to ease gradually to a halt, before gradually starting up again. By establishing the relations between words, punctuation establishes the relations between the people using words. That may be one reason why schoolteachers exalt it and lovers defy it ("We love each other and belong to each other let's don't ever hurt each other Nicole let's don't ever hurt each other," wrote Gary Gilmore to his girlfriend). A comma, he must have known, "separates inseparables," in the clinching words of H. W. Fowler, King of English Usage.

3   Punctuation, then, is a civic prop, a pillar that holds society upright. (A run-on sentence, its phrases piling up without division, is as unsightly as a sink piled high with dirty dishes.) Small wonder, then, that punctuation was one of the first proprieties of the Victorian age, the age of the corset, that the modernists threw off: the sexual revolution might be said to have begun when Joyce's Molly Bloom spilled out all her private thoughts in 36 pages of unbridled, almost unperioded and officially censored prose; and another rebellion was surely marked when E. E. Cummings first felt free to commit "God" to the lower case.

4   Punctuation thus becomes the signature of cultures. The hot-blooded Spaniard seems to be revealed in the passion and urgency of his doubled exclamation points and question marks ("¡Caramba! ¿Quién sabe?"), while the impassive Chinese traditionally added to his so-called inscrutability by omitting directions from his ideograms. The anarchy and commotion of the '60s were given voice in the exploding exclamation marks, riotous capital letters and Day-Glo italics of Tom Wolfe's spray-paint prose; and in Communist societies, where the State is absolute, the dignity—and divinity—of capital letters is reserved for Ministries, Sub-Committees and Secretariats.

5   Yet punctuation is something more than a culture's birthmark; it scores the music in our minds, gets our thoughts moving to the rhythm of our hearts. Punctuation is the notation in the sheet music of our words, telling us when to rest, or when to raise our voices; it acknowledges that the meaning of our discourse, as of any symphonic composition, lies not in the units but in the pauses, the pacing and the phrasing. Punctuation is the way one bats one's eyes, lowers one's voice or blushes demurely. Punctuation adjusts the tone

and color and volume till the feeling comes into perfect focus: not disgust exactly, but distaste; not lust, or like, but love.

6   Punctuation, in short, gives us the human voice, and all the meanings that lie between the words. "You aren't young, are you?" loses its innocence when it loses the question mark. Every child knows the menace of a dropped apostrophe (the parent's "Don't do that" shifting into the more slowly enunciated "Do not do that"), and every believer, the ignominy of having his faith reduced to "faith." Add an exclamation point to "To be or not to be . . ." and the gloomy Dane has all the resolve he needs; add a comma, and the noble sobriety of "God save the Queen" becomes a cry of desperation bordering on double sacrilege.

7   Sometimes, of course, our markings may be simply a matter of aesthetics. Popping in a comma can be like slipping on the necklace that gives an outfit quiet elegance, or like catching the sound of running water that complements, as it completes, the silence of a Japanese landscape. When V. S. Naipaul, in his latest novel, writes, "He was a middle-aged man, with glasses," the first comma can seem a little precious. Yet it gives the description a spin, as well as a subtlety, that it otherwise lacks, and it shows that the glasses are not part of the middle-agedness, but something else.

8   Thus all these tiny scratches give us breadth and heft and depth. A world that has only periods is a world without inflections. It is a world without shade. It has a music without sharps and flats. It is a martial music. It has a jackboot rhythm. Words cannot bend and curve. A comma, by comparison, catches the gentle drift of the mind in thought, turning in on itself and back on itself, reversing, redoubling and returning along the course of its own sweet river music; while the semicolon brings clauses and thoughts together with all the silent discretion of a hostess arranging guests around her dinner table.

9   Punctuation, then, is a matter of care. Care for words, yes, but also, and more important, for what the words imply. Only a lover notices the small things: the way the afternoon light catches the nape of a neck, or how a strand of hair slips out from behind an ear, or the way a finger curls around a cup. And no one scans a letter so closely as a lover, searching for its small print, straining to hear its nuances, its gasps, its sighs and hesitations, poring over the secret messages that lie in every cadence. The difference between "Jane (whom I adore)" and "Jane, whom I adore," and the difference between them both and "Jane—whom I adore—" marks all the distance between ecstasy and heartache. "No iron can pierce the heart with such force as a period put at just the right place," in Isaac Babel's lovely words; a comma can let us hear a voice break, or a heart. Punctuation, in fact, is a labor of love. Which brings us back, in a way, to gods.

• Vocabulary

pedant (1)
ideograms (4)
aesthetics (7)
martial (8)

proprieties (3)
enunciated (6)
heft (8)
nuances (9)

inscrutability (4)
ignominy (6)
inflections (8)

The Facts

1. How does Iyer define *punctuation?* Which definition seems most helpful, and which least? Give reasons for your answers.
2. The author never gives a formal definition of the comma. What reason can you offer for this omission?
3. What does the author mean when he suggests that punctuation is the "signature of cultures"?
4. In the author's view, how is punctuation related to music?
5. According to the author, what would writing be like if it were deprived of the comma?

The Strategies

1. Why does the author entitle his essay *In Praise of the Humble Comma* when most of the essay deals with punctuation in general?
2. What is the author's style in this essay? How effective do you consider it?
3. What is the author's tone when he uses the word "humble" in connection with the comma?
4. What technique does the author use in closing his essay? How effective is it?
5. How does the author establish coherence between paragraphs 5 and 6?

The Issues

1. If the author is correct that punctuation is "the signature of cultures," then how would you define our culture in terms of the way we use punctuation?
2. In your own writing, which punctuation mark gives you the most trouble? Which do you find the most helpful?
3. Review paragraph 3. What is your reaction to the author's view that our modern age has thrown off the Victorian restrictions of punctuation? If the author's view is true, has our new freedom improved writing? Why or why not?
4. How important is it for students to learn how to write with care? Support your answer with reasons.
5. What examples can you provide to support Isaac Babel's opinion that "[n]o iron can pierce the heart with such force as a period put at just the right place"? Use your imagination to create appropriate sentences.

Suggestions for Writing

1. Write an essay in which you create your own definition of *punctuation.*
2. Write an essay in which you either support or attack the author's view that punctuation is a matter of care for what words imply.
3. Write an essay in which you assign responsibility for teaching punctuation to the proper educational institution.

Kitsch

Gilbert Highet

Gilbert Highet (1906–1978) was born in Glasgow, Scotland, educated at the University of Glasgow and at Oxford, and became an American citizen in 1951. A classicist, Highet was known for his scholarly and critical writing, including *The Classical Tradition* (1949) and *The Anatomy of Satire* (1962).

You probably have had some experience with "kitsch" even if you do not know what the word means. You may have friends or relatives whose furniture, curios, or even favorite books are clearly kitschy. Gilbert Highet draws mainly on literary examples to define kitsch; *but, as you shall see, the concept applies to nearly all matters of bad taste.*

• • •

1 If you have ever passed an hour wandering through an antique shop (not looking for anything exactly, but simply looking), you must have noticed how your taste gradually grows numb, and then—if you stay—becomes perverted. You begin to see unsuspected charm in those hideous pictures of plump girls fondling pigeons, you develop a psychopathic desire for spinning wheels and cobblers' benches, you are apt to pay out good money for a bronze statuette of Otto von Bismarck, with a metal hand inside a metal frock coat and metal pouches under his metallic eyes. As soon as you take the things home, you realize that they are revolting. And yet they have a sort of horrible authority; you don't like them; you know how awful they are; but it is a tremendous effort to drop them in the garbage, where they belong.

2 To walk along a whole street of antique shops—that is an experience which shakes the very soul. Here is a window full of bulbous Chinese deities; here is another littered with Zulu assagais, Indian canoe paddles, and horse pistols which won't fire; the next shopfront is stuffed with gaudy Italian majolica vases, and the next, even worse, with Austrian pottery—tiny ladies and gentlemen sitting on lace cushions and wearing lace ruffles, with every frill, every wrinkle and reticulation translated into porcelain: pink; stiff; but fortunately not unbreakable. The nineteenth century produced an appalling amount of junky art like this, and sometimes I imagine that clandestine underground factories are continuing to pour it out like illicit drugs.

3 There is a name for such stuff in the trade, a word apparently of Russian origin, *kitsch*[1]: it means vulgar showoff, and it is applied to anything that took a lot of trouble to make and is quite hideous.

4 It is paradoxical stuff, kitsch: It is obviously bad: so bad that you can scarcely understand how any human being would spend days and weeks making it, and how anybody else would buy it and take it home and keep it and dust it and leave it to her heirs. It is terribly ingenious, and terribly ugly, and utterly useless;

---

[1]The Russian verb *keetcheetsya* means "to be haughty and puffed up."

and yet it has one of the qualities of good art—which is that, once seen, it is not easily forgotten. Of course it is found in all the arts: think of Milan Cathedral, or the statues in Westminster Abbey, or Liszt's settings of Schubert songs. There is a lot of it in the United States—for instance, the architecture of Miami, Florida, and Forest Lawn Cemetery in Los Angeles. Many of Hollywood's most ambitious historical films are superb kitsch. Most Tin Pan Alley love songs are perfect 100 per cent kitsch.

5   There is kitsch in the world of books also. I collect it. It is horrible, but I enjoy it.

6   The gem of my collection is the work of the Irish novelist Mrs. Amanda McKittrick Ros, whose masterpiece, *Delina Delaney,* was published about 1900. It is a stirringly romantic tale, telling how Delina, a fisherman's daughter from Erin Cottage, was beloved by Lord Gifford, the heir of Columbia Castle, and—after many trials and even imprisonment—married him. The story is dramatic, not to say impossible; but it is almost lost to view under the luxuriant style. Here, for example, is a sentence in which Mrs. Ros explains that her heroine used to earn extra cash by doing needlework:

> She tried hard to assist in keeping herself a stranger to her poor old father's slight income by the use of the finest production of steel, whose blunt edge eyed the reely covering with marked greed, and offered its sharp dart to faultless fabrics of flaxen fineness.

Revolting, but distinctive: what Mr. Polly called "rockockyo" in manner.

7   For the baroque vein, here is Lord Gifford saying goodbye to his sweetheart:

> My darling virgin! my queen! my Delina! I am just in time to hear the toll of a parting bell strike its heavy weight of appalling softness against the weakest fibers of a heart of love, arousing and tickling its dormant action, thrusting the dart of evident separation deeper into its tubes of tenderness, and fanning the flame, already unextinguishable, into volumes of blaze.

8   Mrs. Ros had a remarkable command of rhetoric, and could coin an unforgettable phrase. She described her hero's black eyes as "glittering jet revolvers." When he became ill, she said he fell "into a state of lofty fever"—doubtless because commoners have high fever, but lords have lofty fever. And her reflections on the moral degeneracy of society have rarely been equaled, in power and penetration:

> Days of humanity, whither hast thou fled? When bows of compulsion, smiles for the deceitful, handshakes for the dogmatic, and welcome for the tool of power live under your objectionable, unambitious beat, not daring to be checked by the tongue of candour because the selfish world refuses to dispense with her rotten policies. The legacy of your

forefathers, which involved equity, charity, reason, and godliness, is beyond the reach of their frivolous, mushroom offspring—deceit, injustice, malice and unkindness—and is not likely to be codiciled with traits of harmony so long as these degrading vices of mock ambition fester the human heart.

9   Perhaps one reason I enjoy this stuff is because it so closely resembles a typical undergraduate translation of one of Cicero's finest perorations: sound and fury, signifying nothing. I regret only that I have never seen Mrs. Ros's poetry. One volume was called *Poems of Puncture* and another *Bayonets of Bastard Sheen*: alas, jewels now almost unprocurable. But at least I know the opening of her lyric written on first visiting St. Paul's Cathedral:

> Holy Moses, take a look,
> Brain and brawn in every nook!

10   Such genius is indestructible. Soon, soon now, some earnest researcher will be writing a Ph.D. thesis on Mrs. Amanda McKittrick Ros, and thus (as she herself might put it) conferring upon her dewy brow the laurels of concrete immortality.

11   Next to Mrs. Ros in my collection of kitsch is the work of the Scottish poet William McGonagall. This genius was born in 1830, but did not find his vocation until 1877. Poor and inadequate poets pullulate in every tongue, but (as the *Times Literary Supplement* observes) McGonagall "is the only truly memorable bad poet in our language." In his command of platitude and his disregard of melody, he was the true heir of William Wordsworth as a descriptive poet.

12   In one way his talents, or at least his aspirations, exceeded those of Wordsworth. He was at his best in describing events he had never witnessed, such as train disasters, shipwrecks, and sanguinary battles, and in picturing magnificent scenery he had never beheld except with the eye of the imagination. Here is his unforgettable Arctic landscape:

> Greenland's icy mountains are fascinating and grand,
> And wondrously created by the Almighty's command;
> And the works of the Almighty there's few can understand:
> Who knows but it might be a part of Fairyland?

> Because there are churches of ice, and houses glittering like glass,
> And for scenic grandeur there's nothing can it surpass,
> Besides there's monuments and spires, also ruins,
> Which serve for a safe retreat from the wild bruins.

> The icy mountains they're higher than a brig's topmast,
> And the stranger in amazement stands aghast
> As he beholds the water flowing off the melted ice
> Adown the mountain sides, that he cries out, Oh! how nice!

13   McGonagall also had a strong dramatic sense. He loved to tell of agonizing adventures, more drastic perhaps but not less moving than that related in Wordsworth's "Vaudracour and Julia." The happy ending of one of his "Gothic" ballads is surely unforgettable:

> So thus ends the story of Hanchen, a heroine brave,
> That tried hard her master's gold to save,
> And for her bravery she got married to the miller's eldest son,
> And Hanchen on her marriage night cried Heaven's will be done.

14   These scanty selections do not do justice to McGonagall's ingenuity as a rhymester. His sound effects show unusual talent. Most poets would be baffled by the problem of producing rhymes for the proper names General Graham and Osman Digna, but McGonagall gets them into a single stanza, with dazzling effect:

> Ye sons of Great Britain, I think no shame
> To write in praise of brave General Graham!
> Whose name will be handed down to posterity without any stigma,
> Because, at the battle of El-Tab, he defeated Osman Digna.

15   One of McGonagall's most intense personal experiences was his visit to New York. Financially, it was not a success. In one of his vivid autobiographical sketches, he says, "I tried occasionally to get an engagement from theatrical proprietors and music-hall proprietors, but alas! 'twas all in vain, for they all told me they didn't encourage rivalry." However, he was deeply impressed by the architecture of Manhattan. In eloquent verses he expressed what many others have felt, although without adequate words to voice their emotion:

> Oh! Mighty City of New York, you are wonderful to behold,
> Your buildings that magnificent, the truth be it told;
> They were the only thing that seemed to arrest my eye,
> Because many of them are thirteen stories high.
>
> And the tops of the houses are all flat,
> And in the warm weather the people gather to chat;
> Besides on the house-tops they dry their clothes,
> And also many people all night on the house-tops repose.

16   Yet McGonagall felt himself a stranger in the United States. And here again his close kinship with Wordsworth appears. The Poet Laureate, in a powerful sonnet written at Calais, once reproached the English Channel for

delaying his return by one of those too frequent storms in which (reckless tyrant!) it will indulge itself:

> Why cast ye back upon the Gallic shore,
> Ye furious waves! a patriotic Son
> Of England?

17   In the same vein McGonagall sings with rapture of his return to his "ain countree":

> And with regard to New York, and the sights I did see,
> One street in Dundee is more worth to me,
> And, believe me, the morning I sailed from New York,
> For bonnie Dundee—my heart it felt as light as a cork.

18   Indeed, New York is a challenging subject for ambitious poets. Here, from the same shelf, is a delicious poem on the same theme, by Ezra Pound:

> My City, my beloved
> Thou art a maid with no breasts
> Thou art slender as a silver reed.
> Listen to me, attend me!
> And I will breathe into thee a soul,
> And thou shalt live for ever.

19   The essence of this kind of trash is incongruity. The kitsch writer is always sincere. He really means to say something important. He feels he has a lofty spiritual message to bring to an unawakened world, or else he has had a powerful experience which he must communicate to the public. But either his message turns out to be a majestic platitude, or else he chooses the wrong form in which to convey it—or, most delightful of all, there is a fundamental discrepancy between the writer and his subject, as when Ezra Pound, born in Idaho, addresses the largest city in the world as a maid with no breasts, and enjoins it to achieve inspiration and immortality by listening to him. This is like climbing Mount Everest in order to carve a head of Mickey Mouse in the east face.

20   Bad love poetry, bad religious poetry, bad mystical prose, bad novels both autobiographical and historical—one can form a superb collection of kitsch simply by reading with a lively and awakened eye. College songs bristle with it. The works of Father Divine[2] are full of it—all the more delightful because in him it is usually incomprehensible. One of the Indian mystics, Sri Ramakrishna, charmed connoisseurs by describing the Indian scriptures (in a phrase which almost sets itself to kitsch-music) as fried in the butter of knowledge and steeped in the honey of love.

---

[2] A black evangelist of New York.—Ed.

21   Bad funeral poetry is a rich mine of the stuff. Here, for example, is the opening of a jolly little lament, "The Funeral" by Stephen Spender, apparently written during his pink period:

> Death is another milestone on their way,
> With laughter on their lips and with winds blowing round
> Them
> They record simply
> How this one excelled all others in making driving belts.

22   Observe the change from humanism to communism. Spender simply took Browning's "Grammarian's Funeral," threw away the humor and the marching rhythm, and substituted wind and the Stakhanovist[3] speed-up. Such also is a delicious couplet from Archibald MacLeish's elegy on the late Harry Crosby:

> He walks with Ernest in the streets in Saragossa
> They are drunk their mouths are hard they saw qué cosa.

23   From an earlier romantic period, here is a splendid specimen. Coleridge attempted to express the profound truth that men and animals are neighbors in a hard world; but he made the fundamental mistake of putting it into a monologue address to a donkey:

> Poor Ass! Thy master should have learnt to show
> Pity—best taught by fellowship of Woe!
> Innocent foal! thou poor despised forlorn!
> I hail thee brother. . . .

24   Once you get the taste for this kind of thing it is possible to find pleasure in hundreds of experiences which you might otherwise have thought either anesthetic or tedious: bad translations, abstract painting, grand opera . . . Dr. Johnson, with his strong sense of humor, had a fancy for kitsch, and used to repeat a poem in celebration of the marriage of the Duke of Leeds, composed by "an inferiour domestick . . . in such homely rhimes as he could make":

> When the Duke of Leeds shall married be
> To a fine young lady of high quality,
> How happy will that gentlewoman be
> In his Grace of Leed's good company.
>
> She shall have all that's fine and fair,
> And the best of silk and sattin shall wear;
> And ride in a coach to take the air,
> And have a house in St. James's Square.

---

[3] Alexei Stakhanov, a Russian miner who devised a worker incentive system.—Ed.

25   Folk poetry is full of such jewels. Here is the epitaph on an old gentleman from Vermont who died in a sawmill accident:

> How shocking to the human mind
> The log did him to powder grind.
> God did command his soul away
> His summings we must all obey.

26   Kitsch is well known in drama, although (except for motion pictures) it does not usually last long. One palmary instance was a play extolling the virtues of the Boy Scout movement, called *Young England*. It ran for a matter of years during the 1930's, to audiences almost wholly composed of kitsch-fanciers, who eventually came to know the text quite as well as the unfortunate actors. I can still remember the opening of one magnificent episode.

> Scene: a woodland glade. Enter the hero, a Scoutmaster, riding a bicycle, and followed by the youthful members of his troop. They pile bicycles in silence. Then the Scoutmaster raises his finger, and says (accompanied fortissimo by most of the members of the audience):
> Fresh water must be our first consideration.

27   In the decorative arts kitsch flourishes, and is particularly widespread in sculpture. One of my favorite pieces of bad art is a statue in Rockefeller Center, New York. It is supposed to represent Atlas, the Titan condemned to carry the sky on his shoulders. That is an ideal of somber, massive tragedy: greatness and suffering combined as in Hercules or Prometheus. But this version displays Atlas as a powerful moron, with a tiny little head, rather like the panfried young men who appear in the health magazines. Instead of supporting the heavens, he is lifting a spherical metal balloon: it is transparent, and quite empty; yet he is balancing insecurely on one foot like a furniture mover walking upstairs with a beach ball; and he is scowling like a mad baboon. If he ever gets the thing up, he will drop it; or else heave it onto a Fifth Avenue bus. It is a supremely ridiculous statue, and delights me every time I see it.

28   Perhaps you think this is a depraved taste. But really it is an extension of experience. At one end, Homer. At the other, Amanda McKittrick Ros. At one end, Hamlet. At the other, McGonagall, who is best praised in his own inimitable words:

> The poetry is moral and sublime
> And in my opinion nothing could be more fine.
> True genius there does shine so bright
> Like unto the stars of night.

Vocabulary

psychopathic (1)	frock coat (1)	bulbous (2)
Zulu (2)	assagais (2)	majolica (2)
reticulation (2)	appalling (2)	illicit (2)
paradoxical (4)	ingenious (4)	luxuriant (6)
perorations (6)	unprocurable (6)	pullulate (11)
platitude (11)	sanguinary (12)	rapture (17)
incongruity (19)	enjoins (19)	mystical (20)
incomprehensible (20)	connoisseurs (20)	anesthetic (24)
palmary (26)	extolling (26)	fortissimo (26)
spherical (27)	depraved (28)	inimitable (28)

The Facts

1. Where in his essay does Highet give a succinct definition of *kitsch?* After reading the essay, how would you explain this term to a friend who has never heard it?
2. What examples of kitsch does Highet provide? Name the three that impressed you most. Give reasons for your choice.
3. What metaphor does Mrs. Ros use to describe her hero's black eyes? Provide a metaphor or simile that would not be kitsch.
4. What characteristics of William McGonagall's poetry make it kitsch? Give a brief critique of two or three excerpts reprinted by Highet.
5. What is the essence of kitsch, according to the author? In what paragraph is this essence revealed?

The Strategies

1. What is the predominant tone of the essay? Supply appropriate examples of this tone.
2. Point out some examples of striking figurative language in the essay. Are they serious or humorous?
3. What mode of development does Highet use more than any other? How does this method help his definition?
4. In the final paragraph, what is the irony of using McGonagall's own words to praise him?

The Issues

1. Can you think of some well-known examples of kitsch in the United States besides those cited by Highet? What makes them kitsch?
2. Highet admits that certain kitsch items delight him. Explain how a person of taste might feel such delight.
3. How do you explain the overwhelming popularity of kitsch?

4. Popular lyrics are always a good source of kitsch. What lines from one of today's well-known songs can you quote as an example of kitsch? Do you still like the song even though it is kitsch? Give reasons for your answer.
5. Following are excerpts from two love poems (A and B). Which of them might be considered kitsch? Why?

> A.
>
> The time was long and long ago,
> And we were young, my dear;
> The place stands fair in memory's glow,
> But it is far from here.
>
> The springtimes fade, the summers come,
> Autumn is here once more;
> The voice of ecstasy is dumb,
> The world goes forth to war.
>
> But though the flowers and birds were dead,
> And all the hours we knew,
> And though a hundred years had fled,
> I'd still come back to you.
>
> B.
>
> Ah, love, let us be true
> To one another! for the world, which seems
> To lie before us like a land of dreams,
> So various, so beautiful, so new,
> Hath really neither joy, nor love, nor light,
> Nor certitude, nor peace, nor help for pain;
> And we are here as on a darkling plain
> Swept with confused alarms of struggle and flight,
> Where ignorant armies clash by night.

- ## Suggestions for Writing

1. Using Gilbert Highet's definition of kitsch, choose one area of popular taste today and show how it fits the definition.
2. Write a paragraph in which you compare or contrast the meaning of *camp* with that of *kitsch*.

Ars Poetica

Archibald MacLeish

Archibald MacLeish (1892–1982), poet and playwright, was born in Glencoe, Illinois, and educated at Yale University. Trained as a lawyer, MacLeish served as librarian of Congress and as an adviser to President

Franklin D. Roosevelt. A recurrent theme in his poetry was his deep apprehension about the rise of fascism. MacLeish won a Pulitzer Prize for a poetry collection, *Conquistador* (1932), and another for his play *J. B.* (1958).

In this famous poem, MacLeish proposes a succinct definition of poetry. The poem comes from a collection of poems spanning the years 1917 to 1982.

• • •

  1 A poem should be palpable and mute
     As a globed fruit,

     Dumb
     As old medallions to the thumb,

  5 Silent as the sleeve-worn stone
     Of casement ledges where the moss has grown—

     A poem should be wordless
     As the flight of birds.

     A poem should be motionless in time
10 As the moon climbs,

     Leaving, as the moon releases
     Twig by twig the night-entangled trees,

     Leaving, as the moon behind the winter leaves,
     Memory by memory the mind—

15 A poem should be motionless in time
     As the moon climbs.

     A poem should be equal to:
     Not true

     For all the history of grief
20 An empty doorway and a maple leaf.

     For love
     The leaning grasses and two lights above the sea—

     A poem should not mean
     But be.

● Vocabulary

palpable (1)   medallions (4)   casement (6)

● The Facts

1. The translation of the poem's Latin title is "The Art of Poetry." Why is the title in Latin? How does the title relate to the poem?

2. Where does MacLeish give an explicit definition of poetry? How does he convey to the reader what poetry is?
3. In lines 17 and 18, what does MacLeish mean by the words "equal to: / Not true"?
4. The final stanza contains MacLeish's summarized view of poetry. What is your interpretation of the stanza?

● The Strategies

1. *Ars Poetica* is developed through a series of paradoxes. Analyze and interpret each.
2. MacLeish suggests that all the history of grief could be summarized by "an empty doorway and a maple leaf." Do you consider this an appropriate image? Can you suggest another equally appropriate image?
3. What image does MacLeish suggest for love? Do you find this image appropriate? Explain.
4. What synonyms for *mute* does the poet use? Cite them all.
5. What is the significance of repeating the fifth stanza in the eighth stanza?

● The Issues

1. What are some other definitions of *poetry*? What is your own definition? How does it compare to or contrast with MacLeish's definition?
2. How do you interpret MacLeish's statement that "A poem should be equal to: / Not true"? Provide an example to clarify this statement.
3. What does the author mean when he writes in stanza 4 that "A poem should be wordless / As the flight of birds"? How does this statement relate to Highet's notion of kitsch? (See Highet's essay on pages 393–400.)
4. Find a short poem that, in your view, perfectly exemplifies MacLeish's view that a poem should "not mean / But be." Do you like this poem? Why or why not?

● Suggestions for Writing

1. Consult a collection of the works of Wordsworth, Coleridge, Keats, or Shelley, for a definition of poetry. Contrast that definition with the one in *Ars Poetica*. State which definition you like best and why.
2. Write a paragraph in which you give a definition of *love,* and support that definition with appropriate images. Then write another paragraph in which you do the same thing for *hate*.

ISSUE FOR CRITICAL THINKING AND DEBATE: IMMIGRATION

Some years ago we took an airplane trip from Atlanta to Zürich, Switzerland, aboard a Swissair jet. During the long crossing, we felt sorry for the poor pilot. Every time he made an announcement, he had to repeat it in English, French, German, and Swiss German. For most of the eight-hour flight, the pilot quite sensibly remained mute. But his behavior brought to mind one predicted effect of immigration that Americans fear the most—the tendency of new arrivals to settle in communities where they can speak their mother tongue rather than learn English. Miami, and much of Florida, has virtually become a bilingual land, with Spanish as the primary language. California and Texas are in a similar predicament. Countries whose people are polyglot rather than sharing one common language have a tendency to develop profound divisions and differences based on linguistic groupings. One has only to think of Québec and the deep antagonisms that exist between French and English-speaking Canadians. The lack of a common language is one reason the European Union is faltering in its attempt to unite that deeply divided continent.

When it comes to immigrants and immigration, Americans are truly a deeply conflicted people. The vast majority of us are the descendants of immigrants, some with fathers and mothers who came here from other countries, others with foreign great ancestors. It is a rare American whose origin one or two or three generations back does not lie abroad. One of this book's authors, for example, is a Jamaican immigrant who became a naturalized American citizen many years ago. The other was born to American parents living abroad and grew up speaking French within her immediate family, coming to the United States to attend college as a teenager. The wife of the male author is the granddaughter of a Polish immigrant who spoke mainly Polish and, even at the end of her life, only badly fractured English. The wife's own mother speaks both Polish and English; the wife herself speaks only English, and has some regrets about not learning her grandmother's language. In this evolution of language, the family is almost stereotypical, with the experience being repeated throughout millions of American households.

Is immigration good for America? The answer you get depends on whom you ask. In 2004, National Public Radio, collaborating with Harvard's Kennedy School of Government and the Kaiser Family Foundation, undertook a survey of 1,100 native Americans and nearly 800 immigrants and found deep divisions in the opinion of those polled, with 37% saying that immigration should be kept the same, 41% that it should be decreased, and only 18% saying that it should be increased. Those Americans who had direct contact with some immigrant group were, as a whole, less negative about immigrants. Among the strongest fears of the native population was that immigrants would displace Americans from jobs. Another fear was that America would be changed by the influx of immigrants. Yet even the most rabid opponent of immigration has to admit that immigrants do much of the dirty work in our communities, such as digging ditches, cleaning houses, sweeping streets, picking fruit, and other kinds of manual labor that natives do not like to do.

Immigrants bring blessings to America, not the least of which is a variegated cuisine and a unique outlook. What would American cuisine be like without pizza, Chinese food, gyro sandwiches, or enchiladas? The infusion

- Why is the life of migrant farmworkers often backbreaking labor under the hot sun?

of cultural richness into the melting pot is the primary contribution of successive waves of immigrants. There are other benefits as well, one of which is pointed out by writer Eduardo Porter. Immigrants, many of whom are on shaky legal footing, contribute billions of dollars to Social Security, yet they draw no benefits. Without them, Social Security would be in even worse shape than presently reported. As for the charge often made that the country is being overrun by immigrant groups, writer Bill Bryson points out a fact often overlooked: that the vast continent of America is really underpopulated and with far fewer immigrants than European countries such as France and England. It really is an oddity that so many of us, the children and grandchildren of immigrants, would take such a negative attitude toward what is, in effect, a nearly universal common background of immigration roots.

Aside from their contributions of crafts and foods, immigrants bring to the table a fresh perspective of wonderment to the grand experiment that is America. They do not whine as natives are likely to, for they are not used to the manifold opportunities in business and education and to the social advancement that are available to the hardworking newcomer and that many natives take for granted. This, of all the immigrant's endowments, is probably the greatest and the least appreciated of all gifts: namely, the gift of fresh eyes to see anew for us and to remind us that no matter what our difficulties or passing worries might be, all in all we have it pretty good.

Illegal Immigrants Are Bolstering Social Security with Billions

EDUARDO PORTER

Eduardo Porter is a journalist and prolific contributor to the business section of *The New York Times,* writing dozens of articles each year. He has covered subjects ranging from the effect of oil demand on the U.S. trade deficit to an essay on why Monaco is a country. The essay below was published in the *Times* on April 5, 2005.

The limits of compassion are being severely tested in states like Arizona, California, and Texas where as many as 4,000 illegal immigrants per day cross into the U.S. from Mexico. Add to that number the illegals who enter from Canada, and the flood is massive. Many citizens consider this constant flow of illegals a danger to U.S. homeland security and complain that they will vote only for congressmen and presidents who address this chronic problem. The essay that follows gives us another perspective on the uncounted contributions of immigrants.

* * *

1 STOCKTON, Calif. - Since illegally crossing the Mexican border into the United States six years ago, Angel Martínez has done backbreaking work, harvesting asparagus, pruning grapevines and picking the ripe fruit. More recently, he has also washed trucks, often working as much as 70 hours a week, earning $8.50 to $12.75 an hour.

2 Not surprisingly, Mr. Martínez, 28, has not given much thought to Social Security's long-term financial problems. But Mr. Martínez—who comes from the state of Oaxaca in southern Mexico and hiked for two days through the desert to enter the United States near Tecate, some 20 miles east of Tijuana—contributes more than most Americans to the solvency of the nation's public retirement system.

3 Last year, Mr. Martínez paid about $2,000 toward Social Security and $450 for Medicare through payroll taxes withheld from his wages. Yet unlike most Americans, who will receive some form of a public pension in retirement and will be eligible for Medicare as soon as they turn 65, Mr. Martínez is not entitled to benefits.

4 He belongs to a big club. As the debate over Social Security heats up, the estimated seven million or so illegal immigrant workers in the United States are now providing the system with a subsidy of as much as $7 billion a year.

5 While it has been evident for years that illegal immigrants pay a variety of taxes, the extent of their contributions to Social Security is striking: the money added up to about 10 percent of last year's surplus—the difference between what the system currently receives in payroll taxes and what it doles out in pension benefits. Moreover, the money paid by illegal workers and their employers is factored into all the Social Security Administration's projections.

6   Illegal immigration, Marcelo Suárez-Orozco, co-director of immigration studies at New York University, noted sardonically, could provide "the fastest way to shore up the long-term finances of Social Security."

7   It is impossible to know exactly how many illegal immigrant workers pay taxes. But according to specialists, most of them do. Since 1986, when the Immigration Reform and Control Act set penalties for employers who knowingly hire illegal immigrants, most such workers have been forced to buy fake ID's to get a job.

8   Currently available for about $150 on street corners in just about any immigrant neighborhood in California, a typical fake ID package includes a green card and a Social Security card. It provides cover for employers, who, if asked, can plausibly assert that they believe all their workers are legal. It also means that workers must be paid by the book—with payroll tax deductions.

9   IRCA, as the immigration act is known, did little to deter employers from hiring illegal immigrants or to discourage them from working. But for Social Security's finances, it was a great piece of legislation.

10   Starting in the late 1980's, the Social Security Administration received a flood of W-2 earnings reports with incorrect—sometimes simply fictitious—

11   Social Security numbers. It stashed them in what it calls the "earnings suspense file" in the hope that someday it would figure out whom they belonged to.

12   The file has been mushrooming ever since: $189 billion worth of wages ended up recorded in the suspense file over the 1990's, two and a half times the amount of the 1980's.

13   In the current decade, the file is growing, on average, by more than $50 billion a year, generating $6 billion to $7 billion in Social Security tax revenue and about $1.5 billion in Medicare taxes.

14   In 2002 alone, the last year with figures released by the Social Security Administration, nine million W-2's with incorrect Social Security numbers landed in the suspense file, accounting for $56 billion in earnings, or about 1.5 percent of total reported wages.

15   Social Security officials do not know what fraction of the suspense file corresponds to the earnings of illegal immigrants. But they suspect that the portion is significant.

16   "Our assumption is that about three-quarters of other-than-legal immigrants pay payroll taxes," said Stephen C. Goss, Social Security's chief actuary, using the agency's term for illegal immigration.

- Vocabulary

solvency (2)   subsidy (4)   doles (5)
factored (5)   sardonically (6)   shore up (6)
plausibly (8)   deter (9)   fictitious (10)

- The Facts

1. How accurate are the figures reported concerning illegal entries into the United States?

2. How did Angel Martinez find his way to the United States? Do you think his journey is typical of that of other illegal immigrants?

3. How much money did Martinez contribute in 2004? What is ironic about his contribution? Did this figure surprise you? Explain your answer.

4. What amazing fact about how much money illegal immigrants pay toward social security is brought to light in this essay? Does this fact change your views on illegal immigration?

5. What is the IRCA? What was its intent? What has been the unforeseen result?

The Strategies

1. Where does the author place the thesis of his essay? What advantage does this placement have?

2. How does the author grab the reader's attention while introducing his subject? What is your reaction to his technique?

3. According to the author, what is happening while "the debate over Social Security heats up"? Who is participating in this debate? Where do you stand on the issue?

4. What is the importance of the reference to Marcelo Suárez-Orozco in paragraph 6?

5. What is the role of statistics in this essay? Do they help or hinder? Support your opinion with examples from the essay.

The Issues

1. Did Porter's essay in any way change your opinion about illegal immigrants? What was your opinion before reading the essay, and what is it now?

2. Porter describes the backbreaking work of harvesting asparagus, pruning grapevines, picking the ripe fruit, and washing trucks performed by Angel Martinez. What other kinds of work have you watched illegal immigrants perform? Has any of this work been rewarded with high wages? What sort of work do they typically carry out?

3. Why is it that illegal immigrants contribute so heftily to Social Security and Medicare? Should the situation be changed? If so, how? If not, why not?

4. What is the government doing with all of the phony Social Security numbers they discover because of the fake IDs purchased by illegal immigrants? How can this situation be corrected? Suggest some corrective measures.

5. Why has the term "other than legal immigrants" (OTLI) evolved? What is your reaction to this term? What better term, if any, can you suggest?

Suggestions for Writing

1. Write an essay in which you describe how you feel about the many immigrant workers who help grow our food and keep our cities clean. Begin with a vivid description of their tasks and then explain how you feel about these workers. Ask yourself these questions: Do I show enough respect for these immigrants?

• Why are pride and belonging such a powerful part of the swearing-in ceremony for immigrants who receive U.S. citizenship?

Do I think they should receive appropriate medical and social benefits? Support your view with documentary evidence—by quoting an expert on the subject of immigrant workers.

2. Write a vivid portrait of an acquaintance or loved one who has spent his or her life doing physical labor. Make sure that your portrait reflects how you feel about this person. For instance, if Aunt Julia cleans houses as a living, indicate how she does her job and what kind of person she is.

Wide-Open Spaces
BILL BRYSON

Bill Bryson (b. 1952) was born in Des Moines, Iowa, but spent twenty years in England, working as a journalist for *The Independent* and *The Times*. He moved to the USA in 1995 and returned to England in 2003. He continues to delight audiences with books that are not only perceptive but also hilariously funny. Among his bestsellers are the following: *African Diary* (2002), *A Short History of Nearly Everything* (2003), *A Walk in the Woods* (1998), and *I'm a Stranger Here Myself* (1999), from which the essay below was excerpted.

The writer is American born and reared but at heart an Englishman. After a stay of twenty years in England, he returned to America with a point of view informed by an English perspective. As you read this essay, try to keep an open mind and to remember that the author has a reputation for a snide sense of humor.

• • •

1   Here are a couple of things to bear in mind as you go through life: Daniel Boone was an idiot, and it's not worth trying to go to Maine for the day from Hanover, New Hampshire. Allow me to explain.

2   I was fooling around with a globe the other evening and was mildly astounded to discover that here in Hanover I am much closer to our old house in Yorkshire than I am to many other parts of the United States. Indeed, from where I sit to Attu, the westernmost of Alaska's Aleutian Islands, is almost four thousand miles. Put another way, a person in London is closer to Johannesburg than I am to the outermost tip of my own country.

3   Of course, you could argue that Alaska is not a fair comparison because there is so much non-U.S. territory between here and there. But even if you confine yourself to the mainland United States, the distances are imposing, to say the least. From my house to Los Angeles is about the same as from London to Lagos. We are, in a word, talking big scale here.

4   Here is another arresting fact to do with scale. In the past twenty years (a period in which, let the record show, I was doing my breeding elsewhere), the population of the United States increased by almost exactly the equivalent of Great Britain's. I find that quite amazing, not least because I don't know where all these new people are.

5   A remarkable thing about America, if you have been living for a long time in a crowded little place like the United Kingdom, is how very big and very empty so much of it is. Consider this: Montana, Wyoming, and North and South Dakota have an area twice the size of France but a population less than that of south London. Alaska is bigger still and has even fewer people. Even my own adopted state of New Hampshire, in the relatively crowded Northeast, is 85 percent forest, and most of the rest is lakes. You can drive for very long periods in New Hampshire and never see anything but trees and mountains—not a house or a hamlet or even, quite often, another car.

6   I am constantly caught by this. Not long ago, I had a couple of friends over from England and we decided to take a drive over to the lakes of western Maine. It had the makings of a nice day out. All we had to do was cross New Hampshire—which is, after all, the fourth tiniest state in America—and go a little way over the state line into our lovely, moose-strewn neighbor to the east. I figured it would take about two hours—two and a half tops.

7   Well, of course you have anticipated the punchline. Six hours later we pulled up exhausted at the shore of Rangeley Lake, took two pictures, looked at each other, and wordlessly got back in the car and drove home. This sort of thing happens all the time.

8 The curious thing is that a very great many Americans don't seem to see it this way. They think the country is way too crowded. Moves are constantly afoot to restrict access to national parks and wilderness areas on the grounds that they are dangerously overrun. Parts of them *are* unquestionably crowded, but that is only because 98 percent of visitors arrive by car, and 98 percent of those venture no more than a couple of hundred feet from their metallic wombs. Elsewhere, however, you can have whole mountains to yourself, even in the most popular parks on the busiest days. Yet I may soon find myself barred from hiking in many wilderness areas unless I had the foresight to book a visit weeks beforehand, because of perceived overcrowding.

9 Even more ominously, there is a growing belief that the best way of dealing with this supposed crisis is by expelling most of those not born here. There is an organization whose name escapes me (it may be "Dangerously Small-Minded Reactionaries for a Better America") that periodically runs earnest, carefully reasoned ads in the *New York Times, Atlantic Monthly,* and other important and influential publications, calling for an end to immigration because, as one of its ads explains, it "is devastating our environment and the quality of our lives." Elsewhere it adds, "Primarily because of immigration we are rushing at breakneck speed toward an environmental and economic disaster." Oh, give me a break, please.

10 You could, I suppose, make an economic or even cultural case for cutting back on immigration, but not on the grounds that the country is running out of room. Anti-immigration arguments conveniently overlook the fact that America already expels a million immigrants a year and that those who are here mostly do jobs that are too dirty, low-paying, or unsatisfying for the rest of us to do. Getting rid of immigrants is not suddenly going to open employment opportunities for those born here; all it's going to do is leave a lot of dishes unwashed, a lot of beds unmade, and a lot of fruit unpicked. Still less is it going to miraculously create a lot more breathing space for the rest of us.

11 America already has one of the lowest proportions of immigrants in the developed world. Just 6 percent of people in the United States are foreign born, compared with, for instance, 8 percent in Britain and 11 percent in France. America may or may not be heading for an environmental and economic disaster, but if so it certainly isn't because six people in every hundred were born somewhere else.

12 There aren't many human acts more foolishly simplistic or misguided, or more likely to lead to careless evil, than blaming general problems on small minorities, yet that seems to be quite a respectable impulse where immigration is concerned these days. Two years ago, Californians voted overwhelmingly for Proposition 187, which would deny health and education services to illegal immigrants. Almost immediately upon passage of the proposition, Governor Pete Wilson ordered the state health authorities to stop providing prenatal care to any woman who could not prove that she was here legally. Now please correct me by all means, but does it not seem just a trifle harsh—a trifle barbaric

even—to imperil the well-being of an unborn child because of the actions of its parents?

13   No less astounding in its way, the federal government recently began removing basic rights and entitlements even from legal immigrants. We are in effect saying to them: "Thank you for your years of faithful service to our economy, but things are a little tough at the moment, so we aren't prepared to help you. Besides, you have a funny accent."

14   I'm not arguing for unlimited immigration, you understand, just a sense of proportion in how we treat those who are here already. The fact is, America is one of the least crowded countries on earth, with an average of just 68 people per square mile, compared with 256 in France and over 600 in Britain. Altogether, only 2 percent of the United States is classified as "built up."

15   Of course, Americans have always tended to see these things in a different way. Daniel Boone famously is supposed to have looked out his cabin window one day, seen a wisp of smoke rising from a homesteader's dwelling on a distant mountain, and announced his intention to move on, complaining bitterly that the neighborhood was getting too crowded.

16   Which is why I say Daniel Boone was an idiot. I just hate to see the rest of my country going the same way.

● Vocabulary

arresting (4)   punchline (7)   venture (8)
ominously (9)   periodically (9)   prenatal (12)
barbaric (12)   imperil (12)   entitlements (13)

● The Facts

1. What major fact does Bryson try to bring out in his essay? Is this a disputable fact? Explain your answer.
2. According to the author, how fast has the population of the United States grown? What comparison does the author make?
3. What impression do people from European countries get when they visit the United States?
4. According to the author, most Americans disagree with his view. What is their perception?
5. From Bryson's point of view, what causes the most beautiful wilderness areas to be overcrowded? What statistic does the author cite to support his declaration?

● The Strategies

1. Early in the essay, the author calls Daniel Boone an "idiot." What dangerous ground is he treading on when he uses such a demeaning label? Who is Daniel Boone? How do you feel about his being called an "idiot"?
2. What strategy is the author using when he mentions an organization that may be called "Dangerously Small-Minded Reactionaries for a Better America"?

3. How does the author underscore the fact that the United States has one of the lowest proportions of immigrants in the developed world? Do you consider his strategy effective? Give reasons for your answer.
4. At what point in the essay does the author shift from writing about the geography of the United States to the problem of immigration? What good reason is there for not attacking the immigration issue earlier?
5. What is the tone of the quotation used by the author in paragraph 13? What is your response to this paragraph?

● The Issues

1. For the author, an American who spent twenty years in England, what is the "remarkable thing" about America? Do you, too, find it remarkable? Explain your answer.
2. The author dislikes the thought that someday he may have to make a reservation in order to hike in a certain wilderness area. To him this would be a ridiculous requirement considering how most mountainous areas remain free of human visitors. How do you feel about forest rangers who require a reservation for hiking along certain trails? What logical reason can you suggest for such a requirement?
3. According to the author, what is the only result that will come from expelling all the immigrants who work in our country? Do you agree with Bryson on this point? Explain yourself.
4. How strongly does the author feel about blaming our general problems on the minorities in our country? What is your reaction?
5. Is the author for or against unlimited immigration? What approach does he propose? Does his idea appeal to your sense of justice, or do you think the author goes overboard one way or another? Explain your view.

● Suggestions for Writing

1. Write a journal entry in which you dream about the most beautiful, pristine vacation spot in the United States. Then describe an ideal vacation there. Indicate whether you would want to be alone or have company during this retreat. If your choice is to be alone, explain why you want seclusion. If your choice is to have company, then describe the company you would choose.
2. Bryson draws our attention to the absurdity of being paranoid about allowing foreigners into our country with its thousands of miles of open spaces. Write an essay in which you refute Bryson's view. Like Bryson, use some appropriate quotations and examples to shore up your case.

Stumped by ending an essay? Exit on page 696, at the **Editing Booth!**

Punctuation Workshop
The Apostrophe (')

The apostrophe shows ownership, the omission in a contraction, and certain plurals.

1. Use an apostrophe + *s* to show ownership.

    Pete's baseball bat

    Someone's mistake

    This bicycle is Katie's. (A possessive can follow the word to which it belongs.)

    Venus's beauty

    For a plural that ends in *s*, omit an additional *s*.

    The Dodgers' baseball camp (rather than *Dodgers's*)

2. Use an apostrophe to show an omission in a contraction.

    don't (for *do not*)

    can't (for *cannot*)

    High school class of '52

CAUTION: Don't confuse the contraction *who's* with the pronoun *whose*.

3. Use the apostrophe to form certain plurals.

    He crossed all of his *t*'s and dotted all of his *i*'s.

    I love to read about the 1800s (*1800's* is sometimes acceptable).

    Her *l*'s are written in bold strokes

CAUTION: Do not use an apostrophe to form plural nouns that don't show ownership. (The lions were restless—not *lion's*. The Goldmans were out of town—not *Goldman's*.)

STUDENT CORNER

Immigrants in America
Dave Herman, Georgia State University

An immigrant is a person whose ancestral roots lie in another country. By that definition nearly all Americans are immigrants or the descendants of immigrants. Even the Native Americans, the so-called American Indians, are immigrants whose ancestors came to the new world via the Bering Straits, which geologists tell us was once connected to the North American continent by a land bridge. Ours, like it or not, is an immigrant society.

One disadvantage of this widespread immigrant influence is an attitude of snobbery that some American citizens have, depending on when their ancestors came to the United States. The most conspicuous example of this is an organization called Daughters of the American Revolution (DAR for short). To be a member of this snobbish group, you have to prove that one of your ancestors fought in the American Revolution. The guidelines for eligibility declare that membership is open to any woman who can prove "lineal, bloodline descent from an ancestor who aided in achieving American independence," adding that the applicant "must provide documentation for each statement of birth, marriage, and death."

The children of immigrants sometimes hold a condescending or embarrassed attitude toward their parents, especially if the parents have a strong foreign accent from a language other than English. Often the children make excuses for the way their parents mispronounce words or ignore grammar rules. Once the third generation emerges, the language of the first generation has usually been lost, with only nostalgic scraps of idioms and quaint sayings surviving.

In my own family, for example, my grandmother speaks Spanish, which is her native tongue, and so does my mother. An aunt or two understand a few words. But only my mother has mastered the language, probably because she has a good ear. The third generation, of which I'm

---

DAR Web site. July 7, 2005. Online at http://www.dar.org/natsociety/content.cfm?ID=145&hd=n&FO=Y.

a member, speaks no Spanish. One cousin can understand a phrase here and there if the speaker enunciates clearly and slowly. But for the most part, the language is Greek to my generation. Because the cultural emphasis in those days was on instant adaptation to a new society, the children were encouraged to speak English everywhere, even at home. Those who fear that immigrants will introduce and cling to the mother tongue of their parents don't understand the tremendous pressure immigrants and their children are subjected to by American society. Even Miami, which has a majority Hispanic population and where Spanish seems to be the language of the majority, has a bilingual population that speaks both English and Spanish fluently.

I think immigration has been good for America. Wherever there is a brain drain going on in some foreign country of our world, it is likely that the brains leaving their homeland are flowing into America. My uncle, for example, went to school with a boy who later became an astrophysicist for NASA. This boy become so important to the space program that when he came back to the village where my father and he came from, he was in the company of two Secret Service agents as his personal bodyguards.

In my neighborhood are three families from what used to be Armenia. The children have all done well at the University. One is a neurosurgeon, one a gynecologist, and one a successful businessman. Several of the other children are still at the University pursuing advanced degrees. It is impossible to estimate in dollars alone what these three families have or will contribute to the society in which they were born because their parents had migrated to America.

We are a society of immigrants. And we're better off for it. The problems of adjustment to a new culture, or a new culture adjusting to the influx of immigrants, are minor compared to the richness and blessings that immigration bestows on America. There's a reason why the inscription of the base of the Statue of Liberty says,

> Give me your tired, your poor,
> Your huddled masses yearning to breathe free,

Herman 3

The wretched refuse of your teeming shore,
Send these, the homeless, tempest-tost to me,
I lift my lamp beside the golden door!

Emma Lazarus, the poet who wrote this jingle, was no fool. She knew a good thing when she saw it.

How I Write

I write late at night or early in the morning. I cannot write during the day because my thoughts race too fast for writing. I have to be in a slower mode in order to write effectively. Mostly, I rewrite everything over two or three times just to make it smooth.

How I Wrote This Essay

I tried to personalize the topic by thinking of immigrants I knew who contributed some substance to America. I didn't want to just recite statistics, which tends to be boring anyway. Plus, by using examples within my reach, I thought that would make the essay easier to read and more interesting.

My Writing Tip

Go over your work again and again. Sometimes when you can't get something just right, an idea will occur to you if you keep going over the material. I know this sounds boring, but it's the technique that works for me.

CHAPTER WRITING ASSIGNMENTS

1. In an essay, define *history*.
2. Define yourself in an essay.
3. Write a definition of *superstition*.
4. Choose one of the following terms and write an essay in which you first define the term as a dictionary would. Then give an extended definition, using the development most suitable for answering the question, "What is it?"

    curiosity   mecurial
    genetic   pratfall

WRITING ASSIGNMENTS FOR A SPECIFIC AUDIENCE

1. Define the term *authority* for a seven-year-old child.
2. Write an essay defining *failure* to an audience of your peers.

COLLABORATIVE WRITING PROJECT

Form a group with five other students. Brainstorm on the topic of explorers such as Christopher Columbus who discovered the New World. Because there were people already living on the newly discovered land, write a definition of "discovered" as it applies to the findings of explorers. Define the term from Columbus's point of view and from the point of view of the people he "discovered."

IMAGE GALLERY WRITING ASSIGNMENT

Visit pages 659–661 of our image gallery and study all three images dealing with immigration. Then choose the image that most appeals to you. Answer the questions and do the writing assignment.

12

Comparison/Contrast

ROAD MAP TO COMPARISON/CONTRAST

What Comparison/Contrast Does

To *compare* is to point out how two things are similar; to *contrast* is to stress how they are dissimilar. To say that both John Calvin and Martin Luther were persecuted by the Catholic Church, opposed to conservative theology, and personally against materialistic self-indulgence is to make a comparison. A contrast between the two men, however, might stress that Luther wanted the Church to return to the primitive simplicity of the apostles, whereas Calvin heartily supported the advancement of capitalism. The following passage from a student essay draws a contrast, indicated by the use of the underlined contrasting words and expressions, between Egyptian and Greek mythologies.

>   A brief consideration of Egyptian mythology contrasted with the mythology of the Greeks is enough to convince us of the revolution in thought that must have taken place from one age to the other. The Egyptian gods had no resemblance to anything in the real world, whereas the Greek gods were fashioned after real Greek people. In Egypt the gods typically worshiped consisted of a towering colossus, so immobile and so distorted that no human could imagine it alive; or a woman with a cat's head, suggesting inflexible, inhuman cruelty; or a monstrous mysterious sphinx, aloof from anything we might consider human. The Egyptian artists' interpretations of the divine were horrid bestial shapes that combined men's heads with birds' bodies or portrayed lions with eagle wings—creatures that could inhabit only terrifying nightmares. The monstrosities of an invisible world were what the Egyptians worshiped. The Greek interpretation of divinity stands in <u>opposition</u> to this dark picture. The Greeks were preoccupied with the visible world. <u>Unlike</u> the Egyptians, they found their desires satisfied in what they could actually see around them. The ancient statues of Apollo, for instance, resemble the strong young bodies of athletes contending in the Olympic games. Homer describes Hermes as if he were a splendid Greek citizen. Generally the Greek artists found their gods in the idealized beauty or intelligence of

actual human counterparts. In direct contrast to the Egyptians, they had no wish to create some hideous fantasy that they then called God.

On the other hand, the following passage finds similarities between whales and human beings:

> Whales and human beings are like two nations of individuals who have certain characteristics in common. As mammals they both are warm-blooded, giving milk and breathing air. As social creatures they both have basic urges for privacy as well as for fraternization. As species bent on reproduction they both show similar patterns of aggression during courtship, the male trying to gain the female's attention and the female responding. Finally, as mystical beings they both are caught in the net of life and time, fellow prisoners of the splendor, travail, and secrets of earth.

Comparisons that take the form of extended analogies are frequently used to clarify abstract or complex ideas. One of the most famous examples of this use comes from the biblical accounts of Jesus' remarks:

> The kingdom of heaven is like unto a grain of mustard seed, which a man took and sowed in his field: which indeed is less than all seeds; but when it is grown, it is greater than the herbs, and becometh a tree, so that the birds of the heaven come and lodge in the branches thereof.
>
> —Matthew 13:31–32

By comparing the kingdom of heaven to a mustard seed, which would have been familiar to his agrarian listeners, Jesus explains the power and the influence that a life dedicated to God can exert.

When to Use Comparison/Contrast

The odds are that you will not get through college without having to write a comparison/contrast, either in an essay exam or in a research paper. An English exam may typically ask for a contrast between the tragic flaws of Oedipus and Othello. A sociology question may call for a comparison between the demands of the feminist and civil rights movements. You may be asked to catalogue the differences between substances of organic and inorganic chemistry, or you may be asked to write an essay contrasting the traits of apes in captivity with those of apes who live in the wild. Comparison/contrast questions, in fact, commonly arise in every imaginable discipline.

How to Use Comparison/Contrast

1. **Use logical bases of contrast.** Suppose you want to develop the key thought "My college experience is teaching me that good instructors are a different breed from bad ones." You must first decide on your bases for

contrast. You must ask yourself in which areas of instruction you wish to contrast the activities of good teachers with bad teachers. The following three could be your choice: (1) time spent on lesson preparation; (2) willingness to tolerate dissent; (3) personal relationship with students. Having chosen your bases, write down the three areas under consideration on the left side of a sheet of paper and then create two columns (one for good instructors, the other for bad instructors) in which you will place comments, as follows:

	Good instructors	**Bad instructors**
1. **Time spent on lesson preparation**	Good instructors constantly revise lessons, including up-to-date reviews, newspaper clippings, research results, and other relevant material. They refer to more than one source work and give suggestions for further reading. Lectures and discussions are the result of clear objectives.	Bad instructors give the same lectures year in and year out, including the same dead jokes. They do nothing but spell out rudimentary facts, to be memorized verbatim for final tests. They often spend class time on dull workbook assignments. They show as many movies as possible, during which they nap.
2. **Willingness to tolerate dissent**	Good instructors welcome arguments as a way of bringing life into the classroom and of pointing out alternatives. Like Socrates, they believe the classroom dialectic is a valid teaching method.	Bad instructors see dissent or discussion as a threat to discipline and to their authority, so they avoid both. They feel safe only when they are parroting themselves or the textbook.
3. **Personal relationships with students**	Good instructors spend time beyond office hours listening to student questions or complaints. They willingly clarify difficult problems. They never embarrass or patronize students.	Bad instructors are usually too busy off campus to spend time in personal consultation with students. They make students who ask for special help feel inferior.

2. **Use either the alternating or block method of contrast.** Once you have made a preliminary sketch, you can develop it simply by adding a few

transitional words and phrases, as has been done in the following passage (transitions are underlined):

My college experience is teaching me that good instructors are a different breed from bad ones. <u>In terms of time spent on lesson preparation,</u> good instructors constantly revise their lessons, including such items as up-to-date reviews, newspaper clippings, research results, or any other relevant material. They refer to more than one source work and give suggestions for further reading. Their lectures and discussions are the obvious result of clear objectives. <u>In contrast, bad instructors</u> give the same lectures year in and year out, including the same dead jokes. Only the rudimentary facts are spelled out in class, to be memorized verbatim and regurgitated on final tests. They often spend classroom time on dull workbook assignments or, as often as possible, a movie, during which they take a nap.

<u>Another big difference between good and bad instructors is in their willingness to tolerate dissent.</u> Good instructors welcome arguments as a way of bringing life into the classroom and of pointing out alternatives. Like Socrates, they believe that the classroom dialectic is a valid learning method. <u>Bad instructors, however, take the opposite tack.</u> They see dissent or discussion as a threat to their discipline and to their authority, so they avoid both. They feel safe only when they are parroting themselves or their textbooks.

<u>Good and bad instructors differ markedly in their relationship to students.</u> Good instructors spend time beyond office hours listening to student questions or complaints. They willingly clarify difficult problems, and they never embarrass or patronize students. Bad instructors, <u>on the contrary,</u> are usually too busy off campus to spend time in personal consultation with students. They deliver their lecture and disappear. The student who asks for special help is made to feel inferior.

The preceding example demonstrates the *alternating* method of comparison/contrast. The paragraph is written to alternate back and forth from one side of an issue to the other. Another system—called the *block* method—uses separate paragraphs for each side of the issue, as illustrated in the following passage that contrasts two views of Jewish history:

On the one hand, the Diaspora Jews can say that this talk of a predestination drama is a lot of nonsense. What has happened is only an interesting constellation of accidental, impersonal events, which some people have distorted out of all proportions to reality. We were defeated in war, they could say, we lost our land, we were exiled, and now it is our turn to disappear, just as under similar circumstances the Sumerians, the Hittites, the Babylonians, the Assyrians, the Persians—yes, even the Jews in the Kingdom of Israel—disappeared.

On the other hand, they can say that their ancestors could not have been pursuing a mere illusion for 2,000 years. They could say that if we are God's Chosen People as our forefathers affirmed, if we have been placed in an exile to accomplish a divine mission as our Prophets predicted, and since we did receive the Torah, then we must survive to fulfill our Covenant with God.

—Max I. Dimont, *The Indestructible Jews*

The alternating and block methods of comparison/contrast are further clarified in the following two outlines contrasting the Toyota Camry and the Volkswagen Jetta on the basis of cost, performance, and looks:

Alternating Outline

First paragraph	I. Cost
	A. Camry
	B. Jetta
Second paragraph	II. Performance
	A. Camry
	B. Jetta
Third paragraph	III. Looks
	A. Camry
	B. Jetta

Block Outline

First paragraph	I. Camry
	A. Cost
	B. Performance
	C. Looks
Second paragraph	II. Jetta
	A. Cost
	B. Performance
	C. Looks

3. **Make sure that the items to be compared/contrasted belong to the same class.** Some common ground must exist between items in order for a comparison/contrast to be meaningful. For example, a comparison between a hummingbird and a cement mixer or between backgammon and Dutch Cleanser would be silly. On the other hand, some usefulness can be derived from a comparison between the Chinese and Japanese languages or between golf and tennis—pairings that belong to common groups: Asian languages and sports, respectively. Moreover, the expression of the comparison/contrast must be grammatically accurate:

> **Wrong:** Our telephone system is better than Russia.
>
>   Here, a telephone system is contrasted with all of Russia.

Right: Our telephone system is better than *that* of Russia.
or
Our telephone system is better than Russia's.

Wrong: Ed's income is less than his wife.

Here, Ed's income is contrasted with his wife.

Right: Ed's income is less than that of his wife.
or
Ed's income is less than his wife's.

4. **Deal with both sides of the question.** All comparisons and contrasts are concerned with two sides, and you must deal equally with both. Do not mention one side and assume that your reader will fill in the other side. If you are contrasting the summer weather in Death Valley with the summer weather at Donner Pass, you cannot say:

   In Death Valley the heat is so intense that even lizards wilt.

   and assume that your reader will fill in "but at Donner Pass the summers remain cool." You must draw the contrast fully, as in the following:

   In Death Valley the heat is so intense that even lizards wilt, whereas at Donner Pass a cool breeze freshens even the hottest day.

5. **Use expressions indicating comparison/contrast.** Although comparison requires less back-and-forth movement than does contrast, you must nevertheless take both sides into account by stating exactly what traits they have in common. For instance, in pointing out that in some ways high schools are like prisons, you cannot restrict yourself to discussing the domineering principal, the snoopy truant officer, the pass required to leave campus, or the punitive grading system. You must mention both sides, indicating that the domineering principal in high school is *like* the stern warden in prison; that the snoopy truant officer who makes sure that students attend school has much *in common with the prison guards* who make sure that inmates stay in prison; that the pass required to leave campus is *similar* to the formal permission required to leave a locked ward; and that the punitive grading system of high schools is *like* the demerit system of prisons. These expressions serve as signposts in your text, telling your reader how your different points relate.

The following expressions indicate comparison:

also	as well as
bears resemblance to both . . .	and in common with
in like manner	like
likewise	neither . . . nor
similar	too

The following expressions indicate contrast:

although this may be true	at the same time
but	for all that
however	in contrast to
in opposition to	nevertheless
on the contrary	on the one hand . . . on the other hand
otherwise	still
unlike	whereas
yet	

Contrast emphasizes the separate sides of an issue by pulling them apart as much as possible in order to clarify their differences. Comparison is less two-sided because it tries to draw together both sides of an issue in order to reveal what they have in common. In short, *contrasts diverge, comparisons converge*. Refer back to the contrast example on page 421, and note how Egyptian mythology and Greek mythology are placed far apart so that their ideological differences stand out. Note also how the underlined expressions indicating contrast clarify the shift from one side to the other.

Warming Up to Write a Comparison/Contrast

Comparing and contrasting are normal ways people think, so you should not have too much difficulty completing these exercises.

1. For the item on the left of each column, write in three or four characteristics that describe the item; then write contrasting characteristics for the item at the right.

   Example:

   Teacher Smith
   Pleasant
   Always prepared
   Fascinating in his presentations

   Teacher Brown
   Grouchy
   Sometimes disorganized
   Usually boring

   a. Historical romances — Myths
   b. Tornadoes — Cyclones
   c. Friend with bad ethics — Friend with good ethics
   d. Working in a restaurant — Working in a hospital
   e. Watching a movie on TV — Watching a movie in a theater

2. Write down three bases of contrast (not comparison) for each of the following subjects.

   a. Two close friends
   b. Two church services

  c. Two holidays

  d. Two sports teams (or persons)

  e. Two attitudes toward work

 3. Write down at least three aspects in which each of the following pairs are similar.

  a. A farm and a garden

  b. A storm and a lover's quarrel

  c. An ant hill and city government

  d. Fishing and looking for a wife

  e. An eagle and a lion

EXAMPLES

That Lean and Hungry Look

Suzanne Jordan

Suzanne Jordan (b. 1946), formerly a university teacher of English, is now a feature writer for the Raleigh, North Carolina, *News and Observer.*

Flying in the face of today's admiration for slimly elegant people, Jordan gives the winning edge to the chubbies, favorably comparing them point by point with "that lean and hungry look" so mistrusted by Shakespeare.

• • •

1 Caesar was right. Thin people need watching. I've been watching them for most of my adult life, and I don't like what I see. When these narrow fellows spring at me, I quiver to my toes. Thin people come in all personalities, most of them menacing. You've got your "together" thin person, your mechanical thin person, your condescending thin person, your tsk-tsk thin person, your efficiency-expert thin person. All of them are dangerous.

2 In the first place, thin people aren't fun. They don't know how to goof off, at least in the best, fat sense of the word. They've always got to be a-doing. Give them a coffee break, and they'll jog around the block. Supply them with a quiet evening at home, and they'll fix the screen door and lick S&H green stamps. They say things like "there aren't enough hours in the day." Fat people never say that. Fat people think the day is too damn long already.

3 Thin people make me tired. They've got speedy little metabolisms that cause them to bustle briskly. They're forever rubbing their bony hands together and eyeing new problems to "tackle." I like to surround myself with sluggish, inert, easygoing fat people, the kind who believe that if you clean it up today, it'll just get dirty again tomorrow.

4   Some people say the business about the jolly fat person is a myth, that all of us chubbies are neurotic, sick, sad people. I disagree. Fat people may not be chortling all day long, but they're a hell of a lot nicer than the wizened and shriveled. Thin people turn surly, mean and hard at a young age because they never learn the value of a hot-fudge sundae for easing tension. Thin people don't like gooey soft things because they themselves are neither gooey nor soft. They are crunchy and dull, like carrots. They go straight to the heart of the matter while fat people let things stay all blurry and hazy and vague, the way things actually are. Thin people want to face the truth. Fat people know there is no truth. One of my thin friends is always staring at complex, unsolvable problems and saying, "The key thing is . . ." Fat people never say that. They know there isn't any such thing as the key thing about anything.

5   Thin people believe in logic. Fat people see all sides. The sides fat people see are rounded blobs, usually gray, always nebulous and truly not worth worrying about. But the thin person persists. "If you consume more calories than you burn," says one of my thin friends, "you will gain weight. It's that simple." Fat people always grin when they hear statements like that. They know better.

6   Fat people realize that life is illogical and unfair. They know very well that God is not in his heaven and all is not right with the world. If God was up there, fat people could have two doughnuts and a big orange drink anytime they wanted it.

7   Thin people have a long list of logical things they are always spouting off to me. They hold up one finger at a time as they reel off these things, so I won't lose track. They speak slowly as if to a young child. The list is long and full of holes. It contains tidbits like "get a grip on yourself," "cigarettes kill," "cholesterol clogs," "fit as a fiddle," "ducks in a row," "organize" and "sound fiscal management." Phrases like that.

8   They think these 2,000-point plans lead to happiness. Fat people know happiness is elusive at best and even if they could get the kind thin people talk about, they wouldn't want it. Wisely, fat people see that such programs are too dull, too hard, too off the mark. They are never better than a whole cheesecake.

9   Fat people know all about the mystery of life. They are the ones acquainted with the night, with luck, with fate, with playing it by ear. One thin person I know once suggested that we arrange all the parts of a jigsaw puzzle into groups according to size, shape and color. He figured this would cut the time needed to complete the puzzle by at least 50 per cent. I said I wouldn't do it. One, I like to muddle through. Two, what good would it do to finish early? Three, the jigsaw puzzle isn't the important thing. The important thing is the fun of four people (one thin person included) sitting around a card table, working a jigsaw puzzle. My thin friend had no use for my list. Instead of joining us, he went outside and mulched the boxwoods. The three remaining fat people finished the puzzle and made chocolate, double-fudged brownies to celebrate.

10   The main problem with thin people is they oppress. Their good intentions, bony torsos, tight hips, neat corners, cerebral machinations and pat solutions loom like dark clouds over the loose, comfortable, spread-out, soft world of the fat. Long after fat people have removed their coats and shoes and put their feet up on the coffee table, thin people are still sitting on the edge of the sofa, looking neat as a pin, discussing rutabagas. Fat people are heavily into fits of laughter, slapping their thighs and whooping it up, while thin people are still politely waiting for the punch line.

11   Thin people are downers. They like math and morality and reasoned evaluation of the limitations of human beings. They have their skinny little acts together. They expound, prognose, probe and prick.

12   Fat people are convivial. They will like you even if you're irregular and have acne. They will come up with a good reason why you never wrote the great American novel. They will cry in your beer with you. They will put your name in the pot. They will let you off the hook. Fat people will gab, giggle, guffaw, galumph, gyrate and gossip. They are generous, giving and gallant. They are gluttonous and goodly and great. What you want when you're down is soft and jiggly, not muscled and stable. Fat people know this. Fat people have plenty of room. Fat people will take you in.

● Vocabulary

metabolism (3)
surly (4)
mulched (9)
rutabagas (10)
guffaw (12)
gluttonous (12)

inert (3)
nebulous (5)
boxwoods (9)
prognose (11)
galumph (12)

wizened (4)
elusive (8)
machinations (10)
convivial (12)
gyrate (12)

● The Facts

1. In a nutshell, what bothers the author most about thin people?
2. What is your view of the myth about the "jolly fat person" mentioned in paragraph 4? What evidence is there for your view?
3. In paragraph 9, what is the "list" objected to by the thin person? What is ironic about this objection?
4. The thesis of Jordan's essay is obvious, but what is her underlying purpose? Because the essay is humorous, you might say that she simply wants to entertain the reader; but what more serious purpose is revealed?
5. In paragraph 10, Jordan claims that thin people "oppress." What evidence does she cite to support this claim?

● The Strategies

1. The title of the essay is a literary allusion that is echoed in the opening sentence. What is the origin of the allusion? What other allusion can you identify in the essay?

2. What rhetorical organization does the author use to develop her essay? What advantage does her organization present? What other type of organization could be used to contrast thin and fat people?
3. Paragraph 5 and other paragraphs open with short, declarative sentences. What is the effect?
4. Here and there throughout the essay, Jordan uses figurative language. Find three examples and label the kind of figure of speech used in each.
5. How does the author achieve humor in her essay? Cite appropriate examples of her techniques.

● The Issues

1. "Thin is in" is irrefutably one of the maxims of today. Why have we placed such emphasis on the slim look?
2. Reread John Leo's essay *Mirror, Mirror, on the Wall* on pages 356–358. What does Leo say about the slim-hipped look of today? Does your answer to question 1 fit in with his view? Why or why not?
3. Are you convinced by Jordan's logic about the superiority of fat people? How does it strike you? Be specific in your answer.
4. If you were to play devil's advocate, how would you describe the thin person as desirable and the fat person as undesirable? Give specific examples as does Jordan.
5. How much should a person's appearance affect his or her success on the job?

● Suggestions for Writing

1. Write an essay in which you compare two people you know—one fat, one thin.
2. Using Jordan's piece as a model, write a 500-word essay in which you contrast tall and short people.

Diogenes and Alexander
Gilbert Highet

Gilbert Highet (1906–1978) was born in Glasgow, Scotland, educated at the University of Glasgow and at Oxford, and became an American citizen in 1951. A classicist, Highet was known for his scholarly and critical writing, including *The Classical Tradition* (1949) and *The Anatomy of Satire* (1962).

This essay describes a meeting between two sharply contrasting personalities in Greek history—the Greek Cynic philosopher Diogenes (c. 412–323 B.C.) and Alexander the Great (356–323 B.C.), King of Macedonia. As Highet shows, although the two men occupied strikingly different positions in Greek society, they shared at least one quality that made them unique among the people of their time.

* * *

1   Lying on the bare earth, shoeless, bearded, half-naked, he looked like a beggar or a lunatic. He was one, but not the other. He had opened his eyes with the sun at dawn, scratched, done his business like a dog at the roadside, washed at the public fountain, begged a piece of breakfast bread and a few olives, eaten them squatting on the ground, and washed them down with a few handfuls of water scooped from the spring. (Long ago he had owned a rough wooden cup, but he threw it away when he saw a boy drinking out of his hollowed hands.) Having no work to go to and no family to provide for, he was free. As the market place filled up with shoppers and merchants and gossipers and sharpers and slaves and foreigners, he had strolled through it for an hour or two. Everybody knew him, or knew of him. They would throw sharp questions at him and get sharper answers. Sometimes they threw jeers, and got jibes; sometimes bits of food, and got scant thanks; sometimes a mischievous pebble, and got a shower of stones and abuse. They were not quite sure whether he was mad or not. He knew they were mad, each in a different way; they amused him. Now he was back at his home.

2   It was not a house, not even a squatter's hut. He thought everybody lived far too elaborately, expensively, anxiously. What good is a house? No one needs privacy; natural acts are not shameful; we all do the same things, and need not hide them. No one needs beds and chairs and such furniture: the animals live healthy lives and sleep on the ground. All we require, since nature did not dress us properly, is one garment to keep us warm, and some shelter from rain and wind. So he had one blanket—to dress him in the daytime and cover him at night—and he slept in a cask. His name was Diogenes. He was the founder of the creed called Cynicism (the word means "doggishness"); he spent much of his life in the rich, lazy, corrupt Greek city of Corinth, mocking and satirizing its people, and occasionally converting one of them.

3   His home was not a barrel made of wood: too expensive. It was a storage jar made of earthenware, something like a modern fuel tank—no doubt discarded because a break had made it useless. He was not the first to inhabit such a thing: the refugees driven into Athens by the Spartan invasion had been forced to sleep in casks. But he was the first who ever did so by choice, out of principle.

4   Diogenes was not a degenerate or a maniac. He was a philosopher who wrote plays and poems and essays expounding his doctrine; he talked to those who cared to listen; he had pupils who admired him. But he taught chiefly by example. All should live naturally, he said, for what is natural is normal and cannot possibly be evil or shameful. Live without conventions, which are artificial and false; escape complexities and superfluities and extravagances: only so can you live a free life. The rich man believes he possesses his big house with its many rooms and its elaborate furniture, his pictures and his expensive clothes, his horses and his servants and his bank accounts.

He does not. He depends on them, he worries about them, he spends most of his life's energy looking after them; the thought of losing them makes him sick with anxiety. They possess him. He is their slave. In order to procure a quantity of false, perishable goods he has sold the only true, lasting good, his own independence.

5   There have been many men who grew tired of human society with its complications, and went away to live simply—on a small farm, in a quiet village, in a hermit's cave, or in the darkness of anonymity. Not so Diogenes. He was not a recluse, or a stylite, or a beatnik. He was a missionary. His life's aim was clear to him: it was "to restamp the currency." (He and his father had once been convicted for counterfeiting, long before he turned to philosophy, and this phrase was Diogenes' bold, unembarrassed joke on the subject.) To restamp the currency: to take the clean metal of human life, to erase the old false conventional markings, and to imprint it with its true values.

6   The other great philosophers of the fourth century before Christ taught mainly their own private pupils. In the shady groves and cool sanctuaries of the Academy, Plato discoursed to a chosen few on the unreality of this contingent existence. Aristotle, among the books and instruments and specimens and archives and research-workers of his Lyceum, pursued investigations and gave lectures that were rightly named esoteric "for those within the walls." But for Diogenes, laboratory and specimens and lecture halls and pupils were all to be found in a crowd of ordinary people. Therefore he chose to live in Athens or in the rich city of Corinth, where travelers from all over the Mediterranean world constantly came and went. And, by design, he publicly behaved in such ways as to show people what real life was. He would constantly take up their spiritual coin, ring it on a stone, and laugh at its false superscription.

7   He thought most people were only half-alive, most men only half-men. At bright noonday he walked through the market place carrying a lighted lamp and inspecting the face of everyone he met. They asked him why. Diogenes answered, "I am trying to find a man."

8   To a gentleman whose servant was putting on his shoes for him, Diogenes said, "You won't be really happy until he wipes your nose for you: that will come after you lose the use of your hands."

9   Once there was a war scare so serious that it stirred even the lazy, profit happy Corinthians. They began to drill, clean their weapons, and rebuild their neglected fortifications. Diogenes took his old cask and began to roll it up and down, back and forward. "When you are all so busy," he said, "I felt I ought to do something!"

10   And so he lived—like a dog, some said, because he cared nothing for privacy and other human conventions, and because he showed his teeth and barked at those whom he disliked. Now he was lying in the sunlight, as contented as a dog on the warm ground, happier (he himself used to boast) than the Shah of Persia. Although he knew he was going to have an important visitor, he would not move.

11   The little square began to fill with people. Page boys elegantly dressed, spearmen speaking a rough foreign dialect, discreet secretaries, hard-browed

officers, suave diplomats, they all gradually formed a circle centered on Diogenes. He looked them over, as a sober man looks at a crowd of tottering drunks, and shook his head. He knew who they were. They were the attendants of the conqueror of Greece, the servants of Alexander, the Macedonian king, who was visiting his newly subdued realm.

12 Only twenty, Alexander was far older and wiser than his years. Like all Macedonians he loved drinking, but he could usually handle it; and toward women he was nobly restrained and chivalrous. Like all Macedonians he loved fighting; he was a magnificent commander, but he was not merely a military automaton. He could think. At thirteen he had become a pupil of the greatest mind in Greece, Aristotle. No exact record of his schooling survives. It is clear, though, that Aristotle took the passionate, half-barbarous boy and gave him the best of Greek culture. He taught Alexander poetry: the young prince slept with the *Iliad* under his pillow and longed to emulate Achilles, who brought the mighty power of Asia to ruin. He taught him philosophy, in particular the shapes and uses of political power: a few years later Alexander was to create a supranational empire that was not merely a power system but a vehicle for the exchange of Greek and Middle Eastern cultures.

13 Aristotle taught him the principles of scientific research: during his invasion of the Persian domains Alexander took with him a large corps of scientists, and shipped hundreds of zoological specimens back to Greece for study. Indeed, it was from Aristotle that Alexander learned to seek out everything strange which might be instructive. Jugglers and stunt artists and virtuosos of the absurd he dismissed with a shrug; but on reaching India he was to spend hours discussing the problems of life and death with naked Hindu mystics, and later to see one demonstrate Yoga self-command by burning himself impassively to death.

14 Now, Alexander was in Corinth to take command of the League of Greek States which, after conquering them, his father Philip had created as a disguise for the New Macedonian Order. He was welcomed and honored and flattered. He was the man of the hour, of the century: he was unanimously appointed commander-in-chief of a new expedition against old, rich, corrupt Asia. Nearly everyone crowded to Corinth in order to congratulate him, to seek employment with him, even simply to see him: soldiers and statesmen, artists and merchants, poets and philosophers. He received their compliments graciously. Only Diogenes, although he lived in Corinth, did not visit the new monarch. With that generosity which Aristotle had taught him was a quality of the truly magnanimous man, Alexander determined to call upon Diogenes. Surely Diogenes, the God-born, would acknowledge the conqueror's power by some gift of hoarded wisdom.

15 With his handsome face, his fiery glance, his strong supple body, his purple and gold cloak, and his air of destiny, he moved through the parting crowd, toward the Dog's kennel. When a king approaches, all rise in respect. Diogenes did not rise, he merely sat up on one elbow. When a monarch enters a precinct, all greet him with a bow or an acclamation. Diogenes said nothing.

16 There was a silence. Some years later Alexander speared his best friend to the wall, for objecting to the exaggerated honors paid to His Majesty; but now he was still young and civil. He spoke first, with a kindly greeting. Looking at the poor broken cask, the single ragged garment, and the rough figure lying on the ground, he said: "Is there anything I can do for you, Diogenes?"

17 "Yes," said the Dog, "Stand to one side. You're blocking the sunlight."

18 There was silence, not the ominous silence preceding a burst of fury, but a hush of amazement. Slowly, Alexander turned away. A titter broke out from the elegant Greeks, who were already beginning to make jokes about the Cur that looked at the King. The Macedonian officers, after deciding that Diogenes was not worth the trouble of kicking, were starting to guffaw and nudge one another. Alexander was still silent. To those nearest him he said quietly, "If I were not Alexander, I should be Diogenes." They took it as a paradox, designed to close the awkward little scene with a polite curtain line. But Alexander meant it. He understood Cynicism as the others could not. Later he took one of Diogenes' pupils with him to India as a philosophical interpreter (it was he who spoke to the naked *addhus*). He was what Diogenes called himself, a cosmopolités, "citizen of the world." Like Diogenes, he admired the heroic figure of Hercules, the mighty conqueror who labors to help mankind while all others toil and sweat only for themselves. He knew that of all men then alive in the world only Alexander the conqueror and Diogenes the beggar were truly free.

● Vocabulary

expounding (4)   conventions (4)   superfluities (4)
stylite (5)   discoursed (6)   contingent (6)
archives (6)   superscription (6)   suave (11)
supranational (12)   virtuosos (13)

Professor Highet explains the meanings of several words used in the essay. How does he interpret the following?

cynicism (2)   esoteric (6)   Diogenes (14)
cosmopolités (18)

● The Facts

1. What characteristics do Diogenes and Alexander share?
2. In what ways are Diogenes and Alexander different?
3. What is Diogenes's rationale for living so humbly?
4. According to Diogenes, the richer a man is, the more enslaved he becomes. How does he explain this statement?
5. How did the teaching method of Diogenes differ from that of Plato or Aristotle?
6. Paragraph 12 states that Alexander was far older and wiser than his twenty years. How is this maturity indicated?
7. According to the essay, Alexander "understood Cynicism as the others could not." What is Cynicism? Why did Alexander understand it better than others?

The Strategies

1. In what paragraph does the focus shift from Diogenes to Alexander?
2. Does Highet draw his contrast by alternating back and forth between Diogenes and Alexander, or does he first draw a full portrait of Diogenes and then a full portrait of Alexander? What does Highet's method require of the reader?
3. How do you explain the paradox "If I were not Alexander, I should be Diogenes" (paragraph 18)?
4. The opening paragraph contains a sentence characterized by balance and parallelism. What are the opening words of this sentence?
5. What is the literary term for the phrase "to restamp the currency"? What is the meaning?
6. What topic sentence covers paragraphs 7, 8, and 9? How is it developed?

The Issues

1. Which of the two men—Alexander or Diogenes—had a better chance for leading a contented life? Give reasons for your answer.
2. Reread the essay *My Wood* by E. M. Forster, pages 142–145, then make a connection between Alexander's and Diogenes's lives and the essay. Ask yourself which of the two world figures most closely resembles the owner of the wood. Why?
3. Respond to paragraph 2: Do you agree with the idea that man should live naturally and that we have become far too elaborate? Give reasons for your answer.
4. How important are philosophy, poetry, and the principles of scientific investigation—all subjects taught to Alexander by Aristotle—to a modern curriculum? What other subjects, if any, would you add to a balanced curriculum?
5. Which would you prefer to be—a person of power or a person of influence? Be specific in describing yourself, later in life, as having achieved either of these characteristics. What job would you be holding? What kind of family life would you lead?

Suggestions for Writing

1. Write an essay in which you state why you admire Alexander more than Diogenes, or vice versa. Base your essay on the portraits of the two men as drawn by Highet.
2. Choosing one of the pairs listed here, write an essay developed by contrast. Begin with a thesis that summarizes the contrast. Keep in mind the basis of your contrast.
    a. Jealousy/envy
    b. Thoreau/Gandhi
    c. Wisdom/knowledge
    d. Statesman/politician
    e. Old age/youth

Grant and Lee: A Study in Contrasts
BRUCE CATTON

> Bruce Catton (1899–1978) is regarded as one of the most outstanding Civil War historians of the twentieth century. His books include *Mr. Lincoln's Army* (1951), *Glory Road* (1952), *A Stillness at Appomattox* (1953, Pulitzer Prize), and *This Hallowed Ground* (1956).

The following essay contrasts two famous personalities in American Civil War history: Ulysses S. Grant (1822–1885), commander in chief of the Union army and, later, eighteenth president of the United States (1869–1877), and his principal foe in the Civil War, Robert E. Lee (1807–1870), general in chief of the Confederate armies, who surrendered his forces to Grant in April of 1865. The essay illustrates the development of a comparison/contrast between paragraphs, rather than within a paragraph.

• • •

1 When Ulysses S. Grant and Robert E. Lee met in the parlor of a modest house at Appomattox Court House, Virginia, on April 9, 1865, to work out the terms for the surrender of Lee's Army of Northern Virginia, a great chapter in American life came to a close, and a great new chapter began.

2 These men were bringing the Civil War to its virtual finish. To be sure, other armies had yet to surrender, and for a few days the fugitive Confederate government would struggle desperately and vainly, trying to find some way to go on living now that its chief support was gone. But in effect it was all over when Grant and Lee signed the papers. And the little room where they wrote out the terms was the scene of one of the poignant, dramatic contrasts in American history.

3 They were two strong men, these oddly different generals, and they represented the strengths of two conflicting currents that, through them, had come into final collision.

4 Back of Robert E. Lee was the notion that the old aristocratic concept might somehow survive and be dominant in American life.

5 Lee was tidewater Virginia, and in his background were family, culture, and tradition . . . the age of chivalry transplanted to a New World which was making its own legends and its own myths. He embodied a way of life that had come down through the age of knighthood and the English country squire. America was a land that was beginning all over again, dedicated to nothing much more complicated than the rather hazy belief that all men had equal rights and should have an equal chance in the world. In such a land Lee stood for the feeling that it was somehow of advantage to human society to have a pronounced inequality in the social structure. There should be a leisure class, backed by ownership of land; in turn, society itself should be keyed to the land as the chief source of wealth and influence. It would bring forth (according to this ideal) a class of men with a strong sense of obligation to the community; men who lived not to gain advantage for themselves, but to meet the solemn

obligations which had been laid on them by the very fact that they were privileged. From them the country would get its leadership; to them it could look for the higher values—of thought, of conduct, of personal deportment—to give it strength and virtue.

6   Lee embodied the noblest elements of this aristocratic ideal. Through him, the landed nobility justified itself. For four years, the Southern states had fought a desperate war to uphold the ideals for which Lee stood. In the end, it almost seemed as if the Confederacy fought for Lee; as if he himself was the Confederacy . . . the best thing that the way of life for which the Confederacy stood could ever have to offer. He had passed into legend before Appomattox. Thousands of tired, underfed, poorly clothed Confederate soldiers, long since past the simple enthusiasm of the early days of the struggle, somehow considered Lee the symbol of everything for which they had been willing to die. But they could not quite put this feeling into words. If the Lost Cause, sanctified by so much heroism and so many deaths, had a living justification, its justification was General Lee.

7   Grant, the son of a tanner on the Western frontier, was everything Lee was not. He had come up the hard way and embodied nothing in particular except the eternal toughness and sinewy fiber of the men who grew up beyond the mountains. He was one of a body of men who owed reverence and obeisance to no one, who were self-reliant to a fault, who cared hardly anything for the past but who had a sharp eye for the future.

8   These frontier men were the precise opposites of the tidewater aristocrats. Back of them, in the great surge that had taken people over the Alleghenies and into the opening Western country, there was a deep, implicit dissatisfaction with a past that had settled into grooves. They stood for democracy, not from any reasoned conclusion about the proper ordering of human society, but simply because they had grown up in the middle of democracy and knew how it worked. Their society might have privileges, but they would be privileges each man had won for himself. Forms and patterns meant nothing. No man was born to anything, except perhaps to a chance to show how far he could rise. Life was competition.

9   Yet along with this feeling had come a deep sense of belonging to a national community. The Westerner who developed a farm, opened a shop, or set up in business as a trader, could hope to prosper only as his own community prospered—and his community ran from the Atlantic to the Pacific and from Canada down to Mexico. If the land was settled, with towns and highways and accessible markets, he could better himself. He saw his fate in terms of the nation's own destiny. As its horizons expanded, so did his. He had, in other words, an acute dollars-and-cents stake in the continued growth and development of his country.

10   And that, perhaps, is where the contrast between Grant and Lee becomes most striking. The Virginia aristocrat, inevitably, saw himself in relation to his own region. He lived in a static society which could endure almost anything except change. Instinctively, his first loyalty would go to the locality in which that society existed. He would fight to the limit of endurance to defend it,

because in defending it he was defending everything that gave his own life its deepest meaning.

11   The Westerner, on the other hand, would fight with an equal tenacity for the broader concept of society. He fought so because everything he lived by was tied to growth, expansion, and a constantly widening horizon. What he lived by would survive or fall with the nation itself. He could not possibly stand by unmoved in the face of an attempt to destroy the Union. He would combat it with everything he had, because he could only see it as an effort to cut the ground out from under his feet.

12   So Grant and Lee were in complete contrast, representing two diametrically opposed elements in American life. Grant was the modern man emerging; beyond him, ready to come on the stage, was the great age of steel and machinery, of crowded cities and a restless, burgeoning vitality. Lee might have ridden down from the old age of chivalry, lance in hand, silken banner fluttering over his head. Each man was the perfect champion of his cause, drawing both his strengths and his weaknesses from the people he led.

13   Yet it was not all contrast, after all. Different as they were—in background, in personality, in underlying aspiration—these two great soldiers had much in common. Under everything else, they were marvelous fighters. Furthermore, their fighting qualities were really very much alike.

14   Each man had, to begin with, the great virtue of utter tenacity and fidelity. Grant fought his way down the Mississippi Valley in spite of acute personal discouragement and profound military handicaps. Lee hung on in the trenches at Petersburg after hope itself had died. In each man there was an indomitable quality . . . the born fighter's refusal to give up as long as he can still remain on his feet and lift his two fists.

15   Daring and resourcefulness they had, too; the ability to think faster and move faster than the enemy. These were the qualities which gave Lee the dazzling campaigns of Second Manassas and Chancellorsville and won Vicksburg for Grant.

16   Lastly, and perhaps greatest of all, there was the ability, at the end, to turn quickly from war to peace once the fighting was over. Out of the way these two men behaved at Appomattox came the possibility of a peace of reconciliation. It was a possibility not wholly realized, in the years to come, but which did, in the end, help the two sections to become one nation again . . . after a war whose bitterness might have seemed to make such a reunion wholly impossible. No part of either man's life became him more than the part he played in their brief meeting in the McLean house at Appomattox. Their behavior there put all succeeding generations of Americans in their debt. Two great Americans, Grant and Lee—very different, yet under everything very much alike. Their encounter at Appomattox was one of the great moments of American history.

• Vocabulary

poignant (2)
sanctified (6)
diametrically (12)
deportment (5)
obeisance (7)
burgeoning (12)
embodied (6)
tenacity (11)

The Facts

1. What was Lee's background? What ideal did he represent?
2. What was Grant's background? What did he represent?
3. What was Grant's view of the past? What was his attitude toward society and democracy?
4. What was the most striking contrast between Grant and Lee?
5. Catton writes that the behavior of Grant and Lee at Appomattox "put all succeeding generations of Americans in their debt" (paragraph 16). Why?

The Strategies

1. Although the article is entitled *Grant and Lee: A Study in Contrasts,* Catton begins by examining what Lee represented. Why? What logic is there to his order?
2. What function does paragraph 4 serve? Why is this one sentence set off in a separate paragraph?
3. What common contrast phrase does paragraph 11 use?
4. In paragraph 8, the author writes: "These frontier men were the precise opposites of the tidewater aristocrats." What do these types have to do with a contrast between Grant and Lee?
5. What function does paragraph 8 serve?

The Issues

1. Does an aristocracy still survive in our multicultural United States? If you believe it has survived, describe what and where it is. If you believe it has vanished, then describe what has taken its place.
2. Which kind of citizen do you admire most—the aristocrat or the frontiersman? Which do you believe is needed most for the betterment of our society today? Give reasons for your answers.
3. The aristocrat believes in form and tradition. How important are these ideas, in your view? Which traditions would you be willing to part with? Which would you want to keep?
4. What two women from history present an interesting contrast in two cultures? Describe both women and their contrasting cultures.
5. Which US president, besides Ulysses S. Grant, is known for his support of economic growth and expansion? Do you favor continued growth and expansion, or are there other values you cherish more?

Suggestions for Writing

1. Examine and analyze the organization of the contrast in this essay. In what various respects are Grant and Lee contrasted? How does Catton order and structure his contrast?

2. Discuss the idea that a society can benefit from the presence of a privileged class. Or, conversely, take the position that a society can benefit from the presence of an underprivileged class.

Baba and Me
Khaled Hosseini

Khaled Hosseini (b. 1965) became an international sensation with the publication of his first novel, *The Kite Runner* (2003), from which this reading comes. Although the author contends that the novel is pure fiction, the reader cannot help but wonder if Hosseini's youth, lived in Afghanistan, did not imprint itself on this story. Hosseini was born in Kabul, Afghanistan, the oldest of five children. His mother taught Farsi and history at a large girls' high school in Kabul. In 1976, Hosseini's family was relocated to Paris, France, where his father was assigned a diplomatic post in the Afghan embassy. The assignment would have returned the Hosseini family to Afghanistan in 1980, but by then the country had already witnessed the bloody communist coup and the Soviet invasion. Thus, the Hosseini family asked for and was granted political asylum in the United States, where Khaled Hosseini eventually graduated from the UC San Diego School of Medicine. He has been in practice as an internist since 1996. His reading audience eagerly anticipates his next novel.

As you read the narrator's comparison of his father and himself, you might reflect on your own father to see how you were influenced by him, what kind of image he left on your consciousness and in what vital ways he shaped your character.

• • •

1   Lore has it my father once wrestled a black bear in Baluchistan with his bare hands. If the story had been about anyone else, it would have been dismissed as *laaf*, that Afghan tendency to exaggerate—sadly, almost a national affliction; if someone bragged that his son was a doctor, chances were the kid had once passed a biology test in high school. But no one ever doubted the veracity of any story about Baba. And if they did, well, Baba did have those three parallel scars coursing a jagged path down his back. I have imagined Baba's wrestling match countless times, even dreamed about it. And in those dreams, I can never tell Baba from the bear.

2   It was Rahim Khan who first referred to him as what eventually became Baba's famous nickname, *Toophan agha,* or "Mr. Hurricane." It was an apt enough nickname. My father was a force of nature, a towering Pashtun specimen with a thick beard, a wayward crop of curly brown hair as unruly as the man himself, hands that looked capable of uprooting a willow tree, and a black glare that would "drop the devil to his knees begging for mercy," as Rahim Khan used to say. At parties, when all six-foot-five of him thundered into the room, attention shifted to him like sunflowers turning to the sun.

3   Baba was impossible to ignore, even in his sleep. I used to bury cotton wisps in my ears, pull the blanket over my head, and still the sounds of Baba's snoring—so much like a growling truck engine—penetrated the walls. And my room was across the hall from Baba's bedroom. How my mother ever managed to sleep in the same room as him is a mystery to me. It's on the long list of things I would have asked my mother if I had ever met her.

4   In the late 1960s, when I was five or six, Baba decided to build an orphanage. I heard the story through Rahim Kahn. He told me Baba had drawn the blueprints himself despite the fact that he'd had no architectural experience at all. Skeptics had urged him to stop his foolishness and hire an architect. Of course, Baba refused, and everyone shook their heads in dismay at his obstinate ways. Then Baba succeeded and everyone shook their heads in awe at his triumphant ways. Baba paid for the construction of the two-story orphanage, just off the main strip of Jadeh Maywand south of the Kabul river, with his own money. Rahim Kahn told me Baba had personally funded the entire project, paying for the engineers, electricians, plumbers, and laborers, not to mention the city officials whose "mustaches needed oiling."

It took three years to build the orphanage. I was eight by then. I remember the day before the orphanage opened, Baba took me to Ghargha Lake, a few miles north of Kabul. He asked me to fetch Hassan too, but I lied and told him Hassan had the runs. I wanted Baba all to myself. And besides, one time at Ghargha Lake, Hassan and I were skimming stones and Hassan made his stone skip eight times. The most I managed was five. Baba was there, watching, and he patted Hassan on the back. Even put his arm around his shoulder.

5   We sat at a picnic table on the banks of the lake, just Baba and me, eating boiled eggs with *kofta* sandwiches—meatballs and pickles wrapped in *naan*. The water was a deep blue and sunlight glittered on its looking glass-clear surface. On Fridays, the lake was bustling with families out for a day in the sun. But it was mid-week and there was only Baba and me, us and a couple of long-haired, bearded tourists—"hippies," I'd heard them called. They were sitting on the dock, feet dangling in the water, fishing poles in hand. I asked Baba why they grew their hair long, but Baba grunted, didn't answer. He was preparing his speech for the next day, flipping through a havoc of handwritten pages, making notes here and there with a pencil. I bit into my egg and asked Baba if it was true what a boy in school had told me, that if you ate a piece of eggshell, you'd have to pee it out. Baba grunted again.

6   I took a bite of my sandwich. One of the yellow-haired tourists laughed and slapped the other one on the back. In the distance, across the lake, a truck lumbered around a corner on the hill. Sunlight twinkled in its side-view mirror.

7   "I think I have *saratan*," I said. Cancer. Baba lifted his head from the pages flapping in the breeze. Told me I could get the soda myself, all I had to do was look in the trunk of the car.

8   Outside the orphanage, the next day, they ran out of chairs. A lot of people had to stand to watch the opening ceremony. It was a windy day, and I sat behind Baba on the little podium just outside the main entrance of the new building. Baba was wearing a green suit and a caracul hat. Midway through the

speech, the wind knocked his hat off and everyone laughed. He motioned to me to hold his hat for him and I was glad to, because then everyone would see that he was *my* father, *my* Baba. He turned back to the microphone and said he hoped the building was sturdier than his hat, and everyone laughed again. When Baba ended his speech, people stood up and cheered. They clapped for a long time. Afterward, people shook his hand. Some of them tousled my hair and shook my hand too. I was so proud of Baba, of us.

9   But despite Baba's successes, people were always doubting him. They told Baba that running a business wasn't in his blood and he should study law like his father. So Baba proved them all wrong by not only running his own business but becoming one of the richest merchants in Kabul. Baba and Rahim Khan built a wildly successful carpet-exporting business, two pharmacies, and a restaurant.

10   When people scoffed that Baba would never marry well—after all, he was not of royal blood—he wedded my mother, Sofia Akrami, a highly educated woman universally regarded as one of Kabul's most respected, beautiful, and virtuous ladies. And not only did she teach classic Farsi literature at the university, she was a descendant of the royal family, a fact that my father playfully rubbed in the skeptics' faces by referring to her as "my princess."

11   With me as the glaring exception, my father molded the world around him to his liking. The problem, of course, was that Baba saw the world in black and white. And he got to decide what was black and what was white. You can't love a person who lives that way without fearing him too. Maybe even hating him a little.

12   When I was in fifth grade, we had a mullah who taught us about Islam. His name was Mullah Fatiullah Khan, a short, stubby man with a face full of acne scars and a gruff voice. He lectured us about the virtues of *zakat* and the duty of *hadj*, he taught us the intricacies of performing the five daily *namaz* prayers, and made us memorize verses from the Koran—and though he never translated the words for us, he did stress, sometimes with the help of a stripped willow branch; that we had to pronounce the Arabic words correctly so God would hear us better. He told us one day that Islam considered drinking a terrible sin; those who drank would answer for their sin on the day of *Qiyamat*, Judgment Day. In those days, drinking was fairly common in Kabul. No one gave you a public lashing for it, but those Afghans who did drink did so in private, out of respect. People bought their scotch as "medicine" in brown paper bags from selected "pharmacies." They would leave with the bag tucked out of sight, sometimes drawing furtive, disapproving glances from those who knew about the store's reputation for such transactions.

13   We were upstairs in Baba's study, the smoking room, when I told him what Mullah Fatiullah Khan had taught us in class. Baba was pouring himself a whiskey from the bar he had built in the corner of the room. He listened, nodded, took a sip from his drink. Then he lowered himself into the leather sofa, put down his drink, and propped me up on his lap. I felt as if I were sitting on a pair of tree trunks. He took a deep breath and exhaled through his nose, the air hissing through his mustache for what seemed an

444 CHAPTER 12 • Comparison/Contrast

eternity. I couldn't decide whether I wanted to hug him or leap from his lap in mortal fear.

14. "I see you've confused what you're learning in school with actual education," he said in his thick voice.

15. "But if what he said is true then does it make you a sinner, Baba?"

16. "Hmm." Baba crushed an ice cube between his teeth. "Do you want to know what your father thinks about sin?"

17. "Yes."

18. "Then I'll tell you," Baba said, "but first understand this and understand it now, Amir: You'll never learn anything of value from those bearded idiots."

19. "You mean Mullah Fatiullah Khan?"

20. Baba gestured with his glass. The ice clinked. "I mean all of them. Piss on the beards of all those self-righteous monkeys."

21. I began to giggle. The image of Baba pissing on the beard of any monkey, self-righteous or otherwise, was too much.

22. "They do nothing but thumb their prayer beads and recite a book written in a tongue they don't even understand." He took a sip. "God help us all if Afghanistan ever falls into their hands."

23. "But Mullah Fatiullah Khan seems nice," I managed between bursts of tittering.

24. "So did Genghis Khan," Baba said. "But enough about that. You asked about sin and I want to tell you. Are you listening?"

25. "Yes," I said, pressing my lips together. But a chortle escaped through my nose and made a snorting sound. That got me giggling again.

26. Baba's stony eyes bore into mine and, just like that, I wasn't laughing anymore. "I mean to speak to you man to man. Do you think you can handle that for once?"

27. "Yes, Baba jan," I muttered, marveling, not for the first time, at how badly Baba could sting me with so few words. We'd had a fleeting good moment—it wasn't often Baba talked to me, let alone on his lap—and I'd been a fool to waste it.

28. "Good," Baba said, but his eyes wondered. "Now, no matter what the mullah teaches, there is only one sin, only one. And that is theft. Every other sin is a variation of theft. Do you understand that?"

29. "No, Baba jan," I said, desperately wishing I did. I didn't want to disappoint him again.

30. Baba heaved a sigh of impatience. That stung too, because he was not an impatient man. I remembered all the times he didn't come home until after dark, all the times I ate dinner alone I'd ask Ali where Baba was, when he was coming home, though I knew full well he was at the construction site, overlooking this, supervising that. Didn't that take patience? I already hated all the kids he was building the orphanage for; sometimes I wished they'd all died along with their parents.

31. "When you kill a man, you steal a life," Baba said. "You steal his wife's right to a husband, rob his children of a father. When you tell a lie, you steal someone's right to the truth. When you cheat, you steal the right to fairness. Do you see?"

32   I did. When Baba was six, a thief walked into my grandfather's house in the middle of the night. My grandfather, a respected judge, confronted him, but the thief stabbed him in the throat, killing him instantly—and robbing Baba of a father. The townspeople caught the killer just before noon the next day; he turned out to be a wanderer from the Kunduz region. They hanged him from the branch of an oak tree with still two hours to go before afternoon prayer. It was Rahim Khan, not Baba, who had told me that story. I was always learning things about Baba from other people.

33   "There is no act more wretched than stealing, Amir," Baba said. "A man who takes what's not his to take, be it a life or a loaf of *naan* . . . I spit on such a man. And if I ever cross paths with him, God help him. Do you understand?"

34   I found the idea of Baba clobbering a thief both exhilarating and terribly frightening. "Yes, Baba."

35   "If there's a God out there, then I would hope he has more important things to attend to than my drinking scotch or eating pork. Now, hop down. All this talk about sin has made me thirsty again."

36   I watched him fill his glass at the bar and wondered how much time would pass before we talked again the way we just had. Because the truth of it was, I always felt like Baba hated me a little. And why not? After all, I *had* killed his beloved wife, his beautiful princess, hadn't I? The least I could have done was to have had the decency to have turned out a little more like him. But I hadn't turned out like him. Not at all.

37   In school, we used to play a game called *Sherjangi*, or "Battle of the Poems." The Farsi teacher moderated it and it went something like this: You recited a verse from a poem and your opponent had sixty seconds to reply with a verse that began with the same letter that ended yours. Everyone in my class wanted me on their team, because by the time I was eleven, I could recite dozens of verses from Khayyám, Hāfez, or Rumi's famous *Masnawi*. One time, I took on the whole class and won. I told Baba about it later that night, but he just nodded, muttered, "Good."

38   That was how I escaped my father's aloofness, in my dead mother's books. That and Hassan, of course. I read everything, Rumi, Hāfez, Saadi, Victor Hugo, Jules Verne, Mark Twain, Ian Fleming. When I had finished my mother's books—not the boring history ones, I was never much into those, but the novels, the epics—I started spending my allowance on books. I bought one a week from the bookstore near Cinema Park, and stored them in cardboard boxes when I ran out of shelf room.

39   Of course, marrying a poet was one thing, but fathering a son who preferred burying his face in poetry books to hunting . . . well, that wasn't how Baba had envisioned it, I suppose. Real men didn't read poetry—and God forbid they should ever write it! Real men—real boys—played soccer just as Baba had when he had been young. Now *that* was something to be passionate about. In 1970, Baba took a break from the construction of the orphanage and flew to Tehran for a month to watch the World Cup games on television, since at the time Afghanistan didn't have TVs yet. He signed me up for soccer teams to stir the same passion in me. But I was pathetic, a blundering liability

to my own team, always in the way of an opportune pass or unwittingly blocking an open lane. I shambled about the field on scraggy legs, squalled for passes that never came my way. And the harder I tried, waving my arms over my head frantically and screeching, "I'm open! I'm open!" the more I went ignored. But Baba wouldn't give up. When it became abundantly clear that I hadn't inherited a shred of his athletic talents, he settled for trying to turn me into a passionate spectator. Certainly I could manage that, couldn't I? I faked interest for as long as possible. I cheered with him when Kabul's team scored against Kandahar and yelped insults at the referee when he called a penalty against our team. But Baba sensed my lack of genuine interest and resigned himself to the bleak fact that his son was never going to either play or watch soccer.

40 I remember one time Baba took me to the yearly *Buzkashi* tournament that took place on the first day of spring, New Year's Day. Buzkashi was, and still is, Afghanistan's national passion. A *chapandaz*, a highly skilled horseman usually patronized by rich aficionados, has to snatch a goat or cattle carcass from the midst of a melee, carry that carcass with him around the stadium at full gallop, and drop it in a scoring circle while a team of other *chapandaz* chases him and does everything in its power—kick, claw, whip, punch—to snatch the carcass from him. That day, the crowd roared with excitement as the horsemen on the field bellowed their battle cries and jostled for the carcass in a cloud of dust. The earth trembled with the clatter of hooves. We watched from the upper bleachers as riders pounded past us at full gallop, yipping and yelling, foam flying from their horses' mouths.

41 At one point Baba pointed to someone. "Amir, do you see that man sitting up there with those other men around him?"

42 I did.

43 "That's Henry Kissinger."

44 "Oh," I said. I didn't know who Henry Kissinger was, and I might have asked. But at the moment, I watched with horror as one of the *chapandaz* fell off his saddle and was trampled under a score of hooves. His body was tossed and hurled in the stampede like a rag doll, finally rolling to a stop when the melee moved on. He twitched once and lay motionless, his legs bent at unnatural angles, a pool of his blood soaking through the sand.

45 I began to cry.

46 I cried all the way back home. I remember how Baba's hands clenched around the steering wheel. Clenched and unclenched. Mostly, I will never forget Baba's valiant efforts to conceal the disgusted look on his face as he drove in silence.

47 Later that night, I was passing by my father's study when I overheard him speaking to Rahim Khan. I pressed my ear to the closed door.

48 "—grateful that he's healthy," Rahim Khan was saying.

49 "I know, I know. But he's always buried in those books or shuffling around the house like he's lost in some dream."

50 "And?"

51 "I wasn't like that." Baba sounded frustrated, almost angry.

52 Rahim Khan laughed. "Children aren't coloring books. You don't get to fill them with your favorite colors."

53 "I'm telling you," Baba said, "I wasn't like that at all, and neither were any of the kids I grew up with."

54 "You know, sometimes you are the most self-centered man I know," Rahim Khan said. He was the only person I knew who could get away with saying something like that to Baba.

55 "It has nothing to do with that."

56 "Nay?"

57 "Nay."

58 "Then what?"

59 I heard the leather of Baba's seat creaking as he shifted on it. I closed my eyes, pressed my ear even harder against the door, wanting to hear, not wanting to hear. "Sometimes I look out this window and I see him playing on the street with the neighborhood boys. I see how they push him around, take his toys from him, give him a shove here, a whack there. And, you know, he never fights back. Never. He just . . . drops his head and . . ."

60 "So he's not violent," Rahim Khan said.

61 "That's not what I mean, Rahim, and you know it," Baba shot back. "There is something missing in that boy."

62 "Yes, a mean streak."

63 "Self-defense has nothing to do with meanness. You know what always happens when the neighborhood boys tease him? Hassan steps in and fends them off. I've seen it with my own eyes. And when they come home, I say to him, 'How did Hassan get that scrape on his face?' And he says, 'He fell down.' I'm telling you, Rahim, there is something missing in that boy."

64 "You just need to let him find his way," Rahim Khan said.

65 "And where is he headed?" Baba said. "A boy who won't stand up for himself becomes a man who can't stand up to anything."

66 "As usual you're oversimplifying."

67 "I don't think so."

68 "You're angry because you're afraid he'll never take over the business for you."

69 "Now who's oversimplifying?" Baba said. "look, I know there's a fondness between you and him and I'm happy about that. Envious, but happy. I mean that. He needs someone who . . . understands him, because God knows I don't. But something about Amir troubles me in a way that I can't express. It's like . . ." I could see him searching, reaching for the right words. He lowered his voice, but I heard him anyway. "If I hadn't seen the doctor pull him out of my wife with my own eyes, I'd never believe he's my son."

70 The next morning, as he was preparing my breakfast, Hassan asked if something was bothering me. I snapped at him, told him to mind his own business.

71 Rahim Khan had been wrong about the mean streak thing.

Vocabulary

lore (1)	penetrated (3)	skeptics (4)
obstinate (4)	lumbered (6)	caracul (7)
virtuous (8)	mullah (10)	intricacies (10)
furtive (10)	mortal (11)	chortle (23)
exhilarating (32)	moderated (35)	opportune (37)
shambled (37)	squalled (37)	aficionados (38)
bellowed (38)	melee (42)	valiant (44)

The Facts

1. What is the lore circulating about the narrator's father? What does this lore establish immediately? Do you believe it? Of what other famous story does it remind you?
2. What happened to the narrator's mother? What bearing does this fact have on the relationship between son and father?
3. What characteristics, in addition to being athletic and physically powerful, describe Baba? What is Amir's reaction to his father?
4. According to Baba, what is the most hideous sin in life? What standard does Baba use to evaluate this sin? Do you agree with him? What do you consider the worst sin on earth?
5. What excuse for drinking, despite the Koran's admonition against it, does Baba give? To what extent do you agree with Baba?
6. To whom does Baba confide his feelings about Amir? How do you know that Amir knows how his father feels about his lack of athletic ability? How typical is Baba's attitude toward his son? What is the source of Amir's love of poetry and books?
7. Why is Baba so frustrated about Amir's approach to life? Does this frustration seem justified? Explain your answer.

The Strategies

1. Which paragraph best describes Baba's sense of obligation and selfless generosity to his country? Who explains to Amir how outstanding his father is? Is this an accurate source to describe Baba's reputation?
2. What is the meaning of the figure of speech "mustaches needed oiling"?
3. What does the reference to "hippies" contribute to the narration? What reference later on makes the same contribution?
4. Why are paragraphs 52 through 56 so short?
5. What figures of speech are found throughout the essay? Point out two that captured your attention. What do these figures of speech add to the essay?

Stumped by rhetorical questions? Exit on page 689, at the **Editing Booth!**

The Issues

1. What is the essential theme of this narration? What is the story about? Try to formulate the theme in one sentence.
2. How do you know that Baba is a passionate patriot? Point to specific places in the story that reveal his concern for civic duties.
3. How does Baba's orphanage affect Amir's relationship with his father? What are some specific results?
4. Why is Baba so passionate about the sin of stealing? What is revealed in the narrative that gives a clue to his passion?
5. What is Baba's opinion of the mullahs, which eventually formed the Taliban in Afghanistan? What about them is particularly disgusting to Baba? Do you think he was justified in his attitude?

Suggestions for Writing

1. Write an essay in which you contrast a son and his father who are thoroughly different one from the other. Begin your contrast by stating the overall difference, such as, "Ben's father is determined to control his entire family and does not allow Ben to make any major decisions on his own." Then establish the bases of the contrast, considering such aspects as looks, hobbies, educational level, attitude toward money, and capacity for affection.
2. Write an essay in which you contrast yourself with one of your closest friends. Be sure to state an overall contrast and to choose three or four bases of contrast. Use vivid details that will increase the appeal of your essay.

ISSUE FOR CRITICAL THINKING AND DEBATE: THE EXISTENCE OF GOD

"God is dead. Nietzsche," wrote some unknown wit on a bathroom wall, to which another unknown writer replied, "Nietzsche is dead. God." As an example of the everyday debate that has long raged about the existence of God, this exchange is a classic. Yet, what Friedrich Nietzsche, the German philosopher, actually wrote was considerably more complex: "God is dead, but considering the state species Man is in, there will perhaps be caves, for ages yet, in which his shadow will be shown." The shorthand version of what Nietzsche actually said is perhaps catchier, but the fuller version is a more accurate summation about the condition of God among modern thinkers. Even today, and not only in caves, the shadow of God is everywhere around us. God may or may not be dead, but the argument about his alleged death is very much alive.

Of all the questions we ask about our world, none is more profound than "Does God exist?" Every generation asks this question anew and answers it in its own way. Every generation has its own attitudes and its own relationship with the concept of a divinity. But one truth is constant: Wherever human beings have made history, they have talked about or written about God. Rare indeed is

- Why is a connection with God through prayer still an important spiritual refuge for many Americans?

the mythology that does not contain some story of creation, of the origin of evil, and of an ultimate power ruling the universe and directing its destiny.

The variations of belief or nonbelief in God are also staggering. Some highly educated people base their faith on a simple acceptance of the four biblical Gospels. Others base complex beliefs on astronomical numbers, Cabalistic mysteries, or prophetic interpretations. Some people who think themselves moral are staunch atheists, whereas others who profess to be religious behave in ways that strike many of us as immoral. Some people follow the teachings of Jesus, some of Buddha, some of Mohammed, and some of latterday prophets like Scientology's L. Ron Hubbard. Still others search for God in nature, in mystery, or in coincidence and tea leaves.

Regardless of who we are, all of us occasionally experience a twinge of wonder about where we came from, about who made our world, and where it and we are headed. It also mystifies us to contemplate that so far, in peering out with gigantic telescopes into the endless expanse of space, we still have not found any evidence of other civilizations. The speculations and beliefs go on as they have throughout the ages, with many of us—believers or nonbelievers—hovering between acceptance of an all-powerful, all-knowing, and ever-present force—God—and the aloneness of believing in a Godless universe in which we make our own destiny. Whether or not there is a God is a question that lies at the core of our being.

This chapter offers two viewpoints on whether or not God exists. First, there is a reasoned sermon from a minister of religion in which he gives ten reasons for believing in immortality and therefore in God. This is followed by a systematic listing by a secular humanist of quotations by the famous who denied that God existed. In the Student Corner, a student writer weighs in with his own opinion about the existence of God.

Ten Reasons for Believing in Immortality
JOHN HAYNES HOLMES

John Haynes Holmes (1897–1964) was an American minister and social activist, known for fearlessly defending many controversial causes, including pacifism and civil liberties for all. He was a prolific writer who wrote twenty books, including *Religion for Today* (1917), *My Gandhi* (1953), *The Collected Hymns of John Haynes Holmes* (1960), and an autobiography, *I Speak for Myself* (1959).

• • •

1   Nobody can speak on the immortality of the soul at this late date without being acutely conscious of the fact that there is nothing new that can be said. Since the time of Plato, at least, five hundred years before the birth of Jesus, the discussion of immortality has been conducted by the greatest minds upon the highest levels of human thought. Theology, philosophy, psychology and science have all been called upon to make their contributions to the theme. Poetry has offered its voice and religion its faith, with the result that every corner of knowledge has been explored, every depth of truth uncovered and revealed! There is always the possibility, of course, that the veil which hangs over every grave to divide this life from the mystery that lies beyond, may some day be lifted to our gaze. There are those who claim—not without some reason, it seems to me—that they have penetrated this veil, and thus have looked upon the reality of survival after death. But short of some such remarkable discovery as this, there is nothing new to be anticipated in this field. Everything has been said that can be said. The case for immortality is in!

2   Now it is this case which I want to present to you this morning. Since I cannot hope to say anything that is new, I want to see what I can do in the way of saying something that is old. I cannot say much, to be sure, for no discourse however merciless in length, can compass the range and beauty of the argument for immortality. But since ten is a goodly number, I take ten of the reasons which have brought conviction to the minds of men and offer these as the case for immortality today. I trust that it may be interesting, and also persuasive, especially to the members of our younger generation, to be reminded of what has been thought upon this question for many years.

3   By way of introduction, may I make mention of some two or three reasons for believing in immortality which do not concern me. I speak of these not

because they are important, but because some of you may wonder, if I am silent, why they do not appear in my list of ten.

4   Thus I do not see any reason for believing in immortality because Jesus is reputed to have risen from the dead. In the first place, I do not believe that he rose from the dead. There is no evidence to substantiate this miracle. In the second place, even if he did break the barriers of the tomb, I fail to see what the resurrection of the body has to do with the immortality of the soul. The two things are irrelevant, the one to the other. What we have here is one of the myths of Christianity which, even if it were true, would have nothing seriously to do with our question.

5   Again, I find no argument for immortality in the succession of the seasons, the revival of nature of the spring, the blossoming of the flowers after the winter's cold. Poets are fond of this idea, as Shelley, for example, when he wrote his famous line,

6   If winter comes, can spring be far behind?

7   I think we may see in it a pretty parable, a rather beautiful poetic concept.

8   But as an argument for immortality, it is what Ruskin called an instance of the "pathetic fallacy." The flowers that blossom in the spring are not the flowers that died the preceding autumn. The tide of life that flows on through nature, season after season, is the tide that flows on through humanity, generation after generation, and it touches as little in the one case as in the other the survival of the individual. Like most parables, this does not hold when applied rigorously to the issue that is involved.

9   Again, I must confess that I am not convinced by the argument that men must be immortal because the heart demands it. It is natural that we should cling to those we love. It is inevitable that we should believe that providence, if it be beneficent, must give answer to our plea that we have not permanently separated from our friends and kindred. Whittier was yielding to the deepest impulses of the soul when he suggested in his "Snow Bound" that "Life is ever Lord of Death," because "Love can never lose its own." This is the cry of the human heart, and I personally believe that it is not destined to go unanswered. But a longing is one thing, and a reason is another. I see no evidence, in the scheme of things, that what we want we are therefore going to have. On the contrary, Felix Adler has taught us that frustration is the basic principle of life, that experience is "permeated with the sense of incompleteness," and that this "sense of incompleteness" is a perpetual doom that is laid upon us as "a necessary instrument of spiritual development." Whether this be true or not I do not know, but in either case I still believe that love gives no guarantee of its own survival.

10   But there are arguments for immortality which seem to suggest that it is true. Surveying all the field, I find myself agreeing with William James that, while we are under no compulsion to believe in immortality, as we are under a compulsion, for example, to believe that "things equal to the same thing are equal to each other," yet we are free to believe, if we so desire, without being guilty of superstition. "You may believe henceforward;" said Professor James,

"whether you care to profit by the permission or not." There are perfectly good and sufficient reasons, in other words, why an intelligent man may intelligently believe in immortality. Ten of these reasons I propose to submit to you this morning, beginning with those which open up the question, so to speak, and ending with those which close it as a conviction of the soul.

11 (1) First of all, may I offer the suggestion, not important in itself and yet of real significance to the thinking mind, that we may believe in immortality because there is no reason for not believing in it. In discussions of this question we are constantly reminded that immortality has never been proved. To which there is the immediate and inevitable reply that immortality has never been disproved! As there is no positive testimony to prove it true, so is there no negative testimony to prove it untrue. What we have here is an absence of testimony, and such "absence of testimony," says John Fiske, "does not even raise a negative presumption, except in cases where testimony is accessible." In this case, testimony is not accessible. Therefore the question is open "for those general considerations of philosophic analogy and moral probability which are the grounds upon which we can call for help in this arduous inquiry." As the question is open, so must our minds be open. My first reason, therefore, for believing in immortality or for being ready to believe in immortality, is the primarily interesting fact that there is no reason for not believing in immortality. My mind is absolutely at one with that of John Stuart Mill when he said upon this question, "To anyone who feels it conducive either to his satisfaction or to his usefulness to hope for a future state, . . . there is no hindrance to his indulging that hope."

12 (2) My second reason for believing in immortality is to be found in the universality of the idea. In saying this, I am not seeking to substantiate my position by taking a majority vote upon the question. I am not arguing that a proposition is necessarily true because most persons have believed it. All too many beliefs have clung pertinaciously to the human mind, only in the end to be revealed as superstitions, and it may very well be that this concept of immortality is one of them.

13 What I have in mind here is the very different consideration that immortality is not merely a belief to be accepted but an idea to be explained. "Here is this wonderful thought," says Emerson, "Wherever man ripens, this audacious belief presently appears. . . . As soon as thought is exercised, this belief is inevitable. . . . Whence came it? Who put it in the mind?" In itself it is remarkable, this idea that the death of the body is not the extinction of personality. Who has ever looked upon a dead body without marveling that man has ever thought of survival beyond the grave? Emerson could not explain the fact, as it has appeared in all ages and among all peoples, except upon the supposition that the thought of immortality is "not sentimental" but "elemental"—elemental in the sense that it is "grounded in the necessities and forces we possess."

14 That this idea is something more than idle speculation is shown by the whole philosophy of evolution, which has given to us that fundamental interpretation of life as "the continuous adjustment of inner relations to outer

relations." An organism lives by successfully adjusting itself to the conditions of its environment, by developing itself inwardly in such a way as to meet the conditions of reality. When we find in plant or animal some inner faculty or attitude which is universally present, and which persists from generation to generation, we may be perfectly sure that it represents some correspondence with reality which has made survival possible. Life, in other words, is so definitely a matter of the successful coordination of inner relations with outer relations, that it is altogether impossible to conceive that in any specific relation the subjective term is real and the objective term is non-existent. What exists within is the sign and symbol, and guarantee, of what exists without.

15   Now man has never existed without the thought of immortality. From the earliest period of his life upon the earth, he has been profoundly concerned with this idea. He has never been able to live without it; even when he has tried to deny it, he has not been able to get rid of it. The immortal life is part of his being, as a line on the surface of a coin is a part of the pattern of its design. And as the line upon the coin could not have been set there except as the impression of the die which stamped its mark upon the metal, so the idea of immortality could not have appeared within the consciousness of man, except as the impression of the reality which made it what it is. Our faculties, our attributes, our ideas, as we have seen, are the reflection of the environment to which we adapt ourselves as the condition of survival. What we feel within is the reaction upon what exists without. As the eye proves the existence of light, and the ear the existence of sound, so the immortal hope may not unfairly be said to prove the existence of the immortal life. It is this that we mean when we say that the universality of the idea is an argument for the acceptance of the idea. In his great essay on "Immortality," Emerson tells us of two men who early in life spent much of their time together in earnest search for some proof of immortality. An accident separated them, and they did not meet again for a quarter of a century. They said nothing, "but shook hands long and cordially. At last his friend said, 'Any light, Albert?' 'None', replied Albert. 'Any light, Lewis?' 'None,' he replied." And Emerson comments "that the impulse which drew these two minds to this inquiry through so many years was a better affirmative evidence for immortality than their failure to find a confirmation was a negative."

16   This universal diffusion of the idea of immortality takes on an added significance when I come to my third reason for believing in immortality. I refer to the fact so memorably stated by Cicero. "There is in the minds of men," he says, "I know not how, a certain presage, as it were, of a future existence; and this takes deepest root in the greatest geniuses and the most exalted souls." The leaders of the race, in other words, have always believed in immortality. They are not separated in this case, as in so many cases, from the masses of ignorant and superstitious men by doctrines of dissent. On the contrary, in this case the ideas of the highest are at one with the hopes of the humblest among mankind.

17   In referring thus to the great names that are attached to the idea of immortality, I would not have you believe that I am making any blind appeal to

the concept of authority. I have never seen any reason for arbitrarily separating our minds from the companionship of other minds. There is such a thing, even for the independent thinker, as a consensus of best opinion which cannot be defied without the weightiest of reasons. And in this matter of immortality there is a consensus of best opinion which constitutes, to my mind, one of the most remarkable phenomena in the whole history of human thinking. I have no time this morning to list the names of those who have believed in the immortality of the soul. If I did so, I should have to include the names of scientists from Aristotle to Darwin and Eddington, of philosophers from Plato to Kant and Bergson, of poets from Sophocles to Goethe and Robert Browning, of ethical teachers and public leaders from Socrates to Tolstoi and Mahatma Gandhi. There are dissenters from the doctrine, like Epictetus yesterday and Bernard Shaw today, but the consensus of opinion the other way is remarkable. Even the famous heretics stand in awe before this conception of eternity. Thus, Voltaire declared that "reason agrees with revelation . . . that the soul is immortal." Thomas Paine affirmed that he did not "trouble (himself) about the manner of future existence," so sure he was that "the Power which gave existence is able to continue it in any form." Even Robert G. Ingersoll confessed, as he stood by his brother's grave, that love could "hear the rustle of an angel's wing:" In the light of such testimony as this, are we not justified in believing that there is reason for believing in immortality? If not, then we know, with James Martineau, "who are those who are mistaken. Not the mean and grovelling souls who never reached to so great a thought. . . . No, the deceived are the great and holy, whom all men revere; the men who have lived for something better than their happiness and spent themselves on the altar of human good. Whom are we to reverence, and what can we believe, if the inspirations of the highest nature are but cunningly-devised fables?"

18   (4) This conviction of immortality as rooted in the minds of men, and the greatest men, brings us immediately to the consideration of human nature itself as evidence for its own survival. Thus, my fourth reason this morning for believing in immortality is found in what I would call man's over endowment as a creature of this earth, his surplus equipment for the adventure of his present life. If we want to know what is needed for successful existence upon this planet, we have only to look at any animal. His equipment of physical attributes and powers seems perfectly adapted to the necessities of his natural environment. The outfit of man, on the contrary, seems to constitute something like "a vast over-provision" for his necessities. If this life is all, in other words, what need has man for all these mental faculties, moral aspirations, spiritual ideals, which make him to be distinctly a man as contrasted with the animal? If existence upon the earth is his only destiny, why should man not prefer the swiftness of the deer, the strength of the lion, the vision of the eagle, to any endowment of mind and heart, as more adequate provision for the purely physical task of physical survival in a physical world? What we have here is a fundamental discrepancy between the endowment of man and the life he has to live; and this constitutes, if this life be all, an unparalleled

violation of the creative economy of the universe. In every other form of life, an organism is equipped to meet the exactions of its immediate environment. Man is equipped for this environment, and also for something more. Why is this not proof that he is destined for something more? As we estimate the length of the voyage of a ship by the character of its equipment, never confusing a little coasting vessel with a transatlantic liner or an arctic exploration steamer, why should we not estimate the length of man's voyage upon the seas of life in exactly the same way? What man bears within himself is evidence that he is destined for some farther port than any upon these shores. What he is in mind and heart and spirit, in the range of his interests and the lift of his soul, can only be explained on the supposition that he is preparing for another and a vaster life. I believe that man is immortal because already the signs of immortality are upon him.

19 (5) This consideration is basic, and sums up our whole case for immortality as rooted in human nature. But it opens out into other considerations which may well be taken as other reasons for believing in immortality. Thus, I would specify as my fifth reason for believing in immortality the lack of co-ordination, or proportion, between a man's body and a man's mind. If these two are to be regarded as aspects of a single organism, adapted only to the conditions of this present life, why do they so early begin to pull apart, and the weakness of the one to retard and at last to defeat the other? For a while, to be sure, there seems to be a real coordination between soul and body, between the personality, on the one hand, and the physical frame which it inhabits, on the other. Thus the child is in nothing so delightful as in the fact that it is a perfect animal. Then, as maturity approaches, two exactly opposite processes begin to take place within the life of the human being. On the one hand, the body begins to lose its resiliency and harden, to stop its growth and become static, then to decay and at last to dissolve. There is a definite cycle, in other words, in the physical life of the individual. There is a beginning, then a pause, and then an end. It is from first to last a process of completion. But there is no completion in the life of the soul. "Who dares speak the word 'completed,'" says Professor Munsterberg, the great psychologist. "Do not our purposes grow? Does not every newly-created value give us the desire for further achievement? Is our life ever so completely done that no desire has still a meaning?" The personality of man is an enduring thing. As the body weakens through the years, so the soul only grows the stronger and more wonderful. As the body approaches irrevocably to its end, so the soul only mounts to what seems to be a new beginning. We come to death, in other words, only to discover within ourselves exhaustless possibilities. The aged have testified again and again to this amazing truth that as the body turns to ashes, the spirit mounts as to a flame. Victor Hugo, protesting against the waning of his powers, said, "For half a century I have been writing my thoughts in prose and verse . . . but I feel that I have not said a thousandth part of what is in me." Said James Martineau, on his 80th birthday, "How small a part of my plans have I been able to carry out! Nothing is so plain as that life at its fullest on earth is but a fragment." Robert

Browning catches this thought in his poem, "Cleon," where he makes his hero say,

> . . . Every day my sense of joy
> Grows more acute, my soul . . . enlarged, more keen,
> While every day my hairs fall more and more,
> My hand shakes, and the heavy years increase
> The horror quickening still from year to year,
> When I shall know most, and yet least enjoy.
> What to do, in such emergency, except what Cleon did,
> . . . imagine to (our) need Some future state . . .

20   (6) But there is a lack of coordination not only between our personalities and our physical bodies, but also between our personalities and the physical world. This is my sixth reason for believing in immortality—that our souls have potentialities and promises which should not, as indeed they cannot, be subject to the chance vicissitudes of earthly fortune. What are we going to say, for example, when we see some life of eminent utility, of great achievement, of character and beauty and noble dedication to mankind, not merely borne down by the body, but cut off sharply before its time by an automobile accident, a disease germ, a bit of poisoned food? What shall we think when we see a Shelley drowned in his thirtieth year by the heedless sea, a Phillips Brooks stricken in the prime of his manhood by a diphtheric sore-throat, a Captain Scott frozen in mid-career by an accident of weather? Is it possible that these lives of ours are dependent upon a fall of snow, a grain of dust, a passing breeze upon the sea? Is it conceivable that our personalities, with all their potencies of spirit, can be destroyed, as our bodies can be broken, by the material forces of the world? Are we to believe that eternal powers can be annihilated by transient accidents? I cannot think so! Rather must I think, as Professor George Herbert Palmer thought, as he looked upon the dead body of his wife, one of the greatest and most beautiful women of her time, stricken ere her years were ripe. "Though no regrets are proper for the manner of her death," said this noble husband, "yet who can contemplate the fact of it and not call the world irrational if, out of deference to a few particles of disordered matter, it excludes so fair a spirit?"

21   (7) But this question of the irrationality of a world which would allow death to exercise mastery over a radiant spirit, has application not merely to the individual but also to the race. This brings me to my seventh reason for believing in immortality—a reason drawn from the logic of evolution. There is nothing more familiar, of course, than the fact that this world is the result of a natural process of development which has been going on for unnumbered millions of years. If this process is rational, as man's processes are rational, it must have been working all these eons of time to the achievement of some permanent and worthy end. What is this end? It is not the physical world itself, for the day must come when this earth will be swallowed up by the sun, and all the universe be merged again into the original fire-mist from which it

sprang. It is not the works of man, for these perish even as man lives, and must vanish utterly in the last cataclysm of ruin. It is not man himself, for man, like the earth on which he lives, must finally disappear. Is there nothing that will remain as the evidence and vindication of this cosmic process? Or must we believe that, from the beginning, it has been like a child's tower of blocks built up only to be thrown down?

22   It was the challenge of this contingency, of evolution coming in the end to naught that moved no less a man than Charles Darwin, agnostic though he was, to proclaim the conviction that "it is an intolerable thought that man and all other sentient beings are doomed to complete annihilation after such long continued slow process." Unless the universe is crazy, something must remain. The process must justify itself by producing something that endures. And what can this thing be but the spiritual essence of man's nature—the soul which is immortal? "The more thoroughly we comprehend the process of evolution," says John Fiske in an unforgettable statement, "the more we are likely to feel that to deny the everlasting persistence of the spiritual element in man is to rob the whole process of its meaning. Its goes far toward putting us to permanent intellectual confusion." Which led him to his famous verdict upon all the evidence: "I believe in the immortality of the soul as a supreme act of faith in the reasonableness of God's work."

23   (8) This leads us deep into the realm of science—to a fundamental principle that provides my eighth reason for believing in immortality. I refer to the principle of persistence or conservation. The gist of this doctrine is that nothing in the universe is ever lost. All energy is conserved. No matter what changes take place in any particular form of energy, that energy persists, if not in the old form then in a new, and the sum total of energy in the universe remains the same. "Whatever is," says Sir Oliver Lodge, speaking of forms of energy in the physical universe, "whatever is, both was and shall be." And he quotes the famous statement of Professor Tait, that "persistence, or conservation, is the test or criterion of real existence."

24   Now if this principle applies to the "real existence" of the material world, why not to the "real existence" of the spiritual world as well? If it is impossible to think of physical energy as appearing and disappearing, coming into and going out of existence, why is it not equally impossible to think of intellectual or moral or spiritual energy as acting in this same haphazard fashion? We would laugh at a man who contended that the heat in molten metal, which disappears under the cooling action of air or water, had thereby been destroyed. Why should we not similarly laugh at a man who argues that the personality of a human being, which disappears under the chilling influence of death, has thereby been annihilated? What the personality may be, I do not know. Whether it is a form of energy itself, as some scientists assert, or "belongs to a separate order of existence," as Sir Oliver Lodge, for example, argues, I cannot say. But of this thing I am sure—that the soul of man is just as much a force in the world as magnetism or steam, or electricity, and that if the cosmic law of conservation forbids the destruction of the latter, it must as well forbid the destruction of the former. Anything else is inconceivable. The

universe cannot be so thrifty of its physical, and so wasteful of its spiritual, resources. It is madness to conceive that the heat of an engine must be preserved, while the love of a heart may be thrown away. What prevails in the great realm of matter can be only an anticipation of what must equally prevail in the greater realm of spirit. For the universe is one. Its laws are everywhere the same. What science has discovered about the conservation of energy is only the physical equivalent of what religion has discovered about the immortality of the soul.

(9) We are coming now to ultimate things—to those first and last questions of origins and meanings. This brings me to my ninth reason for believing in immortality—the fact, namely, that all the values of life exist in man, and in man alone. For the world as we know it and love it is not the world as we receive it, but the world as we make it by the creative genius of the inward spirit. Consider this earthly scene with man eliminated! The sun would be here, and the stars. Mountains would still lift themselves to the skies, and oceans spread afar to vast horizons. Birds would sing, and leaves rustle, and sunsets glow. But what would it all mean without man to see and hear, to interpret? What do the stars mean to the eagle, or the sea to the porpoise, or the mountain to the goat? It is man's ear which has heard the cuckoo as a "wandering voice," his eye which has seen "the floor of heaven thick inlaid with patines of bright gold," his mind which has found "sermons in stone, books in the running brooks, and good in everything." All that is precious in the world—all its beauty, its wonder, its meaning—exists in man, and by man, and for man. The world is what man has done with it in the far reaches of his soul. And we are asked to believe that the being who sees and glorifies shall perish, while the world which he has seen and glorified endures! Such a conclusion is irrational. The being who created the world must himself be greater than the world. The soul which conceives Truth, Goodness and Beauty, must itself be as eternal as the Truth, Goodness, and Beauty which it conceives. Nothing has any value without man. Man, therefore, is the supreme value. Which is the essence of the Platonic philosophy of eternal life for man!

"Tell me, then," says Socrates in the *Phaedo,* "what is that the inherence of which renders the body alive?"

"The soul," Cebes replied.

"Then whatever the soul possesses, to that she comes bearing life?"

"Yes, certainly."

"And is there any opposite to life?"

"There is—Death."

"And will the soul ever receive the opposite of what she brings?"

"Impossible," replied Cebes.

"Then," said Socrates, "the soul is immortal!"

(10) These, now, are my main reasons for believing in immortality. I have but one more, the tenth to add. It is the pragmatic argument that faith in an eternal life beyond the grave justifies itself in terms of the life that we are now living upon this side of the grave. For immortality does not concern the future alone; it

concerns, also, the present. We are immortal today, if we are ever going to be immortal tomorrow. And this means that we have the chance to put to the test, even now and here, the belief to which we hold. It is the essence of the pragmatic philosophy that what is true will conduce to life, as food conduces to health, and that what is false will destroy life, as poison the body. Whatever is true enlarges and lifts and strengthens the life of man; whatever is false represses and weakens and disintegrates his life. Now what does immortality do when we put its affirmation to this test? What are the consequences which follow if we live as though we were eternal spirits? Can there be any doubt as to the answer?

36   We see a universe where spiritual values, not material forces, prevail; where personality, whether in ourselves or in others, is precious, and therefore to be conserved; where principles, not possessions, are the supreme concern of life; where man is equal to his task, and labors not in vain for the high causes of humanity; where sacrifice is not foolish but wise, and love "the greatest thing in the world." The man who lives an immortal life takes on immortal qualities. His character assumes the proportions of his faith, and his work the range of his high destiny. "Immortality makes great living;" says Dr. Fosdick. Therefore I believe in immortality.

37   Ten reasons! Are these all? No, they are not all! They are simply ten of the many reasons for the most persistent faith which has ever beset the heart of man. In choosing these ten, I have sought to gather reasons which were reasons, and not mere superstitions—arguments which appeal to intellect rather than emotion, and which are based upon experience rather than credulity. That these reasons prove the idea of immortality to be true, I cannot claim. But there is many an idea which we accept for good reasons, even though it be not proved, as there is many a verdict in court which is returned for good reasons, even though it be not proved, and immortality is one of them. What impresses me, as I follow the course of this great argument through the ages, is what impressed the mind of James Martineau when he said, "We do not believe immortality because we have proved it, but we forever try to prove it because we believe it." Hence the judgment of the poet, Tennyson—

> O, yet we trust that somehow good
> Will be the final goal of ill,
> pangs of nature, sins of will,
> Defects of doubt, and taints of blood.
>
> That nothing walks with aimless feet;
> That not one life shall be destroyed,
> cast as rubbish to the void,
> When God hath made the pile complete. . . .
>
> I stretch lame hands of faith, and grope
> And gather dust and chaff, and call
> To what I feel is Lord of all,
> And faintly trust the larger hope.

Vocabulary

immortality (title)
parable (5)
permeated (6)
pertinaciously (9)
correspondence (11)
consensus (14)
constitutes (15)
economy (15)
vindication (18)
sentient (19)
annihilated (21)
credulity (34)

penetrated (1)
providence (6)
testimony (8)
speculation (11)
diffusion (13)
endowment (15)
unparalleled (15)
transient (17)
contingency (19)
persistence (20)
pragmatic (32)

discourse (2)
beneficent (6)
presumption (8)
organism (11)
presage (13)
discrepancy (15)
violation (15)
cataclysm (18)
naught (19)
conservation (20)
disintegrates (32)

The Facts

1. Does the author offer proof of immortality or does he base his argument on other claims? In what way does he compare the belief in immortality to experience in a courtroom? Explain how he achieved his belief in immortality.

2. Does the author come up with some telling, new ideas in support of immortality? If so, what are they; if not, why not?

3. What three existing reasons favoring immortality does the author dismiss? Why do these reasons not concern him?

4. What is the first reason the author presents for believing in immortality? How strong do you consider the logic behind this reason? Offer your own reaction.

5. What idea from the evolutionary theory does the author borrow in order to strengthen his second reason for believing in immortality—namely, that whenever human beings think deeply, the idea of immortality surfaces?

The Strategies

1. How does the author assure that the reader can follow his ten reasons for believing in immortality without getting lost in the catalogue? What advantage does this system have? What other system could he have used?

2. Who are "those who claim," referred to in paragraph 1? What do you make of this reference? Does it help the author's argument? Why or why not? Explain yourself.

3. Compared with the other essays in this book, what level of English does this essay use? How easy or difficult was it for you to follow the argument? Analyze the style and voice. Consider such matters as vocabulary, allusions, figurative language, and sentence structure.

4. Which paragraph begins the author's reasons for believing in immortality? How does he indicate that this is where he intends to start? What other purpose does the paragraph serve?

5. In paragraph 17, the author alludes to Shelley, Phillips Brooks, and Captain Scott—all men with lives of great promise cut off by early deaths. Who are these men and what were their contributions to history? What other talented young people can you cite who died while they were young?

● **The Issues**

1. What is your response to the author's view that because immortality cannot be disproved, anyone who feels that a belief in immortality would bring satisfaction and hope should hold such a belief with impunity? How logical is this argument?

2. How comfortable are you with the author's third reason for believing in immortality—that because the leaders and greatest geniuses of the human race have always believed in immortality, therefore such a belief is rational? How does the author support this reason?

3. Do you agree that if human beings were not immortal, they would not be so overendowed with mental and spiritual faculties not necessary to a successful existence? Why, in your view, do we not have the swiftness of the deer, the strength of the lion, or the vision of the eagle? Would you prefer more brawn and less brain? Explain your answer.

4. Do you agree with the author's view that as human beings age and lose their physical abilities they develop deeper desires for spiritual gifts? What distinction do you see between the life of the body and the life of the soul? Explain your answer.

5. Do you agree with the author's view that because nothing is ever destroyed in the physical world, this same law can apply to the spiritual world as well? An answer to this question requires that you closely evaluate the similarities of the physical and spiritual worlds. In other words, are these two realms really alike or are there significant differences between them?

● **Suggestions for Writing**

1. Using Alfred Lord Tennyson's lines at the end of the essay as a springboard, write an essay on the subject of hope beyond this life.

2. Write an essay in which you use the seasonal cycles—spring, summer, autumn, and winter—as symbols of either hope or fate.

Breaking the Last Taboo
JAMES A. HAUGHT

James A. Haught (b. 1932) is an editor and writer who has won many awards, including the National Headliner Award (1971). He is the author of several books, among them *Holy Horrors: An Illustrated History of Religious Murder and Madness* (1990) and *Two Thousand Years of Disbelief: Famous People with the Courage to Doubt* (1996).

Few Americans know that Thomas Jefferson wrote, in a letter to John Adams:

> "The day will come when the mystical generation of Jesus, by the supreme being as his father in the womb of a virgin, will be classed with the fable of the generation of Minerva in the brain of Jupiter."

Or that Albert Einstein wrote in the *New York Times* in 1930:

> "I cannot imagine a God who rewards and punishes the objects of his creation, whose purposes are modeled after our own—a God, in short, who is but a reflection of human frailty. Neither can I believe that the individual survives the death of his body, although feeble souls harbor such thoughts through fear or ridiculous egotism."

Or that Mark Twain wrote in his journal:

> "I cannot see how a man of any large degree of humorous perception can ever be religious—unless he purposely shut the eyes of his mind and keep them shut by force."

Or that Emily Brontë wrote in 1846:

> "Vain are the thousand creeds that move men's hearts, unutterably vain, worthless as withered weeds."

Or that Sigmund Freud wrote, in a letter to a friend:

> "Neither in my private life nor in my writings, have I ever made a secret of being an out-and-out unbeliever."

Or that Thomas Paine wrote in *The Age of Reason*:

> "All national institutions of churches, whether Jewish, Christian or Turkish, appear to me no other than human inventions, set up to terrify and enslave mankind, and monopolize power and profit."

Or that Thomas Edison told the *New York Times* in 1910:

> "I cannot believe in the immortality of the soul.... No, all this talk of an existence for us, as individuals, beyond the grave is wrong. It is born of our tenacity of life—our desire to go on living—our dread of coming to an end."

Or that Voltaire wrote, in a letter to Frederick the Great:

> "Christianity is the most ridiculous, the most absurd, and bloody religion that has ever infected the world."

16. Or that Beethoven shunned religion and scorned the clergy.
17. Or that Abraham Lincoln never joined a church, and once wrote a skeptical treatise, which friends burned in a stove, to save him from wrecking his political career.
18. Or that the motto of Margaret Sanger's birth-control newsletter was: "No gods, no masters."
19. Or that Clarence Darrow said, in a 1930 speech in Toronto:

20. "I don't believe in God because I don't believe in Mother Goose."

21. Or that President William Howard Taft said, in a letter declining the presidency of Yale University:

22. "I do not believe in the divinity of Christ, and there are many other of the postulates of the orthodox creed to which I cannot subscribe."

23. Or that Luther Burbank told a newspaper interviewer in 1926:

24. "As a scientist, I cannot help feeling that all religions are on a tottering foundation.... I am an infidel today. I do not believe what has been served to me to believe. I am a doubter, a questioner, a skeptic. When it can be proved to me that there is immortality, that there is resurrection beyond the gates of death, then I will believe. Until then, no."

25. Or that Bertrand Russell wrote in 1930:

26. "My own view of religion is that of Lucretius. I regard it as a disease born of fear and as a source of untold misery to the human race."

27. Or that George Bernard Shaw wrote, in the preface to one of his plays:

28. "At present there is not a single credible established religion in the world."

29. Or that Leo Tolstoy wrote, in response to his excommunication by the Holy Synod of the Russian Orthodox church:

30. "To regard Christ as God, and to pray to him, are to my mind the greatest possible sacrilege."

31. Or that Charles Darwin said:

32. "The mystery of the beginning of all things is insoluble by us, and I for one must be content to remain an agnostic."

33   Or that Kurt Vonnegut said:

34   "Say what you will about the sweet miracle of unquestioning faith, I consider a capacity for it terrifying and absolutely vile."

35   Or that Gloria Steinem said:

36   "By the year 2000, we will, I hope, raise our children to believe in human potential, not God."

37   Many, perhaps most, of the world's outstanding thinkers, scientists, writers, reformers—people who changed Western life—have been religious skeptics. But this fact is little known in America. Why?

38   Because our nation has one last taboo, one unmentionable topic: religious doubt.

39   In the daily tumult, it's permissible to challenge any idea, save one. Supernatural religion—invisible gods and devils, heavens and hells—is off limits. It's acceptable to write that Elvis is alive on a UFO, but not that God is a figment of the imagination. A few "freethought" journals do so, but mainstream media mostly stay mum.

40   There's an unspoken consensus that the subject is too touchy, that it is "impolite" to question anyone's religion. In a nation of 100 million church members, with an upsurge of fundamentalism, too many feelings would be hurt.

41   Why are some believers angered by disbelief? Bertrand Russell offered this explanation:

42   "There is something feeble and a little contemptible about a man who cannot face the perils of life without the help of comfortable myths. Almost inevitably, some part of him is aware that they are myths, and that he believes them only because they are comforting. But he dares not face this thought! Moreover, since he is aware, however dimly, that his opinions are not rational, he becomes furious when they are disputed."

43   Maybe that's the reason why, for many centuries, you could be killed for doubting dogmas. Believers killing non-believers was a pattern long before the Ayatollah Khomeini ordered a holy hit on Salman Rushdie.

44   In the fifth century B.C.E., the Greek teacher Protagoras wrote:

45   "As to the gods, I have no way of knowing either that they exist or do not exist, or what they are like."

46   Protagoras was charged with impiety, as were other Greek thinkers. Unlike Socrates and Anaxagoras, who were sentenced to death, Protagoras merely

was banished from Athens, and his books were burned. As he sailed into exile, he drowned.

47   In the year 415, the woman scientist Hypatia, head of the legendary Alexandria library, was beaten to death by Christian monks who considered her a pagan. The leader of the monks, Cyril, was canonized a saint.

48   In the eleventh century, Omar Khayyam wrote his exquisite Persian verses on the futility of trying to discern any purpose of life. He scoffed at believers yearning for heaven—"Fools, your reward is neither here nor there"—and belittled divine prophecies:

49
> The revelations of the devout and learn'd
> Who rose before us and as prophets burn'd
> Are all but stories, which, awoke from sleep
> They told their comrades, and to sleep return'd.

50   How did Omar escape execution in the Muslim world, which is known for beheading "blasphemers"? Actually, Omar is a mystery, and the verses attributed to him didn't begin surfacing until two centuries after his death.

51   In the 1500s, Michel de Montaigne, who created the essay as a literary form, wrote comments such as:

52
> "Man is certainly stark mad: he cannot make a worm, yet he will make gods by the dozen."

53   Although Montaigne lived at a time when "heretics" were burned, he eluded prosecution. Other thinkers weren't so lucky. In 1553, the physician Michael Servetus, who discovered the pulmonary circulation of blood, was burned alive in John Calvin's Geneva for doubting the Trinity. (In my Unitarian church, the youth group holds a yearly "Michael Servetus Wiener Roast" in his memory.)

54   In 1600, the philosopher Giordano Bruno was burned for teaching that the earth circles the sun, and that the universe is infinite. He was among thousands of Inquisition victims.

55   Later in the 1600s, the Englishman Thomas Hobbes, generally deemed the first major thinker in what is now called the Age of Reason, wrote:

56
> "Opinion of ghosts, ignorance of second causes, devotion to what men fear, and taking of things casual for prognostics, consisteth the natural seeds of religion."

57   A bishop accused Hobbes of atheism. Parliament ordered an investigation. Hobbes hastily burned his manuscripts, and escaped with only a ban against future writings.

58   Baruch Spinoza, a Jew in Amsterdam, doubted theological dogmas and wrote lines such as:

59
> "Popular religion may be summed up as a respect for ecclesiastics."

60   He was excommunicated by the Dutch synagogue, and lived as a semi outcast.

61   Gradually, the iron fist of religion lost its grip in the West, and disbelief became a bit safer. But there were relapses. For example, a French teen-ager was beheaded and burned in 1766 for marring a crucifix, singing irreverent songs, and wearing his hat while a church procession passed. Voltaire tried to save him, but the clergy demanded death, and the French parliament decreed it.

62   And Denis Diderot, creator of the first encyclopedia, was jailed for skepticism, and his writings burned. And English publishers who printed Thomas Paine's *The Age of Reason* were jailed for blasphemy.

63   Despite the risks, thinkers kept on questioning, and the right to doubt gradually was established—in the West, but not in the Muslim world, where "blasphemers" still face death today.

64   Although the right was won, it remains partly muzzled in America. What schoolchild is taught that Thomas Jefferson wrote many sneers at "priestcraft"—that he was denounced as a "howling atheist"—and that his famous vow of "eternal hostility against every form of tyranny over the mind of man," which is engraved in his memorial in Washington, was written of the clergy?

65   What student hears scientific explanations of religion, such as this one: Sigmund Freud said the widespread belief in a father-god arises from psychology. Each tiny child is awed by his or her father as a seemingly all-powerful protector and punisher. As maturity comes, the real father grows less awesome. But the infantile image remains hidden in the subconscious, and becomes attached to an omnipotent, magical father in an invisible heaven. Unknowingly, Freud said, believers worship the loner forgotten toddler impression of the biological father, "clothed in the grandeur in which he once appeared to the small child."

66   Although open agnosticism is a no-no in America—and although fundamentalism is booming—supernatural religion is fading among educated people. America's mainline Protestant churches, formerly the domain of the elite, have lost millions of members since the 1960s. Intelligent people don't take miracles seriously, and realize there's no evidence of a spirit realm.

67   The old church "thou shalt nots" against sex, liquor, gambling, birth control, dancing, Sunday shopping, etc., have subsided in our lifetime. Fundamentalism may be rising, but so is secularism. Educated Americans are becoming like Europeans, who have mostly abandoned religion. In England, for example, only a tiny fringe attends church today.

68   Soon it may be acceptable to challenge the supernatural, as so many great figures have done. The tacit code of silence—the last taboo—may be near an end. I certainly hope so.

Sources of Quotations (in sequence as they appear in the article)

Thomas Jefferson—letter to John Adams, April 11, 1823

Albert Einstein—*New York Times* commentary, November 9, 1930

Mark Twain—*Mark Twain's Notebooks and Journals,* edited by Frederick Anderson, 1979, notebook 27, August 1887–July 1888

Emily Brontë—*No Coward Soul,* January 1846

Sigmund Freud—letter to Charles Singer

Thomas Paine—*The Age of Reason,* 1794

Thomas Edison—interview in the *New York Times,* October 2, 1910, front of magazine section, by Edward Marshall

Voltaire—letter to Frederick the Great, quoted in the *Encyclopedia of Unbelief,* Prometheus Books, 1985, p. 715

Margaret Sanger—masthead of her newsletter, *The Woman Rebel,* quoted in the 1994 *Women of Freethought Calendar* by Carole Gray, Columbus, Ohio

Clarence Darrow—speech at Toronto, 1930, cited in *The Great Quotations* by George Seldes, Lyle Stuart publisher, 1960, p. 190

William Howard Taft—*The Life and Times of William Howard Taft,* by Harry F. Pringle, Farrar & Rinehart, Inc., New York, 1939, p. 373

Luther Burbank—*San Francisco Bulletin,* January 22, 1926, p. 1, by Edgar Waite, headline: "I'm an Infidel, Declares Burbank, Casting Doubt on Soul Immortality Theory"

Bertrand Russell—opening lines of essay "Has Religion Made Useful Contributions to Civilization?" 1930

George Bernard Shaw—*Major Barbara,* preface, final paragraph

Leo Tolstoy—letter April 4, 1901, to the Holy Synod of the Russian Orthodox church, in response to his excommunication, cited in *Tolstoy,* by Henri Troyat, Doubleday, 1967, p. 591; and *In The Life of Lyof N. Tolstoy,* by Nathan Haskell Dole, Scribner's, 1923, pp. 371–372

Charles Darwin—*Life and Letters,* cited in Peter's *Quotations,* by Laurence J. Peter, Wm. Morrow & Co., 1977, p. 45

Kurt Vonnegut—*Peter's Quotations,* p. 191

Gloria Steinem—*Peter's Quotations,* p. 103

Russell again—*Human Society in Ethics and Politics,* 1954

Protagoras—*On the Gods*

Omar Khayyam—*The Rubaiyat of Omar Kiayyam,* translated by Edward Fitzgerald, fifth translation, *1889,* verse 65, reprinted by Dover Thrift Editions, 1990, p. 41

Michel de Montaigne—*Apology to Raimond Sebond.* 1580, Essays book 2, chapter 12

Thomas Hobbes—quoted by Rufus K. Noyes in *Yews of Religion,* L. K. Washburn publisher, Boston, 1906, p. 30

Baruch Spinoza—quoted by Eugene Brussell in *The Dictionary of Quotable Definitions,* Prentice Hall, 1970, p. 490

Thomas Jefferson—vow against tyranny, letter to Dr. Benjamin Rush, September 23, 1800

Sigmund Freud—father-God explanation from "The Future of an Illusion," in *The Freud Reader,* edited by Peter Gay, W. W. Norton, 1989, pp. 694–696; quote is from *New Introductory Lectures on Psychoanalysis,* cited by Seldes in *The Great Quotations,* p. 261

Vocabulary

mystical (2)
creeds (7)
tenacity (13)
orthodox (22)
sacrilege (30)
tumult (39)
contemptible (42)
futility (48)
pulmonary (53)
tacit (68)

fable (2)
unutterably (7)
treatise (17)
infidel (24)
insoluble (32)
mum (39)
disputed (42)
discern (48)
dogmas (58)

perception (6)
monopolize (11)
postulates (22)
excommunication (29)
taboo (38)
consensus (40)
impiety (46)
eluded (53)
ecclesiastics (59)

The Facts

1. What is a *taboo?* Look up the word if you don't understand it. What is the particular taboo about which the author writes?

2. Who is Clarence Darrow, referred to in paragraph 19? Do you consider him a viable reference for the author's position on the supernatural? What is the meaning of Darrow's reference to Mother Goose?

3. Charles Darwin called himself an *agnostic.* What are the differences among an *agnostic,* a *skeptic,* and an *atheist?* Look up each word in a dictionary so that you understand its meaning. Which of these attitudes is most likely to develop into a *believer?*

4. According to Bertrand Russell, believers are dangerous because they get deeply angered by disbelief. Why are they so angered? Do you agree with this opinion? Explain your answer.

5. What explanation does Sigmund Freud, the father of psychiatry, give for the widespread belief in a father-God? What is your response to Freud's explanation?

The Strategies

1. What is the main rhetorical mode used by the author to support his thesis that a belief in God is going out of style? Do you think this same mode could be used to support a thesis stating the opposite view?

2. Which quotation impressed you the most—either positively or negatively? Explain your answer.

3. Who is the first person quoted by the author at the start of his essay? Why do you think he placed this particular reference at the outset of his essay? What is your personal reaction to the allusion?

4. Why is the allusion to Hypatia (paragraph 47) rather unusual in this essay? What irony does it point out?

5. What is the purpose of repeating the word "or" so often in the first part of the essay? What effect does this repetition have? Where does the author express his own view of "the last taboo"? How effective is this placement?

The Issues

1. How important is it to live in a country that allows its citizens to question sacred beliefs? How is this right guaranteed in the United States? What dangers, if any, might be associated with freedom of expression?

2. If you are a believer, how do you feel about unbelievers? If you are an unbeliever, how do you feel about believers?

3. In your view, what happens when scientific discoveries are suppressed as soon as they disagree with truths that are held sacred? Give examples that support your answer.

4. What would it take for a person like Luther Burbank to believe in immortality? What proof would he need? Is this kind of proof available?

5. For most believers, what is the crux of their belief? Is this an intelligent approach? Why or why not? How do you think unbelievers should be treated in our country?

Suggestions for Writing

1. After comparing the essay by John Haynes Holmes with that of James A. Haught, write an essay in which you support one view or the other. Write a clear thesis in the opening paragraph of your essay; then support that thesis with appropriate reasoning and evidence.

2. Write an essay in which you state your own approach to the existence of God and immortality. Whatever your position, state it clearly as a thesis and then support it with appropriate evidence.

Children's Letters to God

Dear God, Thank you for the baby brother but what I asked for was a puppy. You can look it up.
Joyce

Dear God, It rained for our whole vacation and is my father mad! He said some things about you that people are not supposed to say, but I hope you will not hurt him anyway. Your friend (I am not going to tell you who I am).
Unsigned

Dear God, How did you know you were God?
Charlene

Dear God, What does it mean you are a jealous God? I thought you had everything.
Jane

Dear God, We read Thomas Edison made light. But in Sunday School they said you did it. I bet he stoled your Idea.
Sincerely, Donna

Dear God, I am doing the best I can. It's hard sometimes.
Frank

Dear God, I didn't think orange went with purple until I saw the sunset you made on Tuesday. That was Cool. Thank you.
Eugene

Dear God, I do not think anybody could be a better God. Well, I just want you to know that. And I am not just saying that because you are God.
Charles

Punctuation Workshop
The Question Mark (?)

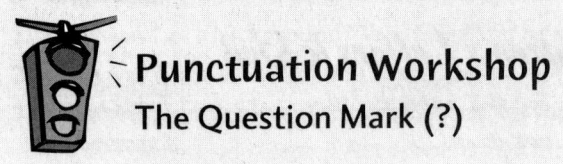

Put a question mark after a direct question, but not after an indirect question:

> **DIRECT:** What is keeping the catcher from reading the pitcher's signals?
>
> **INDIRECT:** We asked what was keeping the catcher from reading the pitcher's signals.
>
> **DIRECT:** Did you understand the insulting question, "Do you have a low I.Q.?"
>
> (A question within a question contains only one question mark, inside the closing quotation mark.)
>
> **INDIRECT:** They were asked if they understood the insulting question.

A series of direct questions having the same subject can be treated as follows:

> What on earth is little Freddy doing? Laughing? Crying? Screaming?

Sometimes a declarative sentence contains a direct question that requires a question mark:

> He asked his neighbor, "Have you seen the raccoon?" (The question mark goes inside the quotation mark.)

CAUTION: Do not write an indirect question as if it were a direct question:

> **WRONG:** He asked her would she join the team?
>
> **RIGHT:** He asked her if she would join the team.

STUDENT CORNER

The Existence of God
Ara Babaian, Loyola Law School of Los Angeles

Whether viewed as a single deity or a collection of deities, God used to perform a larger role in society than he (or she) does today. In fact, human beings of bygone eras would plead to God for everything in their lives, giving him the power to rule over them in every situation. When something good happened, these people explained the good as God's favor. Conversely, when something bad happened, they understood it to be God's wrath, punishing humans for being sinful, or sometimes God's fickleness, done for no apparent reason. For instance, the cavemen begged God for a successful hunt. The Greeks pleaded to their gods and goddesses for a bountiful harvest of grapes. In the middle ages, Europeans and Middle Easterners alike prayed to God to prevail in war. However, as people began to better understand the science of things, they reduced the role that God played in their lives. They no longer needed to pray to God for rain, because they understood how water evaporates and turns into clouds which, in turn, make rain. They understood that it was not the devil who possessed certain individuals, but chemical and psychological disturbances that produce schizophrenia, manic depression, and other personality disorders. As such, science made God smaller.

Now, people still invoke God's name in times of despair, as when natural disaster strikes or when someone dies, and also in times of celebration, as when a child is born or when two people marry. Of course, many sectors of society remain devout followers of one religion or another. These people uphold traditions, old and new, and call to God more regularly than most other people for spiritual support and guidance. Still, many people are not as fervent in their religious practice as were humans in the past.

Nevertheless, it would be false to say that Americans lack spirituality in today's world. During the 1990s, "religions" have gained a certain popularity. People study religions like Buddhism, the Cabbala, and New Age philosophies. They pick and choose tenets from these and other doctrines to form their own, idiosyncratic faith. Even die-hard Christians, at the very least, use terms in their daily vocabulary that stem from other religions, terms like *karma, nirvana,* and *yin* and *yang.*

Thus, although many Americans are no longer religious in the traditional sense, we are nevertheless spiritual in a more organic and all-inclusive sense. True, parts of American society stand firm in their belief in one God or another, and there is definitely a good share of new religions that may or may not deserve merit. It is doubtful that these phenomena will change in the future. However, in this highly technological world where the role of God has essentially atrophied to a smaller stature, Americans are looking to a variety of beliefs not only for spiritual nourishment, but also to contemplate the final, unanswerable question—death.

How I Write

I admit it: I enjoy writing. Writing is a difficult process; you have to sit alone and pull words from your mind, put them in an intelligible sequence, and hopefully do it in an interesting way. When I write an essay, I go around for days or, if I have time, weeks just thinking about the topic. Most people call this procrastination, but it's really not because I am constantly thinking about the things I want to say. When I finally sit in front of my computer, I write whatever comes to my mind, however it comes. I then go back and rewrite portions, copy and paste parts of my essay to other parts, and just generally make it better.

How I Wrote This Essay

Writing this essay was like going to the dentist. I didn't pick the topic, and I don't like writing about "The Existence of God." The topic just sounds too daunting—but then again so is going to the dentist. Nevertheless, I went around for a month thinking about what I wanted to say, with the deadline of when I had to turn in the essay in mind. Finally, I sat in front of my computer, wrote, rewrote, and finalized the essay.

My Writing Tip

Write about a topic that you like and want to learn more about. Write after you have thought about your topic for at least a couple of days. When you write, do not be afraid of making typographical, punctuation, or grammatical errors. Just write. Later, you will have plenty of time to edit your paper. Always make several drafts; nobody's first product is a final product. If you have the time, put what you've written away for a couple of days (or at least hours) and read it again with a "fresh eye," making any necessary edits. Make your edits on a hard copy of the essay, not on the computer screen. Read your essay aloud; awkward sentences sound awkward. I strongly urge you to use your spell check, but after you do, read your essay again for spelling errors; your computer can't tell the difference between "here" and "hear" or "their" and "there." Finally, if you like what you wrote, try to publish it in a school or community magazine. It's worth the effort.

● CHAPTER WRITING ASSIGNMENTS

1. Write an essay in which you contrast one of the following pairs of concepts:
   a. Hearing–Listening
   b. Liberty–License
   c. Servant–Slave

d. Democracy–Demagoguery
   e. Art–Craft
   f. Having an opinion–Being opinionated
   g. Talent–Ability
2. Write an essay comparing any two jobs you've ever had.

● WRITING ASSIGNMENTS FOR A SPECIFIC AUDIENCE

1. Write a letter to a younger brother or sister—or an imaginary one—contrasting college with high school. Be sure to choose appropriate bases for the contrast, such as academic rigor, social life, relationships with teachers, and independence.
2. Write an essay to one of your parents contrasting your former boss with your present one.

● COLLABORATIVE WRITING PROJECT

Assemble students who are literature lovers into two groups. Each group will select a modern author for a study. By consensus, choose one short work from the author for reading and study. In an oral session, compare and contrast the single representative work of both authors using mutually agreed upon bases of comparison/contrast. From your notes, team-write a comparison/contrast of the chosen authors.

● IMAGE GALLERY WRITING ASSIGNMENT

Visit pages 662–664 of our image gallery and study all three images dealing with the existence of God. Then choose the image that most appeals to you. Answer the questions and do the writing assignment.

13

Division/Classification

ROAD MAP TO DIVISION/CLASSIFICATION

What Division/Classification Does

To write a division/classification essay means to break down a subject into its constituent types. If you write a paragraph on the kinds of books in your library, the types of cars in your miniature-car collection, or the varieties of humor in Mark Twain's works, you are classifying. A prime purpose of a division/classification is to discover the nature of a subject by a study of its parts and their relationship to the larger whole. For example, the following paragraph tries to explain and understand people by grouping them together into two primary categories:

> A simple experiment will distinguish two types of human nature. Gather a throng of people and pour them into a ferry-boat. By the time the boat has swung into the river you will find that a certain proportion have taken the trouble to climb upstairs in order to be out on deck and see what is to be seen as they cross over. The rest have settled indoors to think what they will do upon reaching the other side, or perhaps lose themselves in apathy or tobacco smoke. But leaving out those apathetic, or addicted to a single enjoyment, we may divide all the alert passengers on the boat into two classes: those who are interested in crossing the river, and those who are merely interested in getting across. And we may divide all the people on the earth, or all the moods of people, in the same way. Some of them are chiefly occupied with attaining ends, and some with receiving experiences. The distinction of the two will be more marked when we name the first kind practical, and the second poetic, for common knowledge recognizes that a person poetic or in a poetic mood is impractical, and a practical person is intolerant of poetry.
>
> —Max Eastman, "Poetic People"

Division and classification are common to the way we think. We divide and classify the plant and animal kingdoms into phyla, genera, families, and species; we divide the military into the Army, Navy, Air Force, Marines, and Coast Guard. We divide and classify people into kinds and types. When we ask, "What kind of person is he?" we are asking for information developed by division and classification. An assignment asking for an essay developed by division, therefore, is an exercise in this common mode of thinking.

When to Use Division/Classification

Division/classification is especially useful in analyzing big, complex subjects. All of us draw on categories—some accurate, some prejudicial—in our attempts to understand the world around us. We wonder what type of person a certain man or woman is, and when we think we know, we react accordingly. This is not necessarily bad, so long as we do not hold false categories about people that function as prejudices. We speculate on the experiences that happen to us and try to sort them into understandable types. We say that yesterday was that kind of day and that last year was that sort of year. We have theories about kinds of love, types of friends, varieties of personalities. Science, philosophy, and even the practical arts are largely based on classifications. Biology sorts animals and plants into genera and species; medicine organizes diseases into types; chemistry classifies substances; and literature classifies writing. The concept of types rescues us from the tyranny of uniqueness and spares us from having to individually study every event, object, person, or thing. Without categories that tell us that this is like that, experience would have no predictive value and we would be overwhelmed by the uniqueness of every butterfly, thunderstorm, or love affair.

How to Use Division/Classification

1. **All good writing is based on clear thinking, but division/classification most decidedly so.** To classify is to think and analyze, to see relationships between individual items where none are obvious. You are, in a sense, superimposing your mind's filing cabinet onto the world. To classify accurately, then, you must base your typing and sorting on a single principle. This means that your sorting must be done on the basis of one criterion or your scheme will be a muddle. A simple example would be if you were to classify sports by whether or not they involve physical contact and lumped tennis in with football. Obviously, tennis is a noncontact sport, and your sorting would be inaccurate. Likewise, if you were writing a paper on the works written by Samuel Johnson and came up with the following list:

    a. Johnson's poetry
    b. Johnson's prose
    c. Johnson's dictionary
    d. Boswell's *Life of Johnson*

your division/classification would also be false. Boswell's *Life of Johnson* is not by Johnson but about him and, therefore, does not belong in your list. In a more formal context, we see this error repeated in the following paragraph, whose division/classification is not based on a single principle:

> Mass production in American industry is made up of four distinct elements: division of labor, standardization through precision tooling, assembly line, and consumer public. First is the division of labor, which means that a complicated production process is broken down into specialized individual tasks that are performed by people or machines who concentrate on these tasks only. Second is the standardization of parts as a result of precision tooling. This means that each part can be produced by machines both for interchangeability and for assembly by semiskilled workers. Third is the assembly line, which is a method of moving the work from one person to another in a continual chain of progress until the item is completed. This is a way of moving the work to the person, instead of the person to the work. The last element is the consumer public. Without it mass production would be a futile endeavor, for it is the public that buys up all the mass-produced items as fast as they roll off the assembly line.

Clearly, the division/classification is not based on a single principle. Division of labor, standardization through precision tooling, and the use of an assembly line may be part of the mass-production process, but the consumer public plainly is not. Only after production has been completed and an item is ready to be marketed does the consumer enter into the picture. As it stands, the paragraph has misrepresented the elements involved in mass production.

2. **Make your division/classification complete.** A complete division/classification is one that includes all the parts of the subject being divided. If you were to classify sports by whether or not they involve the use of a ball and left out soccer, your division/classification would be incomplete. If you omitted the short story from an essay classifying types of literature, you would likewise be guilty of this error. Similarly, if you were to divide the family of Equidae into its main categories, you would have to include the horse, the ass, and the zebra. Leave out any of these, and your division/classification would be incomplete.

3. **Avoid the overlapping of categories.** Here is an example of an overlapping division in the division/classification of literature according to genres:
   a. Poetry
   b. Short story
   c. Humor
   d. Drama
   e. Novel

Humor is not a genre but a characteristic of poetry, a short story, a drama, or a novel. Therefore, it does not belong in this list.

Warming Up to Write a Division/Classification

1. Here's a good exercise to get your brain to think in terms of classification—that is, inventing categories into which to divide a subject and then placing items into each category. As quickly as possible, divide each of the following subjects into as many categories as seems sensible. Keep a list of the categories. If, after rereading your list, a category doesn't fit, delete it.
   a. Books
   b. Clothing
   c. Friends
   d. Weather
   e. TV programs
   f. Pets
   g. Music

2. In the following classifications, check the category that does not fit and write down the reasons why it should be excluded.
   a. Dreams
      _____1. sexual
      _____2. paralyzing
      _____3. imagining
      _____4. replaying the day
   b. Cars
      _____1. SUVs
      _____2. trucks
      _____3. sedans
      _____4. electric cars
   c. Family games
      _____1. card games
      _____2. ping pong
      _____3. domino games
      _____4. board games
   d. Houses in which to live
      _____1. sheds
      _____2. cottages
      _____3. mansions
      _____4. tract homes

e. Jobs
   _____1. technical
   _____2. waiter
   _____3. professional
   _____4. hard labor

3. Looking back at Exercise 1, choose one of the subjects you classified into categories; then pick one of the categories and place at least three items in it. For instance, if you classified meals into *hors d'oeuvres, main dishes, side dishes,* and *desserts,* you might choose "main dishes" as your category and then list the following items as belonging to it: meat, poultry, fish, and vegetarian substitute. Make sure that your items are appropriately related to the category.

EXAMPLES

Move Over, Teams
PAUL M. MUCHINSKY

Paul M. Muchinsky is a psychology professor at the University of North Carolina, Greensboro. He was educated at Iowa State University, Kansas State University, and Purdue University, from which he received a Ph.D. in Industrial Organizational Psychology. Dr. Muchinsky was a recipient of the Distinguished Teaching Award for outstanding contributions to Industrial and Organizational Psychology. The essay that follows first appeared in the January 2005 issue of the magazine of the Society for Industrial and Organizational Psychology, Inc.

This hilarious essay was published in 2005 in The Industrial Organizational Psychologist—*a magazine whose readership is hardly associated with humor. Keeping a straight face, the writer comes up with hilarious names that divide groups into some unusual categories.*

• • •

1 I am rarely wrong. But when I am wrong, I am really wrong. I couldn't have been more wrong about this "team" thing. I thought the team concept would be like a rain event (as my local TV meteorologist calls it): something that blows into town, does its thing, then leaves. No way. I am convinced that teams are here to stay. I-O psychology might as well bury the individual as an object of study and embrace our new love object, the collectivity.

2 I believe in the value of diversity. Not long ago I successfully passed a diversity training workshop. Diversity means differentness. If we are now doing the collective thing, at the very least let's dignify the whole affair by studying a diversity of collectivities, not just teams. Here are 10 other collectivities that deserve their place and space as objects of study by I-O psychologists.

1. Here's a group we don't know much about. Monks. If you run a key word search on monks, I bet you won't come up with much. That's primarily because the *Journal of Monk Behavior* is not in our computerized literature base. A group of monks is an *abomination*. I always thought an abomination was a bad thing, but not necessarily so. What if a particular group of monks had and needed no contact with the outside world? They selected their own members, did their own plumbing and electrical work, baked their own bread, raised their own crops, and so on. Do you think they would refer to themselves as a *total abomination?*

2. Here's a group you simply won't believe. Morons don't have their own group. Neither do imbeciles. But idiots do. Do you know what a bunch of idiots are called? *A thicket*. It's bad enough when you encounter one idiot at work, but can you imagine running into several of them?

Spouse: "Hi honey. Welcome home. How was your day at the office? Can I make you a drink?"

I-O: "What a day I had! I ran into these idiots. I don't know where they came from. They said black was white, up was down, and in was out. I nearly lost it."

Spouse: "These idiots, were they like, a group?"

I-O: "No."

Spouse: "A bunch?"

I-O: "No."

Spouse: "A bevy?"

I-O: "No."

Spouse: "A crew?"

I-O: "No."

Spouse: "A squad?"

I-O: "No."

Spouse: "A thicket?"

I-O: "Yeah, that's it. A thicket of idiots."

Spouse: "Would you like your drink now?"

I-O: "Yes, and please make it a double."

3. I'm not surprised this group has a name, but I was surprised to learn what it is. A group of lawyers is called a *huddle*. Maybe it's because at recess in a trial they always huddle up. I can't help but think of football when I think of a huddle of lawyers. Something like this. "Before entering the huddle, attorney Schwartz looks over at the CEO for any last-second signals. Schwartz then calls the play. Attorneys Robinson and Davis will run interference for attorney Smith, who will deliver the motion to dismiss on the unsuspecting defense. All right, *habeas corpus* on two. Let's go."

4. Even philosophers have their own name. They are called a *ponder*. Maybe it's because philosophers like to ponder weighty issues. I bet this group knows how to party. I envision a meeting of the Southern Philosophical Association holding their annual meeting in Natchez, Mississippi. Out on the veranda are two veteran philosophers, Rhett and Beauregard. Amidst the honeysuckle and jasmine, they are sipping on mint juleps. They are observing

clusters of their colleagues engaged in passionate conversations about such topics as the meaning of meaning. Just then the weather turns inclement. Rhett turns to his colleague and says, "Bo, I wonder if we should wander over yonder to take a gander at that ponder. They seem to be lost in their own thoughts. They appear not to realize it is starting to hail."

23   5. If any group has a perfect name, it is this group. A bunch of bureaucrats is called a *shuffle*. How many times have you been shuffled around when trying to get a straight answer from bureaucrats? Trying to get your driver's license renewed with the Department of Motor Vehicles would be a prime example. The clerk says, "If your birthday falls on an odd-numbered day in an even-numbered year, get in Line 1. However, if you were born in a year that was a leap year, ignore this direction. But if this year is a leap year, then reinstate that direction. If the last thing I told you is false, but the first thing I told you is true, should you believe me? Now, if your birthday falls on an even-numbered day in an odd-numbered year, get in Line 2. However,...." Do the shuffle!

24   6. Here is one that just doesn't make much sense. Not only do I not understand why this group rates a name, but how did they get this name? A group of nudists is called a *hangout*. I can see a hangdown, but not a hangout.

25   7. Here's a tricky one. A bunch of car dealers is called a *lot*. You probably thought it is the cars themselves that are positioned on a lot. Well, it's also the people who sell them to you. A commercial: "So what do you like most about the sales department at Jayhawk Chrysler, Dodge, Mitsubishi Motors?" Satisfied customer: "Their attentiveness to customer needs. They have lots of lots on their lots."

26   8. Not to be outdone, car mechanics also have their own name. A bunch of car mechanics is called a clutch. Not a brake, or an accelerator, but a *clutch*. Maybe this group got itself named after what it works on much of the day. Remember when we were 15 and were taking driving lessons? Some grizzled old driving instructor was trying to teach us how to brake, steer, accelerate, and use the clutch, all at the same time. By now we must have realized, looking back, that this poor slob must have drawn the short straw in getting this work assignment. Just about any work assignment involving cars, including changing the oil, has got to be better than teaching 15-year-olds how to drive one. Remember when the car started to stall, and the driving instructor screamed, "Release the clutch!"? Maybe he really wasn't yelling at us. Maybe he was wishing aloud for someone to lay off the car mechanics about whom he was envious.

27   9. A group of widows is called an *ambush*. I can see something like this: A heavy manufacturing company is under a lot of pressure to produce orders. The HR director is sympathetic to the need for further production, but he is also concerned about the welfare of the workforce. The HR director addresses the production supervisors. "Fellows, I know you have to meet your production schedules, but I'm telling you that you are pushing your men too hard. They're coming to me complaining about being overworked, stressed-out, and on the verge of collapse. I'm telling you that you gotta ease up a bit. If you don't, you're just setting this company up for an ambush."

28   10. This group has a rather predictable name. A group of mathematicians is called a *number*. I think they could have been more original than that, but who am I to judge? Suppose there is a national association of mathematicians, organized by state associations of mathematicians, each being a number. But there is dissent among some of the groups of mathematicians. At the national conference, the president intones the danger of splinter groups within the association. "I understand some of our numbers are up while other numbers are down, yet other numbers are difficult to interpret. I only hope when we add all the numbers together, their sum total will achieve unity for our association." What if one particular number was repeatedly successful in winning raffles and contests. Would we call it a "lucky number?" You could have fun with this one.

29   My point is simple. We can't pick and choose which collectivities we will study. As I-O psychologists, our tent should be inclusive and we should welcome any and all parties. That means we give equal and fair treatment to abominations, thickets, huddles, ponders, shuffles, hangouts, lots, clutches, ambushes, and numbers, as well as teams. We will not exhibit bias or preferential treatment toward any one group over any other. I can't wait to read the first meta-analysis on clutchwork.

30   I feel it is only fair that if I-O psychology is now in the business of studying collectivities, we should have our own name. The mathematicians have theirs, the philosophers have theirs, but I-O psychologists have none. The bird kingdom has many collective nouns for its respective members. The most linguistically evocative collective noun refers to a group of larks. Larks are beautiful, graceful, and agile creatures, who collectively are called an *exaltation*. I-O psychologists are also beautiful, graceful, and agile. I decree that we shall, from here on out, refer to ourselves as an exultation of I-O psychologists. The most beautiful of all the beautiful I-O psychologists are those who serve on the Executive Committee of SIOP. They shall now be known as the Executive Exultation. What a euphonious name. I propose the members of the Executive Exultation shall have their ID badges at our national conference adorned with long flowing streamers to indicate their special status. Embossed on the streamers will be the outline of a lark. That's the least we can do to honor the larks. After all, we stole their name.

31   I understand SIOP is considering changing its name. Some people want to jettison the old industrial prefix. That only solves half the problem. If we are now going to be studying collectivities and not individuals, our name should reflect what we are. SIOP should change its name to SOS: The Society for Organizational Sociologists.

● Vocabulary

meteorologist (1)	collectivity (1)	diversity (2)
abomination (3)	ponder (22)	inclement (22)
shuffle (23)	nudists (24)	grizzled (26)
ambush (27)	HR (Human Resources) (27)	predictable (28)
dissent (28)	raffles (28)	linguistically (30)
evocative (30)	exultation (30)	euphonious (30)

● The Facts

1. How factual is this essay? Is this an essay that will teach you the major "facts" about the groups the author categorizes? Explain your answers.
2. How many teams does the author categorize, and in what paragraph does he list them all?
3. What does the opening paragraph indicate about the author? What aspect of his profession had he misjudged?
4. The author begins his classification with the category of monks. Why do you suppose he placed them at the head of his list?
5. What is the name he suggests for the group of psychologists who want to study collectivities? What connotations go along with this name?

● The Strategies

1. What is the purpose of Muchinsky's overall strategy? In other words, what purpose is served by his language, his examples, and his categories? What reaction does he expect from his readers?
2. What rhetorical mode does the author use? How does the mode suit the purpose of this essay?
3. Why is the essay so humorous? Point out what you think is the most humorous passage and state why it made you laugh.
4. Why are paragraphs 7 through 20 so short? Explain the reason.
5. What humorous ploy does the author use in describing the nudists in paragraph 24? Is the humor in good taste, or might some readers be offended?

● The Issues

1. If a serious message is contained within this humorous essay, what might it be? Does the essay support a serious message? Why or why not?
2. What is the author's definition of an idiot? How effective is this definition in terms of the average reader? Do you have a better or different definition? If so, what is it? How does the term "thicket" fit this group?
3. How does the author's description of the philosopher category fit the popular impression of philosophers? How does the author connect the name for the group to the subject matter with which they deal? How does the author maintain a humorous stance? Is the humor gentle or vitriolic? Explain your answer.
4. Why do you think the author calls a group of widows an ambush? What popular view is he exploiting? What better name can you suggest?
5. The final paragraph may be confusing to most readers, who may not understand its context, but what is the main point that is clearly understandable?

● Suggestions for Writing

1. Using Muchinsky's formula for classification, try to think of other groups that deserve to be classified under a heading you humorously supply. If you

can't think of any human groups, see if you can come up with groups of animals or objects.
2. Choosing one of Muchinsky's groups, divide it into appropriate subcategories. You may be either humorous or serious. For example, you might choose the category of bureaucrats and subdivide them as follows: (1) educators, (2) church officials, (3) politicians, and (4) accountants. The point is to create a classification.

Thinking as a Hobby
WILLIAM GOLDING

English novelist William Golding (1911–1993) was educated at Oxford. Golding once described his hobbies as "thinking, classical Greek, sailing, and archaeology." His works include *The Pyramid* (1964), *The Scorpion God* (1971), and *Paper Work* (1984), but he is best known for his novel *Lord of the Flies* (1954). In 1983, Golding won the Nobel Prize for Literature.

Division and classification are often creative thinking exercises in which the essayist looks for patterns and relationships that are not immediately obvious. In this essay, for example, William Golding concludes that there are three grades of thinking, which he explains with examples and anecdotes. Are there really only three grades of thinking? That is beside the point. The essayist is not a scientific researcher, but an expresser and shaper of opinion. As a professional writer, Golding takes liberties with his classification and does here what any essayist should do: He makes us think.

• • •

1   While I was still a boy, I came to the conclusion that there were three grades of thinking; and since I was later to claim thinking as my hobby, I came to an even stranger conclusion—namely, that I myself could not think at all.

2   I must have been an unsatisfactory child for grownups to deal with. I remember how incomprehensible they appeared to me at first, but not, of course, how I appeared to them. It was the headmaster of my grammar school who first brought the subject of thinking before me—though neither in the way, nor with the result he intended. He had some statuettes in his study. They stood on a high cupboard behind his desk. One was a lady wearing nothing but a bath towel. She seemed frozen in an eternal panic lest the bath towel slip down any farther, and since she had no arms, she was in an unfortunate position to pull the towel up again. Next to her, crouched the statuette of a leopard, ready to spring down at the top drawer of a filing cabinet labeled A–AH. My innocence interpreted this as the victim's last, despairing cry. Beyond the leopard was a naked, muscular gentleman, who sat, looking down, with his chin on his fist and his elbow on his knee. He seemed utterly miserable.

3   Some time later, I learned about these statuettes. The headmaster had placed them where they would face delinquent children, because they symbolized to him the whole of life. The naked lady was the Venus of Milo. She was

Love. She was not worried about the towel. She was just busy being beautiful. The leopard was Nature, and he was being natural. The naked, muscular gentleman was not miserable. He was Rodin's Thinker, an image of pure thought. It is easy to buy small plaster models of what you think life is like.

4   I had better explain that I was a frequent visitor to the headmaster's study, because of the latest thing I had done or left undone. As we now say, I was not integrated. I was, if anything, disintegrated; and I was puzzled. Grownups never made sense. Whenever I found myself in a penal position before the headmaster's desk, with the statuettes glimmering whitely above him, I would sink my head, clasp my hands behind my back and writhe one shoe over the other.

5   The headmaster would look opaquely at me through flashing spectacles. "What are we going to do with you?"

6   Well, what *were* they going to do with me? I would writhe my shoe some more and stare down at the worn rug.

7   "Look up, boy! Can't you look up?"

8   Then I would look up at the cupboard, where the naked lady was frozen in her panic and the muscular gentleman contemplated the hindquarters of the leopard in endless gloom. I had nothing to say to the headmaster. His spectacles caught the light so that you could see nothing human behind them. There was no possibility of communication.

9   "Don't you ever think at all?"

10 No, I didn't think, wasn't thinking, couldn't think—I was simply waiting in anguish for the interview to stop.

11 "Then you'd better learn—hadn't you?"

12 On one occasion the headmaster leaped to his feet, reached up and plonked Rodin's masterpiece on the desk before me.

13 "That's what a man looks like when he's really thinking."

14 I surveyed the gentleman without interest or comprehension.

15 "Go back to your class."

16 Clearly there was something missing in me. Nature had endowed the rest of the human race with a sixth sense and left me out. This must be so, I mused, on my way back to the class, since whether I had broken a window, or failed to remember Boyle's Law, or been late for school, my teachers produced me one, adult answer: "Why can't you think?"

17 As I saw the case, I had broken the window because I had tried to hit Jack Arney with a cricket ball and missed him; I could not remember Boyle's Law because I had never bothered to learn it; and I was late for school because I preferred looking over the bridge into the river. In fact, I was wicked. Were my teachers, perhaps, so good that they could not understand the depths of my depravity? Were they clear, untormented people who could direct their every action by this mysterious business of thinking? The whole thing was incomprehensible. In my earlier years, I found even the statuette of the Thinker confusing. I did not believe any of my teachers were naked, ever. Like someone born deaf, but bitterly determined to find out about sound, I watched my teachers to find out about thought.

18 There was Mr. Houghton. He was always telling me to think. With a modest satisfaction, he would tell me that he had thought a bit himself. Then why

did he spend so much time drinking? Or was there more sense in drinking than there appeared to be? But if not, and if drinking were in fact ruinous to health—and Mr. Houghton was ruined, there was no doubt about that—why was he always talking about the clean life and the virtues of fresh air? He would spread his arms wide with the action of a man who habitually spent his time striding along mountain ridges.

19 "Open air does me good, boys—I know it!"

20 Sometimes, exalted by his own oratory, he would leap from his desk and hustle us outside into a hideous wind.

21 "Now, boys! Deep breaths! Feel it right down inside you—huge draughts of God's good air!"

22 He would stand before us, rejoicing in his perfect health, an open-air man. He would put his hands on his waist and take a tremendous breath. You could hear the wind, trapped in the cavern of his chest and struggling with all the unnatural impediments. His body would reel with shock and his ruined face go white at the unaccustomed visitation. He would stagger back to his desk and collapse there, useless for the rest of the morning.

23 Mr. Houghton was given to high-minded monologues about the good life, sexless and full of duty. Yet in the middle of one of these monologues, if a girl passed the window, tapping along on her neat little feet, he would interrupt his discourse, his neck would turn of itself and he would watch her out of sight. In this instance, he seemed to me ruled not by thought but by an invisible and irresistible spring in his nape.

24 His neck was an object of great interest to me. Normally it bulged a bit over his collar. But Mr. Houghton had fought in the First World War alongside both Americans and French, and had come—by who knows what illogic?—to a settled detestation of both countries. If either country happened to be prominent in current affairs, no argument could make Mr. Houghton think well of it. He would bang the desk, his neck would bulge still further and go red. "You can say what you like," he would cry, "but I've thought about this—and I know what I think!"

25 Mr. Houghton thought with his neck.

26 There was Miss Parsons. She assured us that her dearest wish was our welfare, but I knew even then, with the mysterious clairvoyance of childhood, that what she wanted most was the husband she never got. There was Mr. Hands—and so on.

27 I have dealt at length with my teachers because this was my introduction to the nature of what is commonly called thought. Through them I discovered that thought is often full of unconscious prejudice, ignorance and hypocrisy. It will lecture on disinterested purity while its neck is being remorselessly twisted toward a skirt. Technically, it is about as proficient as most businessmen's golf, as honest as most politicians' intentions, or—to come near my own preoccupation—as coherent as most books that get written. It is what I came to call grade-three thinking, though more properly, it is feeling, rather than thought.

28 True, often there is a kind of innocence in prejudices, but in those days I viewed grade-three thinking with an intolerant contempt and an incautious

mockery. I delighted to confront a pious lady who hated the Germans with the proposition that we should love our enemies. She taught me a great truth in dealing with grade-three thinkers; because of her, I no longer dismiss lightly a mental process which for nine-tenths of the population is the nearest they will ever get to thought. They have immense solidarity. We had better respect them, for we are outnumbered and surrounded. A crowd of grade-three thinkers, all shouting the same thing, all warming their hands at the fire of their own prejudices, will not thank you for pointing out the contradictions in their beliefs. Man is a gregarious animal, and enjoys agreement as cows will graze all the same way on the side of a hill.

29   Grade-two thinking is the detection of contradictions. I reached grade two when I trapped the poor, pious lady. Grade-two thinkers do not stampede easily, though often they fall into the other fault and lag behind. Grade-two thinking is a withdrawal, with eyes and ears open. It became my hobby and brought satisfaction and loneliness in either hand. For grade-two thinking destroys without having the power to create. It set me watching the crowds cheering His Majesty the King and asking myself what all the fuss was about, without giving me anything positive to put in the place of that heady patriotism. But there were compensations. To hear people justify their habit of hunting foxes and tearing them to pieces by claiming that the foxes like it. To hear our Prime Minister talk about the great benefit we conferred on India by jailing people like Pandit Nehru and Gandhi. To hear American politicians talk about peace in one sentence and refuse to join the League of Nations in the next. Yes, there were moments of delight.

30   But I was growing toward adolescence and had to admit that Mr. Houghton was not the only one with an irresistible spring in his neck. I, too, felt the compulsive hand of nature and began to find that pointing out contradiction could be costly as well as fun. There was Ruth, for example, a serious and attractive girl. I was an atheist at the time. Grade-two thinking is a menace to religion and knocks down sects like skittles. I put myself in a position to be converted by her with an hypocrisy worthy of grade three. She was a Methodist—or at least, her parents were, and Ruth had to follow suit. But, alas, instead of relying on the Holy Spirit to convert me, Ruth was foolish enough to open her pretty mouth in argument. She claimed that the Bible (King James Version) was literally inspired. I countered by saying that the Catholics believed in the literal inspiration of Saint Jerome's Vulgate, and the two books were different. Argument flagged.

31   At last she remarked that there were an awful lot of Methodists, and they couldn't be wrong, could they—not all those millions? That was too easy, said I restively (for the nearer you were to Ruth, the nicer she was to be near to) since there were more Roman Catholics than Methodists anyway; and they couldn't be wrong, could they—not all those hundreds of millions? An awful flicker of doubt appeared in her eyes. I slid my arm round her waist and murmured breathlessly that if we were counting heads, the Buddhists were the boys for my money. But Ruth had really wanted to do me good, because I was so nice. She fled. The combination of my arm and those countless Buddhists was too much for her.

32   That night her father visited my father and left, red-cheeked and indignant. I was given the third degree to find out what had happened. It was lucky we were both of us only fourteen. I lost Ruth and gained an undeserved reputation as a potential libertine.

33   So grade-two thinking could be dangerous. It was in this knowledge, at the age of fifteen, that I remember making a comment from the heights of grade two, on the limitations of grade three. One evening I found myself alone in the school hall, preparing it for a party. The door of the headmaster's study was open. I went in. The headmaster had ceased to thump Rodin's Thinker down on the desk as an example to the young. Perhaps he had not found any more candidates, but the statuettes were still there, glimmering and gathering dust on top of the cupboard. I stood on a chair and rearranged them. I stood Venus in her bath towel on the filing cabinet, so that now the top drawer caught its breath in a gasp of sexy excitement. "A-ah!" The portentous Thinker I placed on the edge of the cupboard so that he looked down at the bath towel and waited for it to slip.

34   Grade-two thinking, though it filled life with fun and excitement, did not make for content. To find out the deficiencies of our elders bolsters the young ego but does not make for personal security. I found that grade two was not only the power to point out contradictions. It took the swimmer some distance from the shore and left him there, out of his depth. I decided that Pontius Pilate was a typical grade-two thinker. "What is truth?" he said, a very common grade-two thought, but one that is used always as the end of an argument instead of the beginning. There is a still higher grade of thought which says, "What is truth?" and sets out to find it.

35   But these grade-one thinkers were few and far between. They did not visit my grammar school in the flesh though they were there in books. I aspired to them, partly because I was ambitious and partly because I now saw my hobby as an unsatisfactory thing if it went no further. If you set out to climb a mountain, however high you climb, you have failed if you cannot reach the top.

36   I did meet an undeniably grade-one thinker in my first year at Oxford. I was looking over a small bridge in Magdalen Deer Park, and a tiny mustached and hatted figure came and stood by my side. He was a German who had just fled from the Nazis to Oxford as a temporary refuge. His name was Einstein.

37   But Professor Einstein knew no English at that time and I knew only two words of German. I beamed at him, trying wordlessly to convey by my bearing all the affection and respect that the English felt for him. It is possible—and I have to make the admission—that I felt here were two grade-one thinkers standing side by side; yet I doubt if my face conveyed more than a formless awe. I would have given my Greek and Latin and French and a good slice of my English for enough German to communicate. But we were divided; he was as inscrutable as my headmaster. For perhaps five minutes we stood together on the bridge, undeniable grade-one thinker and breathless aspirant. With true greatness, Professor Einstein realized that any contact was better than none. He pointed to a trout wavering in midstream.

38   He spoke: "Fisch."

39   My brain reeled. Here I was, mingling with the great, and yet helpless as the veriest grade-three thinker. Desperately I sought for some sign by which I

might convey that I, too, revered pure reason. I nodded vehemently. In a brilliant flash I used up half of my German vocabulary. *"Fisch. Ja. Ja."*

40   For perhaps another five minutes we stood side by side. Then Professor Einstein, his whole figure still conveying good will and amiability, drifted away out of sight.

41   I, too, would be a grade-one thinker. I was irreverent at the best of times. Political and religious systems, social customs, loyalties and traditions, they all came tumbling down like so many rotten apples off a tree. This was a fine hobby and a sensible substitute for cricket, since you could play it all the year round. I came up in the end with what must always remain the justification for grade-one thinking, its sign, seal and charter. I devised a coherent system for living. It was a moral system, which was wholly logical. Of course, as I readily admitted, conversion of the world to my way of thinking might be difficult, since my system did away with a number of trifles, such as big business, centralized government, armies, marriage . . .

42   It was Ruth all over again. I had some very good friends who stood by me, and still do. But my acquaintances vanished, taking the girls with them. Young women seemed oddly contented with the world as it was. They valued the meaningless ceremony with a ring. Young men, while willing to concede the chaining sordidness of marriage, were hesitant about abandoning the organizations which they hoped would give them a career. A young man on the first rung of the Royal Navy, while perfectly agreeable to doing away with big business and marriage, got as red-necked as Mr. Houghton when I proposed a world without any battleships in it.

43   Had the game gone too far? Was it a game any longer? In those prewar days, I stood to lose a great deal, for the sake of a hobby.

44   Now you are expecting me to describe how I saw the folly of my ways and came back to the warm nest, where prejudices are so often called loyalties, where pointless actions are hallowed into custom by repetition, where we are content to say we think when all we do is feel.

45   But you would be wrong. I dropped my hobby and turned professional.

46   If I were to go back to the headmaster's study and find the dusty statuettes still there, I would arrange them differently. I would dust Venus and put her aside, for I have come to love her and know her for the fair thing she is. But I would put the Thinker, sunk in his desperate thought, where there were shadows before him—and at his back, I would put the leopard, crouched and ready to spring.

- ### Vocabulary

statuettes (2)
opaquely (5)
impediments (22)
clairvoyance (26)
proposition (28)
flagged (30)
inscrutable (37)
amiability (40)

integrated (4)
ruinous (18)
monologues (23)
disinterested (27)
solidarity (28)
restively (31)
veriest (39)

penal (4)
draughts (21)
detestation (24)
proficient (27)
skittles (30)
libertine (32)
revered (39)

The Facts

1. Into what three types does Golding divide all thinking? Describe each type in your own words. Is there a value judgment implied in the division?
2. Why does Golding take up so much time describing some of his grade-school teachers? How are they related to the purpose of the essay?
3. Why is it so difficult to find grade-one thinkers? Describe someone whom you consider a grade-one thinker.
4. How do you interpret Golding's last two paragraphs? Has the author reverted to grade-three or grade-two thinking, or is he still a grade-one thinker? Comment.
5. What does the encounter between Golding and Albert Einstein indicate?

The Strategies

1. In paragraph 2, the author describes three statuettes on a cupboard behind the headmaster's desk. In what paragraph is each of the statuettes explained? Why is the explanation necessary?
2. Much of the article reflects a young boy's point of view. How is this point of view achieved? Point to some specific passages.
3. Paragraphs 24, 25, and 27 refer to the word *neck* repeatedly. What has the neck come to symbolize in this context?
4. What is the analogy used in paragraph 28 to describe grade-three thinkers? Is the analogy effective? Explain.
5. What is Golding's purpose in alluding to the jailing of Nehru and Gandhi, and to the Americans' refusal to join the League of Nations?

The Issues

1. To be a grade-one thinker, must one do away with big business, centralized government, armies, marriages, and so on? How could one be a grade-one thinker without wanting to destroy these?
2. Golding seems to indicate that his teachers were conformists, hypocrites, or men of prejudice. What kinds of thinkers do you remember your grade-school teachers to have been? Give examples of their thinking.
3. What groups in our society reveal typical grade-three thinking? Give reasons for your choices.
4. What, if anything, is important about grade-two thinking? Does one need to be a grade-two thinker before going on to grade one?
5. How does nature assist or resist grade-one thinking?

Suggestions for Writing

1. Write an essay in which you answer the question "Does a college education help to eliminate prejudice and hypocrisy?" Support your answer with examples from your own experience.

2. Write an essay in which you divide your acquaintances into types according to the kinds of behavior they project. Be sure that your categories are mutually exclusive and that they take in as many of your acquaintances as possible.

Kinds of Discipline
JOHN HOLT

John Holt (1923–1985), education theorist, was born in New York. He taught at Harvard University and the University of California, Berkeley. His works include *How Children Fail* (1964), *How Children Learn* (1967), *Freedom and Beyond* (1972), from which this selection was taken, *Escape from Childhood* (1974), *Instead of Education* (1976), and *Teach Your Own* (1981).

Because discipline *is an ambiguous and often misunderstood word, the author attempts to give it a clearer meaning by focusing on three specific kinds of discipline.*

• • •

1   A child, in growing up, may meet and learn from three different kinds of disciplines. The first and most important is what we might call the Discipline of Nature or of Reality. When he is trying to do something real, if he does the wrong thing or doesn't do the right one, he doesn't get the result he wants. If he doesn't pile one block right on top of another, or tries to build on a slanting surface, his tower falls down. If he hits the wrong key, he hears the wrong note. If he doesn't hit the nail squarely on the head, it bends, and he has to pull it out and start with another. If he doesn't measure properly what he is trying to build, it won't open, close, fit, stand up, fly, float, whistle, or do whatever he wants it to do. If he closes his eyes when he swings, he doesn't hit the ball. A child meets this kind of discipline every time he tries to do something, which is why it is so important in school to give children more chances to do things, instead of just reading or listening to someone talk (or pretending to). This discipline is a great teacher. The learner never has to wait long for his answer; it usually comes quickly, often instantly. Also it is clear, and very often points toward the needed correction; from what happened he can not only see that what he did was wrong, but also why, and what he needs to do instead. Finally, and most important, the giver of the answer, call it Nature, is impersonal, impartial, and indifferent. She does not give opinions, or make judgments; she cannot be wheedled, bullied, or fooled; she does not get angry or disappointed; she does not praise or blame; she does not remember past failures or hold grudges; with her one always gets a fresh start, this time is the one that counts.

2   The next discipline we might call the Discipline of Culture, of Society, of What People Really Do. Man is a social, a cultural animal. Children sense around them this culture, this network of agreements, customs, habits, and rules binding the adults together. They want to understand it and be a part of it. They watch very carefully what people around them are doing and want to do the same.

They want to do right, unless they become convinced they can't do right. Thus children rarely misbehave seriously in church, but sit as quietly as they can. The example of all those grownups is contagious. Some mysterious ritual is going on, and children, who like rituals, want to be part of it. In the same way, the little children that I see at concerts or operas, though they may fidget a little, or perhaps take a nap now and then, rarely make any disturbance. With all those grownups sitting there, neither moving nor talking, it is the most natural thing in the world to imitate them. Children who live among adults who are habitually courteous to each other, and to them, will soon learn to be courteous. Children who live surrounded by people who speak a certain way will speak that way, however much we may try to tell them that speaking that way is bad or wrong.

3   The third discipline is the one most people mean when they speak of discipline—the Discipline of Superior Force, of sergeant to private, of "you do what I tell you or I'll make you wish you had." There is bound to be some of this in a child's life. Living as we do surrounded by things that can hurt children, or that children can hurt, we cannot avoid it. We can't afford to let a small child find out from experience the danger of playing in a busy street, or of fooling with the pots on the top of a stove, or of eating up the pills in the medicine cabinet. So, along with other precautions, we say to him, "Don't play in the street, or touch things on the stove, or go into the medicine cabinet, or I'll punish you." Between him and the danger too great for him to imagine we put a lesser danger, but one he can imagine and maybe therefore wants to avoid. He can have no idea of what it would be like to be hit by a car, but he can imagine being shouted at, or spanked, or sent to his room. He avoids these substitutes for the greater danger until he can understand it and avoid it for its own sake. But we ought to use this discipline only when it is necessary to protect the life, health, safety, or well-being of people or other living creatures, or to prevent destruction of things that people care about. We ought not to assume too long, as we usually do, that a child cannot understand the real nature of the danger from which we want to protect him. The sooner he avoids the danger, not to escape our punishment, but as a matter of good sense, the better. He can learn that faster than we think. In Mexico, for example, where people drive their cars with a good deal of spirit, I saw many children no older than five or four walking unattended on the streets. They understood about cars, they knew what to do. A child whose life is full of the threat and fear of punishment is locked into babyhood. There is no way for him to grow up, to learn to take responsibility for his life and acts. Most important of all, we should not assume that having to yield to the threat of our superior force is good for the child's character. It is never good for anyone's character. To bow to superior force makes us feel impotent and cowardly for not having had the strength or courage to resist. Worse, it makes us resentful and vengeful. We can hardly wait to make someone pay for our humiliation, yield to us as we were once made to yield. No, if we cannot always avoid using the Discipline of Superior Force, we should at least use it as seldom as we can.

4   There are places where all three disciplines overlap. Any very demanding human activity combines in it the disciplines of Superior Force, of Culture, and of Nature. The novice will be told, "Do it this way, never mind asking

why, just do it that way, that is the way we always do it." But it probably is just the way they always do it, and usually for the very good reason that it is a way that has been found to work. Think, for example, of ballet training. The student in a class is told to do this exercise, or that; to stand so; to do this or that with his head, arms, shoulders, abdomen, hips, legs, feet. He is constantly corrected. There is no argument. But behind these seemingly autocratic demands by the teacher lie many decades of custom and tradition, and behind that, the necessities of dancing itself. You cannot make the moves of classical ballet unless over many years you have acquired, and renewed every day, the needed strength and suppleness in scores of muscles and joints. Nor can you do the difficult motions, making them look easy, unless you have learned hundreds of easier ones first. Dance teachers may not always agree on all the details of teaching these strengths and skills. But no novice could learn them all by himself. You could not go for a night or two to watch the ballet and then, without any other knowledge at all, teach yourself how to do it. In the same way, you would be unlikely to learn any complicated and difficult human activity without drawing heavily on the experience of those who know it better. But the point is that the authority of these experts or teachers stems from, grows out of their greater competence and experience, the fact that what they do works, not the fact that they happen to be the teacher and as such have the power to kick a student out of the class. And the further point is that children are always and everywhere attracted to that competence, and ready and eager to submit themselves to a discipline that grows out of it. We hear constantly that children will never do anything unless compelled to by bribes or threats. But in their private lives, or in extracurricular activities in school, in sports, music, drama, art, running a newspaper, and so on, they often submit themselves willingly and wholeheartedly to very intense disciplines, simply because they want to learn to do a given thing well. Our Little-Napoleon football coaches, of whom we have too many and hear far too much, blind us to the fact that millions of children work hard every year getting better at sports and games without coaches barking and yelling at them.

- ## Vocabulary

    wheedled (1)   ritual (2)   impotent (3)
    autocratic (4)

- ## The Facts

    1. What principle or basis of division does Holt use?
    2. How does Holt clarify for the reader what he means by "Discipline of Nature or of Reality"? Is this method of clarification effective? Why?
    3. What are the advantages of learning from nature or reality?
    4. According to the author, when should the discipline of superior force be used? Do you agree?
    5. At the end of his essay, Holt identifies the most successful motivation for discipline. What is it?

496 CHAPTER 13 • Division/Classification

● **The Strategies**

1. In the last sentence of paragraph 1, the author uses the feminine pronouns *she* and *her* in referring to nature. What is his purpose?
2. What transitional guideposts does the author use to gain coherence and organization?
3. What is the effect of labeling certain football coaches "Little Napoleons"?

● **The Issues**

1. What additional examples can you supply of the ways in which children submit to the discipline of culture or society?
2. What tips can you provide for someone who has no discipline in studying college courses? What method has worked best for you?
3. Holt warns adults that the use of superior force in order to punish children is never good for the children's characters (see paragraph 3) and should therefore be used as little as possible. What, in your opinion, is the result of never using this superior force in the training of children? Give examples to support your point.
4. Our society is witnessing the self-destruction of many young people through chemical abuse of one kind or another. How is this abuse tied to Holt's idea of discipline?
5. How important is discipline in your life? Do you choose friends who are strongly disciplined, or do you prefer those who are more "laid back"? Give reasons for your answers.

● **Suggestions for Writing**

1. Write an essay in which you divide discipline according to the kinds of effects it produces: for example, discipline that results in strong study habits.
2. Develop the following topic sentence into a three-paragraph essay: "To be successful, a person must have three kinds of discipline: of the intellect, of the emotions, and of the body." Use Holt's essay as a model for your organization.

The Idols

Francis Bacon

Francis Bacon (1561–1626) was born in London and educated at Trinity College, Cambridge, and Gray's Inn. Bacon is generally credited with applying the inductive method of logic to scientific investigation. His essays, which are notable for their aphoristic style, are his best-known works.

This excerpt comes from Novum Organum *(1620), possibly Bacon's most famous work. Bacon was struggling against the traditions of medieval scholasticism, which assumed a given and unchangeable set of premises from which, by deductive logic, one could infer truths about the world. Our way of thinking today, especially in science, is just the opposite, thanks in part to*

Bacon. We begin not with givens but with questions. We proceed by gathering data and using induction to draw conclusions. (See the discussion of logic in Chapter 15.) This method of thinking does not completely safeguard us from Bacon's Idols, but it does help keep them at bay.

• • •

1 The *Idols* and false notions which have already preoccupied the human understanding, and are deeply rooted in it, not only so beset men's minds, that they become difficult to access, but even when access is obtained, will again meet and trouble us in the instauration of the sciences, unless mankind, when forewarned, guard themselves with all possible care against them.

2 Four species of *Idols* beset the human mind: to which (for distinction's sake) we have assigned names: calling the first *Idols of the Tribe;* the second *Idols of the Den;* the third *Idols of the Market;* the fourth *Idols of the Theater.*

3 The formation of notions and axioms on the foundations of true induction, is the only fitting remedy, by which we can ward off and expel these *Idols*. It is however of great service to point them out. For the doctrine of *Idols* bears the same relation to the interpretation of nature, as that of the confutation of sophisms does to common logic.

4 The *Idols of the Tribe* are inherent in human nature, and the very tribe or race of man. For man's sense is falsely asserted to be the standard of things. On the contrary, all the perceptions, both of the senses and the mind, bear reference to man, and not to the universe, and the human mind resembles those uneven mirrors, which impart their own properties to different objects, from which rays are emitted, and distort and disfigure them.

5 The *Idols of the Den* are those of each individual. For every body (in addition to the errors common to the race of man) has his own individual den or cavern, which intercepts and corrupts the light of nature; either from his own peculiar and singular disposition, or from his education and intercourse with others, or from his reading, and the authority acquired by those whom he reverences and admires, or from a different impression produced on the mind, as it happens to be preoccupied and predisposed, or equable and tranquil, and the like: so that the spirit of man (according to its several dispositions) is variable, confused, and as it were actuated by chance; and Heraclitus[1] said well that men search for knowledge in lesser worlds and not in the greater or common world.

6 There are also *Idols* formed by the reciprocal intercourse and society of man with man, which we call *Idols of the Market,* from the commerce and association of men with each other. For men converse by means of language; but words are formed at the will of the generality; and there arises from a bad and unapt formation of words a wonderful obstruction to the mind. Nor can the definitions and explanations, with which learned men are wont to guard and protect themselves in some instances, afford a complete remedy: words still manifestly force the understanding, throw everything into confusion, and lead mankind into vain and innumerable controversies and fallacies.

---

[1] Greek philosopher of the sixth century B.C.—Ed.

7   Lastly there are *Idols* which have crept into men's minds from the various dogmas of peculiar systems of philosophy, and also from the perverted rules of demonstration, and these we denominate *Idols of the Theater*. For we regard all the systems of philosophy hitherto received or imagined, as so many plays brought out and performed, creating fictitious and theatrical worlds. Nor do we speak only of the present systems, or of the philosophy and sects of the ancients, since numerous other plays of a similar nature can be still composed and made to agree with each other, the causes of the most opposite errors being generally the same. Nor, again, do we allude merely to the general systems, but also to many elements and axioms of sciences, which have become inveterate by tradition, implicit credence and neglect. We must, however, discuss each species of *Idols* more fully and distinctly in order to guard the human understanding against them.

- ## Vocabulary

  beset (1)   instauration (1)   axioms (3)
  induction (3)   confutation (3)   sophism (3)
  inherent (4)   predisposed (5)   equable (5)
  reciprocal (6)   wont (6)   dogmas (7)
  denominate (7)   sects (7)   inveterate (7)
  implicit (7)   credence (7)

- ## The Facts

  1. Exactly what is being divided in this essay? Why does Bacon use the term *idols*?
  2. Using your own words, describe each idol in the order listed by Bacon. Supply an example for each from your own experience.
  3. According to Bacon, what is the remedy for all these idols? How will this remedy work?

- ## The Strategies

  1. What connection is there between Bacon's thought and his style?
  2. Point out specific words or phrases to show that Bacon's style is archaic.
  3. What method of thinking does Bacon use to conclude that idols preoccupy the human understanding? Trace his use of the method in the essay.
  4. What is the analogy used to illustrate the last idol? Explain how this analogy helps clarify the idol.

- ## The Issues

  1. Compare Bacon's division with some more contemporary ideas on the same subject. Is his essay still valid, or is it out of date? Give reasons for your answer.
  2. What specific examples can you cite to illuminate Bacon's "idols of the tribe"?
  3. How dangerous to present society are "idols of the market"? Give reasons for your opinion.

4. What examples can you cite from your own upbringing to indicate that you have bowed to "idols of the den"?
5. In your view, what ideas marketed publicly today are dangerous but highly seductive—especially for the naïve?

- ## Suggestions for Writing

1. Write an essay in which you divide your bad habits into three or four categories. Make sure that these categories are mutually exclusive and that they include the entire range of your bad habits.
2. Write a brief report on Francis Bacon's major contributions to society. In the report, organize these contributions into separate divisions.

English 101

BART EDELMAN

Bart Edelman (b. 1951) is a contemporary American poet who spent his childhood in Teaneck, New Jersey, the subject of many of his poems. Today he lives in southern California, and he gives poetry readings across the United States. He has been the recipient of numerous grants and fellowships to study literature in India, Egypt, Nigeria, and Poland. He is currently a professor of English at Glendale College in California. His poetry collections include *Crossing the Hackensack* (1993), *Under Damaris' Dress* (1996), *The Alphabet of Love* (1999), *The Gentle Man* (2001), and *The Last Mojito* (2005).

This poem conjures up familiar memories in anyone who has taken freshman composition and remembers the opening session when students are introduced to the requirements and goals of the course. The poet uses concrete language to convey vivid portraits of three kinds of students in class on opening day.

• • •

1   They appear—
    Always—
    That first day,
    Astray;
5   Some wait to fall,
    Others to rise:

    Here rests the tired boy,
    The hour long,
    He drops his brain
10 Upon the desk
    And thinks he'd be better off dead,
    Five worlds away
    From Frost and Twain . . .
    (He'll have no part of 101).

            15 A fair-haired girl in knots
                Twists her braids so tight
                They make her ache;
                She takes good notes,
                Does what she's told,
            20 If asked a quote
                She knows it cold . . .
                (But could a smile unclench those lips?)

                Then the hand,
                One resolute voice
            25 Speaks through the bell
                And the great stampede—
                Engaged in speculation
                We turn wheat to notion,
                Sifting through each tiny grain . . .
            30 (The composition now complete).

● Vocabulary

astray (4)   resolute (24)   stampede (26)

● The Facts

1. Where does the action of the poem take place? How do you know?
2. Who are "They" in the first stanza? Why are they described as "astray"?
3. What is meant by "He drops his brain/Upon the desk" in the second stanza? Explain the figure of speech.
4. What kind of student is described in stanza 3? Describe her in your own words.
5. What is the meaning of the phrase "One resolute voice/Speaks through the bell"?

● The Strategies

1. In what sense is this poem a classification? What is being classified? How many items belong to the classification? List them.
2. After listing the first two students as a boy and a girl, why does the poet then refer to a "hand" and "voice" as the third student?
3. Why do you suppose the author chose the title "English 101" rather than, say, "Math 220" or "Economics 300"?
4. What comparison does the poet draw in stanza 4? What other simile might be used? Use your poetic imagination to find one.

The Issues

1. What is the theme (thesis) of this poem? State it in one sentence.
2. According to the poem, wherein lies a teacher's greatest classroom challenge?
3. If you were a teacher, which student would bother you more—the student of stanza 2 or the student of stanza 3? Give reasons for your answer.
4. What is your opinion on the basic importance of freshman composition? Should it be a requirement? Why or why not?
5. In stanza 2, the poet refers to Frost and Twain. How are these two literary figures related to the theme of the poem?

Suggestions for Writing

1. Write an essay in which you classify the various kinds of teachers who have taught you. For your bases of classification, consider such aspects as ability to communicate, personality, values, and attitude toward the subject matter.
2. Using Edelman's poem as a springboard, choose three or four friends who are representative types to classify your most intimate friends. Try to make each type come to life by using vivid details in describing him or her.

ISSUE FOR CRITICAL THINKING AND DEBATE: RACISM

Even to the casual observer, racism in America remains a festering problem. Its toxic influence ranges from blatant discrimination in the housing market, where minorities are deliberately steered to specific neighborhoods, to subtle hiring practices wherein deserving employees are denied promotions because of skin color. Blacks live shorter lives than whites, earn less money, and make up over half of US murder victims (94% of whom are killed by other blacks). Compared to whites, blacks are also imprisoned more often and are more likely to be executed.

To remedy the inequality between whites and blacks, the US Congress passed the Civil Rights Act of 1964 and set in place laws promoting affirmative action. The effect of this measure was to narrow the educational gap between blacks and whites. Black children today outnumber both white and Hispanic children enrolled in center-based preprimary education. Still, it is sobering to think that nearly one-third of all black families and nearly one-half of all black children still live in poverty. The National Urban League estimated in 2005 that the equality index of blacks stood at 73% when measured against whites, little changed from 2004.

How this inequality is viewed depends as much on the viewer's race as on any facts. Predictably, the explanations for the causes of the inequality are

● *Mexico, Chile, Soweto . . . , 1997, by Rupert Garcia*
Will race hatred ever stop?

divided along liberal/conservative fault lines. Liberals blame white racism and its poisonous legacy, arguing that the remedy for racial inequality is more government intervention. Conservatives argue that the time has come for racially neutral laws, with no affirmative action boost for minorities. Neither side denies the historical effects of racism. But whereas conservatives assert that the past is past and opportunities are now equal, liberals insist that the damage done to black consciousness by past injustices cannot be so casually dismissed.

These two themes are implicit in the pieces we have chosen for this debate. The first is a wrenching chapter from a book, *Warriors Don't Cry*, by an African American woman who helped desegregate Central High School in Little Rock, Arkansas, in 1954. Because this woman dared to want an education equal to what white Americans regard as their birthright, she was hounded with obscene phone calls, pelted with rocks, threatened by mobs, and tormented by her fellow students. The second reading is by a remarkable set of black sisters—Sarah L. and A. Elizabeth Delany—who wrote their memoirs when both were over 100 years old. The artwork of the chapter also reflects the problem of racism. In the painting on page 502, a black victim lies lifeless on the ground as two soldiers walk away, seemingly indifferent to the plight of the slain man. The photo on page 508 emphasizes the choice we all make between love and hate.

The turmoil caused by racism is as unsettling as it is unsettled. The liberal/conservative argument over race boils down to these questions: How much is the past really past? What can we do to ensure that the ugly legacy of racism won't continue to poison the efforts of those men and women who try to make race relations better?

Warriors Don't Cry

Melba Patillo Beals

Melba Patillo Beals (b. 1941) earned a B.A. degree from San Francisco State and a graduate degree from Columbia. She has worked as a reporter for NBC. Today she works as a communications consultant and has written books on public relations and marketing. In 1957, she was one of nine students chosen to integrate Central High School in Little Rock, Arkansas, in the wake of the 1954 Supreme Court decision *Brown v. Board of Education of Topeka, Kansas*, which declared segregated schools illegal. This reading is the opening chapter from her memoir of that traumatic experience, *Warriors Don't Cry* (1994).

1   In 1957, while most teenage girls were listening to Buddy Holly's "Peggy Sue," watching Elvis gyrate, and collecting crinoline slips, I was escaping the hanging rope of a lynch mob, dodging lighted sticks of dynamite, and washing away burning acid sprayed into my eyes.

2   During my junior year in high school, I lived at the center of a violent civil rights conflict. In 1954, the Supreme Court had decreed an end to segregated

schools. Arkansas Governor Orval Faubus and states' rights segregationists defied that ruling. President Eisenhower was compelled to confront Faubus—to use U.S. soldiers to force him to obey the law of the land. It was a historic confrontation that generated worldwide attention. At the center of the controversy were nine black children who wanted only to have the opportunity for a better education.

3   On our first day at Central High, Governor Faubus dispatched gun-toting Arkansas National Guard soldiers to prevent us from entering. Mother and I got separated from the others. The two of us narrowly escaped a rope-carrying lynch mob of men and women shouting that they'd kill us rather than see me go to school with their children.

4   Three weeks later, having won a federal court order, we black children maneuvered our way past an angry mob to enter the side door of Central High. But by eleven that morning, hundreds of people outside were running wild, crashing through police barriers to get us out of school. Some of the police sent to control the mob threw down their badges and joined the rampage. But a few other brave members of the Little Rock police force saved our lives by spiriting us past the mob to safety.

5   To uphold the law and protect lives, President Eisenhower sent soldiers of the 101st Airborne Division, the elite "Screaming Eagles"—Korean War heroes.

6   On my third trip to Central High, I rode with the 101st in an army station wagon guarded by jeeps with turret guns mounted on their hoods and helicopters roaring overhead. With the protection of our 101st bodyguards, we black students walked through the front door of the school and completed a full day of classes.

7   But I quickly learned from those who opposed integration that the soldiers' presence meant a declaration of war. Segregationists mounted a brutal campaign against us, both inside and out of school.

8   My eight friends and I paid for the integration of Central High with our innocence. During those years when we desperately needed approval from our peers, we were victims of the most harsh rejection imaginable. The physical and psychological punishment we endured profoundly affected all our lives. It transformed us into warriors who dared not cry even when we suffered intolerable pain.

9   I became an instant adult, forced to take stock of what I believed and what I was willing to sacrifice to back up my beliefs. The experience endowed me with an indestructible faith in God.

10 I am proud to report that the Little Rock experience also gave us courage, strength, and hope. We nine grew up to become productive citizens, with special insights about how important it is to respect the value of every human life.

11 I am often asked, in view of the state of race relations today, if our effort was in vain. Would I integrate Central if I had it to do over again? My answer is yes, unequivocally yes. I take pride in the fact that, although the fight for equality must continue, our 1957 effort catapulted the civil rights movement forward a giant step and shifted the fight to a more dignified battlefield. For the first time in history, a President took a very bold step to defend civil rights—our civil rights.

12 Back then, I naively believed that if we could end segregation in the schools, all barriers of inequality would fall. If you had asked me in 1957 what I expected, I would have told you that by this time our struggle for human rights would have been won. Not so. But I am consoled by the words my grandmother spoke: "Even when the battle is long and the path is steep, a true warrior does not give up. If each one of us does not step forward to claim our rights, we are doomed to an eternal wait in hopes those who would usurp them will become benevolent. The Bible says, WATCH, FIGHT, and PRAY."

13 Although I am perplexed by the state of race relations in this country today, I am at the same time very hopeful because I have ample evidence that what Grandmother promised me is true. With time and love, God solves all our problems. When we returned to Central High School for our first reunion in 1987, many Little Rock residents, white and black, greeted the nine of us as heroines and heroes. Hometown white folk in the mall smiled and said hello and offered directions even when they did not recognize us from our newspaper photos.

14 During all the fancy ceremonies, some of Arkansas's highest officials and businessmen came from far and wide to welcome us. And perhaps the most astounding evidence that things have indeed changed for the better was the attitude of Governor Bill Clinton.

15 "Call me Bill," he said, extending his hand, looking me in the eye. "You'all come on up to the house and sit a while." He flashed that charming grin of his. A few minutes of conversation assured me that his warm invitation was genuine. He is, after all, a man my brother refers to as "good people," based on their working relationship over the years.

16 So my eight friends and I found ourselves hanging out at the governor's mansion, the one Faubus built. Governor Clinton sauntered about serving soft drinks and peanuts. He and his wife, Hillary, were the kind of host and hostess who could make me feel at home even in the place where Faubus had hatched his devilish strategies to get the nine of us out of Central High School by any means possible.

17 "You'all ought to think about coming on back home now. Things are different," Governor Clinton said. He had been eleven years old when Faubus waged his segregationist battle against us. He displayed genuine respect for our contribution to the civil rights struggle. That visit was to become an evening I shall always treasure. As Chelsea played the piano and Bill and Hillary talked to me as though we'd known each other always, I found myself thinking, "Oh, Mr. Faubus, if only you and your friends could see us now."

18 My grandmother India always said God had pointed a finger at our family, asking for just a bit more discipline, more praying, and more hard work because He had blessed us with good health and good brains. My mother was one of the first few blacks to integrate the University of Arkansas, graduating in 1954. Three years later, when Grandma discovered I would be one of the first blacks to attend Central High School, she said the nightmare that had surrounded my birth was proof positive that destiny had assigned me a special task.

19   First off, I was born on Pearl Harbor Day, December 7, 1941. Mother says while she was giving birth to me, there was a big uproar, with the announcement that the Japanese had bombed Pearl Harbor. She remembers how astonished she was, and yet her focus was necessarily on the task at hand. There was trouble with my delivery because Mom was tiny and I was nine pounds. The doctor used forceps to deliver me and injured my scalp. A few days later, I fell ill with a massive infection. Mother took me to the white hospital, which reluctantly treated the families of black men who worked on the railroad. A doctor operated to save my life by inserting a drainage system beneath my scalp.

20   Twenty-four hours later I wasn't getting better. Whenever Mother sought help, neither nurses nor doctors would take her seriously enough to examine me. Instead, they said, "Just give it time."

21   Two days after my operation, my temperature soared to 106 and I started convulsing. Mother sent for the minister to give me the last rites, and relatives were gathering to say farewell.

22   That evening, while Grandmother sat in my hospital room, rocking me back and forth as she hummed her favorite hymn, "On the Battlefield for My Lord," Mother paced the floor weeping aloud in her despair. A black janitor who was sweeping the hallway asked why she was crying. She explained that I was dying because the infection in my head had grown worse.

23   The man extended his sympathy. As he turned to walk away, dragging his broom behind him, he mumbled that he guessed the Epsom salts hadn't worked after all. Mother ran after him asking what he meant. He explained that a couple of days before, he had been cleaning the operating room as they finished up with my surgery. He had heard the doctor tell the white nurse to irrigate my head with Epsom salts and warm water every two or three hours or I wouldn't make it.

24   Mother shouted the words "Epsom salts and water" as she raced down the hall, desperately searching for a nurse. The woman was indignant, saying, yes, come to think of it, the doctor had said something about Epsom salts. "But we don't coddle niggers," she growled.

25   Mother didn't talk back to the nurse. She knew Daddy's job was at stake. Instead, she sent for Epsom salts and began the treatment right away. Within two days, I was remarkably better. The minister went home, and the sisters from the church abandoned their death watch, declaring they had witnessed a miracle.

26   So fifteen years later, when I was selected to integrate Central High, Grandmother said, "Now you see, that's the reason God spared your life. You're supposed to carry this banner for our people."

- Vocabulary

decreed (2)
usurp (12)
convulsing (21)

endowed (9)
benevolent (12)

unequivocally (11)
sauntered (16)

The Facts

1. What president ordered in the troops to ensure the integration of the high school that the author attended?
2. What does the author admit she naively believed would happen if the segregation of schools could be ended?
3. Who was governor of Arkansas when the author returned to her former high school for her reunion?
4. What happened to the author when she was born?
5. Whose muttered remark resulted in the author's getting the treatment that saved her life?

The Strategies

1. The author wrote her memoir some forty years after the actual event. What kinds of problems do you think she encountered in writing this piece so many years after it happened?
2. How would you characterize the person who is telling the story? How old do you think she is? What characteristics of her language help project her onto the page?
3. What technique does the writer use to grab our interest in the opening paragraph?
4. The author tells the story of how she almost died when she was a baby, but does so with little or no editorial comment. Why is this an effective technique?
5. In addition to the author's religious convictions, what does the story about her illness as a newborn dramatically illustrate?

The Issues

1. What effect do you think living through such a traumatic experience is likely to have on someone? How does it seem to have affected the author?
2. The author says that she is perplexed by the state of race relations today. How do you feel about the relationship between the races in the United States today?
3. What do you regard as the most pressing issue in race relations today? What solution do you have for that issue?
4. The author says that the experience of desegregating Central High made her an "instant adult." What do you think she meant by that? What is an *instant adult*?
5. What, in your opinion, is necessary to end racism in the United States?

Suggestions for Writing

1. Write an essay about a personal encounter you have had with prejudice.
2. Write an essay about any side of racism.

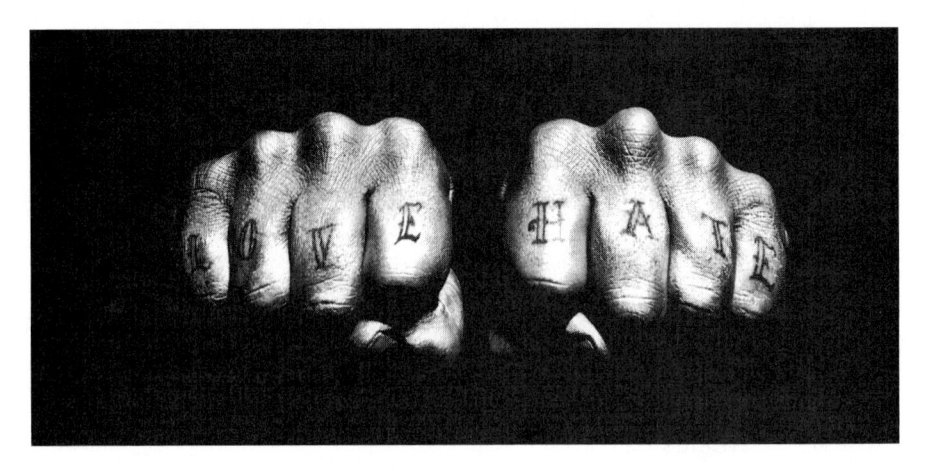

• Why do love and hate coexist in life's great controversy between good and evil?

Incidents with White People
SARAH L. AND A. ELIZABETH DELANY

Sarah (Sadie) L. Delany (1890–1999) and Dr. A. Elizabeth (Bessie) Delany (1891–1995) were African American centenarian sisters who found fame and fortune in 1993 with the publication of their co-authored memoirs *Having Our Say: The Delany Sisters' First 100 Years,* written in collaboration with Amy Hill Hearth. The book was on the *New York Times* bestseller list for two years and has been translated into seven languages. The Delany sisters left one million dollars to St. Augustine College, on whose campus they were born, lived, and were educated.

In this excerpt from Having Our Say, *Bessie tells of leaving home in 1911 at age twenty to teach school in Boardman, North Carolina, where she boarded with a couple, Mr. and Mrs. Atkinson. We learn of her reaction to the news that the* Titanic *had sunk (1912) and how she narrowly escaped being lynched in Georgia. As you read the essay, ask yourself how you would have reacted if you had been in Bessie's shoes during the encounter with the drunken white man.*

• • •

1   Mr. Atkinson was the ugliest man I ever saw, and not at all well educated, but he was an absolute gentleman. He never bothered me once. His first name was Spudge, which was short for Spudgeon, or so he told me. He said he was named after a Baptist preacher who was legendary in those parts, and he was just appalled that this little Episcopalian girl had never heard of him.

2   There was no Episcopal Church in Boardman, so I attended Baptist or Methodist services. They were poor and had no hymnals. The Methodists had

the words to their hymns scratched out in the margins of old pieces of paper, like the Sears catalog.

3   The food we ate in Boardman was about the worst diet I have ever been on. I have always been a slim thing, but Honey, I got fat while I was there! When I came home at Christmas I weighed 153 pounds, and people came from everywhere to see this fat Bessie. But I lost that weight eventually, and never gained it back. Sadie says it was from eating all that fatback and collards and sweet potatoes in Boardman.

4   Those people didn't know the first thing about vitamins or minerals. They were so poor and ignorant. It was the same thing Sadie was running into as Jeanes Supervisor in Wake County. Mama was worried about me, and she would send me these little care packages. She would go to a store in Raleigh called the California Fruit Company, and buy some grapefruits and ship them to me.

5   Well, Mr. Spudge Atkinson had never seen a grapefruit before. He said, "Miss Delany, what is that ugly-looking piece of fruit?" Now, I gave him a piece and he just puckered up and spit it out and said it was the worst, most sour, miserable thing he'd ever put in his mouth! And I said, "Mr. Atkinson, if you're just going to waste my grapefruit, then please give it back to me." And he gave me the rest back, gladly. He sure did think that Miss Delany from Raleigh was peculiar, sitting on his porch sucking down grapefruit.

6   Mr. Atkinson tended to be a rather dramatic man. One time he came into my classroom and said, "Oh, Miss Delany! Miss Delany!" And I said, "What's the matter, Mr. Atkinson?" And he fell to the ground and said, "It's terrible, it's just terrible!" And I said, "What's terrible?" And he said, "That ship they said could not sink, well, it's done sunk! And all those rich white people have gone down with it, in that icy water!"

7   I didn't say it out loud, but I remember thinking, Too bad the *Titanic* didn't take more rich white people down with it, to its watery grave! Especially some of the rebby boys around here! Now, isn't that awful of me? Isn't it vicious? You see why this child is worried about getting into Heaven? Sadie is just shocked by me sometimes. Sadie just says, "Live, and let live."

8   But in a way, I was a sweet child, too. You know, when I was in Boardman and got my first paycheck—$40 a month—I paid nine dollars for my room and board and sent the rest home to Papa immediately. No one had asked me to do that. It just seemed like the right thing to do.

9   Well, I got a letter back from Mama. She thanked me for the money but she told me not to send any more. She told me to save it for myself, or I'd never get to college.

10   I saved most of my money, but I will admit that I spent some on a silk dress, yes, sir! Papa wouldn't let me have a silk dress—I guess because it was so expensive but also kind of sexy. So, when I was in Boardman I ordered several yards of silk. I think it was blue, with a thin white stripe. And I made myself a dress. Skirts were going up, and you could see the ankle when you walked. And when the men would see a glimpse of ankle they would say,

"Ooooohweeee!" Papa didn't like that at all. When Sadie and I would wear those dresses, he would just scowl at us!! Today women show everything. They're crazy. Trust me, you can get in enough trouble just with a little ankle showing.

11   Now, after two years in Boardman, it was time for me to move on to a new teaching assignment. The people didn't want to see me go, but I was ready for a new challenge. So in 1913 I went to Brunswick, Georgia, to teach at Saint Athanasius, an Episcopal school for colored children. I wanted to see the world!

12   Brunswick was a sophisticated place compared to Boardman. The faculty lived together in a dormitory, and that is how I met my lifelong friend, Elizabeth Gooch. "Gooch," as I always called her, was the oldest one of us, and I was the youngest, and so the principal assigned the two of us to room together. I guess he thought Gooch would be a good influence on me, but I think I was a good influence on Gooch!

13   I didn't like Gooch that much at first. She didn't treat me the way I would have liked to be treated. For instance, she took the bed away from the window, so that I'd get the draft at night. But after a while, Gooch and I became good friends. Sometimes, we'd go to the beach and see the turtles come in from the sea to nest.

14   Now, Georgia was a mean place—meaner than North Carolina. You know that song about Georgia, that sentimental song? Well, they can have it! They can have the whole state as far as I'm concerned.

15   In Georgia, they never missed a chance to keep you down. If you were colored and you tried on a hat or a pair of shoes, Honey, you owned 'em. What a rebby state! To be fair, I can understand why they didn't want Negroes to try on hats without buying them: because in those days, Negroes would grease their hair. And the store couldn't sell the hat if it got grease on it. So, to be fair, I think that was OK.

16   But it was on my way to my job in Brunswick in 1913 that I came close to being lynched. You see, I had to change trains in Waycross, Georgia. I was sitting in the little colored waiting room at the station, and I took my hair down and was combing it. I was fixing myself up. I was going to my new job, and I wanted to look nice.

17   Well, there I was with my long hair down when this white man opened the door, to the colored waiting room. There was no one in there except me and two colored teachers from New York who were traveling with me to Brunswick. The white man stuck his head in and started, well, leering at me. He was drunk, and he smelled bad, and he started mumbling things. And I said, "Oh, why don't you shut up and go wait with your own kind in the white waiting room?"

18   What happened next was kind of like an explosion. He slammed the door and I could hear him shouting at the top of his lungs outside, "The nigger bitch insulted me! The nigger bitch insulted me!"

19   The two colored teachers traveling with me slipped out the back without a word and made a beeline for the woods. They hid in the woods! I guess I

can't blame them. A colored porter came in to see what this was all about, and he whispered to me, "Good for you!" But then he ran out on me, too. He left me there by myself.

20   Well, I could see a crowd begin to gather on the platform, and I knew I was in big trouble. Papa always said, "If you see a crowd, you go the other way. Don't even hang around long enough to find out what it's about!" Now, this crowd was outside, gathering for me.

21   By now, there were dozens of white people in the crowd, and the white man kept yelling, "Nigger bitch insulted me!" I was just waiting for somebody to get a rope. Thousands of Negroes had been lynched for far less than what I had just done. But I just continued to sit on the bench, combing my hair, while that white man was a-carrying on! I realized that my best chance was to act like nothing was happening. You see, if you acted real scared, sometimes that spurred them on.

22   Two things saved me: That glorious, blessed train rounded the bend, breaking up the crowd and giving me my way to get on out of there. And it helped that the white man was drunk as a skunk, and that turned off some of the white people.

23   But I wasn't afraid to die! I know you ain't got to die but once, and it seemed as good a reason to die as any. I was ready. Lord, help me, I was ready.

24   You know what Sadie says? Sadie says I was a fool to provoke that white man. As if I provoked him! Honey, he provoked me! Sadie says she would have ignored him. I say, how do you ignore some drunk, smelly white man treating you like trash? She says, child, it's better to put up with it, and live to tell about it. She says at the very least I should have run off into the woods with those other two teachers. She says I am lucky to be alive. But I would rather die than back down, Honey.

Vocabulary

legendary (1)   appalled (1)   vicious (7)
sophisticated (12)   lynched (16)   spurred (21)

The Facts

1. Which of the three religions in Boardman—Methodist, Baptist, Episcopalian—had the poorest membership? How was the poverty revealed? Who do you think made up the membership of the churches mentioned by the narrator?
2. What kind of diet made Bessie gain weight? What do we find out about Bessie's family and its knowledge of healthy foods? What kinds of foods should be blamed today for making so many youngsters obese?
3. What was your reaction to Bessie's admission that she wished more rich white people had sunk with the *Titanic?*
4. What is the difference between Bessie's personality and that of the rest of her family? Which attitude do you admire most? Explain your answer.

5. According to Bessie, what saved her from being lynched? Do you think she really was in danger of being lynched? Give reasons for your answer.

● The Strategies

1. How does the author keep this story a dramatic monologue in which the speaker is telling her story to an unseen, trusted interviewer? Give examples of the author's technique.
2. The title of the story is "Incidents with White People." How do the incidents portray the white people? Is the portrait flattering or not? Support your answer with examples from the narration.
3. What is the reference to "that sentimental song about Georgia" that Bessie discredits? What is the title of the song? Why does Bessie dislike Georgia?
4. How does Bessie refer to black people in this narration? Is this how blacks refer to themselves today in most American locations or do they use other terminologies? Cite examples.
5. How well does the narrator handle the scene with the white drunk? What strategies does she use to keep the reader interested in the scene?

● The Issues

1. How is Mr. Atkinson portrayed in the narrative? How does the narrator seem to feel about him? Does the portrayal seem realistic or fantastic? Give reasons for your answer.
2. What reputation did silk dresses have among the conscientious parents of black girls at the time of this story? What might the equivalent be today?
3. What is your view of the black teachers who slipped out the back without a word and made a beeline for the woods? What is your view of the black porter who said, "Good for you!" and then ran away? What kinds of people today are fearless and stand up to be counted? Give examples.
4. What is your reaction to the advice from Bessie's father—"If you see a crowd, you go the other way. Don't even hang around long enough to find out what it's about!"? Is this sound advice, even today?
5. Bessie felt that she would rather die than back down in front of this crowd of whites when she had been insulted. She also felt that she could not just ignore the white drunk. Do you think she was right? Would you be willing to lay your life on the line if you were in a similar situation? What issue would you be willing to die for?

● Suggestions for Writing

1. Write an essay in which you offer your opinion as to why blacks were treated the way they were at the time Bessie and Sadie lived in the South.
2. In an ideal world, how would ethnic, economic, religious, and gender differences be treated? Answer this question in an essay.

Punctuation Workshop
The Colon (:)

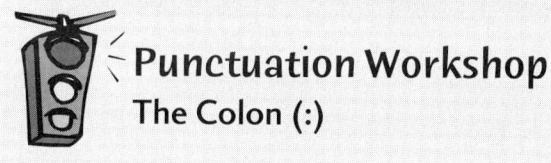

1. Put a colon after a complete statement followed by a list or long quotation:

    > These are the reading assignments for next week: Hawthorne's *Scarlet Letter,* two magazine articles about women today, and three books about feminism.

    > This is what Stanley J. Randall said about perfection: "The closest to perfection a person ever comes is when he fills out an application form."

    Use a comma instead of a colon if the quotation is not introduced by a complete statement:

    > It was Thomas Jefferson who said, "One generation cannot bind another."

    Do not use a colon between a verb and its object or after *such as:*

    > **WRONG:** The contest winners were: Jerry Meyer, Ani Hossein, and Franco Sanchez.

    > **RIGHT:** The contest winners were Jerry Meyer, Ani Hossein, and Franco Sanchez.

    > **WRONG:** People no longer believe in evil spirits, such as: ghosts, witches, and devils.

    > **RIGHT:** People no longer believe in evil spirits, such as ghosts, witches, and devils.

2. Use a colon between figures that express time:

    > Professor Stern entered the classroom at exactly 2:10 p.m.

3. Use a colon between titles and subtitles:

    > The Golden Years: Telling the Truth about Aging

4. Use a colon after the salutation of a formal letter:

    > Dear Mrs. Smith:

The colon also appears in bibliographic data. (See the student paper on page 709.)

STUDENT CORNER

Racial Justice: How Far Have We Come?
Nancey Phillips, California State University at Long Beach

"I have a dream my four little children will one day live in a nation where they will not be judged by the color of their skin but by the content of their character." —Martin Luther King, Jr.

Dr. Martin Luther King, Jr. had great hopes for racial harmony in this country. The 1960s saw many advancements toward that end; the destruction of segregation and the passage of the Civil Rights Amendment were giant steps toward equality. But today, at the beginning of the twenty-first century, the state of race relations could still be defined by one sensational trial that split the country along racial lines and revealed the continuing problem of deep-seated racism in the United States. This was the 1995 trial of O. J. Simpson for the double murder of Nicole Kidman and Ronald Goldman, and it sparked heated debate at every level of American society, proving that there still remains a great divide between black and white.

No impartial observer surveying the racial situation in the United States today can deny that since Dr. King's groundbreaking speech progress has been made in race relations. Blacks are better off now than they were then. One striking difference between the 1960s and now is in the improvement in earnings of blacks versus whites. Blacks with the same level of educational achievement as whites used to earn significantly less than their white counterparts. Statistics now show a narrowing of the gap in wages. Many attribute gains made in the earning capacity of blacks to civil rights legislation passed in the 1960s and 1970s.

Not every study paints a rosy picture, however. In a report entitled "The State of The Dream 2004" an organization called United for a Fair Economy found that unemployment for blacks was nearly double that for whites—10.8 percent versus 5.2 percent in 2003. This figure reflects a wider gap in unemployment between the races than existed in 1972. Nor has there been any improvement in black infant mortality, which the report claims is greater today than in 1970. Among blacks in 2001 the mortality rate was 14 per 1,000 live births, almost $1^1/_2$ times that of whites.

Statistics do not tell the entire story. The evidence from our own observations confirms the obvious gains made by blacks. For example, Condoleezza Rice is the first black Secretary of State ever. Colin Powell, the son of Jamaican immigrants, served a term under the Bush administration as Secretary of Defense, distinguishing himself in the process. There is now speculation that one or the other of these two is likely to become a credible candidate for president in the 2008 presidential election.

Some blacks feel that the outstanding among them are often targeted by spiteful white administrations. Whether or not this is so is unprovable. But if it is, some recent victories by prominent black achievers in the courts tell a different story. For example, on June 13, 2005, pop icon Michael Jackson was found innocent of all charges, which some black commentators feel were spitefully brought against him by an overzealous white prosecutor. Edgar Ray Killen, an aged and former KKK member, was on June 21, 2005, convicted of killing three civil rights workers in Mississippi 41 years ago. Similarly, Byron de la Beckwith was convicted in 1994 of the 1963 sniper killing of Medgar Evers, the leader of the Mississippi NAACP. Granted, it took 31 years, but eventually justice won out.

Improvements in racial justice cannot be measured by court cases alone. Other observational evidence of the gains in race relations may seem trivial but in fact is quite momentous. The neighborhood I live in has always been a white-bread neighborhood up until recently. Several black families now live in it and are accepted like any other family, their kids playing in Little League and joining Boy Scout troops. The fact that this has happened indicates two implicit truths: one, since my neighborhood is quite expensive, that there are now many black families able to afford substantial homes; two, that blacks and other minorities are free to buy and live in any neighborhood they can afford, even one like mine that has traditionally always been white. That is, without question, progress toward the dream.

Phillips 3

The murder of Nicole Brown Simpson and Ronald Goldman in 1994 and the subsequent trial of a black celebrity, O. J. Simpson, for the crime became a national obsession as millions tuned in television to watch the thrust and parry of the lawyers. Instead of setting off hostility between the genders, the O. J. Simpson trial divided the country by race, with black America crying "innocent" and white America crying "guilty." Even those black people who believed Simpson was guilty felt that he should be set free to make up for the injustices that African Americans have suffered through the years in the biased courts. But if the court system is used for a vengeful settling of scores between the races rather than as a forum for determining truth and promoting justice, we are truly in trouble as a nation.

And so, more than forty years after Dr. King's landmark speech, Americans find themselves still in the midst of racial crisis. O. J. Simpson illuminated the ongoing problem of racial injustice in this country, not because of his guilt or innocence, but because of America's polarized reaction to the case.

How I Write

I need absolute quiet when I write, so I usually lock myself away in my bedroom to work. My list of necessary tools is quite succinct: my PowerBook and a strong cup of tea. Inspiration tends to strike late at night . . . and very often the night before the assignment is due. (I suppose that would be desperation rather than inspiration.) Nevertheless, you can now understand my need for the tea; the PowerBook, of course, is self-explanatory. My writing tends to be highly structured, and so I simply cannot begin a paper without having a clear outline in my head. I rarely write down a formal outline, but I will jot down on paper my main points and the order in which I will use them. Once I know where I'm going with a paper, I sometimes write the body paragraphs first, and go back to construct the introduction later. I find it difficult to give my reader a preview of coming attractions when I'm not even sure what's ahead; once the body is done, the introduction practically writes itself. I compose very slowly, agonizing over each sentence as I go, instead of simply getting the basic idea down and rewriting later. As a result, my first draft is generally pretty close to the final product. I know plenty of people who can breeze through their first draft and then spend time perfecting their work; but I simply cannot write that way. My time on a project is spent mentally categorizing and organizing my points, and then physically sitting at the computer, choosing the best words to express my ideas. Once I start writing, I don't like to stop until I'm finished with the project or until I run out of tea . . . and actually it appears that my cup is now empty.

How I Wrote This Essay

The most difficult part of writing this essay was narrowing down the topic. Volumes and volumes have been written on the topic of racism, and so I had to find the one small area that I could manage in an essay of this length. I found using the Internet quick and easy compared to digging through microfiche at the library. After compiling my information, I jotted down a few main points and went to work on writing the essay. I spent about four hours writing the first draft and another hour revising it.

My Writing Tip

My best writing tip is to have someone else read your paper before you print the final draft. I mean ANYONE! It doesn't have to be a tutor or an English major; even your Mom or Dad will suffice. I find that after writing a paper, I am too used to looking at the words to be objective, and I often miss simple spelling or punctuation errors. An outsider will give you a fresh perspective and often find errors that you missed.

CHAPTER WRITING ASSIGNMENTS

1. In an essay, divide and classify one of the following subjects:
   a. Your friends
   b. Your relatives
   c. Things or activities that give you pleasure
   d. Classes you like to take
   e. Classes you don't like to take
2. Write an essay dividing and classifying the various techniques you have used over the years to make yourself a better writer.

WRITING ASSIGNMENTS FOR A SPECIFIC AUDIENCE

1. Pretending that you're writing to a prospective employer, divide and classify your life into various stages leading up to the present.
2. Write a letter to anyone you admire, dividing and classifying into stages the changes you have undergone in your career ambitions since you were young.

COLLABORATIVE WRITING PROJECT

Get together with a panel of eight other students in your class. The purpose of the panel is to gather crime statistics for the neighborhood around your school. Go through the public records available either online or through your police department and classify the crimes by any basis agreed on by a panel—whether by frequency, severity, or any other yardstick. Assemble and report on the results of your investigation in a team-written essay that you present to the class.

IMAGE GALLERY WRITING ASSIGNMENT

Visit pages 665–668 of our image gallery and study all four images dealing with racism. Then choose the image that most appeals to you. Answer the questions and do the writing assignment.

14

Causal Analysis

ROAD MAP TO CAUSAL ANALYSIS

What Causal Analysis Does

Causal analysis focuses specifically on explanations that show a connection between a situation and its cause or effect. It either answers the question "Why did this happen?" or "What will this do?" An answer to the first question will result in an explanation of cause; an answer to the second, a prediction of effect. An essay based on the controlling idea that "The lack of tough antipollution laws is the cause of multiple illnesses, including cancer, in the United States" is analyzing cause. If the essay was based on the controlling idea that "A law to stiffen penalties against toxic polluters will clear our drinking water from cancer-causing chemicals," it would be forecasting effect.

As the diagram illustrates, cause points to past occurrences, whereas effect predicts future consequences.

$$\text{cause} \leftarrow \text{situation} \rightarrow \text{effect}$$

Here, for example, is a causal analysis written to answer the question "Why are so many couples unable to discuss their marital problems?"

> Barriers between husbands and wives are often caused by timidity. Many couples are embarrassed to discuss intimate problems, such as sexual maladjustment, personal hygiene, or religious beliefs. They prefer to let their discontent fester rather than confront it openly. A wife says, "I wouldn't hurt my husband by telling him that his dirty hands offend me." A husband says, "I dislike the way my wife compares me to her father in everything I do, from mowing the lawn to smoking my pipe, but I could never tell her so." Guilt feelings can reinforce this sort of timidity. If a wife or husband knows that a frank talk about sex, for instance, will uncover some past indiscretion, he or she will avoid the confrontation either out of personal guilt or fear of knowing about the other partner's past. The longer this silence is kept, the stronger and more destructive it

becomes. Many a broken marriage can trace the break back to barriers in communication.

On the other hand, a slight shift in the approach to this topic leads naturally to a discussion of effect. An essay based on the question, "What happens when two people no longer discuss their marital problems?" would now focus on the effect, rather than the cause, of no communication in a marriage:

> Barriers between husband and wife result in a tension-filled home. When marriage partners constantly overlook a problem or pretend it does not exist, they eventually become frustrated and angry. They develop feelings of isolation and rejection, as their unfulfilled yearnings become a gnawing hunger. Lacking communication, the marriage is left without an emotional safety valve to let off pent-up frustration. The ensuing strain increases as the angry partners take out hidden, unexpressed resentments on their children, using them as scapegoats for their own great void. In the beginning the tension may show itself only in minor misunderstandings or brief pout sessions, but as the barriers remain, these little hurts turn into large wounds. The husband may become belligerent toward the wife, belittling her in front of friends or ignoring her until she retreats in cold indignation. The wife may feel so rejected and worthless that she seeks another man to comfort her or to treat her with sensitivity. The tension grows. Soon the home has become a place of bitter hostility, where love and warmth are impossible.

When to Use Causal Analysis

Use causal analysis when you are trying to explain why something happened or to predict the likely results if an event does or does not occur. Throughout your college study you will probably be given many assignments that require writing in the causal analysis mode of development. A history paper might ask you to analyze the causes of the Louisiana Purchase in 1803; an astronomy exam, to explain the cause of the aurora borealis. In economics, you might be asked to predict what will happen to the American economy if oil prices surge. A psychology exam might require you to examine three results on the work of Carl Jung caused by his break with Sigmund Freud. Causal analysis is also commonly employed in argumentative papers written in all fields and disciplines.

How to Use Causal Analysis

Know the Differences among Necessary, Sufficient, and Contributory Cause
Three kinds of cause can create a given effect:

1. **A necessary cause is one that must be present for the effect to occur, but it alone cannot make the effect occur.** For instance, irrigation is necessary for a crop of good grapes, but irrigation alone will not cause a

good crop. Enough sunshine, correct pruning, proper pesticides, and good soil are also required.

2. **A sufficient cause is one that can produce a given effect by itself.** For instance, an empty gasoline tank alone can keep a car from running, even though other problems such as a bad spark plug, a leaking hose, or ignition trouble may also be present.

3. **A contributory cause is one that might produce an effect but cannot produce the effect by itself.** For instance, vitamin E may help a long-distance runner win a race but cannot by itself determine the performance of a runner who got a bad start, trained haphazardly, or is not properly conditioned. The runner may also win the race without the help of vitamin E.

Understanding the differences among these three causes will help you in your investigations of cause and effect and keep you from making dogmatic statements such as these:

> A vegetarian diet will prevent cancer.
>
> Acupuncture is the answer to anesthesiology problems in America.
>
> Violence on television is the cause of today's growing criminal violence.

Rather, you will soften your statements by inserting such phrases as "may be," "is a contributing factor," "is one of the reasons," or "is a major cause." A careful study of cause and effect teaches that few causes are sufficient; most are merely necessary or contributory.

Make Your Purpose Clear The excerpt from Jim Corbett's book, reprinted later in this chapter, opens with this clear statement: "As many of the stories in this book are about man-eating tigers, it is perhaps desirable to explain why these animals develop man-eating tendencies." It proceeds to explain exactly that. This sort of definiteness early in the piece adds a guiding focus to any explanation of cause.

Be Modest in Your Choice of Subject It is difficult enough to analyze the causes of simple effects without compounding your problem through the choice of a monstrously large subject. The student who tries to write an essay on the causes of war is already in deep trouble; such a complex phenomenon bristles with thousands of causes. Selecting a more manageable subject for causal analysis will make your task much easier.

Concentrate on Immediate Rather than Remote Cause It is easy in analysis of cause to become entangled in the infinite. In a series of causations, the most likely cause is always the nearest. For example, take the case of a student—John Doe—who gets a poor grade on a test. Why? Probably because he failed to study. On the other hand, perhaps John failed to study because he thought he was doomed to fail anyway, and didn't see the point in exerting himself. Why? Probably because the instructor scared him with a lecture on how high her standards were and how hard it was to pass her class. Why did she do that? Probably because of pressure from the Regents, who accused her and her department of grading too easily. Why? The Regents, in turn, may have gotten tough because of an article critical of the department's standards that appeared in a newspaper and was written by a cub reporter who played loose with the facts. This story, in turn, was approved by an editor who had a toothache caused by a badly filled tooth. Yet, in spite of this chain of events, it is a stretch to claim that John Doe failed the test because of sloppy dentistry. Common sense must guide your thinking in this sort of analysis; but because infinity lies behind even the reason why someone purchases a popsicle, it is safer, as a rule of thumb, to stay with immediate cause and ignore the remote.

Don't Be Dogmatic about Cause Institutions of learning rigorously demand that students analyze cause with caution and prudence. The reasoning is simple enough: Colleges and universities are quite determined to impress on their students the complexity of the world. It is advisable, therefore, that you be modest in your claims of causation. You can easily temper a dogmatic statement by interjecting qualifiers into your claims. Instead of writing:

> Violence in America is *caused* by violent television programs.

you could more prudently write:

> Violence in America is *influenced* by television programs.

If a student had written the following paragraph, it would no doubt have drawn the instructor's criticism:

> This brings me to the major cause of unhappiness, which is that most people in America act not on impulse but on some principle, and that principles upon which people act are usually based upon a false psychology and a false ethic. There is a general theory as to what makes for happiness and this theory is false. Life is conceived as a competitive struggle in which felicity consists in getting ahead of your neighbor. The joys which are not competitive are forgotten.

Yet this paragraph is from a Bertrand Russell article, "The Unhappy American Way," which readers have read with much sagacious head-nodding. Bertrand Russell was a Nobel laureate, a mathematician, and a noted philosopher when he wrote this. No doubt it is unfair, but his obvious accomplishments gain for him a temporary suspension of the rules against dogmatizing. Students, however, are not readily granted such license. We advise that, for the time being, anyway, you generalize about cause prudently.

Use Common Sense in Asserting Cause Most writers do not rigidly follow the principles of causal analysis except when they argue a technical question that must be explained according to the rules of logic. The following passage is an example of the free use of the principles of causal analysis:

> The association of love with adultery in much of medieval love poetry has two causes. The first lies in the organization of feudal society. Marriages, being matters of economic or social interest, had nothing whatever to do with erotic love. When a marriage alliance no longer suited the interests of the lord, he got rid of his lady with as much dispatch as he got rid of a horse. Consequently, a lady who might be nothing more than a commodious piece of property to her husband, could be passionately desired by her vassal. The second cause lies in the attitude of the medieval Christian church, where the desire for erotic, romantic love was considered wicked and a result of Adam's sin in the Garden of Eden. The general impression left on the medieval mind by the church's official teachers was that all erotic pleasure was wicked. And this impression, in addition to the nature of feudal marriage, produced in the courtly poets the perverse desire to emphasize the very passion they were told to resist.

The student who wrote this paragraph does not demonstrate cause according to precise rules, but rather shows the commonsense result of her research into why medieval poetry emphasized adulterous love.

Warming Up to Write a Causal Analysis

Remember that causes look backward to the source of an event whereas effects look forward to consequences. Here are some warm-up exercises that will help you focus on cause and effect.

1. List at least three causes for each of the following situations:
   a. Teenage smoking
   b. Recent increase in obesity
   c. Deadlock between executives and strong labor unions
   d. Children's feelings of guilt during a divorce
   e. Grownups not knowing how to use a computer
2. List at least three effects that result from the following situations:
   a. Loss of a parent while one is still young
   b. Having one's car stolen
   c. The fear of further terrorist attacks in the United States and other countries
   d. Listening to classical music
   e. Discovering a rat infestation in one's cellar

3. Write a thesis for each of the answers you gave to Exercise 1. Then pick the thesis that you think would lead to the best essay.

4. Write a thesis for each of the answers you gave to Exercise 2. Then pick the thesis that you think would lead to the best essay.

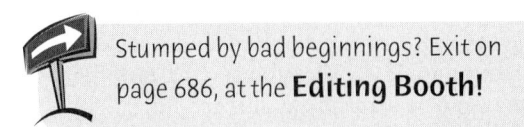

> Stumped by bad beginnings? Exit on page 686, at the **Editing Booth!**

EXAMPLES

A Peaceful Woman Explains Why She Carries a Gun
LINDA M. HASSELSTROM

Linda M. Hasselstrom (b. 1943) is a writer and teacher who grew up in rural South Dakota. Her works include *Roadkill* (1984), a collection of her poetry, and *Land Circle* (1991), a collection of her essays.

Living alone on an isolated ranch may seem romantic to some who love nature or solitude, but it can involve some hair-raising encounters, as we find out from the close calls related in the essay that follows. Embedded within the story line is the issue of who, if anyone, should have legal access to a gun.

• • •

1   I am a peace-loving woman. But several events in the past 10 years have convinced me I'm safer when I carry a pistol. This was a personal decision, but because handgun possession is a controversial subject, perhaps my reasoning will interest others.

2   I live in western South Dakota on a ranch 25 miles from the nearest town: for several years I spent winters alone here. As a free-lance writer, I travel alone a lot—more than 100,000 miles by car in the last four years. With women freer than ever before to travel alone, the odds of our encountering trouble seem to have risen. Distances are great, roads are deserted, and the terrain is often too exposed to offer hiding places.

3   A woman who travels alone is advised, usually by men, to protect herself by avoiding bars and other "dangerous situations," by approaching her car like an Indian scout, by locking doors and windows. But these precautions aren't always enough. I spent years following them and still found myself in dangerous situations. I began to resent the idea that just because I am female, I have to be extra careful.

4   A few years ago, with another woman, I camped for several weeks in the West. We discussed self-defense, but neither of us had taken a course in it. She

was against firearms, and local police told us Mace was illegal. So we armed ourselves with spray cans of deodorant tucked into our sleeping bags. We never used our improvised Mace because we were lucky enough to camp beside people who came to our aid when men harassed us. But on one occasion we visited a national park where our assigned space was less than 15 feet from other campers. When we returned from a walk, we found our closest neighbors were two young men. As we gathered our cooking gear, they drank beer and loudly discussed what they would do to us after dark. Nearby campers, even families, ignored them: rangers strolled past, unconcerned. When we asked the rangers pointblank if they would protect us, one of them patted my shoulder and said, "Don't worry girls. They're just kidding." At dusk we drove out of the park and hid our camp in the woods a few miles away. The illegal spot was lovely, but our enjoyment of that park was ruined. I returned from the trip determined to reconsider the options available for protecting myself.

5   At that time, I lived alone on the ranch and taught night classes in town. Along a city street I often traveled, a woman had a flat tire, called for help on her CB radio, and got a rapist who left her beaten. She was afraid to call for help again and stayed in her car until morning. For that reason, as well as because CBs work best along line-of-sight, which wouldn't help much in the rolling hills where I live, I ruled out a CB.

6   As I drove home one night, a car followed me. It passed me on a narrow bridge while a passenger flashed a blinding spotlight in my face. I braked sharply. The car stopped, angled across the bridge, and four men jumped out. I realized the locked doors were useless if they broke the windows of my pickup. I started forward, hoping to knock their car aside so I could pass. Just then another car appeared, and the men hastily got back in their car. They continued to follow me, passing and repassing. I dared not go home because no one else was there. I passed no lighted houses. Finally they pulled over to the roadside, and I decided to use their tactic: fear. Speeding, the pickup horn blaring, I swerved as close to them as I dared as I roared past. It worked: they turned off the highway. But I was frightened and angry. Even in my vehicle I was too vulnerable.

7   Other incidents occurred over the years. One day I glanced out at a field below my house and saw a man with a shotgun walking toward a pond full of ducks. I drove down and explained that the land was posted. I politely asked him to leave. He stared at me, and the muzzle of the shotgun began to rise. In a moment of utter clarity I realized that I was alone on the ranch, and that he could shoot me and simply drive away. The moment passed: the man left.

8   One night, I returned home from teaching a class to find deep tire ruts in the wet ground of my yard, garbage in the driveway, and a large gas tank empty. A light shone in the house: I couldn't remember leaving it on. I was too embarrassed to drive to a neighboring ranch and wake someone up. An hour of cautious exploration convinced me the house was safe, but once inside, with the doors locked, I was still afraid. I kept thinking of how vulnerable I felt, prowling around my own house in the dark.

9   My first positive step was to take a kung fu class, which teaches evasive or protective action when someone enters your space without permission.

I learned to move confidently, scanning for possible attackers. I learned how to assess danger and techniques for avoiding it without combat.

10   I also learned that one must practice several hours every day to be good at kung fu. By that time I had married George: when I practiced with him, I learned how close you must be to your attacker to use martial arts, and decided a 120-pound woman dare not let a six-foot, 220-pound attacker get that close unless she is very, very good at self-defense. I have since read articles by several women who were extremely well trained in the martial arts, but were raped and beaten anyway.

11   I thought back over the times in my life when I had been attacked or threatened and tried to be realistic about my own behavior, searching for anything that had allowed me to become a victim. Overall, I was convinced that I had not been at fault. I don't believe myself to be either paranoid or a risk-taker, but I wanted more protection.

12   With some reluctance I decided to try carrying a pistol. George had always carried one, despite his size and his training in martial arts. I practiced shooting until I was sure I could hit an attacker who moved close enough to endanger me. Then I bought a license from the county sheriff, making it legal for me to carry the gun concealed.

13   But I was not yet ready to defend myself. George taught me that the most important preparation was mental: convincing myself I could actually shoot a person. Few of us wish to hurt or kill another human being. But there is no point in having a gun; in fact, gun possession might increase your danger unless you know you can use it. I got in the habit of rehearsing, as I drove or walked, the precise conditions that would be required before I would shoot someone.

14   People who have not grown up with the idea that they are capable of protecting themselves—in other words, most women—might have to work hard to convince themselves of their ability, and of the necessity. Handgun ownership need not turn us into gunslingers, but it can be part of believing in, and relying on, ourselves for protection.

15   To be useful, a pistol has to be available. In my car, it's within instant reach. When I enter a deserted rest stop at night, it's in my purse, with my hand on the grip. When I walk from a dark parking lot into a motel, it's in my hand, under a coat. At home, it's on the headboard. In short, I take it with me almost everywhere I go alone.

16   Just carrying a pistol is not protection; avoidance is still the best approach to trouble. Subconsciously watching for signs of danger, I believe I've become more alert. Handgun use, not unlike driving, becomes instinctive. Each time I've drawn my gun—I have never fired it at another human being—I've simply found it in my hand.

17   I was driving the half-mile to the highway mailbox one day when I saw a vehicle parked about midway down the road. Several men were standing in the ditch, relieving themselves. I have no objection to emergency urination, but I noticed they'd dumped several dozen beer cans in the road. Besides being ugly, cans can slash a cow's feet or stomach.

18   The men noticed me before they finished and made quite a performance out of zipping their trousers while walking toward me. All four of them gathered around my small foreign car, and one of them demanded what the hell I wanted.

19   "This is private land. I'd appreciate it if you'd pick up the beer cans."

20   "What beer cans?" said the belligerent one, putting both hands on the car door and leaning in my window. His face was inches from mine, and the beer fumes were strong. The others laughed. One tried the passenger door, locked; another put his foot on the hood and rocked the car. They circled, lightly thumping the roof, discussing my good fortune in meeting them and the benefits they were likely to bestow upon me. I felt very small and very trapped and they knew it.

21   "The ones you just threw out," I said politely.

22   "I don't see no beer cans. Why don't you get out here and show them to me, honey?" said the belligerent one, reaching for the handle inside my door.

23   "Right over there," I said, still being polite. "—there, and over there." I pointed with the pistol, which I'd slipped under my thigh. Within one minute the cans and the men were back in the car and headed down the road.

24   I believe this incident illustrates several important principles. The men were trespassing and knew it: their judgment may have been impaired by alcohol. Their response to the polite request of a woman alone was to use their size, numbers, and sex to inspire fear. The pistol was a response in the same language. Politeness didn't work: I couldn't match them in size or number. Out of the car, I'd have been more vulnerable. The pistol just changed the balance of power. It worked again recently when I was driving in a desolate part of Wyoming. A man played cat-and-mouse with me for 30 miles, ultimately trying to run me off the road. When his car passed mine with only two inches to spare, I showed him my pistol, and he disappeared.

25   When I got my pistol, I told my husband, revising the old Colt slogan, "God made men *and women*, but Sam Colt made them equal." Recently I have seen a gunmaker's ad with a similar sentiment. Perhaps this is an idea whose time has come, though the pacifist inside me will be saddened if the only way women can achieve equality is by carrying weapons.

26   We must treat a firearm's power with caution. "Power tends to corrupt, and absolute power corrupts absolutely," as a man (Lord Acton) once said. A pistol is not the only way to avoid being raped or murdered in today's world, but, intelligently wielded, it can shift the balance of power and provide a measure of safety.

Vocabulary

improvised (4)   angled (6)   evasive (9)
assess (9)   martial (10)   paranoid (11)
reluctance (12)   urination (17)   trespassing (24)

The Facts

1. How many times did the author actually use her pistol? In each case, what was the pistol's role? How do you feel about her use of a pistol?

2. Why is a woman who travels alone believed to be more vulnerable than a man who does the same? What other precautions besides avoiding bars, approaching her car carefully, and locking doors and windows can a woman traveling alone observe?
3. Why did the author have to go to town at night when she lived on a ranch out in the country? Could she have avoided the regular trips to town?
4. According to the author, why is the martial art of kung fu not an ideal deterrent to anyone with a criminal intent?
5. Why did the author buy a license from the county sheriff after she had practiced shooting and had purchased a gun? Do you think all gun owners should follow her example? Why or why not?

The Strategies

1. Where is the thesis of the essay most clearly stated? Evaluate the merits of this particular position.
2. What rhetorical strategy does the author use to convince her readers that she did the appropriate thing by purchasing a pistol that she could easily hide from view? Were you convinced by her argument? Why or why not?
3. At what point in the essay does the author seem to be in the most danger? Explain your answer.
4. Which paragraphs of the essay constitute a fascinating drama with an exciting climax and a happy ending? What technique makes this passage so absorbing?
5. What is the purpose of the famous quotation by Lord Acton? In what context is this quotation usually used? Why does it fit the context of this essay as well?

The Issues

1. How do you interpret the author's revision of the old Colt slogan, "God made men, but Sam Colt made them equal"? What do you think of the notion that carrying a gun is one way for women to achieve equality with men? Why does the author express sorrow at the thought that carrying weapons might be the only way women can achieve equality with men?
2. Do you believe the author was paranoid or an excessive risk taker? Did she in any way contribute to her own insecurity while living at the ranch? What, if anything, could she have done to better protect herself?
3. What are some useful ways in which women in general can learn to protect themselves when they are forced to be in an environment where they could be victims of criminals?
4. What is the most frightening encounter you have ever had? If you were a victim, how did you handle the situation?
5. What is your opinion of gun control? Support your opinion with logic and strong evidence.

Suggestions for Writing

1. Write an essay in which you propose an effective solution for the crime of rape.
2. Using Hasselstrom's essay as a counterpoint, write an essay entitled *The Dangers of Carrying a Gun*.

Coming into Language

JIMMY SANTIAGO BACA

Jimmy Santiago Baca (b. 1952) is one of several admired "Barrio" writers, so-called because they emerged from the poverty and squalor of barrio life to portray their background with power and vividness. An ex-convict, Baca taught himself to read and write while in prison, eventually winning the American Book Award of 1988. Part Chicano and part Indian, he was abandoned by his parents when he was two and lived with his grandparents. By the time he was five, his mother had been murdered by her second husband, his father had died of alcoholism, and Baca had lived in an orphanage, from which he escaped to survive on the streets. In time, he landed in prison on a drug charge (which he claimed was false) and was sent to maximum security and later placed in isolation because of his combative nature. Through an outside mentor, his writings gradually received international attention, and he was released from prison Despite his tragic life, his writing—mostly poetry—dwells on rebirth rather than bitterness. Among his works are *Immigrants in Our Own Land* (1979), *Swords of Darkness* (1981), *What's Happening?* (1982), *Martin and Meditations on the South Valley* (1987), *Black Mesa Poems* (1989), and *Working in the Dark: Reflections of a Poet of the Barrio* (1990), from which the following essay is taken.

What follows is a horrifying yet heartwarming autobiographical account of the author's personal journey toward poetic birth. We are allowed an intimate glance into a man's scarred and demon-filled soul and we witness how he faces the horrors of prison life, including solitary confinement and the mental ward. We see and feel his torment and hellish despair, but we also watch his slow development as a writer as he is purged of crime and violence through an appreciation of the beauty of language.

• • •

1 On weekend graveyard shifts at St. Joseph's Hospital I worked the emergency room, mopping up pools of blood and carting plastic bags stuffed with arms, legs, and hands to the outdoor incinerator. I enjoyed the quiet, away from the screams of shotgunned, knifed, and mangled kids writhing on gurneys outside the operating rooms. Ambulance sirens shrieked and squad car lights reddened the cool nights, flashing against the hospital walls: gray–red, gray–red. On slow nights I would lock the door of the administration office, search the reference library for a book on female anatomy and, with my feet propped on the desk, leaf through the illustrations, smoking my cigarette. I was seventeen.

2   One night my eye was caught by a familiar-looking word on the spine of a book. The title was *450 Years of Chicano History in Pictures.* On the cover were black-and-white photos: Padre Hidalgo exhorting Mexican peasants to revolt against the Spanish dictators; Anglo vigilantes hanging two Mexicans from a tree; a young Mexican woman with rifle and ammunition belts crisscrossing her breast; César Chávez and field workers marching for fair wages; Chicano railroad workers laying creosote ties; Chicanas laboring at machines in textile factories; Chicanas picketing and hoisting boycott signs.

3   From the time I was seven, teachers had been punishing me for not knowing my lessons by making me stick my nose in a circle chalked on the blackboard. Ashamed of not understanding and fearful of asking questions, I dropped out of school in the ninth grade. At seventeen I still didn't know how to read, but those pictures confirmed my identity. I stole the book that night, stashing it for safety under the slop-sink until I got off work. Back at my boardinghouse, I showed the book to friends. All of us were amazed; this book told us we were alive. We, too, had defended ourselves with our fists against hostile Anglos, gasping for breath in fights with the policemen who outnumbered us. The book reflected back to us our struggle in a way that made us proud.

4   Most of my life I felt like a target in the cross hairs of a hunter's rifle. When strangers and outsiders questioned me I felt the hang-rope tighten around my neck and the trapdoor creak beneath my feet. There was nothing so humiliating as being unable to express myself, and my inarticulateness increased my sense of jeopardy, of being endangered. I felt intimidated and vulnerable, ridiculed and scorned. Behind a mask of humility, I seethed with mute rebellion.

5   Before I was eighteen, I was arrested on suspicion of murder after refusing to explain a deep cut on my forearm. With shocking speed I found myself handcuffed to a chain gang of inmates and bused to a holding facility to await trial. There I met men, prisoners, who read aloud to each other the works of Neruda, Paz, Sabines, Nemerov, and Hemingway. Never had I felt such freedom as in that dormitory. Listening to the words of these writers, I felt that invisible threat from without lessen—my sense of teetering on a rotting plank over swamp water where famished alligators clapped their horny snouts for my blood. While I listened to the words of the poets, the alligators slumbered powerless in their lairs. Their language was the magic that could liberate me from myself, transform me into another person, transport me to other places far away.

6   And when they closed the books, these Chicanos, and went into their own Chicano language, they made barrio life come alive for me in the fullness of its vitality. I began to learn my own language, the bilingual words and phrases explaining to me my place in the universe. Every day I felt like the paper boy taking delivery of the latest news of the day.

7   Months later I was released, as I had suspected I would be. I had been guilty of nothing but shattering the windshield of my girlfriend's car in a fit of rage.

8   Two years passed. I was twenty now, and behind bars again. The federal marshals had failed to provide convincing evidence to extradite me to Arizona on a drug charge, but still I was being held. They had ninety days to prove I was guilty. The only evidence against me was that my girlfriend had been at the scene of the crime with my driver's license in her purse. They had to come up with something else. But there was nothing else. Eventually they negotiated a deal with the actual drug dealer, who took the stand against me. When the judge hit me with a million-dollar bail, I emptied my pockets on his booking desk: twenty-six cents.

9   One night in my third month in the county jail, I was mopping the floor in front of the booking desk. Some detectives had kneed an old drunk and handcuffed him to the booking bars. His shrill screams raked my nerves like a hacksaw on bone, the desperate protest of his dignity against their inhumanity. But the detectives just laughed as he tried to rise and kicked him to his knees. When they went to the bathroom to pee and the desk attendant walked to the file cabinet to pull the arrest record, I shot my arm through the bars, grabbed one of the attendant's university textbooks, and tucked it in my overalls. It was the only way I had of protesting.

10   It was late when I returned to my cell. Under my blanket I switched on a pen flashlight and opened the thick book at random, scanning the pages. I could hear the jailer making his rounds on the other tiers. The jangle of his keys and the sharp click of his boot heels intensified my solitude. Slowly I enunciated the words . . . p-o-n-d, ri-pple. It scared me that I had been reduced to this to find comfort. I always had thought reading a waste of time, that nothing could be gained by it. Only by action, by moving out into the world and confronting and challenging the obstacles, could one learn anything worth knowing.

11   Even as I tried to convince myself that I was merely curious, I became so absorbed in how the sounds created music in me and happiness, I forgot where I was. Memories began to quiver in me, glowing with a strange but familiar intimacy in which I found refuge. For a while, a deep sadness overcame me, as if I had chanced on a long-lost friend and mourned the years of separation. But soon the heartache of having missed so much of life, that had numbed me since I was a child, gave way, as if a grave illness lifted itself from me and I was cured, innocently believing in the beauty of life again. I stumblingly repeated the author's name as I fell asleep, saying it over and over in the dark: Words-worth, Words-worth.

12   Before long my sister came to visit me, and I joked about taking her to a place called Kubla Khan and getting her a blind date with this *vato* named Coleridge who lived on the seacoast and was *malias* on morphine. When I asked her to make a trip into enemy territory to buy me a grammar book, she said she couldn't. Bookstores intimidated her, because she, too, could neither read nor write.

13   Days later, with a stub pencil I whittled sharp with my teeth, I propped a Red Chief notebook on my knees and wrote my first words. From that moment, a hunger for poetry possessed me.

14 Until then, I had felt as if I had been born into a raging ocean where I swam relentlessly, flailing my arms in hope of rescue, of reaching a shoreline I never sighted. Never solid ground beneath me, never a resting place. I had lived with only the desperate hope to stay afloat; that and nothing more.

15 But when at last I wrote my first words on the page, I felt an island rising beneath my feet like the back of a whale. As more and more words emerged, I could finally rest: I had a place to stand for the first time in my life. The island grew, with each page, into a continent inhabited by people I knew and mapped with the life I lived.

16 I wrote about it all—about people I had loved or hated, about the brutalities and ecstasies of my life. And, for the first time, the child in me who had witnessed and endured unspeakable terrors cried out not just in impotent despair, but with the power of language. Suddenly, through language, through writing, my grief and my joy could be shared with anyone who would listen. And I could do this all alone; I could do it anywhere. I was no longer a captive of demons eating away at me, no longer a victim of other people's mockery and loathing, that had made me clench my fist white with rage and grit my teeth to silence. Words now pleaded back with the bleak lucidity of hurt. They were wrong, those others, and now I could say it.

17 Through language I was free. I could respond, escape, indulge; embrace or reject earth or the cosmos. I was launched on an endless journey without boundaries or rules, in which I could salvage the floating fragments of my past, or be born anew in the spontaneous ignition of understanding some heretofore concealed aspect of myself. Each word steamed with the hot lava juices of my primordial making, and I crawled out of stanzas dripping with birth-blood, reborn and freed from the chaos of my life. The child in the dark room of my heart, that had never been able to find or reach the light switch, flicked it on now; and I found in the room a stranger, myself, who had waited so many years to speak again. My words struck in me lightning crackles of elation and thunderhead storms of grief.

18 When I had been in the county jail longer than anyone else, I was made a trustee. One morning, after a fist fight, I went to the unlocked and unoccupied office used for lawyer-client meetings, to think. The bare white room with its fluorescent tube lighting seemed to expose and illuminate my dark and worthless life. And yet, for the first time, I had something to lose—my chance to read, to write; a way to live with dignity and meaning, that had opened for me when I stole that scuffed, second-hand book about the Romantic poets. In prison, the abscess had been lanced.

19 "I will never do any work in this prison system as long as I am not allowed to get my G.E.D." That's what I told the reclassification panel. The captain flicked off the tape recorder. He looked at me hard and said, "You'll never walk outta here alive. Oh, you'll work, put a copper penny on that, you'll work."

20 After that interview I was confined to deadlock maximum security in a subterranean dungeon, with ground-level chicken-wired windows painted gray. Twenty-three hours a day I was in that cell. I kept sane by borrowing books from the other cons on the tier. Then, just before Christmas, I received a

letter from Harry, a charity house Samaritan who doled out hot soup to the homeless in Phoenix. He had picked my name from a list of cons who had no one to write to them. I wrote back asking for a grammar book, and a week later received one of Mary Baker Eddy's treatises on salvation and redemption, with Spanish and English on opposing pages. Pacing my cell all day and most of each night, I grappled with grammar until I was able to write a long true-romance confession for a con to send to his pen pal. He paid me with a pack of smokes. Soon I had a thriving barter business, exchanging my poems and letters for novels, commissary pencils, and writing tablets.

21   One day I tore two flaps from the cardboard box that held all my belongings and punctured holes along the edge of each flap and along the border of a ream of state-issue paper. After I had aligned them to form a spine, I threaded the holes with a shoestring, and sketched on the cover a hummingbird fluttering above a rose. This was my first journal.

22   Whole afternoons I wrote, unconscious of passing time or whether it was day or night. Sunbursts exploded from the lead tip of my pencil, words that grafted me into awareness of who I was; peeled back to a burning core of bleak terror, an embryo floating in the image of water, I cracked out of the shell wide-eyed and insane. Trees grew out of the palms of my hands, the threatening otherness of life dissolved, and I became one with the air and sky, the dirt and the iron and concrete. There was no longer any distinction between the other and I. Language made bridges of fire between me and everything I saw. I entered into the blade of grass, the basketball, the con's eye and child's soul.

23   At night I flew. I conversed with floating heads in my cell, and visited strange houses where lonely women brewed tea and rocked in wicker rocking chairs listening to sad Joni Mitchell songs.

24   Before long I was frayed like a rope carrying too much weight, that suddenly snaps. I quit talking. Bars, walls, steel bunk and floor bristled with millions of poem-making sparks. My face was no longer familiar to me. The only reality was the swirling cornucopia of images in my mind, the voices in the air. Mid-air a cactus blossom would appear, a snake-flame in blinding dance around it, stunning me like a guard's fist striking my neck from behind.

25   The prison administrators tried several tactics to get me to work. For six months, after the next monthly prison board review, they sent cons to my cell to hassle me. When the guard would open my cell door to let one of them in, I'd leap out and fight him—and get sent to thirty-day isolation. I did a lot of isolation time. But I honed my image-making talents in that sensory-deprived solitude. Finally they moved me to death row, and after that to "nut-run," the tier that housed the mentally disturbed.

26   As the months passed, I became more and more sluggish. My eyelids were heavy, I could no longer write or read. I slept all the time.

27   One day a guard took me out to the exercise field. For the first time in years I felt grass and earth under my feet. It was spring. The sun warmed my face as I sat on the bleachers watching the cons box and run, hit the handball, lift weights. Some of them stopped to ask how I was, but I found it impossible to utter a syllable. My tongue would not move, saliva drooled from the corners

of my mouth. I had been so heavily medicated I could not summon the slightest gesture. Yet inside me a small voice cried out, I am fine! I am hurt now but I will come back! I am fine!

28   Back in my cell, for weeks I refused to eat. Styrofoam cups of urine and hot water were hurled at me. Other things happened. There were beatings, shock therapy, intimidation.

29   Later, I regained some clarity of mind. But there was a place in my heart where I had died. My life had compressed itself into an unbearable dread of being. The strain had been too much. I had stepped over that line where a human being has lost more than he can bear, where the pain is too intense, and he knows he is changed forever. I was now capable of killing, coldly and without feeling. I was empty, as I have never, before or since, known emptiness. I had no connection to this life.

30   But then, the encroaching darkness that began to envelop me forced me to re-form and give birth to myself again in the chaos. I withdrew even deeper into the world of language, cleaving the diamonds of verbs and nouns, plunging into the brilliant light of poetry's regenerative mystery. Words gave off rings of white energy, radar signals from powers beyond me that infused me with truth. I believed what I wrote, because I wrote what was true. My words did not come from books or textual formulas, but from a deep faith in the voice of my heart.

31   I had been steeped in self-loathing and rejected by everyone and everything—society, family, cons, God and demons. But now I had become as the burning ember floating in darkness that descends on a dry leaf and sets flame to forests. The word was the ember and the forest was my life.

32   I was born a poet one noon, gazing at weeds and creosoted grass at the base of a telephone pole outside my grilled cell window. The words I wrote then sailed me out of myself, and I was transported and metamorphosed into the images they made. From the dirty brown blades of grass came bolts of electrical light that jolted loose my old self; through the top of my head that self was released and reshaped in the clump of scrawny grass. Through language I became the grass, speaking its language and feeling its green feelings and black root sensations. Earth was my mother and I bathed in sunshine. Minuscule speckles of sunlight passed through my green skin and metabolized in my blood.

33   Writing bridged my divided life of prisoner and free man. I wrote of the emotional butchery of prisons, and of my acute gratitude for poetry. Where my blind doubt and spontaneous trust in life met, I discovered empathy and compassion. The power to express myself was a welcome storm rasping at tendril roots, flooding my soul's cracked dirt. Writing was water that cleansed the wound and fed the parched root of my heart.

34   I wrote to sublimate my rage, from a place where all hope is gone, from a madness of having been damaged too much, from a silence of killing rage. I wrote to avenge the betrayals of a lifetime, to purge the bitterness of injustice. I wrote with a deep groan of doom in my blood, bewildered and dumbstruck; from an indestructible love of life, to affirm breath and laughter and the abiding innocence of things. I wrote the way I wept, and danced, and made love.

Vocabulary

incinerator (1)   inarticulateness (4)   lairs (5)
extradite (8)   enunciated (10)   primordial (17)
subterranean (20)   Samaritan (20)   treatises (20)
regenerative (30)   creosoted (32)   metamorphosed (32)

The Facts

1. Why did the author drop out of school in the ninth grade?
2. What reason does the author offer for his having been sent to prison on a murder charge?
3. Who are Wordsworth and Coleridge? How do they relate to the author?
4. What was the "island" on which the author finally could rest while he was in jail? (See paragraph 15.)
5. When a prison guard finally took the author out to the exercise field, why couldn't he talk or even make the slightest gesture?

The Strategies

1. Who is the voice in this essay? What kind of person is revealed? How do you feel about him? What do you think are his reasons for writing the essay?
2. The author's experience is rendered in separate steps that could be called "the process of regeneration." What are the steps?
3. Where in this essay does the author reveal his poetic talent? Find specific examples of poetic utterances.
4. How does the author indicate the passage of time?
5. What do you think the author meant when he made the following statement: "Most of my life I felt like a target in the cross hairs of a hunter's rifle"? Explain this statement in your own words.

The Issues

1. Which aspect of the author's artistic journey do you consider the climax of his experience as related in this essay? In other words, at which point does he recognize the possibilities inherent in language? Give reasons for your choice.
2. How can you explain the author's grasp of English grammar despite the fact that he was a school dropout?
3. How would you characterize the essence of Baca's life before he became a writer? How was it possible for him to become a writer?
4. What is your opinion of the punishment meted out by the author's teachers from the time he was seven years old? What typical results does this kind of pedagogy produce?
5. Do you consider it a good idea to encourage prison inmates to develop their talents while in prison? Why or why not? If you believe the idea to have merit,

Suggestions for Writing

1. Language reached Baca in a way nothing else had. Write an essay that answers these questions: "Can every criminal be 'reached' on some level?" "Is there a good person inside even the most violent and apparently unrepentant criminal?"
2. Write an essay either attacking or defending our prison system in the way it helps inmates to improve themselves intellectually.

Why Tigers Become Man-Eaters

Jim Corbett

James Edward Corbett (1875–1955) was born in Nainital, India, and worked with a railroad company for twenty years. He served first as a captain and then as a major during World War I. From 1907 to 1938, he was a tiger hunter in the remote regions of India, where he was often summoned to destroy man-eaters preying on villagers. His memoirs, *Man-Eaters of Kumaon*, was first published in 1944 in India.

The big-game hunter has dwindled into something of a movie spoof. But not so many years ago, such a figure was a godsend to helpless remote villagers being preyed upon by rogue animals. Although he has hunted many such predators, the author tells us in an opening note to his famed book, Man-Eaters of Kumaon, *that when an animal becomes a man-eater, the transformation is rare, unnatural, and never without cause. In this, his opening chapter, the author explains why tigers change suddenly into man-eaters, giving us a sympathetic view of the tiger, which has today been hunted by humans to the brink of extinction.*

• • •

1   As many of the stories in this book are about man-eating tigers, it is perhaps desirable to explain why these animals develop man-eating tendencies.

2   A man-eating tiger is a tiger that has been compelled, through stress of circumstances beyond its control, to adopt a diet alien to it. The stress of circumstances is, in nine cases out of ten, wounds, and in the tenth case old age. The wound that has caused a particular tiger to take to man-eating might be the result of a carelessly fired shot and failure to follow up and recover the wounded animal, or be the result of the tiger having lost his temper when killing a porcupine. Human beings are not the natural prey of tigers, and it is only when tigers have been incapacitated through wounds or old age that, in order to live, they are compelled to take to a diet of human flesh.

3   A tiger when killing its natural prey, which it does either by stalking or lying in wait for it, depends for the success of its attack on its speed and, to a lesser extent, on the condition of its teeth and claws. When, therefore, a tiger is

suffering from one or more painful wounds, or when its teeth are missing or defective and its claws worn down, and it is unable to catch the animals it has been accustomed to eating, it is driven by necessity to killing human beings. The changeover from animal to human flesh is, I believe, in most cases accidental. As an illustration of what I mean by "accidental" I quote the case of the Muktesar man-eating tigress. This tigress, a comparatively young animal, in an encounter with a porcupine lost an eye and got some fifty quills, varying in length from one to nine inches, embedded in the arm and under the pad of her right foreleg. Several of these quills after striking a bone had doubled back in the form of a U, the point and the broken-off end being quite close together. Suppurating sores formed where she endeavored to extract the quills with her teeth, and while she was lying up in a thick patch of grass, starving and licking her wounds, a woman selected this particular patch of grass to cut as fodder for her cattle. At first the tigress took no notice, but when the woman had cut the grass right up to where she was lying the tigress struck once, the blow crushing in the woman's skull. Death was instantaneous, for, when found the following day, she was grasping her sickle with one hand and holding a tuft of grass, which she was about to cut when struck, with the other. Leaving the woman lying where she had fallen, the tigress limped off for a distance of over a mile and took refuge in a little hollow under a fallen tree. Two days later a man came to chip firewood off this fallen tree, and the tigress who was lying on the far side killed him. The man fell across the tree and, as he had removed his coat and shirt and the tigress had clawed his back when killing him, it is possible that the smell of the blood trickling down his body as he hung across the bole of the tree first gave her the idea that he was something that she could satisfy her hunger with. However that may be, before leaving him she ate a small portion from his back. A day later she killed her third victim deliberately, and without having received any provocation. Thereafter she became an established man-eater and had killed twenty-four people before she was finally accounted for.

4   A tiger on a fresh kill, or a wounded tiger, or a tigress with small cubs will occasionally kill human beings who disturb them; but these tigers cannot, by any stretch of imagination, be called man-eaters, though they are often so called. Personally I would give a tiger the benefit of the doubt once, and once again, before classing it as a man-eater, and whenever possible I would subject the alleged victim to a post-mortem before letting the kill go down on the records as the kill of a tiger or a leopard, as the case might be. This subject of post-mortems of human beings alleged to have been killed by either tigers or leopards or, in the plains, by wolves or hyenas, is of great importance, for, though I refrain from giving instances, I know of cases where deaths have wrongly been ascribed to carnivora.

5   It is a popular fallacy that all man-eaters are old and mangy, the mange being attributed to the excess of salt in human flesh. I am not competent to give any opinion on the relative quantity of salt in human or animal flesh; but I can, and I do, assert that a diet of human flesh, so far from having an injurious effect on the coat of man-eaters, has quite the opposite effect, for all the man-eaters I have seen have had remarkably fine coats.

6   Another popular belief in connection with man-eaters is that the cubs of these animals automatically become man-eaters. This is quite a reasonable supposition; but it is not borne out by actual facts, and the reason why the cubs of a man-eater do not themselves become man-eaters is that human beings are not the natural prey of tigers, or of leopards.

7   A cub will eat whatever its mother provides, and I have even known of tiger cubs' assisting their mothers to kill human beings; but I do not know of a single instance of a cub, after it had left the protection of its parent, or after that parent had been killed, taking to killing human beings.

8   In the case of human beings killed by carnivora, the doubt is often expressed as to whether the animal responsible for the kill is a tiger or leopard. As a general rule—to which I have seen no exceptions—tigers are responsible for all kills that take place in daylight, and leopards are responsible for all kills that take place in the dark. Both animals are semi-nocturnal forest-dwellers, have much the same habits, employ similar methods of killing, and both are capable of carrying their human victims for long distances. It would be natural, therefore, to expect them to hunt at the same hours; and that they do not do so is due to the difference in courage of the two animals. When a tiger becomes a man-eater it loses all fear of human beings and, as human beings move about more freely in the day than they do at night, it is able to secure its victims during daylight hours and there is no necessity for it to visit their habitations at night. A leopard on the other hand, even after it has killed scores of human beings, never loses its fear of man; and, as it is unwilling to face up to human beings in daylight, it secures its victims when they are moving about at night, or by breaking into their houses at night. Owing to those characteristics of the two animals, namely, that one loses its fear of human beings and kills in the daylight, while the other retains its fear and kills in the dark, man-eating tigers are easier to shoot than man-eating leopards.

9   The frequency with which a man-eating tiger kills depends on (a) the supply of natural food in the area in which it is operating; (b) the nature of the disability which has caused it to become a man-eater; and (c) whether it is a male or a female with cubs.

10   Those of us who lack the opportunity of forming our own opinion on any particular subject are apt to accept the opinions of others, and in no case is this more apparent than in the case of tigers—here I do not refer to man-eaters in particular, but to tigers in general. The author who first used the words "as cruel as a tiger" and "as bloodthirsty as a tiger," when attempting to emphasize the evil character of the villain of his piece, not only showed a lamentable ignorance of the animal he defamed, but coined phrases which have come into universal circulation, and which are mainly responsible for the wrong opinion of tigers held by all except that very small proportion of the public who have the opportunity of forming their own opinions.

11   When I see the expression "as cruel as a tiger" and "as bloodthirsty as a tiger" in print, I think of a small boy armed with an old muzzle-loading gun—the right barrel of which was split for six inches of its length, and the stock and barrels of which were kept from falling apart by lashings of brass wire—wandering

through the jungles of the terai and bhabar in the days when there were ten tigers to every one that now survives; sleeping anywhere he happened to be when night came on, with a small fire to give him company and warmth, wakened at intervals by the calling of tigers, sometimes in the distance, at other times near at hand; throwing another stick on the fire and turning over and continuing his interrupted sleep without one thought of unease; knowing from his own short experience and from what others, who like himself had spent their days in the jungles, had told him, that a tiger, unless molested, would do him no harm; or during daylight hours avoiding any tiger he saw, and when that was not possible, standing perfectly still until it had passed and gone, before continuing on his way. And I think of him on one occasion stalking half-a-dozen jungle fowl that were feeding in the open, and, on creeping up to a plum bush and standing up to peer over, the bush heaving and a tiger walking out on the far side and, on clearing the bush, turning round and looking at the boy with an expression on its face which said as clearly as any words, "Hello, kid, what the hell are you doing here?" and, receiving no answer, turning round and walking away very slowly without once looking back. And then again I think of the tens of thousands of men, women, and children who, while working in the forests or cutting grass or collecting dry sticks, pass day after day close to where tigers are lying up and who, when they return safely to their homes, do not even know that they have been under the observation of this so-called "cruel" and "bloodthirsty" animal.

12 Half a century has rolled by since the day the tiger walked out of the plum bush, the latter thirty-two years of which have been spent in the more or less regular pursuit of man-eaters, and though sights have been seen which would have caused a stone to weep, I have not seen a case where a tiger has been deliberately cruel or where it has been bloodthirsty to the extent that it has killed, without provocation, more than it has needed to satisfy its hunger or the hunger of its cubs.

13 A tiger's function in the scheme of things is to help maintain the balance in nature and if, on rare occasions when driven by dire necessity, he kills a human being, or when his natural food has been ruthlessly exterminated by man he kills two percent of the cattle he is alleged to have killed, it is not fair that for these acts a whole species should be branded as being cruel and bloodthirsty.

14 Sportsmen are admittedly conservative, the reason being that it has taken them years to form their opinions, and as each individual has a different point of view, it is only natural that opinions should differ on minor, or even in some cases on major, points, and for this reason I do not flatter myself that all the opinions I have expressed will meet with universal agreement.

15 There is, however, one point on which I am convinced that all sportsmen—no matter whether their point of view has been a platform on a tree, the back of an elephant, or their own feet—will agree with me, and that is, that a tiger is a largehearted gentleman with boundless courage and that when he is exterminated—as exterminated he will be unless public opinion rallies to his support—India will be the poorer by having lost the finest of her fauna.

16   Leopards, unlike tigers, are to a certain extent scavengers and become man-eaters by acquiring a taste for human flesh when unrestricted slaughter of game has deprived them of their natural food.

17   The dwellers in our hills are predominantly Hindu, and as such cremate their dead. The cremation invariably takes place on the bank of a stream or river in order that the ashes may be washed down into the Ganges and eventually into the sea. As most of the villages are situated high up on the hills, while the streams or rivers are in many cases miles away down in the valleys, it will be realized that a funeral entails a considerable tax on the manpower of a small community when, in addition to the carrying party, labor has to be provided to collect and carry the fuel needed for the cremation. In normal times these rites are carried out very effectively; but when disease in epidemic form sweeps through the hills and the inhabitants die faster than they can be disposed of, a very simple rite, which consists of placing a live coal in the mouth of the deceased, is performed in the village and the body is then carried to the edge of the hill and cast into the valley below.

18   A leopard, in an area in which his natural food is scarce, finding these bodies very soon acquires a taste for human flesh, and when the disease dies down and normal conditions are established, he very naturally, on finding his food supply cut off, takes to killing human beings.

19   Of the two man-eating leopards of Kumaon, which between them killed five hundred and twenty-five human beings, one followed on the heels of a very severe outbreak of cholera, while the other followed the mysterious disease which swept through India in 1918 and was called "war fever."

● Vocabulary

incapacitated (2)   suppurating (3)   ascribed (4)
carnivora (4)   fallacy (5)   semi-nocturnal (8)
habitations (8)   defamed (10)   fauna (15)
entails (17)

● The Facts

1. In nine cases out of ten, what is the cause of a tiger's suddenly becoming a man-eater? What is the cause in the tenth case?
2. What animal was responsible for wounding the Muktesar tigress, making her incapable of hunting her natural prey?
3. What popular fallacy does the author cite about the condition of man-eaters?
4. In the author's opinion, what are the chances that a tiger cub whose mother has become a man-eater will also prey on humans?
5. What phrases often applied to the tiger does the author find untrue and objectionable? Why?

● The Strategies

1. Aside from explaining why tigers become man-eaters, what do the early paragraphs do? Why is this task necessary to the author's purpose?

2. What kinds of support does the author offer for most of his assertions about tigers?
3. In paragraph 11, the author relates his boyhood experiences with tigers, using the third-person singular rather than the first person. Why do you think he makes this odd choice of pronouns? What effect does this usage have on the story?
4. The author is a big-game hunter, not a writer, and his style reflects an expected roughness. What example of this roughness can you cite from paragraph 12?
5. Throughout the explanation of why tigers become man-eaters, the author subtly contrasts the tiger with the leopard. Why? What effect does that contrast have on his explanation?

● The Issues

1. What can you infer about the author's childhood from his writing?
2. What would you imagine would be the author's initial reaction if he were asked to hunt down a tiger that had allegedly become a man-eater?
3. Considering that, by the author's own admissions, tigers and leopards have killed hundreds of humans, why should these animals be saved from extinction?
4. The author says in paragraph 14 that sportsmen are conservative. What is your opinion of sportsmen?
5. Of the two animals, tigers and leopards, which has the greater claim on the public imagination? How do you account for this difference?

● Suggestions for Writing

1. Find a poem or short work about the tiger and write an essay on the way the work depicts the animal.
2. Write an essay for or against hunting as a sport.

Why I Went to the Woods

HENRY DAVID THOREAU

Henry David Thoreau (1817–1862), essayist, lecturer, and moralist, was born in Concord, Massachusetts, and educated at Harvard University. He is regarded as one of the seminal influences on American thought and literature. His most famous work is *Walden* (1854), which grew out of the journal recording his solitary existence in a cabin beside Walden Pond, near Concord. His essay *Civil Disobedience* (1849) has been enormously influential since it was first published and has affected the actions and thoughts of such men as Mahatma Gandhi and Martin Luther King, Jr.

In this excerpt from Walden, *Thoreau explains why he went to the woods to live by himself. Unlike many of the writers in this section, Thoreau writes in a voice rich with metaphors, allusions, and images.*

● ● ●

1. I went to the woods because I wished to live deliberately, to front only the essential facts of life, and see if I could not learn what it had to teach, and not, when I came to die, discover that I had not lived. I did not wish to live what was not life, living is so dear; nor did I wish to practice resignation, unless it was quite necessary. I wanted to live deep and suck out all the marrow of life, to live so sturdily and Spartanlike as to put to rout all that was not life, to cut a broad swath and shave close, to drive life into a corner, and reduce it to its lowest terms, and, if it proved to be mean, why then to get the whole and genuine meanness of it, and publish its meanness to the world; or if it were sublime, to know it by experience, and be able to give a true account of it in my next excursion. For most men, it appears to me, are in a strange uncertainty about it, whether it is of the devil or of God, and have somewhat hastily concluded that it is the chief end of man here to "glorify God and enjoy him forever."

2. Still we live meanly, like ants; though the fable tells us that we were long ago changed into men; like pygmies we fight with cranes; it is error upon error, and clout upon clout, and our best virtue has for its occasion a superfluous and evitable wretchedness. Our life is frittered away by detail. An honest man has hardly need to count more than his ten fingers, or in extreme cases he may add his ten toes, and lump the rest. Simplicity, simplicity, simplicity! I say, let your affairs be as two or three, and not a hundred or a thousand; instead of a million count half a dozen, and keep your accounts on your thumbnail. In the midst of this chopping sea of civilized life, such are the clouds and storms and quick sands and thousand-and-one items to be allowed for, that a man has to live, if he would not founder and go to the bottom and not make his port at all, by dead reckoning, and he must be a great calculator indeed who succeeds. Simplify, simplify. Instead of three meals a day, if it be necessary eat but one; instead of a hundred dishes, five; and reduce other things in proportion. Our life is like a German Confederacy, made up of petty states, with its boundary forever fluctuating, so that even a German cannot tell you how it is bounded at any moment. The nation itself, with all its so-called internal improvements, which, by the way are all external and superficial, is just such an unwieldy and overgrown establishment, cluttered with furniture and tripped up by its own traps, ruined by luxury and heedless expense, by want of calculation and a worthy aim, as the million households in the lands; and the only cure for it, as for them, is in a rigid economy, a stern and more than Spartan simplicity of life and elevation of purpose. It lives too fast. Men think that it is essential that the Nation have commerce, and export ice, and talk through a telegraph, and ride thirty miles an hour, without a doubt, whether they do or not; but whether we should live like baboons or like men, is a little uncertain. If we do not get our sleepers, and forge rails, and devote days and nights to the work, but go to tinkering upon our lives to improve them, who will build railroads? And if railroads are not built, how shall we get to heaven in season? But if we stay at home and mind our business, who will want railroads? We do not ride on the railroad; it rides upon us. Did you ever think what those sleepers[1] are

---
[1] Cross ties; Thoreau is playing on the word.—Ed.

that underlie the railroad? Each one is a man, an Irishman, or a Yankee man. The rails are laid on them, and they are covered with sand, and the cars run smoothly over them. They are sound sleepers, I assure you. And every few years a new lot is laid down and run over; so that, if some have the pleasure of riding on a rail, others have the misfortune to be ridden upon. And when they run over a man that is walking in his sleep, a supernumerary sleeper in the wrong position, and wake him up, they suddenly stop the cars, and make a hue and cry about it, as if this were an exception. I am glad to know that it takes a gang of men for every five miles to keep the sleepers down and level in their beds as it is, for this is a sign that they may sometimes get up again.

3   Why should we live with such hurry and waste of life? We are determined to be starved before we are hungry. Men say that a stitch in time saves nine, and so they take a thousand stitches to-day to save nine to-morrow. As for work, we haven't any of any consequence. We have the Saint Vitus' dance, and cannot possibly keep our heads still. If I should only give a few pulls at the parish bell-rope, as for a fire, that is, without setting the bell, there is hardly a man on his farm in the outskirts of Concord, notwithstanding that press of engagements which was his excuse so many times this morning, nor a boy, nor a woman, I might almost say, but would forsake all and follow that sound, not mainly to save property from the flames, but, if we will confess the truth, much more to see it burn, since burn it must, and we, be it known, did not set it on fire,—or to see it put out, and have a hand in it, if that is done as handsomely; yes, even if it were the parish church itself. Hardly a man takes a half-hour's nap after dinner, but when he wakes he holds up his head and asks, "What's the news?" as if the rest of mankind had stood his sentinels. Some give directions to be waked every half-hour, doubtless for no other purpose; and then, to pay for it, they tell what they have dreamed. After a night's sleep the news is as indispensable as the breakfast. "Pray tell me anything new that has happened to a man anywhere on this globe,"—and he reads it over his coffee and rolls, that a man has had his eyes gouged out this morning on the Wachito River; never dreaming the while that he lives in the dark unfathomed mammoth cave of this world, and has but the rudiment of an eye himself.

4   For my part, I could easily do without the post-office. I think that there are very few important communications made through it. To speak critically, I never received more than one or two letters in my life—I wrote this some years ago—that were worth the postage. The penny-post is, commonly, an institution through which you seriously offer a man that penny for his thoughts which is so often safely offered in jest. And I am sure that I never read any memorable news in a newspaper. If we read of one man robbed, or murdered, or killed by accident, or one house burned, or one vessel wrecked, or one steamboat blown up, or one cow run over on the Western Railroad, or one mad dog killed, or one lot of grasshoppers in the winter,—we never need read of another. One is enough. If you are acquainted with the principle, what do you care for a myriad instances and applications? To a philosopher all news, as

it is called, is gossip, and they who edit and read it are old women over their tea. Yet not a few are greedy after this gossip. There was such a rush, as I hear, the other day at one of the offices to learn the foreign news by the last arrival, that several large squares of plate glass belonging to the establishment were broken by the pressure,—news which I seriously think a ready wit might write a twelvemonth, or twelve years, beforehand with sufficient accuracy. As for Spain, for instance, if you know how to throw in Don Carlos and the Infanta, and Don Pedro and Seville and Granada, from time to time in the right proportions,—they may have changed the names a little since I saw the papers,—and serve up a bullfight when other entertainments fail, it will be true to the letter, and give us as good an idea of the exact state or ruin of things in Spain as the most succinct and lucid reports under this head in the newspapers: and as for England, almost the last significant scrap of news from that quarter was the revolution of 1649; and if you have learned the history of her crops for an average year, you never need attend to that thing again, unless your speculations are of a merely pecuniary character. If one may judge who rarely looks into the newspapers, nothing new does ever happen in foreign parts, a French revolution not excepted.

5   What news! how much more important to know what that is which was never old! "Kieou-he-yu (great dignitary of the state of Wei) sent a man to Khoung-tseu to know his news. Khoung-tseu caused the messenger to be seated near him, and questioned him in these terms: What is your master doing? The messenger answered with respect: My master desires to diminish the number of his faults, but he cannot come to the end of them. The messenger being gone, the philosopher remarked: What a worthy messenger! What a worthy messenger!" The preacher, instead of vexing the ears of drowsy farmers on their day of rest at the end of the week,—for Sunday is the fit conclusion of an ill-spent week, and not the fresh and brave beginning of a new one,—with this one other draggle-tail of a sermon, should shout with thundering voice, "Pause! Avast! Why so seeming fast, but deadly slow?"

6   Shams and delusions are esteemed for soundest truths, while reality is fabulous. If men would steadily observe realities only, and not allow themselves to be deluded, life, to compare it with such things as we know, would be like a fairy tale and the Arabian Nights' Entertainments. If we respected only what is inevitable and has a right to be, music and poetry would resound along the streets. When we are unhurried and wise, we perceive that only great and worthy things have any permanent and absolute existence, that petty fears and petty pleasures are but the shadow of the reality. This is always exhilarating and sublime. By closing the eyes and slumbering, and consenting to be deceived by shows, men establish and confirm their daily life of routine and habit everywhere, which still is built on purely illusory foundations. Children, who play life, discern its true law and relations more clearly than men, who fail to live it worthily, but who think that they are wiser by experience, that is, by failure. I have read in a Hindoo book, that "there was a king's son, who, being expelled in infancy from his native city, was brought up by a forester, and, growing up to maturity in that state, imagined himself to belong to the barbarous

race with which he lived. One of his father's ministers having discovered him, revealed to him what he was, and the misconception of his character was removed, and he knew himself to be a prince. So soul," continues the Hindoo philosopher, "from the circumstances in which it is placed, mistakes its own character, until the truth is revealed to it by some holy teacher, and then it knows itself to be Brahme." I perceive that we inhabitants of New England live this mean life that we do because our vision does not penetrate the surface of things. We think that that is which appears to be. If a man should walk through this town and see only the reality, where, think you, would the "Milldam" go to? If he should give us an account of the realities he beheld there, we should not recognize the place in his description. Look at the meetinghouse, or a court-house, or a jail, or a shop, or a dwelling-house, and say what that thing really is before a true gaze, and they would all go to pieces in your account of them. Men esteem truth remote, in the outskirts of the system, behind the farthest star, before Adam and after the last man. In eternity there is indeed something true and sublime. But all these times and places and occasions are now and here. God himself culminates in the present moment, and will never be more divine in the lapse of all the ages. And we are enabled to apprehend at all what is sublime and noble only by the perpetual instilling and drenching of the reality that surrounds us. The universe constantly and obediently answers to our conceptions; whether we travel fast or slow, the track is laid for us. Let us spend our lives in conceiving then. The poet or the artist never yet had so fair and noble a design but some of his posterity at least could accomplish it.

7   Let us spend one day as deliberately as Nature, and not be thrown off the track by every nutshell and mosquito's wing that falls on the rails. Let us rise early and fast, or breakfast, gently and without perturbation; let company come and let company go, let the bells ring and the children cry,—determined to make a day of it. Why should we knock under and go with the stream? Let us not be upset and overwhelmed in that terrible rapid and whirlpool called a dinner, situated in the meridian shallows. Weather this danger and you are safe, for the rest of the way is down hill. With unrelaxed nerves, with morning vigor, sail by it, looking another way, tied to the mast like Ulysses.[2] If the engine whistles, let it whistle till it is hoarse for its pains. If the bell rings, why should we run? We will consider what kind of music they are like. Let us settle ourselves, and work and wedge our feet downward through the mud and slush of opinion, and prejudice, and tradition, and delusion, and appearance, that alluvion which covers the globe, through Paris and London, through New York and Boston and Concord, through Church and State, through poetry and philosophy and religion, till we come to a hard bottom and rocks in place, which we can call reality, and say, This is, and no mistake; and then begin, having a

---

[2]tied . . . Ulysses: In Homer's *Odyssey,* Ulysses had himself tied to the mast of his boat so that he could listen, but not respond, to the irresistible songs of the sirens, who were believed to lure ships to their doom.—Ed.

point d'appui,[3] below freshet and frost and fire, a place where you might found a wall or a state, or set a lamp-post safely, or perhaps a gauge, not a Nilometer, but a Realometer, that future ages might know how deep a freshet of shams and appearances had gathered from time to time. If you stand right fronting and face to face to a fact, you will see the sun glimmer on both its surfaces, as if it were a cimeter, and feel its sweet edge dividing you through the heart and marrow, and so you will happily conclude your mortal career. Be it life or death, we crave only reality. If we are really dying, let us hear the rattle in our throats and feel cold in the extremities; if we are alive, let us go about our business.

8   Time is but the stream I go a-fishing in. I drink at it; but while I drink I see the sandy bottom and detect how shallow it is. Its thin current slides away, but eternity remains. I would drink deeper; fish in the sky, whose bottom is pebbly with stars. I cannot count one. I know not the first letter of the alphabet. I have always been regretting that I was not as wise as the day I was born. The intellect is a cleaver; it discerns and rifts its way into the secret of things. I do not wish to be any more busy with my hands than is necessary. My head is hands and feet. I feel all my best faculties concentrated on it. My instinct tells me that my head is an organ for burrowing, as some creatures use their snout and fore paws, and with it I would mine and burrow my way through these hills. I think that the richest vein is somewhere hereabouts; so by the divining-rod and thin rising vapors, I judge; and here I will begin to mine.

- ## Vocabulary

    superfluous (2)   evitable (2)   supernumerary (2)
    rudiment (3)   myriad (4)   succinct (4)
    pecuniary (4)   culminates (6)   posterity (6)
    perturbation (7)   meridian (7)   alluvion (7)
    freshet (7)

- ## The Facts

    1. Why did Thoreau go to the woods? What, in his opinion, was wrong with the nation?
    2. Thoreau writes: "We do not ride on the railroad; it rides upon us." What does he mean?
    3. What is Thoreau's definition of "news"? What is his definition of "gossip"? According to Thoreau, how does news differ from gossip?
    4. What does Thoreau mean when he says that the "universe constantly and obediently answers to our conceptions" (paragraph 6)? How, then, is truth possible?
    5. Where, according to Thoreau, is truth to be found? What prevents us from finding it?

---

[3]point d'appui: point of stability.—Ed.

The Strategies

1. Reread the final sentence of paragraph 1. What tone does Thoreau use?
2. Thoreau uses two anecdotes in this excerpt (paragraphs 5 and 6). What do these have in common? What do they indicate about the writer's philosophy?
3. "We have the Saint Vitus' dance, and cannot possibly keep our heads still" (paragraph 3). What figure of speech is this? Can you find other examples of this same figure of speech in the text? What effect do they have on Thoreau's writing?
4. "Our life is like a German Confederacy, made up of petty states, with its boundary forever fluctuating, so that even a German cannot tell you how it is bounded at any moment" (paragraph 2). What figure of speech is this? How does it differ from the example in the preceding question?
5. An allusion is a figure of speech in which some famous historical or literary figure or event is casually mentioned. Can you find an allusion in Thoreau's text? (*Hint:* Examine paragraph 7.) What effect does the allusion have on the writer's style?

The Issues

1. Reread the essay *Diogenes and Alexander,* on pages 431–435. What views about society do Diogenes and Thoreau share? Do you agree with these views? Why or why not?
2. Thoreau witnessed the creation of the railroad and felt that it was an intrusion on life. In paragraph 2, he states, "We do not ride on the railroad; it rides upon us." What new industrial creation of your time might evoke a similar statement from some social commentator like Thoreau?
3. Do you agree with Thoreau that few important communications reach you through the post office? Why or why not?
4. In paragraph 6, Thoreau follows in Plato's footsteps when he tells us that only great and worthy things have absolute existence, but that petty things are a mere shadow of reality. Imagine yourself to be like Thoreau, living alone out in the woods. What would be essential to your life? What would seem petty? Give examples.
5. What memorable experience, if any, have you had of being alone in nature? How did this experience affect you? What did you learn from it?

Suggestions for Writing

1. Write an essay describing the clutter of petty affairs in your life. Suggest some ways of simplifying your affairs.
2. Pretend that you are Thoreau and that you have just been brought back to life and introduced to twentieth-century America. Write a diary putting down your first impressions.

Term Paper Suggestion

Thoreau was once sent to jail for refusing to pay his taxes. Research this episode and write about it.

The Storm
Kate Chopin

Kate O'Flaherty Chopin (1851–1904) was an American author of Creole-Irish descent, born in St. Louis. In 1870, she married a Louisiana businessman and lived with him in Natchitoches parish and New Orleans, where she acquired an intimate knowledge of Creole and Cajun life, on which she based most of her best stories. After her husband's death in 1883, she returned with their six children to St. Louis and began to write seriously. Her novel *The Awakening* (1899) caused a furor among readers because of its treatment of feminine sexuality that seemed to ignore the mores of the time. For the next sixty years, Chopin was virtually ignored. Today, her work is praised for its regional flavor and for its remarkable independence of mind and feeling. Among her works are two collections of short stories, *Bayou Folk* (1894) and *A Night in Acadie* (1897).

This story, The Storm, *makes light of an adulterous episode that takes place during a storm. Notice the parallels between the passion of the lovers and the ferocity of the storm as well as the serenity in both human and nature that follows afterwards. As you read this story, ask yourself if it seems to represent a particular feminist ideology toward sexuality.*

* * *

I

1   The leaves were so still that even Bibi thought it was going to rain. Bobinôt, who was accustomed to converse on terms of perfect equality with his little son, called the child's attention to certain sombre clouds that were rolling with sinister intention from the west, accompanied by a sullen, threatening roar. They were at Friedheimer's store and decided to remain there till the storm had passed. They sat within the door on two empty kegs. Bibi was four years old and looked very wise.

2   "Mama'll be 'fraid, yes," he suggested with blinking eyes.

3   "She'll shut the house. Maybe she got Sylvie helpin' her this evenin'," Bobinôt responded reassuringly.

4   "No; she ent got Sylvie. Sylvie was helpin' her yistiday," piped Bibi.

5   Bobinôt arose and going across to the counter purchased a can of shrimps, of which Calixta was very fond. Then he returned to his perch on the keg and sat stolidly holding the can of shrimps while the storm burst. It shook the wooden store and seemed to be ripping great furrows in the distant field. Bibi laid his little hand on his father's knee and was not afraid.

II

6   Calixta, at home, felt no uneasiness for their safety. She sat at a side window sewing furiously on a sewing machine. She was greatly occupied and did not

notice the approaching storm. But she felt very warm and often stopped to mop her face on which the perspiration gathered in beads. She unfastened her white sacque[1] at the throat. It began to grow dark, and suddenly realizing the situation she got up hurriedly and went about closing windows and doors.

7   Out on the small front gallery she had hung Bobinôt's Sunday clothes to air and she hastened out to gather them before the rain fell. As she stepped outside, Alcée Laballière rode in at the gate. She had not seen him very often since her marriage, and never alone. She stood there with Bobinôt's coat in her hands, and the big rain drops began to fall. Alcée rode his horse under the shelter of a side projection where the chickens had huddled and there were plows and a harrow piled up in the corner.

8   "May I come and wait on your gallery till the storm is over, Calixta?" he asked.

9   "Come 'long in, M'sieur Alcée."

10 His voice and her own startled her as if from a trance, and she seized Bobinôt's vest. Alcée, mounting to the porch, grabbed the trousers and snatched Bibi's braided jacket that was about to be carried away by a sudden gust of wind. He expressed an intention to remain outside, but it was soon apparent that he might as well have been out in the open: the water beat in upon the boards in driving sheets, and he went inside, closing the door after him. It was even necessary to put something beneath the door to keep the water out.

11 "My! what a rain! It's good two years sence it rain' like that," exclaimed Calixta as she rolled up a piece of bagging and Alcée helped her to thrust it beneath the crack.

12 She was a little fuller of figure than five years before when she married; but she had lost nothing of her vivacity. Her blue eyes still retained their melting quality; and her yellow hair, dishevelled by the wind and rain, kinked more stubbornly than ever about her ears and temples.

13 The rain beat upon the low, shingled roof with a force and clatter that threatened to break an entrance and deluge them there. They were in the dining room—the sitting room—the general utility room. Adjoining was her bed room, with Bibi's couch alongside her own. The door stood open, and the room with its white, monumental bed, its closed shutters, looked dim and mysterious.

14 Alcée flung himself into a rocker and Calixta nervously began to gather up from the floor the lengths of a cotton sheet which she had been sewing.

15 "If this keeps up, Dieu sait[2] if the levees goin' to stan' it!" she exclaimed.

16 "What have you got to do with the levees?"

17 "I got enough to do! An' there's Bobinôt with Bibi out in that storm—if he only didn' left Friedheimer's!"

18 "Let us hope, Calixta, that Bobinôt's got sense enough to come in out of a cyclone."

19 She went and stood at the window with a greatly disturbed look on her face. She wiped the frame that was clouded with moisture. It was stiflingly hot. Alcée

---

[1] Work dress, house dress.—Ed.
[2] French for "God knows."—Ed.

got up and joined her at the window, looking over her shoulder. The rain was coming down in sheets obscuring the view of far-off cabins and enveloping the distant wood in a gray mist. The playing of the lightning was incessant. A bolt struck a tall chinaberry tree at the edge of the field. It filled all visible space with a blinding glare and the crash seemed to invade the very boards they stood upon.

20   Calixta put her hands to her eyes, and with a cry, staggered backward. Alcée's arm encircled her, and for an instant he drew her close and spasmodically to him.

21   "Bonté!"[3] she cried, releasing herself from his encircling arm and retreating from the window, "the house'll go next! If I only knew w'ere Bibi was!" She would not compose herself; she would not be seated. Alcée clasped her shoulders and looked into her face. The contact of her warm, palpitating body when he had unthinkingly drawn her into his arms, had aroused all the old-time infatuation and desire for her flesh.

22   "Calixta," he said, "don't be frightened. Nothing can happen. The house is too low to be struck, with so many tall trees standing about. There! aren't you going to be quiet? say, aren't you?" He pushed her hair back from her face that was warm and steaming. Her lips were as red and moist as pomegranate seed. Her white neck and a glimpse of her full, firm bosom disturbed him powerfully. As she glanced up at him the fear in her liquid blue eyes had given place to a drowsy gleam that unconsciously betrayed a sensuous desire. He looked down into her eyes and there was nothing for him to do but to gather her lips in a kiss. It reminded him of Assumption.

23   "Do you remember—in Assumption, Calixta?" he asked in a low voice broken by passion. Oh! she remembered; for in Assumption he had kissed her and kissed and kissed her; until his senses would well nigh fail, and to save her he would resort to a desperate flight. If she was not an immaculate dove in those days, she was still inviolate; a passionate creature whose very defenselessness had made her defense, against which his honor forbade him to prevail. Now—well, now—her lips seemed in a manner free to be tasted, as well as her round, white throat and her whiter breasts.

24   They did not heed the crashing torrents, and the roar of the elements made her laugh as she lay in his arms. She was a revelation in that dim, mysterious chamber; as white as the couch she lay upon. Her firm, elastic flesh that was knowing for the first time its birthright, was like a creamy lily that the sun invites to contribute its breath and perfume to the undying life of the world.

25   The generous abundance of her passion, without guile or trickery, was like a white flame which penetrated and found response in depths of his own sensuous nature that had never yet been reached.

26   When he touched her breasts they gave themselves up in quivering ecstasy, inviting his lips. Her mouth was a fountain of delight. And when he possessed her, they seemed to swoon together at the very borderland of life's mystery.

27   He stayed cushioned upon her, breathless, dazed, enervated, with his heart beating like a hammer upon her. With one hand she clasped his head, her lips lightly touching his forehead. The other hand stroked with a soothing rhythm his muscular shoulders.

---

[3] French for "goodness."—Ed.

28   The growl of the thunder was distant and passing away. The rain beat softly upon the shingles, inviting them to drowsiness and sleep. But they dared not yield.

29   The rain was over; and the sun was turning the glistening green world into a palace of gems. Calixta, on the gallery, watched Alcée ride away. He turned and smiled at her with a beaming face; and she lifted her pretty chin in the air and laughed aloud.

III

30   Bobinôt and Bibi, trudging home, stopped without at the cistern to make themselves presentable.

31   "My! Bibi, w'at will yo' mama say! You ought to be ashame'. You oughtn' put on those good pants. Look at 'em! An' that mud on yo' collar! How you got that mud on yo' collar, Bibi? I never saw such a boy!" Bibi was the picture of pathetic resignation. Bobinôt was the embodiment of serious solicitude as he strove to remove from his own person and his son's the signs of their tramp over heavy roads and through wet fields. He scraped the mud off Bibi's bare legs and feet with a stick and carefully removed all traces from his heavy brogans. Then, prepared for the worst—the meeting with an overscrupulous housewife, they entered cautiously at the back door.

32   Calixta was preparing supper. She had set the table and was dripping coffee at the hearth. She sprang up as they came in.

33   "Oh, Bobinôt! You back! My! but I was uneasy. W'ere you been during the rain? An' Bibi? he ain't wet? he ain't hurt?" She had clasped Bibi and was kissing him effusively. Bobinôt's explanations and apologies which he had been composing all along the way, died on his lips as Calixta felt him to see if he were dry, and seemed to express nothing but satisfaction at their safe return.

34   "I brought you some shrimps, Calixta," offered Bobinôt, hauling the can from his ample side pocket and laying it on the table.

35   "Shrimps! Oh, Bobinôt! you too good fo' anything!" and she gave him a smacking kiss on the cheek that resounded. "J'vous réponds,[4] we'll have a feas' to night! umph-umph!"

36   Bobinôt and Bibi began to relax and enjoy themselves, and when the three seated themselves at table they laughed much and so loud that anyone might have heard them as far away as Laballière's.

IV

37   Alcée Laballière wrote to his wife, Clarisse, that night. It was a loving letter, full of tender solicitude. He told her not to hurry back, but if she and the babies liked it at Biloxi, to stay a month longer. He was getting on nicely; and though he missed them, he was willing to bear the separation a while longer—realizing that their health and pleasure were the first things to be considered.

---

[4]French for "I answer you."—Ed.

V

38 As for Clarisse, she was charmed upon receiving her husband's letter. She and the babies were doing well. The society was agreeable; many of her old friends and acquaintances were at the bay. And the first free breath since her marriage seemed to restore the pleasant liberty of her maiden days. Devoted as she was to her husband, their intimate conjugal life was something which she was more than willing to forego for a while.

39 So the storm passed and every one was happy.

● Vocabulary

sombre (1)	projection (7)	harrow (7)
gallery (8)	deluge (13)	monumental (13)
levees (15)	incessant (19)	spasmodically (20)
palpitating (21)	sensuous (22)	immaculate (23)
inviolate (23)	revelation (24)	enervated (27)
cistern (30)	resignation (31)	embodiment (31)
solicitude (31)	brogans (31)	effusively (33)
conjugal (38)		

● The Facts

1. What relationship exists between Calixta and Alcée? What do you infer from their past?
2. How does the storm contribute to the love tryst that takes place?
3. What caused the lovers to act so impetuously? Do you consider the cause valid and acceptable?
4. How do the lovers react to their mates after the love affair? Does the reaction seem plausible? Give reasons for your answer.
5. In paragraph 13, what is the significance of describing Calixta's bedroom as "dim and mysterious"? Explain the reference.

● The Strategies

1. What setting forms the backdrop for this story? What does the setting contribute?
2. What is the purpose of the Roman numerals dividing the story?
3. What kind of language does the author resort to in describing the passion of the two lovers? Point to specific examples.
4. What do you think of the title of this story? Is the story really about a storm? Explain your answer.
5. Where does the climax of the story take place? Explain your answer.

● The Issues

1. In your opinion, did the lovers handle the situation as morally as possible, given that they yielded to the temptation of the situation? If you disagree with their reactions, what should they have done?

2. The narrator tells us that Calixta's flesh "was knowing for the first time its birthright" (paragraph 24). What is meant by this statement? What similar comment is made about Alcée?
3. As indicated in the biographical headnote about Kate Chopin, the author's work was criticized for its "feminine sexuality." What do you think readers of her day thought about a story like "The Storm"? How does your view of the story compare with the view of Chopin's contemporaries?
4. What kind of conjugal life do the couples described seem to share? What, if anything, is good about it?
5. What is the theme (main point) of the story? Express it in one sentence.

Suggestions for Writing

1. Write an analysis of what happens when people lose control of their passions. Use examples to prove your point.
2. Write an essay offering your views about the causes of the widespread marital infidelity so common in our society today.

Design

Robert Frost

Robert Frost (1874–1963) was a lecturer, poet, and teacher. When he was nineteen and working in a mill in Lawrence, Massachusetts, the *Independent* accepted and published "My Butterfly, an Elegy"—the poem that began Frost's career as one of America's great poets. Rugged New England farm life was the inspiration for many of his poems.

Like much of Frost's poetry, "Design" appears on the surface to be simple and plain, but a closer study reveals subtleties and depth. The speaker observes nature with a philosophic mind.

• • •

1   I found a dimpled spider, fat and white,
    On a white heal-all, holding up a moth
    Like a white piece of rigid satin cloth—
    Assorted characters of death and blight
5   Mixed ready to begin the morning right,
    Like the ingredients of a witches' broth—
    A snow-drop spider, a flower like a froth,
    And dead wings carried like a paper kite.

10 What had that flower to do with being white,
    The wayside blue and innocent heal-all?
    What brought the kindred spider to that height,
    Then steered the white moth thither in the night?
    What but design of darkness to appall?—
    If design govern in a thing so small.

Vocabulary

characters (4) blight (4) kindred (11)
appall (13)

The Facts

1. The heal-all is a wildflower—usually blue or violet, but occasionally white—commonly found blooming along footpaths and roads. The name derives from the belief that this flower possessed healing qualities. As described in the first stanza, what do the spider, the heal-all, and the moth have in common?
2. Three questions are asked in the second stanza. How can these be condensed into one question? What answer is implied in the poem?
3. The "argument from design" was a well-known eighteenth-century argument for the existence of God. It proposed a broad view of history and the cosmos, which revealed that some divine intelligence fashioned and then sustained existence. What twist does Frost give this argument?
4. Is the poem probing a sufficient, a necessary, or a contributory cause?

The Strategies

1. What five examples of figurative language are used in the first stanza? Tell what effect each has.
2. In the second stanza, why does the poet use the adjective *kindred* in connection with the spider?
3. In the second stanza, what synonyms does the poet use to repeat the concept of design?

The Issues

1. The question of whether or not our destinies are controlled by some higher intelligence concerns many thinking people. Why do you suppose human beings wrestle so often with this question?
2. How would you argue against Frost's theme? Use an example from nature to take the opposite viewpoint.
3. Judging from your experience, which of your intimate acquaintances are better able to cope with life—those with a strong belief in a God who controls human destiny, or those with the belief that existence is simply experience and that no God controls any aspect of the universe?

Suggestions for Writing

1. Using an example from nature, write a brief essay showing how an incontrovertible harmony seems to regulate the activities of the world as a whole.
2. Write a brief essay in which you explain what in the poem causes you to like or dislike it.

ISSUE FOR CRITICAL THINKING AND DEBATE: THE STATUS OF WOMEN

Women in the United States are better off today than ever before. We can make that statement boldly on the evidence of statistics and from our own experience. In 1900, women could not vote, could not own property, and derived their legal status from whether or not they had husbands. Women, who did not win the right to vote until 1920, now vote in larger numbers than men. In a recent poll conducted by *USA Today,* 81% of the sampled women predicted the election of a woman president within the next twenty-five years.

Today, women work in as varied a range of occupations as men. Some are senators, CEOs, TV anchors, stockbrokers, and university presidents. Some have made financial fortunes while their husbands took care of the children. Only a few years ago, when a woman's place was thought to be in the home and her job to care for her husband and family, such achievements would have been unthinkable.

In spite of these victories, the war for equality between men and women in the workplace and in society at large continues. One lingering bone of contention is the disparity between the salaries of men and the salaries of women for the same work. The 2000 census showed that for 1999, the median income of men was $35,922, in contrast to $26,292 for women. This inequality has persisted since record keeping began.

Anyone with even a scant knowledge of history would have to admit that the significant gains made in the status of woman were mainly won by the feminist movement. It is therefore a paradox that feminism has lost its appeal to many women of the upcoming generation. Daughters who today enjoy the benefits won by yesterday's militants regard feminism as their mother's movement, not theirs. In an ironic way, that attitude is a triumph for feminism, whose central aim has always been the empowerment of the individual to do, say, and think as he/she feels.

The change in the status of women, however, comes at a price. Women now face a world that no longer regards them as delicate and needing protection. If the *Titanic* disaster had happened in our era, the cry heard on deck would not be the chivalrous one that rang out in 1912 aboard the doomed ship, "Women and children first!" It would more likely be, "Every person for himself/herself!" For some conservative women, this has been too high a price to pay. For many other women, it's a bargain. The photo on page 556 is a declaration of what women have gained in the race for equality with men—the right to hold high executive jobs. Conversely, the cartoon on page 559 argues that the price of equality for some women is an overburdened life.

Our essayists take predictably different tacks on the subject. Kate Gubata declares firmly that women should continue to work toward achieving total equality with men in every nook of life—from politics to economics. Rebecca E. Rubins believes that women have already achieved equality with men, making the feminist movement obsolete. The student essay, written by Paula Rewa of East Tennessee State University, argues that the word *woman* now mainly

- In business and politics, are women today reaching rungs on the success ladder previously reserved only for men?

functions as an adjective—as in *woman* lawyer—but should be reclaimed as a noun. *Woman*—used as a noun—remains a woman, no matter how she dresses or what she does.

The New Feminism
KATE GUBATA

Kate Gubata writes a column for the Brown University student newspaper.

1   Jane is pro-choice. Jane loves chocolate. She backs candidates who strive to change the wages inequity that exists in this country. She likes boys who wear Abercrombie & Fitch. She wishes she looked a little more like Jennifer Lopez. She believes in human rights and equality for men and women.

2   Is she a feminist? Possibly. Is she a young woman in America? Without a doubt.

3   At a time when the term *feminism* often suggests the impression of the radical, almost militantly liberal rival of the male-dominated status quo, many young women are hesitant, if not outright opposed, to associate themselves with this exclusive group.

4   After all, that is feminism, right? Feminism defines my mother's generation. It represents at one extreme the assemblage of hairy-legged, men-hating

conspirators to overthrow professional men's sports; on the softer side, feminists gather together to hold hands and listen to Helen Reddy. Why on earth would a young woman today deny herself the title of feminist?

5   One of the greatest barriers opposing the feminist movement today is the lack of interest of young women due to their misconceptions of the feminists' aims. Feminism is a progressive movement that seeks to bring about the change that will embed equality for men and women in all aspects of life, from the larger spheres of political, social and economic structure, to the ways in which men and women perceive each other throughout the course of common interaction. Feminism is not an abstract, ideological construct. It represents not an exclusive body of individual motivations but a movement that reaches everyone who believes in human rights.

6   How can we bridge the gap between feminist rhetoric and everyday life? How can feminists illuminate the aspects of the movement that affect the ways in which we on this campus live our lives?

7   Feminism is a movement of action. The goal of feminism today is to stimulate men and women to transform the aims of equality into reality. This is not an ideological mission. The causes of feminism are about action; as Brown students we can all become active participants. Choice, pay inequity, the recent passage of mifeprestone—"the abortion drug"—by the FDA, and the legal battles over homosexual marriage are some of the issues pertinent to feminists today. The various on-campus events intend to educate the Brown community as a whole and to promote a sense of unity among students who have an interest in these types of issues. The movements both on campus and in the local community to promote change are the mechanisms by which young people can use their ideas and energies to fuel united action.

8   Feminism does not have a feminist-checklist. Feminists embody the characteristics of free thought, openness to ideas, and the desire to pool resources with all people willing to work for equality. Feminism represents an inclusive, not exclusive assembly. The key to encompassing a wide range of interest is the resolution of the conflict many people sense between the abstract concepts of feminism and their personal emotions and ideas. A young woman who does not identify with her impression of the radical image of a feminist must not deny herself the opportunity to share her opinions and ideas with a group that is in fact more than willing to listen and learn. There is no dress code or behavior code for a feminist; the term *feminist* characterizes anyone who aspires to achieve equality and who believes in the power of the united fight for human rights.

9   What's the solution for Jane and others seeking the balance between the persona of the radical feminist ideology and feminism's role in the modern lifestyle? Get involved. Keep an eye out for campus and community events that pertain to important feminist issues and goals. If a group interests you, dive in and make yourself heard; but leave your preconceptions at the door. Be prepared to find a diverse group of people who may share nothing but the will to achieve equality. Move over Helen Reddy; a new group of activists is ready to roar.

Vocabulary

feminism (title) militantly (3) assemblage (4)
ideological (5) illuminate (6) persona (9)
preconceptions (9)

The Facts

1. At the time of writing this essay, where is the author? What does her location bring to the essay?
2. According to the author, what is the goal of feminism today? What other goal(s), if any, do you consider important for women to pursue?
3. In paragraph 5 and again in paragraph 7, the author insists that feminism must not be an "ideological" movement. Why does the author shun ideology? What is more important to her than ideology? Do you agree with her? Explain your position.
4. According to the author, what issues should be of major concern to feminists today? Respond to each issue by evaluating its importance within the total social fabric of your environment.
5. What does the author mean when she writes that "Feminism does not have a feminist-checklist"? Do you think the movement *should* have a checklist? Explain your answer.

The Strategies

1. In what paragraph does the author define feminism by stating what it is not? Is this a good technique to use when defining a term?
2. In what paragraph does the author associate feminism with a past generation? What effect does the association have? Offer your personal response.
3. What is the purpose of the question posed at the start of paragraph 9? Is the question ever answered? If yes, what is the answer; if no, why is no answer given?
4. Who is the "Jane" referred to at the beginning and at the end of the essay? Explain her function in the essay.
5. What is the author's tone in the final sentence of the essay? Explain why you think the author uses this tone to end her essay.

The Issues

1. What does the term *feminist* conjure up in your mind? Do you react favorably or unfavorably to this term? Explain your answer.
2. In your view, what have women gained so far and what have they lost as a result of the feminist movement? Whom does the movement favor most? Whom does it favor least?
3. Do you agree with the author that one of the greatest barriers opposing the feminist movement today is the lack of interest on the part of young women? If the author is right, what do you think are the reasons for today's apathy on the part of young women? If you think the author is wrong, give reasons why you think so.

4. If a woman prefers to stay home and be a housewife once she is married, does she still have an obligation to get involved in feminist issues? Or should she focus more on matters of family values? Give reasons for your stand.

5. If you are a man, do you want your wife to have her own career, or would you prefer to have her be a full-time homemaker? Explain your choice. If you are a woman, would you prefer to have a career or to be a full-time homemaker? Explain your choice. Consider also the possibility of combining a career with homemaking.

Suggestions for Writing

1. Write an essay in which you define the term *feminism* as you understand it. Clarify your definition by using illustration, comparison/contrast, causal analysis, or any other rhetorical mode that helps you answer the question, "What is feminism?"

2. Re-read the question at the beginning of paragraph 9 to make sure you understand what is meant by feminist ideology and by the feminist's role in today's lifestyle. Then write an essay answering the question. Be sure to formulate a thesis that you support with appropriate evidence. For instance, you might write "The true feminist will support human rights while remaining

"Now that I've moved my files down here to the basement, we'll be able to spend a lot more time together."

Why is multitasking a concept with which many working mothers are familiar?

nonmasculine in her manner." Or, if you really detest feminism, your thesis might read: "The feminist movement has done nothing but destroy family values, which are the foundation of a strong nation."

The Farce of Feminism

Rebecca E. Rubins

Rebecca E. Rubins wrote this column for the Harvard Crimson.

1   Strolling through the Freshman Week Activities Fair, I was accosted by an energetic young woman from a women's issues group who asked me fiercely, "Do you support women?"—As I took my time answering, my interrogator laughingly remarked, "It'd be really sad if you didn't."

2   Although at the time I shrugged my shoulders and signed my name to the mailing list, the feeling of having been grouped into a general category against my will simply because of my sex haunted me. For the question being asked was not "Do I support women?"—which I certainly do—but "Do I support feminism?"—which I emphatically do not. Feminism is an outdated, misdirected ideology that perpetuates the very ills it condemns and harms women much more than it helps them.

3   Perhaps there was once a time when feminism was warranted, when its name was not synonymous with self-pitying whining but with active efforts toward positive change. In the early 20th century, when women still had not gained the right to vote, the suffragettes showed remarkable dedication in bringing the system's inherent inequality to the forefront of public awareness.

4   In recent years, however, feminism in America has found itself hopelessly bereaved of a cause for which to fight. Women in this country are now on an entirely equal footing with men and are sometimes even given preferential treatment. Instead of focusing on areas of the world where women are truly being oppressed, where they cannot show their ankles on the street without fear of being shot and killed, feminists of today spend their time creating support groups for one another and debating the relative disadvantages faced by girls in science and math classrooms. Feminism keeps women from naturally asserting their equality to men in an environment which is now conducive to such equality.

5   Feminism also creates a double standard for men and women, thus promoting the societal ills it supposedly opposes. Feminists laud women-only discussion groups, dance teams and drama clubs, but when men try to create or maintain similar men-only groups, they are accused of discrimination. The feminist movement operates on the principle that past wrongs done to women can be remedied by preferential treatment now—that two wrongs will make a right. This reverse discrimination is not only unethical but also belies their alleged opposition to judgment or exclusion based on gender alone.

6   Finally, and most importantly, feminism accomplishes the exact opposite of what it intends. Instead of raising women's social status, it burdens them with a weighty sense of victimization that neither empowers them nor motivates men

to view them as equals. Girls are not born feeling inferior to boys. Rather, it is their exposure to feminism that causes them to develop a slavelike mentality.

7   This is particularly evident in school, where the "feminist aspect" of every subject is now played up, thereby bringing social activism into the classroom where it only detracts from the learning process. English teachers ask students to apply feminist criticism to books with no semblance of a feminist outlook. History textbooks try to compensate for the fact that women were in the kitchen for most of recorded time by highlighting the life of one particular female or another regardless of how little she matters to history. Other programs, such as Take Your Daughter to Work Day, also impress upon young girls the notion that they are inherently inferior citizens who need rewritten history books and politically correct semi-holidays to raise them up to the level of their male peers who, incidentally, seem to do just fine without such support. In this way, the movement marginalizes women by reminding them constantly of their former subservient status and instilling in them at a very young age a dependency on the support of other women and on feminism to "survive" in a horribly male-dominated world.

8   If feminists were to take a step back and view the current situation of women in the country objectively, they might realize that women no longer need interest groups, support networks, activism and doctored curriculae—that they, in fact, are better off without feminists' supposed help. But that objective view would leave feminists without a viable *raison d'etre*, and so they continue to ignore, for example, the possibility that the average female college student walking through an activities fair might support women but not support feminism, that she might instead consider feminism a threat to her own sense of self and empowerment.

9   Maybe feminists should start asking themselves the question, "Do we support women?" And maybe it's time someone said, "It's sad, but you don't."

● Vocabulary

farce (title)   accosted (1)   interrogator (1)
ideology (2)   inherent (3)   preferential (4)
conducive (4)   discrimination (5)   belies (5)
alleged (5)   victimization (6)   marginalizes (7)
subservient (7)   curriculae (curriculum) (8) empowerment (8)

● The Facts

1. Why does the author entitle her essay *The Farce of Feminism*? Look up the word *farce* to make sure you understand its full meaning. In what way is the feminist movement a farce in the eyes of the author?

2. The author states that feminism promotes the very ills it condemns and thus harms women (see paragraph 2). To what ills is the author referring? Can you name other ills promoted by feminism?

3. According to the author, why do women no longer need feminism? Do you agree with her reasoning? Why or why not?

4. What is the difference between *feminine* and *feminism*? How important is it for the reader to be aware of the distinction?
5. What activities of feminism does the author particularly discredit? How do you feel about these activities? How important are they today? Evaluate them critically.

The Strategies

1. What grabber does the author use to capture the reader's attention? How effective is it in keeping you interested in what follows?
2. Where does the author place her thesis? Why is it not in the opening or final paragraph? Is the placement effective? Explain your opinion.
3. How does the author make a transition from the past to the present as it concerns feminism? What is the purpose of such a transition? Where does it take place?
4. Paragraph 5 refers to a "double standard" created by feminism. What example does the author use to illustrate the double standard? In what other areas in politics or society do double standards occur? Provide some examples.
5. Why does the author return to the activities fair at the end of the essay? Is she being redundant or is there a good reason for the repeated reference? Explain your answer.

The Issues

1. Do you agree that feminism has reached the point at which it perpetuates the very ills it condemns? If you agree, what are some of the ills that feminism perpetuates? Provide examples. If you believe that feminism must continue to fight for women's rights, what are these rights?
2. Do you think that women who have not had the advantage of a higher education and women with advanced degrees hold different attitudes toward feminism?
3. What is *reverse discrimination* as the author uses the term? What are some of the examples of reverse discrimination not mentioned in the essay? How can it be prevented?
4. Do you agree with the author that women today are better off without the help of feminism? What contribution might feminism still make to the cause of women?
5. What would your answer be to the question, "Do you support feminism?" What would your answer be to the question, "Do you support women?"

Suggestions for Writing

1. Using the Internet as your research source, find out what contributions the suffragettes (see paragraph 3) made to the cause of feminism and write an essay using the information you uncovered.
2. Write an essay in which you contrast the position of Kate Gabata with that of Rebecca Rubins concerning feminism. Be sure to find some clear bases for the contrast. Review the *Road Map to Comparison/Contrast* in Chapter 12, p. 421.

Punctuation Workshop
The Exclamation Point (!)

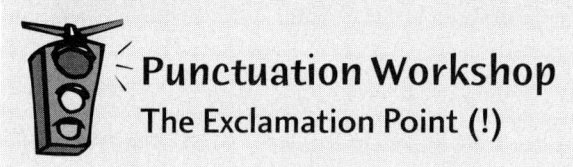

1. Use the exclamation point after expressions of strong emotion, such as joy, surprise, disbelief, or anger:

    Hooray! You beat the last record!

    Amazing! The snake is still alive.

    How dark the sky has suddenly become!

    Get out of my sight, you monster!

    "Stop that yelling immediately!" he shouted. (The comma or period that normally follows a direct quotation is omitted when the quotation has an exclamation point.)

2. Use the exclamation point sparingly. Overuse will diminish its impact. Often a comma will suffice after a mild interjection, and a period will suffice after a mild exclamation or command:

    Oh, now I see the difference in their attitude.

    How desperately he tried to please his mother.

    Please sit down and buckle your seat belt.

STUDENT CORNER

"Woman" Is a Noun
Paula Rewa, East Tennessee State University

From a local playground, a brave voice yells, "Are you a boy or a girl?" A cluster of children grin as they wait for my answer. They think they've caught me. "I'm a girl," I answer with a forced but friendly smile. I picture myself as they must see me . . . my stubble hair, my chunky black glasses and overloaded backpack. In my standard jeans and plain t-shirt, I'm not the collegiate Barbie they expect. I'm a curious blur as I walk past their games—an oddity.

In a restaurant, an older man at the bar asks me, "What are you, a man or a woman?" I wonder, if he thought I was a man, would he have asked? "I am a woman," I answer as he looks me over. I feel his eyes on me as I leave.

In the mirror, I ask myself, "Who am I?" I know the answer. I am a woman.

No matter what advances women have made in present-day society, we are still restricted by cultural expectations. If we choose to pursue a career, we become women in the workplace. If we have a family and a job, we become working mothers. We are women bankers, women lawyers, and women plumbers.

Today, it seems "woman" is used as an adjective. Defined positively, "woman" means feminine in appearance, even while wearing a suit. A woman person exists in a male world while retaining female qualities. Ideally, she is someone's wife. She is never taken for a "man."

Defined negatively, "woman" also means potentially bossy, overzealous, or emotionally driven (. . . the phrase "woman lawyer" makes more sense now, doesn't it?).

The adjective "woman" confers many, if not all, of these qualities. So where does this leave the woman person who does not fit? She is stripped of her womanhood. Her sexual orientation often is questioned. It may be said that she is trying to be a man. Society pressures her to become the adjectival "woman."

The image of the working woman is simply a modern version of the homemaker dress of the fifties. The codes of womanly appearance dictate what is appropriate. It is acceptable for a woman to have short hair if she wears cosmetics. If she chooses not to wear cosmetics, she should have a naturally pretty face and wear feminine clothing. We may now have access to the world of business, but we are still put in our place as much as ever. Our suit jackets proclaim us as equals, while our skirts hint that we are really just women underneath.

Codes of appearance apply not only in corporate America but also in society in general. The look has changed, but we are still expected to conform. Today, women can wear anything that men wear. In fact, many popular stores carry only clothing that can be worn by both men and women. Yet the expectations persist: when a woman wears it, she must still look "woman."

Our culture must reclaim "woman" as a noun, and recognize that women remain women, regardless of what they wear or what they do. If they are accountants, call them accountants. To say "woman accountant" is unnecessary, and the implications of such a title are not appreciated. If a woman has short hair and prefers suits to skirts, do not assume that she wants to be a man. Instead, consider how secure she must be to feel comfortable without conforming to society's expectations.

Women must learn to cherish themselves without being slaves to femininity. Many women enjoy wearing dresses, and they should be applauded for their own expression of self. But dresses should not be mandatory, and neither should long hair, painted nails, or push-up bras. The true woman is the person inside, not the image she projects.

I have been asked many times if I am a man or a woman. Children ask out of curiosity, men ask with mockery. I answer without hesitation, because I know that "woman" is a noun. I may have very short hair. I may wear cosmetics only occasionally. But I am proud to be a woman, just as I am proud to be myself.

How I Write

When I sit down to write, the most important factor in my productivity is comfort. I do all my writing on a computer, but I don't sit directly in front of the screen, feet flat on the floor, and all that jazz. My high school typing teacher would probably be appalled to see me lounging on my couch with my keyboard on my knees, an extension cord reaching across the living room to my PC.

I never have any music playing when I need to concentrate. I used to play my favorite artists as inspiration, but I tended to get carried away. As a result, the flavor of my writing was often influenced by the mood of the music.

I like to do all my writing on a computer, because it is much easier to revise over and over. I tend to revise as I write, and then over again several times as my essay develops. I find that this helps me maintain clarity and stay connected to what I'm writing. I find it frustrating to do first, second, and third drafts, because I feel I should wait for the next official "draft" to change something I don't like. In order to write effectively, it is essential that I give myself permission to change things any time I want. I do save different versions of my paper as it evolves, for reference and in case I decide I like something better the way it was. I also print out my paper several times, in order to make notes for necessary changes.

How I Wrote This Essay

When I get a new assignment or idea, I try to get something on paper immediately. Even if I don't end up using any of it, the writing gets my mind moving in a direction. It also solidifies the images and phrases that fly through my head when I'm excited about a new project.

For this essay, I was given the subject of "Women's Status: Gains or Losses?" I started by breaking down the subject. My first thought was "why not gains and losses?" Other questions followed, such as "What is our status?" "How are women perceived?" "What does 'woman' really mean?" I recorded these questions and others at the top of my paper, and kept them there for reference throughout the writing process.

The first time I sat down to work on this essay, I had so many thoughts swimming around in my head that the result was five different introductory paragraphs, all strung together with no connections. Instead of worrying about this, I set the essay aside for a few days and thought about what it was that I truly wanted to say. When I came back to my computer, my thoughts were much clearer, and I was able to mold what I had into a clear idea.

My Writing Tip

Above all, don't get frustrated when you start writing. I have my bouts with writer's block, but I try to keep writing: Write anything that pops into your head. Don't worry about if it's in the right place.

I tend to have three or four good sentences pushing along ahead of my cursor, just waiting for a good place for me to stick them in.

The trick is to keep going. Eventually, you'll hit on an idea, a sentence, or even a combination of words that say just what you want it to say, and the rest will flow from there.

Good luck!

● CHAPTER WRITING ASSIGNMENTS

1. Write a causal analysis for one of the following conditions:
   a. The poor writing habits of today's students
   b. The lack of popular financial support for museums, concerts, and other art forms
   c. The decline of the stock market
   d. The need for prison reform
   e. The worldwide popularity of rock music
   f. The rise in child pornography
   g. The failure of the rapid transit system in most large cities
   h. The need to conserve our beaches
   i. Our tendency to buy throwaway items

2. Write a causal analysis explaining the reason behind the breakup of a relationship.

● WRITING ASSIGNMENTS FOR A SPECIFIC AUDIENCE

1. Write a letter to a teacher you once had (but don't send it!) analyzing why you did badly or well in his/her class.
2. Write an essay explaining why you chose a certain major in college.

● COLLABORATIVE WRITING PROJECT

Join a group of four other students. After reviewing all the material in this chapter on women's status today, brainstorm about why the steam has gone out of the feminist movement. Assign research on the topic to the group's members and work together to team-write an essay entitled: *Why the Feminist Movement Has Lost Its Punch*.

● IMAGE GALLERY WRITING ASSIGNMENT

Visit pages 669–672 of our image gallery and study all four images dealing with the status of women. Then choose the image that most appeals to you. Answer the questions and do the writing assignment.

15

Argumentation and Persuasion

ROAD MAP TO ARGUMENTATION AND PERSUASION

What Argumentation and Persuasion Do

Argumentation and persuasion are the fraternal twins of rhetoric. The difference between them is this: An argument appeals strictly by reason and logic; persuasion appeals by both logic and emotion. If you're pleading for more funding for diabetes research and you base your appeal primarily on numbers, you're making an argument. If you supplement the number crunching with testimony from diabetes sufferers who have been horribly affected by the disease, you're being persuasive. The forum in which the argument takes place will determine which tactic you should adopt. A formal paper for a philosophy class should be worded as an argument. An essay or article written for your student newspaper, depending on the topic, should be both logical and persuasive.

Argumentation, unlike the other modes of writing, is a term of rhetorical intent, not of form. It refers to any essay or speech whose aim is to sway or persuade a reader or listener. Because writers resort to many techniques and devices to achieve this aim, the argumentation essay tends to be a mixture of rhetorical forms; that is, you are likely to find the writer defining, describing, narrating, or even dividing during the course of the argument. The tone of the essay can vary from the savage sarcasm of Jonathan Swift's *A Modest Proposal* to the chilling, matter-of-fact tone of Andrew Vachss's *Sex Predators Can't Be Saved*. The subject matter can include any topic from the nearly infinite spectrum of issues about which people argue.

When to Use Argumentation and Persuasion

Some people think that all writing is persuasive. Their reasoning is that even if you're describing a scene, what you're really doing is trying to persuade your reader to see through your eyes. If you are comparing two friends, you are hoping to convince your reader that your observations about them are true. Trace elements of the techniques of persuasion are no doubt present in other kinds of writing, but we formally apply the techniques of argumentation and persuasion when we're trying to bring someone around to our opinion or point of view. This may be in a debate or in an essay on a topic that requires you to advocate one side over another.

How to Use Argumentation and Persuasion

What elements are most likely to sway us in an argumentative essay—to make us change our minds and believe a writer's arguments? Research suggests some clues. First, there is our perception of the writer's credentials to hold an opinion on the subject. If we think the writer is competent and qualified on the subject—a medical doctor writing on a medical topic, for example—we are more likely to believe the advocated opinion. If you hold a particular qualification to write on the subject, then mentioning it will probably help. You do not have to blare out your credentials, but you can do it subtly. For example, in his essay on the sexual predators, Vachss tells us that he has interviewed many sex predators over the years—a revelation that leaves us more likely to accept his views of them. If you are not an expert yourself, quoting an expert can certainly lend weight to your view.

Another element that inclines us to believe an argumentative essay is the quality of its reasoning. If the writer's logic is sound, if the facts and supporting details strike us as reasonable and strong, then we are likely to be swayed by the conclusions. Presenting your facts in all their glory, while making the links between the propositions of your argument instantly clear, will make it difficult for anyone to easily dismiss your conclusions.

Finally, arguments are persuasive if they appeal to our self-interests. We are more likely to believe an argument if we think there is something in it for us. This insight explains why arguers huff and puff to portray themselves and their views as if they agreed exactly with our self-interests, even if the correspondence is far-fetched. The underlying appeal of Jonathan Swift's ironic proposal, for instance, is to the self-interests of Irish citizens who Swift thinks would be better off in a unified Ireland free from British exploitation.

If your argument is not reasoned logically, it is unlikely to be effective. And if it is not backed with solid evidence, its claims will most likely arouse disbelief. When the issue at stake is a practical one, these two elements—logical reasoning and solid evidence—are basic requirements for any effective argument.

There are, in addition, some common strategies that writers use to make their arguments persuasive. Being persuasive involves more than being strictly logical; it takes in the whole range of writing skills—conciseness, clarity, and the ability to infuse a prose style with a distinctive personality. To write a persuasive argument, then, you should try to use the following techniques:

1. **Begin your argument at the point of contention.** This means that your initial paragraph should immediately focus on the issue being argued. Consider this opening from an argument:

> *"We have room for but one language here, and that is the English language, for we intend to see that the crucible turns our people out as Americans and not as dwellers in a polyglot boarding house."* Theodore Roosevelt
> In the store windows of Los Angeles, gathering place of the world's aspiring peoples, the signs today ought to read, "English spoken here." Supermarket price tags are often written in Korean, restaurant menus in Chinese, employment-office signs in Spanish. In the new city of dreams, where gold can be earned if not found on the sidewalk, there are laborers and businessmen who have lived five, ten, 20 years in America without learning to speak English. English is not the common denominator for many of these new Americans. Disturbingly, some of them insist it need not be.
>
> —William A. Henry III, "Against a Confusion of Tongues"

As you can see, the writing begins with a quotation from Theodore Roosevelt and a pointed paragraph that makes it immediately clear what he is arguing against: immigrants who refuse to learn English. He wastes no time in pointless preamble or beating around the bush.

Here are two openings from student essays arguing against offshore drilling. One begins with an ominous drift; the other gets immediately to the point.

> **Unfocused:** I oppose offshore drilling for oil. But before I give my reasons for making this statement, I would like to review the various present sources of crude oil in our country....
>
> **Focused:** I oppose offshore drilling for oil because such a project could, in the name of energy, destroy thousands of square miles of our oceans and add to the already staggering amount of pollution on the earth...

Your opening sentence or sentences should underscore your stand as well as your preliminary reasoning.

2. **Draw your evidence from multiple sources.** This is a self-evident observation. If your argument is based on a single book or the testimony of one expert, it will be invariably weaker than if it draws support from many sources. Ideally, the direction and force of your research should lead you to different kinds and sources of evidence. However, we often get papers that are based on the writer's devotion to a single book or the point of view of one expert. This can be a crippling limitation, especially if your one book or one expert hold views that turn out to be wrong. The antidote for overreliance on a single source of evidence is to find a topic you're truly interested in.

3. **Pace your argument with some obvious movement.** Don't allow your argument to become clogged with a dreary recital of evidence or bogged down with pointless hairsplitting. We suggest that you imagine the typical reader's reactions to any argumentative essay or speech:

Reader or Listener	Your Response
Ho hum!	Wake up the reader with a provocative introduction.
Why bring that up?	State your argument in clear, forceful language.
For instance?	Supply evidence and facts.
So what?	Restate the thesis, say what you expect the reader to do.

Responding to these four imagined reader/listener attitudes will give your argument a discernible movement.

4. **Begin your argument with an assumption that is either grounded in evidence or defensible.** You should not attempt to argue the unarguable or prove the unprovable. While the realm of the arguable is constantly expanding before an onslaught of mysticism and fantasy, many instructors would nevertheless find the following theses entirely unacceptable in an argumentative essay:

> Hell exists as a place of punishment for sinners to atone for wrongdoing committed on earth.
> The Great Depression of the 1930s was caused by a destructive astrological conjunction between the planets Venus and Mars.
> Cats and all manner of feline creatures are despicable, nauseating beasts.
> Arthur Conan Doyle, creator of Sherlock Holmes, was the greatest detective-story writer of all times.

All four propositions are based on personal belief and, therefore, unprovable in a strictly logical sense.

5. **Anticipate the opposition.** For instance, if you are arguing that a controversial cancer drug should be legalized, you must not only marshal evidence to show the effectiveness of the drug, you must also answer the arguments of those opposed to its legalization. You might, for instance, introduce these arguments this way:

> Opponents to the legalization of this drug claim that its use will prevent the cancer patient from using other remedies proven effective against cancer. This claim, however, misses the point.

Then get down to the point that has been missed.

A frequent tactic used in arguments is not only to sum up the opposition's viewpoint but also to point out any inconsistencies in it. Here is an example of this tactic from an argument in favor of using animals in medical research:

> Extremists within the animal-rights movement take the position that animals have rights equal to or greater than those of humans. It follows from this that even if humans might benefit from animal research, the cost to animals is too high. It is ironic that despite this moral position, the same organizations condone—and indeed sponsor—activities that appear to violate the basic rights of animals to live and reproduce. Each year 10,000,000 dogs are destroyed by public pounds, animal shelters and humane societies. Many of these programs are supported and even operated by animal-protectionist groups. Surely there is a strong contradiction when those who profess to believe in animal rights deny animals their right to life. A similar situation exists with regard to programs of pet sterilization, programs that deny animals the right to breed and to bear offspring and are sponsored in many cases by antivivisectionists and animal-rights groups. Evidently, animal-rights advocates sometimes recognize and subscribe to the position that animals do not have the same rights as humans. However, their public posture leaves little room for examining these subtleties or applying similar standards to animal research.
>
> —Frederick A. King, "Animals in Research: The Case for Experimentation"

Moral logic requires us to practice what we preach; if it can be shown that the opposition is more likely to preach than to practice, that is grounds for calling into question the sincerity of its views.

6. **Supplement your reasoning and evidence with an emotional appeal.** This tactic must, however, be used with discretion and caution—as we said, depending on the topic and the forum. Emotional appeal is no substitute for reasoned argument or solid evidence. However, used in supplementary doses, emotional appeal can be highly persuasive in dramatizing an outcome or condition in a way that evidence and facts alone cannot. Here is an example: A speaker is trying to persuade an audience to donate blood for the benefit of hemophiliacs. A hemophiliac himself, he spends the first half of his speech explaining factually what hemophilia is—reciting statistics about its incidence and discussing its symptoms. Then, to dramatize the awfulness of the disease, he resorts to an emotional appeal, using his own experience with the pain of hemophilia:

> Because medical science had not advanced far enough, and fresh blood was not given often enough, my memories of childhood and adolescence are memories of pain and heartbreak. I remember missing school for weeks and months at a stretch—of being very proud because I attended school once for four whole weeks without missing a single day. I remember the three long years when I couldn't even walk because repeated hemorrhages had twisted my ankles and knees to pretzel-like forms. I remember being pulled to school in a wagon while other boys rode their bikes, and being pushed to my table. I remember sitting in the

dark empty classroom by myself during recess while the others went out in the sun to run and play. And I remember the first terrible day at the big high school when I came on crutches and built-up shoes carrying my books in a sack around my neck.

But what I remember most of all is the pain. Medical authorities agree that a hemophilic joint hemorrhage is one of the most excruciating pains known to mankind.

To concentrate a large amount of blood into a small compact area causes a pressure that words can never hope to describe. And how well I remember the endless pounding, squeezing pain. When you seemingly drown in your own perspiration, when your teeth ache from incessant clenching, when your tongue floats in your mouth and bombs explode back of your eyeballs; when darkness and light fuse into one hue of gray; when day becomes night and night becomes day and time stands still—and all that matters is that ugly pain. The scars of pain are not easily erased.

—Ralph Zimmerman, "Mingled Blood"

The appeal is moving and effective and contributes to the persuasiveness of the speaker's plea.

7. **Avoid common logical fallacies.** A logical fallacy occurs when you draw a conclusion that is false or deceptive. Often an argument may seem to be moving in the right direction, but on closer inspection, it has veered off the reasonable course and ends in confusion. Here are the most common logical fallacies to avoid:

Ad hominem (Latin for "to the man") Here the writer mounts a personal attack on an individual rather than dealing with the argument under consideration. *Example:* "Senator X's proposal to cut inflation is nonsensical; however, that should not surprise us since the senator flunked economics in college."

Ad populum (Latin for "to the public") The writer appeals to feelings, passions, or prejudices shared by large segments of the population. *Example:* "The illegal immigrants crossing our borders will bring in gangs, dope, and vile beliefs or habits that will eventually ruin our country." This logical fallacy overlooks the valuable skills and labor provided by many of the illegal immigrants who have entered our country.

False analogy The writer mistakenly compares two situations that have some characteristics in common, treating them as if they were alike in all respects. *Example:* "Since we have legalized cigarettes, we should legalize marijuana, which does not cause lung cancer the way cigarettes do." The writer overlooks a major difference between the two drugs: marijuana impairs a person's powers of perception and judgment, whereas cigarettes do not.

Begging the question An argument that "begs the question" is one that moves in circles rather than forward. *Example:* "I am against prostitution because it dehumanizes women by having them sell themselves." The writer is saying that prostitution is wrong because it involves women prostituting themselves.

Ignoring the question (also known as the "red herring") This logical fallacy involves shifting the focus of discussion to points that have nothing to do with the basic argument. *Example*: "We must not re-elect Congressman X because he does not believe in subsidizing our farmers during droughts. Moreover, the congressman wants to get rid of Christmas crèches in the lobbies of all city halls. Do we really want an atheist to represent us in Congress?" Remember that the original argument was about farm subsidies, not religion.

Either-or reasoning Here the writer sees an issue in black or white, with no shades of gray in between. *Example*: "If the administration gets rid of our Music Appreciation and German classes in order to balance the college budget, we shall soon become a technological school rather than a well-balanced undergraduate college." Many colleges with good reputations have had to cut certain nonrequired courses during temporary budget crises.

Hasty generalization It is human to draw conclusions before adequately sampling a situation. But in writing an argument, it is important that your evidence be sufficient and representative. *Example*: "Embryonic stem cell research offers hope to millions of people suffering from diabetes, Parkinson's, and spinal injuries. In the next election, do not vote for those narrow-minded religious fanatics who oppose embryonic stem cell research." Not everyone who is opposed to stem cell research is a narrow-minded religious fanatic.

Non sequitur **(Latin for "it does not follow")** An argument based on a non sequitur has a faulty premise. *Example*: "All women who have dark skin and wear head scarves hate Americans and support any Jihad that will annihilate us. The counselor of our honor students, Miriam Hussein, has dark skin and always wears a head scarf; therefore, she is to be suspected of disloyalty to the United States." In this example, the major premise ("all women who have dark skin and wear head scarves hate Americans and support any Jihad that will annihilate us") is false; therefore, the conclusion will be false.

All of the logical fallacies mentioned above can crop up when writers do not use solid evidence to support their arguments but instead rely on flimsy hearsay, illogical connections, or improperly tested assumptions to force agreement on their readers.

Warming Up to Write an Argument

1. Write down at least three objections to each of the following propositions:
   a. Women should be drafted into the military.
   b. The United Nations should have its own army.

576 CHAPTER 15 • Argumentation and Persuasion

    c. The Euro should now be used in every country of the world.
    d. Every official meeting of Congress should begin with prayer.
    e. "I am not responsible for saving the world."

2. For each of the following areas, list three topics you think you could develop into a persuasive argument:
    a. Something in your personal life you would like to change
    b. A social or political problem that needs solving
    c. An area of education you would like to see improved

3. Sketch out some ideas you would use to support the following quotations:
    a. "Opinions founded on prejudice are always sustained with the greatest violence."
                                    —Francis Jeffrey

    b. "The most tragic paradox of our time is to be found in the failure of nation-states to recognize the imperatives of internationalism."
                                    —Chief Justice Earl Warren

    c. "There is no greater lie than a truth misunderstood."
                                    —William James

    d. "The drive toward complex technical achievement offers a clue to why the U.S. is good at space gadgetry and bad at slum problems."
                                    —John Kenneth Galbraith

EXAMPLES

In Defense of Gender
Cyra McFadden

Cyra McFadden (b. 1937) is a freelance writer and teacher who lives in California. She is a contributor of articles to many popular magazines such as *Nation*, *McCall's*, and *Smithsonian*. Among her works is the novel *The Serial* (1977).

English is sexist in its use of pronouns. The third-person singular pronoun, when a specific person is not identified, is always "he." One result of this is a prejudice against women. In the 1960s, with the rise of the feminist movement, came a determined attempt to correct this inequity, leading to strange coinages such as "mailpersons" and "salespersons." Predictably, this sparked a backlash, particularly among highly literary people such as the author. Even today, a solution to satisfy everyone has not yet been found, and writers continue to muddle their way through on a case-by-case basis, sometimes saying "he/she" or putting the sentence in the plural to avoid having to use a sexist pronoun.

• • •

1   So pervasive is the neutering of the English language on the progressive West Coast, we no longer have people here, only persons: male persons and female persons, chairpersons and doorpersons, waitpersons, mailpersons—who may be either male or female mailpersons—and refuse-collection persons. In the classified ads, working mothers seek childcare persons, though one wonders how many men (archaic for "male person") take care of child persons as a full-time occupation. One such ad, fusing nonsexist language and the most popular word in the California growth movement, solicits a "nurtureperson."

2   Dear gents and ladies, as I might have addressed you in less troubled times, this female person knows firsthand the reasons for scourging sexist bias from the language. God knows what damage was done me, at fifteen, when I worked in my first job—as what is now known as a newspaper copyperson—and came running to the voices of men barking, "Boy!"

3   No aspirant to the job of refuse-collection person myself, I nonetheless take off my hat (a little feathered number, with a veil) to those of my own sex who may want both the job and a genderless title with it. I argue only that there must be a better way, and I wish person or persons unknown would come up with one.

4   Defend it on any grounds you choose; the neutering of spoken and written English, with its attendant self-consciousness, remains ludicrous. In print, those "person" suffixes and "he/she's" jump out from the page, as distracting as a cloud of gnats, demanding that the reader note the writer's virtue. "Look what a nonsexist writer person I am, voiding the use of masculine forms for the generic."

5   Spoken, they leave conversation fit only for the Coneheads on "Saturday Night Live." "They have a daily special," a woman at the next table told her male companion in Perry's, a San Francisco restaurant. "Ask your waitperson." In a Steig cartoon, the words would have marched from her mouth in the form of a computer printout.

6   In Berkeley, Calif., the church to which a friend belongs is busy stripping its liturgy of sexist references. "They've gone berserk," she writes, citing a reading from the pulpit of a verse from 1 Corinthians. Neutered, the once glorious passage becomes "Though I speak with the tongues of persons and of angels...." So much for sounding brass and tinkling cymbals.

7   The parson person of the same church is now referring to God as "He/She" and changing all references accordingly—no easy undertaking if he intends to be consistent. In the following, the first pronoun would remain because at this primitive stage of human evolution, male persons do not give birth to babies: "And she brought forth her firstborn son/daughter, and wrapped him/her in swaddling clothes, and laid him/her in a manger; because there was no room for them in the inn...."

8   As the after-dinner speaker at a recent professional conference, I heard a text replete with "he/she's" and "his/hers" read aloud for the first time. The

hapless program female chairperson stuck with the job chose to render these orally as "he-slash-she" and "his-slash-her," turning the following day's schedule for conference participants into what sounded like a replay of the Manson killings.

9   Redress may be due those of us who, though female, have answered to masculine referents all these years, but slashing is not the answer; violence never is. Perhaps we could right matters by using feminine forms as the generic for a few centuries, or simply agree on a per-woman lump-sum payment.

10 Still, we would be left with the problem of referring, without bias, to transpersons. These are not bus drivers or Amtrak conductors but persons in transit from one gender to the other—or so I interpret a fund-drive appeal asking me to defend their civil rights, along with those of female and male homosexuals.

11 Without wishing to step on anyone's civil rights, I hope transpersons are not the next politically significant pressure group. If they are, count on it, they will soon want their own pronouns.

12 In the tradition of the West, meanwhile, feminists out here wrestle the language to the ground, plant a foot on its neck and remove its masculine appendages. Take the local art critic Beverly Terwoman.

13 She is married to a man surnamed Terman. She writes under "Terwoman," presumably in the spirit of *vive la différence*. As a letter to the editor of the paper for which she writes noted, however, "Terwoman" is not ideologically pure. It still contains "man," a syllable reeking of all that is piggy and hairy-chested.

14 Why not Beverly Terperson? Or better, since "Terperson" contains "son," Terdaughter"? Or a final refinement, Beverly Ter?

15 Beverly Terwoman did not dignify this sexist assault with a reply. The writer of the letter was a male person, after all, probably the kind who leaves his smelly sweat socks scattered around the bedroom floor.

16 No one wins these battles anyway. In another letter to the same local weekly, J. Seibert, female, lets fire at the printing of an interview with Phyllis Schlafly. Not only was the piece "an offense to everything that Marin County stands for," but "it is even more amusing that your interview was conducted by a male.

17 "This indicates your obvious assumption that men understand women's issues better than women since men are obviously more intelligent (as no doubt Phyllis would agree)."

18 A sigh suffuses the editor's note that follows: "The author of the article, Sydney Weisman, is a female."

19 So the war of the pronouns and suffixes rages, taking no prisoners except writers. Neuter your prose with all those clanking "he/she's," and no one will read you except Alan Alda. Use masculine forms as the generic, and you have joined the ranks of the oppressor. None of this does much to encourage friendly relations between persons, transpersons or—if there are any left—people.

20 I also have little patience with the hyphenated names more and more California female persons adopt when they marry, in the interests of retaining

their own personhood. These accomplish their intention of declaring the husband separate but equal. They are hell on those of us who have trouble remembering one name, much less two. They defeat answering machines, which can't handle, "Please call Gwendolyn Grunt-Messerschmidt." And in this culture, they retain overtones of false gentility.

21   Two surnames, to me, still bring to mind the female writers of bad romances and Julia Ward Howe.

22   It's a mug's game, friends, this neutering of a language already fat, bland and lethargic, and it's time we decide not to play it. This female person is currently writing a book about rodeo. I'll be dragged behind a saddle bronc before I will neuter the text with "cowpersons."

● Vocabulary

pervasive (1)   archaic (1)   scourging (2)
aspirant (3)   generic (4)   replete (8)
hapless (8)   redress (9)   suffuses (18)
gentility (20)   lethargic (22)

● The Facts

1. What is the author's main complaint against the movement to neuter English of its sexist pronouns?
2. To what popular television characters does the author think neutered English is suited?
3. In Berkeley, California, what has the movement to neuter English led to? What have been the results, according to the author?
4. According to the author, what is due to women for having had to endure centuries of pronouns with masculine referents?
5. What solution does the author propose? Do you agree with her solution?

● The Strategies

1. Very early in her essay, as if we couldn't tell from her name, the author tells us that she is female. What rhetorical advantage you think she gets from doing this?
2. Where in the first three paragraphs does the author assert what is the closest thing to a thesis? What is this sentence?
3. What technique of tone does the author use repeatedly to get her opinions across?
4. In paragraph 2, the author tells us about her experience with sexist language in her first job. Why do you think she shares this experience with us? What does it add to her argument?
5. Although this essay definitely makes an argument against gender neutering of the language, the author draws heavily on one of the modes of development. Which one is it, and how does it suit her purpose?

The Issues

1. What are your views on the neutering of English? Do you agree with the author or do you think she's being hypercritical and extraordinarily fussy?
2. What do you think the English language will lose if all of its pronouns become nonsexist?
3. Reread paragraph 8. What metaphor here would strike some as being in bad taste?
4. What does the author propose in paragraph 9? Do you think she's serious? What is your opinion of this proposal?
5. Assuming that the movement to neuter English began with the feminist movement of the 1960s, what changed circumstances of women would seem to make that issue irrelevant? Or, do you believe that the change is still necessary? Why?

Suggestions for Writing

1. Find a piece of writing from an old magazine or newspaper that uses "he" as a generic pronoun and commits other sexist-language sins. Rewrite it to make the passage completely nonsexist. Compare the two and say which one is better.
2. In an essay, argue for or against McFadden's opinion that neutering the language has led to some ludicrous constructions.

A Modest Proposal

For Preventing the Children of Poor People from Being a Burden to Their Parents or the Country and for Making Them Beneficial to the Public

JONATHAN SWIFT

Considered one of the greatest satirists in the English language, Jonathan Swift (1667–1745) was born in Dublin and educated at Trinity College. His satirical masterpiece, *Gulliver's Travels,* was published in 1726, by which time Swift was already regarded by the Irish as a national hero for his *Drapier's Letters* (1724). Originally published as a pamphlet, *A Modest Proposal* first appeared in 1729.

In this famous satire, Swift, assuming the role of a concerned and logical citizen, turns society's indifference to the value of human life into an outraged attack against poverty in Ireland.

• • •

1   It is a melancholy object to those who walk through this great town, or travel in the country, when they see the streets, the roads, and cabin doors crowded with beggars of the female sex followed by three, four, or six children, all in rags and importuning every passenger for an alms. These mothers, instead of

being able to work for their honest livelihood, are forced to employ all their time in strolling, to beg sustenance for their helpless infants, who, as they grow up, either turn thieves for want of work or leave their dear native country to fight for the Pretender in Spain or sell themselves to the Barbadoes.[1]

2   I think it is agreed by all parties that this prodigious number of children, in the arms or on the backs or at the heels of their mothers and frequently of their fathers, is in the present deplorable state of the kingdom a very great additional grievance, and therefore whoever could find out a fair, cheap, and easy method of making these children sound and useful members of the commonwealth would deserve so well of the public as to have his statue set up for a preserver of the nation.

3   But my intention is very far from being confined to provide only for the children of professed beggars; it is of a much greater extent, and shall take in the whole number of infants at a certain age who are born of parents in effect as little able to support them as those who demand our charity in the streets.

4   As to my own part, having turned my thoughts for many years upon this important subject and maturely weighed the several schemes of other projectors, I have always found them grossly mistaken in their computation. It is true, a child just dropped from its dam may be supported by her milk for a solar year, with little other nourishment, at the most not above the value of two shillings, which the mother may certainly get, or the value in scraps, by her lawful occupation of begging; and it is exactly at one year old that I propose to provide for them in such a manner as, instead of being a charge upon their parents or the parish or wanting food and raiment for the rest of their lives, they shall on the contrary contribute to the feeding, and partly to the clothing, of many thousands.

5   There is likewise another great advantage in my scheme, that it will prevent those voluntary abortions and that horrid practice of women murdering their bastard children, alas! too frequent among us, sacrificing the poor innocent babes, I doubt more to avoid the expense than the shame, which would move tears and pity in the most savage and inhuman breast.

6   The number of souls in this kingdom being usually reckoned one million and a half, of these I calculate there may be about two hundred thousand couple whose wives are breeders, from which number I subtract thirty thousand couple who are able to maintain their own children (although I apprehend there cannot be so many, under the present distresses of the kingdom); but this being granted, there will remain a hundred and seventy thousand breeders. I again subtract fifty thousand for those women who miscarry or whose children die by accident or disease within the year. There only remain a hundred and twenty thousand children of poor parents annually born. The question therefore is how this number shall be reared and provided for, which, as I

---

[1]Swift refers to the exiled Stuart claimant of the English throne, and to the custom of poor emigrants to commit themselves to work for a number of years to pay off their transportation to a colony.—Ed.

have already said, under the present situation of affairs is utterly impossible by all the methods hitherto proposed. For we can neither employ them in handicraft or agriculture; we neither build houses (I mean in the country) nor cultivate land; they can very seldom pick up a livelihood by stealing, till they arrive at six years old, except where they are of towardly parts, although I confess they learn the rudiments much earlier, during which time they can, however, be properly looked upon only as probationers; as I have been informed by a principal gentleman in the County of Cavan who protested to me that he never knew above one or two instances under the age of six, even in a part of the kingdom so renowned for the quickest proficiency in that art.

7   I am assured by our merchants that a boy or a girl before twelve years old is no saleable commodity, and even when they come to this age they will not yield above three pounds or three pounds and a half a crown at most on the exchange, which cannot turn to account either to the parents or the kingdom, the charge of nutriment and rags having been at least four times that value.

8   I shall now, therefore, humbly propose my own thoughts, which I hope will not be liable to the least objection.

9   I have been assured by a very knowing American of my acquaintance in London that a young, healthy child well nursed is, at a year old, a most delicious, nourishing, and wholesome food, whether stewed, roasted, baked, or boiled; and I make no doubt that it will equally serve in a fricassee or a ragout.

10 I do therefore humbly offer it to public consideration that of the hundred and twenty thousand children already computed, twenty thousand may be reserved for breed, whereof only one fourth part to be males, which is more than we allow to sheep, black cattle, or swine; and my reason is that these children are seldom the fruits of marriage, a circumstance not much regarded by our savages; therefore one male will be sufficient to serve four females. That the remaining hundred thousand may, at a year old, be offered in sale to the persons of quality and fortune through the kingdom, always advising the mother to let them suck plentifully in the last month, so as to render them plump and fat for a good table. A child will make two dishes at an entertainment for friends; and when the family dines alone, the fore-or hind-quarter will make a reasonable dish, and seasoned with a little pepper or salt, will be very good boiled on the fourth day, especially in winter. I have reckoned, upon a medium, that a child just born will weigh twelve pounds, and in a solar year, if tolerably nursed, will increase to twenty-eight pounds.

11 I grant this food will be somewhat dear, and therefore very proper for the landlords, who, as they have already devoured most of the parents, seem to have the best title to the children.

12 Infant's flesh will be in season throughout the year, but more plentifully in March and a little before and after; for we are told by a grave author, an eminent French physician, that fish being a prolific diet, there are more children born in Roman Catholic countries about nine months after Lent than at any other season; therefore, reckoning a year after Lent, the markets will be more glutted than usual, because the number of Popish infants is at least three to one in this kingdom; and therefore it will have one other collateral advantage,

by lessening the number of Papists among us. I have already computed the charge of nursing a beggar's child (in which list I reckon all cottagers, laborers, and four fifths of the farmers) to be about two shillings per annum, rags included; and I believe no gentleman would repine to give ten shillings for the carcass of a good fat child, which, as I have said, will make four dishes for excellent nutritive meat, when he has only some particular friend or his own family to dine with him. Thus the squire will learn to be a good landlord and grow popular among his tenants; the mother will have eight shillings net profit and be fit for work till she produces another child.

13 Those who are more thrifty (as I must confess the times require) may flay the carcass, the skin of which, artificially dressed, will make admirable gloves for ladies and summer boots for fine gentlemen.

14 As to our city of Dublin, shambles[2] may be appointed for this purpose in the most convenient parts of it; and butchers, we may be assured, will not be wanting, although I rather recommend buying the children alive than dressing them hot from the knife as we do roasting pigs.

15 A very worthy person, a true lover of his country, and whose virtues I highly esteem, was lately pleased in discoursing on this matter to offer a refinement upon my scheme. He said that many gentlemen of his kingdom having of late destroyed their deer, he conceived that the want of venison might be well supplied by the bodies of young lads and maidens, not exceeding fourteen years of age nor under twelve, so great a number of both sexes in every country being now ready to starve for want of work and service; and these to be disposed of by their parents if alive, or otherwise by their nearest relations. But with due deference to so excellent a friend and so deserving a patriot, I cannot be altogether in his sentiments; for as to the males, my American acquaintance assured me, from frequent experience, that their flesh was generally tough and lean, like that of our schoolboys, by continual exercise, and their taste disagreeable; and to fatten them would not answer the charge. Then as to the females, it would, I think, with humble submission, be a loss to the public, because they would soon become breeders themselves, and besides, it is not improbable that some scrupulous people might be apt to censure such a practice (although indeed very unjustly) as a little bordering upon cruelty, which, I confess, has always been with me the strongest objection against any project, however so well intended.

16 But in order to justify my friend, he confessed that this expedient was put into his head by the famous Psalmanazar, a native of the island Formosa, who came from thence to London above twenty years ago and in conversation told my friend that in his country, when any young person happened to be put to death, the executioner sold the carcass to persons of quality as a prime dainty and that in his time the body of a plump girl of fifteen, who was crucified for an attempt to poison the emperor, was sold to his imperial Majesty's prime minister of state and other great mandarins of the court in joints from the gibbet at four hundred crowns. Neither, indeed, can I deny that if the same use were made of several plump young girls in this town who, without one single

---
[2]Slaughterhouses—Ed.

groat to their fortunes, cannot stir abroad without a chair, and appear at playhouse and assemblies in foreign fineries which they never will pay for, the kingdom would not be the worse.

17   Some persons of a desponding spirit are in great concern about that vast number of poor people who are aged, diseased, or maimed, and I have been desired to employ my thoughts what course may be taken to ease the nation of so grievous an encumbrance. But I am not in the least pain upon the matter, because it is very well known that they are every day dying and rotting by cold, and famine, and filth, and vermin, as fast as can be reasonably expected. And as to the young laborers, they are now in almost as hopeful a condition; they cannot get work and consequently pine away for want of nourishment to a degree that if at any time they are accidentally hired to common labor, they have not strength to perform it; and thus the country and themselves are happily delivered from the evils to come.

18   I have too long digressed and therefore shall return to my subject. I think the advantages by the proposal which I have made are obvious and many, as well as of the highest importance.

19   For first, as I have already observed, it would greatly lessen the number of Papists, with whom we are yearly overrun, being the principal breeders of the nation as well as our most dangerous enemies, and who stay at home on purpose to deliver the kingdom to the Pretender, hoping to take their advantage by the absence of so many good Protestants, who have chosen rather to leave their country than stay at home and pay tithes, against their conscience, to an Episcopal curate.

20   Secondly, the poorer tenants will have something valuable of their own which by law may be made liable to distress and help to pay their landlord's rent, their corn and cattle being already seized and money a thing unknown.

21   Thirdly, whereas the maintenance of a hundred thousand children from two years old and upward cannot be computed at less than ten shillings apiece per annum, the nation's stock will thereby be increased fifty thousand pounds per annum, beside the profit of a new dish introduced to the tables of all gentlemen of fortune in the kingdom who have any refinement in taste. And the money will circulate among ourselves, the goods being entirely of our own growth and manufacture.

22   Fourthly, the constant breeders, beside the gain of eight shillings sterling per annum by the sale of their children, will be rid of the charge of maintaining them after the first year.

23   Fifthly, this food would likewise bring great custom to taverns, where the vintners will certainly be so prudent as to procure the best receipts for dressing it to perfection and consequently have their houses frequented by all the fine gentlemen who justly value themselves upon their knowledge in good eating; and a skillful cook who understands how to oblige his guests will contrive to make it as expensive as they please.

24   Sixthly, this would be a great inducement to marriage, which all wise nations have either encouraged by rewards or enforced by laws and penalties. It would increase the care and tenderness of mothers toward their children when they were sure of a settlement for life to the poor babes, provided in

some sort by the public, to their annual profit or expense. We could see an honest emulation among the married women, which of them could bring the fattest child to the market. Men would become as fond of their wives during the time of their pregnancy as they are now of their mares in foal, their cows in calf, or sows when they are ready to farrow, nor offer to beat or kick them (as is too frequent a practice) for fear of a miscarriage.

25   Many other advantages might be enumerated. For instance, the addition of some thousand carcasses in our exportation of barreled beef; the propagation of swine's flesh and improvement in the art of making good bacon, so much wanted among us by the great destruction of pigs, too frequent at our table, which are no way comparable in taste or magnificence to a well-grown fat yearling child, which, roasted whole, will make a considerable figure at a lord mayor's feast or any other public entertainment. But this and many others I omit, being studious of brevity.

26   Supposing that one thousand families in this city would be constant customers for infant's flesh, beside others who might have it at merry-meetings, particularly at weddings and christenings, I compute that Dublin would take off annually about twenty thousand carcasses and the rest of the kingdom (where probably they will be sold somewhat cheaper) the remaining eighty thousand.

27   I can think of no one objection that will possibly be raised against this proposal unless it should be urged that the number of people will be thereby much lessened in the kingdom. This I freely own, and it was indeed one principal design in offering it to the world. I desire the reader will observe that I calculate my remedy for this one individual kingdom of Ireland and for no other that ever was, is, or I think ever can be, upon earth. Therefore let no man talk to me of other expedients; of taxing our absentees at five shillings a pound; of using neither clothes nor household furniture except what is of our own growth and manufacture; of utterly rejecting the materials and instruments that promote foreign luxury; of curing the expensiveness of pride, vanity, idleness, and gaming in our women; of introducing a vein of parsimony, prudence, and temperance; of learning to love our country, in the want of which we differ even from Laplanders and the inhabitants of Tupinamba; of quitting our animosities and factions, nor acting any longer like the Jews, who were murdering one another at the very moment their city was taken; of being a little cautious not to sell our country and conscience for nothing; of teaching landlords to have at least one degree of mercy toward their tenants; lastly, of putting a spirit of honesty, industry, and skill into our shop-keepers, who, if a resolution could now be taken to buy only our native goods, would immediately unite to cheat and exact upon us in the price, the measure, and the goodness, nor could ever yet be brought to make one fair proposal of just dealing, though often and earnestly invited to it.

28   Therefore, I repeat, let no man talk to me of these and the like expedients till he has at least some glimpse of hope that there will be ever some hearty and sincere attempt to put them in practice.

29   But as to myself, having been wearied out for many years with offering vain, idle, visionary thoughts and at length utterly despairing of success, I fortunately fell upon this proposal, which, as it is wholly new, so it has something

solid and real, of no expense and little trouble, full in our own power, and whereby we can incur no danger in disobliging England. For this kind of commodity will not bear exportation, the flesh being of too tender a consistence to admit a long continuance in salt, although perhaps I could name a country which would be glad to eat up our whole nation without it.

30   After all, I am not so violently bent upon my own opinion as to reject any offer proposed by wise men which shall be found equally innocent, cheap, easy, and effectual. But before some thing of that kind shall be advanced in contradiction to my scheme and offering a better, I desire the author or authors will be pleased maturely to consider two points: first, as things now stand, how they will be able to find food and raiment for a hundred thousand useless mouths and backs; and secondly, there being a round million of creatures in human figure throughout this kingdom whose whole subsistence, put into a common stock, would leave them in debt two millions of pounds sterling, adding those who are beggars by profession to the bulk of farmers, cottagers, and laborers, with the wives and children who are beggars in effect, I desire those politicians who dislike my overture, and may perhaps be so bold as to attempt an answer, that they will first ask the parents of these mortals whether they would not at this day think it a great happiness to have been sold for food at a year old in the manner I prescribe, and thereby have avoided such a perpetual scene of misfortunes as they have since gone through by the oppression of landlords, the impossibility of paying rent without money or trade, the want of common sustenance, with neither house nor clothes to cover them from the inclemencies of the weather, and the most inevitable prospect of entailing the like of greater miseries upon their breed forever.

31   I profess in the sincerity of my heart that I have not the least personal interest in endeavoring to promote this necessary work, having no other motive than the public good of my country, by advancing our trade, providing for infants, relieving the poor, and giving some pleasure to the rich. I have no children by which I can propose to get a single penny, the youngest being nine years old and my wife past childbearing.

- Vocabulary

    importuning (1)   sustenance (1)   prodigious (2)
    proficiency (6)   collateral (12)   censure (15)
    gibbet (16)   encumbrance (17)   digressed (18)
    propagation (25)   parsimony (27)   overture (30)
    inclemencies (30)

- The Facts

1. On what premise is *A Modest Proposal* based? What is the chief assumption of its argument?
2. Reread paragraph 11. Why do the landlords have "the best title to the children"?
3. Swift's satire redefines children in economic terms. What does this say about his view of the society in which he lived?

4. What does the satire imply about religious feelings in Ireland during Swift's time?
5. Given the state of affairs as the author describes them, is his argument logical? Explain.

The Strategies

1. What is the effect of the word *Modest* in the title?
2. Swift describes people with words like *breeder, dam, carcass,* and *yearling child.* What are the effects of these words?
3. Satire usually provides hints of the true state of things as it proposes its own alternatives. How does Swift hint at the true state of things? Give examples.
4. How would you characterize the tone of this piece?
5. Reread the final paragraph. What is its purpose?

The Issues

1. Do you consider satire an effective way to call attention to social ills? Why or why not?
2. Which paragraphs reveal Swift's real suggestions for improving the economic condition of the Irish? How do these paragraphs fit into the general scheme of Swift's essay?
3. How persuasive do you consider this essay? Would a straightforward essay be more effective? Why or why not?
4. Is Swift's essay simply a literary masterpiece to be studied within its context, or does it have a message for us today?
5. What condition existing in our country today would make an excellent subject for the kind of satire used by Swift? What satirical proposal can you suggest?

Suggestions for Writing

1. Infer from *A Modest Proposal* the state of life in Ireland during Swift's time. Make specific references to the article to justify your inferences.
2. Using your answer to question 5, write a satirical proposal for curing some aspect of today's society.

I Want a Wife

JUDY SYFERS-BRADY

Judy Syfers-Brady (b. 1937) is a freelance writer who espouses the feminist cause. Born in San Francisco, she studied at the University of Iowa, where she earned a B.F.A. in painting (1962). In 1973, her feminist convictions led her to Cuba to study class relationships as a means of understanding how social change can occur. She is best known for the essay reprinted here, which has become a classic and has been hailed as the feminist manifesto of the modern woman's emancipation from male domination.

Syfers-Brady's argument is based on the premise that all wives are completely devoted to their husbands and ardently diligent about promoting their husbands' causes and tending to their needs while remaining glamorous and sexual. Once you accept that premise, Syfers's argument makes perfect sense and seems incontrovertible. But more critical reading reveals some flaws in the argument. Pay particular attention to tone.

• • •

1   I belong to that classification of people known as wives. I am a Wife. And, not altogether incidentally, I am a mother.

2   Not too long ago a male friend of mine appeared on the scene fresh from a recent divorce. He had one child, who is, of course, with his ex-wife. He is obviously looking for another wife. As I thought about him while I was ironing one evening, it suddenly occurred to me that I, too, would like to have a wife. Why do I want a wife?

3   I would like to go back to school so that I can become economically independent, support myself, and, if need be, support those dependent on me. I want a wife who will work and send me to school. And while I am going to school I want a wife to take care of my children. I want a wife to keep track of the children's doctor and dentist appointments. And to keep track of mine, too. I want a wife to make sure that my children eat properly and are kept clean. I want a wife who will wash the children's clothes and keep them mended. I want a wife who is a good nurturant attendant to my children, who arranges for their schooling, makes sure they have an adequate social life with their peers, takes them to the park, the zoo, etc. I want a wife who takes care of the children when they are sick, a wife who arranges to be around when the children need special care, because, of course, I cannot miss classes at school. My wife must arrange to lose time at work and not lose the job. It may mean a small cut in my wife's income from time to time, but I guess I can tolerate that. Needless to say, my wife will arrange and pay for the care of the children while my wife is working.

4   I want a wife who will take care of my physical needs. I want a wife who will keep the house clean. A wife who will pick up after me. I want a wife who will keep my clothes clean, ironed, mended, replaced when need be, and who will see to it that my personal things are kept in their proper place so that I can find what I need the minute I need it. I want a wife who cooks the meals, a wife who is a *good* cook. I want a wife who will plan the menus, do the necessary shopping, prepare the meals, serve them pleasantly, and then do the cleaning up while I do my studying. I want a wife who will care for me when I am sick and sympathize with my pain and loss of time from school. I want a wife to go along when our family takes a vacation so that someone can continue to care for me and my children when I need a rest and change of scene.

5   I want a wife who will not bother me with rambling complaints about a wife's duties. But I want a wife who will listen to me when I feel the need to

explain a rather difficult point I have come across in my course of studies. And I want a wife who will type my papers for me when I have written them.

6   I want a wife who will take care of the details of my social life. When my wife and I are invited out by my friends, I want a wife who will take care of the babysitting arrangements. When I meet people at school that I like and want to entertain, I want a wife who will have the house clean, prepare a special meal, serve it to me and my friends, and not interrupt when I talk about the things that interest me and my friends. I want a wife who will have arranged that the children are fed and ready for bed before my guests arrive so that the children do not bother us. I want a wife who takes care of the needs of my guests so that they feel comfortable, who makes sure that they have an ashtray, that they are passed the hors d'oeuvres, that they are offered a second helping of the food, that their wine glasses are replenished when necessary, that their coffee is served to them as they like it.

7   And I want a wife who knows that sometimes I need a night out by myself.

8   I want a wife who is sensitive to my sexual needs, a wife who makes love passionately and eagerly when I feel like it, a wife who makes sure that I am satisfied. And, of course, I want a wife who will not demand sexual attention when I am not in the mood for it. I want a wife who assumes the complete responsibility for birth control, because I do not want more children. I want a wife who will remain sexually faithful to me so that I do not have to clutter up my intellectual life with jealousies. And I want a wife who understands that *my* sexual needs may entail more than strict adherence to monogamy. I must, after all, be able to relate to *people* as fully as possible.

9   If, by chance, I find another person more suitable as a wife than the wife I already have, I want the liberty to replace my present wife with another one. Naturally, I will expect a fresh, new life; my wife will take the children and be solely responsible for them so that I am left free.

10   When I am through with school and have a job, I want my wife to quit working and remain at home so that my wife can more fully and completely take care of a wife's duties.

11   *My God, who wouldn't want a wife?*

Vocabulary

nurturant (3)   replenished (6)   entail (8)
adherence (8)

The Facts

1. According to Syfers-Brady, what dual role does a wife play in the family?
2. What physical needs of the husband does the wife take care of?
3. What does Syfers-Brady say about the sexual expectations and behavior of husbands?
4. According to the author, for what details of a husband's social life are wives responsible?

5. According to the essay, what should happen if a more suitable wife comes along?

- ## The Strategies
1. What part does hyperbole or exaggeration play in this essay? What flaws do you detect in Syfers-Brady's argument?
2. How would you characterize the tone of this essay?
3. What pronoun does the author use to refer to a "wife"? Why?
4. How and where does the author use italics in this essay? To what effect?
5. What kinds of evidence does the author use to support her argument?

- ## The Issues
1. Do you think Syfers-Brady has fairly characterized the expectations men have of their wives or has she grossly exaggerated?
2. Syfers-Brady's article was first published in 1970. Do you think her criticisms still apply today or has the relationship between men and women changed so much that they are now dated?
3. Would you want a spouse, male or female, as obliging and eager to please as the one Syfers-Brady parodies in her essay? Why or why not?
4. What qualities and characteristics would you expect to find in the perfect spouse?

- ## Suggestions for Writing
1. Write a similar essay, from a man's point of view, about wanting a husband.
2. Write a serious essay describing your ideal mate.
3. Write an essay telling why you would not want a wife like the one Syfers-Brady has described.

Sex Predators Can't Be Saved
ANDREW VACHSS

Andrew Vachss (b. 1942) is a New York–based lawyer whose professional focus has been representing children. From 1965 to 1966, he served as a field interviewer and investigator for the Task Force on the Eradication of Syphilis for the US Public Health Service in Ohio. He also worked for numerous community organizations concerned with youth problems. Since 1976, he has been in private law practice and has been a lecturer at numerous law schools in New York. His writing includes a book, *Life-Style Violent Juvenile: The Secure Treatment Approach* (1979), and two novels—*Flood* (1985) and *Strega* (1996). He has written numerous magazine articles.

All of us have seen and read media accounts of violent sexual crimes, which force us to wonder what a fitting punishment for violent offenders should be. In Vachss's essay, a criminal lawyer provides what he considers the only possible solution to violent sex offenses.

• • •

1   Westley Allan Dodd was scheduled to be hanged at 12:01 a.m. this morning at the Washington State Penitentiary in Walla Walla. Sentenced to execution for the torture-murder of three boys, Mr. Dodd has refused all efforts to appeal his case. He may not have exhausted his legal remedies, but he has certainly exhausted society's efforts at "rehabilitation."

2   A chronic, calcified sexual sadist, Mr. Dodd stated in a recent court brief, "If I do escape, I promise you I will kill and rape again, and I will enjoy every minute of it."

3   Mr. Dodd's threat demands a response because we know he is not unique. There can be no dispute that monsters live among us. The only question is what to do with them once they become known to us.

4   The death penalty is not a response. Racially and economically biased and endlessly protracted, it returns little for its enormous economic and social costs. Though it is effective—the killer will not strike again—the death penalty is limited to murderers; it will not protect us from rapists and child molesters who are virtually assured of release and who are almost certain to commit their crimes again.

5   If we do not intend to execute sex criminals, does our hope lie in killing their destructive impulses? Mr. Dodd and his ilk are sociopaths. They are characterized by a fundamental lack of empathy. All children are born pure egoists. They perceive their needs to the exclusion of all others. Only through socialization do they learn that some forms of gratification must be deferred and others denied. When a child's development is incomplete or perverted—and child abuse is the most dominant cause in that equation—he or she tends not to develop empathy. There's a missing card, one that cannot be put back in the deck once the personality is fully formed.

6   While early childhood experiences may impel, they do not compel. In the end, evil is a matter of choice. Sociopaths can learn to project a veneer of civilization—for predators, it is part of their camouflage—but they will always lack the ability to feel any pain but their own, pursuing only self-gratification. Not all sociopaths choose sexual violence. For some, the outlet can be political or economic skullduggery. But those for whom blood or pain is the stimulus act no less efficiently and at a terrible and unacceptable cost.

7   Some predatory sociopaths can be deterred. None can be rehabilitated, since they cannot return to a state that never existed. The concept of coercive therapy is a contradiction; successful psychiatric treatment requires participants, not mere recipients. What makes sexual predators so intractable and dangerous is that, as Mr. Dodd candidly acknowledged, they like what they do and intend to keep doing it.

8   The obsession of sexual predators is typified in the case of Donald Chapman, a New Jersey rapist who was released in November after serving

12 years, the maximum for his crime. He underwent continual therapy in prison, and was utterly unaffected by it. He vows to continue to attack women—a threat that reflects his total absorption with sexual torture. As a result of his threat, he sits in his house in Wyckoff, N.J., surrounded by a 24-hour police guard.

9   A 1992 study of 767 rapists and child molesters in Minnesota found those who completed psychiatric treatment were arrested more often for new sex crimes than those who had not been treated at all. A Canadian survey that tracked released child molesters for 20 years revealed a 43 percent recidivism rate regardless of the therapy. The difference between those simply incarcerated and those subjected to a full range of treatment appears statistically negligible. And the more violent and sadistic the offense, the more likely it is to be repeated.

10   Another factor that thwarts rehabilitation is the need for offenders to seek higher and higher levels of stimulation. There is no observable waning of their desires over time: sexual predators do not outgrow their behavior. Thus, while most sadistic sex offenders are not first arrested for homicide, they may well try to murder someone in the future.

11   What about a traditional self-help program? Should we concentrate on raising their self-esteem? Imprisoned predators receive as much fan mail as rock stars. They are courted by the news media, studied by devoted sociologists, their every word treasured as though profound. Their paintings are collected, their poetry published. Trading cards celebrate their bloody passage among us.

12   I recently received a letter from a young woman who gushed that, after a long exchange of letters, she was "granted visiting privileges" with Mr. Dodd and subsequently appeared on "Sally Jessy Raphael" "due to my relationship" with "Wes," who she believes is "sincere." So do I. We simply disagree about the object of his sincerity.

13   Sexual predators are already narcissistic; they laugh behind their masks at our attempts to understand and rehabilitate them. We have earned their contempt by our belief that they can change—by our confusion of "crazy" with "dangerous," and "sick" with "sickening."

14   If we don't intend to execute sexual predators, and we have no treatment, what is our final line of defense? Washington State has a so-called sexual predator law permitting indefinite confinement of sex offenders deemed to be dangerous if released. The law's critics argue that psychiatry has been a woefully inadequate forecaster. Others cite the constitutional problems of imprisonment based on prospective conduct.

15   Recently there has been much discussion of voluntary castration. Such a "remedy" ignores reality. Sexual violence is not sex gone too far, it is violence with sex as its instrument. Rage, sadism and a desire to control or debase others are the driving forces. Castration can be reversed chemically with black-market hormones, and sex murders have been committed by physically castrated rapists. People have been raped by blunt objects. And how do you castrate female offenders?

16   Our response to sexual predators must balance the extent and intensity of the possible behavior with the probability of its occurrence. An ex-prisoner

likely to expose himself on a crowded subway may be a risk we are willing to assume. A prisoner with even a moderate probability of sexual torture and murder is not. Such violence is like a rock dropped into a calm pool—the concentric circles spread even after the rock has sunk. More and more victims will be affected.

17   When it comes to sexual violence, the sum of our social and psychiatric knowledge adds up to this: Behavior is the truth.

18   Chronic sexual predators have crossed an osmotic membrane. They can't step back to the other side—our side. And they don't want to. If we don't kill or release them, we have but one choice: Call them monsters and isolate them.

19   When it comes to the sexual sadist, psychiatric diagnoses won't protect us. Appeasement endangers us. Rehabilitation is a joke.

20   I've spoken to many predators over the years. They always exhibit amazement that we do not hunt them. And that when we capture them, we eventually let them go. Our attitude is a deliberate interference with Darwinism—an endangerment of our species.

21   A proper experiment produces answers. Experiments with sexual sadists have produced only victims. Washington State's sexual predator law will surely be challenged in the courts and it may take years before constitutional and criminological criteria are established to incarcerate a criminal beyond his or her sentence.

22   Perhaps no-parole life sentences for certain sex crimes would be a more straightforward answer. In any event, such laws offer our only hope against an epidemic of sexual violence that threatens to pollute our society beyond the possibility of its own rehabilitation.

● Vocabulary

rehabilitation (1)   calcified (2)   protracted (4)
ilk (5)   sociopaths (5)   empathy (5)
impel/compel (6)   predators (6)   camouflage (6)
skullduggery (6)   intractable (7)   recidivism (9)
narcissistic (13)   castration (15)   osmotic (18)
appeasement (19)

● The Facts

1. What particular crime does the essay analyze? How does this crime differ from other crimes?
2. What are the main causes that lead human beings to become sex offenders? When are these causes developed?
3. According to the author, do sex offenders have a choice in the way they act?
4. According to Westley Allan Dodd's testimony, why will he continue to kill and rape?
5. According to the author, what has research found out about the efficacy of psychiatric treatment for violent sex criminals?

The Strategies

1. Where does the author place the proposition (main point) of his argument? How does this placement affect his argument?
2. What kinds of argumentative strategies does the author use to support his proposition? Cite specific strategies.
3. What is the point of view from which the essay is written? How effective is this point of view? Give reasons for your answer.
4. How soon in the essay is the audience introduced to the idea that sex offenders cannot be rehabilitated?
5. Where does the author use figurative language? Is this helpful, or does it detract from the seriousness of the topic? For instance, how apt is the analogy of the missing card in paragraph 5?

The Issues

1. Do you agree completely with the author's view that there is no hope for the rehabilitation of sex offenders, or do you believe the author has neglected some aspect of healing? Explain your answer.
2. How important is self-esteem in the socialization of human beings? Provide examples from your own experience to show what happens when individuals lack self-esteem and also examples to show the effect of having self-esteem.
3. What do you think of the idea of castrating violent sex offenders? Does such a policy seem logical, humane, and appropriate for our times? Explain your answers.
4. Why do you think the woman who befriended Westley Allan Dodd while he was in prison could possibly have been attracted to such a man?
5. What is your own solution to the problem of sex predators? How do you propose that we protect society from their heinous crimes?

Suggestions for Writing

1. Write an essay in which you argue for your own solution to the social menace posed by sex predators. Use facts, statistics, experience, and expert testimony to bolster your proposition. Also, be sure to take into account any opposition to your argument.
2. Write a letter to a person—real or imaginary—who is in prison because of a violent sex crime. Even though the letter will not be mailed, it should reveal your honest thoughts.

Dooley Is a Traitor

JAMES MICHIE

James Michie (b. 1927), British poet and translator, is director of The Bodley Head Ltd. publishers, London, and a former lecturer at London University. His works include *Possible Laughter* (1959), *The Odes of Horace* (trans. 1964), and *The Epigrams of Martial* (trans. 1973).

In this humorous poem, a murderer makes a spirited defense against being compelled to fight a war not of his own making.

• • •

"So then you won't fight?"
"Yes, your Honour," I said, "that's right."
"Now is it that you simply aren't willing,
Or have you a fundamental moral objection to killing?"
5   Says the judge, blowing his nose
And making his words stand to attention in long rows.
I stand to attention too, but with half a grin
(In my time I've done a good many in).
"No objection at all, sir," I said
10 "There's a deal of the world I'd rather see dead—
Such as Johnny Stubbs or Fred Settle or my last landlord,
    Mr. Syme.
Give me a gun and your blessing, your Honour, and I'll be
    killing them all the time.
But my conscience says a clear no
To killing a crowd of gentlemen I don't know.
15 Why, I'd as soon think of killing a worshipful judge,
High-court, like yourself (against whom, God knows, I've got
    no grudge—
So far), as murder a heap of foreign folk.
If you've got no grudge, you've got no joke
To laugh at after."
20 Now the words never come flowing
Proper for me till I get the old pipe going.
And just as I was poking
Down baccy, the judge looks up sharp with "No smoking,
Mr. Dooley. We're not fighting this war for fun.
25 And we want a clearer reason why you refuse to carry a gun.
This war is not a personal feud, it's a fight
Against wrong ideas on behalf of the Right.
Mr. Dooley, won't you help to destroy evil ideas?"
"Ah, your Honour, here's
30 The tragedy," I said. "I'm not a man of the mind.
I couldn't find it in my heart to be unkind
To an idea. I wouldn't know one if I saw one. I haven't one of
    my own.
So I'd best be leaving other people's alone."
"Indeed," he sneers at me, "this defence is
35 Curious for someone with convictions in two senses.
A criminal invokes conscience to his aid
To support an individual withdrawal from a communal crusade
Sanctioned by God, led by the Church, against a godless,
    churchless nation!"

I asked his Honour for a translation.
40 "You talk of conscience," he said. "What do you know of the
     Christian creed?"
"Nothing, sir, except what I can read,
That's the most you can hope for from us jail-birds.
I just open the Book here and there and look at the words.
And I find when the Lord himself misliked an evil notion
45 He turned it into a pig and drove it squealing over a cliff into
     the ocean,
And the loony ran away
And lived to think another day.
There was a clean job done and no blood shed!
Everybody happy and forty wicked thoughts drowned dead.
50 A neat and Christian murder. None of your mad slaughter
Throwing away the brains with the blood and the baby with
     the bathwater.
Now I look at the war as a sportsman. It's a matter of choosing
The decentest way of losing.
Heads or tails, losers or winners,
55 We all lose, we're all damned sinners.
And I'd rather be with the poor cold people at the wall that's
     shot
Than the bloody guilty devils in the firing-line, in Hell and
     keeping hot."
"But what right, Dooley, what right," he cried,
"Have you to say the Lord is on your side?"
60 "That's a dirty crooked question," back I roared.
"I said not the Lord was on my side, but I was on the side of the
     Lord."
Then he was up at me and shouting,
But by and by he calms: "Now we're not doubting
Your sincerity, Dooley, only your arguments,
65 Which don't make sense."
('Hullo,' I thought, 'that's the wrong way round.
I may be skylarking a bit, but my brainpan's sound.')
Then biting his nail and sugaring his words sweet:
"Keep your head, Mr. Dooley. Religion is clearly not up your
     street.
70 But let me ask you as a plain patriotic fellow
Whether you'd stand there so smug and yellow
If the foe were attacking your own dear sister."
"I'd knock their brains out, mister,
On the floor," I said. "There," he says kindly, "I knew you were
     no pacifist.
75 It's your straight duty as a man to enlist.
The enemy is at the door." You could have downed

Me with a feather. "Where?" I gasp, looking round.
"Not this door," he says angered. "Don't play the clown.
But they're two thousand miles away planning to do us down,
80 Why, the news is full of the deeds of those murderers and rapers.
"Your Eminence," I said, "my father told me never to believe the papers
But to go by my eyes,
And at two thousand miles the poor things can't tell truth from lies."
His fearful spectacles glittered like the moon: "For the last time what right
85 Has a man like you to refuse to fight?"
"More right," I said, "than you.
You've never murdered a man, so you don't know what it is I won't do.
I've done it in good hot blood, so haven't I the right to make bold
To declare that I shan't do it in cold?"
90 Then the judge rises in a great rage
And writes DOOLEY IS A TRAITOR in black upon a page
And tells me I must die.
"What, me?" says I.
"If you still won't fight."
95 "Well, yes, your Honour," I said, "that's right."

● The Facts

1. Dooley is an admitted murderer, yet he refuses to fight. Why? What is his primary objection to war?
2. How many arguments does the judge use in trying to persuade Dooley? What are they, and in what order are they used?
3. Are the judge's arguments logical? Do they appeal to reason and evidence or to emotion?

● The Strategies

1. The poem is written in rhyming couplets. What does the rhyme contribute to the poem's tone?
2. How is Dooley characterized? What techniques are used?
3. How is the judge characterized? What techniques are used?

● The Issues

1. Evaluate critically the saying "All's fair in love and war." Has this attitude prevailed throughout history? Is it morally valid?

2. What is the poet's point in reflecting a pacifist view through a criminal rather than, say, a minister or a respected private citizen?
3. Do you perceive a difference between killing a rapist who attacked your sister and killing an unknown enemy during war? Explain your answer.

- Suggestions for Writing
1. Analyze the logic in the exchanges between Dooley and the judge. Pinpoint the difference between their respective ways of thinking.
2. Assume that you are in Dooley's position and must argue against your participation in a war. Formulate an argument in your defense.

ISSUE FOR CRITICAL THINKING AND DEBATE: HOMELESSNESS

Homelessness would seem to be a nondebatable issue. Everyone is against it, at least in principle. The debate begins not on whether or not homelessness is terrible—everyone agrees that it is—but on its causes. The division of opinion is predictably political: Conservatives, as a whole, blame homelessness on lapses and addictions in the individual; liberals tend to blame economic causes.

Adding to the muddle is the blurry definition of homelessness. Is a person who lives in a government-funded shelter, such as a hotel that houses the poor through a system of voucher payments from the state, homeless? Or is the homeless person one with no permanent residence, who sleeps on the street, in a car, or in a bus station? Most government statistics count both groups among the homeless. Yet, government-funded housing, as some critics point out, may be drawing people who had been doubling up with family members into the ranks of the counted homeless. The result is the more the government funds shelters for the homeless, the greater the homeless population seems to grow (Robert Ellickson, "The Homelessness Muddle," *Public Interest,* April 1990).

How many people are homeless in America? No one knows for sure. Homelessness advocates say there are 3 million. Other studies have put the figure at around 400 thousand. The Department of Housing and Urban Development estimated in 1994 that there were about "600,000 people on the streets on any given night and that 7 million Americans experienced homelessness at some point in the latter half of the 1980s" ("Who's Homeless and Why, *Christian Century,* September 7, 1994). One recent report claims that nearly 1 percent of American families, even in a robust economy, will go through episodes of homelessness within a year (The Urban Institute: available online at http://www.urban.org/news/pressrel/pr000201.html). These figures—whether high or low—are difficult to trust because they are always based on different methods of counting. Added to the roster of the uncountable are the so-called "invisible homeless," who have no residence of their own but live in makeshift arrangements with relatives.

The two essays in this section typify the debate about homelessness. The first essay, "Homeless: Expose the Myths," by a conservative writer, argues that

- *Migrant Mother, Nipomo Valley, 1936, by Dorothea Lange*
  Being worn out and worried, in addition to being homeless, is the migrant mother's lot.

the individual, not the system or the economy, is to blame for homelessness. Having spent a night in New York's Grand Central Station, the author reports that he saw no dispossessed yuppies, only dysfunctional people. The other point of view is represented by a columnist who examines the complexities behind the homeless problem and shows us an example, Greg, who ended up being homeless because of a change in Boston's rent control laws. Here, the author lays the blame at the doorstep of a badly run government bureaucracy and an out-of-kilter economy. The photos in this chapter offers a concrete view of the problem. Above a homeless migrant worker, holding a child, sends a look of anguished despair from her tired eyes. The photo on page 602 makes the viewer wonder what this homeless woman will be thinking when she wakes up from her nap.

Which view of the causes of homelessness is accurate? It is impossible to say. Certainly, one can imagine a scenario where an individual, even a family, can fall on hard times that result in homelessness. Yet, anyone who lives in a city also knows from plain observation that many dysfunctional, tormented souls haunt the streets. Why homelessness exists in such an affluent country as ours may be impossible to explain, but one thing is certain: It should not exist.

Homeless: Expose the Myths
JOSEPH PERKINS

Joseph Perkins (b. 1960) is a regular columnist for *The San Diego Union-Tribune.*

According to the author, the homeless people out on our streets do not suffer from poverty as much as they suffer from mental illness or substance abuse.

• • •

1. Back in the days when the homeless problem was in vogue, I decided to investigate for myself whether economic policies were to blame for the growing legions of street people who seemed to have invaded America's cities.
2. So I spent a night at New York's Grand Central Station, which was a favorite gathering place for many of the city's homeless.
3. I quickly discovered that contrary to the news reportage at that time, the homeless were not "people like you and me" who simply had fallen upon hard times. I saw no yuppies in threadbare suits sifting through the trash bins. I saw no middle-class families huddled on benches.
4. What I did see were dozens upon dozens of pitiable men and women who were suffering from some dysfunction or another. Some were afflicted with mental problems. Others were drug or alcohol abusers. Clearly their homelessness owed not to economic dislocation, but simply to self-destruction.
5. It is now eight years later, yet homeless advocates continue to promulgate the myth that homelessness is primarily an economic problem rather than a mental health and substance-abuse problem.
6. Among the more prominent purveyors of this misinformation is the National Law Center on Homelessness and Poverty. It notes that 40 percent of poor people spend two-thirds of their income on housing. "This means that for growing millions of Americans, a missed paycheck, a health crisis or a high utility bill brings the threat of homelessness," the lawyers assert.
7. The law center advocates were less than happy with President Clinton's recent executive order calling for a homeless plan to be developed within nine months. They saw no reason why he shouldn't have given his imprimatur to a plan that they already have drawn up.

8   So what is the lawyers' solution? Have the federal government turn over former military bases and other vacant property to the homeless. Create a jobs program for them. Give them income assistance. Offer them day care and health care.

9   It's the typical liberal response to a problem—spend more money, create programs. They miss the boat. In 1963, there were as many poor people as there are today. Yet, in 1963, the only homeless people were the occasional bums and hobos.

10   Two things happened between 1963 and 1993 to give us today's homeless population: All but the most dangerous patients were disgorged from state mental hospitals, and illegal drug use exploded.

11   This is borne out by a 1992 survey conducted by the U.S. Conference of Mayors. The mayors found that 28 percent of the homeless population in the cities were mentally ill and 41 percent substance abusers.

12   This means that at least seven of 10 street people have either a mental or chemical problem. Even if the economy were booming, jobs were plentiful and affordable housing abundant, these unfortunates probably would still be out on the streets.

13   By linking homelessness to poverty, advocates obscure the real root of the problem. If we really wanted to help the homeless, we would pay far more attention to their mental health and substance abuse problems.

Vocabulary

vogue (1)
promulgate (5)
disgorged (10)
legions (1)
purveyors (6)
dysfunction (4)
imprimatur (7)

The Facts

1. How did the author find out whether government policies were really to blame for the growing number of street people—as often claimed by liberals?
2. What was the author's first discovery? How long did this discovery take?
3. What about the National Law Center on Homelessness and Poverty annoys the author?
4. According to the author, what happened between 1963 and the present to change the statistics concerning the homeless population?
5. What is the author's answer to our desire to help the homeless?

The Strategies

1. In your view, how does the brevity of the essay affect its ability to convince? Why or why not?
2. Why does the author word his proposition as a conditional clause ("If we really wanted to help the homeless . . .")? What might an alternate wording be?

- Why does a shopping cart become "home"?

3. How does the author maintain coherence between paragraphs 10 and 11?
4. What does the word *myths* refer to in the title of the essay?
5. How would you describe the author's style of writing?

The Issues

1. The author says that in 1963, the only homeless people were occasional bums and hobos. How are bums and hobos different from today's homeless?
2. How much influence do economic policies have on people's standard of living?
3. What is the author's most compelling support for his proposition?
4. In your opinion, which is more effective—the liberals' response of spending more money on programs for the homeless or the conservatives' response of tending to their mental illnesses? Give reasons for your stance.
5. What is your opinion of the suggestion that military bases be turned into housing for the poor? What other solution would you propose?

Suggestions for Writing

1. Write an essay in which you propose a solution to the problem of begging that is so prevalent in our cities today. Support your argument with facts, experience, expert testimony, and logic.
2. Write an essay in which you detail what you would do should you suddenly find yourself homeless and foodless. Base your plan on reality, not fantasy.

The Homeless Lack a Political Voice, But Not American Ideals

Matt Lynch

Matt Lynch writes a column for *University Wire*.

Exactly who are the homeless and how did they get that way? The answer you get depends on whom you ask. Conservatives maintain that the homeless mainly consist of people with addiction problems or those who are mentally ill. Liberals reply that anyone can become homeless during difficult economic times, that elements of bad luck and bad timing are often responsible for homelessness. These two points of view have a radical effect not only on our attitudes toward the homeless but on government policy. If we believe that people become homeless because of bad economics, we are inclined to help. If we think that addiction is to blame, we are more inclined to punish. This writer demonstrates that the stereotypes about the homeless are often off the mark and hollow.

...

1 Greg is a conservative's dream.

2 He wakes up every morning before 6:00 a.m., showers, eats breakfast, and dons a suit and tie. He goes to his office job every day, puts in more than forty hours per week, saves his money and doesn't drink. He gets back in time for dinner, watches the news and is in bed by 10:00 p.m.

3 Greg is not his real name. Homeless shelter volunteers are not permitted to give out the names of those staying in the facility, for fear of discrimination. It's a fear that is well-founded.

4 The prevailing attitudes toward the homeless in America are not particularly sympathetic. Most people view them as a minor annoyance; their only exposure to the homeless comes when someone on the street bothers them for change. Many would characterize them as a bunch of degenerates and alcoholics, fully deserving of their unfortunate fate.

5 If they would only get themselves together and get a job like everyone else, most say, they wouldn't find themselves in this predicament.

6 But it's a bit more complicated than that.

7 Homelessness in the wealthiest nation on earth is caused by a variety of factors and they are not always the result of repeated bad judgment by those who are homeless. For Greg, it came from the skyrocketing rents and housing prices in Boston, which did away with rent-control laws in 1997.

8 For others, it comes from an untimely lay-off and a lack of close relatives to take them in. Some, like a former Boston College basketball player and account coordinator whose story appeared in a recent *Boston Globe* column, just made one mistake—in his case, incurring the wrath of the I.R.S.

9 Walking into a homeless shelter in Cambridge, Massachusetts, the shelter where Greg sleeps, is not setting foot into the armpit of society. It's more akin to walking into a hospital waiting room: residents play cards, watch the news or read magazines. At dinnertime, they are as orderly and polite as anyone else.

10 The shelter is dry; anyone who is intoxicated is turned away at the door. Fights and rude language are no more common than in the rest of society.

Residents are early to bed and early to rise, and strive to look as presentable as everyone else.

11   For most at this shelter, homelessness is not a career. They have fallen on hard times, and are trying to pull themselves up by their bootstraps. Anyone who buys into the American work ethic, particularly politicians, should be proud.

12   Yet efforts to help the homeless remain woefully under-funded, and the only legislation that deals with homelessness—the oft-amended McKinney-Vento Bill of 1987—addresses the effects rather than the causes of the problem. The National Coalition for the Homeless called for $4.3 billion for their efforts in the 2002 budget, an amount it says will still leave many of its programs without adequate funding. Bush requested just over half that amount for efforts to help the homeless.

13   In today's political climate, this is not surprising. Requests for homeless programs are seen as bleeding-heart-liberal garbage, further evidence of the liberals' tax-and-spend nature. They do not understand that efforts to help the homeless are compatible with the historical, mythical allure of America: the opportunity to start over, to begin anew. It brought colonists here as the continent was being settled, and it brought them to the frontier as the country grew.

14   But the frontier is gone; those with economic troubles can no longer escape to the West. Greg will probably escape homelessness through his shelter's progressive work-contract program, but he is one of the lucky ones.

15   Today's economy is struggling, and most homeless shelters do not have enough beds to go around. Not all of them have the resources for the kind of work-contract program Greg takes part in. Few can offer the necessary treatment for diseases that sometimes contribute to homelessness, namely mental illness and alcoholism.

16   Unfortunately, the problem will probably not be addressed until stereotypes disappear, until those begging on the street are no longer taken to represent the group as a whole, until people understand that those who are homeless often appear no different than anyone else. Most strive for the same goals and possess the same virtue, but do not have the same luck.

17   Politicians must change their attitudes, as well. They do deal with the effects of homelessness; no one enjoys hearing stories of the homeless freezing to death in winter months, and usually there are places for them to stay for some period of time. But the politicians need to get over their instinctive reactions against funding programs and address the roots of homelessness by helping people out of it.

18   The cause is not a hopeless one; it has simply never been given the resources it needs and deserves. Republicans and Democrats alike must recognize that though the homeless lack a strong political voice in this country, most do not lack its ideals.

- ## Vocabulary

    prevailing (4)   degenerates (4)   woefully (12)
    mythical (13)   allure (13)   stereotypes (16)

- ## The Facts

    1. What is it that makes Greg a conservative's dream? Do you agree that he is a conservative's dream? Why or why not?

2. What is the prevailing attitude toward homelessness, according to the author? What is your own attitude?
3. What is the reason for Greg's homeless condition? What other reasons, besides irresponsibility and drug abuse, can you cite for the homelessness of certain people?
4. What institution does Greg's shelter resemble? What factors contribute to the resemblance?
5. According to the author, programs to help the homeless reflect the American Dream. What is the American Dream, and how can government programs help the homeless achieve it?

The Strategies

1. What is the author's thesis, and where is it stated?
2. How does the author try to capture your attention at the start of his essay? How successful is he? What other effective introduction can you suggest?
3. What figures of speech does the author use to enliven his language? Name at least two and explain the meaning of each.
4. In paragraph 13, what effect does the expression "historical, mythical allure" create? Explain why you think the author used this phrase.
5. Why does the author insist that real help for the homeless cannot come until we get rid of stereotyping? What does stereotyping do to retard the general cause of helping the homeless?

The Issues

1. What plan for helping people like Greg would you propose if you were mayor of your city or governor of your state? How would you propose to fund your plan?
2. What is the best method of demolishing established stereotypes—whether of the homeless, of certain ethnic groups, or of class levels?
3. In paragraph 12, the author mentions that current legislation deals with the effects, rather than the roots, of homelessness. What effects does he have in mind? What is the difference between cause and effect in this case?
4. How is the pursuit of the American Dream different today from, say, two centuries ago? What can we do to help the homeless pursue the American Dream?
5. Do you agree with the notion that anyone in a homeless shelter has the right to live there anonymously in order to avoid discrimination? Explain your answer.

Suggestions for Writing

1. Write a proposal in which you suggest practical ways of helping the homeless reestablish themselves.
2. Write an essay in which you describe how a friend, relative, or acquaintance lost all possessions and the living conditions that this person was forced to accept. If help was offered, mention that as well.

Punctuation Workshop
Quotation Marks ("")

1. Put quotation marks around the exact words of a speaker:

   He said, "I'll buy the house."

2. Begin every quotation with a capital letter. If a quotation is broken, the second part does not begin with a capital letter unless it is a new sentence:

   "You are an angel," Guido whispered, "and I want to marry you."
   "Some people feel," said the woman. "Others think."

   Set off with a comma the identification of the person who is speaking unless a question mark or exclamation mark is needed:

   "You need to learn how to use a computer," he told his grandfather.
   "Are you satisfied with your life?" she asked.

3. When you are writing a dialogue, begin a new paragraph with each change of speaker:

   "It never occurred to me that I might have a half brother," he muttered.
   "Why not? It seemed so obvious to us," she said.

   If a speaker takes up more than one paragraph, put quotation marks at the beginning of each new paragraph. Use one set of quotation marks at the end of the last paragraph.

STUDENT CORNER

People Out on a Limb
Antoinette Poodt, Furman University

Homelessness is an epidemic in our country, but just how many people are homeless is unclear. One estimate says that 600,000 people are chronically homeless and another 700,000 sometimes homeless. A large number of the homeless are blacks and some 40% are veterans. The homeless are not lazy as some people think. Ninety percent of them once held jobs, and 15–20% of them are currently employed but unable to afford a home. In another chilling statistic, it was found that 40% of the homeless are entire families (National Mental Health Association, "Ending Homelessness in America" 2005. <http://www.nmha.org/homeless/index.cfm.> June 22, 2005).

So what is the cause of homelessness? Some of the explanations suggest it is economic, and some suggest it is individual circumstances. But one cause of homelessness is almost certainly deinstitutionalization, or the releasing of patients from mental hospitals. In the early 70s with the emergence of psychoactive drugs, deinstitutionalizing the homeless appeared to be a good way to save money and a way of giving freedom to people whose mental illnesses had trapped them in institutions such as asylums. Unfortunately, releasing the mentally ill into the streets and expecting them to function as responsible citizens, turned out to be a pipe dream. Many of the mentally ill had developed "institutionalism," which means they had become used to living a life that had been over-regulated (H. Richard Lamb, "Deinstitutionalization and the Homeless Mentally Ill." June 2005. Online at http://www.interactivist.net/housing/deinstitutionalization_2.html. June 22, 2005). In a nutshell, people were released on the streets who were incapable of taking care of themselves.

Poodt 2

    As a society, many of us are unsure what we think about the homeless. The typical reaction is either one of pity or of condemnation. Yet, if we live in an urban area, the likelihood is great that our lives will intersect with the homeless people who hang out around our neighborhood. For the past year, for example, an elderly woman who was obviously mentally ill, had been sleeping in a public garage near where I park. Some of my coworkers were so familiar with her that they would greet her by name. Some brought her food; some gave her money. When I worked late, I often saw her curled up asleep on pieces of cardboard laid out on the floor. One morning she was found dead in the same spot where she had always slept.

    The attitude of my town towards the homeless is mixed. Because many of the homeless are dirty and smell from living outdoors, and because many of them are aggressive panhandlers, the city council often instructs the police to jail the homeless for vagrancy and keep them out of sight of the tourists. The police, themselves, are inconsistent in their treatment of the homeless. For example, there's a post office near work with two rooms filled with only post boxes. A homeless man sleeps in one of the rooms when the weather is bad. An older police officer cruising past will often turn a blind eye, but will make certain that the man is gone before daybreak. On the other hand, when the older police officer is off duty, other police officers drive the homeless man away from this makeshift shelter.

    Not so long ago Americans had an extended family in place that acted as a safety net against homelessness. If a family member fell on bad times, the unfortunate one would be welcomed into the home of an aunt or uncle or cousin and given shelter until he/she got on his/her feet. That sense of obligation to the extended family is rarely practiced anymore. Today's family generally consists of mom, pop, and children. We do not always feel a sense of obligation or responsibility for anyone else in the family. This shift has made the government a last resort. But government benefits have taken more cuts in the past three years than in the past 25 years. Rent has also risen substantially in the past few years, making the issue hit closer to home than many ever imagined. As a college student, who is earning below the poverty line, who cannot afford housing on her own, and who receives little or no government benefits, I can empathize with the homeless. When it comes right down to it, the only difference between me and a homeless person is that I have a family who cares.

It is easy for me to sit in judgment when I see a "bum" on the side of the street and think to myself that he should get a job, because I am not in his position. Usually as I walk past this helpless-looking unkempt creature, whose possessions are bundled in crude wrapping, I mutter to myself, "There, but for the grace of God, go I." And I sometimes even add a more secular thanksgiving, "There, but for the love of my family, go I."

How I Write

Writing has always been a challenge for me, and it is usually very difficult for me to get started. Once I get the introduction down, however, the rest of the paper usually flows. Before I begin writing, I gather information about my topic, which I get from the Internet or the library. Then I go to my computer and begin typing. I cannot write in pen or pencil, and then type a paper. Instead, I type as I write. This is easier for me because it is simple to make corrections as I go along. When writing a paper or essay, I usually begin with a story, quote, or statement that will grab the reader's attention. Then, taking into account the audience and depending on the type of writing I am to do, I follow with an outline covering specific points. If the paper is a story about me, or something I am very familiar with, I do not follow an outline.

After I write the first draft, I begin with a spell check followed by a computer grammar check. Then I print out the paper and do at least three to five revisions. Once I think the paper is good, I give it to someone else to read. I feel that I do much better on a paper when I spend a few days revising it instead of writing, revising, and turning it in all in one day. When I leave a paper for a while, and then go back to look at it, I see new things that I can do to improve it. Once I have made all the revisions, I read it over one more time and then turn it in.

How I Wrote This Essay

I began this paper by doing research to get some facts on the homeless. It took me a while to figure out what spin I was going to take. I actually started this essay three or four times before I found the spin I wanted to use. Once I got started on the one I wanted, the essay flowed for me. After a very rough first draft, I revised the paper six times. Then I had my mom read over it to make any last-minute changes. While doing my corrections, my improvements were more instinctive than for any specific reason. When I thought I could not change the paper any more, I printed out the last copy.

My Writing Tip

One word of wisdom I can give to fellow writers is to learn to type on a computer as they write. Being a college student, I do not know where I would find the time if I had to write, say in pen or pencil, and then type. Corrections are so much quicker and easier to make when you can see them on the computer screen. It saves so much time, leading to less stress and hence better writing.

Another tip I would give is not to follow a cookie-cutter style of writing. Find your style, become comfortable with it, and use it whenever you write. Do not let one teacher discourage your writing ability because he or she doesn't like your style. We all have our own style. Write in your own style and your paper will turn out better than if you try to write like everyone else. In other words, trust your own personality.

● CHAPTER WRITING ASSIGNMENTS

1. Write an essay arguing the point that religion is a conditioned reflex.
2. Analyze the logic in *Dooley Is a Traitor*.
3. Construct an argument for or against competitiveness in business.
4. Should a belief in intelligent creation be taught along with Darwin's theory of evolution? Write an essay arguing for or against this question.
5. Write an essay suggesting ways of achieving sexual equality.

● TERM PAPER SUGGESTIONS

Investigate the major arguments related to any one of the following subjects:
a. The influence of the church in our country today
b. Animal experimentation
c. Better care for the poor
d. Increased emphasis on physical fitness
e. Careful monitoring of the ecosystems on our planet
f. Equal rights for women (or some other population group)
g. Maintaining ethnic identities in a pluralistic environment
h. Improved local and federal response to natural disasters
i. The need for a national health program that provides funding for long-term health care

● WRITING ASSIGNMENTS FOR A SPECIFIC AUDIENCE

1. Write an essay arguing for a campus completely free from smoking. Your audience consists of the readers of your college paper. State your proposition clearly and support it with convincing evidence about the hazards of secondhand smoke.
2. Write an essay in which you argue that movies often portray minorities inaccurately or offensively. Be specific with your facts and examples.

● COLLABORATIVE WRITING PROJECT

This assignment requires a minimum of three students, each researching one aspect of homelessness in our cities: (1) homelessness due to job loss, (2) homelessness due to illness or some other catastrophe, or (3) homelessness due to laziness or irresponsibility or drug and alcohol abuse. The bulk of the research should represent specific statistics and examples. The three students should make copies of their research for distribution to each other.

After the members of your group have read each other's work, prepare a group paper offering solutions to the problem and arguing that as citizens of a civilized and compassionate democracy, we have a sacred duty to end homelessness.

CHAPTER 15 • Argumentation and Persuasion

● **IMAGE GALLERY WRITING ASSIGNMENT**

Visit pages 673–675 of our image gallery and study all three images dealing with homelessness. Then choose the image that most appeals to you. Answer the questions and do the writing assignment.

16

Combining the Modes

EDITORS' NOTE

What Combining the Modes Does

The rhetorical modes are an idealization. In the rough-and-tumble writing of the everyday world, they exist only in hit-or-miss practice. It is possible to find a paragraph or even an entire essay that is written strictly in one mode; it is far more typical to find essays that blend the modes rather than observe them faithfully. Writing, a creative art, is nothing if not unpredictable.

Here are two examples that illustrate what we mean. The first is a paragraph that we would say was developed by *illustration*. It opens with the traditional topic sentence (underlined), which it then supports with a series of examples.

> <u>Considerations of what makes for good English or bad English are to an uncomfortably large extent matters of prejudice and conditioning.</u> Until the eighteenth century it was correct to say "you was" if you were referring to one person. It sounds odd today, but the logic is impeccable. *Was* is a singular verb and *were* a plural one. Why should *you* take a plural verb when the sense is clearly singular? The answer—surprise, surprise—is that Robert Lowth[1] didn't like it. "I'm hurrying, are I not?" is hopelessly ungrammatical, but "I'm hurrying, aren't I?"—merely a contraction of the same words—is perfect English. *Many* is almost always a plural (as in "Many people were there"), but not when it is followed by *a,* as in "Many a man was there." There's no inherent reason why these things should be so. They are not defensible in terms of grammar. They are because they are.
>
> —Bill Bryson, *The Mother Tongue: English and How It Got That Way*

---

[1] An amateur grammarian whose influential book, *A Short Introduction to English Grammar* (1762), enshrined many of the stupid rules of English usage still observed today.

Here, however, is an example of a mixed-mode paragraph that is even more typical of everyday writing:

causal analysis
illustration

comparison

argument

English grammar is so complex and confusing for the one very simple reason that its rules and terminology are based on Latin—a language with which it has precious little in common. In Latin, to take one example, it is not possible to split an infinitive. So in English, the early authorities decided, it should not be possible to split an infinitive either. But there is no reason why we shouldn't, any more than we should forsake instant coffee and air travel because they weren't available to the Romans. Making English grammar conform to Latin rules is like asking people to play baseball using the rules of football. It is a patent absurdity. But once this insane notion became established grammarians found themselves having to draw up ever more complicated and circular arguments to accommodate the inconsistencies. As Burchfield notes in *The English Language,* one authority, F. Th. Visser, found it necessary to devote 200 pages to discussing just one aspect of the present participle. That is as crazy as it is amazing.

—Bill Bryson, *The Mother Tongue: English and How It Got That Way*

The writer begins with a causal analysis, gives an illustration, makes a comparison, and then develops an argument.

This is exactly how writers actually write. They treat the rhetorical modes the way a baker might treat a cookie cutter. The object is to produce cookies, not exalt the cutter. It is the same with the rhetorical modes—they exist to make writing easier for beginners. When you're no longer a beginner, you will discard them.

When to Combine the Modes

Combining modes is a tactic many writers follow, especially for long and complex subjects. You should use a combination of modes only when you feel comfortable with it and when your subject is a particularly demanding one that requires a complex form. If you're ranging far afield on an unfamiliar topic, you may not wish to follow any strict pattern and might prefer to improvise as you go along. This is the ideal time to combine the rhetorical modes.

How to Use Combined Modes

The key in writing a mixed-mode essay is to stick to the point and use ample transitions. Essays that are written in a combination of modes have a tendency to either drift from the point or to be herky-jerky rather than smooth. Writers overcome these tendencies by using the techniques of paragraph writing covered in Chapter 6 (now would be a good time to review this material). If you use transitions to guide the reader from one point to the next and if you faithfully stick to your announced topic, your mixed-mode essays will read as smoothly as anything you've ever written in any single pattern. Here is an example of a mixed-mode paragraph that sticks to the point. The writer is discussing the implements that the Arawak Indians, who lived in Jamaica at the time of Columbus, used in their daily lives. He begins with a description, moves to a process, and ends with a definition. He is able to do all of these things without losing the reader because his focus is so tight and his transitions skillful.

> Apart from earthen pots and other utensils, the main items of furniture were hammocks and wooden stools. The hammock was an Indian invention (even the original name, which was *hamac*), one which was not known in Europe before the discovery of the West Indies. These hammocks were made either of cotton string "open-work," or of a length of woven cotton cloth, sometimes dyed in bright colours. Jamaica was well known at that period for the cultivation of cotton, and much of the women's time was spent spinning and weaving it. In fact Jamaica supplied hammocks and cotton cloth to Cuba and Haiti for some time after those islands had been occupied by Spain, and the Spaniards themselves had sail-cloth made in Jamaica. Because of this, one of the many suggested origins of the name *Jamaica* attempts to link it with the Indian word for hammock and to prove that it means "land of cotton." The name Jamaica is of great interest. Some of the early Spanish historians, substituting X for J as they often did, write the name *Xaymaca,* but it also appears in its present form in a work published as early as 1511. Columbus called the island *St. Jago* (Santiago), but as with the other islands of the Greater Antilles, the Indian name has survived the Spanish. It is commonly thought that Xaymaca in the Arawak language meant "land of springs," but since the discoverers do not give the meaning of the name (as they do in the case of various place-names in Haiti) it is possible that the meaning had already been forgotten by the Indians themselves.
>
> —Clinton V. Black, *The Story of Jamaica*

Notice the repetition of the word *hammocks*, the variant forms of *Jamaica*, and the writer's use of the transitional sentence "The name Jamaica is of great interest." These little transitional touches are designed to nudge the reader along the writer's line of thought.

To sum up, if you do not now do it, eventually you will find yourself commonly writing essays that conform more to the mixed-mode pattern than to any other. The rhetorical modes are useful tools for the beginning writer, but less so for the veteran. As you make your way through school, you, too, will become a practiced writer who has outgrown them.

EXAMPLES

Shrew—The Littlest Mammal
ALAN DEVOE

Alan DeVoe (1909–1955) wrote many naturalist essays that were much admired by his readers. He also contributed widely to numerous magazines, among them the *American Mercury, Audubon,* and *Readers' Digest.* Additionally, he was the author of numerous books, including *Phudd Hill* (1937), *Down to Earth* (1940), and *This Fascinating Animal World* (1951).

DeVoe's description of the tiniest mammal, the shrew, tells us how this frenzied little beast got its reputation for ferocity. The shrew, having features similar to those of a mouse, is so rabid about pursuing its one mission in life—to eat—that it will attack animals twice its size. DeVoe uses paragraphs of different modes to portray the life cycle of this tiny creature whose nature is driven by a giant appetite.

• • •

1   The zoological Class to which we human beings belong is the Mammalia. There has been some dispute as to whether we possess immortal souls and the capacity for a unique kind of intellection, but we do possess unquestionably the " . . . four-chambered heart, double circulatory system, thoracic cavity separated from abdominal cavity by muscular diaphragm, and habit of bearing the young alive and nursing them at the breast" which classically establish our membership in that group of warm-blooded animals which are guessed to have come into being on the planet some hundred-odd million years ago.

2   It is today a large and various group, this mammalian kindred. With some of our fellow-mammals it is not hard to feel relationship: with apes, for instance, or with the small sad-eyed monkeys that we keep for our beguilement as flea-bitten captives in our pet shops. But with others of the group our tie is less apparent; and the reason, often enough, is disparity of size and shape. It is such disparity, no doubt, that prevents our having much fellow-feeling for the hundred-ton sulphur-bottomed whales that plunge through the deep waters of both Pacific and Atlantic, though whales' blood is warmed as ours is, and the females of their kind have milky teats; and likewise it is doubtless in part because we have two legs and attain to some seventy inches of height that we do not take as much account as otherwise we might of the little animal that is at the opposite end of the mammal size-scale: the little four-footed mammal that is rather smaller than a milkweed pod and not as heavy as a cecropia cocoon.

3   This tiniest of mammals is the minute beast called a shrew. A man need go to no great trouble to look at it, as he must to see a whale; he can find it now in the nearest country woodlot. Despite its tininess a shrew is still after a fashion a relative of ours; and on that account, even if on no other, should merit a little knowing.

4   In the narrow twisting earth-burrow dug by a mouse or a mole the least of the mammals is usually born. Its fellows in the litter may number four or five, and they lie together in the warm subterranean darkness of their tiny nest chamber in a little group whose whole bulk is scarcely that of a walnut. The infant shrew, relative of whales and elephants and us, is no more than a squirming pink speck of warm-fleshed animal aliveness. Totally defenseless and unequipped for life, it can only nuzzle the tiny dugs of its mother, wriggle tightly against its brothers to feel the warmth of the litter, and for many hours of the twenty-four lie asleep in the curled head-to-toes position of a minuscule foetus.

5   The baby shrew remains a long time in the birth-chamber. The size of even an adult shrew is very nearly the smallest possible for mammalian existence, and the young one cannot venture out into the world of adult activity until it has almost completely matured. Until then, therefore, it stays in the warm darkness of the burrow, knowing the universe only as a heat of other little bodies, a pungence of roots and grasses, a periodic sound of tiny chittering squeakings when its mother enters the burrow after foraging-trips, bringing food. She brings in mostly insects—small lady-beetles whose brittle spotted wing-covers must be removed before they can be eaten, soft-bodied caterpillars, ants, and worms. The young shrew, after its weaning has come about, acquires the way of taking this new food between its slim delicate forepaws, fingered like little hands, and in the under-earth darkness nibbles away the wing-covers and chitinous body-shells as adroitly as a squirrel removes the husk from a nut.

6   When at last the time comes for the young shrew to leave its birthplace, it has grown very nearly as large as its mother and has developed all the adult shrew-endowments. It looks, now, not unlike a mouse, save that its muzzle is more sharply pointed, but a mouse reduced in size to extreme miniature. The whole length of its soft-furred little body is only a fraction more than two inches, compared to the four-inch length of even the smallest of the white-footed woods-mice; its tail is less than half as long as a mouse's. The uniquely little body is covered with dense soft hair, sepia above and a paler buffy color underneath—a covering of fur so fine and close that the shrew's ears are nearly invisible in it, and the infinitesimal eyes are scarcely to be discerned. The shrew's hands and feet are white, smaller and more delicate than any other beast's; white also is the underside of the minute furry tail. The whole body, by its softness of coat and coloring and its tininess of bulk, seems far from kinship with the tough strong bodies of the greater mammals. But it is blood-brother to these, all the same; warm blood courses in it; the shrew is as much mammal as a wolf. It sets forth, with its unparalleledly tiny physical equipments, to live as adventurous a life as any of its greater warm-blooded relatives.

7   The life-adventure of Man, "the medium-sized mammal," is shaped by such diverse motives and impulsions that it is difficult to say what may be the most powerful of the driving urges that direct it. In the life-adventure of the littlest mammal, the shrew, the driving urge is very plain and single: it is hunger. Like hummingbirds, smallest of the aves, this smallest of the mammals lives at a tremendous pitch of nervous intensity. The shrew's little body quite literally quivers with the vibrance of life-force that is in it; from tiny

pointed snout to tailtip the shrew is ever in a taut furor of aliveness. Its body-surface, like a hummingbird's, is maximally extensive in relation to its minimal weight; its metabolism must proceed with immense rapidity; to sustain the quivering nervous aliveness of its mite of warm flesh it must contrive a food-intake that is almost constant. It is possible on that account to tell the shrew's life-story almost wholly in terms of its feeding. The shrew's life has other ingredients, of course—the seeking of its small mate, the various rituals of copulating and sleeping and dung-dropping and the rest, that are common to all mammal lives—but it is the process of feeding that is central and primary, and that is the distinguishing preoccupation of the littlest mammal all its days.

8   The shrew haunts mostly moist thick-growing places, the banks of streams and the undergrowth of damp woods, and it hunts particularly actively at night. Scuttling on its pattery little feet among the fallen leaves, scrabbling in the leaf-mould in a frenzy of tiny investigation, it looks ceaselessly for food. Not a rodent, like a mouse, but an insectivore, it seizes chiefly on such creatures as crickets, grasshoppers, moths, and ants, devouring each victim with nervous eagerness and at once rushing on with quivering haste, tiny muzzle incessantly a-twitch, to look for further provender.

9   Not infrequently the insects discoverable in the shrew's quick scampering little sallies through the darkness are inadequate to nourish it, so quick is its digestion and so intense the nervous energy it must sustain. When this is the case, the shrew widens its diet-range, to include seeds or berries or earthworms or any other sustenance that it can stuff with its little shivering forepaws into its tiny muzzle. It widens its diet to include meat; it becomes a furious and desperate carnivore. It patters through the grass-runways of the meadow-mice, sniffing and quivering; it darts to the nest of a deer-mouse. And presently, finding deer-mouse or meadowmouse, it plunges into a wild attack on this "prey" that is twice its size. The shrew fights with a kind of mad recklessness; it becomes a leaping, twisting, chittering, squeaking speck of hungering fury. Quite generally, when the battle is over, the shrew has won. Its thirty-two pinpoint teeth are sharp and strong, and the wild fury of its attack takes the victim by surprise. For a little while, after victory, the shrew's relentless body-needs are appeased. For a little while, but only a little; and then the furry speck must go pattering and scuttling forth into the night again, sniffing for food and quivering with need.

10   That is the pattern of shrew-life: a hunting and a hungering that never stops, an endless preoccupied catering to the demands of the kind of metabolism which unique mammalian smallness necessitates. The littlest mammal is a mammal in all ways; it breathes and sleeps and mates and possibly exults, as others do; but chiefly, as the price of unique tininess, it engages in restless never-ending search for something to eat.

11   The way of a shrew's dying is sometimes curious. Sometimes, of course, it dies in battle, when the larger prey which it has tackled proves too strong. Sometimes it dies of starvation; it can starve in a matter of hours. But often it is set upon by one of the big predators—some fox or lynx or man. When that happens, it is usually not the clutch of fingers or the snap of the carnivorous

jaws that kills the shrew. The shrew is usually dead before that. At the first instant of a lynx's pounce—at the first touch of a human hand against the shrew's tiny quivering body—the shrew is apt to shiver in a quick violent spasm, and then lie still in death. The littlest of the mammals dies, as often as not, of simple nervous shock.

Vocabulary

beguilement (2)
chitinous (5)
discerned (6)
extensive (7)
exults (10)

disparity (2)
adroitly (5)
diverse (7)
contrive (7)

minuscule (4)
infinitesimal (6)
impulsions (7)
provender (8)

The Facts

1. About which zoological fact is the author sure? About which element is he less sure? Why is he so much more sure about one than the other?
2. Where is the shrew usually born? What does this tell us about shrew parents?
3. In terms of its impulses, how does the shrew differ from its other mammal relatives? What causes this difference?
4. If the shrew can't find enough insects to feed its hunger, what will it do?
5. If insects and vegetation are not available, what will the shrew do to get the food it so badly needs to stay alive? What attitude does the shrew convey? How do you view this attitude?

The Strategies

1. This essay reveals the use of more than one rhetorical mode. What other modes are used? Try to name these modes paragraph by paragraph.
2. What dominant impression of the shrew did you receive from this essay?
3. What is the purpose of the quotation in the opening paragraph? What, if anything, does it add to the essay?
4. Of what help is paragraph 10 as you learn about the shrew?
5. Why does the author sprinkle specialized terms throughout the essay (e.g., *cecropia, cocoon, chitinous body shells*)? How do these terms affect the author's style?

The Issues

1. The author declares a kinship among whales, monkeys, shrews, and humans. Of the nonhuman mammals, which do you feel closest to? Why? Of all animals, which one would you prefer to have as a pet? Why?
2. Do you agree with the author that because the shrew is related to us, we should know something about this mammal? Give reasons for your answer. What other reasons are there to encourage us to learn more about animals?
3. If a woman is called a "shrew," what is meant by the label? What connection can you see between this metaphor and the tiniest mammal?

Suggestions for Writing

1. Describe the most interesting animal you have ever observed. If needed, use more than one rhetorical mode for this assignment.
2. Choose one of the following creatures and write an essay describing in what ways it is superior to human beings: lion, tiger, cat, dog, eagle, snake, or ant.

Will Spelling Count?
Jack Connor

Jack Connor grew up in New Jersey and received his Ph.D. from the University of Florida. For many years he taught English in the Department of Humanities and Communications at Drexel University in Philadelphia. It is interesting to note that in 2003, the freshman composition teachers of Drexel University created a *Handbook for Freshman Writing* to help new teachers teach their classes effectively.

For those students who have always been anxious about the mechanics in their compositions, Connor offers an answer. Although his essay mainly focuses on the importance of spelling, his journey of discovery can be applied to other aspects of writing, such as grammar, organization, clarity of purpose, and style. The point is that writing requires meticulous effort, so keep that in mind as you read about Connor's experiences in the college classroom.

• • •

1   "Will spelling count?" In my first year of teaching freshman composition I had a little act I performed whenever a student asked that inevitable question. Frowning, taking my pipe out of my mouth, and hesitating, I would try to look like a man coming down from some higher mental plane. Then, with what I hoped sounded like a mixture of confidence and disdain, I would answer, "No. Of course it won't."

2   In that first year, I was convinced that to have a significant effect on my students' writing I had to demonstrate that I was not the stereotypical English teacher: a fussbudget who would pick through their essays in search of misspellings and trivial errors. I intended to inspire students in my classes to write the kinds of papers the unconventional teachers I had read about—John Holt, A. S. Neill, Herbert Kohl, and Ken Macrorie—had inspired: papers bristling with life, written by the students with their inner voices.

3   It was not to be. Week after week students handed in papers that had obviously been dashed off in 30 or 40 minutes. By the end of the year I realized my mistake: I had been too subtle; I had not made it clear enough that mine was a revolutionary way to teach writing.

4   So, in my second year, I answered the question with a 50-minute lecture. I quoted education theories, told several semifictional stories of my student days, and recited some entirely fictional statistics—all of which argued that people write better when they don't worry about spelling.

5   "What you have to do is write honestly about things you care about," I told them. "Don't interrupt your thoughts to check your spelling."

6   That lecture—and other strategic changes I made in my teaching style that second year—had no noticeable effect. Once again, almost all the papers were dull, predictable, and carelessly done. My students didn't understand that writing could be an act of self-exploration and discovery.

7   They wrote essays of two kinds: unorganized narratives with such titles as "My First Drunk" or "How to Roll a Joint at 70 m.p.h." and fourth-hand, insipid arguments with such titles as "Capital Punishment = Murder" or "The Space Race—What a Waste."

8   Since assigning topics or imposing organizational schemes would mark me as just another conventional English teacher, killing any chance I had to inspire my students to discover their inner voices, I tried to proceed indirectly—with class discussions on subjects I thought would make good topics: the latest editorial in the student newspaper, the problems of communicating with parents and friends, political apathy, the sights and sounds of the campus. However, although I could sometimes get a "lively" discussion going, it was obvious that the students saw these exchanges not as relevant to their writing but as a painless way to spend the 50 minutes. They sat up and took note only to ask me about the mechanical details of the next assignment: "How many words does it have to be?" "How much do you take off for late papers?" "Is it O.K. to write in blue ink?"

9   It was in that year that I began to be embarrassed by my students' course evaluations. They usually gave me top grades in every category and then wrote something such as, "This was a great class because the teacher understood that students in this university have a lot of other things to worry about besides his particular course."

10 By the start of the third year, I was wondering whether the education theorists had known what they were taking about. When the usual question came, I equivocated and told them they could decide questions about spelling for themselves.

11 It was a low point. By that time a couple of hundred freshmen had passed through my composition classes, but I could not have named one who had discovered himself as a writer because of my teaching. Of the few A+ papers in my files, half were written by students who could have written an A+ paper the first day of class; the rest were happy accidents, written by students in moments of inspiration they were unable to repeat.

12 That year, one student wrote in his evaluation, "This was a very good course because the teacher believed college students are mature enough to make their own decisions about things like whether spelling is important. It isn't important to me. I'm going to let my secretary take care of my spelling."

13 I knew it was time for a radical change. I was going to have to give up trying to teach my students that writing could be an act of self-exploration;

I would have to concentrate on teaching a truth more essential to their education: Writing is hard work.

14   In the summer before my fourth year, I wrote a ten-page syllabus, two pages of which were given over to the old questions and my new answers:

Q: Is blue ink acceptable?
A: No. In fact, handwriting is unacceptable. All papers in this course must be typed.
Q: What about students who can't type?
A: This course will provide them with an opportunity to learn.
Q: Why do papers have to be typed?
A: Because in the real world adults type when they want to put serious communications in writing.
Q: What if we can't hand a paper in on time?
A: Hand it in as soon as possible. It will be marked "late."
Q: What if we have a legitimate excuse?
A: Keep it to yourself. My job is to evaluate your writing, not your excuses.

15   Knowing the eternal question would come up the first day, I had my best answer in reserve. When one of the students asked it after my introductory talk, I crossed my arms and let them have it.

16   "The best answer to that question is an analogy: Imagine a team of college basketball players meeting their coach for the first time. The coach distributes a book outlining the plays he will be teaching them, and then talks to them about how the practices will be organized, what he thinks his role should be, and what he considers their responsibilities to be. When he has finished, the first question is, 'Will dribbling count?'"

17   The student who asked the question dropped the course, as did a couple of others who didn't like their first impressions of me and my nasty syllabus. But my new tone, and the classroom style if forced me to adopt, had several excellent consequences:

18   I stopped trying to make the class interesting. No more lively discussions on the sights and sounds of the campus—or anything else that wasn't directly related to helping my students write better this week than they had last week.

19   I learned to keep oral analysis and commentary to a minimum, because it disappeared into the air over my classroom. I put all directions and suggestions in writing, and tried to note on each of the papers submitted where the writer had followed my advice and where he had not.

20   The students spent more and more time pushing their pens across paper in class: writing thesis statements, writing drafts of introductory paragraphs, listing ten concrete words (five from last week's essay, five they thought they could use in next week's), working to arrange a sentence or two from their last essay into a parallel structure.

21   I stopped hoping to find in the weekly pile of papers evidence of some student writing with his inner voice. Inspired papers continued to appear at the old rate (about one in a hundred), but I no longer looked to them for proof of my effectiveness as a teacher.

22   A new kind of paper appeared in the weekly pile: well organized, mechanically polished, and clearly a second or third draft. Although some of them were titled "My First Drunk" and "The Space Race—What a Waste," I could read them attentively and praise their strengths sincerely.

23   Finally, I received some negative comments in the course evaluations: "I did not enjoy this class. The teacher was too finicky and graded too hard."

24   After four years of teaching I had learned that, given my particular skills, I had to leave consciousness-raising to other teachers. My first three years had been unsuccessful because I had been too intent on playing the guru, and I couldn't pull it off. The role I adopted that fourth year was not one I was comfortable with—Ken Macrorie is a hero of mine, not Vince Lombardi—but I could pull it off. And, more important, the tyrannical coach was a character my students recognized, and they understood what would be expected of them.

25   Last year, on my way to a different university, I decided to modify the role a little. The new syllabus has the old rules, but—while still playing the traditional authoritarian—I have changed my tone to that of a man sure of what he wants his students to do, certain they can do it, but too cool to be nasty about it.

26   This year, I have a little act I perform whenever a student asks, "Will spelling count?" Frowning, taking my pipe out of my mouth, and hesitating a moment, I try to look like a man coming down from some higher plane. Then, with what I hope sounds like a mixture of confidence and disdain, I reply, "Yes. Of course it will."

● Vocabulary

inevitable (1)   disdain (1)   stereotypical (2)
strategic (6)   insipid (7)   apathy (8)
equivocated (10)   radical (13)   legitimate (14)
analogy (16)   oral (19)   guru (24)
authoritarian (25)

● The Facts

1. What conspicuous change did the author make in his approach to teaching composition? How long did it take him to make that change?
2. What were the typical questions asked by students about their essays? Try to add some current questions to the list.
3. What two kinds of essays did Connor receive from his students? Do you think teachers still receive these kinds of essays today? Explain your answer.
4. What is Connor's ultimate answer to the question posed in the title of the essay? Do you think most composition teachers today would give the same answer?
5. What reason does Connor offer for his requirement that students type their papers? Does his reason still hold true today?

The Strategies

1. How does the author's essay come full circle in the end? How effective is this strategy? What does it bring to the essay?
2. How is paragraph 14 different from the other paragraphs? What does it do for the essay?
3. What is the purpose of paragraphs 19 to 23? What would the essay lose if these paragraphs were deleted?
4. What descriptive details in Connor's essay no longer fit the current group of English teachers? What details could be added that probably did not exist at the time of Connor's writing? Which of Connor's observations are still prevalent in composition classes?
5. How does Connor indicate the passage of time? What is remarkable about his pacing?

The Issues

1. What is the thesis of Connor's essay? Is it entirely limited to spelling? If not, what more expanded thesis does he develop?
2. Do you agree with Connor that writing is hard work? (See paragraph 13.) Or does writing for you flow easily as your fingers fly across the computer keyboard? Evaluate the ease or difficulty with which you write.
3. Which kind of professor do you value most—the cool guru who helps you through self-discovery or the teacher who teaches with lucid objectives that he or she tries to achieve in class? Describe the kind of English teacher you consider ideal.
4. Do you think that lively class discussions are useful to the writing process or are they "a painless way to spend 50 minutes"? (See paragraph 8.) Explain your answer with appropriate evidence to support your point.
5. After studying this essay, how convinced are you by the author's views? Is his essay still relevant to today's freshman composition students? Or has the computer rendered his ideas beside the point? Do not simply answer yes or no, but give reasons for each of your answers.

Suggestions for Writing

1. Write an essay offering your opinion on the importance of mechanics and grammar in writing English. In other words, ask yourself if it is more important to express a profound and important thought than to write correctly. Support your thesis with strong examples.
2. Write an essay in which you describe the changes that have taken place in freshman composition courses over the last ten years. Consider these innovations: (1) interactive computers that allow you to communicate after class with your teacher; (2) submitting your papers electronically to the teacher; (3) doing library research on the Internet; (3) using spelling and grammar checks on your computer.

Once More to the Lake

E. B. WHITE

Elwyn Brooks White (1899–1985) was one of the wittiest and most admired observers of contemporary American society. As a member of *The New Yorker* magazine staff, he wrote a number of essays for the section called "Talk of the Town"; some of these essays have been collected in *The Wild Flag* (1946) and *Writings from The New Yorker* (1991). With James Thurber, White wrote *Is Sex Necessary?* (1929). His other well-known works include *One Man's Meat* (1942), *Here Is New York* (1949), and two beloved children books, *Stuart Little* (1945) and *Charlotte's Web* (1952).

This essay ends with a bang, not a whimper. The writer tackles what might seem at first glance a humdrum subject—an annual vacation trip to a lake—and describes in evocative and lovely prose the carefree summer days he spent hiking and fishing with his son. Then, at the very end, the trap is sprung and the true meaning of the essay is revealed.

• • •

August 1941

1   One summer, along about 1904, my father rented a camp on a lake in Maine and took us all there for the month of August. We all got ringworm from some kittens and had to rub Pond's Extract on our arms and legs night and morning, and my father rolled over in a canoe with all his clothes on; but outside of that the vacation was a success and from then on none of us ever thought there was any place in the world like that lake in Maine. We returned summer after summer—always on August 1 for one month. I have since become a salt-water man, but sometimes in summer there are days when the restlessness of the tides and the fearful cold of the sea water and the incessant wind that blows across the afternoon and into the evening make me wish for the placidity of a lake in the woods. A few weeks ago this feeling got so strong I bought myself a couple of bass hooks and a spinner and returned to the lake where we used to go, for a week's fishing and to revisit old haunts.

2   I took along my son, who had never had any fresh water up his nose and who had seen lily pads only from train windows. On the journey over to the lake I began to wonder what it would be like. I wondered how time would have marred this unique, this holy spot—the coves and streams, the hills that the sun set behind, the camps and the paths behind the camps. I was sure that the tarred road would have found it out, and I wondered in what other ways it would be desolated. It is strange how much you can remember about places like that once you allow your mind to return into the grooves that lead back. You remember one thing, and that suddenly reminds you of another thing. I guess I remembered clearest of all the early mornings, when the lake was cool and motionless, remembered how the bedroom smelled of the lumber it was made of and of the wet woods whose scent entered through the screen. The partitions in the camp were thin and did not extend clear to the top of the

rooms, and as I was always the first up I would dress softly so as not to wake the others, and sneak out into the sweet outdoors and start out in the canoe, keeping close along the shore in the long shadows of the pines. I remembered being very careful never to rub my paddle against the gunwale for fear of disturbing the stillness of the cathedral.

3   The lake had never been what you would call a wild lake. There were cottages sprinkled around the shores, and it was in farming country although the shores of the lake were quite heavily wooded. Some of the cottages were owned by nearby farmers, and you would live at the shore and eat your meals at the farmhouse. That's what our family did. But although it wasn't wild, it was a fairly large and undisturbed lake and there were places in it that, to a child at least, seemed infinitely remote and primeval.

4   I was right about the tar: it led to within half a mile of the shore. But when I got back there, with my boy, and we settled into a camp near a farmhouse and into the kind of summertime I had known, I could tell that it was going to be pretty much the same as it had been before—I knew it, lying in bed the first morning smelling the bedroom and hearing the boy sneak quietly out and go off along the shore in a boat. I began to sustain the illusion that he was I, and therefore, by simple transposition, that I was my father. This sensation persisted, kept cropping up all the time we were there. It was not an entirely new feeling, but in this setting it grew much stronger. I seemed to be living a dual existence. I would be in the middle of some simple act, I would be picking up a bait box or laying down a table fork, or I would be saying something and suddenly it would be not I but my father who was saying the words or making the gesture. It gave me a creepy sensation.

5   We went fishing the first morning. I felt the same damp moss covering the worms in the bait can, and saw the dragonfly alight on the tip of my rod as it hovered a few inches from the surface of the water. It was the arrival of this fly that convinced me beyond any doubt that everything was as it always had been, that the years were a mirage and that there had been no years. The small waves were the same, chucking the rowboat under the chin as we fished at anchor, and the boat was the same boat, the same color green and the ribs broken in the same places, and under the floorboards the same fresh water leavings and débris—the dead helgramite, the wisps of moss, the rusty discarded fishhook, the dried blood from yesterday's catch. We stared silently at the tips of our rods, at the dragonflies that came and went. I lowered the tip of mine into the water, tentatively, pensively dislodging the fly, which darted two feet away, poised, darted two feet back, and came to rest again a little farther up the rod. There had been no years between the ducking of this dragonfly and the other one—the one that was part of memory. I looked at the boy, who was silently watching his fly, and it was my hands that held his rod, my eyes watching. I felt dizzy and didn't know which rod I was at the end of.

6   We caught two bass, hauling them in briskly as though they were mackerel, pulling them over the side of the boat in a businesslike manner without any landing net, and stunning them with a blow on the back of the head. When we got back for a swim before lunch, the lake was exactly where we had

left it, the same number of inches from the dock, and there was only the merest suggestion of a breeze. This seemed an utterly enchanted sea, this lake you could leave to its own devices for a few hours and come back to, and find that it had not stirred, this constant and trustworthy body of water. In the shallows, the dark, water-soaked sticks and twigs, smooth and old, were undulating in clusters on the bottom against the clean ribbed sand, and the track of the mussel was plain. A school of minnows swam by, each minnow with its small individual shadow, doubling the attendance, so clear and sharp in the sunlight. Some of the other campers were in swimming, along the shore, one of them with a cake of soap, and the water felt thin and clear and unsubstantial. Over the years there had been this person with the cake of soap, this cultist, and here he was. There had been no years.

7   Up to the farmhouse to dinner through the teeming dusty field, the road under our sneakers was only a two-track road. The middle track was missing, the one with the marks of the hooves and the splotches of dried, flaky manure. There had always been three tracks to choose from in choosing which track to walk in; now the choice was narrowed down to two. For a moment I missed terribly the middle alternative. But the way led past the tennis court, and something about the way it lay there in the sun reassured me; the tape had loosened along the backline, the alleys were green with plantains and other weeds, and the net (installed in June and removed in September) sagged in the dry noon, and the whole place steamed with midday heat and hunger and emptiness. There was a choice of pie for dessert, and one was blueberry and one was apple, and the waitresses were the same country girls, there having been no passage of time, only the illusion of it as in a dropped curtain—the waitresses were still fifteen; their hair had been washed, that was the only difference—they had been to the movies and seen the pretty girls with the clean hair.

8   Summertime, oh, summertime, pattern of life indelible with fade-proof lake, the wood unshatterable, the pasture with the sweetfern and the juniper forever and ever, summer without end; this was the background, and the life along the shore was the design, the cottages with their innocent and tranquil design, their tiny docks with the flagpole and the American flag floating against the white clouds in the blue sky, the little paths over the roots of the trees leading from camp to camp and the paths leading back to the outhouses and the can of lime for sprinkling, and at the souvenir counters at the store the miniature birch-bark canoes and the postcards that showed things looking a little better than they looked. This was the American family at play, escaping the city heat, wondering whether the newcomers in the camp at the head of the cove were "common" or "nice," wondering whether it was true that the people who drove up for Sunday dinner at the farmhouse were turned away because there wasn't enough chicken.

9   It seemed to me, as I kept remembering all this, that those times and those summers had been infinitely precious and worth saving. There had been jollity and peace and goodness. The arriving (at the beginning of August) had been so big a business in itself, at the railway station the farm wagon drawn up, the first smell of the pine-laden air, the first glimpse of the smiling farmer, and the

great importance of the trunks and your father's enormous authority in such matters and the feel of the wagon under you for the long ten-mile haul, and at the top of the last long hill catching the first view of the lake after eleven months of not seeing this cherished body of water. The shouts and cries of the other campers when they saw you, and the trunks to be unpacked, to give up their rich burden. (Arriving was less exciting nowadays, when you sneaked up in your car and parked it under a tree near the camp and took out the bags and in five minutes it was all over, no fuss, no loud wonderful fuss about trunks.)

10   Peace and goodness and jollity. The only thing that was wrong now, really, was the sound of the place, an unfamiliar nervous sound of the outboard motors. This was the note that jarred, the one thing that would sometimes break the illusion and set the years moving. In those other summertimes all motors were inboard; and when they were at a little distance, the noise they made was a sedative, an ingredient of summer sleep. They were one-cylinder and two-cylinder engines, and some were make-and-break and some were jumpspark, but they all made a sleepy sound across the lake. The one-lungers throbbed and fluttered, and the twin-cylinder ones purred and purred, and that was a quiet sound, too. But now the campers all had outboards. In the daytime, in the hot mornings, these motors made a petulant, irritable sound; at night in the still evening when the afterglow lit the water, they whined about one's ears like mosquitoes. My boy loved our rented outboard, and his great desire was to achieve single-handed mastery over it, and authority, and he soon learned the trick of choking it a little (but not too much), and the adjustment of the needle valve. Watching him I would remember the things you could do with the old one-cylinder engine with the heavy flywheel, how you could have it eating out of your hand if you got really close to it spiritually. Motorboats in those days didn't have clutches, and you would make a landing by shutting off the motor at the proper time and coasting in with a dead rudder. But there was a way of reversing them, if you learned the trick, by cutting the switch and putting it on again exactly on the final dying revolution of the flywheel, so that it would kick back against compression and begin reversing. Approaching a dock in a strong following breeze, it was difficult to slow up sufficiently by the ordinary coasting method, and if a boy felt he had complete mastery over his motor, he was tempted to keep it running beyond its time and then reverse it a few feet from the dock. It took a cool nerve, because if you threw the switch a twentieth of a second too soon you would catch the flywheel when it still had speed enough to go up past center, and the boat would leap ahead, charging bull-fashion at the dock.

11   We had a good week at the camp. The bass were biting well and the sun shone endlessly, day after day. We would be tired at night and lie down in the accumulated heat of the little bedrooms after the long hot day and the breeze would stir almost imperceptibly outside and the smell of the swamp drift in through the rusty screens. Sleep would come easily and in the morning the red squirrel would be on the roof, tapping out his gay routine. I kept remembering everything, lying in bed in the mornings—the small steamboat that had a long rounded stern like the lip of a Ubangi, and how quietly she ran on the moonlight

sails, when the older boys played their mandolins and the girls sang and we ate doughnuts dipped in sugar, and how sweet the music was on the water in the shining night, and what it had felt like to think about girls then. After breakfast we would go up to the store and the things were in the same place—the minnows in a bottle, the plugs and spinners disarranged and pawed over by the youngsters from the boys' camp, the Fig Newtons and the Beeman's gum. Outside, the road was tarred and cars stood in front of the store. Inside, all was just as it had always been, except there was more Coca-Cola and not so much Moxie and root beer and birch beer and sarsaparilla. We would walk out with the bottle of pop apiece and sometimes the pop would backfire up our noses and hurt. We explored the streams, quietly, where the turtles slid off the sunny logs and dug their way into the soft bottom; and we lay on the town wharf and fed worms to the tame bass. Everywhere we went I had trouble making out which was I, the one walking at my side, the one walking in my pants.

12   One afternoon while we were at that lake a thunderstorm came up. It was like the revival of an old melodrama that I had seen long ago with childish awe. The second-act climax of the drama of the electrical disturbance over a lake in America had not changed in any important respect. This was the big scene, still the big scene. The whole thing was so familiar, the first feeling of oppression and heat and a general air around camp of not wanting to go very far away. In midafternoon (it was all the same) a curious darkening of the sky, and a lull in everything that had made life tick; and then the way the boats suddenly swung the other way at their moorings with the coming of a breeze out of the new quarter, and the premonitory rumble. Then the kettle drum, then the snare, then the bass drum and cymbals, then crackling light against the dark, and the gods grinning and licking their chops in the hills. Afterward the calm, the rain steadily rustling in the calm lake, the return of light and hope and spirits, and the campers running out in joy and relief to go swimming in the rain, their bright cries perpetuating the deathless joke about how they were getting simply drenched, and the children screaming with delight at the new sensation of bathing in the rain, and the joke about getting drenched linking the generations in a strong indestructible chain. And the comedian who waded in carrying an umbrella.

13   When the others went swimming my son said he was going in, too. He pulled his dripping trunks from the line where they had hung all through the shower and wrung them out. Languidly, and with no thought of going in, I watched him, his hard little body, skinny and bare, saw him wince slightly as he pulled up around his vitals the small, soggy, icy garment. As he buckled the swollen belt, suddenly my groin felt the chill of death.

● Vocabulary

incessant (1)
transposition (4)
undulating (6)
indelible (8)
premonitory (12)

desolated (2)
tentatively (5)
unsubstantial (6)
sedative (10)

primeval (3)
pensively (5)
cultist (6)
imperceptibly (11)

630 CHAPTER 16 • Combining the Modes

● The Facts

1. How old was White when he first went to the lake with his father? How old was he when he took his own son there?
2. What illusion did White begin to sustain on hearing his own son sneaking out to go down to the boat on the lake?
3. What changes did the author notice in the road leading from the lake to the farmhouse? What did these changes say about the passing of time?
4. What difference did the author note between the way guests arrived at the lake in his own boyhood days and their arrival now?
5. What experience precipitated White's realization that time had passed, that he was no longer young, that he was mortal?

● The Strategies

1. Aside from description, what other mode of development is implicitly part of the structure of this essay? What is the purpose of holding back the true meaning of the essay until the final paragraph?
2. In paragraph 2, White writes that he "was sure that the tarred road would have found it [the lake] out." What is odd about the phrasing of this sentence? What do you think White was trying to achieve in phrasing it that way?
3. Examine the author's boyhood recollections of the lake (paragraph 2). To which of our senses do his details and images appeal?
4. Examine the description of the fishing boat in paragraph 5. How does White manage to convey such a vivid picture of the boat?
5. In what part of his body did White feel the chill of death? In the context of the essay, why is this such an appropriate place?

● The Issues

1. In paragraph 2, why does White refer to the lake as a "holy spot"? What is the connotation of this term, given that the place was not a religious shrine? What, in your life, would be a similar spot? Give reasons for your choice.
2. The author states that he missed the "middle track" of the road leading up to the farmhouse for dinner. Try to imagine yourself in a similar situation forty years hence. What vehicles of transportation, not yet commonly used, might invade your road then?
3. What is the social implication of the words *common* and *nice* in paragraph 8? Have times changed, or are these distinctions still made?
4. Not everyone would have reacted in the way the author describes his own reaction in the final sentence of the essay. What might be another realistic reaction?
5. What are some clear signs in your life to indicate that you are not immortal? What are your feelings about these signs?

Suggestions for Writing

1. Write a mixed-mode essay about anything you really like to do. Be specific in your details.
2. Write an essay in any mode about your favorite author.

ISSUE FOR CRITICAL THINKING AND DEBATE: SAME-SEX MARRIAGE

Of all the issues for critical thinking and debate, none is more polarizing in this country than same-sex marriages. Opponents of same-sex unions are adamant that marriage should be allowed only between members of opposite sexes Proponents, on the other hand, contend that prohibiting same-sex marriage unfairly deprives committed gay couples of the practical benefits of inheritance, visitation, and community property rights enjoyed by heterosexual couples. In many states gay couples who have lived together for years have no official status in each others' lives and in times of crisis or emergency have no say whatsoever in treatment options for their partners. Health insurance benefits, for example, are often not available to the domestic partner of a gay employee but only to a husband or wife.

In the history of marriage, the concept of same-sex unions is a relatively recent development. Up until the late twentieth century, such marriages did not exist anywhere in the world. In April 2001, Holland set a precedent by expanding the definition of marriage to include both heterosexual and homosexual relationships. Belgium did likewise in 2003, followed in rapid succession by Québec and by many Canadian provinces, including Manitoba, Saskatchewan, and British Columbia.

Behind this debate is a profound disagreement over the nature of homosexuality. Opponents argue that to allow gay couples to marry is to put homosexuality and heterosexuality on an equal footing, as if marrying a member of the same sex were no different from marrying one of the opposite sex. Many religions not only reject this implied equivalence but also have deep taboos and historical prohibitions against homosexuality. The Catholic Church, in particular, is staunchly against homosexual relationships and profoundly opposed to recognizing them in marriage. As Pope Benedict XVI, in one of his first pronouncements after being elected, put it, "Marriage is not just a casual sociological construction" but is based on "the most profound essence of the human being." This essence, of course, includes heterosexuality.

Underlying this attitude is the belief that there is something unnatural about being gay. In the view of opponents to same-sex marriages, to allow gays to marry would not only demean the value of marriage, it would also legitimize what is an unnatural relationship. Moreover, opponents of same-sex marriage fear that such marriages would produce gay adopted children. However, gay

● Should same-sex couples have the right to be parents?

marriages are no more likely to produce only gay children than are straight marriages to produce only straight children.

Are homosexuals making a conscious but perverse choice of sex partners, or are they driven by psychological and genetic forces beyond their control? The evidence from nature is that homosexuality exists among primates, the species to which we belong, and is not restricted to human beings. Some researchers have even suggested that homosexuality is nature's experimentation with birth control.

The issue is a complex one that generates volumes of bumper sticker slogans and exposes society's contradictory expectations of homosexuals. On the one hand, we lament homosexual promiscuity; on the other hand, we encourage it by denying homosexuals the stable relationship and commitment of marriage. Far from settled in the public debate is the troubling question of the origin of homosexuality. But should the civil rights of citizens of a free country hinge on whether their sexual destiny is freely chosen or genetically hard-wired into their nature? That, perhaps, is the primal and yet unanswered question behind this entire debate.

The Case against Homosexual Marriage
R. ALBERT MOHLER

R. Albert Mohler has served as president of the Southern Baptist Theological Seminary, the flagship school of the Southern Baptist Convention and one of the largest seminaries in the world. He is a theologian and ordained minister, as well as an author, speaker, and host of his own radio program, *The Albert Mohler Program*. The essay below is a reprint of Dr. Mohler's opening statement during a debate on homosexual marriage sponsored by the Louisville Forum on January 14, 2004.

Is same-sex marriage right or wrong? That is the question before us in this debate and one that in the upcoming years will be bitterly contested in the courts. The issue is a troubling one that drives to the core of many religious principles and beliefs. The two essays that follow take dramatically opposite points of views on this significant question.

• • •

1   The question of homosexual marriage presents the American people with an inescapable moral challenge. The words *homosexual* and *marriage* are inherently contradictory. The very fact that these terms are in public conflict demonstrates the radical character of the social revolutionaries that now demand the legalization of homosexual marriage.

2   For at least the last one hundred years, America has experienced an unprecedented season of social transformation. Now, this transformation has been extended to experimentation with the most basic institutions and cherished principles of our common life. A conversation about "homosexual marriage" is only possible if the concept of marriage is completely redefined and severed from its historic roots and organic meaning.

3   Civilization requires the regulation of human sexuality and relationships. No society—ancient or modern—has survived by advocating a *laissez faire* approach to sex and sexual relationships. Every society, no matter how liberal, sanctions some sexual behaviors and proscribes others. Every society establishes some form of sexual norm.

4   Pitirim Sorokin, the founder of sociology at Harvard University, pointed to the regulation of sexuality as the essential first mark of civilization. According to Sorokin, civilization is possible only when marriage is normative and sexual conduct is censured outside of the marital relationship. Furthermore, Sorokin traced the rise and fall of civilizations and concluded that the weakening of marriage was a first sign of civilizational collapse.

5   We should note that Sorokin made these arguments long before anything like homosexual marriage had been openly discussed. Sorokin's insight was the realization that civilization requires men to take responsibility for their offspring. This was possible, he was convinced, only when marriage was held to be the unconditional expectation for sexual activity and procreation. Once individuals—especially males—are freed for sexual behavior outside of marriage,

civilizational collapse becomes an inevitability. The weakening of marriage—even on heterosexual terms—has already brought a harvest of disaster to mothers and children abandoned in the name of sexual liberation.

6   The regulation of sexuality is thus a primary responsibility of any civilization. In their review of Western civilization, Will and Ariel Durant noted that sex is "a river of fire that must be banked and cooled by a hundred restraints." The primary restraint has always been the institution of marriage itself—an institution that is inescapably heterosexual and based in the monogamous union of a man and a woman as husband and wife. In postmodern America, the fires of sex are increasingly unbanked and uncooled.

7   In a very real sense, marriage becomes the civilizational DNA of our social genetic structure. Beyond this, marriage serves as the basic molecular structure for human social organization. Though the family is extended through children and other bonds of kinship, the basic "molecule" of human society is marriage. This molecular reality implies that the structure cannot be changed without destroying the molecule—and the organism—itself.

8   This is precisely the challenge we now face on the issue of what is called homosexual marriage and the legalization of same-sex relationships. The "molecule" of marriage has always defined human relatedness, and this most venerable institution is rooted in its inherent *heterosexuality*.

9   The family has undergone transformations throughout time, but at the core of any enduring family structure stands the integrity of marriage as an institution and the stability of marriage as an expectation both within and without the marital unit. Marriage is always both a private and a public matter, and in Western cultures, it has stood as both a civil and religious institution. As such, it has been recognized as inherently and indisputably *heterosexual.*

10 The unique role of marriage in civilization is rightly attributed to the social value any culture must place on stable long-term monogamous pairings of men and women. The institution of marriage has been invested with both rights and responsibilities directly tied to the social importance of long-term commitment.

11 The heterosexual union of a man and a woman in monogamous marriage is the rightful context for procreation. When reproduction is severed from marriage, the society reaps the breakdown of both kinship and parental responsibility. Put most simply, even secular historians are aware that marriage is what explains why a father remains committed to the care of his own children. Societies that devalue marriage provide an automatic incentive for young males to act irresponsibly, fathering children without ever assuming responsibility as father.

12 Marriage is indispensable for the successful nurture and raising of children. Both boys and girls define themselves and establish their own identity and expectations based upon their observation of both father and mother, husband and wife—male and female.

13 The extension of the family through other kinship relations links one marriage to another, with the entire family finding its identity and security in the integrity of those marital bonds. The breaking of these bonds leads to social dissolution as well massive economic, legal, and psychological ills. The

integrity of marriage is essential for children to know the security necessary for their own self-identity and sense of belonging.

14 The central function of marriage has been reflected in law, custom, and an entire set of practices deeply embedded in the structures of society. These range from implications in the tax code to various legal supports and cultural expectations extended to the married couple. Society invests both rights and responsibilities in the institution of marriage and by its various incentives and disincentives, points towards a cultural expectation. When that expectation is something other than marriage, problems immediately arise.

15 In its own interest, the government must value stability and reward the healthy raising of children and fulfillment of parental responsibility. To this end, the government does discriminate in order to reward and to support marriage as the centerpiece of self-government and the commonweal.

16 Government has within its power the ability to institutionalize its own expectation in the form of laws, regulations, and a cultural approach that either strengthens or weakens the institution of marriage. Just as the tax code discriminates in favor of homeowners (because the government rationally sees homeownership as a common social interest), a set of financial and legal incentives is directed towards a social preference for marriage. In the same way, even as the law protects corporations in order to encourage financial activity, the government also favors marriage (and thus married couples) in order to encourage procreation, childrearing, and cultural stability.

17 Nevertheless, government does not have the right to reorder this most basic institution of human organization. Marriage predates the establishment of government, and any governmental authority that would presume to redefine marriage apart from its inherently heterosexual nature will do so at great peril. Furthermore, advances toward legal recognition of same-sex relationships have been propelled by the action of courts, rather than legislatures. This is another example of the "judicial usurpation of politics" that threatens the integrity of democracy itself. A government that would claim the right to redefine marriage in this way demonstrates an arrogance that would cause Rome to blush and Babylon to quiver.

18 Inevitably, once marriage is redefined as something other than a heterosexual pair, there is nothing to stop further redefinition but sheer arbitrariness. Once marriage is no longer "one thing," but now "another thing" as well, there is nothing to stop marriage from becoming virtually "everything." Put simply, if marriage can be redefined so as to allow same-sex pairings, there is nothing in the logic of this transformation that could justify discrimination against those who would transform marriage in other ways. Why just two people? If the consent of all partners is all that is requisite, why laws against incest, polygamy, or any number of other alternative arrangements? We can be certain that proponents of these transformations will be waiting in line for their turn to use the courts to reverse what they claim to be unlawful discrimination.

19 Marriage has already been weakened to the point of dire social peril. The acceptance of "no-fault" divorce laws, the ethic of sexual liberation, and even the rise of new reproductive technologies have weakened the foundation

and superstructure of marriage to the point that this most basic molecule is hanging together by a thread. The redefinition of marriage in order to accommodate same-sex relationships would not mean the mere transformation of marriage—but its dissolution. The very concept of marriage cannot survive such a denial of its inherent meaning and historic structure.

20   Of course, I speak as a Christian theologian. Based upon divine revelation, I believe and teach that God created man and woman in His image, created us as male and female to His glory, and gave us the institution of marriage for our health, our happiness, and our holiness. Furthermore, based upon this same revelation—the Holy Scriptures—I am absolutely bound to declare the inherent sinfulness of all sexual activity outside of the marital bond. Procreation, reproduction, child-rearing, and other essential rights and functions are divinely invested in the institution of marriage. Thus, to tamper with this divinely-established institution is to risk not only social peril but the divine judgment that will most surely come.

21   Nevertheless, even those who do not share my Christian commitment must recognize the cultural wisdom and historic knowledge that points to the primacy of marriage and the disaster which will befall a society that would weaken—much less destroy—this most precious institution. The historic wisdom of human happiness and moral knowledge points to the centrality of marriage. A review of history proves its necessity to civilization itself. Marriage is a given—and is therefore not infinitely negotiable. Marriage cannot be severed from heterosexuality without dissolving into meaninglessness. Social experimentation must meet some limitation—and the controversy over same-sex marriage presents us with that limitation.

22   Homosexual couples cannot fulfill the functions of marriage. They cannot procreate. Severed from even the possibility of natural procreation, their relationship is inescapably unnatural. Rather than reinforcing heterosexual responsibility and sanctioning heterosexual monogamy, same-sex sexual pairings undermine the very notion of a sexual norm. Acceptance of homosexual marriage flies in the face of both biblical revelation and millennia of accumulated moral wisdom.

23   This nation stands at a dramatic moment of decision. Our stewardship of this question—our decision on the question of same-sex marriage—will determine the future state of our society, the moral status of our culture, the health and well being of our children, and the inheritance we leave to the world. The choice before us is not between two visions of marriage—but between marriage and madness.

- Vocabulary

inescapable (1)	contradictory (1)	unprecedented (2)
redefined (2)	severed (2)	proscribes (3)
norm (3)	censured (4)	procreation (5)
inevitability (5)	monogamous (6)	molecular (7)
venerable (8)	indisputably (9)	dissolution (13)
commonweal (15)	peril (17)	propelled (17)
usurpation (17)	arbitrariness (18)	proponents (18)
dissolution (19)	stewardship (23)	

The Facts

1. According to the author, why are the terms *homosexual* and *marriage* inherently contradictory? Do you agree with this paradox? Why or why not?
2. What does Pitirim Sorokin have to say about the regulation of sexuality? Why would anyone listen to his opinion?
3. According to the essay, how is one marriage linked to another? What happens when the links are broken?
4. According to Mohler, what is the role of government in the debate over homosexual marriage? Do you believe the government has taken this role seriously? Explain your answer.
5. According to Mohler, what are some factors that have already seriously weakened marriage? In your view, who or what has had the worst effect on marriage within the last century?

The Strategies

1. What metaphor did the historians Will and Ariel Durant use to describe sex? What other metaphor might be appropriate?
2. In which paragraph does the author use the terms of modern geneticists? What effect do the terms have?
3. How soon were you able to see on which side of the same-sex marriage debate the author stands?
4. How does the author make the transition from paragraph 16 to paragraph 17?
5. How forceful is the ending of the essay? Analyze its effect on the reader.

The Issues

1. When you respond to the author's argument, what underlying bias in his argument must you consider? Do you agree or disagree with his bias? Explain your answer.
2. Why, for the first time in history, has the issue of same-sex marriage come to dominate religious, social, and political debates? Why did this issue not surface earlier?
3. Do you agree with Sorokin that the regulation of sexuality is necessary in order to prevent the collapse of civilization? What would happen if sexuality were not regulated? Could we still be civilized as long as we remained kind and tolerant toward each other?
4. In paragraph 12, Mohler insists that "marriage is indispensable for the successful nurture and raising of children" because both girls and boys define themselves by observing their fathers and mothers. What is the meaning of this idea? Do you agree with the author? Give examples from your personal experience to either support or refute the author's view.
5. Mohler writes that "homosexual couples cannot fulfill the functions of marriage because they cannot procreate." He feels that their inability to procreate naturally undermines the idea of sexual standards. What do you think will

happen to a society that approves same-sex marriage? Describe how it would function.

- ## Suggestions for Writing
  1. Write a rebuttal to Mohler's essay, establishing your own moral authority and quoting thinkers who reflect your view. Title your essay "The Case for Homosexual Marriage."
  2. Write an essay in which you imagine what it would be like to be the son or daughter of a same-sex couple. You might write this assignment in the form of a diary entry.

Same-Sex Marriage: Just Say No to Prohibition
Susan Block

Susan Block is a sex educator, cultural commentator, and host of the *Dr. Susan Block Show*. The article that follows was reprinted from the February 3, 2005, issue of *Dr. Susan Block's Journal*. Her outspoken articles about the war in Iraq and other cultural issues have won her praise as well as criticism.

At the heart of the essay below is the belief that the American Constitution provides for equal rights to all American citizens, including the right to marry a person of the same sex. It is the point of view taken by most people who support same-sex marriage.

• • •

1   Like many Americans, I grew up learning a "queer" was a criminal, a pervert, or, probably, both. Not that I was taught this directly. I just picked it up from the embarrassment of my elders, the cruelty of my peers, and the writing on the restroom walls.

2   I also learned, like the President, that marriage was a "union between a man and a woman." Like Adam and Eve. There was no Adam and Steve. I didn't see this as a problem. After all, I liked boys. I was so clueless, I didn't know my favorite cousin Brandon and his buddy Jake weren't just "roommates." What I didn't know didn't hurt me . . . at first.

3   In high school, I learned the truth about Brandon and Jake. By then, I could relate to all kinds of love, and considered their relationship "cool." But I couldn't fathom them being married like my parents were married, or like I expected to get married. Nor could I imagine why they'd want to be.

4   Years later, Jake contracted Lou Gehrig's disease. Soon, he could barely move, only capable of communicating with Brandon. Jake's caretakers understood. But in emergencies, paramedics refused Brandon the right to see Jake. Only "immediate family" allowed. That's parents, children, siblings and spouses. No friends. No lovers. No roommates-for-life. When a nurse wouldn't let Brandon see Jake because their 22-year-old relationship lacked a marriage certificate, I realized why everyone needs the right to marry.

5   Of course, there are happier, "gayer" reasons not to prohibit same-sex marriage, like the radiant newlyweds of San Francisco's "Winter of Love." That historic moment, when a courageous mayor gave the right to marry to people who love people of the same sex, ignited acts of romantic civil disobedience reminiscent of Rosa Parks and the Greensboro sit-ins. The comparison isn't perfect. You can't hide your skin color, while you can closet your sexual orientation. Yet there are parallels. Slaves couldn't marry. After emancipation, most states outlawed interracial marriage. Racists called for constitutional amendments prohibiting black-white marriage with the same sanctimony the anti-same-sex-marriage set utilizes today.

6   Both invoke the "sanctity" of marriage. "Gays can't bear children together," same-sex detractors intone. "God commanded, 'Be fruitful and multiply!'" But that was Genesis, when the desert was vast, and the population small. By Ecclesiastes, God wasn't ordering rampant reproduction anymore. By now, the Earth is overpopulated. Couples who marry not to reproduce, but to stabilize their lives and contribute to their communities, should be applauded, not ostracized.

7   What constitutes marital sanctity anyway? Anti-same-sex marriage fundamentalists are free to believe what they like about it. What they shouldn't be free to do is force those beliefs on everyone. America separates Church and State. Individual churches needn't perform same-sex marriages. Individual states needn't recognize them. But our federal government must not discriminate. Our Constitution, always amended to extend human rights, shouldn't take them away. Remember, America's one attempt at Constitutional Prohibition (anti-alcohol) failed miserably.

8   The President calls marriage civilization's "most fundamental institution." But notions of the proper spouse keep changing. In times past, marriage meant holy union between a man and his chattel. Or one husband and multiple wives. Brothers wed sisters in ancient royal families. In Victorian times, 13-year-old brides married 45-year-old grooms.

9   So why not same-sex marriage? The sexes aren't really "opposite." Men aren't from Mars. Women aren't from Venus. We're all from Earth. We all need sex. We all need love. We all need the right to marry.

10   Even hermaphrodites do.

11   Why not just let gays have civil unions? Because, as anti-segregationists have long known, "separate but equal" is never really equal.

12   Do gay weddings threaten straight ones? Perhaps we'll have fewer opposite-sex marriages wherein one spouse is living a lie. My friend Nikki was devastated to learn her husband Mark was having unsafe sex with men. Mark always preferred men, but he wanted to be "normal," so he'd married Nikki. If Mark had the same-sex marriage option, this unhappy hetero union might have been avoided.

13   As for me, I eventually married (a man). Celebrating our 12th anniversary, I think marriage strengthens our love, though who knows? Marriage isn't for everybody. For many, it's a passion-killer, or torture worse than any homophobe could conjure as the hellfire awaiting the queer. Some left-leaning critics

deplore same-sex marriage as "assimilation, not liberation." Maybe so, but everybody should have the right to enjoy, or endure it.

14   With all the same-sex couples getting hitched nowadays, we can expect plenty of same-sex divorces. That, too, should be their right.

- ## Vocabulary

fathom (3)	ignited (5)	emancipation (5)
sanctimony (5)	intone (6)	ostracized (6)
sanctity (7)	chattel (8)	hermaphrodites (10)
homophobe (13)	conjure (13)	

- ## The Facts

    1. Where in the essay does the author reveal her own sexual preference and her opinion of marriage? How does this revelation affect your opinion on same-sex marriage?
    2. What was the author's attitude toward homosexuals as she was growing up? Do you think her attitude is still common among young people today? Or has society changed in its attitude toward homosexuals? Support your answer with examples.
    3. Where did the expression "Just Say No" originate? Does it suit the author's thesis? Explain your answer.
    4. What appalled the author about the emergency and hospital care given to Jake? What is your reaction to what happened?
    5. In paragraph 11, to what other historical prohibition does the author compare the prohibition against same-sex marriage? What is her main point in making the comparison? What is your reaction to her argument?

- ## The Strategies

    1. What is the purpose of Block's autobiographical introduction? Do you consider it useful or irrelevant? Give reasons for your answer.
    2. What is the effect of paragraph 10?
    3. Paragraphs 7, 9, 11, and 12 begin with a question. What is the purpose of these questions? How do they affect the argument of the essay?
    4. What rhetorical strategy does the author use in paragraph 6? Where does she leave the reader at the end of the paragraph?
    5. What ammunition does paragraph 8 add to Block's arsenal to fight arguments that same-sex marriage destroys the sanctity of marriage as it has existed throughout civilization? What is your reaction to this paragraph?

- ## The Issues

    1. After reading Block's argument, what do you think is the major reason why same-sex marriages should be forbidden or allowed legally? What about church weddings? Should they be allowed? Support your answers with the best evidence you can present.

2. What are some of the "gayer" and "happier" reasons for supporting same-sex marriage—other than making it possible for one partner to visit another partner hospitalized with some terminal disease? Which example does Block offer? What other examples can you add?
3. What is the author's answer to the assertion that since homosexuals cannot create children together, they violate the sanctity of God's command to "be fruitful and multiply"? What is your own answer?
4. Since the author herself is heterosexual, what seems to be her main concern in the matter of homosexual marriage? What is your main concern?
5. In paragraph 12, the author asks the question, "Do gay weddings threaten straight ones?" What is her answer to the question? If you have a different answer, what is it?

Suggestions for Writing

1. Write an essay in which you describe our society a decade from now if it were to support same-sex marriage. Focus on such matters as neighborhood social events, school classroom activities, inheritance problems, and church ceremonies. Try to imagine specific details to vivify your essay.
2. Write a rebuttal to Block's essay, refuting her ideas one by one. Entitle your essay "Same-Sex Marriage: Just Say Yes to Prohibition!" Use evidence that is reasonable and accurate.

Stumped by monotonous sentences? Exit on page 694, at the **Editing Booth!**

Punctuation Workshop
Using Other Punctuation with Quotation Marks

1. Periods and commas go inside quotations marks; semicolons and colons go outside.

   "Gilberto," she insisted, "let's do some rope climbing."

   He lectured on "Terrorism in Spain"; I immediately thought of the story "Flight 66": It seemed to follow the lecturer's claims.

2. Question marks, exclamation points, or dashes that apply only to the quoted material go inside the quotation marks. Otherwise, they go outside:

   INSIDE: The Senator asked, "Who will pay for it?"

   OUTSIDE: Which of the senators asked, "Who will pay for it"?

   INSIDE: The crowd shouted, "No more lies!"

   OUTSIDE: Stop playing Bob Marley's "Crazy Baldhead"!

   INSIDE: "Materialism—the greed for things—" insists my father, "is bad."

   OUTSIDE: The article said, "You may be at risk for cancer"—something to think about.

3. Put quotation marks around titles of small works, such as stories, essays, newspaper or magazine articles, poems, songs, and book chapters.

4. Either quotation marks or italics can be used in definitions:

   The word "aquiline" means "related to eagles."

   or

   The word *aquiline* means *related to eagles*.

Will Same-Sex Marriages Change the Constitution?
Adam Winkler, Georgia College & State University

On May 17, 2004, in Cambridge City Hall, Massachusetts became the first state in the United States to grant same-sex couples marriage licenses, leveling the playing field for its gay and lesbian citizens. By granting same-sex couples the same marital rights as heterosexual couples, Massachusetts dismissed the notion that a marriage commitment can only exist between individuals of different sex. It is fitting that Cambridge, across the river from Boston—the city that represents American freedom—was the first city to grant same-sex marriage licenses, thus setting into motion the gradual legitimization of homosexual marriages.

What has followed since then is a state-by-state, federalist sanctioning of homosexual marriage that makes its opponents cringe. In fact, the issue makes people so uneasy that many wish to amend the Constitution. Will we the people really change the Constitution to read that only citizens of heterosexual orientation have the right to life, liberty, and the pursuit of happiness? Such a constitutional change seems on the surface preposterous. Yet this is an issue that polarizes people and inspires fear.

Many people fear that homosexual marriages cheapen or threaten traditional family values. Opponents of homosexual marriage argue that once gay marriage is permitted, same-sex relationships will have a sort of legitimacy that forces the opposition to acknowledge their rights. However, the opposition does not want to acknowledge the rights of these individuals; instead, they want matters to remain legally as they are or for the government to denounce the topic entirely. This is where our society has stood on the subject for the past several decades—stymied in censorship, without civil discourse, and out of the mainstream consciousness. In recent years, however, homosexuals have infiltrated mainstream pop culture in television mini-series and sit-coms, and it is no longer possible to deny their presence.

Families who seek to restrict marriage to traditional heterosexual families defend their position by arguing that they do not want their children to see gay people expressing their affections on picnic blankets in the park, because many think children will get the mistaken idea that homosexuality is merely another option in sexual orientation. Yet, as we know, this sort of interaction between homosexual couples will occur with or without state-sanctioned marriage licenses. Additionally, I do not think that homosexuality is a choice, anymore than I think heterosexuality is a choice. It just is what it is—nothing more, nothing less.

Other opponents of same-sex marriages fear that insurance premiums will go up if employers will have to grant insurance benefits to the spouses of homosexuals, that children will learn about gay marriage in public schools, and that more socially deviant people will become American citizens through the process of homosexual marriages. Indeed, these are all possible dilemmas that must be evaluated through rational civil discourse that removes the blinding hatred of homophobia.

Personally, I do not oppose same-sex marriages. I figure that they will lead to less promiscuity because gay and lesbians will have official marriage contracts and the legal bindings that accompany them. Further, same-sex marriages will more than likely reduce the number of divorces attributed to homosexual men marrying straight women, having children, then coming out of the closet. And if married same-sex couples wish to adopt and rear children, I think that they should be evaluated, scrutinized, and treated the same way as any other compassionate family who seeks to adopt. There is no need to change the Constitution.

How I Write

Like most students, I am very self-conscious about my writing, but it does me more harm than good. To detach myself from what I am writing I often write from points of view other than my own. Sometimes I will start my writing on a napkin or just a scrap piece of paper, because it doesn't count there. If it is good, I will type it out, but I cannot ever start writing by mashing buttons on a keyboard. I always start by using a pen.

How I Wrote This Essay

I wrote this essay from the point of view opposite from my own. I did this to make it challenging and to practice letting go—not allowing my personal feelings to get in the way of my student responsibilities. I sat down and brainstormed a list of pros and cons about same-sex marriages and then I tried to defend the weaker side of the list.

Tips For Writing

Brainstorming is key! I suggest making a big list of ideas that you want to write about: lists, catalogues, pros & cons, etc. . . . Once you have the list it's all about organization, and the paper will write itself from there. Once it's complete, I revise it for language errors and try to make it flow.

● CHAPTER WRITING ASSIGNMENTS

1. Write an essay about your favorite Internet site.
2. Write an imaginative essay that predicts and describes useful gadgets yet to be invented.
3. Who is your favorite actor for playing the "heavy" or a villain in movies? Write an essay on that theme.
4. Write an essay about the job you would least like to have.
5. Write an essay about your favorite board game.

● WRITING ASSIGNMENTS FOR A SPECIFIC AUDIENCE

1. Write to the Internal Revenue Service outlining your expenses for a semester of school.
2. Explain baseball to a foreigner who has never heard of the game.

● COLLABORATIVE WRITING PROJECT

Get together with five or six students who hold different views about the separation of church and state. Discuss your positions and make a note of the differences of opinion. Then write a report to the class suggesting a compromise that could be worked out to the satisfaction of both sides.

● IMAGE GALLERY WRITING ASSIGNMENT

Visit pages 676–678 of our image gallery and study all three images dealing with same-sex marriage. Then choose the image that most appeals to you. Answer the questions and do the writing assignment.

TERRORISM

● STUDYING THE IMAGE

1. What underlying contradiction do you see in this image? What feelings does it evoke in you?
2. What is the effect of the mask worn by the terrorist? Why is the mask black?
3. What stereotype of terrorism does the photo suggest?
4. How do you think a law-abiding, devout Muslim would feel about this photo? How would you react if you were a Muslim?

● WRITING ASSIGNMENT

Write an essay in which you point out the perils of a religious sect that calls for the elimination of innocent citizens believed to be "infidels."

648   IMAGE GALLERY

Bombed bus in London, England, after a terrorist attack on July 7, 2005.

● STUDYING THE IMAGE

1. What one word would you use to describe this scene?
2. What story do the ruins of the bus tell about any passengers who might have been sitting on the upper deck?
3. What is the effect of showing the scene without any people present?
4. What title would you give to this picture?

● WRITING ASSIGNMENT

Write an essay describing this scene and explaining how viewing it made you feel.

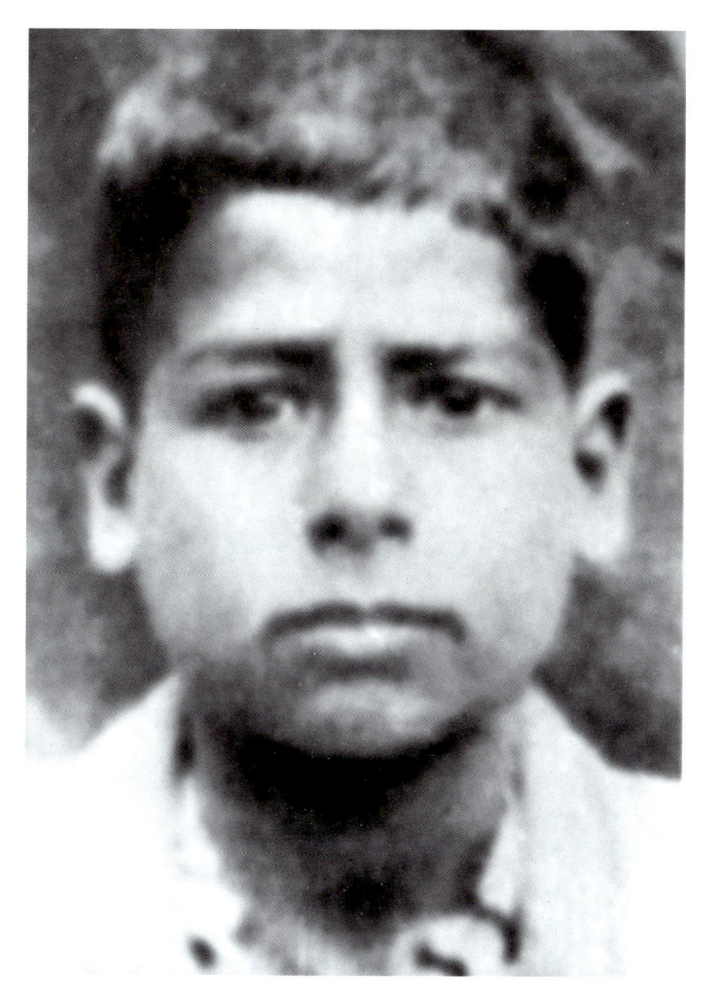

Former Iraqi leader Saddam Hussein as a young boy.

- **STUDYING THE IMAGE**
1. How old would you guess Saddam Hussein to be in this photo?
2. What do the boy's eyes communicate? What is your reaction to these eyes?
3. How would a smile change this portrait?
4. How do you react to knowing that this boy was destined to become a ruthless dictator?

- **WRITING ASSIGNMENT**

Using this photo as your source, write an essay that explores the meaning of innocence.

BODY IMAGE

● STUDYING THE IMAGES

1. What do the two figures share in common? Why do you suppose anyone would want to be so muscle-bound?
2. Explain the symbolism of the woman standing on the world and looking toward the moon.
3. As the male flexes his muscles, his face remains expressionless. Why do you think his face is so deadpan?
4. Does either of these images fit your ideal of the male and female bodies? Why or why not?
5. What do you think is the attitude of society toward female bodybuilders? What is your opinion of muscular women?

● WRITING ASSIGNMENT

Write an essay in which you describe how to achieve and maintain the kind of body you personally admire.

Body Image   651

Before and after photos of socialite Jocelyn Wildenstein.

● STUDYING THE IMAGES

1. The newspaper gossip is that Jocelyn Wildenstein wanted plastic surgery that would make her look more like a cat or panther. How well did she succeed based on the above images?
2. Before her plastic surgery, Wildenstein looked like her little boy, but after her surgery, the resemblance faded. Does the loss seem important, or was the result of the surgery more important than family resemblance?
3. Why do you think people put themselves through the painful process of radical makeovers? What goal do they hope to achieve?
4. What alternatives to plastic surgery have been suggested by beauty experts? Under what circumstances is plastic surgery ever strongly suggested?

● WRITING ASSIGNMENT

It is a common belief that women are more likely to resort to plastic surgery than men are. Write an essay in which you explore the reasons why.

Singer Carnie Wilson before and after her gastric by-pass surgery to help her lose weight.

● STUDYING THE IMAGES

1. Carnie Wilson, daughter of Beach Boy Brian Wilson, spent most of her life struggling with being overweight. In August 1999, weighing nearly 300 pounds, she underwent gastric by-pass surgery, losing 150 pounds and almost 20 dress sizes. What adjective or adjectives might you use to describe her transformation?

2. What is the nature of gastric by-pass surgery? What changes does it make in a person's intake and absorption of food? Use the Internet to find answers to these questions.

3. Carnie Wilson struggled with being overweight most of her life and became a sort of "poster child" for gastric by-pass surgery. What is your opinion of taking such drastic measures to lose weight? Under what circumstances do you think such radical surgery is justified?

4. Why do you think people are willing to risk their lives to be thin? How much do societal pressures to be thin play into a person's decision to have the surgery?

● WRITING ASSIGNMENT

After researching gastric by-pass surgery on the Internet, write an essay in which you cite the possible losses as well as rewards connected with this modern operation. Use examples to help your reader understand why certain people are willing to undergo such a drastic alteration.

AGEISM

● **STUDYING THE IMAGE**

1. How would you characterize the mood of the dancing couple? What does this photo imply about aging?
2. What strong but rather predictable contrast exists between the man and the woman dancing? (*Hint:* Look at their grooming.) Which one looks younger to you? Why?
3. Judging by her jewelry, his shirt, and the general appearance of the couple, to what level of society do you think they belong? How do you think social class affects people in their old age?
4. How do you feel about people who try desperately to look younger than they really are? How do you think you will feel when you grow old?

● **WRITING ASSIGNMENT**

Write an essay using this couple as an example of how getting older does not have to stifle all the fun in life. You might add examples of elderly acquaintances in your life who are still active traveling, attending concerts, or throwing parties.

● STUDYING THE IMAGE

1. Which details in the portrait indicate that the woman is quite old?
2. How would you describe this woman? Do you see beauty in her face? Why or why not?
3. Do you find the portrait depressing or reassuring? What are the reassuring as well as depressing elements?
4. What is your attitude toward old people? Do you take time to visit with them, or do you find them irrelevant to your life? What valuable lessons, if any, can we all learn from the old?

● WRITING ASSIGNMENT

Using your imagination, write a brief biographical sketch of this woman's life, describing her work, her philosophy or religion, and her outlook on her present condition. Your sketch should reflect your personal opinion of the kind of woman you see portrayed.

● **STUDYING THE IMAGE**

1. Ponder the advantages the older physician might have over the younger ones surrounding him, but think also about some possible disadvantages. Which side do you think outweighs the other?
2. Would you trust an older physician like the one in the image? Why or why not?
3. Why do you think older people often want to continue to work? Do you think it is strictly economic necessity that motivates them? Are there other rewards that come from working?
4. Some observers of the job market say that companies are going out of their way to hire older workers. What do you think is the rationale for this trend? What do you think older workers bring to the table that younger ones do not?

● **WRITING ASSIGNMENT**

Write an essay arguing that mandatory retirement at the age of 65 is not necessarily a positive factor for our communities. Or, if you prefer, argue that mandatory retirement at age 65 is appropriate.

656   IMAGE GALLERY

DRUG ABUSE

● STUDYING THE IMAGE

1. What details make this image of a five-year-old girl peering over a drug-filled ashtray so sad and haunting?
2. According to the original caption of this photograph, the little girl had had an argument with her mother before heading to the ashtray. Why do you think the little girl did this?
3. What kinds of drugs appear to be in the ashtray? What might this indicate about the lifestyle of her parent(s)? What might this indicate about the kind of life this little girl lives?
4. What future problems might this child encounter due to the environment in which she grew up?

● WRITING ASSIGNMENT

Write an essay in which you argue for the protection of children whose parents commonly use drugs. What role should the government play in this matter? What remedial action do you recommend? A little research on the Internet about children and drug abuse may be helpful in fulfilling this writing assignment. See what the experts say about this issue.

Drug Abuse 657

- **STUDYING THE IMAGE**

1. Spend several minutes just looking at these cadaverous figures, examining all the details on the canvas. Pay attention to color, line, and perspective. As a symbolic representation of what drugs do, how would you personally interpret the two figures?
2. What difference do you see between the figure in the foreground and the one behind him? What meaning do you attribute to the shadow figure?
3. Where are these two figures? What does the setting contribute to the impact of the painting?
4. What would be an appropriate title for the painting? How would you sum up the theme of the painting?

- **WRITING ASSIGNMENT**

Develop an essay based on the following thesis, derived from the painting: "Death is the ultimate drug seducer."

● STUDYING THE IMAGE

1. With so much public information in the media about the dangers of smoking, what do you think motivates young children to smoke?
2. As you study the expressions on the faces of these young boys, what do you think the one offering the cigarette is telling the other boy? What does the other boy's facial expression tell you about his thoughts? Do you think he will accept or reject the cigarette offered him?
3. What role do grownups play in the upsurge or prevention of youthful smoking?
4. Experts agree that smoking for the beginner is a harsh and unpleasant experience to which the body violently reacts. Why do people persist in smoking in spite of the initial unpleasantness? Do you think that cigarettes are a drug? Why or why not?

● WRITING ASSIGNMENT

Various commercials and ad campaigns have tried to persuade children not to pick up smoking, but with only marginal success. Write an essay in which you discuss an appeal to children not to smoke that is likely to work. How would you word such an appeal? What facts and specific details would you bring up? Personalize your appeal by directing it to a specific child that you know.

IMMIGRATION

Illegal immigrants climbing over a wall at sunset to get into the United States.

● STUDYING THE IMAGE

1. What makes this image seem almost unreal?
2. How does the picture preserve the anonymity of the illegal immigrants? Why?
3. How do you personally regard these men? Be specific in whether you view them as law-breakers, a good source of labor, unwanted intruders, or otherwise.
4. Aside from providing the United States with a source of manual labor, what other good do illegal immigrants contribute to American society? Think of the intangibles that such men and women bring to the culture.

● WRITING ASSIGNMENT

Write an essay in which you explain the causes that lead certain people to risk their lives to enter the United States. Try to keep your personal biases out of the essay.

Early immigrants entering the United States through Ellis Island.

● STUDYING THE IMAGE

1. What general impression of these immigrants does this old photo give?
2. Why do all the immigrants, even the children, seem glum? Why is there no frivolity along the line?
3. Contrast the placidity of this scene with the frantic depiction of the illegal immigrants climbing the wall that blocks them from entry into the United States. What differences can you see between the people shown here and those climbing over the wall? What part do you think racial differences play in the society's attitude toward the two groups?
4. Where is Ellis Island? What reputation does it have in its treatment of immigrants?

● WRITING ASSIGNMENT

Write an essay comparing and contrasting the Ellis Island immigrants with the illegal immigrants entering our country today. Consider such differences as their countries' histories, ethnic differences, and levels of poverty.

● **STUDYING THE IMAGE**

1. Up to 95% of the children available for adoption in China are girls. Why do you think this is? (If you don't know, do a quick online search for the answer.)

2. With thousands of children in the United States waiting to be adopted, why do you think individuals and families go outside the United States to adopt? Do you agree or disagree with this choice?

3. What is your opinion of interracial adoptions? What difficulties do participants in such adoptions face?

4. Looking again at the image above, what is the significance of the little girl's cheongsam and how does it relate to the American flag?

● **WRITING ASSIGNMENT**

Write an essay in which you state your feelings about parents who choose to adopt children from China, Russia, or other foreign countries. Try to be fair in your evaluation of the rewards or hardships of such an adoption, taking into account the parents, the adopted child, and the community.

662 IMAGE GALLERY

THE EXISTENCE OF GOD

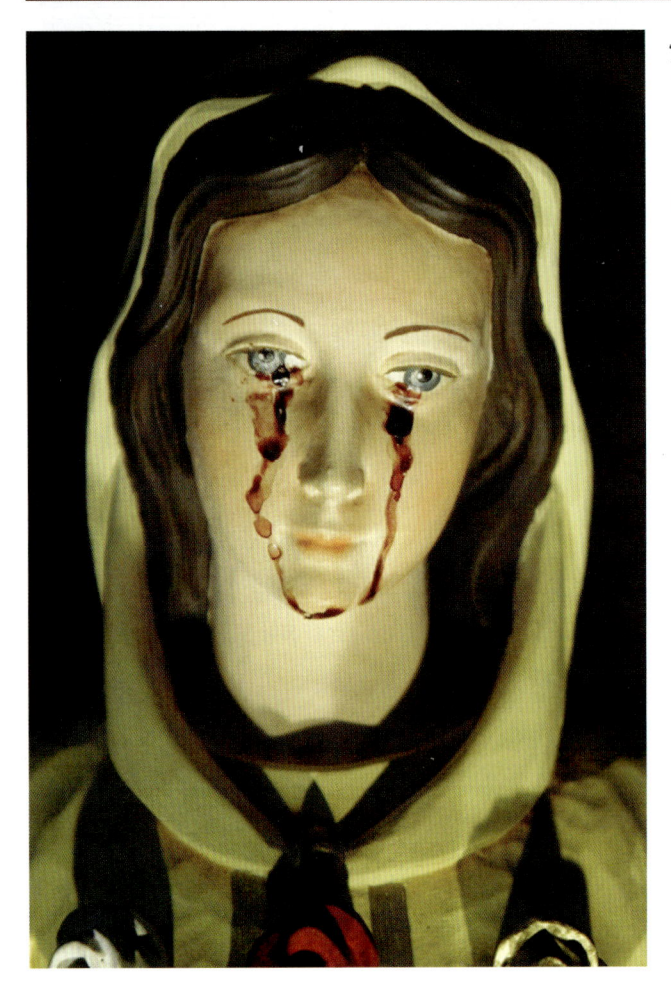

Statue of a weeping Virgin Mary.

● STUDYING THE IMAGE

1. The presence of apparent bloody tears on the face of this statue of the Virgin Mary was hailed by some as a miracle. What is your opinion? What other explanation can be given?

2. Which details of the statue make it physically appealing? What effect would the tears have if the Virgin were old and worn-looking?

3. What role does the Virgin Mary play in the lives of people who believe in her miraculous conception and virgin birth? What do you think is the value of such beliefs to them?

4. What consolation does a belief in the world of science and nature offer the nonreligious believer?

● WRITING ASSIGNMENT

Write an essay about how the belief in Mary, the mother of Jesus, is comforting and fortifying. Or, write an essay in which you put in plain words what comforts you most when disaster hits. Or, write an essay giving examples of a miracle you have witnessed.

The Existence of God   663

Abraham ready to fulfill God's command to offer up his beloved son, Isaac, as a sacrifice.

● **STUDYING THE IMAGE**

1. Why is Abraham looking up? What is he expecting? What do the golden rays mean? From where do they come?

2. What expressions are on the face of Abraham and on that of Isaac? What do these expressions add to the depiction of the moment?

3. What other details in the painting seem important? Explain them as you understand them. Consider such details as the boiling pot, the ram in the thicket, the altar, and Isaac's pose.

4. How do you imagine modern psychology would view the story of Abraham and Isaac? What conflicts do you see between the Holy Scriptures and the teachings of psychology?

● **WRITING ASSIGNMENT**

The biblical story of Abraham's willingness to sacrifice his own son when God asked him to do so has been a source of deep faith for some readers, but a source of revulsion for others. Many theologians have seen this story as pointing forward to another great sacrificial son, Jesus Christ, the Son of God. Others have interpreted it as a lesson in faith, yet others have judged it an incomprehensible myth. Review this story in the book of Genesis, Chapter 22, and then write an essay about what role, if any, faith should play in human life. You do not need to get into complex theological explications. Just write from your own experience and wisdom.

664 IMAGE GALLERY

The Crystal Cathedral in Garden Grove, California.

● STUDYING THE IMAGE

1. Based strictly on appearances, what would you think this building is? Would you think it was a church? Why or why not?
2. In the Middle Ages, the beautiful gothic or baroque churches were paid for by indulgences (church members paying to make sure that their dead relatives went to heaven, not hell). Who do you think pays for modern churches like the one shown?
3. What is your conception of God? How does God benefit from being worshiped in a splendid environment? Do you agree with this or not? Why or why not?
4. What feelings does the Crystal Cathedral evoke in you? Is it conducive to reverence, spirituality, holiness, and intimacy with other worshipers? Or does it seem vast, impersonal, and cold?

● WRITING ASSIGNMENT

Write a vivid description of an ideal place of worship or meditation. Be sure to describe the setting, the size of the place, and its look. Consider also the type of worship it would encourage.

Racism **665**

RACISM

Old ink sketch of black woman on auction block, being sold as a slave.

● STUDYING THE IMAGE

1. How do you think this picture would make you feel if you were the member of a race for whom enslavement, as depicted in this scene, is a historical truth? If your ancestors were once slaves, how do you react to this picture?
2. What do you think the woman to whom the child clings for help is feeling? What does her body language reveal?
3. Many Southern white women insisted that house slaves were often treated like family members. Based on the cruelty implicit in this picture, what is your opinion of that assertion?
4. What effect might a history of enslavement have on the descendents of slaves? How do you feel about the proposal that is occasionally brought up to pay financial reparations to those whose ancestors were once slaves?
5. Why are there no Southern white women in this sketch?

● WRITING ASSIGNMENT

Write an essay on the proposal to pay reparations to the descendents of slaves in the United States. Take a position for or against the proposal and explain the reasons behind your stand. You may need to do a little research on this topic in order to strengthen your assertions.

Painting by Norman Rockwell of Ruby Bridges, the first girl to attend a desegregated school in New Orleans, Louisiana, over the objections of whites, first published in Look *magazine in 1964.*

- **STUDYING THE IMAGE**

1. This painting, by one of America's most beloved artists who is known for his realistic but patriotic depiction of people and events, offended vast numbers of people when it was first published. What do you think so many people who had formerly admired Rockwell's work found offensive in this painting?
2. Who are the men accompanying Ruby Bridges? Why are they headless? What point is made by not showing their heads?
3. From her body language, how would you describe the attitude of the little girl? What is special about her looks?
4. Does the painting support, oppose, or remain neutral to desegregation? What evidence can you cite from the painting itself to support your answer?
5. Depending on your answer to the previous question, what apt title can you think of for this painting?

- **WRITING ASSIGNMENT**

Write an essay in which you analyze the effects on society of segregated public schools. Do not be afraid to take a stand on the issue. Ask yourself what segregation did to blacks and other minorities and what advantages are offered by public schools that encourage ethnic variety.

Racism   667

● STUDYING THE IMAGE

1. Given the participants in the attack on New York and Washington, D.C., on September 11, 2001, how do you think the police would feel about an obviously Middle Eastern passenger who wears a turban at an airport?
2. What argument can you make in favor of racial profiling? What argument can you make against it?
3. What does the picture imply will be the next move of the police? Would a thorough search of this man be justified? Why or why not?
4. How would you feel if you had a turbaned passenger as a seatmate aboard an airplane?

● WRITING ASSIGNMENT

Write an essay about our government's use of racial profiling. Is this practice appropriate considering the political climate of today? Is it constitutional? Take a position for or against racial profiling.

● STUDYING THE IMAGE

1. The tragedy of the September 11, 2001, along with other terrorist suicide bombings committed by Middle Eastern men, have made many US citizens fearful of any male who looks Arabic. How can this fear lead to racism?
2. If a particular race of people are associated with a campaign of terrorism, why is it racism if the authorities targeted those people for special scrutiny? What can the authorities do?
3. What facial traits might make this male suspect? When does this suspiciousness pass the boundary of common sense and become racist?
4. If you looked Middle Eastern, what steps would you take to allay the fears of the public that you might be a terrorist?

● WRITING ASSIGNMENT

Write an essay exploring the racial prejudices—subtle or blatant—that exist among you, members of your family, and your friends. If you feel you have no prejudices, write how you have been able to avoid these feelings.

STATUS OF WOMEN

Susan B. Anthony (1820–1906)

Harriet Tubman (1820–1913)

Eleanor Roosevelt (1884–1962)

Rosa Parks (1913–2005)

- **STUDYING THE IMAGES**

1. Susan B. Anthony was a leader in the women's suffrage movement. How has the right to vote changed the status of women in the United States?

2. Harriet Tubman was a runaway slave who led more than 300 slaves to freedom during the American Civil War. How much did the abolitionist movement help the civil rights cause?

3. Eleanor Roosevelt, the wife of US President Franklin Delano Roosevelt, was a social activist. Should a first lady remain in the background while her husband is in office or involve herself in her favorite causes?

4. Rosa Parks inspired the black civil rights movement by refusing to give up her seat to a white man on a bus in 1955, as was the law in Alabama. How much courage did this take? Was the result worth the rebellion?

- **WRITING ASSIGNMENT**

Do the necessary research then write an essay on woman leaders who through their exemplary performance have opened leadership doors to others of their gender.

670   IMAGE GALLERY

● **STUDYING THE IMAGE**

1. In which part of the world do you think this photo was taken? What clues of the woman's origin does the image provide?
2. Where do you think the woman is headed? What might she be carrying in the basket on her head?
3. What does the picture suggest about the lifestyle of this woman?
4. How does this woman measure up to your expectations of femininity? Explain your answer.

● **WRITING ASSIGNMENT**

Write an essay proposing what we in the United States can do to promote better working conditions among the women in third-world countries. Consider such organizations as the United Nations, the Red Cross, and certain international religious institutions.

Status of Women 671

● **STUDYING THE IMAGE**

1. What is your reaction to seeing these women dressed in burkhas?
2. In what country might they live? For what reason do you think they are wearing burkhas? (If you are not sure, do an Internet search of the word *burkha*.)
3. If you could see the expressions on the women's faces, what emotions would they reveal? Joy or sadness? Determination or humility?
4. How would you deal with a government that would force you to wear clothing that totally hides your body?

● **WRITING ASSIGNMENT**

Write a letter to one of the women in the photo, telling her just how you feel about the way she is forced to hide her identity whenever she appears in public.

● STUDYING THE IMAGE

1. Under what circumstances do you think it appropriate for a woman to take her baby to work with her? How long do you think the mother should be allowed to do that? At what point would she need to find a caregiver for the baby?
2. How would you have reacted if the parent taking a baby to work had been a father? Why is that more, or less, appropriate?
3. What do this woman's looks tell you about her work? What kind of job do you think she has?
4. What alternative plan can women who must work use to assure good care for their children?

● WRITING ASSIGNMENT

Write an essay either defending or attacking the idea of women taking their children to work with them. Try to see the issue from both the employer's and the worker's point of view.

HOMELESSNESS

● **STUDYING THE IMAGE**

1. What title would you give this photo if it were to appear on a city poster?
2. What are some contrasts between the beggar and the passersby? How would you sum up the expression in the face of the first woman passing by?
3. In what geographic areas do you think this scene is typical? What are the conditions that lead to such a scene? Who is responsible?
4. What is the gender of the homeless beggar? How does knowing that affect your response to the picture?

● **WRITING ASSIGNMENT**

Nearly all of us have either passed, or had casual encounters with, homeless people. Write an essay describing the homeless person and saying how he or she made you feel.

Victims of Hurricane Katrina in Louisiana being evacuated by buses, September 2005.

● STUDYING THE IMAGE

1. What is the dominant impression of this photo? Study the details of garbage strewn about, cots piled with goods and people, and the apparent lack of organization.
2. After Hurricane Katrina had leveled whole neighborhoods in New Orleans and the surrounding area, various government and relief agencies were accused of being slow to respond to the devastation because most of the victims were poor and black. What is your opinion of this accusation?
3. What irony exists in the American flag being used to shade one evacuee?
4. Should people made homeless by a catastrophic hurricane be regarded with greater sympathy than those who are homeless because of economic conditions? What role should blame or cause have to do with whether or not we extend help to the homeless?

● WRITING ASSIGNMENT

Write an essay about the "new homelessness" due to a major natural disaster. Compare and contrast the plight of these homeless people with the plight of war refugees. In either case, state what society can do to help.

Homelessness

● STUDYING THE IMAGE

1. How can a sympathetic bystander tell whether this family is really in financial distress or simply trying to make some easy money?
2. What economic or social problems can actually cause a family to become destitute and unable to cope?
3. How do you feel about the child in the picture? Why would some authorities interpret the child's presence as a form of abuse?
4. Which details in the picture reveal that the family is not completely deprived? What arguments can you give to urge someone to help this family? What arguments can you give that this is probably a hoax?

● WRITING ASSIGNMENT

Write an essay in which you propose a way other than legislation to assure that no family in our country is forced to sit outdoors and beg for food to survive. Consider the backing of personal charities, churches, community clubs, and the like. If you do not believe in helping the poor, then explain your position.

676   IMAGE GALLERY

SAME-SEX MARRIAGE

● **STUDYING THE IMAGE**

1. What formalities of a traditional marriage ceremony does this picture contain? Why are these formalities important to what's happening?
2. Is the sex of the minister significant? Would a male minister change the way you view the scene?
3. How would you characterize the facial expressions of the two men being married? How do they differ from the expressions one would expect to find in a photo of a heterosexual marriage ceremony?
4. How old do you guess these men to be? Does their age make any difference in your evaluation of what they are doing?

● **WRITING ASSIGNMENT**

Write an essay in which you indicate what a church marriage ceremony should be and what it means to the community. You may support your view with quotations from sources you trust or admire.

● STUDYING THE IMAGE

1. What is your personal reaction to the men in this picture? Do you find them reasonable or irrational? What authority do they quote? Why?
2. What detail in the background gives you a clue as to where these men are standing? What advantage does their choice of gathering place have?
3. What is the purpose of the white masks?
4. What is your reaction to the question posed in the left-hand posters?

● WRITING ASSIGNMENT

Write an essay either defending or attacking these men's approach to the problem of homosexuality. Ask yourself what might result from this kind of public protest.

678   IMAGE GALLERY

Steven Lofton and Roger Croteau and their five foster children, whom the State of Florida forbids them to adopt.

- **STUDYING THE IMAGE**

1. Steven Lofton, 44, and Roger Croteau, 46, have taken in five foster children who were HIV positive. Even though no one else wanted the children, who have never known another home, when the two gay men tried to adopt them, the State of Florida said "no" because of a statewide ban against adoption by gay couples. As you look at this large family, with its diverse makeup, what reaction do you have toward the ban that will keep these children from being adopted by the only parents they have ever had?

2. What arguments do some people make against gay men becoming adopted parents? What is your own opinion?

3. Bert, the 10-year-old foster son, is being put up for adoption because he is no longer HIV positive and is thus deemed "adoptable." How fair is it to take him out of the home in which he feels secure and force him to live with new parents whom he neither knows or loves?

4. Would your attitude toward gay adoption be different if science were able to prove that homosexuality is an inheritance from nature? Why or why not?

- **WRITING ASSIGNMENT**

Write an essay in which you take a strong stand either for or against allowing Steven Lofton and Roger Croteau to adopt the five children whom they have parented since the children were little. To get a better understanding of this Florida adoption case, check the following Web site: <lethimstay.com/loftons.html>.

PART THREE
Rewriting Your Writing

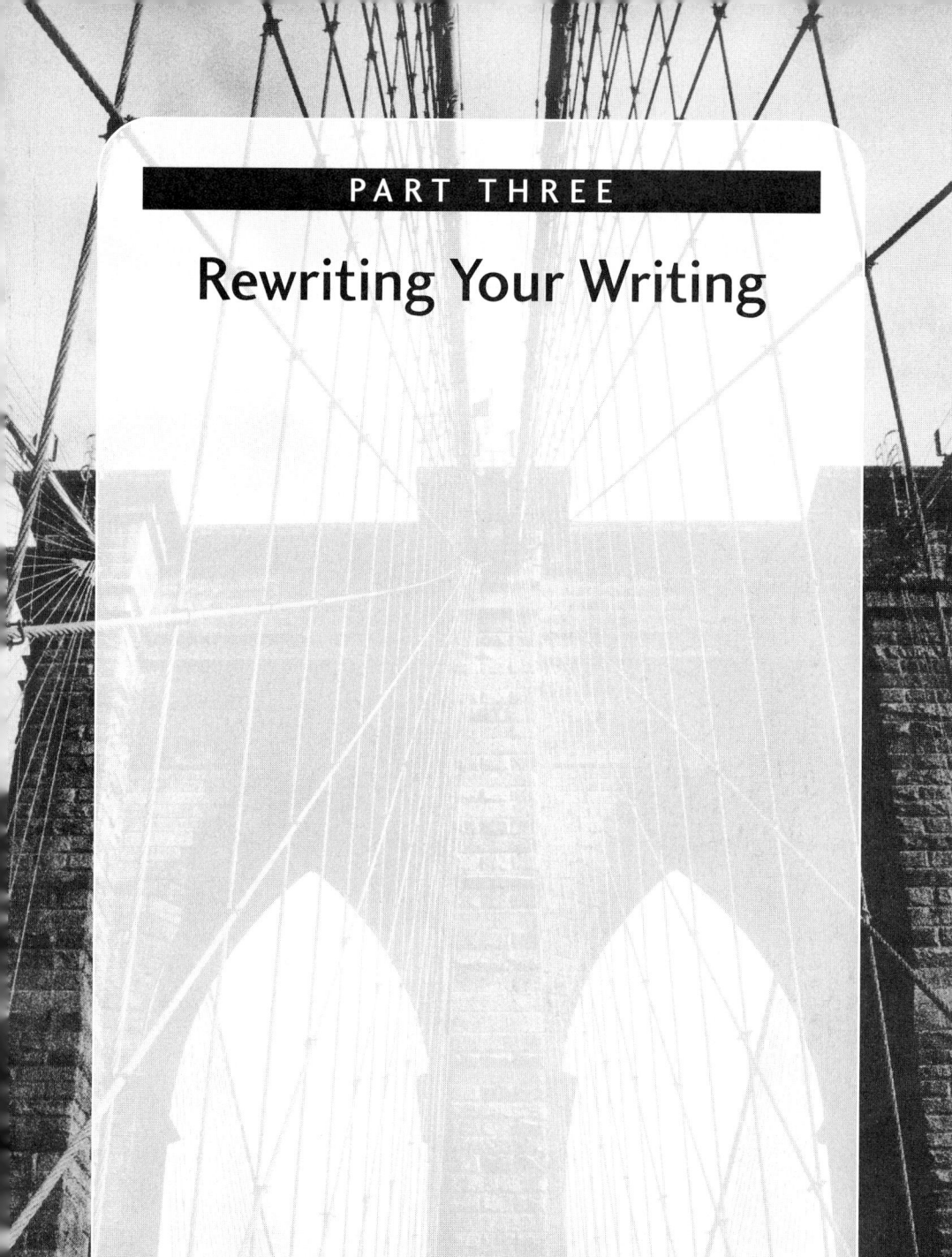

The Editing Booth

Inside the Editing Booth, you will find information on the following topics:

Revising

Editing

    Rule 1: Make Your Title Descriptive
    Rule 2: Begin with a Simple Sentence
    Rule 3: Prune Deadwood
    Rule 4: Do Not Overexplain
    Rule 5: Be Specific
    Rule 6: Avoid Trite Expressions
    Rule 7: Use the Active Voice
    Rule 8: Make Your Statements Positive
    Rule 9: Keep to One Tense
    Rule 10: Place Key Words at the Beginning or End of a Sentence
    Rule 11: Prune Multiple *Of*'s
    Rule 12: Break Up Noun Clusters
    Rule 13: Use Exclamation Points Sparingly
    Rule 14: Vary Your Sentences
    Rule 15: Keep Your Point of View Consistent
    Rule 16: Use Standard Words
    Rule 17: End with Impact

    Revising is part of writing. Few writers are so expert that they can produce what they are after on the first try.

                                      —William Strunk, Jr., and E. B. White

    Rewriting is a necessary part of the composing process. That a writer's best comes gushing out spontaneously at the first and only sitting is true only in some rare instances. Most of the time, it must be coaxed out of the pen, drop by drop (or the computer, keystroke by keystroke), by labored rereading and rewriting. Rewriting means reviewing what you have written and making changes to your text. These steps may be broadly classified as revising and editing.

Revising literally means "seeing again." You take a second look at your paragraphs, sentences, and words and change them until they express your intended meaning. You make major changes to the essay's structure, sentences, and paragraphs. You are trying to stick to a thesis, present evidence in a logical order, and project a tone appropriate to your audience. Accomplishing any of these three tasks may require you to move or insert paragraphs, cut out sentences, add transitions, rewrite your essay's beginning or ending, or even do more research.

Editing, on the other hand, means focusing your rewriting efforts mainly on individual words and sentences. It entails making small changes to the text, often with an eye to improving syntax and overall smoothness. It means choosing a better synonym, correcting a misspelling, inventing a sharper image, improving punctuation, conforming to a specific format, and pruning unnecessary words or phrases.

Both revising and editing are important parts of any rewriting effort. And although it is true that revising usually comes before editing, even this sequence does not necessarily always apply. You may find yourself making small changes to individual words and sentences when you go over your text the first time. On a second reading, you may find an obvious defect missed earlier, causing you to make major changes in the material. As with writing, rewriting is hard to segment into absolute steps.

REVISING

Essential to all rewriting is careful and purposeful rereading. You reread your work with an eye on its intended audience and overall purpose. As you reread what you have written, you ask yourself whether your audience is likely to understand it. You ask yourself whether this paragraph, sentence, or word is appropriate, whether this passage makes your views emphatic and plain. You read with pen in hand or fingers on the keyboard, slashing away here and there, scribbling in the margins, striking out and rewriting some sentences. And as you progress through multiple rereadings, your text will gradually begin to get better.

But the key is rereading, and its importance to a writer cannot be overstated. If you wish to write well, you must be willing to reread your work constantly. You must reread it not only when it is done, but also while you are doing it. If you should even become temporarily stuck—and virtually every writer occasionally does—don't stare vacantly into space or at the ceiling. Reread your work from the beginning. If no new ideas occur to you and you're still stuck, reread your work again. Sooner or later you will see where your text made a lurch in the wrong direction and be able to correct it.

Writing and rewriting are part of the recursive pattern of composing. Some revising to your rough plan or purpose will take place in your head even before you have scribbled a first draft. But most will occur immediately after or during the act of composition. You will set down a sentence or two on the page, glance at it, and see a way to make it better. Or you will write a paragraph, begin another and become stuck, then go back to the first and insert some details or transitional material. Regardless of your personal method of composing, once you have finished your first draft, you should begin the formal process of revising by rereading it. As an example of what we mean by revising, consider the following student paper in its first draft. The writer was asked to indicate through marginal comments the changes she proposed to make. Since this section emphasizes revising, as opposed to editing, we have corrected the errors that would have been caught in the editing process and have left only those that could be improved through revising. In the next part of this chapter, we shall stress editing.

The Exploitation of Endangered Wildlife

The fascination with endangered wildlife within the affluent nations of the world increases the market for illegal poaching and exporting of wildlife goods. Wildlife is big business. Exotic-bird collectors will pay as much as $10,000 for a hyacinth macaw. At Saks Fifth Avenue in New York a pair of cowboy boots, trimmed in lizard skin, will sell for $900. A Christian Dior coat, made from only the belly fur of 17 lynx cats, will cost a staggering $100,000. These are rather mild examples of what is being done with animals stolen from wildlife retreats across the world.

[Move to end of paragraph.]
[For stronger opening, begin here.]

Of course, it's not that anyone cares if people spend their thousands on nonessentials. Instead, the act of murdering innocent and lovely animals for vanity's sake is an irreversible and despicable crime. For example, the baby seals, so prized for their exquisitely soft furs, are repeatedly beaten over the head with heavy clubs until they lie spread out on the ground, unconscious. To the poachers who routinely do the butchering, death is not relevant to this ugly scenario, nor are humane methods of killing. All they care about is the blood money extracted from the skins of these helpless little creatures. Another example is the thousands of wild birds imported live from Brazil and Australia. Since these countries have laws banning such exports, each cage of birds is smuggled aboard the smugglers' boat and has a weight attached to it. In case of being spotted by some police official, the cages can easily be thrown overboard, and no implicating evidence will remain. Still another species of endangered wildlife being exploited is the elephant. Investigators have found as many as twenty of these enormous pachyderms, gunned down with

[Delete: adds nothing. Is too informal.]
[More commentary needed here. Add a transition.]
[of...]
[How often? For what purpose?]
[Where? Add detail.]

automatic weapons or shot with poison darts, lying close together as if they were victims of some cruel genocide. Their tusks have been carved from their heads and carried away, leaving the bloody carcasses to rot and waste away on the plains.

The irreversible effect of this illegal murdering could <u>mean</u> the extinction of many exotic wildlife species. In the 17th century, 13,200 species of mammals and birds were known, but today more than 130 species have gone. An estimated 240 more are considered seriously endangered. Almost all of the cases can be traced to human activity.

It's not because we needed these animals for food, nor because their unique traits could help us find cures for diseases, nor because killing them taught us anything relevant, except that perhaps when they are gone forever, taking with them their natural mystery, beauty, and grace, then we may learn how ignorant we have been.

Be more direct.

Add a transition.

Rewrite to make stronger appeal to reader's sense of fair play. Make more coherent.

Following is the revised version of the first draft:

The Exploitation of Endangered Wildlife

Wildlife is big business. Exotic-bird collectors will pay as much as $10,000 for a hyacinth macaw. At Saks Fifth Avenue in New York a pair of cowboy boots, trimmed in lizard skin, will sell for $900. A Christian Dior coat, made from only the belly fur of 17 lynx cats, will cost a staggering $100,000. These are rather mild examples of what is being done with animals stolen from wildlife retreats across the world. The fascination with endangered wildlife within the affluent nations of the world increases the market for illegal poaching and exporting of wildlife goods.

The act of murdering innocent and lovely animals for vanity's sake is an irreversible and despicable crime. It is a way of saying that animals have no feelings and that human beings have the right to plunder and kill the lower orders if doing so will enhance the human lifestyle. For example, the baby seals, so prized for their exquisitely soft furs, are repeatedly beaten over the head with heavy clubs until they lie spread out on the ground, unconscious. To the poachers who routinely do the butchering, death is not relevant to this ugly scenario, nor are humane methods of killing. All they care about is the blood money extracted from the skins of these helpless little creatures. Another example of this savage and unnecessary rape is the thousands of wild birds imported yearly live from Brazil and Australia—to end up either in cages gracing the living rooms of tycoons who like to collect birds, or as ornaments on sweaters and hats of rich and fashion-conscious women. But since most countries have laws banning such exports, each cage of birds is smuggled aboard the smugglers' boat and has a weight attached to it. In case of being spotted by some police official, the cages can easily be thrown overboard, and no implicating evidence will remain. Still another species of endangered wildlife being exploited is the elephant. Investigators in West Africa have found as many as twenty of these enormous pachyderms, gunned down with automatic weapons or shot with poison darts, lying close together as if they were victims of some cruel genocide. Their tusks have been carved from their heads and carried away, leaving the bloody carcasses to rot and waste away on the plains.

The irreversible effect of this illegal murdering will certainly eventually lead to the extinction of many exotic wildlife species. Already time has witnessed the demise of many exotic animals. In the 17th century, 13,200 species of mammals and birds were known, but today more than 130 species are extinct. An estimated 240 more are considered seriously endangered. In almost all cases, the extinction can be traced to greedy plunder by human beings. And the tragic part is that we did not commit the plunder because we needed these animals for food, nor because their unique traits could help us find cures for diseases, nor because killing them taught us anything useful. But perhaps when they are gone forever—taking with them their natural mystery, beauty, and grace—then we may see how ignorant and foolish we were. Then we will realize, much too late, that we sold our birthright for a mess of pottage.

EDITING

After revising—in most cases—comes editing. You now concentrate on the smaller elements of your writing—on individual words and sentences—with the goal of improving them. Again, careful editing begins with close rereading. You remember whom you are writing for and why, and you use your intended audience and purpose to judge the suitability of both your syntax and diction.

What follows is a checklist of some fundamental rules of editing. Have your own work in front of you as you go over this list. If your writing suffers from mechanical problems, such as fragments, comma splices, and dangling modifiers, you should consult a good grammar handbook.

Rule 1: Make Your Title Descriptive

The title of a paper should describe its content. Avoid puffy, exotic titles like this one on a paper dealing with the use of fantasy in Keats's poetry:

Poor: Keats: The High Priest of Poetry
Rewrite: The Use of Fantasy in Keats's Poetry

Rule 2: Begin with a Simple Sentence

It is stylistically good sense to open your paper with a short and simple sentence. A long and involved opening will repel, rather than attract, a reader:

> **Poor:** The problem that has come up again and again before various workers in the social sciences, and especially before sociologists and anthropologists, and one that has been debated at length in the journals of both disciplines as well as in the classrooms of various universities and colleges across the country, and one to which various answers, none satisfactory, have been proposed, is this: Are social scientists politically neutral, or are they *ipso facto* committed by their research?

To open with such a cumbersome sentence is like compelling a friend to view a landscape through a dirty windowpane. It is better to begin with an easily grasped sentence:

> **Rewrite:** The question is this: Are social scientists politically neutral, or are they committed by their research?

Rule 3: Prune Deadwood

Deadwood refers to any word, phrase, or sentence that adds bulk without meaning. It accumulates wherever the writing is roundabout and indistinct. Some styles of writing are so vested in wordiness that it is impossible to assign blame to any single word or phrase:

> **Poor:** There are many factors contributing to the deficiencies of my writing, the most outstanding being my unwillingness to work.
> **Rewrite:** I write badly mainly because I am lazy.
> **Poor:** Anthropologists carrying their studies of primate behavior deep into the tropical forests of Malaysia contribute, through the pursuit of their specialized interest, to the one field that in fact gives us our broadest perspective of human beings.
> **Rewrite:** Anthropologists add to our knowledge of human beings by studying primate behavior in the forests of Malaysia.

The solution to wordiness is to be plain and direct—to state your ideas without fluff or pretension.

Aside from wordiness there are other, more specific kinds of deadwood:

a. Cut *there are* and *there is* whenever possible, thereby tightening a sentence.

> **Poor:** There are many reasons why businesses fail.
> **Rewrite:** Businesses fail for many reasons.

Poor: There is a cause for every effect.
Rewrite: Every effect has a cause.

b. Cut *I think, I believe,* and *in my opinion.* Such phrases make the writer sound insecure.

Poor: I think that Freud's approach to psychology is too dominated by sex.
Rewrite: Freud's approach to psychology is too dominated by sex.

Poor: I believe that women should be paid as much as men for the same work.
Rewrite: Women should be paid as much as men for the same work.

Poor: In my opinion, marriage is a dying institution.
Rewrite: Marriage is a dying institution.

c. Cut all euphemistic expressions.

Poor: He went to Vietnam and paid the supreme sacrifice.
Rewrite: He was killed in Vietnam.

Poor: Last year for the first time I exercised the right of citizens on election day.
Rewrite: Last year I voted for the first time.

d. Cut *-wise, -ly,* and *-type* word endings. Such words, easily concocted from adverbs and adjectives, have become popular in college writing, but they add bulk, not meaning.

Poor: Moneywise, she just didn't know how to be careful.
Rewrite: She didn't know how to be careful with her money.

Poor: Firstly, let me point out some economic problems.
Rewrite: First, let me point out some economic problems.

Poor: A jealous-type man annoys me.
Rewrite: A jealous man annoys me.

e. Eliminate all redundant phrases or expressions. Here are some typical examples, followed by possible substitutes:

Redundancy	*Rewrite*
bright in color	bright
large in size	large
old in age	old
shiny appearance	shiny
in this day and age	today

true and accurate	accurate (*or* true)
important essentials	essentials
end result	result
terrible tragedy	tragedy
free gift	gift
unexpected surprise	surprise
each and every	each (*or* every)
beginning preparation	preparation
basic and fundamental	basic (*or* fundamental)

In the preceding cases, all you have to do is cross out the words that *do not add* any meaning.

Another kind of redundancy is the use of ready-made phrases that could be replaced by a single word:

Ready-Made Phrase	*Rewrite*
owing to the fact that	because
plus the fact that	and
regardless of the fact that	although
in the event that	if
in a situation in which	when
concerning the matter of	about
it is necessary that	must
has the capacity for	can
it could happen that	may, can, could, might
prior to	before
at the present time	now (*or* today)
at this point in time	now (*or* today)
as of this date	today
in this day and age	nowadays
in an accurate manner	accurately
in a satisfactory manner	satisfactorily
subsequent to	after
along the lines of	like

Unfortunately, we cannot give you an exhaustive list of all unnecessary phrases. Only by a thorough rereading of your text can you spot these redundancies.

However, some chronic redundancies are caused by such words as *process, field, area, systems,* and *subject* being unnecessarily attached by the preposition *of* to certain nouns. Usually these words and the preposition can be eliminated with no damage whatsoever to your meaning and a considerable lightening of your style. Here are some examples:

The *process of law* is not free of faults.

The *field of education* needs creative minds.

Some incompetence exists in the *area of medicine*.

People employed in *systems of management* make good salaries.
They know little about the *subject of mathematics.*

In each case, if you delete the "of" phrase, the redundancy disappears:

The law is not free of faults.
Education needs creative minds.
Some incompetence exists in medicine.
People employed in management make good salaries.
They know little about mathematics.

Context, activity, concept, factor, and *problem* are similar offenders.

f. Cut all preamble phrases such as *the reason why . . . is that.*

Poor: The reason why wars are fought is that nations are not equally rich.
Rewrite: Wars are fought because nations are not equally rich.

Poor: The thing I wanted to say is that history has shown the human being to be a social predator.
Rewrite: History has shown the human being to be a social predator.

Poor: The point I was trying to make is that reality is sometimes confused with fantasy in Keats's poetry.
Rewrite: Reality is sometimes confused with fantasy in Keats's poetry.

In all such cases the rewrite principle is the same: lift out the heart of the idea and state it plainly.

g. Cut most rhetorical questions.

Poor: That illusion, though deceptive, is more consoling and less hostile to human needs than reality appears to be a central theme in Keats's poetry. Why would anyone feel this way? Why did Keats himself feel this way? Possibly because he had tuberculosis and knew he was going to waste away and die.

Rewrite: That illusion, though deceptive, is more consoling and less hostile to human needs than reality appears to be a central theme in Keats's poetry. Keats possibly felt this way because he had tuberculosis and knew he was going to waste away and die.

Rule 4: Do Not Overexplain

Poor: Some critics sneered at Keats for being an apothecary-surgeon, which is what he was trained for.
Rewrite: Some critics sneered at Keats for being an apothecary-surgeon.

If Keats was an apothecary-surgeon, then that is obviously what he was trained to be.

> **Poor:** As president of the company, which is an executive-type position, he never scheduled work for himself during April.
>
> **Rewrite:** As president of the company, he never scheduled work for himself during April.

The term *president* already lets the reader know that the position is an executive one.

> **Poor:** The car is blue in color and costs $15,000 in price.
>
> **Rewrite:** The car is blue and costs $15,000.

That blue is a color and that $15,000 is the price are self-evident.

Rule 5: Be Specific

Lack of specific detail will infect your prose with a pallid vagueness.

> **Poor:** The effect of the scenery was lovely and added a charming touch to the play.
>
> **Rewrite:** The scenery, which consisted of an autumn country landscape painted on four flats extended to cover the entire background of the stage, added a charming touch to the play.

Being specific is simply calling things by their proper names. In speech, it might pass as cute to call things *thingamajigs* or *thingamabobs* or *widgets,* but in prose, any sort of vagueness caused by the writer's not calling things by their proper names will leave a bad impression. Consider the following examples:

> **Poor:** James Boswell, the famous writer, died from living badly.
>
> **Rewrite:** James Boswell, the famous *biographer,* died of *uremia following a gonorrheal infection.*

The writer of the second sentence, who has simply named Boswell's terminal infection, appears more competent than the writer of the first.

> **Poor:** Browning wrote poetry in which a speaker talked either to himself or to someone else.
>
> **Rewrite:** Browning wrote *dramatic monologues.*

In the first sentence, for want of a name, the writer is forced into a roundabout description of the kind of poetry Browning wrote. A little research on Browning would have yielded the term *dramatic monologue.*

Rule 6: Avoid Trite Expressions

Some words, phrases, or expressions through overuse have become unbearably hackneyed and should be avoided. Following are some of the most glaring offenders.

> in conclusion, I wish to say
> last, but by no means least
> slowly but surely
> to the bitter end
> it goes without saying
> by leaps and bounds
> few and far between
> in the final analysis

Rule 7: Use the Active Voice

The active voice is more vigorous and understandable than the passive because it allows the subject of a sentence to stand in its familiar position in front of the verb: for example, "I took a walk." The subject *I* occupies the position immediately in front of the verb *took*. The same sentence in the passive voice denies this familiar immediacy between subject and verb, "A walk was taken by me." The subject and verb stand at opposite ends of the sentence, with *by* intervening between them. In some passive constructions, the subject is even dropped:

> Information about the suspect could not be obtained.

By whom, you might ask. The answer is not evident in this sentence. Because of this tendency to implicate no one as the doer of an action, the passive voice enjoys widespread use among bureaucratic writers. Notice how converting the above sentence to the active voice not only makes the sentence more vigorous, but also makes some agency or person its subject and, therefore, responsible:

> The police could not obtain any information about the suspect.

The strongest argument to be given for using the active instead of the passive voice, however, is the simplest one: the active voice is easier to read and understand. Here are some more examples of the passive voice, followed by appropriate revisions:

> **Passive:** Her makeup was applied in thick, daubing strokes by her.
> **Active:** She applied her makeup in thick, daubing strokes.

Passive: To see their hero in person was the fans' most cherished dream.

Active: The fans' most cherished dream was to see their hero in person.

Passive: It was determined by the committee that the new tax law would benefit middle-income people.

Active: The committee determined that the new tax law would benefit middle-income people.

Passive: My last trip to Jamaica will always be remembered.

Active: I shall always remember my last trip to Jamaica.

The use of the passive voice is stylistically justified only when an action or the object of an action is more important than the subject:

> There, before our eyes, two human beings were burned alive by gasoline flames.

In this case the object, *human beings,* is more important than the subject, *gasoline flames,* and the passive voice is therefore effective. Here are two more examples of the passive voice appropriately used:

> Cancer-producing particles are released into the atmosphere by spray guns applying asbestos during building construction.

In this context, cancer-producing particles are more important than spray guns.

> Widespread death and injury were caused when 20,000 tons of TNT were dropped on Hiroshima in an atomic bomb.

Obviously the human dead and injured are more important than the atomic bomb.

Rule 8: Make Your Statements Positive

Statements that hedge, hesitate, or falter in the way they are worded tend to infuse your style with indecision. Whenever possible, word your statements positively:

Poor: He was not at all a rich man.

Rewrite: He was a poor man.

Poor: *The Cherry Orchard* is not a strong play; it does not usually sweep the audience along.

Rewrite: *The Cherry Orchard* is a weak play that usually bores its audience.

Poor: A not uncommon occurrence is for rain to fall this time of the year.

Rewrite: It commonly rains this time of the year.

Rule 9: Keep to One Tense

Once you have decided to summarize an action or event in one tense, you must thereafter stick to that tense. Don't start in the past and shift to the present, nor start in the present and shift to the past. Notice the corrections in the following passage.

> Here is what I saw: For two acts the ballerina pirouetted, leapt, and floated like a silver swallow; then suddenly, she ~~falls~~ *fell* to the ground like a heavy boulder. Her leg ~~is~~ *was* fractured. For years before I observed this spectacular drama, I ^ *had* often heard of this artist's brilliant career. Now I ~~am~~ *was watching* watching her final performance.

Rule 10: Place Key Words at the Beginning or End of a Sentence

Poor: Workers today have forgotten the meaning of the word *quality,* so most craftsmen tell us.

Rewrite: Workers today, so most craftsmen tell us, have forgotten the meaning of the word *quality.*

Poor: Generally speaking, *wars* turn civilized nations into barbaric tribes.

Rewrite: *Wars,* generally speaking, turn civilized nations into barbaric tribes.

Rule 11: Prune Multiple *Of*s

A double *of* construction is tolerable; a triple *of* construction is not.

Poor: The opinions *of* the members *of* this panel *of* students are their own.

Rewrite: The opinions expressed by this panel of students are their own.

A good way to break up an *of* construction is to add another verb. In the preceding example the verb *expressed* is inserted in the sentence.

Rule 12: Break Up Noun Clusters

A noun cluster is any string of noun + adjective combinations occurring at length without a verb. The cluster is usually preceded by either *the* or *a.* Noun clusters contribute a tone of unarguable objectivity to prose and have consequently found favor in the writing styles of textbooks, the government, and the social sciences. Note the italicized noun clusters in the following:

Poor: We therefore recommend *the use of local authorities for the collection of information on this issue.*

Poor: *The increased specialization and complexity of multicellular organisms* resulted from *evolution according to the principles of random variation and natural selection.*

Poor: The *general lessening of the work role in our society* does not mean that we have abandoned *the work basis for many of our values.*

Poor: One cannot doubt *the existence of polarized groups in America.*

The test for a noun cluster is whether or not it can be replaced by a single pronoun. Each of the above can be.

To rewrite noun clusters, convert one or more of the nouns to an equivalent verb form:

Better: We therefore recommend *using* local authorities *to collect* information on this issue.

Better: Multicellular organisms *specialized and evolved* in complexity by the principles of random variation and natural selection.

Better: Because people today *work* less than they used to is no reason to believe that we have abandoned work as a basis for many of our values.

Better: One cannot doubt that polarized groups *exist* in America.

Noun clusters clot the flow of a sentence. Avoid them by being generous in your use of verbs.

Rule 13: Use Exclamation Points Sparingly

The exclamation point should be used rarely and only when urgency or strong emotion is being expressed, as in the following:

This is what we fought our wars for!

Hooray! They found the prize!

Otherwise, it adds a forced breeziness to your prose.

We must have urban renewal; and we must have it now!

One cannot construct a science with unreliable instruments!

Rule 14: Vary Your Sentences

Do not begin two sentences in a row with the same word or phrase unless you are deliberately aiming for an effect.

Poor: The true Keats scholar is as familiar with the poet's life as with his poetry and can instantly relate any stage of the two. The true Keats scholar has a tendency to use Keats's poetry to explicate his life, and to use his life to explicate his poetry.

Rewrite: Scholars of Keats know the poet's life as well as they know his poetry and can instantly relate any stage of the two. They use Keats's poetry to explain his life, and his life to explain his poetry.

In addition to varying the words, vary the length of your sentences.

Poor: The man was angry and wanted his money back. But the officer would not give it back and told him to leave. That made the man angrier, and he threatened to call the police.

Rewrite: The man was angry; he wanted his money back. But the officer would not give it back to him, and told him to leave, which made the man angrier. He threatened to call the police.

The rewrite is more effective because the sentences have a greater variety in length and style.

Rule 15: Keep Your Point of View Consistent

If you begin a sentence by referring to yourself first as "I" and then as "one," you have made the error known as shift in point of view. Such shifts can occur because of the several ways in which you can refer to yourself, your audience, and people in general. You can refer to yourself as *the writer, I,* or *we.* You can refer to your audience as *you, we,* or *all of us.* You can refer to people in general as *people, one,* and *they.* The rule is that once you have chosen your point of view, it must remain consistent:

Poor: Do not buy Oriental rugs at an auction, because if we do, we may get cheated.

Better: Do not buy Oriental rugs at an auction, because if you do, you may get cheated.

Poor: I try to take good care of my car, for when one does not, they usually pay a big price.

Better: I try to take good care of my car, for when I do not, I usually pay a big price.

Poor: Everyone stood aghast when I told them about the accident.

Better: They all stood aghast when I told them about the accident.

Rule 16: Use Standard Words

College students can be unrelenting in their invention of newfangled vocabulary and often fall prey to the excesses of neologisms—new or coined words. Voguish words fade as quickly as they appear. By the time this book sees print, such words as *tight, trippin',* and *skeezy* will have begun to sound dated and old-fashioned. You should use neologisms sparingly—if at all—in your writing. Instead, draw your primary stock of words from the vocabulary established over the centuries. Remember, too, standard words must be written in standard spelling. Double-check any doubtful spelling in a dictionary.

Rule 17: End with Impact

The ending of your essay should either clinch your argument, summarize your main point, reassert your thesis, urge some kind of action, or suggest a solution. Avoid committing the following common errors in your ending:

a. Endings that are trite:

> In conclusion I wish to say . . .
> And now to summarize . . .

Such endings are too obvious. If your essay has been properly developed, no special announcement of the conclusion is necessary.

b. Endings that introduce a new idea:

> Wealth, position, and friends, then, made him what he is today, although his father's death may also have influenced him.

If an idea has not been covered earlier, do not give in to the temptation to introduce it as a novelty item in the final paragraph.

c. Endings that are superfluous:

> And so these are my thoughts on the subject.
> As you can see, my essay proves that carbohydrates are bad for our health.
> From these thoughts you will clearly see that Diaghilev was a dominant figure in modern ballet.

These endings do not reflect thoughtfulness on the part of the writer; they are useless in an essay.

EDITING AN ACTUAL ESSAY

Following is the first draft of a student paper, with revisions marked in boldface. In the left margin is the corresponding number of the rule in this section that has been broken.

The Loss of Horror in Horror Movies
~~Goose Pimples, Where Are You?~~

Rule 1

Rule 6 ~~For various and sundry reasons,~~ Audiences are no longer scared as they once were by the old-fashioned horror movies. Over the years people have been exposed to so

Rule 5 many ~~monsters~~ vampires, werewolves, zombies, and mummies that such creatures have lost their

Rule 3g effectiveness as objects of terror. ~~Why do you think this happened?~~

Lack of novelty has produced indifference. Originally, a movie monster, such as the one created by Frankenstein, terrified audiences simply because the concept of a man

Rules 9/3e creating human life ~~is~~ was new. ~~Plus the fact that~~ Frankenstein's monster had a sinister plausibility that people of the 1930s had not experienced. But then the public was inundated by a deluge of other film monsters as studios tried to capitalize on the success of the original. Gradually audiences grew bored as these creations became trite and shopworn. Fearing loss of business, ambitious movie producers tried to

Rule 3d invent fresh ~~type,~~ grisly shapes that would lure moviegoers back into the theaters. But their attempts had no effect on a public surfeited with horror, so Frankenstein's monster,

Wolfman, and Dracula eventually became comic creatures in Abbott and Costello films.

Rule 3e — Most modern horror films fail ~~in the production of~~ to produce genuine, goose-pimply terror in their audiences. Of course, it may be argued that films like *The Exorcist* and *Jaws*

Rule 5 — scared many people—even to the point of ~~great fear~~ hysterical screams. But these films relied heavily on shock rather than on fear.

Rule 8 — Shock ~~and fear are not the same~~ differs from fear. Genuine fear involves the unknown or the unseen. ~~Genuine fear~~ It seduces the

Rule 14 — imagination into fantastic realms, and appeals ~~Genuine fear appeals~~ to our innate store of nightmares. But shock is merely synonymous with repulsion. People are shocked when they see something they don't want to see. For example, the scene of a man being devoured by a shark will shock. The flaw here is that the shock value of such a scene serves

Rule 16 — more to ~~give the creeps or the heebie jeebies~~ repulse or offend than to frighten.

Today shock devices are used far too frequently in motion pictures; yet, the sad truth is that these graphic displays of blood and gore lack imagination. In older horror movies, the audience was not privy to the horrible details

Rule 7	of murder. Scenes ~~which~~ merely suggested evil ~~were used~~
	instead, and the ~~details were supplied by the audience's~~ *audience's imagination supplied the details.*
Rule 4	~~imagination.~~ This approach is more effective ~~in its results~~
	than shock because it spurs the viewers to conjure up their
	own images of the unseen. The old movie formulas did not
	have to use shock devices, such as bloody murders, to
	achieve a pinnacle of horror. Unfortunately, today's
	audiences have become "shockproof" in the sense that it
Rule 5	takes ~~more and more~~ *bigger and more bizarre doses of horror* to scare them. ~~In conclusion, horror~~
Rule 17a	~~movies have truly lost their effect.~~ *One wonders what the ultimate horror movie will be.*

Here is the polished version of the paper, ready to be submitted to the instructor.

The Loss of Horror in Horror Movies

Audiences are no longer scared as they once were by the old-fashioned horror movies. Over the years people have been exposed to so many vampires, werewolves, zombies, and mummies that such creatures have lost their effectiveness as objects of terror.

Lack of novelty has produced indifference. Originally, a movie monster, such as the one created by Frankenstein, terrified audiences simply because the concept of a man creating a human life was new. Frankenstein's monster had a sinister plausibility that people of the 1930s had not experienced. But then the public was inundated by a deluge of other film monsters as studios tried to capitalize on the success of the original. Gradually audiences grew bored as these creations became trite and shopworn. Fearing loss of business, ambitious movie producers tried to invent fresh, grisly shapes that would lure moviegoers back into the theaters. But their attempts had no effect on a public surfeited with horror, so Frankenstein's monster, Wolfman, and Dracula eventually became comic creatures in Abbott and Costello films.

Most modern horror films fail to produce genuine, goose-pimply terror in their audiences. Of course, it may be argued that films like *The Exorcist* and *Jaws* scared many people—even to the point of hysterical screams. But these films relied heavily on shock rather than on fear. Shock differs from fear. Genuine fear involves the unknown or the unseen. It seduces the imagination into fantastic realms and appeals to our innate store of nightmares. But shock is merely synonymous with repulsion. People are shocked when they see something they don't want to see. For example, the scene of a man being devoured by a shark will shock. The flaw here is that the shock value of such a scene serves more to repulse or offend than to frighten.

2

    Today shock devices are used far too frequently in motion pictures; yet, the sad truth is that these graphic displays of blood and gore lack imagination. In older horror movies, the audience was not privy to the horrible details of murder. Scenes merely suggested evil instead, and the audience's imagination supplied the details. This approach is more effective than shock because it spurs the viewers to conjure up their own images of the unseen. The old movie formulas did not have to use shock devices, such as bloody murders, to achieve a pinnacle of horror. Unfortunately, today's audiences have become "shockproof" in the sense that it takes bigger and more bizarre doses of horror to scare them. One wonders what the ultimate horror movie will be.

Exercises

1. What follows is the opening paragraph of a student essay. Revise it to improve its effectiveness. Remember that your lead sentence should captivate your audience.

   > Wars are always destructive and rarely worth the devastation they cause. Today, Europe is still recuperating from World War II. Endless statistics attempt to project what would happen if a nuclear war were to break out today; yet, nobody really knows the actual effects. The most accurate picture to date was provided by the bombing of Hiroshima in 1945. This terrible historical event provided actual evidence of what a super weapon has the capability of accomplishing. For the first time the world saw the greatest disaster ever created by man. The effects were unforgettably horrifying and disastrous. No one had bargained for the ensuing nightmare.

2. From the following pairs, choose the more descriptive title.
   a. (1) The Dreadful Nightmare of 1945
      (2) The Crippling Effects of the Atom Bomb on Hiroshima
   b. (1) Whence Did We Come and Why Are We Here?
      (2) What Is Philosophy?
   c. (1) China and Europe: Two Different Cultures
      (2) Dynamic Growth versus Static Social Principles
   d. (1) The People of the Black Moccasin
      (2) The Plains Culture of the Blackfoot Indians
   e. (1) Francisco Pizarro, Conqueror of Peru
      (2) Mighty Conquistador of the New World

3. Rid the following sentences of all deadwood:
   a. There are many ways in which light can be diffracted.
   b. No one has the right, in my opinion, to dictate to another human being whom to worship.
   c. Educationwise Will Rogers never did go to college.
   d. It has been said many times that power corrupts.
   e. There were thousands of teachers who attended the conference.
   f. The attitude-adjustment hour will begin at 5:00 p.m. and will be "no host."

4. Eliminate all redundant or imprecise phrases from the following sentences. Rewrite passages if necessary.
   a. Owing to the fact that it rained, Napoleon was defeated at Waterloo.
   b. We asked for a full and complete list of the passengers.
   c. One-man-one-vote should be a basic and fundamental reality of any political system.
   d. The room is square in shape, pale blue in color, and cheerful in appearance.
   e. The custodian was fired on the grounds that he slept on the job.
   f. A huge celebration marked the occasion of Martin Luther King's birthday.
   g. Those engaged in the profession of writing should be the guardians of grammar.

5. Rewrite the following sentences in the active voice:
   a. From early times on stucco was used by the Romans as a finish for important buildings.
   b. Immortality was not believed in by the Sadducees of Jerusalem.
   c. The *Brahmanas,* originally written in Sanskrit, were produced by Indian priests.
   d. Chewing mouths are used by termites to eat wood.
   e. A good time was had by all of us.
   f. Sometimes no symptoms are exhibited by victims of trichinosis.
6. Rewrite the following sentences to break up the noun clusters:
   a. The way to avoid a future fuel crisis is the construction of a mass transportation system and the investing in quality insulation.
   b. The inspecting of the chemical-disposal plant was never accomplished.
   c. One can hope for the existence of an afterlife.
   d. The making of great strides by medical technology gives hope to people with incurable heart diseases.
   e. The development of a good ear is necessary to the writing of effective prose.
7. Rewrite the following sentences to correct an inconsistent point of view or shift in tense:
   a. They left early for the big city of San Francisco. Once there, they take the cable car to the top of Nob Hill. At five in the evening, they eat at a restaurant on the wharf.
   b. One must have respect for the flag of our country. If you don't, how can we expect others to respect it?
   c. Swarms of bees attacked him, so he quickly hides his face inside his heavy wool jacket.
   d. If one has ever lived by the sea, you always tend to miss the roar of the waves and the sound of seagulls.

PART FOUR

Special Writing Projects

ASSIGNMENT 1: THE RESEARCH PAPER

Why English Instructors Assign Research Papers

Students rarely greet the research paper with joy, but it still remains one of the most important college assignments. Writing one entails thinking critically about a subject, tracking down and evaluating facts for relevance and truth, organizing materials in support of a thesis, and cultivating a readable style. Success in college depends largely on the acquisition of these skills, which are also essential for accomplishment in business, the major professions, and even in private life. Salespeople often research a market and analyze it for trends; lawyers track down facts and organize them when preparing briefs and contracts; journalists depend on investigative research to gather material for stories. Engineers, nurses, secretaries, actors, architects, insurance agents—members of virtually all the professions—rely on the research techniques exemplified in this chapter.

How to Choose Your Topic

Typically, English instructors grant students the freedom to choose their own research topics, thus promoting exploration and self-discovery. If such a choice is indeed available to you, we recommend some preliminary browsing through the library until you come across a subject that arouses your curiosity—be it primitive Indians, the reign of the last empress of China, some influential sports figure, the complexities of the New York Stock Exchange, children's psychological problems, or the fiction or poetry of a modern writer. Here are some tips on finding a suitable topic:

1. **Work with a familiar subject.** For instance, you may have been fascinated by historical attempts of the super rich to manipulate the US economy, such as the Gould-Fisk scheme to corner gold in 1869, with the consequent Black Friday market panic. Now you must find out more about Jay Gould, who became symbolic of autocratic business practices and was hated by most American businesspeople. Research will supply the necessary information.

2. **If familiarity fails, try an entirely new area.** Perhaps you have always wanted to learn about Lenin's philosophy of government, genetic engineering, stem cell technology, evolution in the Paleozoic era, the Roman empress Galla Placidia, the causes of earthquakes, pre-Columbian art, or the historical causes for the political unrest in the Middle East. A research paper finally gives you the opportunity to do so.

3. **Books, magazines, newspapers, and the Internet can suggest possible topics.** The library is a gold mine of hidden information. Browse through book stacks, magazine racks, and newspapers. Some topic of interest is bound to leap out at you. Looking at secondary sources online is probably today's most popular way of finding research material. However, since anyone—from a well-known writer to a smart elementary school student—can place material on the Web, it is best to base your research on databases that are maintained by professionals. Some of these databases may even contain indexes that will allow you to download interesting material at no charge. The process of finding information on the Internet is always the same: access a search engine such as Google and enter a topic in the search slot. The computer will then search databases and Web sites on your topic and present a list of matching items. For example, we did a Google search on "illegal immigrants" and in less than a second got 2,380,000 hits. If you are new to computer research, ask for assistance from the librarian.

Avoid topics for which a single source can provide all the needed information; those that require no development but end as soon as started; those so popular that virtually everything about them has already been written and said; those so controversial that you have only fresh fuel to add to the already raging fire; or those decidedly unsuited to your audience, such as a paper advocating radical revision of the US Constitution written for an instructor who is a conservative Republican.

How to Narrow Your Subject

Good research papers deal with topics of modest and workable proportions. To attempt a paper on the galaxies of the universe or on World War II is to attempt the impossible. A simple but practical way to narrow your subject is to subdivide it into progressively smaller units until you reach a topic specific enough for a paper. The following diagram on the sport of fencing illustrates what we mean:

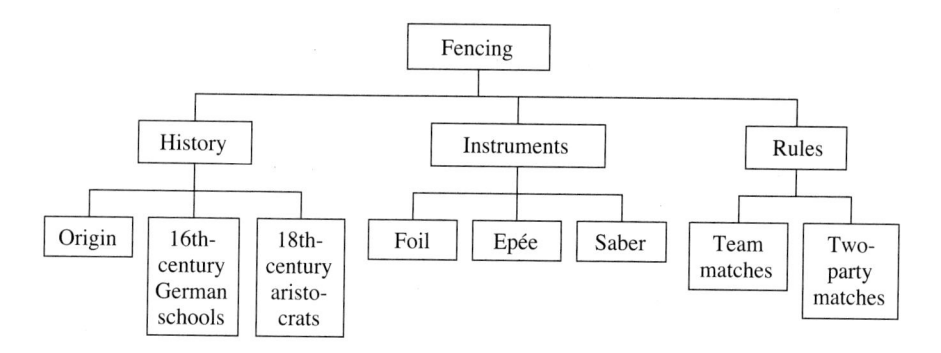

```
                          ┌─────────┐
                          │ Fencing │
                          └────┬────┘
         ┌─────────────────────┼─────────────────────┐
    ┌────┴────┐          ┌─────┴─────┐          ┌────┴────┐
    │ History │          │Instruments│          │  Rules  │
    └────┬────┘          └─────┬─────┘          └────┬────┘
    ┌────┼────┐       ┌────────┼────────┐        ┌───┴───┐
┌───┴──┐┌┴───┐┌┴───┐ ┌┴──┐  ┌──┴──┐  ┌──┴──┐  ┌──┴──┐ ┌──┴──┐
│Origin││16th││18th│ │Foil│ │Epée │  │Saber│  │Team │ │Two- │
│      ││cent││cent│ │    │ │     │  │     │  │match│ │party│
│      ││Germ││aris│ │    │ │     │  │     │  │es   │ │match│
│      ││schl││crat│ │    │ │     │  │     │  │     │ │es   │
└──────┘└────┘└────┘ └────┘ └─────┘  └─────┘  └─────┘ └─────┘
```

Any of the entries found on the lowest subdivision are properly narrowed subjects. For instance, you could write a useful paper on the sixteenth-century German schools that taught fencing to European gentlemen, on the use of the saber in fencing, or on the rules of modern team fencing. But a paper just on fencing would be overambitious and tricky to write.

Another point to bear in mind is that unlike the typical class-written paper, in which you must first formulate a thesis and then write the text, in the research paper you gather evidence, study it, and only then deduce a thesis. The assembled facts, statistics, graphs, schematics, arguments, expert testimony, and so on, will suggest a topic that will be your thesis. What you learn in this process of writing the research paper is not only how to write but also how to infer a reasonable conclusion from a body of evidence.

The Process of Writing the Paper

You have narrowed your subject. You do not yet have a thesis or a definite topic, but you have a likely subject area to explore. You can do it in these simple steps:

Find and Evaluate Sources To do this, you must spend time in a library, which is your systematized retrieval network. Materials for your subject will be listed in the card catalog, in appropriate indexes, in reference works, on shelves, in files, and—in most libraries—on a computer screen. Evaluate each source by scanning titles, tables of contents, chapter headings, or article summaries. Check the date of publication to make sure the information in the source is still valid. Ask the reference librarian for help. As you work, list each possible source on its own bibliography card, providing the information necessary for easy retrieval.

Take a look at the bibliography card on the next page.

The most important part of Internet research is to evaluate the accuracy and dependability of sources. Here are some guidelines for evaluating Internet sources:

- Check the reliability of the source. Since the World Wide Web grows bigger and more complex daily, some of the sources are bogus. We suggest that

> 813.409　　　　　　　　　　　　　　　　　College Library
>
> Sch.
>
> Schneider, Robert W. *Five Novelists of the*
>   *Progressive Era.*
>   New York: Columbia University Press, 1965
> Chapter 5 evaluates the novels of Winston Churchill, stating why
> they were loved by contemporaries but scorned by succeeding generations.

you stick to Web sites that end in *.org* (nonprofit organization), *.gov* (government entity), or *.edu* (educational body), since they are usually reliable.

- Check the dates of the sources to make sure that the information is not outdated.
- Check the authors of the material you have found by logging in their names on the Internet. Their biographies will tell you about their credentials, contributions, and reputations. For instance, if the author is a seasoned journalist reporting for *The New York Times,* you can be reassured that he or she is most likely a credible source.

Take Notes Using your pile of bibliography cards, retrieve the books, magazines, pamphlets, and other identified sources and place them in front of you. Skim each source to get the drift of its content. Decide if it contains material relevant enough to warrant a more detailed reading. Once you have skimmed your sources, you can start taking four basic kinds of notes:

1. **summary**—record the gist of a passage;
2. **paraphrase**—restate in your own words what the source says;
3. **direct quotation**—copy the exact words of a source;
4. **personal comments**—express your own views on the subject or source.

Write or type your notes on cards, which can be easily shuffled or discarded when you get down to the business of writing the paper. For easier reorganization of your notes, restrict each card to a single idea. To guard against unintentional plagiarism, copy down only exact quotations from your sources while digesting and expressing all other ideas in your own words. At some point in this stage (it varies from paper to paper), a thesis will occur to you. When it does, write it down on a card for permanent reference. This will be the starting point for your paper.

Plagiarism Plagiarism is the willful or accidental stealing of someone else's writing. To help you understand the ins and outs of plagiarism, here are three passages about the American poet Walt Whitman, two of them plagiarized and one of them not.

Original Passage

Even when Whitman was working at his career as a newspaperman, his casualness threatened his advancement. As the owners of the New York *Aurora* fired him from the editorial staff, they accused him in print of "loaferism," describing him as "the laziest fellow who ever undertook to edit a city paper." Whitman never reformed. It remained his custom as editor to have the paper made up and ready for printing by noon, then to be off for a swim, a stroll, or a ride down Broadway on a horse-car. Even when working at that leisurely pace, he was complaining in the columns of the Brooklyn *Daily Eagle* that "most editors have far, far too much to do."

Plagiarized (Version 1)

During his career as a newspaperman, Walt Whitman was considered a loafer because his bosses felt that he didn't spend enough time in the newspaper office. In fact, he was fired from the editorial staff of the *Aurora* and labeled "the laziest fellow who ever undertook to edit a city paper." Being fired did not change Whitman, who always felt that editors worked much too hard. It remained his custom as editor to have the paper made up and ready for printing by noon, then to be off for a swim, a stroll, or a ride down Broadway on a horse car.

This is blatant plagiarism. The student has not acknowledged any source for the comments made about Whitman, in effect taking credit for them himself. Even the quotation is not documented.

Plagiarized (Version 2)

Whitman was considered a lazy loafer by the owners of the New York *Aurora* who employed him. They even fired him from their editorial staff and called him "the laziest fellow who ever undertook to edit a city paper." Whitman never reformed. He continued his habit of having the newspaper ready for printing by noon so that he could be off on some adventure of his own—a swim, a stroll, or a ride down Broadway in a horse carriage (Bridgman vii, viii).

This is the "Works Cited" information:

Bridgman, Richard. Introduction. <u>Leaves of Grass</u>. By Walt Whitman. San Francisco: Chandler, 1968.

Despite correct documentation, this passage is still plagiarized because the student has retained too much of the original source's wording, leaving the impression that it is his own.

Not Plagiarized

According to most of Walt Whitman's biographers, the poet did not have a compulsive or ambitious personality as far as his career as a journalist was concerned. In fact, "as the owners of the New York *Aurora* fired him from the editorial staff, they accused him in print of 'loaferism,' describing him as 'the laziest fellow who ever undertook to edit a city paper'" (Bridgman vii, viii).

Reading Whitman's own letters to friends or studying his poetry makes one aware that part of Whitman's philosophy was that a worthwhile life included both partying and working.

The "Works Cited" page then contains this entry:

Bridgman, Richard. Introduction. Leaves of Grass. By Walt Whitman. San Francisco: Chandler, 1968.

This passage is not plagiarized. The documentation is accurate and the ideas found in the original source are properly paraphrased. Remember that it is not enough to simply cite a source. If you're quoting from it, you should use quotation marks. If you're paraphrasing its material, you must do a true paraphrase. Whether you find material on the Internet or in a library book, you should never plagiarize. To avoid plagiarism, follow these rules meticulously:

- Acknowledge any idea taken from another source.
- Place quoted passages inside quotation marks.
- Provide a bibliographic entry at the end of the paper for every source used in your text.

You do not, however, have to document everything. Facts that are common knowledge need no documentation (example: "Abraham Lincoln was shot by John Wilkes Booth"). As a rule, a piece of information that has appeared in five standard sources can be considered common knowledge and needs no documentation.

Write the First Draft With a jumble of notes strewn on your desk, you may feel bewildered about what to include or exclude as you tackle your first draft. This may be the time for an outline, which can be adjusted later to fit your paper, or your paper can subsequently be adjusted to fit your outline.

In any case, by now you should have become something of an expert on your subject. Using your outline, start composing your first draft. As you write, you will be backing up your own opinions and views with source material uncovered by your research and recorded in your notes.

Use Proper Documentation Except for statements that are common knowledge, all information taken from your sources—whether quoted, paraphrased, or summarized—must be accompanied by a source citation given in parentheses and conforming to the proper format. We provide two sample papers in this chapter—one in the Modern Language Association (MLA) format, the other in the American Psychological Association (APA) format. Use the MLA author-work format if your instructor tells you to do so or if your paper is on a subject in the liberal arts, such as literature, philosophy, history, religion, or fine arts. For a paper in a more scientific field, such as psychology, sociology, or anthropology, the APA author-date format should be used. In any event, check with your instructor about the documentation format that is expected and appropriate. One caution: Do *not* mix styles.

The two annotated student papers represented in this part serve as general models and illustrate most of the documenting problems you are likely to encounter. For more complex citations, we recommend that you consult a style sheet or a research paper handbook. Both MLA and APA have gone to a system of parenthetical documentation, which gives brief but specific information about the sources within the text itself. The MLA style cites the author's surname or the title of a work, followed by a page number; the APA style cites the author's surname, followed by a date and a page number. In both styles, the author's name, work, and date can be omitted from the parentheses if they have already been supplied within the text. The rule of thumb is this: If the citation cannot be smoothly worked into the text, it should be supplied within parentheses. This kind of parenthetical documentation is obviously simpler than footnotes or endnotes because the citation can be given as the paper is being written rather than being tediously repeated in the text, the note, and the bibliography.

Flexibility in citations is a characteristic of both the MLA and APA styles. For example, you might choose to cite the author's name in the text while putting the page (MLA) or year and page (APA) in parentheses:

MLA Example

In her autobiography, Agatha Christie admits that often she felt the physical presence of Hercule Poirot (263).

APA Example

According to *800-Cocaine* by Mark S. Gold (1985, p. 21), cocaine has exploded into a business with brand names.

Or you might choose to include the title or author(s) of the citation in the parentheses:

MLA Example

The author began to realize how much she liked Poirot and how much a part of her life he had become (Christie, 263).

APA Example

During the airing of ABC's *Good Morning, America* (Ross & Bronkowski, 1986), case histories were analyzed in an extremely serious tone.

In any case, the overriding aim should be to cite the necessary information without interrupting the flow of the text. What cannot be worked elegantly into the text is cited within parentheses.

Preparing "Works Cited" or "References"

The sources cited in your text must be alphabetically listed in full at the end of your paper. In the MLA style of documentation, the list is titled "Works Cited"; in the APA style, it is titled "References." Both styles require the same general information, but differ slightly in details of capitalization and order. MLA entries, for example, begin with a surname, followed by the author's full (first) name; on the other hand, APA requires a surname, followed only by the initial letters of the author's first and middle names. In MLA entries, the author's name is followed by the title of the work, whereas in APA entries, the author's name is followed by the date. Both APA and MLA entries use hanging indentations (second and subsequent lines are indented one-half inch (or five spaces). Other differences are also minor: MLA requires titles of books or periodicals to be underlined, articles or chapters to be placed within quotation marks, and all principal words of a title to be capitalized (articles, prepositions, coordinating conjunctions, and the "to" in infinitives are not capitalized if they fall in the middle of a title). On the other hand, APA italicizes the titles of books and magazines but uses no quotation marks around the titles of chapters or articles within these longer works. For titles of articles, APA capitalizes only the first word of a book or article title, the first word of a subtitle (if there is one), and any proper nouns; all other words are lowercase. For titles of periodicals, APA capitalizes all principal words. See the sample student papers for specific examples of how to handle various bibliographic matters.

Note: Online sources require a special format. In MLA style the "Works Cited" reference for a Web page should include the following elements: underlined title of the project or database; name of the editor of the project or database, if available; electronic publication information, including version number (if relevant and not part of the title), date of electronic publication or of the latest update, and name of any sponsoring institution or organization; and date of access and electronic address. APA style for online sources requires inclusion of a retrieval statement at the end of the reference item, such as the following: "Retrieved January 23, 2006, from http://apa.org/journals/webref.html" or "Retrieved November 21, 2005, from the PsycARTICLES database."

Writing the Final Copy

Revising and editing your paper is the final step. Do not be easy on yourself. Pretend that the paper is someone else's and badly in need of work. Check for logical progression, completeness of development, and mechanical correctness. The only way to produce an excellent paper is to pore over it paragraph by paragraph looking for weaknesses or faults. After careful review and editing, prepare the final copy using one of the formats exemplified by the two student papers. If you are following the APA format, you will also need to write an abstract summarizing your findings (see student sample, pages 715–745). Remember that the appearance of a paper can add to or detract from its quality. Here are some important tips on manuscript appearance:

1. Use 8½-by-11 white paper. Double-space throughout the paper.
2. Except for page numbers, use one-inch margins at the top, bottom, and sides of the paper. (For page numbers, see item 6.)
3. Avoid fancy fonts such as script.
4. Place a balanced and uncluttered outline before the text of the paper. Double-space throughout the outline. (See item 6 for paginating the outline.)
5. Do not use a title page unless your instructor specifies otherwise. Instead, put your name, instructor's name, course number, and date on the first page of the outline, repeating this information in the upper left-hand corner of the first page of the text. The title should be centered and double-spaced below the date. (See sample papers.)
6. Number pages consecutively throughout the paper in the upper right-hand corner. Do not follow page numbers with hyphens, parentheses, periods, or other characters. Number the pages of the outline with lower-case Roman numerals (i, ii, iii, and so on). Number the first page of the paper itself with an Arabic 1, and continue numbering pages consecutively throughout the paper, including "Works Cited" or "Reference List."
7. Double-check the appropriate format (MLA or APA) for citing and documentation.
8. Note that APA papers feature an abstract and a running header. See the sample paper for a model.

ANNOTATED STUDENT RESEARCH PAPER
Modern Language Association (MLA) Style

(1) The first page seen by your reader is the outline of your paper. Paginate the outline with small Roman numerals. Put your name in the top left-hand margin, followed by your instructor's name, the course title and number, and the date the paper is due.

(2) Center the title of your paper. A good title should tell the reader what the paper is about. Double-space throughout the outline.

(3) The thesis consists of a single declarative sentence preceded by the word *Thesis*. The rest of the outline follows the rules for correct sentence outlining. Some instructors allow topic outlines, which consist of phrases rather than full sentences. Do not make the outline too long. A rule of thumb is to have one page of outline for every five pages of writing. The outline leaves out the details of the paper, mentioning only major points.

---

*The Arabic numerals in the left margins of the student paper correspond to the comments on the facing page.

Hollingsworth i

Stephanie Hollingsworth
Dr. Ronald Dekker
English 101
September 30, 2006

Choosing Single Motherhood: A Sign of Modern Times?

Thesis: Increases in educational and career opportunities for women, advances in medical technology, and diminishing social stigma all contribute to the rising number of women who are choosing to become single mothers.

I. Women are waiting longer to start families.
   A. A shift in women's consciousness has occurred since the 1960s.
      1. Marriage is no longer a necessary component to childbearing.
      2. The use of birth control gave women more choices over when or even if to get pregnant.
   B. There are more opportunities for women today.
      1. More women are taking advantage of higher education.
      2. The number of career opportunities for women has increased.
   C. Women are more willing to wait for the right partner.
      1. Personal fulfillment plays a higher role in the consciousness of today's woman.

2. Many of today's women are children of divorce and would like to avoid that situation in their own marriages.
   D. Waiting longer creates concern for some women who fear the biological clock's ticking.
II. Advances in fertility technology are providing women with more options as to when and how to have a child.
   A. Women can have children later in life.
   B. Single women have the option of conceiving a child through donor insemination.
III. The social stigma of a single woman having a child has diminished.
   A. More adults today are children of divorce and therefore more tolerant of single parenting.
   B. The formation of support groups for single mothers has given single parenting a boost.
IV. Although many critics argue that single mothering by choice represents a breakdown of traditional family values, some studies indicate otherwise.
   A. Critics fear that the traditional nuclear family is quickly becoming the exception.
   B. Some studies argue that a father is not necessary for the healthy upbringing of a child.
      1. These studies show that children do not necessarily fare better when a father is present.
      2. Many fathers spend less than two and a half hours a day with their children.

(4) College papers require no title page. Simply put your name in the top left-hand margin of the first page, your teacher's name, followed by the course title and number, and the date the paper is due—all of this information double-spaced, with each entry on a separate line. Then double-space again, center the title (capitalizing only the first, last, and principal words and without underlining). Continue double-spacing throughout the paper. Number all pages in the upper right-hand corner, one-half inch from the top and adjacent to the right margin. Place your name followed by a space before each page number (so that misplaced pages can be easily found). A one-inch margin is required on all sides. Do not staple the paper or place it in a folder; just use a large paper clip to hold the pages together.

(5) The first paragraph grabs the reader by drawing attention to the difference between the traditional view of having babies and some modern women's views. The last sentence of the paragraph is the thesis. It is placed in the classic position at the end of the opening paragraph, where it controls the remainder of the paper. The parenthetical citation refers the reader to the bibliographic "Works Cited" list at the end of the paper. The abbreviation "qtd. in" means that the person whose words are cited is quoted in someone else's work. Integrating documentary sources into the flow of the paper takes considerable skill. Notice that the final period follows the closing parenthesis of the citation except in case of a long quotation set off from the main text. Study the parenthetical documentation of this paper to see the various possibilities for handling source citations.

Hollingsworth 1

(4) Stephanie Hollingsworth
Dr. Ronald Dekker
English 101
September 30, 2006

(5) Choosing Single Motherhood: A Sign of Modern Times?

First comes love, then comes marriage, then comes baby in the baby carriage ... not necessarily so. Today, an increasing number of children are being reared in single-parent households, usually headed by the mother. These are women who, for whatever reason, have remained single and decided to have a child but don't believe that a husband is necessary for them to achieve motherhood. This trend is boosted by increased career opportunities for women that lessen the need for a husband's financial support. Consequently, the notion that a woman must be married in order to have a child is becoming less and less true. In an article written for Time, Dr. Nachtigall, a fertility specialist, captured the new trend in these words: "The biological drive to reproduce may be stronger than the cultural yearning to get married" (qtd. in Stonesifer 130–31). With increases in educational and career opportunities for women, advances in medical technology making single motherhood a safe and relatively affordable choice, and diminishing social stigma, America's rising number of single mothers by choice comes as little surprise.

(6) The second paragraph introduces the student writer's first major sub-idea, that women are waiting longer to start families. Along with this change has come a substantial rise in the number of children born to unmarried women. The writer observes research convention by introducing the source of a long or important quotation, especially when referring to the source for the first time. A prose quotation longer than four lines should be indented one inch or 10 spaces (left-hand margin only) and should not be enclosed in quotation marks. Also, do not single-space quotations. The parenthetical citation follows the final period of the quotation.

(7) A parenthetical citation is not necessary at the end of the indented quotation for two reasons: the corporate author of this source is mentioned in the introduction to the indented quotation, and the source is a Web site with no pagination (see pp. 727 and 729 for other examples of indented quotations). The superscript "1" at the end of the paragraph refers the reader to the "Notes" heading on p. 10 of the paper. On p. 6, superscript "2" appears. It, too, refers the reader to the "Notes" heading on p. 10.

(8) Because the author and title of the work have been introduced, only the page number needs to be placed in parentheses. Notice how in this sentence and the following paragraphs the quoted material is so well integrated into the grammatical structure of the text that it does not interrupt the natural flow of the ideas.

Hollingsworth 2

According to the National Center for Health Statistics, there has been a substantial rise in the number of children born to unmarried mothers:

> Out-of-wedlock childbearing has been increasing in the United States for over half a century. The rate of non-marital births in 1993 was more than six times the rate in 1940, and the proportion of births that occur outside marriage has risen from four to thirty-one percent. By most measures, the increase has accelerated sharply over the past fifteen years.[1]

Some of this new attitude can be attributed to the dramatic shift in the consciousness of women since the 1960s. The women's movement created feelings of empowerment and self-sufficiency, and the advent of the birth control pill gave a woman control over when to become a mother, if at all. These twin events also emboldened women to challenge the established paradigms on marriage and childbearing. Marriage became more optional as having a child on one's own became possible.

In her book, Going Solo: Single Mothers by Choice, Jean Renvoize claims that it is "impossible to look at the subject of single parenting by choice without considering what effect the women's movement has had and is continuing to have on women all over the world" (3).

The movement also opened a myriad of job opportunities for women, which many took advantage of, resulting in the postponement or relinquishment of marriage and children. In fact, it has been found that there is a direct correlation between the amount of education a

(9) The parenthetical citation indicates that this information is found on pages 116 and 117 in the source authored by Ludtke and fully documented in the "Works Cited."

woman has and her likelihood of having children. A survey conducted by Molly McKaughan in her book, <u>The Biological Clock</u>, reported that ". . . only a third of the women who did not attend college are childless, whereas over half of the college grads are in this position and over two thirds of the MBAs and women with PhDs or MDs hear the clock ticking" (3).

More women are pursuing higher education and professional occupations before beginning families, resulting in a higher median age for first-time brides and mothers, with some women forgoing marriage altogether and opting for single motherhood. The National Center for Health Statistics reports that among all unmarried women aged 35–39, the increase in birthrates from 1984–1994 was 82% (Ludtke 116–17).

Many women come from families of divorce and are waiting longer to get married, if only to avoid becoming involved in a messy divorce themselves. Women whose mothers married right after high school are pursuing academic and career ambitions rather than setting those aside and beginning a family immediately. The increase in opportunities has restructured women's priorities, and because fulfillment of personal goals has become more important to women than in previous years, many are willing to wait for their ideal partner. Today's woman doesn't need to rush into a marriage for reasons of financial security alone. She is often more economically independent than her mother and doesn't feel the pressure to succumb to society's antiquated convention of marrying a good provider. Instead, today's woman feels she deserves

more and is willing to wait for it. The National Center for Health Statistics indicates the following:

> Among . . . women in the early childbearing ages, the decline in the married population largely reflects delays in the timing of first marriage. The percent of women aged twenty-five to twenty-nine who had never been married tripled from eleven to thirty-three percent, between 1950 and 1992. (The Demography)

Consequently, because of these choices, more women are finding themselves approaching middle age unmarried and childless—a situation that can create feelings of disappointment in women who want to have a family. Melissa Ludtke, author of On Our Own: Unmarried Motherhood in America, offers the following assessment:

> Today, because cultural and economic forces encourage women to delay marriage and childbearing, many more women, married and single, arrive at their middle to late thirties feeling that they've missed out on a big part of what their lives were meant to include. (104)

Unfortunately a woman's childbearing years are finite and a "biological clock panic" may hit when a single woman who wants children nears forty. In an article titled "Saga of a Midlife Single Mom," one woman is quoted as making the following observation:

> I was starting to approach my 40th birthday. Up until then I was never around kids very much and, frankly, preferred the idea of a house full of dogs and cats. The 40th approach must have made

my biological clock start ticking more loudly. I didn't want to
be one of those women who at age 50 said, "Oops, I forgot
to have a baby." I began to feel like I was missing something
that was a really important experience—something that
would really mean something.

Concerned about their ability to conceive as they grow older, a number of these women begin to think about the possibility of having a child on their own. As Molly McKaughan states the case, "If a woman hears the clock ticking and is filled with anxiety about how much time she has left, she is more likely to consider going ahead on her own" (89). A study conducted by The Institute for Social Science Research in Los Angeles found that "half the women surveyed said they would consider having and rearing a child by themselves if they were childless by the time they reached their forties" (Ludtke 22).

The decision to opt for single motherhood is rarely taken lightly, and it is often not the woman's first choice. According to author Molly McKaughan,

> Eighty percent of women who say they are considering
> single motherhood plan on waiting three to five years
> before going ahead. Most are hoping that the elusive
> right man for them will show up and they will be able to
> have babies under normal circumstances. (104)

Many of these women have not disregarded marriage; however, they do not feel they must hinge their childbearing future on whether or not the right man comes along, and most are unwilling to settle for an

(10) The second major sub-idea is introduced—namely that advances in fertility technology are providing women with more options as to when and how to have children (see item II of outline). This assertion is then supported through documented evidence.

Hollingsworth 6

inadequate partner and potential father of their children merely to fulfill this desire. Cynthia, "one of the first in the wave of single professional women to choose deliberately to birth and raise a child without a partner," sums up her decision in these words: "I'm a single mother by choice, which doesn't mean that I'm choosing not to be in relationship with a man. It means that I was not in a relationship with a man and I chose to have a child. That's different" (Alexander 26).[2]

(10) Technology today is moving at an incredible pace, and some of the most amazing scientific discoveries have dealt with reproduction. Advances in fertility technology are providing women with numerous options, including when and how to conceive a child. Older women who have delayed pregnancy are not faced with the medical risks taken by earlier generations. In the past, single women who had chosen to conceive were forced to engage in risky sexual behavior, but sperm banks now offer a safe alternative along with a myriad of potential donors. Women can screen for everything from cultural background to IQ. California Cryobank, a Los Angeles sperm bank, estimates that 25% of the women seeking donor insemination are single. According to <u>When Baby Makes Two: Single Mothers by Chance or by Choice</u>, authored by Jene Stonesifer, "increasingly, single women who don't have a steady are turning to artificial insemination as a way to experience motherhood. Its appeal lies in that it is relatively safe, simple and affordable" (128–29). For costs ranging from $50.00 to $150.00 a day, donor insemination allows a woman to choose a deliberate pregnancy

11 Sub-idea number 3 is introduced (see item III of outline). Here the writer shows that the social stigma of being a single mother has diminished.

12 The source of the quotation is given as having been found on the Internet, its author's last name being Thornton. The full reference, of course, is found in "Works Cited."

in a safe, accessible fashion (*Donor Insemination Resources*). Moreover, there has been a dramatic alteration of society's perception of single mothers. In an article titled "Attitudes, Values and Norms Related to Non-marital Fertility," Arland Thornton gives this description:

> Recent data reveal fundamental shifts in values, attitudes, and norms concerning a wide range of family issues, including marriage, sexuality, and childbearing . . . In addition, attitudes and norms prohibiting . . . premarital sexual relationships, and childbearing outside of marriage have dramatically receded. Thus, many behaviors that were previously restricted by prevailing social norms and personal attitudes have become accepted by substantial fractions of Americans.

Whereas previously a woman who found herself unmarried and pregnant would either try to hide the fact from society or rush to get married, today's single mother experiences less societal opposition to her lifestyle. Because the single-parent phenomenon has become so widespread, its stigma has lessened dramatically and many Americans "agree that there is no reason why single women shouldn't have children and rear them if they want to" (Thornton).

No longer is the single mother regarded as a social deviant, and many single mothers are finding support from family, friends, and organized groups. This is true also for women who are consciously choosing this lifestyle. Single Mothers By Choice, a nationwide group devoted to providing information and support to single mothers, was

(13) The fourth and final sub-idea is introduced (see outline item IV). Here the writer deftly indicates that she realizes that some opposition exists to the modern idea of single mothers. But she quickly minimizes the opposing point of view by offering documentation supporting her thesis that single motherhood is here to stay and is a sign of the times.

described by one member as a group of "single women who chose to become single mothers; single mothers who are mature and responsible and who feel empowered rather than victimized" (Mattes xxi).

There are, however, opponents to the single-mother phenomenon. Critics argue that single motherhood signals a breakdown of traditional family values; yet these same critics fail to recognize that the traditional nuclear family is quickly becoming a thing of the past and that "in an era in which close to one half of all marriages end in divorce, belief in marriage as a secure, supportive relationship has greatly diminished" (Ludtke 117). By the mid-1990s, three of every ten families with young children had only one parent (usually the mother) living with them (25). Critics also argue that the absence of a father in the house causes harm to children growing up. However, they neglect to mention that the father, even if he still lives at home, often spends little time actually caring for the child. A study by Karl Zinsmeister, a DeWitt Wallace Fellow at the American Enterprise Institute, found that three-fourths of modern dads do not take regular responsibility for the daily care of their children; studies of children from kindergarten to tenth grade found that daily father-child interaction averages only between thirty minutes and two and a half hours (Stonesifer ii). And author Trish Wilson, in a critique of "Deconstructing the Essential Father," an article written by Louise B. Silverstein and Carl F. Auerbach, found that "Mothers, not fathers, continue to take on the bulk of the day-to-day childrearing and housekeeping, whether or not they work outside the home" (qtd. in Wilson).

(14) Like all good research papers, this one reflects mostly the ideas of outside sources, not the writer's own. Nevertheless, the student provides enough commentary of her own to make a convincing case for her thesis. As is proper in a formal research paper, the writer expresses her opinions without using the personal pronouns *I, me,* and *my.*

(14) On the whole, women's lives have changed dramatically in the last few decades, with one of the most significant lifestyle changes being the increasing numbers of women who are choosing the single-motherhood lifestyle. Pursuing her own goals and unwilling to settle for an unsatisfactory partner, today's single-mother-by-choice is truly a sign of the times.

(15) Both notes are listed on a separate page, under the "Notes" heading (not underlined and without quotation marks), centered and one inch from the top of the page. The Notes page appears at the end of the paper but before the "Works Cited" page. The notes are double-spaced throughout.

Hollingsworth 10

Notes

¹ An informal poll of my female friends indicated that the majority of them would not consider giving birth to a baby without a father to help in his or her upbringing.

² It must be noted that some sociologists see a backlash occurring and predict that the difficulties of being the sole breadwinner and parent are leading women to return to the traditional approach of waiting until they have a husband before planning to give birth.

16 The heading "Works Cited" (not underlined and without quotation marks) is centered on the page one inch from the top. The entire page is double-spaced. Notice that the second and subsequent lines of each entry are indented one-half inch. The entries appear in alphabetical order according to the first letter of the entry. Left and right margins are one inch.

17 Typical entry for a book.

18 Typical entry for a source found on the Internet.

Works Cited

Alexander, Shoshana. In Praise of Single Parents: Mothers and Fathers Embracing Challenges. New York: Houghton, 1994.

The Demography of Out-of-Wedlock Childbearing. 11 Sept. 2003. National Center for Health Statistics. 18 Sept. 2003 <http://www.cdc.gov/nchswww/data/Wedlock.pdf>.

Donor Insemination Resources. 6 Sept. 2003. <http://www.parentsplace.com/family/singleparent/gen/0,3375,10660,00.html>.

Fabe, Marilyn, and Norma Wikler. Up Against the Clock: Career Women Speak on the Choice to Have Children. New York: Random House, 1979.

Ludtke, Melissa. On Our Own: Unmarried Motherhood in America. New York: Random House, 1997.

Mattes, Jane. Single Mothers by Choice: A Guidebook for Single Women Who Are Considering or Have Chosen Single Motherhood. New York: Random House, 1994.

McKaughan, Molly. The Biological Clock. New York: Doubleday, 1987.

Renvoize, Jean. Going Solo: Single Mothers by Choice. New York: Routledge, 1985.

"Saga of a Midlife Single Mom." 15 September 1999. Midlife Mommies. 20 Sept. 2003. <http://www.midlifemommies.com/singlemompart1.html>.

Stonesifer, Jene. When Baby Makes Two: Single Mothers by Chance or by Choice. Los Angeles: Lowell, 1994.

(19) Typical entry for a periodical with an annual volume as well as issue number.

Thornton, Arland. <u>Attitudes, Values and Norms Related to Non-marital Fertility</u>. 20 Sept. 2003. Institute for Social Research, Department of Sociology and Population Studies Center at the University of Michigan. 25 Sept. 2003. <http://www.cdc.gov/nchswww/data/Wedlock.pdf>.

Wilson, Trish. "Deconstructing Fatherhood Propaganda." <u>Feminista</u> 3.4 (1999): 34–38.

ANNOTATED STUDENT RESEARCH PAPER

American Psychological Association (APA) Style

Development of a Scale to
Detect Sexual Harassers:
The Potential Harasser Scale (PHS)
Leanne M. Masden
and
Rebecca B. Winkler
DePaul University

(1) The Abstract should not exceed 120 words. Any numbers present in the Abstract should appear as Arabic numerals (except a number that begins a sentence).

Development of a Scale 2

Abstract

(1) The current study was an attempt to design a scale to detect one's propensity to sexually harass women. The Likelihood to Sexually Harass (LSH) scale designed by Pryor (1987) was used as a starting point in probing the characteristics held by men who sexually harass women. Using existing research, an initial scale was designed and tested on a pilot sample of men known to the authors. After the scale was completed by the participants, statistics were calculated and explored to determine which items needed to be retained and which needed to be dropped. Following these analyses, the Potential Harasser Scale (PHS) was determined to be statistically sound and ready for future use.

(2) This is a typical citation, appearing at the sentence's conclusion and followed by a period. This work has three authors.

(3) Because the information mentioned in this sentence is derived from three different sources, the paper's authors have chosen to place each citation adjacent to the corresponding element. Note that the first citation identifies a source with two authors, the second citation has three authors, and the third citation has one author.

Development of a Scale to Detect Sexual Harassers:
The Potential Harasser Scale (PHS)

Our interest in the current topic was first sparked as a result of sexual harassment being the focus of one team member's master's thesis. Current estimates state that approximately one out of every two women will be sexually harassed at least once during her working or educational life (Fitzgerald, Swan, & Magley, 1997). But why do so many women experience sexual harassment? Researchers have found evidence to support a power threat motive for offenders, whereby women who possess certain characteristics that would put them in direct competition with men for resources are more likely to be harassed, apparently in an attempt to dissuade them from entering the male-dominated sphere of privilege and power. Some such female characteristics are having egalitarian sex-role attitudes (Dall'Ara & Maass, 1999), being single, having more education and longer tenure within the organization (DeCoster, Estes, & Mueller, 1999), and being young (Gruber, 1998). However, there is not pure consensus in the field regarding the effect of age on the risk of being sexually harassed (O'Connell & Korabik, 2000). Because men are more likely than women to be perpetrators of sexual harassment (Fitzgerald, Magley, Drasgow, & Waldo, 1999), this particular population will be the focus of the present study.

During the initial research process, we discovered the Likelihood to Sexually Harass (LSH) scale, originally developed by Pryor (1987). This scale was designed to measure one's propensity to sexually harass based on the possession of certain characteristics that perpetrators of sexual

4. Because the authors are mentioned in the sentence, a citation is not necessary at the sentence's conclusion.

5. The paper's first-level internal heading appears centered, using uppercase and lowercase.

6. The paper's second-level internal heading appears flush with the left margin, using italicized uppercase and lowercase.

harassment tend to have. This scale gave us the direction we needed to conduct further research in order to identify the relevant constructs this topic contained. Luckily, the LSH scale has generated a fair amount of research as a result of others attempting to find exactly what constructs this scale measures. For example, Driscoll, Kelly, and Henderson (1998) found that men who scored high on the LSH also held more traditional views toward women, more negative views toward women, and had a more masculine personality. Other researchers also found that aggression, acceptance of interpersonal violence, fraternity affiliation, and sex-role stereotyping were related to scoring high on the LSH (Lackie & de Man, 1997). In addition, Pryor (1987) showed that men scoring high on the LSH found it more difficult to view things from another's perspective and had higher authoritarian beliefs. As a result of this research, we now knew what we needed to include when we started to develop our own Potential Harasser Scale (PHS).

Method

Item and Scale Development

After reading the relevant research on our topic, we decided that our scale should include eight dimensions plus a few demographic questions. We also decided that each dimension should have four items. Our eight dimensions were as follows: aggression, sex role stereotyping (i.e., holding traditional views toward women), egalitarianism/negative views toward women, masculinity, acceptance of interpersonal violence, lack of empathy, authoritarianism, and hostile environment behaviors.

The first seven dimensions were derived from the current literature on the topic of sexual harassment and related concepts. However, the last dimension was developed to fill a gap in the existing LSH scale. The LSH scale is designed to detect sexual harassers who exhibit *quid pro quo* behaviors, meaning those who attempt to exchange sexual favors for work-related promotions or other advantages (Pryor, 1987). However, this focus fails to address other forms of sexual harassment, such as hostile environment behaviors. This type of sexual harassment is considered to be less severe but even more pervasive (Fitzgerald, Gelfand, & Drasgow, 1995). Therefore, we thought it would be important to attempt to capture this dimension in our PHS instrument.

We also included a few demographic questions to see if age, race, or marital status were related to one's potential to sexually harass. In addition, a short section about fraternity membership and extent of one's involvement were included as a result of this affiliation being significantly related in previous research (Lackie & de Man, 1997). Therefore, our total scale had 37 items, 32 in the actual scale and 5 demographic questions. Furthermore, we renamed our instrument the *Personal Beliefs Questionnaire* so that those who completed our instrument would not be alerted to what it was attempting to measure.

Characteristics of the Pilot Sample

We recruited male classmates, co-workers, fathers, and significant others to complete our scale. As a result of our efforts, we had 14 respondents. All of them were Caucasian with the exception of one Hispanic. In addition, three individuals in our sample were married, five were single, and six currently

lived with a partner. Our respondents ranged in age from 23 to 60, with a mean age of 30.28. Concerning fraternity affiliation, 35.7% of our sample were members of a fraternity, and 40% reported being "very involved."

Results

Results of Preliminary Item Analyses

First, we cleaned the data by looking at the frequencies and descriptive statistics. All values were within the expected range, so we considered our data to be clean. By taking a closer look at our means and standard deviations, we immediately noticed some items had extremely low standard deviations. For example, item 11 asks about one's acceptance of domestic violence. Whether the answers reflected socially desirable responses due to lack of anonymity with only 14 respondents or true beliefs, everyone in our sample strongly disagreed with the appropriateness of hitting one's spouse.

We scanned the correlation matrix including all of our items, and with the exception of item 11, which had no correlations due to its lack of variance, every other item exhibited at least one theoretically meaningful correlation with another item. For example, two items relating to aggression were significantly correlated (i.e., "I am an aggressive driver" and "I enjoy playing sports with a lot of physical contact"). The only items that were not significantly correlated with anything else on the scale were those that tapped into fraternity affiliation and involvement.

We also ran an intraclass correlation analysis to determine our scale's internal consistency. As a result, our Cronbach's alpha was $r = .8069$, which shows that our scale had high internal consistency.

(7) The authors refer the reader to the Appendix, which appears at the paper's conclusion and following the References.

Final Scale Revision
Based on our initial item analyses, we determined that a few changes could be made that would improve our scale's psychometric properties. Therefore, we removed the items on fraternity affiliation and involvement. Although previous research has shown these constructs to be related to one's likelihood to sexually harass (Lackie & de Man, 1997), our analyses showed that these items were the only ones that were not significantly correlated to any other item in our scale. Since these items were in the demographics section, they were not included in the intraclass correlation analysis. Therefore, this analysis was not re-run, because no improvement would have been noted here.

Although traditional scale construction theory would normally guide us to remove a few other items due to their low standard deviations, we decided that the low variance on these items was most likely due to the restrictions placed on us by our small sample. If we were to administer our scale to more people in a more anonymous setting, perhaps we would not see the same restricted variance due to the greater chance of people answering truthfully. In our small and familiar sample, we found many answers that may have been driven by a socially desirable and appropriate manner of responding. See the Appendix for the final version of the PHS.

Discussion

This project taught us many valuable lessons. To begin with, we were pleased with the fact that we were able to construct a theoretically

meaningful instrument that also displayed desirable psychometric properties, such as our high Cronbach's alpha. In addition, it was an interesting experience to design items that fit into our proposed dimensions. We also had a fun time piloting it on our sample and gathering the reactions from our participants, in addition to analyzing their answers to draw the relevant conclusions on our new tool. However, there are also many things we would have done differently had this been a "real world" project.

First, merely masking our scale's true intent by designing a new label did not do much to mask the content and what we were trying to measure. Our participants (especially our classmates) could tell by the transparency of many of our items what we were aiming for. In addition, although we believe our sample to be well-educated and fairly liberal overall in their views toward women, they all still knew that we would be analyzing their responses and would probably be able to tell who was who if we really wanted to. Therefore, there may have been some socially desirable responding that caused many of our items to have low variances.

Some improvements in methodology could prevent this type of responding from occurring. For example, administering this scale in a more anonymous format with many other respondents (e.g., in an auditorium setting) would probably allow more truthful answers to emerge. Furthermore, if the scale items could be embedded within a larger instrument, the aim of the Potential Harasser Scale would also be less obvious. Overall, however, we were pleased with both the process and the results.

During the course of this project, we each also attempted to contact a publisher who had designed a relevant scale. One person contacted the

company Risk and Needs Assessment, Inc., to obtain their Sexual Adjustment Inventory. The other person contacted Sigma Assessment Systems to obtain their Sex-Role Egalitarianism Scale.

Both of us were successful in our endeavors and did not have to endure any trouble at all. One team member simply called the publisher and received a sample packet in a matter of days that included one test book, two answer sheets, one training manual, one example report, and a computer disk that provided the scoring key program. The other person e-mailed the publisher and received a sample brochure in the mail a few days later. Therefore, the ease in contacting the publishers was about equal between the two team members, but the amount of scale information given varied greatly.

In summary, working on this project allowed us to put into action much of the theory that we have spent the past 10 weeks learning. It was interesting to us to experience the process of developing a scale as well as learning to deal with some of the pitfalls that inevitably occur with not having a large group of people we don't know to pilot our instrument on.

However, all in all, we think we will be better survey and test developers in the future as a result of constructing the Potential Harasser Scale.

(8) The list of references appears on a separate page (or pages), with the heading "References" centered at the top of the page. All references cited in the text must appear in the Reference list; and each entry in the Reference list must be cited in the text of the paper. Note that APA now prefers italicizing titles of books, magazines and journals over underlining.

(9) References with the same first author and different second, third, or fourth authors are alphabetized by the surname of the second author (or, if the second author is the same in the two references, the surname of the third).

Development of a Scale 10

References

Dall'Ara, E., & Maass, A. (1999). Studying sexual harassment in the laboratory: Are egalitarian women at higher risk? *Sex Roles, 41*(9/10), 681–704. Retrieved December 9, 2002, from Proquest Education Complete database.

DeCoster, S., Estes, S. B., & Mueller, C.W. (1999). Routine activities and sexual harassment in the workplace. *Work and Occupations, 26*(1), 21–49.

Driscoll, D. M., Kelly, J. R., & Henderson, W. L. (1998). Can perceivers identify likelihood to sexually harass? *Sex Roles, 38*(7/8), 557–588.

Fitzgerald, L. F., Gelfand, M. J., & Drasgow, F. (1995). Measuring sexual harassment: Theoretical and psychometric advances. *Basic and Applied Social Psychology, 17,* 425–427.

Fitzgerald, L. F., Magley, V. J., Drasgow, F., & Waldo, C. R. (1999). Measuring sexual harassment in the military: The sexual experiences questionnaire (SEQ-DoD). *Military Psychology, 11*(3), 243–263. Retrieved December 9, 2002, from Academic Search Elite database.

Fitzgerald, L. F., Swan, S., & Magley, V. J. (1997). But was it really sexual harassment? Legal, behavioral, and psychological definitions of the workplace victimization of women. In W. O'Donohue (Ed.), *Sexual harassment: Theory, research, and treatment* (pp. 5–28). Boston: Allyn & Bacon.

Gruber, J. E. (1998). The impact of male work environments and organizational policies on women's experiences of sexual harassment. *Gender and Society, 12*(3), 301–320.

Lackie, L., & de Man, A. F. (1997). Correlates of sexual aggression among male university students. *Sex Roles, 37*(5/6), 451–457.

O'Connell, C. E., & Korabik, K. (2000). Sexual harassment: The relationship of personal vulnerability, work context, perpetrator status, and type of harassment to outcomes. *Journal of Vocational Behavior, 56,* 299–329.

Pryor, J. B. (1987). Sexual harassment proclivities in men. *Sex Roles, 17*(5/6), 269–290.

(10) If the paper has only one appendix, label it Appendix. If your paper has more than one appendix, label each one with a capital letter (e.g., Appendix A, Appendix B). Provide a title for each appendix.

Development of a Scale 12

(10) → Appendix

Personal Beliefs Questionnaire

Please rate how strongly you agree or disagree with the following statements using the scale provided below. Please answer all questions honestly; note that all of your answers will remain anonymous.

1 = Strongly Disagree
2 = Disagree
3 = Neither Agree nor Disagree
4 = Agree
5 = Strongly Agree

1. Being around strong women makes me uncomfortable.	1	2	3	4	5
2. I am an aggressive driver (e.g., I cut people off, honk the horn often).	1	2	3	4	5
3. I believe some women are to blame for being raped (e.g., by wearing sexy clothes, flirting, etc.).	1	2	3	4	5
4. I believe that every citizen should have the right to carry a gun.	1	2	3	4	5
5. I believe that it is important for a woman to take care of her body so that she looks good for her man.	1	2	3	4	5
6. I believe that it is important to volunteer time or donate money to help others in need.	1	2	3	4	5

Development of a Scale 13

1 = Strongly Disagree
2 = Disagree
3 = Neither Agree nor Disagree
4 = Agree
5 = Strongly Agree

7. I believe that men should be the primary breadwinners for their families.	1	2	3	4	5
8. I believe that most homeless people are still homeless because they are lazy.	1	2	3	4	5
9. I believe that people should respect their place within an organizational hierarchy.	1	2	3	4	5
10. I believe that some women are still paid less than men for doing the same work.	1	2	3	4	5
11. I believe that sometimes it is OK for a husband to hit his wife.	1	2	3	4	5
12. I believe that too many women are focusing too much on their careers, to the detriment of their families.	1	2	3	4	5
13. I believe that too many women are trying to enter occupations that are better suited for men.	1	2	3	4	5
14. I believe that women should be primarily responsible for taking care of children.	1	2	3	4	5
15. I believe that women should not play sports with a lot of physical contact (e.g., football).	1	2	3	4	5

Development of a Scale 14

1 = Strongly Disagree
2 = Disagree
3 = Neither Agree nor Disagree
4 = Agree
5 = Strongly Agree

16. I display pictures of naked/near naked women at work/school.	1	2	3	4	5
17. I do not question the decisions made by the President.	1	2	3	4	5
18. I enjoy cooking for others.	1	2	3	4	5
19. I enjoy magazines that display pictures of scantily clad women.	1	2	3	4	5
20. I enjoy participating in cultural events (e.g., attending dramatic plays, museums, poetry readings).	1	2	3	4	5
21. I enjoy playing sports with a lot of physical contact.	1	2	3	4	5
22. I enjoy playing video games that allow you to fight and kill others.	1	2	3	4	5
23. I enjoy watching action movies with scenes involving car crashes, fights, and guns.	1	2	3	4	5
24. I flirt with women at my place of work/school.	1	2	3	4	5
25. I often get into fights.	1	2	3	4	5
26. I tell lewd jokes at work/school.	1	2	3	4	5

1 = Strongly Disagree

2 = Disagree

3 = Neither Agree nor Disagree

4 = Agree

5 = Strongly Agree

27. I tend to raise my voice when I am upset.	1	2	3	4	5
28. I think it is important to obey authority figures.	1	2	3	4	5
29. I try to put myself in others' shoes to help me understand their situation.	1	2	3	4	5
30. In spousal disagreements, I believe that the man should have the final say.	1	2	3	4	5
31. Watching the nightly news can be depressing.	1	2	3	4	5
32. When it comes to asking a girl for a date, I don't take no for an answer.	1	2	3	4	5

Demographics

33. How old are you? ____

34. What is your race? Check one.

☐ Caucasian ☐ African American ☐ Hispanic
☐ Asian ☐ Native American Other____

35. Please indicate your marital status. Check one.

☐ Married ☐ Single ☐ Divorced
☐ Widowed ☐ Living with partner

36. Did you belong to a fraternity? Circle one.   Yes   No

If so, how involved were you? Circle one.

Not at all involved   Somewhat involved   Very involved

Suggestions for Writing

1. Following the style advocated by your instructor, write a five- to eight-page research paper on one of the following psychological problems:
   a. Anorexia nervosa in teenage girls
   b. Effects of loneliness and alienation on the elderly
   c. The effects of divorce on children under the age of ten
   d. Alcoholism among high school students

   Be sure to document any significant statement that is not your own.

2. Write a paper on the relationship between art and social class. Focus your research on the following queries:
   a. Does art reflect a class bias?
   b. Do different classes hold different standards for judging art?
   c. Are these standards related to the ways different classes perceive the world?
   d. Is there a sociology of art?

3. Choosing any poem or short story in this book, write a literary analysis focusing on theme, character, action, or form.

PART IV WRITING ASSIGNMENTS

Write a research paper, following the format suggested by your instructor. Above all, choose a topic in which you have a genuine interest. The following titles and restricted theses are presented to stimulate your own investigation.

Title	*Thesis*
"A Look at Thomas Wolfe"	The inconsistencies in Thomas Wolfe's writing can be directly attributed to constant family conflicts, to his doubts concerning his country's economic stability, and to his fear of not being accepted by his reading public.
"American Architectural Development"	The development of American architecture was greatly attenuated until the eighteenth century because of the lack of adequate transportation and manufacturing facilities, and because city life had not formed prior to that century.
"Wordsworth and Coleridge: Their Diverse Philosophies"	Although Wordsworth and Coleridge were both Romantic poets, they believed in two completely different philosophies of nature.
"Why Jazz Was What We Wanted"	Various trends led to the rise, development, and recognition of jazz as an important part of

Title	Thesis
	American musical culture during the nineteenth and twentieth centuries.
"The Influence of Imagism on Twentieth-Century Poetry"	Imagism, a self-restricted movement, has greatly influenced twentieth-century poetry.
"Automation and Employment"	The current fear of humans being displaced by machines, or what alarmists term the "automation hysteria," is based on insubstantial reports.
"Needed: A New Definition of Insanity"	Our courts need a better definition of insanity because neither the M'Naghten Rule nor the psychological definition is adequate.
"The Proud Sioux"	The Sioux Indians, although confined to a shabby reservation, still fought on stubbornly against their captors—the white man and his hard-to-accept peace terms.
"Women's Fashions after the World Wars"	The First and the Second World Wars had significant effects on women's fashions in America.
"Charlie Chaplin"	Various factors made Charlie Chaplin the master of silent movies.
"The Funnies"	Today's funnies reflect a change in America's attitude toward violence, ethnic minorities, and ecology.
"The Decline of the Mayans"	The four most popular theories that have been advanced to explain the abrupt end of the Mayan civilization are the effects of natural disaster, physical weaknesses, detrimental social changes, and foreign influence.
"Relief Paintings in Egyptian Mastabas"	The relief paintings found in the mastabas depict the everyday life of the Egyptian people.
"Athena"	The goddess Athena bestowed her favors not on those who worshipped her, but on those who fought for their own beliefs.
"Goldfish"	Originally from China, goldfish have been bred into one of the most beautiful and marketable species of fish.

ASSIGNMENT 2: THE LITERARY PAPER

How to Write a Paper about Literature

Literature is a difficult subject to write about. First, it is a subject about which there is no shortage of opinions; a famous play such as *Hamlet* has been so thoroughly studied and interpreted that it would take a tome or two to collect everything that has been written about it. Beginning writers must therefore always live in dread that what they have to say about a work may be blasphemously contrary to established opinion.

Second, the beginning writer is often unaware of the tradition or era into which a piece of literature falls. Yet to write intelligently about a piece of literature, a student must be able to distinguish the qualities of its literary tradition from the properties singular to the particular work. It is nearly impossible, for instance, to write comprehensibly about the work of a Romantic poet unless one knows something about the disposition of Romanticism.

However, the beginning student is rarely called upon to perform any such feat of interpretation. Instead, what an instructor generally wishes to evoke from a student writer is simply an intelligent exploration of a work's meaning, along with a straightforward discussion of one or two of its techniques. The student might therefore be asked to analyze the meaning of a sonnet and to comment briefly on its prosody, to discuss the theme of a short story and to examine the actions and attitudes of a principal character, or to explain the social customs upon which a certain play is based.

Even so, there are numerous pitfalls awaiting the beginning commentator on literature. The first of these is a tendency to emote over a literary favorite. Students who fall victim to this trait mistake sentimentality for judgment, and write enthusiastically about how much they like a particular work. But this is not what the instructor is generally looking for in a student's essay. What is desired is not an outpouring of affection, but the careful expression of critical judgment.

A second mistake beginning students of literature often make is assuming that one opinion about a literary piece is as valid and as good as another. It is only in literature classes that one finds such extreme democracy. Geologists do not assume that one opinion about a rock is the same as another, nor do chemists or astronomers blithely accept every theory about chemicals and planets. This fallacious view of criticism has its origin in the mistaken belief that one's primary reaction toward literature is emotional. But the emotional response evoked by the literary work is not what a writing assignment is designed to draw out of a student. Instead, what the instructor is looking for is reasoned opinion based on a close reading of the text. Disagreements in interpretation can then be referred to the text, and evidence can be gathered to support one view over another. It is very much like two lawyers getting together to interpret the fine print on a contract. It is not at all like two people trying to reconcile their differing reactions to anchovy pizza. Interpretations that cannot be supported by the text may be judged far-fetched or simply wrong; those that can be supported may be judged *more* right.

But perhaps the most common mistake of the student-critic is a tendency to serve up inconsistent, unproven, and fanciful interpretations of the literary work. Often, these take the guise of rather exotic meanings that the student has inferred and for which scanty (if any) evidence exists. In its most extreme form, this tendency leads to rampant symbol hunting, whereby the writer finds complex and knotty meanings bristling behind the most innocent statements. The only known cure is the insistence that all interpretations be grounded in material taken from the text itself. If you have devised an ingenious explanation or reading of a work, be certain that you can point to specific passages from it that support your interpretations, and always make sure that other passages do not contradict your thesis.

The In-Class Essay on Literature

Often students are asked to analyze and interpret literature in class-written essays. The literary work may consist of a poem, a passage from a novel being read by the class, a short story, or a play. Depending on how the assignment is worded, the student may be required to find and express the theme, analyze an action, interpret a symbol, or comment on form.

Finding and Expressing a Theme The theme of a literary work is its central or dominant idea, its comment on life. Finding and expressing this idea involves a form of literary algebra that requires students to think logically from cause to effect. Of course, writers say more than any summary theme can possibly express; finding a theme should not involve smothering a writer's work under a crude and simplistic summary. Instead, in the summary you should compress into a few brief sentences what you interpret as the emphasis of the work.

Consider the poem "Design" (p. 553). A moth has been found dead in a spider's web spun on a heal-all flower. The poet wonders what could have brought the moth to this particular flower, where a web was spun and a spider was waiting. Why didn't the moth go to another, safer flower? This apparently trivial discovery leads the poem to speculate that destiny operates in random and mysterious ways, which is more or less the central emphasis or theme of the poem.

This theme can, of course, be stated in several ways. So, for that matter, can the theme of any poem or other literary work. What you must do, after you have deciphered the theme of the work, is to make a statement and prove it. Proof can be supplied by quoting lines and passages from the work. The instructor can then reconstruct the process of thinking behind your conclusion. If you have misinterpreted the work, the proof allows the instructor to see how your misreading occurred.

Analyzing Character and Action Fictional characters behave according to the same hopes, fears, hates, and loves that motivate real people, but the characters of fiction are found in exotic dilemmas real people hardly ever encounter. Consequently, fiction provides us with an opportunity to ponder how common people might react in uncommon situations; we can then draw moral lessons, psychological principles, and philosophical insights from their behavior. Without fiction, we would remain hemmed in by the narrow horizons of reality and experience.

By asking you to write an essay explaining why a certain character performed a certain action, your instructor is fostering valuable skills of social analysis. If you can understand the rage and jealousy of Othello or the isolated pride of Hester Prynne, you are better equipped to understand these emotions in yourself or in your acquaintances.

When you state that a certain character behaves a certain way, the burden of proof is on you. It is not enough to say that Hamlet was indecisive or weak, or that Lear was overweening and arrogant, or that the unidentified male character in "Hills Like White Elephants" is petty and selfish. In every instance, you must quote passages that prove your interpretation.

Interpreting Symbols In its most literal sense, a symbol is a thing that stands for something beyond itself. The dove is a symbol of peace; the flag is the symbol of a country. In literature, a symbol is created when an author invests an object, an idea, or an action with a significance far beyond itself. A person may also be treated in such a way as to symbolize a class or a group of people.

Most of the time, symbolism is implicit in literature. The reader is left to unravel the meaning of the symbol. Indeed, the effect of a symbol would otherwise be ruined by preachiness. But occasionally an author will come out and say what a certain symbol means. For instance, in "Ars Poetica" (p. 402), the poet tells us explicitly that "An empty doorway and a maple leaf" are symbols that stand for "all the history of grief." In the interpretation of symbols, it is less a matter of who is right or wrong than of who has proven a point and who has not. Symbols rarely have cut-and-dried, unarguable meanings. Considerable variation in the interpretation of symbols is not only possible, but extremely likely. Whatever your interpretation, however, it must be supported by material quoted from the text.

Commenting on Form For the most part, this type of assignment applies to poetry, where the student has numerous opportunities to express a knowledge of the terms and concepts of prosody. (Fiction and drama contain fewer nameable techniques.) In writing about a poem, you may be asked to describe its verse form or its meter, or to label and identify various tropes and figures of speech.

Wherever possible, use the formal names of any techniques present in a work. If you know that the poem you are analyzing is an Italian sonnet, it does no harm to say so. If you know that a certain action in a play occurs in its *denouement*, you should not be bashful about using that term. If a story begins *in media res* and then proceeds in *flashbacks,* you should say so. Your use of such labels will show an instructor that you have not only mastered the meaning of the work but have also grasped its form.

In summary, when writing about literature, you should do more than simply ascribe a certain interpretation to the literary work. Your prime purpose should be to prove that your reading of the work is reasonable and logical. Passages from the work should be liberally quoted to support your paper's interpretation of it. Above all, never assume that any reading of a work, no matter how unsupported or farfetched, will do.

Bear one thing in mind before you begin to write your paper: Famous literary works, especially works regarded as classics, have been thoroughly studied to the point where prevailing opinion on them has assumed the character of orthodoxy. What may seem to you a brilliant insight may, in fact, be nothing more than what critics have been saying about the writer and his or her works for years. Saying that Hemingway's male characters suffer from *machismo* is a little like the anthropology student opining that humans are bipedal. Both remarks are undoubtedly true, but they are neither original nor insightful. You should, therefore, check out the prevailing critical opinions on a writer before attempting to dogmatize on your own.

ANNOTATED LITERARY PAPER

The following literary paper is one student's response to the following assignment: "Write a 500-word critical analysis of Eudora Welty's 'A Worn Path,' focusing on character, action, mood, setting, and literary techniques such as diction, figurative language, and symbolism. Choose those strategies that best illumine the theme of the narrative." (See this essay on pp. 264–270.)

① The introductory paragraph captures the reader's attention by creating a "jewel" metaphor. It also presents the reviewer's unqualified literary judgment—that "A Worn Path" is an excellent, moving story.

② Paragraph two provides a summary of the story's literal level, allowing even the uninitiated reader to comprehend the reviewer's comments and interpretations.

---

*The Arabic numerals in the left margin of the student paper correspond to the comments on the facing page.

Inman 1

Douglas B. Inman
English 102
Professor McCuen-Metherell
March 15, 2006

A Worn but Lightly Traveled Path

(1) In this day when mediocrity is praised as inspiration and chaos as art, it is refreshing to find among the literary dung heaps a jewel, shining and glittering and making one forget, for the moment, the overwhelming stench and filth that threatens to suffocate and squeeze the very life from one's literary soul. Eudora Welty's "A Worn Path" is such a rare jewel. Here is a story that exudes craftsmanship from every pore. It is filled with finely turned phrases, distinctly vivid imagery, and carefully constructed moods; but, more importantly, it tells its story well, communicating on many different levels. Ms. Welty demonstrates a firm command of the art of storytelling, and the way she weaves this particular tapestry of words will convince the reader that here is a lady who could turn a sow's ear into silk.

(2) "A Worn Path" is the portrait of Phoenix Jackson, an old Negro woman, seen making a trip to town to retrieve badly needed medicine for her ailing grandchild. Burdened by age and faced with obstacles, she nevertheless presses on, stoically pursuing her goal. On the most obvious level, this is the story of an eccentric but delightful woman whose spirit

(3) Paragraph three begins the most important part of this critical review. The student has chosen to focus on the symbolic level of the story. For him, the importance of the narrative lies in its relationship to the history of black freedom in America.

(4) Here, as in several other passages, the reviewer carefully quotes from the story in order to bolster his argument—that the plight of Phoenix Jackson is also the history of blacks in America. Notice that each quotation is smoothly integrated into the main text of the essay. Note also that when Phoenix Jackson, the character, is speaking, the student writer uses single quotation marks within double quotation marks. But when the student is quoting the narrator, he uses double quotation marks only. In this way the reader can distinguish what the narrator says from what the character says in monologue or dialogue.

(5) The reviewer is straightforward in his explication of the thorn bush as a significant individual symbol within the total allegorical framework.

Inman 2

belies her advanced years. She makes the long and arduous trip to town despite the great distance, the many obstacles she encounters, and an encroaching senility that gently touches the soul of the reader. She climbs hills, crosses a creek by way of a suspended log, crawls under a barbed wire fence, marches through fields, confronts a stray dog, and comes to grips with exhaustion, hallucinations, and a failing memory. And throughout these ordeals, the author reveals a character filled with pride and dignity.

But there is another story here, one played out on a much deeper level. It is the story of black people in America, and their struggle for freedom and equality. The path Phoenix follows is the road of life for her people, and the obstacles she encounters on the way become the challenges of being black.

For instance, she comes to a hill. "'Seems like there is chains about my feet, time I get this far,'" she says, and we know that it is the hill out of slavery that she must climb. And she does it, although "'something,'" white people perhaps, "'pleads I should stay.'" And when she gets to the top, she turns and gives a "full, severe look behind her where she had come." Doubtless this action represents the black race scrutinizing in retrospect some especially difficult scene in the drama of their freedom. Phoenix encounters opposition to her newfound freedom in the form of a thorny bush, and here her dress is a symbol of that freedom, as she struggles to free herself from the thorns without tearing her garment. But

(6,7) Two more symbols—the marble cake and the scarecrow—are interpreted.

(8) The reviewer alludes to Egyptian mythology in order to draw attention to the special significance of the heroine's name.

(9) The reviewer points out other bird symbols and interprets them. Even the little grandson is seen as a bird symbol. Again, quotations from the story are used as primary sources to support the reviewer's claims.

Inman 3

she maintains her dignity, showing no spite for the thorns, saying "'you doing your appointed work. Never want to let folks past—.'" And finally, trembling from the experience, "she stood free."

(6) But freedom for blacks is an illusive thing, as the reader understands when a small boy seems to bring Phoenix a slice of marble-cake, "but when she went to take it there was just her own hand in the air." Like the cake, freedom for the blacks has historically often been a seductive picture that seemed real; yet, when the blacks tried to claim it, it dissolved back into fantasy.

Phoenix passes through the childhood of her race when she traverses fields of "withered cotton" and "dead corn." She encounters "something tall, black, and skinny," and it is both a
(7) scarecrow and the image of slavery past. "'Who be you the ghost of?'" she asks, but there is only silence and the scarecrow dancing in the wind. And here Phoenix is the Negro of the past giving way to the future, as she intones, "'Dance, old scarecrow, while I dancing with you.'"

In this story, birds are used repeatedly to symbolize freedom.
(8) The character's very name, Phoenix, is an illustration of this strategy, for the phoenix was a bird in Egyptian mythology which, every five hundred years, would consume itself in fire and then rise renewed from the ashes, as blacks rose from slavery after the Civil War. Other bird symbols occur. For
(9) instance, Phoenix comes to a place where quail are walking about, and she tells then, as she would young Negroes, "'Walk

(10) The reviewer begins to summarize by focusing on the mood of the story, calling it "optimistic." In other words, the summary appraisal is that this is a story of hope and triumph, not of bitterness and despair.

Inman 4

pretty. This is the easy place. This is the easy going,'" referring to the new time of freedom after the Civil War. And when she encounters a white hunter, she sees in his sack a bobwhite, "with its beak hooked bitterly to show it was dead," indicating that even though slavery has been abolished, whites still managed to oppress blacks, and the struggle for black freedom is not yet complete.

Phoenix's grandson represents the new generation of blacks who never knew slavery, but still feel its impact, and he too is portrayed as a bird of freedom. "'He suffer and it don't seem to put him back at all. He got a sweet look. He going to last. He wear a little patch quilt and peep out, holding his mouth open like a little bird,'" she tells a nurse in town.

(10) → Overall, the story is an optimistic outlook on the black experience. Though much of the action focuses on earlier hardship, it ends with hope for the future, as can be seen when Phoenix finally reaches town. There, it is Christmastime, while during her journey it is simply a cold December day. In town, dozens of black children whirl around her in the street, bells are ringing, and colorful lights abound. "'Here I be,'" she says, indicating the end of the journey, the attaining of freedom and new life. And already the past is being forgotten; all the slavery, the fight for freedom, the long and painful road to happiness is but a dim memory. "'It was my memory had left me,'" she says near the end, "'There I sat and forgot why I made my long trip.'"

"'Forgot?'" asks the nurse. " 'After you came so far?'"

11. The final paragraph makes the point that it is Phoenix Jackson, the heroine and major character of the story, who gives the story its meaning and beauty. The concluding sentence brings the analysis full circle by using the same jewel/gem metaphor used in the introduction.

(11) This is the story of a courageous and dignified old woman on a long journey, but it is also the story of a courageous and dignified race, and their long struggle for freedom and equality. With wonderful artistry, Eudora Welty takes the reader along, to travel this worn path of struggle that has been trudged by so many peoples over the ages. She shows the dignity in the struggle and the hope of a new generation. And she does so with the craftsmanship of a fine watchmaker. One cannot help but be changed in some way by this beautiful story. "A Worn Path" is truly a gem.

Glossary

abstract Said of words or phrases denoting ideas, qualities, and conditions that exist but cannot be seen. *Love,* for example, is an abstract term; so are *happiness, beauty,* and *patriotism.* The opposites of abstract terms are concrete ones—words that refer to things that are tangible, visible, or otherwise physically evident. *Hunger* is abstract, but *hamburger* is concrete. The best writing blends the abstract with the concrete, with concrete terms used in greater proportion to clarify abstract ones. Writing that is too steeped in abstract words or terms tends to be vague and unfocused.

ad hominem **argument** A fallacious argument that attacks the integrity or character of an opponent rather than the merits of an issue. (*Ad hominem* is Latin for "to the man.") It is also informally known as "mud-slinging."

ad populum **argument** A fallacious argument that appeals to the passions and prejudices of a group rather than to its reason. (*Ad populum* is Latin for "to the people.") An appeal, for instance, to support an issue because it's "the American Way" is an *ad populum* argument.

allusion A casual reference to some famous literary work, historical figure, or event. For example, to say that a friend "has the patience of Job" means that he is as enduring as the biblical figure of that name. Allusions must be used with care lest the audience miss their meaning.

ambiguity A word or an expression having two or more possible meanings is said to be ambiguous. Ambiguity is a characteristic of some of the best poetry, but it is not a desired trait of expository writing, which should clearly state what the writer means.

analogy A comparison that attempts to explain one idea or thing by likening it to another. Analogy is useful if handled properly, but it can be a source of confusion if the compared items are basically unlike.

argumentation A writer's attempt to convince the reader of a point. It is based on appeals to reason, evidence proving the argument, and sometimes emotion to persuade. Some arguments attempt merely to prove a point, but others go beyond proving to inciting the reader to action. At the heart of all argumentation lies a debatable issue.

audience The group for whom a work is intended. For a writer, the audience is the reader whom the writer desires to persuade, inform, or entertain. Common sense tells us that a writer should always write to the level and needs of the particular audience for whom the writing is meant. For example, if you are writing for an unlettered audience, it is pointless to cram your writing with many literary allusions whose meanings will likely be misunderstood.

balance In a sentence, a characteristic of symmetry between phrases, clauses, and other grammatical parts. For example, the sentence "I love Jamaica for its weather, its lovely scenery, and its people" is balanced. This sentence—"I love Jamaica for its weather, its lovely scenery, and because its people are friendly"—is not. See also **parallelism.**

causal analysis A mode of developing an essay in which the writer's chief aim is to analyze cause or predict effect. For example, in "Why Tigers Become Man-Eaters" (Chapter 14), Jim Corbett's chief aim is to explain why some tigers start to prey on people.

cliché A stale image or expression, and the bane of good expository writing. "White as a ghost" is a cliché; so is "busy as a bee." Some clever writers can produce an effect by occasionally inserting a cliché in their prose, but most simply invent a fresh image rather than cull one from the public stock.

coherence The principle of clarity and logical adherence to a topic that binds together all parts of a composition. A coherent essay is one whose parts—sentences, paragraphs, pages—are logically fused into a whole. Its opposite is an incoherent essay—one that is jumbled, illogical, and unclear.

colloquialism A word or expression acceptable in informal usage but inappropriate in formal discourse. A given word may have a standard as well as a colloquial meaning. *Bug,* for example, is standard when used to refer to an insect, but when it is used to designate a virus—for example, "She's at home recovering from a bug"—the word is a colloquialism.

comparison/contrast A rhetorical mode used to develop essays that systematically match two items for similarities and differences. See the comparison/contrast essay examples in Chapter 12.

conclusion The final paragraph or paragraphs that sum up an essay and bring it to a close. Effective conclusions vary widely, but common tacks used by writers to end their essays include summing up what has been said, suggesting what ought to be done, specifying consequences that are likely to occur, restating the beginning, and taking the reader by surprise with an unexpected ending. Most important of all, however, is to end the essay artfully and quietly in a way that emphasizes your main point without staging a grand show for the reader's benefit.

concrete Said of words or terms denoting objects or conditions that are palpable, visible, or otherwise evident to the senses. *Concrete* is the opposite of *abstract.* The difference between the two is a matter of degree. *Illness,* for example, is abstract; *ulcer* is concrete; "sick in the stomach" falls somewhere between the two. The best writing usually expresses abstract propositions in concrete terms.

connotation The implication or emotional overtones of a word rather than its literal meaning. *Lion,* used in a literal sense, denotes a beast (see **denotation**). But to say that Winston Churchill had "the heart of a lion" is to use the connotative or implied meaning of *lion.*

deduction Something inferred or concluded. Deductive reasoning moves from the general to the specific.

denotation The specific and literal meaning of a word, as found in the dictionary. The opposite of *connotation.*

description A rhetorical mode used to develop an essay whose primary aim is to depict a scene, person, thing, or idea. Descriptive writing evokes the look, feel, sound, and sense of events, people, or things. See Chapter 8 for instructions on writing a descriptive essay.

diction The choice of words a writer uses in an essay or other writing. Implicit in the idea of diction is a vast vocabulary of synonyms—words that have more or less equivalent meanings. If only one word existed for every idea or condition, diction would not exist. But because we have a choice of words with various shades of meaning, a writer can and does choose among words to express ideas. The diction of skilled writers is determined by the audience and occasion of their writing.

division and classification A rhetorical mode for developing an essay whose chief aim is to identify the parts of a whole. A division and classification essay is often an exercise in logical thinking. See, for example, "Thinking as a Hobby," by William Golding, in Chapter 13.

documentation In a research paper, the support provided for an assertion, theory, or idea, consisting of references to the works of other writers. Different styles of documentation exist. Most disciplines now use the parenthetical style of documentation—see the sample research paper, "Choosing Single Motherhood: A Sign of Modern Times," in Part Four—where citations are made within the text of the paper rather than in footnotes or endnotes.

dominant impression The central theme around which a descriptive passage is organized. For example, a description of an airport lobby would most likely use the dominant impression of rush and bustle, which it would support with specific detail, even though the lobby may contain pockets of peace and tranquility. Likewise, a description of Cyrano de Bergerac—the famous dramatic lover whose nose was horrendously long—would focus on his nose rather than on an inconspicuous part of his face.

emotion, appeal to   An appeal to feelings rather than to strict reason; a legitimate ploy in an argument as long as it is not excessively and exclusively used.

emphasis   A rhetorical principle that requires stress to be given to important elements in an essay. Emphasis may be given to an idea in various parts of a composition. In a sentence, words may be emphasized by placing them at the beginning or end or by judiciously italicizing them. In a paragraph, ideas may be emphasized by repetition or by the accumulation of specific detail.

essay   From the French word *essai,* or "attempt," the essay is a short prose discussion of a single topic. Essays are sometimes classified as formal or informal. A formal essay is aphoristic, structured, and serious. An informal essay is personal, revelatory, humorous, and somewhat loosely structured.

evidence   The logical bases or supports for an assertion or idea. Logical arguments consist of at least three elements: propositions, reasoning, and evidence. The first of these consists of the ideas that the writer advocates or defends. The logical links by which the argument is advanced make up the second. The statistics, facts, anecdotes, and testimonial support provided by the writer in defense of the idea constitute the evidence. In a research paper, evidence consisting of paraphrases or quotations from the works of other writers must be documented in a footnote, endnote, or parenthetical reference. See also **argumentation** and/or **documentation**.

example   An instance that is representative of an idea or claim or that otherwise illustrates it. The example mode of development is used in essays that make a claim and then prove it by citing similar and supporting cases. See, for example, the essays in Chapter 10.

exposition   Writing whose chief aim is to explain. Most college composition assignments are expository.

figurative   Said of a word or expression used in a nonliteral way. For example, the expression "to go the last mile" may have nothing at all to do with geographical distance, but may mean to complete a task or job.

focus   In an essay, the concentration or emphasis on a certain subject or topic.

generalization   A statement that asserts some broad truth based on a knowledge of specific cases. For instance, the statement "big cars are gas guzzlers" is a generalization about individual cars. Generalizations are the products of inductive reasoning, whereby a basic truth may be inferred about a class after experience with a representative number of its members. However, one should beware of rash or faulty generalizations—those made on insufficient experience or evidence. It was once thought, for example, that scurvy sufferers were malingerers, which led the British navy to the policy of flogging the victims of scurvy aboard its ships. Later, medical research showed that the lethargy of scurvy victims was an effect rather than the cause of the disease. The real cause was found to be a lack of vitamin C in their diet.

image   A phrase or expression that evokes a picture or describes a scene. An image may be either literal, in which case it depicts what something looks like, or figurative, in which case an expression is used that likens the thing described to something else (e.g., "My love is like a red, red rose").

induction   A form of reasoning that proceeds from specific instances to a general inference or conclusion. Inductive reasoning is the cornerstone of the scientific method, which begins by examining representative cases and then infers some law or theory to explain them as a whole. See Chapter 9.

interparagraph   Between paragraphs. A comparison/contrast, for example, may be drawn between several paragraphs rather than within a single paragraph. For an example of an interparagraph comparison/contrast, see Chapter 6.

intraparagraph   Within a single paragraph. For an example of an intraparagraph comparison/contrast, see Chapter 6.

inversion   The reversal of the normal order of words in a sentence to achieve some desired effect, usually emphasis. Inversion is a technique long used in poetry, although most modern poets shun it as too artificial. For examples of inversion, see Shakespeare's "That Time of Year" (Sonnet 73) in Chapter 5.

irony   The use of language in such a way that apparent meaning contrasts sharply with real meaning. One famous example (in Shakespeare's *Julius Caesar*) is Antony's description of Brutus as "an honorable man": Because Brutus was one of Caesar's assassins, Antony meant just the opposite. Irony is a softer form of sarcasm and shares with it the same contrast between apparent and real meaning.

jargon   The specialized or technical language of a trade, profession, class, or other group of people. Jargon is sometimes useful, but when used thoughtlessly it can become meaningless expression bordering on gibberish, as in the following sentence from a psychology text: "Her male sibling's excessive psychogenic outbursts were instrumental in causing her to decompensate emotionally." A clearer statement would be the following: "Her brother's temper eventually caused her to have a nervous breakdown."

literal   *Literal* and *figurative* are two opposing characteristics of language. Literal meaning is a statement about something rendered in common, factual terms: "Good writers must be aggressive and daring." Figurative meaning is clouded in an image: "Good writers must stick out their necks." See **figurative**.

logical fallacies   Errors in reasoning used by speakers or writers, sometimes in order to dupe their audiences. Most logical fallacies are based on insufficient evidence ("All redheads are passionate lovers") or on irrelevant information ("Don't let him do the surgery; he cheats on his wife") or on faulty reasoning ("If you don't quit smoking, you'll die of lung cancer").

metaphor   A figurative image that implies a similarity between things otherwise dissimilar, such as the poet Robert Frost's statement "I have been acquainted with the night," meaning that he has suffered despair.

mood of a story   The pervading impression made on the feelings of the reader. For instance, Edgar Allan Poe often created a mood of horror in his short stories. A mood can be gloomy, sad, joyful, bitter, frightening, and so forth.

mood of verbs   A verb form expressing the manner or condition of the action. The moods of verbs are *indicative* (statements or questions), *imperative* (requests or commands), and *subjunctive* (expressions of doubt, wishes, probabilities, and conditions contrary to fact).

narrative   An account of events that happened. A narrative organizes material on the basis of chronological order or pattern, stressing the sequence of events and pacing these events according to the emphasis desired. Narration is often distinguished from three other modes of writing: argumentation, description, and exposition. See "How to Write a Narrative" in Chapter 7.

objective and subjective   Two attitudes toward writing. In *objective* writing, the author tries to present the material fairly and without bias; in *subjective* writing, the author stresses personal responses and interpretations. For instance, news reporting should be objective, whereas poetry can be subjective.

pacing   The speed at which a piece of writing moves along. Pacing depends on the balance between summarizing action and representing the action in detail. See "How to Write a Narrative" in Chapter 7.

parallelism   The principle of coherent writing requiring that coordinate elements be given the same grammatical form, as in Daniel Webster's dictum, "I was born an American; I will live an American; I will die an American."

paraphrase A restatement of a text or passage in another form or in other words, often to clarify the meaning. Paraphrase is commonly used in research papers to assimilate the research into a single style of writing and thereby avoid a choppy effect. See also **plagiarism.**

personification Attributing human qualities to objects, abstractions, or animals: "'Tis beauty calls and glory leads the way."

plagiarism Copying words from a source and then passing them off as one's own. Plagiarism is considered dishonest scholarship. Every writer is obligated to acknowledge ideas or concepts that represent someone else's thinking.

point of view The perspective from which a piece of writing is developed. In nonfiction, the point of view is usually the author's. In fiction, the point of view can be first- or third-person. In the first-person point of view, the author becomes part of the narrative and refers to him/herself as "I." In the third-person point of view, the narrator simply observes the action of the story. Third-person narration is either *omniscient* (the narrator knows everything about all of the characters) or *limited* (the narrator knows only those things that might be apparent to a sensitive observer).

premise An assertion or statement that is the basis for an argument. See **syllogism.**

process A type of development in writing that stresses how a sequence of steps produces a certain effect. For instance, explaining to the reader all of the steps involved in balancing a checkbook would be a *process* essay. See Chapter 9 for examples of process writing.

purpose The commitment on the part of authors to explain what they plan to write about. Purpose is an essential part of unity and coherence. Most teachers require students to write a statement of purpose, also called a *thesis*: "I intend to argue that our Federal Post Office needs a complete overhaul."

red herring A side issue introduced into an argument to distract from the main argument. It is a common device of politicians: "Abortion may be a woman's individual right, but have you considered the danger of the many germ-infested abortion clinics?" Here the side issue of dirty clinics clouds the ethical issue of having an abortion.

repetition A final review of all of the main points in a piece of writing; also known as *recapitulation*. In skillful writing, repetition is a means of emphasizing important words and ideas, of binding together the sentences in a passage, and of creating an effective conclusion. Its purpose is to accumulate a climactic impact or to cast new light on the material being presented.

rhetoric The art of using persuasive language. This is accomplished through the author's diction and sentence structure.

rhetorical question A question posed with no expectation of receiving an answer. This device is often used in public speaking to launch or further discussion. For example, a speaker might say, "What is the meaning of life, anyway?" as a way of nudging a talk toward a discussion of ethics.

satire Often an attack on a person. Also the use of wit and humor to ridicule society's weaknesses so as to correct them. In literature, two types of satire have been recognized: *Horatian satire,* which is gentle and smiling, and *Juvenalian satire,* which is sharp and biting.

simile A figure of speech that, like the metaphor, implies a similarity between things otherwise dissimilar. The simile, however, always uses *like, as,* or *so* to introduce the comparison: "My word is like a steel plate, never to be broken."

slanting The characteristic of selecting facts, words, or emphasis to achieve a preconceived intent:

favorable intent: "Although the Senator looks bored, when it comes time to vote, she is on the right side of the issue."

unfavorable intent: "The Senator may vote on the right side of issues, but she always looks bored."

specific A way of referring to the level of abstraction in words; the opposite of *general*. A *general* word refers to a group or class, whereas a *specific* word refers to a member of a group or class. Thus, the word *nature* is general, the word *tree* more specific, and the word *oak* even more specific. The thesis of an essay is general, but the details supporting that thesis are specific. See also **abstract** and **concrete**.

Standard English   The English of educated speakers and writers. Any attempt to define Standard English is controversial because no two speakers of English speak exactly alike. What is usually meant by "Standard English" is what one's grammar book dictates.

statement of purpose   What an author is trying to tell an audience; the main idea of an essay. Traditionally, what distinguishes a statement of purpose from a *thesis* is wording, not content. A statement of purpose includes words such as "My purpose is . . ." and "In this paper I intend to . . ." A statement of purpose is often the lead sentence of an essay. See Chapter 4.

straw man   An opposing point of view, set up so that it can easily be refuted. This is a common strategy used in debate.

style   The expression of an author's individuality through the use of words, sentence patterns, and selection of details. Our advice to fledgling writers is to develop a style that combines sincerity with clarity. See F. L. Lucas's "What Is Style?" in Chapter 10.

subordination   Expressing in a dependent clause, phrase, or single word any idea that is not significant enough to be expressed in a main clause or an independent sentence:

lacking subordination: John wrote his research paper on Thomas Jefferson; he was interested in this great statesman.

with subordination: Because John was interested in Thomas Jefferson, he wrote his research paper on this great statesman.

syllogism   In formal logic, the pattern by which a deductive argument is expressed:

All men are mortal. (major premise)

John Smith is a man. (minor premise)

Therefore John Smith is mortal. (conclusion)

symbol   An object or action that in its particular context represents something else. For instance, in Ernest Hemingway's novel *A Farewell to Arms,* the rain represents impending disaster because when it rains something terrible happens.

synonym   A word or phrase that has the same meaning as another. For instance, the words *imprisonment* and *incarceration* are synonyms. The phrases "fall short" and "miss the mark" are synonymous.

syntax   The order of words in a sentence and their relationships to each other. Good syntax requires correct grammar as well as effective sentence patterns, including unity, coherence, and emphasis.

theme   See **thesis**.

thesis   The basic idea of an essay, usually stated in a single sentence. In expository and argumentative writing, the thesis (or *theme*) is the unifying force that every word, sentence, and paragraph of the essay must support.

tone   The reflection of the writer's attitude toward subject and audience. The tone can be personal or impersonal, formal or informal, objective or subjective, or expressed in irony, sarcasm, anger, humor, satire, hyperbole, or understatement.

topic sentence   The *topic sentence* is to a paragraph what the *thesis* or *theme* is to the entire essay—that is, it expresses the paragraph's central idea.

transition   Words, phrases, sentences, or even paragraphs that indicate connections between the writer's ideas. These transitions provide landmarks to guide readers from one idea to the next. The following are some standard transitional devices:

time: soon, immediately, afterward, later, meanwhile, in the meantime

place: nearby, on the opposite side, further back, beyond

result: as a result, therefore, thus, as a consequence

comparison: similarly, likewise, also

contrast: on the other hand, in contrast, nevertheless, but, yet, otherwise *addition:* furthermore, moreover, in addition, and, first, second, third, finally

example: for example, for instance, to illustrate, as a matter of fact, on the whole, in other words

understatement Deliberately representing something as less than it is in order to stress its magnitude. Also called *litotes*. A good writer will restrain the impulse to hammer home a point and will use understatement instead. An example is the following line from Oscar Wilde's play *The Importance of Being Earnest:* "To lose one parent, Mr. Worthing, may be regarded as a misfortune; to lose both looks like carelessness."

unity The characteristic in writing of having all parts contribute to an overall effect. An essay or paragraph is described as having *unity* when all of its sentences develop one central idea. The worst enemy of unity is irrelevant material. A good rule is to delete all sentences that do not advance or prove the thesis or topic sentence of an essay.

voice The presence or the sound of self chosen by an author. Most good writing sounds like someone delivering a message. The aim in good student writing is to sound natural. Of course, the voice will be affected by the audience and occasion for writing. See Chapter 3, "What Is a Writer's Voice?"

Text Credits

This page constitutes an extension of the copyright page. We have made every effort to trace the ownership of all copyrighted material and to secure permission from copyright holders. In the event of any question arising as to the use of any material, we will be pleased to make the necessary corrections in future printings. Thanks are due to the following authors, publishers, and agents for permission to use the material indicated.

Chapter 1. 8: From the *Journal of the writer's guild.* "A Writer's Fantasy." Reprinted by permission of Tribune Media Services, Inc. **10:** "Excerpts from Education of a Wandering Man," by Louis L'Amour, copyright © 1989 by the Louis D. and Katherine E. L'Amour 1983 Trust. Used by permission of Bantam Books, a division of Random House, Inc.

Chapter 2. 18: © *The new yorker collection 2002* Tom Cheney from cartoonbank.com. All Rights Reserved. **37:** From *The writer* (September 1996). **40:** Reprinted by arrangement with the Estate of Martin Luther King Jr., c/o Writer's House as agent for the proprietor New York, NY. Copyright 1963 Martin Luther King, Jr., copyright renewed 1991 Coretta Scott King. **45:** Letter from *Winston and clementine: the personal letters of the churchills.* Copyright © The Lady Soames DBE 1998. Reprinted by permission of Houghton Mifflin Company. All rights reserved. **48:** From *James herriot's dog stories* by James Herriot. Copyright 1986 by James Herriot. Reprinted by permission of St. Martin's Press, LLC and Harold Ober Associates.

Chapter 3. 61: From *Understanding english* by Paul Roberts. Copyright © 1958 by Paul Roberts. Reprinted by permission of Pearson Education, Inc. **71:** Copyright 1997–2000 by Writer's Write, Inc. Reprinted by permission. **76:** From *Story of mary maclane by herself,* Herbert S. Stone & Company, Chicago, 1902. **81:** Bartolomeo Vanzetti, "Remarks on the Life of Sacco and On His Own Life and Execution." **83:** from "The Big Sea" by Langston Hughes. Copyright 1940 by Langston Hughes. Copyright renewed 1968 by Arna Bontemps and George Houston Bass. Reprinted by permission of Hill and Wang, a division of Farrar, Straus & Giroux, LLC.

Chapter 4. 101: Adaptation of pp. 22–25 from *The complete stylist and handbook,* 3rd Edition, by Sheridan Baker. Copyright 1984 by HarperCollins Publishers, Inc. Reprinted by permission of Pearson Education, Inc. **104:** from *The los angeles times,* June 12, 1996. Copyright © 1996 The Washington Post. Reprinted with permission. **111:** From "A Good Man is Hard to Find and Other Stories," copyright 1953 by Flannery O'Connor and renewed 1981 by Regina O'Connor, reprinted by permission of Harcourt, Inc. **123:** From Collected Poems (New York: HarperCollins Publishers). Copyright 1921 and 1948 by Edna St. Vincent Millay.

Chapter 5. 139: From *How to use the power of the printed word* by Malcolm Forbes, edited by Billings S. Fuess, copyright 1985 by International Paper Company. Used by permission of Doubleday, a division of Random House, Inc. **142:** "My Wood" from *Abinger harvest,* copyright 1936 and renewed 1964 by Edward M. Forster. reprinted by permission of Harcourt, Inc. and The Provost and Scholars of King's College, Cambridge and the Society of Authors as the Literary Representatives of the Estate of E.M. Forster. **146:** From *Modern maturity,* May-June 1999. Reprinted by permission of the author. **148:** From *The thurber carnival* (New York: Harper, 1945). Copyright 1945 by James Thurber, renewed 1973 by Helen Thurber and Rosemary A. Thurber.

Chapter 6. 164: *Time,* January 28, 1980 **174:** Excerpt pp. 82–85 from *Strategies of rhetoric,* Revised by A.M. Tibbetts and Charlene Tibbetts. Copyright © 1974 by Scott, Foresman and Company. Reprinted by permission of Pearson Education, Inc. **178:** Excerpt from The Lessons of the Past by Edith Hamilton **180:** Chief Joseph of the Nez Perce, "I am Tired of Fighting" **181:** From *The atlantic monthly,* September 1948, p. 54 **183:** From *The medusa and the snail,* by Lewis Thomas. Copyright 1979. Used by permission of Viking Penguin, a division of Penguin Putnam, Inc. **184:** From *The poetry of robert frost,* edited by Edward Connery Lathem. Coyright 1928, 1936, 1969 by Henry Holt

and Company, 1956 by Robert Frost, 1964 by Lesley Frost Ballantine. Reprinted by permission of Henry Holt and Company, LLC.
Chapter 7. 196: From *Shooting an elephant* by George Orwell. Copyright 1950 by Harcourt, Inc. and renewed 1979 by Sonia Brownell Orwell. Reprinted by permission of Harcourt, Inc. and by permission of Bill Hamilton as the Literary Executor of the Estate of the Late Sonia Brownell Orwell and Secker & Warburg, Ltd. **206:** From *I know why the caged bird sings* by Maya Angelou. Copyright 1969 and renewed 1997 by Maya Angelou. Used by permission of Random House, Inc. **211:** From *Nigger: an autobiography,* copyright 1964 by Dick Gregory Enterprises, Inc. Used by permission of Dutton, a division of Penguin Putnam, Inc. **215:** From Smithsonian Magazine, January, 2005. Internet version used: www.smithsonianmag.si.edu/smithsonian/issues05/jan05/pdf/boswell.pdf. **228:** Copyright © 1966 by Robert Hayden, from *Collected poems of robert hayden* by Robert Hayden, edited by Frederick Glaysher. Used by permission of Liveright Publishing Corporation. **232:** Reprinted by permission of the author. **237:** From *Inside the kingdom* by Carmen Bin Ladin. Copyright © 2004 by Carmen Bin Ladin. By permission of Warner Books, Inc.
Chapter 8. 257: From *A mencken chrestomathy* by H.L. Mencken, copyright 1916, 1918, 1919, 1920, 1921, 1922, 1924, 1926, 1927, 1929, 1932, 1934, 1942, 1949 by Alfred A. Knopf, a division of Random House, Inc. Used by permission of Alfred A. Knopf, a division of Random House, Inc. **261:** James Joyce, "Hell" from *Portrait of the artist as a young man* **265:** From *A curtain of green and other stories,* Copyright 1941 and renewed 1969 by Eudora Welty, reprinted by permission of Harcourt, Inc. **272:** From *New and selected things taking place* (Boston: Little, Brown and Company). Originally published in *The new yorker,* 1962. Copyright © 1962 by May Swenson. Used with permission of the Literary Estate of May Swenson. **276:** from *Current health* 2, 1998, Weekly Reader Corp. All Rights Reserved. **283:** From *Living out loud.* Copyright © 1987 by Anna Quindlen, published by Random House.
Chapter 9. 299: From *Duel:* Alexander Hamilton, Aaron Burr, and the *Future of america,* by Thomas Fleming. Copyright 1999 by Thomas Fleming. Reprinted by permission of Basic Books, a member of Perseus Books, L.L.C. **309:** From *A pattern of islands.* Reprinted by permission of John Murray Publishers, Ltd. **313:** From *Berlin diary* by William Shirer. Boston: Little, Brown, 1940. Reprinted by permission of Estate of William Shirer. **316:** By Kenneth Patchen, from The Collected Poems of Kenneth Patchen, copyright ©1943 by New Directions Publishing Corp. Reprinted by permission of NewDirections Publishing Corp. **320:** From *The view from 80* by Malcolm Cowley, copyright © 1976, 1978, 1980 by Malcolm Cowley. Used by permission of Viking Penguin, a division of Penguin Putnam Inc. **327:** from *More in anger.* Philadelphia: J.B. Lippincott, 1958. Copyright © 1958 by Marya Mannes.
Chapter 10. 342: From *Holiday* (March 1960). Copyright © 1960 by The Curtis Publishing Company. **351:** From *America west* by Barry Parr. Reprinted by permission of the author. **356:** From *Time magazine,* March 6, 1978. Copyright © 1978 Time Inc. Reprinted by permission. **362:** "Drugs" by Gore Vidal, copyright © 1970 by Gore Vidal, From *Homage to daniel shays: collected essays* by Gore Vidal. Used by permission of Random House, Inc. **365:** From *The new republic* (June 17, 1988). Copyright © 1988 by The New Republic, Inc.
Chapter 11. 380: From *Time magazine,* Special Issue, Fall 1993, Pp. 73–75 **385:** Copyright © Garry Trudeav. Reprinted by permission of Universal Press Syndicate. **387:** Reprinted with the permission of Simon & Schuster Adult Publishing Group, from *Close to home* by Ellen Goodman. Copyright © 1979 by the Washington Post Company. All rights reserved. **390:** From *Time magazine,* June 13, 1988. Copyright © 1988 Time Inc. Reprinted by permission. **394:** From *Harper's magazine,* 1934. Copyright 1934 by Gilbert Highet. Reprinted by permission of Curtis Brown, Ltd. **399:** Stephen Spender, "Funeral". Reprinted by permission of Faber & Faber. **402:** From *Collected poems 1917–1982* by Archibald MacLeish. Copyright © 1985 by The Estate of Archibald MacLeish. Reprinted by permission of Houghton Mifflin Company. All rights reserved. Originally published in *Streets in the moon, 1926* **408:** From *The new york times business section,* April 5, 2005. Copyright © 2005 by the New York Times Co. Reprinted with permission. **411:** from *I'm a stranger here myself,* Copyright © 1999 Broadway Books, New York, a division of Random House.
Chapter 12. 429: From "My Turn," *Newsweek on campus* (October 9, 1978). **432:** Originally published by Horizon Magazine, 1963. Copyright © 1963 by Gilbert Highet. Reprinted by permission of Curtis Brown, Ltd. **438:** From *The american story,* edited by Earl Schenk Miers. Copyright © 1956 by the United States Capitol Historical Society. **442:** From Chapter 3 of "Kite Runner," by Khaled Hosseini. Riverhead Books, NY, 2003. **452:** Reprinted by permission of Adria Holmes Katz. **463:** From *Free inquiry,* Winter

1996–1997. Reprinted by permission of Counsel for Secular Humanism. **472:** Copyright © Stuart Hample & Eric Marshall.
Chapter 13. 481: Paul M. Muchinsky, "Move Over, Teams" **486:** From *Holiday magazine* (July 18, 1961). Copyright © 1961 by William Golding. Reprinted by permission of Curtis Brown, Ltd. **494:** Reprinted by permission from Freedom and Beyond by John Holt. Copyright © 1995, 1972 by Holt Associates. Published by Heinemann, a division of Reed Elsevier, Inc., Portsmouth, NH. All rights reserved. **500:** Bart Edelman, "English 101" from *Under damaris' dress.* Copyright © 1996 by Bart Edelman. Reprinted with the permission of Lightning Publications. **504:** Reprinted with the permission of Atria Books, an imprint of Simon & Schuster Adult Publishing Group, from *Warriors don't cry: a searing memoir of the battle to integrate little rock's central high,* by Melba Pattillo Beals. Copyright © 1994 by Melba Beals. All rights reserved. **509:** Reprinted by permission of Kodansha America, Inc. Excerpted from *Having our say: the delany sisters' first 100 years* by Sarah and A. Elizabeth Delany with Amy Hill Hearth published by Kodansha America, Inc. (1993).
Chapter 14. 524: From *Land circle: writing collected from the land.* Copyright © 1991 by Linda Hasselstrom. Reprinted by permission of Fulcrum Publishing. **529:** From *Working in the dark: reflections of a poet of the barrio.* Copyright © 1992 by Jimmy Santiago Baca. **536:** From *The man-eaters of kumaon,* by Jim Corbett. Reproduced by permission of Oxford University Press, India, New Delhi. **541:** Henry David Thoreau, "Why I Went to the Woods" **548:** Kate Chopin, "The Storm" **553:** From *The poetry of robert frost,* edited by Edward Connery Lathem. Copyright 1969 by Henry Holt and Company. Copyright 1936 by Robert Frost, copyright 1964 by Lesley Frost Ballantine. Reprinted by permission of Henry Holt and Company, LLC **557:** Reprinted by permission of U-Wire. **560:** © *The new yorker collection 2005* Jack Ziegler from cartoonbank.com. All Rights Reserved. **561:** Reprinted by permission of U-Wire.
Chapter 15. 577: Reprinted by permission of U-wire. **581:** Jonathan Swift, "A Modest Proposal" **588:** From *Ms.* (1971). Copyright © 1971 Judy Brady. Reprinted with the permission of the author. **591:** From *The new york times,* January 5, 1993. Copyright © 1993 by The New York Times Co. **595:** *From possible laughter* (London Rupert Hart-Davis, 1959). Copyright © 1976 by James Michie. **601:** From San Diego Union Tribune. June 9, 1993. Reprinted by permission. **604:** From *The badger herald,* February 14, 2002. Reprinted by permission of U-Wire.
Chapter 16. 616: From *This fascinating animal world 1951* **621:** From Chronicle of Higher Education, June 2, 1980. **626:** From *One man's meat,* text copyright © 1941 by E.B. White. Copyright renewed. Reprinted by permission of Tilbury House, Publishers, Gardiner, Maine. **634:** from www.cbmw.org/news/ram150104.php **639:** www.drsusanblock.com/editorial/ terror/terror14.htm.

Photo Credits

1: © Martin Casson/SuperStock; **3:** *Brooklyn Bridge Painters* by Eugene de Salignac 1914; Courtesy NYC Municipal Archives

25: Copyright Estate of George Grosz/Licensed by VAGA, New York, NY. Copyright VAGA Nationalgallerie, Staatliche Museen; Berlin, Germany. Copyright Foto Marburg/Art Resource, NY.; **26:** © 2003 Artists Rights Society (ARS), New York/VG Bild-Kunst, Bonn.; **28:** © Reuters New Media, Inc./CORBIS; **31:** © Bill Aron/PhotoEdit, Inc.

216: © Kate Brooks/Polaris Images; **219:** © Kate Brooks/Polaris Images; **221:** © Scottish National Portrait Gallery/Bridgeman Art Library; **223:** © Bettmann/CORBIS; **226:** © Kate Brooks/Polaris Images; **231:** © Mark M. Lawrence/CORBIS; **238:** Lynsey Addario/CORBIS

276: © Lori C. Diehl/PhotoEdit, Inc.; **278:** © Peter M. Fisher/CORBIS

319: Courtesy of Myron Kunin. The Regis Foundation. Copyright The Curtis Galleries, Inc.; **321:** © Hulton Archive/CORBIS

361: ©Zefa Visual Media-German/Index Stock Imagery; **364:** © Ed Kashi/CORBIS

407: © Kevin Flemming/CORBIS; **411:** © Jeff Greenberg/CORBIS;

451: © David McNew/Getty Images

503: Courtesy of the artist and Rena Gransten Gallery, San Francisco, CA and Galerie Claude Samuel, Paris, France; **509:** © V.C.L./Taxi/ GETTY

557: © Royalty Free/CORBIS

600: Courtesy of The Dorothea Lange Collection, Oakland Museum of California, City of Oakland. **603:** © David Doody/Index Stock Imagery

633: © Peter M. Fisher/CORBIS

647: © Mohammed Abed/Getty Images; **648:** © Mike Finn-Kelcey/Reuters/CORBIS; **649:** ©AP Photo; **650:** *(left)* ©MARVY!/CORBIS, *(right)* © Pete Salutos/CORBIS; **651:** *(left)* © Sygma/CORBIS, *(right)* © Arnaldo Magnani/Getty Images Entertainment; **652:** *(left)* © Dowder/Jeff Dowder/Zuma/CORBIS, *(right)* © Reuters/CORBIS; **653:** © Tom and Dee Ann McCarthy/CORBIS; **654:** © Cynthia Diane Pringle/CORBIS; **655:** © Jeff Cadge/Getty Images; **656:** © Brenda Ann Kenneally/CORBIS; **657:** © Erich Lessing/Art Resource, NY; **658:** © Mary Kate Denny/PhotoEdit, Inc.; **659:** © Todd Bigelow/Aurora/Getty Images; **660:** ©Bettmann/CORBIS; **661:** © Paul A. Souders/CORBIS; **662:** © Getty Image News; **663:** © Hulton Archive Kean Collection/Getty Images; **664:** © Richard Cummins/CORBIS; **665:** © Hulton Archive/Getty Images; **666:** The Norman Rockwell Art Collection Trust. Printed by permission of The Norman Rockwell Family Agency, © The Norman Rockwell Family Entities; **667:** © Paul J. Richards/AFP/Getty Images; **668:** © Ron Krisel/Image Bank/Getty Images; **669:** *(top left)* © Bettmann/CORBIS; *(bottom left)* © Hulton Deutsch Collection/CORBIS; *(top right)* © Time Life Pictures/Getty Images; *(bottom right)* © CORBIS; **670:** © Gallo Images/CORBIS; **671:** © Barbara Davidson/Dallas Morning News/CORBIS; **672:** © Myrlee Ferguson Cate/PhotoEdit, Inc.; **673:** © Viviare Moos/CORBIS; **674:** © Michael Macor/San Francisco Chronicle/CORBIS; **675:** © Tony Freeman/PhotoEdit, Inc.; **676:** © Rick Friedman/CORBIS; **677:** © Carlos Sanchez/Stringer/Reuters/Corbis; **678:** © Tomas Gaspar/The Image Works.

Index

(Bold indicates images.)

A
Abbreviations, 244
Abraham (painting), **663**
Abstract, for research paper, 748–**49**
Abstraction, 65–66
Action, in literary work, 782
Active voice, 691–92
Ad hominem attack, 6, 574
Adler, Felix, 452
Ad populum appeal, 6, 574
Advertisements, writing about, 31–33
Advertising, weight loss (photograph), **277**
"Against a Confusion of Tongues" (Henry), 571
Ageism/aging
    Asian couple dancing (photograph), **653**
    Critical Thinking and Debate, 318–29
    older doctor (photograph), **655**
    old woman knitting (photograph), **654**
    Student Corner, 331–32
"Aging" (Wheeler), 331–32
Alternating method of contrast, 423–25
American Psychological Association (APA) format, 711, 745–77
American Way of Death, The (Mitford), 163
Anecdotes, 142, 195
Angelou, Maya, "My Name Is Margaret," 206–10
"Animals in Research: The Case for Experimentation" (King), 573
Annotated literary paper. *See* Literary papers
Annotation, while reading, 6–7
Anthony, Susan B. (photograph), **669**
Apostrophe, 415
Appeal, to reader's senses, in descriptive writing, 254–55
Appendix, for research paper, 768, **769–77**
Arakelian, Sion
    "How I Write," 247
    "How I Wrote This Paper," 247–48
    "My Writing Tip," 248
    "The Right Moves Against Terrorism," 245–47
Argumentation and persuasion, 614
    in advertising, 31–33
    anticipate the opposition, 572–73
    begin at point of contention, 570–71
    Critical Thinking and Debate, 598–605
    emotional appeal, 573–74
    evidence, 571, 572
    examples, 576–98
    how to use, 570
    logical fallacies, avoiding, 574–75
    pace, 571–72
    Student Corner, 607–09
    warming up to write, 575–76
    what they do, 569
    when to use, 569–70
Argumentative edge, to thesis, 102–3
Arguments
    critical reading guidelines for, 3–7
    formal writing for, 20
    kinds of, 6
    unsubstantiated statements in, 6
    values behind, 6
    weakening of, 98
"Ars Poetica" (MacLeish), 402–3
Artworks, writing about, 24–27
Asian couple dancing (photograph), **653**
Asimov, Isaac, "Of What Use?," 337–38
"Aspects of the Novel" (Forster), 375
Assumptions, hidden, 4
Attitude, voice and, 59
Auchinleck Manor, country home of the Boswells (photograph), **219**
Audience
    of advertisements, 32
    level of English appropriate for, 22, 140
    understanding, 19
Authors, biases and hidden assumptions of, 4

B
"Baba and Me" (Hosseini), 441–47
Babaian, Ara
    "How I Write," 474
    "How I Wrote This Essay," 475
    "My Writing Tip," 475
    "The Existence of God," 473–74
Baca, Jimmy Santiago, "Coming Into Language," 529–34
Bacon, Francis, "The Idols," 496–98
Baker, Sheridan, "The Thesis," 101–4
Beal, Frances M., "Double Jeopardy: To Be Black and Female," 378
Beals, Melba Patillo, "Warriors Don't Cry," 503–06
Beethoven, 464
Begging the question, 6, 574–75
Bias, evaluating, in critical reading, 4
"Bible and the Common Reader, The" (Chase), 162–63
"Big Rock Candy Mountain, The" (Stegner), 377–78

Bin Laden, Carmen, *"Postscript" to Inside the Kingdom: My Life in Saudi Arabia*, 236–42
Black, Clinton V., "The Story of Jamaica," 615
Blair, Eric Arthur. *See* Orwell, George
Block, Susan, "Same-Sex Marriage: Just Say No to Prohibition," 638–40
Block method of contrast, 423–25
Body image
    Critical Thinking and Debate, 273–85
    male and female bodybuilders (photograph), **650**
    piercings and tattoos (photograph), **275**
    Student Corner, 287–92
    weight loss advertisement (photograph), **277**
    Wildenstein, Jocelyn, before and after plastic surgery (photograph), **651**
    Wilson, Carnie, before and after bypass surgery (photograph), **652**
"Body Image" (Maynard), 275–80
"Body Modification—Think About It!" (Taylor), 287–92
Bogus claims, 6
Bombed bus in London (photograph), **648**
Boswell mausoleum and graveyard (photograph), **216**
Boswell's study at Auchinleck estate (painting), **226**
Boy offering another boy a cigarette (photograph), **658**
"Breaking the Last Taboo" (Haught), 462–69
Brevity, 141–42, 347–48
Brontë, Emily, 463
Browning, Robert, "Cleon," 457
Bruno, Giordano, 466
Bryson, Bill
    "The Mother Tongue: English and How It Got That Way," 613–14
    "Wide Open Spaces," 410–13
"Buck Stops Where, The?" (Parr), 351–54
"Bullfight, The" (Hemingway), 161
Bumper sticker philosophizing, 4
Burbank, Luther, 464
Buzzwords, 32

C

Cartoons, writing about, 29–31
"Case Against Homosexual Marriage" (Mohler), 633–36
Castle, Mort, "Tone: The Writer's Voice in the Reader's Mind," 71–75
Casual reading, 3
"Catbird Seat, The" (Thurber), 148–55
Catton, Bruce, "Grant and Lee: A Study in Contrasts," 437–39
Causal analysis, 189, 192–93, 614
    causes in, 520–21
    common sense in, 523
    Critical Thinking and Debate, 555–62
    dogmatic statements, 522
    examples, 524–54
    how to use, 520–23

    immediate vs. remote cause, 521–22
    kinds of causes, 520–21
    make the purpose clear, 521
    Student Corner, 564–65
    subject selection, 521
    in thesis development, 94
    warming up to write, 523–24
    what it does, 519–20
    when to use, 520
Cebes, 459
Character, in literary work, 782
Chase, Mary Ellen
    "The Bible and the Common Reader," 162–63
    "What Is the Bible?," 377
Cheney, Tom, *The New Yorker* cartoon, **30**
Chief Joseph of the Nez Percé, "I Am Tired of Fighting (Surrender Speech)," 180
Child looking at drug-filled ashtray (photograph), **656**
"Children's Letters to God," 471
Chinese girl waving flag (photograph), **661**
Chopin, Kate, "The Storm," 548–52
Chronological order
    in process analysis, 297
    in thesis, 95
Churchill, Clementine, "Letter to My Husband," 45–46
Cicero, 454
Cisneros, Sandra, 39
Citations. *See* American Psychological Association (APA) format; Modern Language Association (MLA) format
Claims
    in advertising, 33
    bogus, 5
Clarity, 348, 377–78
Classification. *See* Division and classification
Clauses. *See* Dependent clause; Independent clause
"Cleon" (Browning), 457
Cloister and the Hearth, The (Reade), 251
Coherence, in paragraphs, 168–69
Colloquial expressions, 21
Colon, 513
Colored, colorful, and colorless words, 69–71
Columbus and the Golden World of the Island Arawaks (Walker), 20
"Coming Into Language" (Baca), 529–34
Coming Up for Air (Orwell), 165
"Coming Up Harlem" (Hellman), 379
Commas, 286, 642
Common Sense in Education (Kemelman), 173
"Company Man, The" (Goodman), 387–89
Comparison and contrast, 189, 192, 614
    alternating method, 423–25
    block method, 423–25
    both sides of question requirement, 426
    common ground requirement, 425–26
    Critical Thinking and Debate, 449–71
    examples, 428–49
    expressions indicating, 426–27

how to use, 422–27
logical bases, 422–23
Student Corner, 473–75
warming up to write, 427, 429
what it does, 421–22
when to use, 422
Completeness, in paragraphs, 169–70
Compound sentence, 97
Concrete poetry, 316–17
Connor, Jack, "Will Spelling Count?," 620–23
Context, 19
Contractions, 20, 21
Contributory cause, 521
Controlling ideas, 163
Converse, Charles Crozat, 9
Corbett, Jim, "Why Tigers Become Man-Eaters," 536–40
Courtesy, 347
Cowley, Malcolm, "The View from Eighty," 319–24
Critical reading, guidelines for, 3–7
Critical Thinking and Debate. *See also* Student Corner
  ageism/aging (process analysis), 318–29
  body image (description), 273–85
  drug abuse (illustration/exemplification), 359–69
  existence of God (comparison/contrast), 449–71
  homelessness (argumentation and persuasion), 598–605
  immigration (definition), 404–14
  racism (division/classification), 501–12
  same-sex marriage (combined rhetorical modes), 631–41
  terrorism (narration), 229–43
  women, status of (casual analysis), 555–62
Crystal Cathedral (photograph; architecture), **664**

D

Darrow, Clarence, 464
Darwin, Charles, 464, 458
Dash, 370, 642
Deadwood, pruning, 686–89
"Death in the Open" (Thomas), 166
Definition, 189, 191–92
  clarify the definition, 377–78
  Critical Thinking and Debate, 404–14
  etymological analysis, 376–77, 378
  examples, 380–404
  expand with examples, 378
  how to use, 376–79
  lexical definition, 376, 378
  Student Corner, 416–18
  warming up to write, 379–80
  what it does, 375
  when to use, 376
Delany, Sarah L., and A. Elizabeth Delany, "Incidents with White People," 508–11
Delina Delaney (McKittrick), 254
Dell, Floyd, "We're Poor," 196

Dependent clause, 96
Description, 189, 190–91
  appeal to all the reader's senses, 254–55
  Critical Thinking and Debate, 273–85
  dominant impression, 252–53
  examples, 256–73
  how to write, 252–55
  images in, 253–54
  Student Corner, 287–93
  warming up to write, 255
  what it does, 251–52
  when to use, 252
  as a word picture, 251
"Design" (Frost), 553
Details
  in narration, 198
  specific, 690
  supporting, in paragraphs, 163–64
DeVoe, Alan, "Shrew—The Littlest Mammal," 616–19
Dictionary of Modern English Usage (Fowler), 7, 9
Diderot, Denis, 467
Dinesen, Isak, *Out of Africa*, 161–62
"Diogenes and Alexander" (Highet), 431–35
Direct quotation, in note-taking, 708
Division and classification, 189, 192
  avoiding overlapping of categories, 479–80
  clear thinking requirement, 478–79
  completeness in, 479
  Critical Thinking and Debate, 501–12
  examples, 481–501
  how to use, 478–80
  Student Corner, 514–17
  warming up to write, 480–81
  what it does, 477–78
  when to use, 478
Documentation, of research papers. *See* American Psychological Association (APA) format; Modern Language Association (MLA) format
Dominant impression, in description, 252–53
"Don't Legalize Drugs" (Kondracke), 364–68
"Dooley Is a Traitor" (Michie), 594–97
"Double Jeopardy: To Be Black and Female" (Beal), 378
"Dr. [Oliver] Goldsmith...has been loose in his principles, but he is coming right" (painting), **223**
Drafts, of research papers, 710, 712–13
Drug abuse
  boy offering another boy a cigarette (photograph), **658**
  child looking at drug-filled ashtray (photograph), **656**
  Critical Thinking and Debate, 359–69
  drug artwork (painting), **657**
  person with drugs (photograph), **363**
  Student Corner, 371–72
  woman with pills (photograph), **360**
"Drugs" (Vidal), 361–62

"Drug Use: The Continuing Epidemic" (Kunze), 371–72
Durant, Will, 295

E
Eastman, Max, "Poetic People," 477
Edelman, Bart, "English 101," 499–500
Edison, Thomas, 463
Editing
   defined, 682
   example, 696–701
   internal reader/editor, 19–20
   rules for, 681, 685–96
"Education of a Wandering Man" (L'Amour), 10–14
Einstein, Albert, 463
Either/or reasoning, 6, 575
Ellis Island (photograph), **660**
Emerson, Ralph Waldo, 453, 454
Emotion, 4, 573–74
"English 101" (Edelman), 499–500
English sonnet, 156
Essay. *See also* Long essay; Short essay
Essay flowchart, 130–**31**
Etymological analysis, 376–77, 378
Euphemisms, 32, 68, 687
Evaluation
   of evidence, in critical reading, 5
   of sources, for research paper, 707–08
Evidence
   in argumentation and persuasion, 571, 572
   common sense in evaluating, 5
   date of as important feature, 5
   evaluating, in critical reading, 5
Examples, in definition writing, 378. *See also* Illustration/exemplification
Exclamation point, 563, 642, 694
Exemplification. *See* Illustration/exemplification
"Existence of God, The" (Babaian), 473–74
Explaining, in process analysis, 297–98

F
Facts
   researching, in critical reading, 5
   separating emotion from, 4
False analogy, 6, 574
"Farce of Feminism, The" (Rubins), 560–61
Figurative language, 98
Fiske, John, 453, 458
"First-degree" words, 141
Flame Trees of Thika, The (Huxley), 254–55
Fleming, Thomas, "This Is a Mortal Wound, Doctor," 299–307
"Flood, The" (Frost), 184–85
Flowchart, for essays, 130–**31**
Form, in poetry, 782–83
Formal English, 20
Forster, E. M.
   "Aspects of the Novel," 375
   "My Wood," 142–45
Fosdick, Harry Emerson, 460

Fowler, Henry Watson (*Dictionary of Modern English Usage*), 7, 9
Fragment (sentence), 96–97
Fragmentary paragraph, 177
Freud, Sigmund, 463, 467
"From The Lessons of the Past" (Hamilton), 178
Frost, Robert, 38
   "Design," 553
   "The Flood," 184–85

G
Galbraith, John Kenneth, 577
Garcia, Rupert, *Mexico, Chile, Soweto . . .* (painting), **502**
Gibbon, Edward, *Memoirs*, 2
God, existence of
   Abraham (painting), **663**
   Critical Thinking and Debate, 449–71
   Crystal Cathedral (photograph; architecture), **664**
   Student Corner, 473–74
   weeping Virgin Mary (sculpture), **662**
God hates Sodomites (photograph), **677**
Golding, William, "Thinking as a Hobby," 486–91
Goodman, Ellen, "The Company Man," 387–89
"Good Man Is Hard to Find, A" (O'Connor), 111–22
Grammar, rhetoric vs., 17–18
"Grant and Lee: A Study in Contrasts" (Catton), 437–39
Graves, Robert, *It Was a Stable World*, 175
Greene, Graham, 38
Gregory, Dick, "Shame," 211–14
"Grieving Never Ends, The" (Roberts), 104–10
Grimble, Arthur, "Hunting Octopus in the Gilbert Islands," 309–12
Grosz, George, *Pillars of Society, The* (painting), **25**
Gubata, Kate, "The New Feminism," 556–57
Gucci (billboard; advertising), **31**

H
Hamilton, Edith, "From The Lessons of the Past," 178
Hasselstrom, Linda M., "A Peaceful Woman Explains Why She Carries a Gun," 524–27
Hasty generalization, 6, 575
Haught, James A., "Breaking the Last Taboo," 462–69
"Have a Cigar" (Herriot), 48–50
Hayden, Robert, "Those Winter Sundays," 228
"Hell" (Joyce), 260–62
Hellman, Peter, "Coming Up Harlem," 379
Hemingway, Ernest, "The Bullfight," 161
Henry, William A., III
   "Against a Confusion of Tongues," 571
   "The Politics of Separation," 380–84, 386
Herman, Dave
   "How I Write," 418
   "How I Wrote This Essay," 418
   "Immigrants in America," 416–18
   "My Writing Tip," 418

Herriot, James, "Have a Cigar," 48–50
Highet, Gilbert
    "Diogenes and Alexander," 431–35
    "How to Write an Essay," 176–77
    "Kitsch," 394–400
"Hitler's Workday" (Shirer), 313–15
Hobbes, Thomas, 466
Holmes, John Haynes, "Ten Reasons for Believing in Immortality," 451–60
Holt, John, "Kinds of Discipline," 337, 493–95
"Homeless: Expose the Myths" (Perkins), 600–1
"Homeless Lack a Political Voice, But Not American Ideals" (Lynch), 603–4
Homelessness
    Critical Thinking and Debate, 598–605
    homeless man (photograph), **673**
    Hurricane Katrina aftermath (photograph), **674**
    man, woman, and child with homeless sign (photograph), **675**
    Migrant Mother (photograph; Lange, Nipomo Valley), **599**
    Student Corner, 607–9
    when a shopping cart is your only home (photograph), **602**
Honesty, 347
Hook, J. N., and E. G. Mathews, *Modern American Grammar and Usage*, 164–65
Hosseini, Khaled, "Baba and Me," 441–47
Howells, W. D., 165
"How I Write" (students)
    Arakelian, Sion, 247
    Babaian, Ara, 474
    Herman, Dave, 418
    Kunze, Linda, 373
    Phillips, Nancey, 516–17
    Poodt, Antoinette, 609–10
    Rewa, Paula, 566
    Taylor, Shelley, 292
    Wheeler, Kimberly Caitlin, 333
    Winkler, Adam, 645
"How I Wrote This Essay" (students)
    Arakelian, Sion, 247–48
    Babaian, Ara, 475
    Herman, Dave, 418
    Kunze, Linda, 373
    Phillips, Nancey, 517
    Poodt, Antoinette, 610
    Rewa, Paula, 566–67
    Taylor, Shelley, 292
    Wheeler, Kimberly Caitlin, 334
    Winkler, Adam, 645
"How to Be An Army" (Patchen), 316–17
"How to Say Nothing in Five Hundred Words" (Roberts), 61–71
"How to Write Clearly" (Thompson), 139–42
"How to Write an Essay" (Highet), 176–77
Hughes, Langston, "Salvation," 83–85
Hugo, Victor, 456
Humor, in advertising, 32
"Hunting Octopus in the Gilbert Islands" (Grimble), 309–12

Huntington, Tom, "James Boswell's Scotland," 215–26
Hurricane Katrina aftermath (photograph), **674**
Hussein, Saddam, as a young boy (photograph), **649**
Huxley, Elspeth, *The Flame Trees of Thika*, 254–55
Hypatia, 466

I
"I Am Tired of Fighting (Surrender Speech)" (Chief Joseph), 180
Iconographic pictures. *See* Concrete poetry
Ideas
    controlling, 163
    occurrence of, 38
    paragraphs and, 161–62
    sources of, 13
"Idols, The" (Bacon), 496–98
Ignoring the question, 6, 575
"I Have a Dream" (King), 40–44
"Illegal Immigrants Are Bolstering Social Security with Billions" (Porter), 407–8
Illustration/exemplification, 189, 191, 613, 614
    Critical Thinking and Debate, 359–69
    examples, 342–58
    how to use, 339–41
    linking to a point, 340–41
    real and specific, 339–40
    relevance to the point, 341
    Student Corner, 371–73
    in thesis development, 94
    warming up to write, 341–42
    what it does, 337–38
    when to use, 338–39
Image Gallery, 647–678
    Ageism, 653
    Body Image, 650
    Drug Abuse, 656
    The Existence of God, 662
    Homelessness, 673
    Immigration, 659
    Racism, 665
    Same-Sex Marriage, 676
    Status of Women, 669
    Terrorism, 647
Imagery, 349
Images. *See also* Visual images, writing about
    advertising portrayals of, 31–33
    in descriptive writing, 253–54. *See also* Description
"Immigrants in America" (Herman), 416–18
Immigration
    Chinese girl waving flag (photograph), **661**
    Critical Thinking and Debate, 404–14
    immigrants going over a wall (photograph), **659**
    migrant farm workers (photograph), **406**
    people in line at Ellis Island (photograph), **660**
    receiving U.S. citizenship (photograph), **410**
    Student Corner, 416–18

Implied topic sentences. *See* Paragraphs
Importance, order of, in process analysis, 297
"Incidents with White People" (Delany and Delany), 508–11
"In Defense of Gender" (McFadden), 576–79
Independent clause, 97
Informal English, 21
Information, reading for, 3
InfoTrac © College Edition, 170
Ingersoll, Robert G., 455
"In Praise of the Humble Comma" (Iyer), 390–92
Internal reader/editor, 19–20
Internet
   as research tool, 25–26
   as source of research paper topic, 706
Interpretation of symbols, in literary work, 782
Inversion of reality, in advertising, 32
"I" point of view, 20, 21, 22
Irrelevancies, in paragraphs, 177
Issues for Critical Thinking and Debate. *See* Critical Thinking and Debate
It Was a Stable World (Graves), 175
"I Want a Wife" (Syfers-Brady), 587–89
Iyer, Pico, "In Praise of the Humble Comma," 390–92

J
James, William, 577
"James Boswell's Scotland" (Huntington), 215–26
Jargon, 68, 141
Jefferson, Thomas, 463, 467
Jeffrey, Francis, 577
Johnson, Samuel, 58, 59
Jordan, Suzanne, "That Lean and Hungry Look," 428–30
Jot list, 129–30
Joyce, James, "Hell," 260–62

K
Kemelman, Harry, *Common Sense in Education*, 173
Key terms, repetition of, in paragraphs, 169
Key words
   ambiguous, 96
   placement of, 693
   in thesis, 93, 96
Khayyam, Omar, 466
"Killing Ants in The Kitchen at 3 a.m. (Winkler), 86–87
"Kinds of Discipline" (Holt), 337, 493–95
King, Frederick A., "Animals in Research: The Case for Experimentation," 573
King, Martin Luther, Jr., "I Have a Dream," 40–44
"King of the Birds, The" (O'Connor), 253
"Kitsch" (Highet), 394–400
Koerner, Henry, *My Parents* (painting), **318**
Kollwitz, Kathe, *Never Again War!* (lithograph), **26**
Kondracke, Morton M., "Don't Legalize Drugs," 364–68
Kunze, Linda
   "Drug Use: The Continuing Epidemic," 371–72

"How I Write," 373
"How I Wrote This Essay," 373
"My Writing Tip," 373

L
L'Amour, Louis, "Education of a Wandering Man," 10–14
Lange, Dorthea, *Migrant Mother, Nipomo Valley* (photograph), **599**
Language
   of advertising, 32
   levels of, 140
      formal, 20
      informal, 21
      technical, 21–22
   reasons for mastering, 344–45
   weak, 98
Leo, John, "Mirror, Mirror, on the Wall . . .," 356–58
"Letter to My Husband" (Churchill), 45–46
Levels of English. *See* Language
Lexical definition, 376, 378
"Libido for the Ugly, The" (Mencken), 256–58
Lincoln, Abraham, 464
Linguistic diffidence, 68
Literary papers. *See also* Research papers
   analyzing character and action, 782
   annotated, 783–93
   finding and expressing a theme, 781
   form in, 782–83
   how to write, 780–81
   in-class essay on literature, 781
   interpreting symbols, 782
Loaded words, 70–71
Lofton family (photograph), **678**
Lodge, Oliver, 458
Logic
   for advertising evaluation, 33
   argument evaluation using, 4
   in comparison/contrast, 422–23
   of steps, in process analysis, 297
Logical fallacies, 6, 574–75
Long essay, 131–32
Love and hate tattooed on fists (photograph), **508**
Lucas, F.L., "What Is Style?," 342–50
Lynch, Matt, "The Homeless Lack a Political Voice, But Not American Ideals," 603–4

M
MacLane, Mary, "Me," 76–79
MacLeish, Archibald, "Ars Poetica," 402–3
Man, woman, and child with homeless sign (photograph), **675**
"Man Against Darkness" (Stace), 181
Man holding gun and Koran (photograph), **647**
Man in turban (photograph), **667**
Mannes, Marya, "Stay Young," 326–28
Markham, Beryl, "Praise God for the Blood of the Bull," 197–98
Martineau, James, 455, 456, 460

Material, sources of, 14
Mathews, E. G., and J. N. Hook, *Modern American Grammar and Usage*, 164–65
Maugham, W. Somerset, 19
  "Pain," 179
Mayer, Jean, "Overweight: Causes, Cost, and Control," 165
Maynard, Cindy, "Body Image," 275–80
McFadden, Cyra, "In Defense of Gender," 576–79
McKittrick, Amanda, *Delina Delaney*, 254
"Me" (MacLane), 76–79
Mechanical writers, 129
"Medusa and the Snail, The" (Thomas), 378
Memoirs (Gibbon), 2
Mencken, H. L., "The Libido for the Ugly," 256–58
Meskill, John T., 36
Mexico, Chile, Soweto. . . (painting; Garcia), **502**
Michie, James, "Dooley Is a Traitor," 594–97
Middle-Eastern man (photograph), **668**
Migrant farm workers (photograph), **406**
Migrant Mother, Nipomo Valley (photograph; Lange), **599**
Millay, Edna St. Vincent, "Spring," 123–24
Mill, John Stuart, 453
"Mingled Blood" (Zimmerman), 573–74
"Mirror, Mirror, on the Wall. . ." (Leo), 356–58
Mitford, Jessica, *The American Way of Death*, 163
Modern American Grammar and Usage (Hook and Mathews), 164–65
Modern Language Association (MLA) format, 711, 715–43
"Modest Proposal, A" (Swift), 580–86
Mohler, R. Albert, "The Case Against Homosexual Marriage," 633–36
Momin, Abdullah, "What Does Islam Say About Terrorism?," 231–34
Montaigne, Michel de, 466
"Mother Tongue: English and How It Got That Way" (Bryson), 613–14
"Motor Car, The" (White), 173–74
"Move Over, Teams" (Muchinsky), 481–84
Muchinsky, Paul M., "Move Over, Teams," 481–84
Multiple ofs, 693
Multi-tasking, status of women and (cartoon), **559**
Munsterberg, Hugo, 456
Murray, Donald, "What—and How—to Write When You Have No Time to Write," 37–40
"My Name is Margaret" (Angelou), 206–10
My Parents (painting; Koerner), **318**
"My Wood" (Forster), 142–45
"My Writing Tip" (students)
  Arakelian, Sion, 248
  Babaian, Ara, 475
  Herman, Dave, 418
  Kunze, Linda, 373
  Phillips, Nancey, 517

Poodt, Antoinette, 610
Rewa, Paula, 567
Taylor, Shelley, 293
Wheeler, Kimberly Caitlin, 334
Winkler, Adam, 645

N
Narration, 189, 190
  Critical Thinking and Debate, 229–43
  examples, 199–229
  how to write, 195–98
  process analysis compared to, 295
  Student Corner, 245–48
  warming up to write, 198–99
  what it does, 195
  when to use, 195
Necessary cause, 520–21
Negative words, 142
Neologisms, 695
Never Again War! (lithograph; Kollwitz), **26**
"New Feminism, The" (Gubata), 556–57
News photographs, writing about, 27–29
New York City firefighter watches smoke from the remains of the World Trade Center (photograph), **230**
Nichols, Beverley, "Twenty-Five," 339
Nietzsche, Friedrich, 449
Non sequitur, 6, 575
Notes, in research paper, 738–**39**
Note-taking, for research paper, 708
Noun clusters, 693–94

O
Oates, Joyce Carol, 197
Objectivity, 22
O'Connor, Flannery
  "A Good Man Is Hard to Find," 111–22
  "The King of the Birds," 253
"Of What Use?" (Asimov), 337–38
Older doctor (photograph), **655**
Old woman knitting (photograph), **654**
"Once More to the Lake" (White), 253, 625–29
"On Disease" (Thomas), 183–84
Online sources, citing, 712
Opinions
  evaluating, in critical reading, 4
  supporting, 27
  verifying, by cross-checking, 5
Organic writers, 129
Organization. *See also* Outline, formal
  ABC order, 141
  advice about, 139–42
  examples, 142–57
  of long essay, 131–32
  planning by listing supporting materials, 132
  in process analysis (steps), 297
  Real-Life Student Writing, 158–59
  of short essay, 129–**31**
  in thesis development, 94–95

Orwell, George
  Coming Up for Air, 165
  "Shooting an Elephant," 196, 199–204
Osborn, *The Vulgarians*, 165
Outline, formal
  creating, 134–35
  defined, 133
  framework for, 133–34
  guidelines for, 135
  research paper example, 716, **717**, **719**
  by sentence, 136–37
  tips for, 140
  by topic, 135–36
  usefulness of, 141
Out of Africa (Dinesen), 161–62
Overexplaining, 689–90
"Overweight: Causes, Cost, and Control" (Mayer), 165

P
Pace
  in argumentation and persuasion, 571–72
  of a story, 196
Padding, deleting, 66–67
"Pain" (Maugham), 179
Paine, Thomas, 455, 463
Palmer, George Herbert, 457
Paragraphs
  advice about, 174–77
  characteristics of, 167–70
  coherence in, 168–69
  completeness of, 169–70
  defined, 175
  developing idea in, 161–62
  examples, 178–85
  fragmentary, 177
  introduction to, 161–62
  irrelevancies in, 177
  paragraph promise, 175–77
  parts of, 162–65
  patterns, 167
  Real-Life Student Writing, 186–87
  in short essay, 130
  summary sentence, 164–65
  supporting details in, 163–64
  topic sentence
    at the beginning, 165–66, 178–81
    defined, 162–63
    at the end, 166, 181–85
    implied, 163
    in the middle, 166–67
  unity in, 167–68
  writing, 170–71, 174–77
Parallelism, 169
Paraphrasing, in note-taking, 708
Parks, Rosa (photograph), **669**
Parr, Barry, "The Buck Stops Where?," 351–54
Passive voice, 691–92
Patchen, Kenneth, "How to Be An Army," 316–17
Pat expressions, 68–69

"Peaceful Woman Explains Why She Carries a Gun, A" (Hasselstrom), 524–27
"People Out on a Limb" (Poodt), 607–9
Period, 244, 642
Perkins, Joseph, "Homeless: Expose the Myths," 600–1
Personal comments, in note-taking, 708
Person with drugs (photograph), **363**
Persuasion. *See* Argumentation and persuasion
Phillips, Nancey
  "How I Write," 516–17
  "How I Wrote This Essay," 517
  "My Writing Tip," 517
  "Racial Justice: How Far Have We Come?," 514–16
Photographs, writing about, 27–29
Phrases, 96, 168
Piercings and self-image (photograph), **277**
"Pigeon Woman" (Swenson), 271–72
Pillars of Society, The (painting; Grosz), **25**
Plagiarism, 709–10
Planning and organizing. *See* Organization
Pleasure reading, 3
Plot, 13
"Poetic People" (Eastman), 477
Poetry, concrete, 317
Point
  illustration linked to the, 340
  sticking to the, 141
  to a story, 111, 195–96
Point of view. *See also* "I" point of view
  consistent, 196–98, 695
  critical reading guidelines for, 4
  in formal English, 20
  omniscient, 197
  shift in, 17
"Politics of Separation, The" (Henry), 380–84, 386
Poodt, Antoinette
  "How I Write," 609–10
  "How I Wrote This Essay," 610
  "My Writing Tip," 610
  "People Out on a Limb," 607–9
Porter, Eduardo, "Illegal Immigrants Are Bolstering Social Security with Billions," 407–8
Portrait of James Boswell as a young man (painting), **221**
Positive statements, 692
"Postscript" to Inside the Kingdom: My Life in Saudi Arabia (bin Laden), 236–42
"Praise God for the Blood of the Bull" (Markham), 197–98
Prayer (photograph), **450**
Preamble phrases, 689
Priestly, J. B., "Romantic Recognition," 338
"Privacy" (Westin), 173
Process analysis, 189, 191
  Critical Thinking and Debate, 318–29
  examples, 299–317
  explain everything, 297–98

how to write, 296–98
narration compared to, 295
organize sequence of steps logically, 297
state the purpose in a clear thesis, 296–97
Student Corner, 331–34
subject selection, 296
warming up to write, 298
what it does, 295–96
when to use, 296
Pronoun reference, in paragraphs, 168
Protagoras, 465–66
Punctuation
apostrophe, 415
colon, 513
comma, 286, 642
dash, 370, 642
exclamation point, 563, 642
period, 244, 642
question mark, 472, 642
quotation marks, 606, 642
semicolon, 330
Purpose. *See also* Thesis
defined, 19
level of English appropriate for, 22
in process analysis, 296–97

Q

Question mark, 472, 642
Quindlen, Anna, "Stretch Marks," 282–84
Quotation marks, 606, 642
Quotations, direct, in note-taking, 708

R

"Racial Justice: How Far Have We Come?" (Phillips), 514–16
Racism
Critical Thinking and Debate, 501–12
man in turban (photograph), **667**
Mexico, Chile, Soweto... (painting; Garcia), **502**
Middle-Eastern man (photograph), **668**
Ruby Bridges (painting; Rockwell), **666**
slave auction (drawing), **665**
Student Corner, 514–16
Reade, Charles, *Cloister and the Hearth, The*, 251
Reading
annotating guidelines, 6–7
casual, 3
critical, guidelines for, 3–7
as influence on writing, 1–188
for information, 3
pleasure, 3
Ready-made phrases, 688
Real-Life Student Writing
application letter, 186–87
e-mail, 52–54
eulogy, 126–27
note, 158–59
thank-you note (voice), 89
Reason, argument evaluation using, 4
"Reason why" thesis, 94
Recursive process, of writing, 23, 683

Red herring, 575
Redundancies, 687–89
References, for research papers, 712, 764, **765**, **767**
"Remarks on the Life of Sacco and on His Own Life and Execution" (Vanzetti), 81–82
Rereading, 682, 685
Research papers. *See also* Literary papers
American Psychological Association (APA) format, 711, 745–77
appearance of, 713
appendix for, 768, **769–77**
choosing the topic, 705–6
documentation, 710–12
finding and evaluating sources, 707–8
first draft, 710
Modern Language Association (MLA) format, 711, 715–43
narrowing the subject, 706–7
notes in, 738–**39**
note-taking for, 708
plagiarism, 709–10
process of writing, 707–12
reason for, 705
References, 712, 764–67, **765**, **767**
suggestions for writing, 705–13
thesis sentence for, 716, **717**, 720, **721**
Works Cited, 712, 740, **741–43**
writing the final copy, 712–13
Revising, 681–85. *See also* Editing
Rewa, Paula
"How I Write," 566
"How I Wrote This Essay," 566–67
"My Writing Tip," 567
"'Woman' Is a Noun," 564–65
Rewriting, 681–82. *See also* Editing; Revising
Rhetoric
advice about, 37–40
audience and purpose, 19
defined, 17
effectiveness of writing and, 17–18
examples, 40–52
grammar vs., 17–18
internal reader/editor, 19–20
levels of English, 20–22, 140
process of writing, 23–24
Real-Life Student Writing, 52–54
visual images and, 24–33
Rhetorical modes. *See also* Argumentation and persuasion; *and individual modes*
causal analysis, 189, 192–93, 519–68
combining the modes, 613–645
comparison and contrast, 189, 192, 421–76
definition, 189, 191–92, 375–419
description, 189, 190–91, 251–94
division and classification, 189, 192, 477–518
illustration/exemplification, 189, 191, 337–74
narration, 189, 190, 195–249
process analysis, 189, 191, 295–335
Rhetorical patterns. *See* Rhetorical modes
Rhetorical questions, 689

"Right Moves Against Terrorism, The" (Arakelian), 245–47
Roberts, Paul, "How to Say Nothing in Five Hundred Words," 61–71
Roberts, Roxanne, "The Grieving Never Ends," 104–10
Robertson, Ian, *Sociology*, 166
Rockwell, Norman, *Ruby Bridges* (painting), **666**
"Romantic Recognition" (Priestly), 338
Rooney, Andy, "A Writer's Fantasy—What I Wish I Had Written," 7–10
Roosevelt, Eleanor (photograph), **669**
Rosenblatt, Roger, "Rules for Aging," 146–47
Rubins, Rebecca E. "The Farce of Feminism," 560–61
Ruby Bridges (painting; Rockwell), **666**
"Rules for Aging" (Rosenblatt), 146–47
Ruskin, John, 452
Russell, Bertrand
  on religion, 464, 465
  "The Unhappy American Way," 169

S
"Salvation" (Hughes), 83–85
Same-sex marriage
  Critical Thinking and Debate, 631–41
  God hates Sodomites (photograph), **677**
  Lofton family (photograph), **678**
  Student Corner, 643–44
  two men getting married (photograph), **676**
  two men with baby carriage (photograph), **632**
"Same-Sex Marriage: Just Say No to Prohibition" (Block), 638–40
Sanger, Margaret, 464
Semicolon, 330
Senior-citizen protesters (photograph), **320**
Sentence outline, 136–37
Sentences. *See also* Thesis
  compound, 97
  fragments, 96–97
  key word placement, 693
  as opener, 686
  period at end of, 244
  varying, 694–95
Sequence, in process analysis, 297
Series, commas in, 286
Servetus, Michael, 466
"Sex Predators Can't Be Saved" (Vachss), 590–93
Shakespeare, William, "That Time of Year," 156–57
Shakespearean sonnet, 156
"Shame" (Gregory), 211–14
Shaw, George Bernard, 464
Shelley, Percy, 452
Shirer, William, "Hitler's Workday," 313–15
"Shooting an Elephant" (Orwell), 196, 199–204
Short essay
  defined, 129
  essay flowchart, 130–**31**
  jot list, 129–30
  organizing, 129–31
  sketch out paragraphs, 130
"Shrew—The Littlest Mammal" (DeVoe), 616–19
Simon, John, 36–37
Sitwell, Sacheverell, *Southern Baroque Art*, 252–53
Slave auction (pen and ink drawing), **665**
Sloganeering, 4
Sociology (Robertson), 166
Socrates, 459
Sonnet, 156
Sources. *See also* American Psychological Association (APA) format; Modern Language Association (MLA) format
  evaluating, for research paper, 707–8
  online, citation style, 712
Southern Baroque Art (Sitwell), 252–53
Specific detail, using, 690
Spinoza, Baruch, 466–67
"Spring" (Millay), 123–24
Stace, W. T., "Man Against Darkness," 181
"Stay Young" (Mannes), 326–28
Stegner, Wallace, "The Big Rock Candy Mountain," 377–78
Steinem, Gloria, 465
"Storm, The" (Chopin), 548–52
"Story of Jamaica, The" (Black), 615
"Stretch Marks" (Quindlen), 282–84
Strunk, William, Jr., 681
Student Corner
  Arakelian, Sion, on terrorism, 245–48
  Babaian, Ara, on the existence of God, 473–75
  Herman, Dave, on immigrants, 416–18
  Kunze, Linda, on drug use, 371–72
  Phillips, Nancey, on racism, 514–16
  Poodt, Antoinette, on homelessness, 607–9
  Rewa, Paula, on women, 564–65
  Taylor, Shelley, on body image, 287–92
  Wheeler, Kimberly Caitlin, on aging, 331–32
  Winkler, Adam, on same-sex marriage, 643–44
Student writing. *See* Real-Life Student Writing
Style, tone vs., 55
Subject, for process analysis, 296
Sufficient cause, 521
Summary
  in note-taking, 708
  in paragraphs, 164–65
Swenson, May, "Pigeon Woman," 271–72
Swift, Jonathan, "A Modest Proposal," 580–86
Syfers-Brady, Judy, "I Want a Wife," 587–89
Symbols, in literary work, 782
Syntax, 58

T
Taft, William Howard, 464
Tattoos and self-image (photograph), **277**
Taylor, Shelley
  "Body Modification—Think About It!," 287–92

"How I Write," 292
"How I Wrote This Essay," 292
"My Writing Tip," 293
Technical English, 21–22
Tennyson, Alfred, Lord, 461
"Ten Reasons for Believing in Immortality" (Holmes), 451–60
Tense, 693
Terrorism
    bombed bus in London (photograph), **648**
    Critical Thinking and Debate, 229–43
    Hussein, Saddam, as a young boy (photograph), **649**
    man holding gun and Koran (photograph), **647**
    New York City firefighter watches smoke from the remains of the World Trade Center (photograph), **230**
    Student Corner, 245–47
Thange, Musaddique. *See* Momin, Abdullah
"That Lean and Hungry Look" (Jordan), 428–30
"That Time of Year" (Shakespeare), 156–57
Theme, of literary work, 781
Thesis
    advice about, 101–4
    characteristics of, 93–96
    defined, 91
    errors to avoid, 96–99
    examples, 22, 104–25
    explicit, 99–101
    finding, 91–93, 102–3
    implicit, 99–101
    key words in, 93
    in process analysis, 296–97
    Real-Life Student Writing, 126–27
    "reason why," 94
    research paper example, 716, **717**
    sharpening, 103–4
"Thesis, The" (Baker), 101–4
"Thinking as a Hobby" (Golding), 486–91
Third trapped coal miner being rescued (photograph), **28**
"This Is a Mortal Wound, Doctor" (Fleming), 299–307
Thomas, Lewis
    "Death in the Open," 166
    "On Disease," 183–84
    "The Medusa and the Snail," 378
Thompson, Edward T., "How to Write Clearly," 139–42
Thoreau, Henry David, "Why I Went to the Woods," 541–46
"Those Winter Sundays" (Hayden), 228
Thurber, James, "The Catbird Seat," 148–55
Tibbets, A.M., and Charlene Tibbetts, "Writing Successful Paragraphs," 174–77
Title, descriptive, 685
Tolstoy, Leo, 464
Tone, 55, 56. *See also* Voice
"Tone: The Writer's Voice in the Reader's Mind" (Castle), 71–75

Topic
    defined, 91–92
    for research paper, choosing, 705–6
Topic outline, 135–36
Topic sentence. *See* Paragraphs
Transition, 340
Transitional words and phrases, in paragraphs, 168
Trite expressions, 691
Trudeau, G. B., political correctness (cartoon), **385**
Tubman, Harriet (photograph), **669**
Twain, Mark, 463
"Twenty-Five" (Nichols), 339
Two fists tattooed with Love and Hate (photograph), **509**
Two men getting married (photograph), **676**

U

"Unhappy American Way, The" (Russell), 169
Unity, in paragraphs, 167–68

V

Vachss, Andrew, "Sex Predators Can't Be Saved," 590–93
Values, 6
Van Doren, Mark, "What Is a Poet?," 182–83
Vanzetti, Bartolomeo, "Remarks on the Life of Sacco and on His Own Life and Execution," 81–82
Verbs, active/passive, 142
Vidal, Gore, "Drugs," 361–62
"View from Eighty, The" (Cowley), 319–24
Visual images, writing about. *See also* Image Gallery
    advertisements, **31**, 31–33
    artworks, 24–27, **25**, **26**
    cartoons, 29–31, **30**
    news photographs, 27–29, **28**
Vocabulary, voice and, 57–58
Voice
    active and passive, 691–92
    advice about, 61–71
    attitude and, 59
    examples, 75–88
    introduction to, 55–57
    Real-Life Student Writing, 89
    syntax and, 58
    vocabulary and, 57–58
    writer's psychology and, 55–56
Voltaire, 455, 463
Vonnegut, Kurt, 465

W

Walker, D. J. R., *Columbus and the Golden World of the Island Arawaks*, 20
Warren, Earl, 577
"Warriors Don't Cry" (Beals), 503–06
Weeping Virgin Mary (sculpture), **662**
Weight loss advertising (photograph), **275**

Welty, Eudora, "A Worn Path," 264–70
"We're Poor" (Dell), 196
Westin, Alan F., "Privacy," 173
"What—and How—to Write When You Have No Time to Write" (Murray), 37–40
"What Does Islam Say About Terrorism?" (Momin), 231–34
"What Is a Poet?" (van Doren), 182–83
"What Is Style?" (Lucas), 342–50
"What Is the Bible?" (Chase), 377
Wheeler, Kimberly Caitlin
    "Aging," 331–32
    "How I Write," 333
    "How I Wrote This Essay," 334
    "My Writing Tip," 334
When a shopping cart is your only home (photograph), **602**
White, E. B., 681
    "Motor Car, The," 173–74
    "Once More to the Lake," 253, 625–29
    "Withholding," 170
Whittier, John Greenleaf, 452
"Why I Went to the Woods" (Thoreau), 541–46
"Why Tigers Become Man-Eaters" (Corbett), 536–40
"Wide Open Spaces" (Bryson), 410–13
Wight, James Alfred. *See* Herriot, James
Wildenstein, Jocelyn, before and after plastic surgery (photograph), **651**
"Will Same-Sex Marriages Change the Constitution?" (Winkler), 643–44
"Will Spelling Count?" (Connor), 620–23
Wilson, Carnie, before and after bypass surgery (photograph), **652**
Winkler, Adam
    "How I Write," 645
    "How I Wrote This Essay," 645
    "My Writing Tip," 645
    "Will Same-Sex Marriages Change the Constitution?," 643–44
Winkler, Anthony C., "Killing Ants in The Kitchen at 3 a.m." 86–87
"Withholding" (White), 170
"'Woman' Is a Noun" (Rewa), 564–65
Woman with pills (photograph), 360

Women, status of
    Critical Thinking and Debate, 555–62
    multi-tasking (cartoon), **559**
    Student Corner, 564–65
    Susan B. Anthony, Harriet Tubman, Eleanor Roosevelt, and Rosa Parks (photograph), **669**
    woman conducting a business meeting (photograph), **556**
    woman with arrow-patterned wrap (photograph), **670**
    woman working with baby in carrier (photograph), **672**
    women in burkhas voting (photograph), **671**
Wordiness, 686–89
Words
    arrangements of. *See* Concrete poetry
    colorful/colored/colorless, 69–71
    familiar combinations of, 141
    "first-degree," 141
    negative, 142
    power of, 344
    standard, 695
    syntax, 58
    transitional, 168
    vocabulary and voice, 57–58
    windy phrases, 142
Works Cited, for research papers, 710, 712, 740, **741–43**
"Worn Path, A" (Welty), 264–70
Writers
    desire of to please, 17
    organic/mechanical, 129
"Writer's Fantasy—What I Wish I Had Written" (Rooney), 7–10
Writing. *See also* Paragraphs; Process analysis; Rhetoric; Visual images, writing about
    dull subjects made interesting, guidelines for, 63–71
    habits for, 38–40
    process of, 23–24
    as a recursive process, 23, 683
"Writing Successful Paragraphs" (Tibbetts and Tibbetts), 174–77

Z
Zimmerman, Ralph, "Mingled Blood," 573–74